Awakening from the Dream

Awakening from the Dream

Civil Rights Under Siege and the New Struggle for Equal Justice

Edited by

Denise C. Morgan, Rachel D. Godsil, and Joy Moses

CAROLINA ACADEMIC PRESS

Durham, North Carolina

Library of Congress Cataloging-in-Publication Data

Morgan, Denise C.
Awakening from the dream : civil rights under siege and the new struggle
for equal justice / by Denise C. Morgan, Rachel D. Godsil, Joy Moses.
p. cm.
Includes index.
ISBN 1-59460-074-0 (alk. paper)
1. Civil rights--United States. I. Godsil, Rachel D. II. Moses, Joy. III.
Title.

KF4749.M637 2005
342.7308'5--dc22

2005013079

Carolina Academic Press
700 Kent Street
Durham, North Carolina 27701
Telephone (919) 489-7486
Fax (919) 493-5668
www.cap-press.com

Printed in the United States of America
Cover Photo © Robert Faber/Corbis
Cover Design: Erin M. Ehman

*We dedicate this book to Bonnie Sanders,
Herb Semmel, and other fallen heroes
in the ongoing struggle for equal justice.*

CONTENTS

FOREWORD

Erwin Chemerinsky[*]

These are bleak times for civil rights. Both houses of Congress are controlled by Republican majorities who show no intention of enacting legislation to advance civil rights. The Supreme Court is conservative, and at least two vacancies on that court will be filled by a president whose model justices are those most hostile to civil rights: Antonin Scalia and Clarence Thomas. Until November 2, 2004, there was hope that a Democrat would win the White House and turn the federal courts in a more progressive direction. Now, however, conservatives are increasingly dominating federal courts, and the Supreme Court will only move further to the Right in the years ahead.

Progressives who care about civil rights have two choices: give up, or fight harder. The former, of course, is not really an option. A strategy for how to proceed with even greater energy and dedication, therefore, is needed. The essays in this collection outline such a plan. First, it is important to assess where we are now in the battle to protect and advance civil rights. Second, we must generate ideas about how to both prevent a further rollback in civil rights and enhance liberty and equality.

The first half of this volume assesses where the country is today in terms of protecting civil rights. The collection is comprehensive; the essays examine a broad spectrum of civil rights issues. The popular perception, maybe even among some academics, is that the Court has not moved all that far Right. What, then, explains the failure to recognize how much the extreme Right has managed to roll back civil rights? First, the incremental nature of constitutional law has allowed the retrenchment of civil rights to go unrecognized. Constitutional law develops case-by-case, not all at once. No single decision changes its nature. Second, the Right's position has not triumphed in some of the most politically visible and controversial areas—the Court, for example, has not ended the constitutional right to abortion, affirmative action, or the restric-

---

[*] Alston & Bird Professor of Law, Duke University School of Law.

tions on school prayers. It is easy to generalize from these examples, failing to recognize the other areas where extremist views have won out. Third, political rhetoric about the Judiciary has not caught up with reality; the Right continues to rail against judicial activism, even while Court activism is taking a right-wing direction. Finally, many of the Rehnquist Court's most dramatic changes have been procedural in nature, such as restricting habeas corpus, limiting access to the courts, and expanding sovereign immunity. These do not capture public attention enough to change perceptions.

The essays in this book show how vulnerable groups are being hurt by the rollback in civil rights. There are excellent articles by leading experts: Emily Martin on the rights of women, Simon Lazarus on older Americans, Caroline Palmer on Americans with disabilities, Arthur Leonard on sexual minorities, Lia Epperson on African Americans, Vincent Eng and Julianna Lee on Asian Americans, Marielena Hincapié and Ana Avendaño-Denier on immigrant workers, Sandra Del Valle on Latinos, Rose Cuison Villazor on language minorities, and Nathan Newman on workers' rights. Reading the essays conveys the reality that every group needing protection from discrimination is suffering in the current climate. More importantly, they reveal the extent to which these groups need increasingly absent legal protections. This book should provide a basis for building coalitions.

Imagine if all these groups worked together to pursue common interests. Separate, the Right is able to marginalize their interests as identity group politics and render the groups relatively powerless politically. The recognition of common interests provides a basis for collective action that could make a real difference. In the coming fights over judicial nominations, for example, a coalition of these groups is the only hope in preventing right wing judges from occupying seats on the federal courts (much like how civil rights groups forged a unified coalition to defeat Robert Bork's nomination for the Supreme Court in 1986). The fight to block Clarence Thomas' confirmation in 1991 failed, in part, because such a coalition never formed. Similarly, new federal civil rights legislation (e.g., to overturn recent Court decisions limiting attorney's fees) will occur only if these groups unite in a coalition.

The essays in this book also describe the problems in particular areas of civil rights law. Again, contributors include top experts: Jane Perkins on health law, Olga Pomar and Rachel Godsil on the environment, Denise Morgan on public education, Barbara Olshansky on civil liberties and the war on terrorism, Michelle Alexander on the criminal justice system, and Lori Nessel and Anjum Gupta on immigration issues. The essays do an excellent job of pointing to serious problems and explaining how things could worsen. Since 9/11, for example, the Bush administration has had a dismal record with regard to the environment, educational reform, and protecting civil liberties.

In identifying the problem and necessary direction for action, these essays offer a basis for both political appeals and litigation strategies. As I read, I kept wishing that John Kerry and John Edwards had used them in their 2004 campaign—the Bush record on issues like the environment, education, and civil liberties should have been a major focus.

The initial essays provide a useful framework for understanding what has occurred over the last decade. Paul Finkelman shows that the Rehnquist Court's federalism decisions must be understood as motivated by traditional right wing hostility to civil rights. Wade Henderson and Janelle Byrd-Chichester provide a terrific history of civil rights legislation, and explain how we arrived at the current dismal situation.

If the book stopped mid-way, it would provide an invaluable collection but would fail to take aim at the question of "What next?" The second half offers suggestions for how to proceed. A key insight is that there cannot be a single strategy to restore civil rights; a multi-front war is essential. Lee Cokorinos and Alfred Ross describe the lessons to be learned from the Right—how in its rhetoric and organizing, the right has done a far better job in getting its message across and its agenda accomplished.

Susan Lerner reminds us that the battle over the federal courts is one of the most important in the fight for civil rights. President George W. Bush's judges will dominate the federal judiciary for decades to come. Progressives must therefore unite to block the most extreme nominees. Such an effort will require both an active public relations campaign to convey how many of Bush's picks are extremists, and a coordinated effort in persuading Democratic senators to filibuster the worst candidates. With fifty-five Republicans dominating the Senate for at least the next two years, success can only come about through unified and coordinated action.

Joy Moses describes the need for new civil rights legislation. It must be remembered that major civil rights laws, such as the Americans with Disabilities Act and the Civil Rights Act of 1991, were adopted with Republicans in the White House.

Marianne Engleman Lado then explains how civil rights litigation succeeded through a coordinated effort culminating in *Brown v. Board of Education* and subsequent decisions ordering desegregation. The challenge she sees is to develop a blueprint for litigation success in advancing civil rights.

Dennis Parker's essay is a crucial reminder that action at the state level is more important than ever. Many states have progressive governors and legislatures. Many state court systems are receptive to civil rights litigation. Many reforms in the foreseeable future, therefore, will have to occur at the state level. For example, while federal constitutional litigation to equalize educational opportunity has little chance for success, there have been successful suits in state courts under state constitutions.

Ultimately, however, success in advancing civil rights requires that people mobilize people. Andrew Friedman, Robert García, Julie Hyman, and their co-authors discuss the need for community activism, and Columbia law students Lisa Zeidner and Luke Blocher consider revitalizing student activism.

As I read the first half of this collection, I found myself increasingly depressed. These are awful times for civil rights—the rollback has touched every area of civil rights law. As I read the second half, however, I found myself increasingly hopeful and energized as I realized that our response to the current bleak state of civil rights must not be despair, but action.

Thirty years ago, I went to law school because I wanted to be a civil rights lawyer. I was inspired by the civil rights lawyers of the late 1960s and early 1970s, and believed law to be the most powerful tool for social change. While I continue to believe this, I never imagined how difficult change would be, or that I would spend my career teaching, writing, and litigating in such a regressive climate.

Yet, as this wonderful collection of essays reveals, history shows the overall trend to be positive. Over the course of American history, there have been enormous advances in equality for groups such as African Americans, women, and sexual minorities. Rights for immigrants and criminal defendants, while not where they should be, have taken some strides. The current era must, therefore, be considered a temporary setback in an overall of advancement of rights and liberties. This book provides a clear picture of where we are, and offers a hopeful direction for action. Everyone who cares about civil rights will benefit from reading its essays.

INTRODUCTION

This book is edited by children of the civil rights era. The three of us came of age in a country that held a strong national commitment—in words, if not always in deeds—to realizing the Constitution's promise of equal justice under law. Dr. Martin Luther King, Jr.'s dream that "one day this nation will rise up and live out the true meaning of its creed: 'We hold these truths to be self-evident, that all men are created equal'" reflected a prevalent aspiration.[1] Yet, even as children, we understood that the day for such equality had not yet come. We experienced discrimination first hand, or witnessed it and felt ashamed. Still, we saw the potential for progress and considered law a vehicle for change.

To us, the term "civil rights" means the bundle of rights that advance inclusion, equal membership, political participation, and economic mobility in our diverse national community. We have never known a United States without federal labor laws and an economic safety net to help prevent the exclusion of working people, the poor, and the elderly from the political and economic mainstream. We take those pieces of 1930s New Deal legislation[2]—which are essential prerequisites to equal citizenship—for granted.

During our youth in the 1960s and 1970s, the federal government worked to establish a national floor on individual rights below which the states could not sink—an endeavor that it had been assigned a century earlier by the Reconstruction amendments.[3] Like the New Deal statutes, these civil rights laws created rights of belonging.[4] We understand them to recognize and proclaim that we all belong to America—therefore, our national identity is imperiled if any one of us is turned down for a job because of our sex, denied access to the ballot because we cannot pass an English literacy test, excluded from public buildings because we are in a wheelchair, or steered away from a white neighborhood because of our race. We take for granted the right to be free from such affronts, and assume that the courts will vindicate those rights—these understandings are central to our conception of a just society.

The civil rights laws of the 1930s, 1960s, and 1970s, and the social justice movements supporting them, reinforced our notion that one of the highest functions of federal authority is "to promote an inclusive vision of who belongs to the national community of the United States and to facilitate equal membership in that community."[5] In some instances, the states have led the way in protecting individual rights.[6] On many more occasions, however, the country has lacked the political will to live up to its ideals: public schools and most neighborhoods have remained racially segregated; Congress has never enacted legislation prohibiting discrimination on the basis of sexual orientation; and the War on Poverty ended long before victory could be declared. Still, we grew up in a country where the federal government, particularly the federal courts, could frequently be relied upon to promote equality and individual rights over private bigotry, corporate malfeasance, and state-enforced exclusion of some groups from social, political, and economic power.

Those childhood memories of America now seem like a dream. Today, our children are growing up in a very different country. Many on the Right now openly question government's role in bettering the lives of Americans. Indeed, our federal courts have abdicated their responsibility to promote equal justice, and the Supreme Court under the leadership of Chief Justice William Rehnquist has issued decisions limiting congressional power to enact progressive legislation, eroding existing civil rights protections, and leaving many vulnerable to exclusion from the social, political, and economic mainstream.

These cases have not received significant media attention and there has been little public discussion regarding the dramatic rollback of civil rights. The few cases in which the Court has ruled in favor of progressive interests—such as those allowing universities to implement race-based affirmative action programs, striking down sodomy statutes, and prohibiting the execution of minors[7]—have garnered far more interest. While important, these victories do not mitigate the many cases in which the Court has targeted the powers of Congress, about which there is almost no debate.

This silence is, in part, because instead of advertising or campaigning against civil rights, the Right has waged a quiet, concerted, and effective crusade to enact changes by dominating the federal courts.[8] Indeed, Justice O'Connor's retirement and Chief Justice Rehnquist's death—as this book goes to press—give the Bush administration an extraordinary opportunity to entrench the Right's control of the Supreme Court and to shape the law for the next generation. The right wing's ideologically-driven judges have already eviscerated Congress's ability to define federal rights and to empower individuals to sue to enforce those rights. The echoes of these cases will continue to reverberate in the lower federal courts as long as those judicial activists remain on the bench.

Another reason for the silence surrounding the civil rights roll back is that the Court has couched many of its decisions in the language of "federalism"—the division of power between the states and the federal government. Such reasoning is not the stuff of breaking news reports because it sounds abstract, innocuous, or even attractive. In theory, federalism allows both the states and the federal government to champion civil rights, and privileging states' rights over the exercise of federal power can at times favor the disempowered and provide greater protection for individuals. In the U.S., however, federalism's progressive potential has frequently been undermined. States' rights have been used to justify such oppression as slavery, Jim Crow segregation, and, most famously, southern resistance to the implementation of *Brown v. Board of Education.*

We use the term "Federalism Revolution"[9] to refer to the current appeal to states' rights that has been used to justify decisions undercutting Congress' ability to create and enforce civil rights. Perhaps the term "Anti-Antidiscrimination Revolution"[10] would be more accurate, as the Court has regularly abandoned its commitment to states' rights in order to advance an anti-civil rights agenda. We have chosen the term, however, to highlight the Court's federalism rhetoric and expose its hypocrisy.

As children of the civil rights era, we have a duty to protect what our parents fought, marched, and lobbied for—and what others died for—both for ourselves and for our children. We hope that this book of essays, which stems from a conference held in 2002 at Columbia Law School to celebrate the founding of the National Campaign to Restore Civil Rights (NCRCR), can serve as a beginning. The contributors—activists, law professors, public interest lawyers, and students—tell of some who have been deprived of justice by the rollback. This book is also intended as a call to arms. Progressives and liberals who share our conception of a just society are engaged in a struggle to reclaim civil rights. We write to bring their work to light, and to invite readers to join in their efforts.

Part I, *The Rehnquist Court's Federalism Revolution and Civil Rights*, explores the historical underpinnings of federalism and the Federalism Revolution. Chapter 1, by legal historian Paul Finkelman, explains how, starting with the battle over slavery, federalism and civil rights have been inextricably linked. Southern states enshrined protections for slavery in the Constitution, while federalism enabled northern states to free their black citizens. The Court undermined federalism's progressive potential, however, when it upheld the right of southern states to maintain slavery in the infamous *Dred Scott* decision in 1857, but hinted that northern states would not have the right to protect free blacks. The balance of power between the states and the federal government was radically transformed by the Civil War, Reconstruction, and the enactment of the Thirteenth, Fourteenth, and Fifteenth Amendments in 1865, 1868, and 1870. These gains in civil rights protections were soon lost when a series of Court decisions struck down many of the federal laws that sought to protect the equal citizenship of newly freed blacks.

In chapter 2, respected civil rights leaders Wade Henderson and Janell Byrd-Chichester canvass the Federalism Revolution cases and begin our discussion of strategies to reverse the rollback. Henderson and Byrd-Chichester first discuss the series of statutes enacted in the 1960s and 1970s to protect civil rights and address the needs of the poor. Many consider those laws more important in dismantling state-enforced segregation and blatant racial discrimination than any Court decisions.[11] Their effectiveness was muted by Court interpretation, however. In the 1970s, the composition of the Court changed and civil rights enforcement waned. By the 1990s, the Rehnquist Court began to roll back civil rights protections in earnest.

Part II, *The Impact of the Federalism Revolution on the Lives of Americans*, explores the effects of the Federalism Revolution on all Americans. Because the Federalism Revolution has been incremental and involves technical legal issues, many are unaware that they have lost civil rights protections. Each chapter begins with a brief narrative to illustrate and personalize the injustices people have experienced.

The perception that civil rights are associated with racial minorities is too narrow. People of all races and nationalities—women, older Americans, people with disabilities, immigrants, gay men and lesbians, and workers—all need civil rights protections. Still, the history and pervasiveness of racial discrimination compels particular attention. Accordingly, the first three chapters of Part II address the impact of the rollback of civil rights on communities of color.

Lia Epperson, a civil rights lawyer with the NAACP Legal Defense and Education Fund, opens chapter 3 with a description of conditions at a segregated public school in Gadsen, Alabama. Focusing on the impact of the Federalism Revolution on African Americans, Epperson discusses educational opportunity, affirmative action, voting, employment, and the provision of government services. Her chapter, like those before it, notes the eerie similarity between the current rollback of civil rights and the civil rights retrenchment that led the country into the Jim Crow era.

Chapter 4, by Sandra Del Valle, a civil rights lawyer with the Puerto Rican Legal Defense and Education Fund, and chapter 5, by Vincent Eng, Deputy Director of the National Asian Pacific American Legal Consortium, and Julianna Lee, a Michigan Law School student, explore the rollback's impact on Latinos and Asian Americans. Del Valle juxtaposes two Court cases affecting Latinos—the first a successful 1966 voting case, and the second, an unsuccessful 1991 jury discrimination case—and argues that the arc of those cases traces the Court's declining protection of civil rights. In contrast, Eng and Lee highlight the Court's consistent denial of Asian American civil rights, citing the Court's decisions upholding the 1882 Chinese Exclusion Act, the internment of Japanese Americans during World War II, and more recent employment discrimination and voting rights cases.

Both the Asian American and Latino communities have been particularly harmed by the Court's treatment of language rights and immigrant workers. These issues are examined in chapter 10 by Rose Cuison Villazor, and in chapter 11 by Marielena Hincapié and Ana Avendaño-Denier. The authors contend that judicial decisions limiting access to the courts have had a dire impact on vulnerable communities. Villazor argues that these decisions tacitly approve government programs that exclude language minorities. Similarly, Hincapié and Avendaño-Denier contend that Court decisions limiting undocumented workers' labor rights create perverse incentives for employers to hire and exploit undocumented workers instead of American workers whose rights are better protected. The Federalism Revolution has, of course, hurt communities of color not addressed in this book. We are particularly sorry not to have addressed the impact of the Rehnquist Court's decisions on Native Americans.

Chapters 6 through 9 demonstrate that civil rights—and the Federalism Revolution—reach beyond racial discrimination. In chapter 6, Emily Martin addresses Congress's attempt to provide national civil rights protection for battered women and the Court decision striking down that statute in the name of federalism. Chapters 7 and 8, by Simon Lazarus and Caroline Palmer respectively, also illustrate the Court's use of federalism to eviscerate civil rights and limit congressional authority. Those chapters describe recent cases limiting the reach of the Age Discrimination in Employment Act, the Americans with Disabilities Act, and Medicaid. As a result of those cases, older Americans and people with disabilities can be subjected to employment discrimination by state employers without a judicial remedy, and individuals who rely on Medicaid for their health care face barriers to enforcing their civil rights in court.

The gay rights movement has had many of its recent success in courts, either in the Court's decision striking down state sodomy laws or in state court decisions sanctioning same-sex marriage.[12] However, the Federalism Revolution may imperil lasting federal protections for this community as well. Chapter 9, by Professor Arthur Leonard, explains that sexual minorities still lack federal protection from employment discrimination and hate crimes, and how the Federalism Revolution has limited Congress's authority to enact such legislation. Accordingly, Leonard urges gay rights advocates to join with other civil rights activists to restore congressional authority to redress discrimination.

Part III builds on Part II by looking more closely at the impact of the Federalism Revolution on the provision of government services, including education, health care, the environment, our criminal justice system, and immigration. In chapter 12, Professor Denise Morgan addresses the continuing racial segregation and fiscal inequities in our public school system, and explores the Court's 1970s decisions that reneged on the promise of *Brown*. She then details how the Federalism Revolution cases restricting access to the courts have undercut recent efforts to achieve equal educational opportunity.

In chapter 13, Jane Perkins similarly contends that the Federalism Revolution has denied the fifty-five million people who rely upon Medicaid (the elderly, low-income, and people with disabilities) access to the courts. Since its inception four decades ago, Medicaid has improved the health of these otherwise vulnerable populations. These successes are now at risk, Perkins contends, because states often ignore federal mandates unless they are ordered to comply.

In chapter 14, Olga Pomar and Professor Rachel Godsil argue that the Federalism Revolution cases doomed litigation that sought to eradicate the link between the lack of environmental protection and race. The chapter begins with the story of how a neighborhood in Camden, New Jersey, won a court injunction to prevent the operation of a toxin-spewing cement factory, only to have the decision overruled by the Supreme Court.

In chapter 15, Professor Michelle Alexander paints an ominous picture of the lack of meaningful access to courts in our criminal justice system, focusing on the mass incarceration of people of color. Alexander draws a connection between the high rate of incarceration—which has serious repercussions on employment, voting, and education—and federalism, because the Court has precluded federal civil rights challenges to state and local criminal enforcement measures, even when those measures have a vastly disproportionate effect on blacks and Latinos.

This part of the book ends with an examination of the rollback of civil rights in the context of the war on terror. In chapter 16, Barbara Olshansky, who has represented detainees at Guantánamo Bay, contends that the Federalism Revolution laid the groundwork for the executive branch's ongoing assault on civil liberties that now threatens our constitutional democracy. In chapter 17, Professors Lori Nessel and Anjum Gupta explore how Congress limited immigrants' rights in the wake of 9/11, and argue that for immigrants, it is Court deference to congressional enactments rather than judicial activism that causes concern.

While many of the preceding chapters hint that the Federalism Revolution is motivated by more than an abstract commitment to adjusting the balance of power between the states and the federal government, Part IV, *Federalism Revolution: Principle or Politics?* makes the argument explicit by contending that the Court's appeal to federalism is a rhetorical veil for a political agenda.

In chapters 18 and 19, the late Herbert Semmel and Nathan Newman conclude that the Court's commitment to states' rights is thin. Semmel finds that the Rehnquist Court has consistently ignored states' rights and the principles of federalism whenever states favor civil rights interests. Newman canvasses the Court's treatment of labor and employment laws since the New Deal, and contends that the Rehnquist Court has regularly betrayed the principle of states' rights in order to limit labor and employment rights.

The 2004 elections should be seen as a clarion call. The Right is in ascendance, and those of us committed to the preservation of civil rights must fight an uphill battle. The final part of the book, *Strategies for Reversing the Rollback*, explores the multiple dimensions of our struggle. In chapter 20, Lee Cokorinos and Alfred Ross describe the Right's blueprint to roll back civil rights. The chapter concludes with ten lessons that civil rights activists and progressive and liberal politicians must learn in order to shift the nation's political mindset.

The remaining chapters each address a specific dimension of the struggle to restore civil rights. In chapter 21, Susan Lerner argues that the extreme Right has pursued its anti-civil rights agenda outside of the public eye by stacking the courts rather than lobbying Congress. Lerner concludes that to halt that trend, political activity must be focused on court appointments. In chapter 22, Joy Moses argues that because the Right's anti-civil rights agenda lacks widespread public support, another first step in reversing the rollback should be to lobby Congress. Many of the rollback cases involve misinterpretations of congressional intent, which can be addressed through new legislation.

While some focus their political energies on fights in Washington, DC, others are engaged in political work closer to home. Indeed, states have provided important forums for successful civil rights work. In chapter 23, Dennis Parker, Bureau Chief for the Civil Rights Bureau in the Office of New York State Attorney General Eliot Spitzer, describes three state civil rights strategies currently being employed in some progressive states: state enforcement of federal civil rights laws, state opposition to efforts to strike down federal laws in the name of states' rights, and state waiver of sovereign immunity (which protects states from lawsuits) in federal civil rights actions.

Grassroots organizing has always been critical to any struggle for social justice. Chapter 24, a compilation of essays by Andrew Friedman, Robert García, Erica Flores Baltodano, Julie Hyman, Brad Williams, and Tracie Crandell, explores grassroots activist strategies by poor people, environmental justice activists, and people with disabilities. These struggles are cause for optimism in an otherwise arid political climate. Chapter 25, by Columbia Law students Lisa Zeidner and Luke Blocher, describes the social theory underlying student activism, and provides as examples the movements supporting affirmative action and the anti-sweatshop movement. Zeidner and Blocher offer specific action items to galvanize student organizing, which is crucial to the national civil rights restoration movement.

Marianne Engelman Lado, General Counsel to the New York Lawyers for the Public Interest and one of the founders of NCRCR, concludes the book by discussing litigation strategies to pursue social justice in the wake of the Federalism Revolution. In chapter 26, Lado examines the historical roles of both the courts and progressive lawyers in the protection of civil rights, concluding that federal courts have played a "crucial but inconsistent role." History teaches us that progressive lawyers must employ flexible strategies such as litigating in state courts, providing technical assistance to community groups, and engaging in creative litigation in federal courts.

We would like to thank Marianne Engelman Lado, NCRCR, New York Law School, Seton Hall University School of Law, and the Open Society Institute, for their generous support of this project, our fantastic copyeditor Penny Austen, and the committee members who solicited and discussed the pieces appearing in this book: Rose Cuison Villazor, Mia Lipsit, Gail Miller, Beth Jacob, and Chris Johnson. Thanks also to Suzanne Leechong for setting up the committee's conference calls. Finally, thanks to our team of researchers and cite checkers: Amanda Kelly, Seton Hall Law '06; Ann Macadangdang, NYLS '05; Mike Merola; Derek Nececkas, Seton Hall Law '06; Jaclyn Okin Barney; and Matthew Smalls, NYLS '04.

This introduction benefited from thoughtful critiques from Michelle Adams, Ellen Chapnick, Jim Freeman, Jim Godsil, Tristin Green, Marianne Engleman Lado, Carlin Meyer, John and Coralee Morgan, Frank Munger, Eva Paterson, Tanina Rostain, Karen Royster, Charlie Sullivan, Jim Walker, Eric Wold, Don Zeigler, and Rebecca Zietlow.

Thanks most of all to our supportive families and to our children, Sylvan Wold and Kate and Rebecca Godsil-Freeman, who remind us daily why this fight is so important.

Denise C. Morgan, Rachel D. Godsil, and Joy Moses
New York City, 2005

Endnotes

1. Martin Luther King, Jr., "I Have a Dream," speech on the steps of the Lincoln Memorial (Aug. 28, 1963).

2. The 1935 National Labor Relations Act (the Wagner Act), the 1935 Social Security Act, the 1938 Fair Labor Standards Act.

3. The civil rights legislation enacted in the 1960s and 1970s included: the 1964 Civil Rights Act (prohibiting race discrimination in public accommodations and by recipients of federal funds, and employment discrimination on the basis of race, color, national origin, sex, or religion), the 1965 Immigration and Nationality Act (abolishing the national origins quotas that restricted Asian immigration), the 1965 Voting Rights Act (prohibiting states from denying or abridging the right to vote), the 1967 Age Discrimination in Employment Act (prohibiting employment discrimination against people age forty and over); the 1968 Fair Housing Act (prohibiting discrimination in the sale and rental of housing), Title IX of the Education Amendments of 1972 (prohibiting sex discrimination in federally funded educational programs), and §504 of the Rehabilitation Act of 1973 (prohibiting discrimination by the federal government against people with disabilities).

4. Denise C. Morgan and Rebecca E. Zietlow, The New Parity Debate: Congress and Rights of Belonging, *73 Cincinnati L. Rev.* (2005) 1347.

5. Id.

6. See, e.g., chapter 1.

7. *Grutter v. Bollinger*, 539 U.S. 306, (2003), *Lawrence v. Texas*, 539 U.S. 558, (2003), *Roper v. Simmons*, 125 S. Ct. 1183 (2005).

8. See chapters 20 and 21 discussing the extreme Right and its efforts to dominate the federal courts.

9. See Erwin Chemerinsky, The Federalism Revolution, *31 N.M. L. Rev.* (2001) 7, 7 (coining the term and describing the "revolution with regard to the structure of the American government because of the Supreme Court decisions in the last few years regarding federalism").

10. See, e.g., Jed Rubenfeld, The Anti-Antidiscrimination Agenda, *111 Yale L.J.* (2002) 1141, 1144 ("some of the Court's federalism cases are not really federalism cases at all... they cannot be intelligently explained or debated in the doctrinal terms in which they present themselves").

11. See Michael J. Klarman, *From Jim Crow to Civil Rights: The Supreme Court and the Struggle for Racial Equality* (2004).

12. See *Lawrence v. Texas*, 539 U.S. 558 (2003), *Goodridge v. Dep't. of Pub. Health*, 440 Mass. 309, 798 N.E. 941 (2003), *Hernandez v. Robles*, 2005 NY Slip Op 25057 2005, NY Misc. LEXIS 248 (NY Sup. Ct. Feb. 4, 2005).

Editor Denise C. Morgan died in the spring of 2006 in Chicago after a long illness. As her leadership role in this volume illustrates, Denise was a leading thinker about how principles of federalism could be shaped to promote or retard human rights. She was also deeply committed to creating an inclusive society in which everyone has an opportunity to flourish. This commitment was reflected in her role as a key litigator in a landmark lawsuit that resulted in New York City public schools receiving billions of dollars in additional state education aid, and in her many scholarly articles exploring equal educational opportunity.

Denise's advocacy and scholarship grew out of her own life experience. The daughter of immigrants from the West Indian island of Montserrat, she was born in Manhattan, grew up in the Bronx and was one of the first African-Americans to graduate from the private, all-girls Chapin School on Manhattan's Upper East Side. Denise graduated from Yale University in 1986 with a B.A. in philosophy and returned to Yale for law school. While in law school, Denise was a founding member of the Yale Journal of Law and Liberation, a student organization dedicated to promoting a progressive vision of the law. During this same period, and soon after law school, she overcame two bouts of cancer.

After graduating from law school in 1990, Denise taught law at Florida State University and clerked for a progressive federal judge, Marilyn Hall Patel, in San Francisco before returning to New York to become an associate at the Manhattan law firm of Cleary Gottlieb Steen & Hamilton. While at her law firm, Denise joined the legal team fighting for equitable education in all New York public schools.

In 1995, Denise joined the faculty of New York Law School, where she was awarded tenure in 2001 and taught until she fell ill. Denise's engagement with civil rights in the world continued. From 1995 to 1997 she served as an adviser to the drafting of Eritrea's constitution. For most of the last decade, she served on the advisory committee of the American Civil Liberties Union Women's Rights Project. Denise was also a leading figure in the National Campaign to Restore Civil Rights.

Along with federalism issues, Denise's legal writing ranged from all-female education to the efforts of Jack Johnson, the first African-American world heavyweight boxing champion, to test America's racial boundaries in the early 1900s.

Denise is survived by her daughter Sylvan, and husband Eric of Manhattan; parents John and Coralee of Bronxville, N.Y., and many, many friends and colleagues in the civil rights community. We hope that this book honors Denise's memory and inspires readers to continue her work.

Awakening from the Dream

Part I
The Rehnquist Court's Federalism Revolution and Civil Rights

CHAPTER 1

WHAT IS FEDERALISM AND WHAT DOES IT HAVE TO DO WITH CIVIL RIGHTS?

Federalism: The Double-Edged Sword of Liberty and Oppression

Paul Finkelman[*]

The term "federalism" refers to the division of power between local entities—the states—and the national government under the Constitution. Federalism has always had a progressive potential; it allowed states to experiment with new ideas and policies that could enhance human freedom. However, throughout American history the Supreme Court's reading of the Constitution has often undermined this progressive potential, especially as it applied to race relations.

Federalism developed because after the American Revolution (in which the colonies fought for their independence from the British monarchy), many leaders in the newly independent states feared a strong central government. At the same time, many other leaders, including some of the major figures at the Constitutional Convention, understood the need for a centralized national power, at least for some governmental action. In creating a "federal republic" under the new Constitution, the framers attempted to balance local needs and interests with national needs and interests.

This chapter explores the relationship between federalism and civil rights from the Founding until the mid-twentieth century. While the Constitution protected slavery from federal regulation, federalism allowed the North to experiment with freedom. Those experiments were ultimately limited by the pro-slavery Constitution, and by a Supreme Court that favored slavery over freedom and supported the subordination of blacks on the national level. The Civil War and the adoption of the Thirteenth, Fourteenth, and Fifteenth

---

[*] Chapman Distinguished Professor of Law, University of Tulsa College of Law.

Amendments to the Constitution expanded the power of Congress to regulate the status of individuals and to protect the civil rights of individuals against state violation. From the 1870s through the 1930s, however, the Court's interpretations of federalism severely limited the power of the federal government to create true racial equality. Indeed, during much of this period the southern states relied on the Court's understanding of federalism to bolster their states' rights claims; this is turn led to a system of de jure segregation and the denial of civil rights. From the 1930s through the 1950s, the Court gradually reevaluated federalism in light of the Reconstruction Amendments (especially the Fourteenth Amendment), and in so doing set the stage for the civil rights revolution of the 1950s and 1960s (discussed in chapter 2).

Under the new system of federalism created in 1787, the Constitution granted Congress exclusive power to regulate some aspects of economic and political life, such as interstate commence or relations with foreign nations and Indian tribes. By creating a government of limited powers, however, the Constitution left many areas of life under state control. Thus, federalism would allow individual states to experiment with social and economic policies while the rest of the nation watched and wondered whether the policies were a good idea. Sometimes the experiments led to wholesale changes in policy at the national level, or to most states adopting the new policies. At other times Americans looked back at state experimentation with embarrassment. The law of personal status offers a good illustration of the changing notions of state experimentation. Fifteen southern states maintained slavery until the Civil War and the Thirteenth Amendment forced them to end the practice. On the other hand, the northern states abolished slavery between 1780 and 1804 through various systems of gradual and immediate abolition. In another example, in the early nineteenth century, Indiana allowed divorces for almost any reason, but then moved away from its system of "no-fault divorce." In 1969, more than a century later, California reintroduced the no-fault divorce, and by 1985 every other state had adopted it in some form.

Under the U.S. federal system, some areas of law such as national defense, foreign relations, and the coining of money have always been entirely in the hands of the federal government, while other areas such as family law, criminal law, and zoning have fallen under state authority.[1] Still other areas that were originally left to the states have come to be shared with the federal government through changing understandings of the Constitution and constitutional amendments. Constitutional history tells the story of the federal and state governments struggling for control of those areas in the middle, where authority is unclear. Different notions of federalism tip the balance of power in favor of one or the other.

For example, voting was originally entirely a state matter. Before the Civil War, some states like Massachusetts and New Hampshire had universal adult male suffrage without regard to race or wealth. New York allowed all property-owning males to vote, without regard to race, and then eliminated the property requirement for whites, but not for blacks, in 1821. Antebellum South Carolina, on the other hand, never allowed blacks or poor whites to vote. After the Civil War, congressional action and three new constitutional amendments led to universal adult male suffrage without regard to race. At the same time, the federalist structure of the nation enabled the states to regulate voter registration, other voter qualifications beyond race, and even how ballots should be cast. This aspect of federalism allowed the South to effectively disfranchise most blacks through literacy tests, poll taxes, and impossibly complex systems for casting ballots. It was only in the 1960s that Congress used its powers under the Fourteenth and Fifteenth Amendments to regulate voting to ensure greater access to the ballot.[2]

Today, the lines between federal and state power have become increasingly blurred. For example, while public education was traditionally the province of the states, federal law has mandated changes to local practices as federal money has poured into local school systems. The "No Child Left Behind" legislation illustrates how education is no longer solely in the hands of local school boards and officials. Similarly, zoning and land development, once the province of the states, are now limited by federal environmental laws. In contrast, the Rehnquist Court has limited the broad authority to regulate interstate commerce that Congress had exercised since the 1930s.[3]

The American founders understood all too well the potential for tensions to arise between local and national concerns. They had just fought a revolution against a centralized empire that, from their perspective, had tried to oppress its settlements. When Tom Paine pointed out the absurdity of an island governing a continent,[4] he indirectly underscored the problem of a central government making rules for a distant province. When the English citizens in North America discovered that they were really *Americans*, they acknowledged that people separated by large distances had different interests and needs.

Americans quickly learned that these tensions were not only an issue for colonies in an Empire situated a great distance from the metropolis. It was also an issue for the newly independent states themselves. The new states had one thing in common: their desire to be rid of British rule. But, they had so much that was not shared. More than 1,200 miles separated Boston, Massachusetts from Savannah, Georgia and the cultural distance was even greater. While most Americans were farmers, the economies of the new states differed sharply, as did religious practices and cultural patterns. Most importantly, they diverged on the issue of race. While slavery was legal in all thirteen states at the beginning of the Revolution, white attitudes about race and bondage differed dramatically between different regions of the country and changed significantly during the War. When George Washington took command of the Continental army in Boston in 1775, he was shocked to see scores of black faces among his troops. By the end of the Revolution, however, Washington would be convinced that blacks deserved freedom; at the end of his life, he would emancipate all of his slaves.[5] Collectively, northerners would take the same route, and within a quarter century after the Revolution slavery was all-but-dead throughout the region.[6] Most southerners did not follow Washington in turning against slavery, and none of the southern states followed the North's lead in abolishing the institution. Instead, slavery expanded rapidly in the South after the War. The conflict over slavery and black rights would help shape the nature of American federalism before the Civil War. In the hundred and forty years since that war ended, conflicts over federalism have often been rooted in the struggle to eliminate racial discrimination and the attempts by states to use federalism to impede the expansion of equality for all Americans.

The Constitution, Federalism, and Slavery

By 1787, the U.S. was becoming, to use Abraham Lincoln's apt phrasing, a nation that was "half slave and half free"[7]—a division that was reflected in the federalism that emerged during the Constitutional Convention. Initially, the delegates seemed certain that the central division within the nation was between large and small states. Certainly, that mattered. Small states opposed representation based on population, insisting on equality in Congress. Ultimately, the Convention provided for population based representation in the House, but equal representation in the Senate—a system that gave small states far greater representation in the national government than they would have otherwise received.

During the heated debates over representation, however, James Madison argued that it was not size that would divide the states. Rather, he argued:

> [T]hat the States were divided into different interests not by their difference of size, but by other circumstances; the most material of which resulted partly from climate, but principally from their having or not having slaves. These two causes concurred in forming the great division of interests in the U. States. It did not lie between the large

and small States: it lay between the Northern and Southern, and if any defensive power were necessary, it ought to be mutually given to these two interests.[8]

Alexander Hamilton made much the same point, although he carefully avoided the issue of slavery. Not surprisingly, he saw the issue solely in economic terms: "The only considerable distinction of interests, lay between the carrying and non-carrying States, which divide instead of uniting the largest States."[9] By "carrying and non-carrying States," Hamilton meant those states involved in international commerce, like Massachusetts, New York, and Pennsylvania, and those states that were more likely to export goods than survive on commercial activities such as Virginia, which exported tobacco, and South Carolina, which exported rice.

In the end, the framers protected the institution of slavery by including a number of provisions in the Constitution:

- The Three-Fifths Clause[10] gave the South extra power in the House of Representatives and the Electoral College by counting slaves for purposes of apportioning congressional representation. This provision did not directly affect the powers of the states or of Congress, and thus can be seen as "neutral" on issues of federalism. It did, however, strengthen the slave states at the expense of the free states.

- The Migration and Importation Clause[11] prohibited Congress from banning the international slave trade before 1808, allowing for the importation of about 100,000 Africans in the two decades before Congress was able to implement the ban. This clause was clearly within the spirit of federalism. It can be understood as a modification of national power and a constitutional tip-of-the-hat to state power—states were free to import or not import slaves, while the federal government was prohibited, for at least twenty years, from regulating this form of international trade. After 1808, Congress was empowered to end the trade, but did not have to do so.

- The Domestic Insurrections Clause[12] also supported federalism by guaranteeing that the national government would suppress slave rebellions only if the states decided that they needed the help.[13]

- The prohibition on export taxes[14] protected slavery from being subject to an indirect tax by prohibiting both the national government and the states from taxing exports (the nation's most important exports were the tobacco and rice produced by slaves). The ban on state export taxes was consistent with other federal powers in that it prevented the states from regulating interstate or international trade through taxation. The ban on federal import taxes, however, was inconsistent with the overall powers of Congress to regulate interstate and international commerce, and can only be understood as a substantial victory for the slave states.

- The Fugitive Slave Clause[15] allowed masters to recover runaway slaves from other states, and prohibited those states from permanently freeing runaway slaves. This provision struck directly at the federalism found in the Constitution because it prevented states from regulating the status of people within their jurisdiction. Until the Constitution was amended in 1865–70, the states were generally free to regulate all aspects of personal status—marriage, divorce, child custody, adoption, apprenticeships, and even whether people were free or slaves. The states could use race, gender, economic status, religion, or nationality to limit or expand rights. The one exception to this was the Fugitive Slave Clause of Constitution which prohibited free states from regulating the status of runaway slaves within their jurisdiction. The clause led to the enactment of the Fugitive Slave Acts,[16] the most intrusive federal laws passed before the Civil War and the first federal laws to provide for national law enforcement at the local level.

Given the many ways that the Constitution protected slavery, it is no wonder that some antebellum abolitionists—mainly followers of William Lloyd Garrison—believed that the Constitution was a "Covenant with Death and an Agreement in Hell."[17] By creating a national government with limited powers, the Constitution protected slavery from federal interference, and, except for in the case of fugitive slaves, allowed the states to regulate slaves and free blacks as they wished. This arrangement would lead to conflicts over the status of slaves and free blacks in the antebellum period, and would raise issues of comity and civil rights in the modern period.

With the exception of the slave trade provision, none of the proslavery clauses enhanced the powers of individual states relative to those of the federal government. In addition, the provisions of Article IV of the Constitution (that required interstate comity) complicated the relationships that individual states had with slavery. The Privileges and Immunities Clause,[18] requiring that the states respect the rights of citizens of other states, created the possibility that slave states would have to recognize the rights of free blacks from other jurisdictions. It also meant that free states might have to recognize the right of slave owners to bring their slaves with them when traveling in the North. Similarly, the Full Faith and Credit Clause[19] meant that states had to enforce the statuses created by the laws and decisions of other states. This meant that if a master brought a slave to a free state, and the courts of that state declared the slave to be free, then the slave state would have to recognize that freedom.

In addition to complicating the status of blacks, the Full Faith and Credit and Privileges and Immunities clauses raised other questions about status and race. By the time of the Civil War, interracial marriages were legal in some northern states (almost all northern states would allow them by 1900). Before the Civil War, the South prohibited those unions; after Reconstruction, all the southern states passed new laws banning interracial marriages. The comity provisions of Article IV might have been used to require states to respect marriages and free status created by state law. Instead, however, the Supreme Court never enforced these provisions to enhance liberty and instead allowed states to apply their own rules. People legally married in one state could therefore be arrested for illegal cohabitation if they entered another state.[20]

The very provisions of the Constitution that were designed to ensure interstate harmony held the seeds of conflict and disharmony. Because of its federal structure, the Constitution provided protection for slavery where it existed while at the same time, except as limited by the Fugitive Slave Clause, allowed the northern states to expand freedom. These different approaches to race and status—to freedom and slavery—led to conflicts between slave states and free states and between free states and the national government. Even as federalism promoted sectional needs and desires, therefore, it had the potential to undermine interstate harmony.

The Constitution of 1787 created a government of limited powers. Before the Civil War, the national government had little power to regulate life at the local level. For slave owners, this was a blessing. Explaining why his fellow South Carolinians should ratify the Constitution, General Charles Cotesworth Pinckney declared:

> We have a security that the general government can never emancipate them [slaves], for no such authority is granted and it is admitted, on all hands, that the general government has no powers but what are expressly granted by the Constitution, and that all rights not expressed were reserved by the several states.[21]

Pinckney's argument was correct: the Constitution did not give the national government the power to regulate any domestic institutions, including slavery. His argument was especially powerful when combined with an understanding of the constitutional amendment process. Under Article V, a constitutional amendment requires support from two-thirds of each house of Congress as well as three-quarters of the states. In 1860, there were fifteen slave states and eighteen free states. It would, therefore, have been impossible to amend the Constitution over the objections of the slave states. This meant that the slave states had a perpetual veto over any amendments dealing with slavery or race. As long as they did not secede from the Union, they could count on their most important social and economic institution being protected.[22]

Federalism, however, is a double-edged sword. While the national government could not interfere with slavery, neither could it intervene when the northern states chose to end slavery, enfranchise free blacks, emancipate visiting slaves and slaves in transit,[23] or allow interracial marriage. Furthermore, the national government was prohibited from requiring state officials to enforce national policy or law. In the late antebellum period, therefore, many free states refused to participate in the return of fugitive slaves. The Supremacy Clause[24] made it impossible for northern states to nullify the federal Fugitive Slave laws,[25] but federalism prevented the national government from commandeering state officials to help with their enforcement.[26]

Exploiting the sovereignty promised by federalism, northern states passed personal liberty laws prohibiting state and local officials from participating in the return of fugitive slaves. Some states barred slave catchers, and even federal marshals, from using state facilities to house alleged slaves awaiting a hearing or while returning fugitives to their owners.[27] At the same time, some northern states gave free blacks full political rights, while others afforded them most other rights.[28] On the eve of the Civil War, blacks could vote in a handful of northern states, practice law in a few, and hold office in Massachusetts, Ohio, and Rhode Island.[29] Just as it allowed for the protection of slavery in the South, federalism also allowed for an expansion of black rights in the North.

Chief Justice Roger B. Taney of the Supreme Court could not, however, accept the symmetry of the federal system. In *Dred Scott v. Sandford*,[30] he held that blacks had no rights under the Constitution, whatever their status in their respective states. While this decision did not prevent free states from treating blacks however they chose, it clarified the limits of federalism: no slave state had to recognize the status of a free black person. The decision did not indicate what would happen if a master brought a slave to a free state, but in his concurring opinion, Justice Samuel Nelson of New York—a proslavery northern Democrat—hinted that the slave owner's rights would be protected:

> A question has been alluded to, on the argument, namely: the right of the master with his slave of transit into or through a free State, on Business or commercial pursuits, or in the exercise of a Federal right, or the discharge of a Federal duty, being a citizen of the United States, which is not before us. This question depends upon different considerations and principles from the one in hand, and turns upon the rights and privileges secured to a common citizen of the republic

under the Constitution of the United States. When that question arises, we shall be prepared to decide it.[31]

In the late 1850s, leaders of the new Republican Party worried about what Abraham Lincoln called "the next *Dred Scott* decision."[32] Lincoln, then the Republican candidate for the U.S. Senate, feared that northerners would "*lie down* pleasantly dreaming that the people of *Missouri* are on the verge of making their state *free*; and we shall awake to the *reality*, instead, that the *Supreme Court* has made *Illinois* a slave state."[33] *Dred Scott*, and the implications of Justice Nelson's concurrence, threatened to turn federalism into a one-way street. The states were free to regulate their domestic institutions, so the South could keep slavery and the North could abolish it. But Nelson's opinion implied that the Supreme Court was prepared to hold that the federal government, or at least the Court, could prevent northern states from protecting their domestic institution of freedom from the encroachment of slavery. If this happened, then southerners who took slavery to the North would be protected in their right of transit. In contrast, if slave hunters seized free black people, claiming they were fugitives, the 1850 Fugitive Slave Law would not allow northern states to intervene to protect their black citizens. Similarly, if free black citizens of northern states ventured into the South, or were mistakenly seized in the North as fugitive slaves and taken to the South, they could not turn to the federal courts to vindicate their liberty. In the 1850s, therefore, slavery was national and freedom was local.

The lawmaking and jurisprudence of the 1850s reflected the original proslavery Constitution. In the decade leading to the Civil War, therefore, proponents of freedom became advocates of states' rights. In *Ableman v. Booth*, the Wisconsin Supreme Court challenged the constitutionality of the Fugitive Slave Law of 1850 and ordered a U.S. marshal, Stephen Ableman, to release the abolitionist Sherman Booth, who had helped a fugitive slave escape federal custody. In the most extreme example of a northern state asserting states' rights in the antebellum decade, the Wisconsin Court defiantly refused the U.S. Supreme Court's demand for the record of the case.[34] The U.S. Supreme Court eventually overturned the Wisconsin Supreme Court's decision.[35] The Court's assertion of federal supremacy in *Ableman* reaffirmed the most important aspect of its holding in *Dred Scott*: northern states did not have the power to protect freedom, and federalism would not trump the proslavery Constitution.

Federalism in Post-Civil War America

The Civil War led to a revolution in federalism and a remaking of the Constitution. General Pinckney had been correct, in 1787, that slavery was secure under the Constitution. However, he could not have predicted the events of 1860–61, when most of the slave states left the Union, thereby abandoning the Constitution that protected their peculiar institution from federal interference. Indeed, by leaving the Union the slave states voluntarily gave up their enormous political power to protect slavery from hostile congressional legislation as well as their ability to veto constitutional amendments that threatened slavery. Thus, it was the secession that created the circumstances that led to an end to slavery.

During the Civil War, the traditional balance of power between the states and the federal government changed—the national government became stronger, and the states, weaker. The nature of federalism then changed as the national government began to regulate the status of people—especially slaves who became former slaves—within the states. In the first and second Confiscation Acts of 1861 and 1862 (which authorized the seizure of confederate property), for example, Congress used its war-making powers to destabilize slavery in the South by declaring that some slaves owned by Confederates were free.[36] Similarly, in the Emancipation Proclamation President Lincoln found power as commander-in-chief to end slavery in most of the South.

One price of defeat in the Civil War for the slave states was that Congress required them to ratify the Thirteenth Amendment in 1865, which ended slavery forever in the U.S. That amendment was followed in 1868 by the Fourteenth Amendment, which made all native-born people citizens of both the nation and the states in which they resided. This amendment reversed the holding in *Dred Scott* that blacks, even if free, could never be citizens of the U.S., even if they were citizens of one of the states. The Fifteenth Amendment was adopted two years later, prohibiting racial discrimination in voting. Not only did the two amendments make former slaves and their descendants citizens with the same right to vote as whites, they also granted the full protection of the Constitution to other non-whites, such as people of Asian ancestry who were born in the U.S.[37]

These three Reconstruction amendments profoundly altered the system of federalism in several ways.[38] First, for the first time in American history, the national government was given the power to regulate the status of people within the states.[39] Second, the amendments gave Congress the power to enforce both freedom and equality within the states. After more than seventy years of proslavery constitutionalism, the federal government would now support freedom, equality, and an end to racial discrimination. Congress exercised its new powers by enacting a number of statutes, including the Civil Rights Acts of 1866 and 1875 (designed to secure freedom and equal citizenship for all Americans) and Enforcement Acts in 1870 and 1871 (designed to protect voting rights by suppressing the Ku Klux Klan and other white terrorist organizations).

In *Blyew v. United States* in 1871,[40] however, the Court began to undermine the promise of the new federalism. John Blyew and his co-defendant, both white men, murdered a black woman in Kentucky. The only witnesses were African Americans, and Kentucky law did not allow blacks to testify against whites. With no chance of a conviction in state court, the U.S. Attorney removed the case to federal court and successfully prosecuted the white men for murder. The federal trial court sentenced the murderers to death. The Supreme Court reversed the convictions, however, asserting that the federal government lacked the power to prosecute a simple murder case under the Civil Rights Act of 1866 or the Fourteenth Amendment. Had the victim been only wounded, the Court explained, she could have brought an action against the men for depriving her of her civil rights under the 1866 Act. Because she was dead, however, there was no cause of action. Justices Joseph Bradley and Noah Swayne dissented, protesting that the majority's reading of the Civil Rights Act and the new amendment was "too narrow, too technical, and too forgetful of the liberal objects [the legislation] had in view."[41] Bradley argued that under the Thirteenth Amendment, the national government had the power to prosecute people who murdered former slaves in racially motivated attacks. Despite the new constitutional amendments, however, the Court reinstated the pre-Civil War understanding of federalism that allowed the states to regulate the lives of their own citizens.

In 1873, in *The Slaughterhouse Cases*[42] the Court dealt another major blow to black civil rights and the promise that the federal government would actively protect its citizens. The *Slaughterhouse* Court undermined the meaning of the Fourteenth Amendment by holding that it did not protect citizens from state violations of most of their fundamental rights. The states were not required, for example, to respect most of the rights guaranteed by the federal Bill of Rights. Justice Samuel Miller, who wrote the opinion, asked rhetorically, "Was it the purpose of the fourteenth amendment…to transfer the security and protection of all the civil rights which we have mentioned from the States to the Federal government?" He similarly wondered: "Was it [the Fourteenth Amendment] intended to bring within the power of Congress the entire domain of civil rights heretofore belonging exclusively to the States?" His answer was no. The *Slaughterhouse* Court held that states, not the national government, were to protect most civil and political rights and fundamental civil liberties. The

Court rejected the understanding held by many Republicans that the Civil War and the Reconstruction amendments had fundamentally changed the government by nationalizing both liberty and freedom. As a result of *Slaughterhouse*, the states were empowered to define—and undermine—the civil rights and liberties of their citizens.[43] For blacks, this was the beginning of the end of the hope that the Civil War would lead not only to freedom, but to equality.

Subsequent cases confirmed that the balance of power had shifted dramatically back to the states. In *United States v. Reese* in 1876,[44] the Court struck down the Enforcement Act of 1870 that was designed to implement the Fifteenth Amendment by criminalizing private interference with the right to vote. In *United States v. Cruickshank* in 1876,[45] the Court prevented the federal prosecution of whites who participated in the Colfax massacre in Louisiana in which more than one hundred blacks had died when they tried to hold a public meeting to discuss political issues. The Court's message was clear: except under very narrow circumstances, the federal government would not be permitted to protect the lives or liberties of blacks. Southern blacks would have to rely on state governments to protect their civil rights and liberties—and their lives—if they tried to exercise political rights. By this time, however, the governments of the southern states were almost entirely run by whites largely opposed to blacks having any political or civil rights. Despite the Reconstruction amendments, therefore, pre-Civil War federalism was now largely restored, and the South was free to persecute the same blacks that had once been enslaved.

Ironically, the Court occasionally interfered with states' rights in instances where the southern states used their autonomy to promote equality. In 1878, *Hall v. DeCuir* involved a Louisiana law prohibiting segregation in public transportation.[46] Louisiana had adopted this law when the state was under the control of an integrated Republican Party. The Court struck down the law on the grounds that a ban on segregation interfered with interstate commerce. In the antebellum period, the Court had allowed the states great latitude in regulating local commerce under the "police powers doctrine." The Court had developed this doctrine, in part, to protect the slave states from an influx of free blacks and to ensure that slave states could regulate any black in their jurisdiction.[47] The *Hall* Court ignored this jurisprudence, striking a blow at integration and black civil rights.

In the 1890s, however, the Court upheld state statutes requiring segregation in *Louisville, New Orleans, and Texas Pacific Railroad v. Mississippi*[48] and *Plessy v. Ferguson*.[49] Once again, federalism seemed like a one-way street, at least in the South where segregation was rapidly becoming the rule. State laws that discriminated against blacks were permitted as valid exercises of the "police powers" implicit in federalism, but state laws prohibiting segregation were struck down.

The Reconstruction amendments occasionally trumped the pre-Civil War understanding of federalism, but only when the discrimination was so blatant that the Court could not avoid acting. In *Strauder v. West Virginia* in 1880,[50] for example, the Court struck down a West Virginia law that prohibited blacks from serving on juries. In *Ex parte Virginia and J.D. Coles*,[51] also decided in 1880, the Court upheld the prosecution of a state judge who had excluded all blacks from serving on the jury in his court. Similarly, in *Neal v. Delaware* in 1881,[52] the Court overturned a conviction because no blacks had ever sat on a jury in Delaware.

These three cases had the potential to revolutionize southern justice and undermine per-Civil War federalism by requiring the states to accept racial equality and civil rights. Unfortunately, this did not happen. The cases were generally ignored and did not reverse the trend against black rights. *Virginia v. Rives* in 1880[53] was a more representative case. Here the Court held that black defendants had no right to expect to have members of their race on a jury, and thus all-white juries did not violate the Constitution as long as Virginia did not explicitly prohibit blacks from serving on juries.

Meanwhile, in *Pace v. Alabama* in 1883,[54] the Court upheld an Alabama law that criminalized interracial marriages. The Court refused to apply the Fourteenth Amendment to protect blacks and whites who married each other. Once again, the states were free to regulate the lives and statuses of those in their jurisdiction. At the same time that the Court decided *Pace*, a number of northern states repealed their anti-miscegenation laws. These repeals, like the personal liberty laws of the pre-Civil War era, illustrated the double-edged aspect of federalism. The Court never had occasion to decide whether southern states had to recognize an interracial marriage that was valid in the northern state where it had taken place. Had it heard such a case, it is likely that the Court would have refused to interfere with the right of the southern states to accept interracial couples and would not have forced the southern states to give full faith and credit to interracial marriages legally performed in other states. Indeed, it was not until *Loving v. Virginia* in 1967[55] that the Court finally concluded that the Fourteenth Amendment protects the right of mixed race couples to marry.

The Court also reaffirmed its support for pre-Civil War federalism in *United States v. Harris*.[56] This case, decided in 1883, involved the federal prosecution of twenty whites who had broken into a jail, beat three black prisoners, and murdered a fourth. Under the old federalism, states had handled most criminal law (unless it involved the violation of specific federal statutes such as the Fugitive Slave laws or laws prohibiting counterfeiting).[57] Despite the Recon-

struction amendments, however, the Court refused to allow the federal government to protect the civil rights of blacks by prosecuting white terrorists.
Relying on antebellum notions of federalism, the Court decided that the protection of civil rights belonged to the states. Justice John Marshall Harlan, a
southerner, vigorously dissented, but to no avail. Justice Harlan also dissented
later that year in the *Civil Rights Cases*,[58] when the Court struck down the Civil
Rights Act of 1875 on the grounds that Congress did not have the power to
prohibit private racial discrimination. Blacks throughout the nation protested
the decision, which some believed was as bad as *Dred Scott*, because it left
them without federal protection from private discrimination. Their protests,
however, were useless. Pre-Civil War federalism had been restored. The states,
not the federal government, would have the power to regulate civil rights.

In 1884, the Court offered one last crumb to blacks. In *Ex parte Yarborough*,[59] also known as the *Ku Klux Klan Cases*, the Court upheld the prosecutions of Jasper Yarborough and other Klansmen who had beaten a former slave
in Georgia to prevent him from voting in a congressional election. The Court
reasoned that the Fifteenth Amendment gave Congress the power to protect
voters from private, as well as state, action. However, the Court would abandon this position two decades later in *James v. Bowman*.[60]

The last decade of the century signaled an end to any remaining hope of
federal civil rights protection coming from the Supreme Court. In *Louisville,
New Orleans, and Texas Pacific Railroad v. Mississippi* in 1890,[61] the Court upheld Mississippi's right to require segregation in trains that traveled between
the states. In *Hall v. DeCuir* the Court had previously denied the right of states
to require integration in interstate transportation on the grounds that such a
law placed a burden on interstate commerce.[62] But now, caving in to the whims
and desires of the deep South, the Court bent its rules to accommodate racism
and accepted Mississippi's claim that its laws only affected trains once they entered the state. Although the state's assertion was true as far as it went, Mississippi's segregation statute nevertheless meant that railroads operating between states had to add separate "colored cars" or had to move black passengers
from the "white cars" when entering Mississippi. *Louisville, New Orleans, and
Texas Pacific Railroad* set the stage for a fully segregated South—and in 1896,
the Court gave racial segregation its blessing in *Plessy v. Ferguson*.

During the last three decades of the nineteenth century, the Court eviscerated the Reconstruction Amendments and, in the southern states, left the fate
of the children of slaves in the hands of the children of the masters. Meanwhile, federalism allowed northern states to protect civil rights. The result was

a stunning change as northern states began to actively protect civil rights within their jurisdiction.

In the last two decades of the nineteenth century, most northern states passed civil rights laws to protect blacks from discrimination. Many of these laws contained significant penalties for violations. Pennsylvania's law of 1887, for example, carried a fine of fifty to one hundred dollars[63] for denying equal access to public transportation, theaters, hotels, restaurants, concerts, "or place[s] of entertainment or amusement."[64] New York and New Jersey passed similar laws rejecting the separate but equal rule for public accommodations.[65] New Jersey's act of 1884[66] carried substantial fines of five hundred to one thousand dollars,[67] provided the complaining witness the right to pursue a private action of debt for up to five hundred dollars,[68] and provided for the possibility of jailing offenders for up to one year.[69] In addition to civil rights, the law protected the right to serve on a jury, providing a fine of up to five thousand dollars for any official who refused to call a black person for jury service. In *Miller v. Stamppul,*[70] the New Jersey Supreme Court upheld the imposition of a five hundred dollar fine against a theater owner who refused to admit blacks on the same basis as whites.[71]

Similarly, legal change in Ohio illustrates the profound difference between the North and the South at the end of the century. It also shows how federalism allowed northern states to expand civil rights even while the Supreme Court denied that power to the national government and gave its blessings to southern states which denied civil rights to blacks. In 1884, Ohio adopted a new civil rights law, declaring that all its citizens were "equal before the law" and that such a status was "essential to just government."[72] The statute prohibited private businesses from discriminating, specifically prohibiting discrimination in all "inns, public conveyances on land or water, theaters and other places of public amusement."[73] A second act passed later that year amended the law to include "inns, restaurants, eating-houses, and barber-shops, and all other places of public accommodation and amusement."[74] Three years later, Ohio repealed its last remaining anti-black laws.[75] In 1894, Ohio strengthened its laws, raising the maximum fines for a violation of the civil rights laws from one to five hundred dollars, raised the maximum jail time from thirty to ninety days, and most importantly, provided for the first time a statutory minimum for violators of fifty dollars or thirty days in jail.[76] In 1896, the same year the Court decided *Plessy,* Ohio passed a tough anti-lynching law[77] that historian David Gerber describes as "the most comprehensive measure against mob violence anywhere up to that time."[78]

Other Midwestern states also passed various civil rights laws legalizing interracial marriage, guaranteeing blacks equal access to public accommodations and other facilities, and requiring that insurance companies charge the same premiums for blacks and whites. In 1883, the year the Court upheld Alabama's law prohibiting interracial marriage, Michigan passed a law allowing such marriages. The year before the Court upheld segregation in *Plessy*, Wisconsin passed a law "to protect all citizens in their civil and legal rights."[79]

Northern states used state autonomy to protect civil rights just as the South used that authority to oppress blacks. Sadly, the majority of the Court did not accept the idea that the Reconstruction amendments had destroyed the pre-Civil War system of federalism that allowed the states to violate the basic civil rights of their citizens.

From the 1870s to the 1930s, the Court continued to seem oblivious to the intent and purpose behind the Reconstruction amendments. The Court acknowledged that those amendments ended all forms of slavery and peonage and prohibited the states from formally denying blacks the right to testify in court, serve on juries, and vote. However, the Court narrowly interpreted the Fourteenth Amendment to prohibit state action, and thus would not allow Congress to intervene to protect blacks from private discrimination or violence by white terrorist organizations such as the Ku Klux Klan. In addition, if states used literacy tests, poll taxes, or other methods not explicitly race-based to stop blacks from voting, the Court did not interfere.[80] The Court allowed the southern states to segregate blacks, and even to force private parties to practice segregation.[81] Under the "separate but equal" doctrine, the Court turned a blind eye to the fact that everything in the South was separate and very unequal. Southern blacks—almost ninety percent of the black U.S. population—faced an entirely segregated and unequal world. While federalism allowed the northern states to implement equality, integrate schools, and permit interracial marriage within their own jurisdictions, segregation and racism remained the rule at the national level just as slavery had been the rule before 1861.

Toward a New Federalism

The Court slowly began to change its jurisprudence in the second decade of the twentieth century. In *Guinn v. United States*,[82] the Court struck down Oklahoma's blatantly racist grandfather clause, which required that everyone take a literacy test to vote unless their grandfathers could have voted in the U.S. before the Civil War. This of course excluded African Americans, because most of their grandfathers had been slaves before the Civil War. Similarly, in 1917, the Court struck down local legislation prohibiting whites and blacks from buying homes in certain neighborhoods.[83] The Court reached this decision through its understanding of the rights of property owners, however, not through the application of the Fourteenth Amendment.

Beginning in 1937, the Court upheld New Deal legislation allowing the federal government to regulate virtually every aspect of the U.S. economy, including manufacturing, local economic activity, and labor relations, which under earlier jurisprudence the Court had said were issues to be regulated by the states. This set the stage for a revolution in federalism, as Congress could now regulate almost anything that affected the national economy, even where the connection to the national economy was minimal. A quarter of a century later, Congress would apply the logic of this jurisprudence to the Civil Rights Act of 1964, which banned discrimination in public accommodations including restaurants, hotels, and transportation, on the grounds that such discrimination harmed interstate commerce. The Court would uphold this act in *Katzenbach v. McClung*,[84] even though it applied to a barbeque restaurant that had few out-of-state customers and whose only real involvement with interstate commerce was its purchase of meat and ketchup produced in other states.

From the 1930s through the 1950s, the Court often sided with black plaintiffs who challenged segregation when the southern states did not provide "separate" institutions. Thus, the Court ordered some southern states to integrate a few graduate and professional schools when there were no similar schools for blacks.[85] Finally, the Court struck a blow at segregation itself in *Brown v. Board of Education* in 1954.[86] Within a relatively short fourteen year period, the Court would strike down all forms of state-mandated segregation, and Congress would pass three major civil rights acts undermining traditional notions of federalism and states' rights. It was a full century after the Civil War amendments had remade the Constitution, therefore, that Congress and the Court finally began to implement them. In the process, the old federalism finally died. The new federalism allowed the national government to dictate the rules of race relations.

Conclusion

The Court's recent decisions trimming the power of Congress to regulate some aspects of American life have strong implications for civil rights. The Justices might believe that the states need to be stronger to preserve local control. A number of Justices—sometimes a majority—accept a view of federalism that delegates more power to the states. This is an ominous trend given that, for most of our nation's history, local control has been associated with states' rights claims that have been intimately tied to slavery, racism, and segregation. It is possible to have federalism and local control without sacrificing civil rights. Finding a way to do so may be the challenge for lawyers and jurists in the twenty-first century.

Endnotes

1. One exception to these rules concerns areas that have been under federal control, and thus the national government was forced to act like a state or municipal government. These include the District of Columbia, Indian reservations, military bases, and federal territories.

2. States have retained enormous powers in regulating the act of voting; some states, therefore, have greater voter participation than others. This state regulation of voting, even where limited by the federal Voting Rights Act, has also led to persistent complaints of attempts by state officials to suppress the political power of minorities by making it difficult for them to register or vote, or by creating political districts that lessen the impact of minority voters in congressional, state, and local elections.

3. *United States v. Lopez*, 514 U.S. 549 (1995), striking down the Gun-Free School Zones Act as not having anything to do with interstate commerce; *United States v. Morrison*, 529 U.S. 598 (2000), striking down portions of the Violence Against Women Act as not being germane to interstate commerce.

4. Tom Paine, *Common Sense* (1776).

5. On Washington's views on slavery see Paul Finkelman, *Slavery and the Founders: Race and Liberty in the Age of Jefferson*, 2nd ed., M.E. Sharpe (2001) and Henry Wiencek, *An Imperfect God: George Washington, His Slaves, and the Creation of America*, Farrar, Straus, Giroux (2003).

6. See generally, Arthur Zilversmit, *The First Emancipation: The Abolition of Slavery in the North*, University of Chicago Press (1967); Paul Finkelman, *An Imperfect Union: Slavery, Federalism, and Comity*, University of North Carolina Press (1981).

7. Abraham Lincoln, Speech at Springfield, Illinois (June 16, 1858), in 3 *The Collected Works of Abraham Lincoln*, Roy P. Basler ed. (1953) at 461–62.

8. Max Farrand, *The Records of the Federal Convention of 1787*, rev. ed., Yale University Press (1966) 1: 486–87.

9. Id. at 466.

10. U.S. CONST. art. I, §2, cl. 3.

11. U.S. CONST. art. 1, §9, cl. 1.

12. U.S. CONST. art. I, §8, cl. 15.

13. Federal troops helped suppress Nat Turner's Rebellion and John Brown's raid.

14. U.S. CONST. art. I, §§9, cl. 5 & 10, cl. 2.

15. U.S. CONST. art. IV, §2, cl. 3.

16. Fugitive Slave Act of 1793, 1 Stat. at L. 305; Fugitive Slave Act of 1850, 9 Stat. at L. 462.

17. On the proslavery Constitution, see generally Finkelman, *Slavery and the Founders*, and William M. Wiecek, *The Sources of Antislavery Constitutionalism in America, 1760–1848*, Cornell University Press (1977). See also Paul Finkelman, The Proslavery Origins of the Electoral College, *23 Cardozo L. Rev.* (2002) 1145–57; Paul Finkelman, The Founders and Slavery: Little Ventured, Little Gained, *13 Yale J.L. & Humanities* (2001) 413–49.

18. U.S. CONST. art. IV, §2, cl. 1.

19. U.S. Const. art. IV, §1.

20. The Supreme Court would strike down these laws in *Loving v. Virginia*, 388 U.S. 1 (1967). See also Peter Wallennstein, *Tell the Court I Love My Wife: Race, Marriage and Law—An American History*, Palgrave (2002).

21. Jonathan Elliot, *The Debates in the Several State Conventions on the Adoption of the Federal Constitution*, 5 vols., Burt Franklin (1987, reprint of 1888 ed.) 4:286.

22. With fifteen slave states it would have taken forty-five free states to amend the Constitution to end slavery.

23. The Supreme Court could have decided that under the Commerce Clause free states could not emancipate slaves brought within their jurisdiction by travelers or visitors. Justice Nelson hinted at this in his concurring opinion in *Dred Scott v. Sandford*, 60 U.S. 393 (1857).

24. U.S. Const. art. VI, cl. 2.

25. See *Ableman v. Booth*, 62 U.S. 506 (1859).

26. See *Prigg v. Pennsylvania*, 41 U.S. 539 (1842). The same is true today: *Printz v. United States*, 521 U.S. 898 (1997). For a discussion of these issues, see Paul Finkelman, The Roots of Printz: Proslavery Constitutionalism, National Law Enforcement, Federalism, and Local Cooperation, 69 *Brooklyn L. Rev.* (2004) 1399.

27. See Thomas D. Morris, *Free Men All: The Personal Liberty Laws of the North, 1780–1861*, Johns Hopkins University Press (1974) 114, 118.

28. For a discussion of black rights in the antebellum North, see Paul Finkelman, Prelude to the Fourteenth Amendment: Black Legal Rights in the Antebellum North, 17 *Rutgers L.J.* (1986) 415–82.

29. Id. On blacks as lawyers see Paul Finkelman, Not Only the Judges Robes Were Black, 47 *Stan. L. Rev.* (1994) 161–290.

30. 60 U.S. 393 (1857).

31. Id. at 468–69. For a more elaborate discussion of this issue, see Finkelman, *An Imperfect Union*, 313–38.

32. Abraham Lincoln, "House Divided Speech," Basler, ed., *Works of Lincoln*, 464–67. For a more elaborate discussion of this fear, see Finkelman, *An Imperfect Union*, 313–38.

33. Id.

34. *Ableman*, 62 U.S. at 510–13.

35. Id.

36. Confiscation Act of 1861, 12 Stat. at L. 255; Confiscation Act of 1862, 12 Stat. at L. 589.

37. Because of the Fourteenth Amendment, American-born children of aliens, even illegal aliens, are citizens of the U.S. and of the states in which they reside.

38. U.S. Const. amend. XIII, XIV, & XV.

39. The one major exception to this in the antebellum period was the status of fugitive slaves. Under the Fugitive Slave Clause of the Constitution, states were prohibited from emancipating runaway slaves, and were required to return them to their owners. Congress enforced this provision with statutes in 1793 and 1850.

40. 80 U.S. 581 (1871).

41. 40 Id. at 599 (Bradley, J. dissenting).

42. 83 U.S. 36 (1873).

43. Ironically, had the *Slaughterhouse* Court followed precedent from the pre-Civil War era, it would have come to a much different result. In *Prigg v. Pennsylvania*, 41 U.S. 539 (1842), the Supreme Court had upheld the Fugitive Slave Law of 1793 and denied the right

of free states to protect black citizens from being kidnapped as fugitive slaves. The *Prigg* Court reasoned that the Fugitive Slave Clause gave southerners a federal right to recover runaway slaves. Justice Story's opinion concluded that Congress had the power to enforce this right with appropriate legislation, and that in the absence of such legislation the Court was prepared to protect the rights of slave owners. Had the *Slaughterhouse* Court been similarly willing to protect fundamental federal rights, it could have relied on *Prigg* to support its analysis. The Justices would have seen that Congress and the Court had an obligation, under the new amendments, to protect civil rights, just as under the antebellum proslavery Constitution, it had an obligation to protect the rights of slave owners.

44. 92 U.S. 214 (1876).

45. 92 U.S. 542 (1876).

46. 95 U.S. 485 (1878).

47. Paul Finkelman, Teaching Slavery in American Constitutional Law, 34 *Akron L. Rev.* (2000) 261–82.

48. 133 U.S. 587 (1890).

49. 163 U.S. 537 (1896).

50. 100 U.S. 303 (1880).

51. 100 U.S. 339 (1880).

52. 103 U.S. 370 (1881).

53. 100 U.S. 313 (1880).

54. 106 U.S. 583 (1883).

55. 388 U.S. 1 (1967).

56. 106 U.S. 629 (1883).

57. Federal laws passed in 1807 and 1819 also made it a felony, punishable by death, to engage in the African slave trade; it was not until the Lincoln administration, however, that the federal government vigorously enforced this law. See *Ex parte Gordon*, 66 U.S. 503 (1861). As noted elsewhere in this chapter, where the federal government had municipal jurisdiction, such as in the District of Columbia, Congress had the power to regulate all those activities usually associated with the states, such as marriage, divorce, criminal law, zoning, and matters involving contract, torts, and real property.

58. 109 U.S. 3 (1883).

59. 110 U.S. 651 (1884)

60. 190 U.S. 127 (1903).

61. *Louisville, New Orleans, & Texas Railway Co*, 133 U.S. at 592.

62. *Hall*, 95 U.S. at 488–89.

63. While this amount seems small today, a hundred dollar fine was substantial for the 1880s. Determining the value of money over time is complicated, but there are a number of ways of calculating the value of one hundred dollars in 1887. Under an "inflation" measure, one hundred dollars was equal to the buying power of almost $2,000 today. Economic History Services "What is Its Relative Value in US Dollars", at http://eh.net/hmit/compare/, finds that as a factor of inflation, a "basket of goods" that cost one hundred dollars in 1887 would cost $1,930 today. Relative to unskilled wages, however, one hundred dollars in 1887 would be worth $11,300 today. Furthermore, relative to the per capita Gross Domestic Product (GDP), one hundred dollars in 1887 would be worth $17,600 today. These disparities illustrate how much more workers make today, relative to the cost of goods, than in 1887.

64. "An Act to Provide Civil Rights For all People, Regardless of Race or Color," Act of 1887, ch. 130, 1887 Pa. Laws 130.

65. See David McBride, Mid-Atlantic State Courts and the Struggle With the "Separate but Equal" Doctrine: 1880–1939, *17 Rutgers L.J.* (1986) 569.

66. "An Act To Protect All Citizens In Their Civil And Legal Rights," 1884 NJ Laws 339 (Chap. CCXIX).

67. This was equivalent to the buying power of between $9,000 and $18,000 today. Economic History Services, *supra* note 62. Relative to unskilled wages, $1000 in 1884 would be worth $57,800 today. Relative to the per capita Gross Domestic Product (GDP), $1000 in 1884 would be worth $87,000 today.

68. "An act to protect all citizens in their civil and legal rights," 1884 NJ Laws 2191. See also McBride, *supra* note 64 at 584–85.

69. Id.

70. 83 NJ Laws 278, 84 A. 201 (NJ Sup. Ct. 1912).

71. For a more detailed discussion of these and similar cases, see Paul Finkelman, Civil Rights in Historical Context: In Defense of Brown, *118 Harv. L. Rev.* (2005) 973.

72. An Act To Protect All Citizens In Their Civil And Legal Rights, Act of February 7, 1884, *81 Laws of Ohio* (1884) 15); See also David A. Gerber, *Black Ohio and the Color Line, 1860–1915,* Univ. of Illinois Press (1976) 46.

73. Id. at § 1.

74. "An Act To Amend Section 1 Of An Act 'To Protect All Citizens In Their Civil And Legal Rights,'" Act of March 27, 1884, *81 Laws of Ohio* (1884) 90.

75. Gerber, *Black Ohio, supra* note 71, 241–42.

76. An act to amend sections 2 and 3 of an act entitled, "An Act To Protect All Citizens In Their Civil And Legal Rights, passed February 7, 1884 and was amended March 27, 1884," Act of Feb. 7, 1894, *Laws of Ohio* (1894).

77. An act for the suppression of Mob Violence, 92 *Laws of Ohio* (1896) 136.

78. Gerber, *Black Ohio, supra* note 71, at 252. See also David A. Gerber, Lynching and Law and Order: The Origin and Passage of the Ohio Anti-Lynching Law of 1896, *83 Ohio Hist.* (1974) 33.

79. Act of April 13, 1895, *Wisconsin Laws*, 1895.

80. *Williams v. Mississippi,* 170 U.S. 213 (1898), holding that blacks were not denied fair trials just because no blacks were in jury pools, because jury service was tied to voting, which was limited by poll taxes and literacy tests. Because the poll taxes and literacy tests were race neutral, the Court found no constitutional violation. In *Guinn v. United States,* 238 U.S. 347 (1915), the Court struck down Oklahoma's "grandfather clause" which allowed people to vote without passing a literacy test if their grandfathers had been able to vote in 1867. The Court concluded that this was in fact a racial barrier, because blacks could not vote at that time. However, disfranchisement was still possible through the literacy tests and poll taxes allowed in *Williams.*

81. In *Berea College v. Kentucky,* 211 U.S. 45 (1908), the Court upheld a Kentucky law that prohibited a private college from integrating its classrooms.

82. *Guinn v. United States,* 238 U.S. 347 (1915).

83. *Buchanan v. Warley,* 245 U.S. 60 (1917), striking down a Louisville, Kentucky ordinance that prohibited blacks from buying houses on streets where a majority of the residents were white, and whites from buying houses where a majority of the residents were black.

84. *Katzenbach v. McClung,* 379 U.S. 294 (1964).

85. See *Missouri ex rel. Gaines v. Canada,* 305 U.S. 337 (1938); *Sipuel v. Bd. of Regents,* 332 U.S. 631 (1948); *Sweatt v. Painter,* 339 U.S. 629 (1950); *McLaurin v. Okla. State Re-*

gents for Higher Educ., 339 U.S. 637 (1950). See also, *Henderson v. United States*, 339 U.S. 816 (1950) (holding that a railroad could not segregate passengers in eating cars because it denies blacks equal service).

    86. 347 U.S. 483 (1954).

CHAPTER 2

THE NATIONAL CAMPAIGN TO RESTORE CIVIL RIGHTS CONFERENCE INTRODUCTION

Reversing the Retreat on Civil Rights

Wade Henderson and Janell Byrd-Chichester[*]

The National Campaign to Restore Civil Rights (NCRCR) Conference marks an important milestone in our fight to counter the increasingly conservative federal courts' attempts to radically restructure constitutional principles, dismantle civil rights laws, and undermine democracy. The Conference brings together a large number of people and organizations for discussion, education, strategizing, and activism. Our collaboration will help people understand what is at stake, which is essential in mounting an effective response to what is now being described as the "conservative constitutional counter-revolution."[1]

What is happening in the federal courts and Congress can and will be reversed provided that real changes occur in the political climate. These changes will only come about when Americans—blacks, whites, Native Americans, Asian Americans, Hispanics, Jews, Muslims, Christians, gays and lesbians, workers, immigrants, the disabled, the aged, youth, women, and men—learn about the degradation of our individual rights and take action.

What I would like to do is provide an overview of the development of civil rights laws, explain how many advances in civil rights have been lost or undermined through governmental action strongly influenced by the conserva-

---

[*] Wade J. Henderson, Executive Director, Leadership Conference on Civil Rights, delivered these opening remarks for the NCRCR Conference, held at Columbia University Law School in New York City on October 4, 2002. The remarks were prepared with assistance from Janell Byrd-Chichester, a civil rights attorney in Washington, DC, and have been edited for publication.

tive right, and suggest strategies for overcoming the retrenchment of our civil rights.

The Development of a National Civil Rights Legal Infrastructure

During the history of the United States, there have been periods when the nation made real progress toward fulfilling the promises of the Constitution and the Declaration of Independence by enacting civil rights laws to protect those harmed by discrimination and to bring into the mainstream those left at the margins of society. In the aftermath of the Civil War and the adoption of the Thirteenth (1866), Fourteenth (1868), and Fifteenth Amendments (1870) to the Constitution, Congress enacted laws to provide former slaves with full rights as citizens. These Reconstruction era laws—the Civil Rights Acts of 1866, 1870, 1871, and 1875[2]—and constitutional amendments provided a foundation for much of the nation's civil rights legal structure.

Many of these laws, however, were quickly limited or invalidated by a hostile Supreme Court. As early as 1873, in the *Slaughter-House Cases*,[3] the Court effectively nullified the Fourteenth Amendment's fundamental promise that "no state shall make or enforce any law which shall abridge the privileges or immunities of citizens of the United States." Throughout the late nineteenth century, the Court repeatedly adopted narrow and regressive interpretations of civil rights laws.[4] Most notably, in *Plessy v. Ferguson* in 1896,[5] the Court locked in America's racial caste system by upholding the so-called separate-but-equal doctrine. In *Cumming v. Board of Education of Richmond County* in 1899,[6] the Court refused a demand for equal schools where racial segregation had left black students with no schools at all. In *Lochner v. New York* in 1905[7] and *Carter v. Carter Coal Company* in the 1930s,[8] the Court restricted the power of Congress to protect workers' rights through labor laws. These decisions and others had substantial and harmful effects for a significant portion of the twentieth century.

Indeed, it wasn't until the 1940s and 1950s, when the growing Civil Rights Movement highlighted the contrast between our efforts to address human rights violations by fighting Nazism and fascism abroad and the racial segregation existing under law in the U.S., that the nation began to adopt more progressive positions.

The Movement began to gain traction in the courts in the late 1940s.[9] With the 1954 groundbreaking decision in *Brown v. Board of Education*,[10] the Movement compelled change not only in the courts, but in Congress and the executive branch. Beginning in the mid-1960s, Congress created a civil rights legal framework by enacting a series of statutes. These statutes included:

- Equal Pay Act of 1963[11]
- Civil Rights Act of 1964 (establishing protections from discrimination in public accommodations and employment, and barring discrimination in federally-funded programs on the basis of race, sex, and national origin)[12]
- Voting Rights Act of 1965[13]
- Age Discrimination in Employment Act (ADEA) of 1967[14]
- Fair Housing Act of 1968[15]
- Title IX of the Education Amendments of 1972 (prohibiting gender discrimination in education)[16]
- The 1972 expansion of the 1964 Civil Rights Act's employment provisions to state actors[17]
- Rehabilitation Act of 1973 (providing protections for people with disabilities)[18]
- Age Discrimination Act of 1975[19]
- Amendments to the Voting Rights Act in 1975 (adding protections for language minorities)[20]
- Civil Rights Attorney's Fees Act of 1976[21]
- Americans with Disabilities Act (ADA) of 1990[22]

Despite these tremendous advancements, significant gaps still exist in our civil rights legal infrastructure—including the absence of protections against discrimination on the basis of sexual orientation. Nonetheless, the passage of these laws was a "revolutionary" exercise in democracy that began to open the nation's political, economic, and social structures to all.

Having created a civil rights legal framework, Congress recognized the futility of creating those rights without providing individuals with a means to enforce them. Congress recognized that exclusive reliance on the federal government for enforcement would fail because of the lack of resources and political will. The Civil Rights Attorney's Fees Act of 1976 reflects the understanding that the enforcement of civil rights laws depends upon private efforts.[23] The existence of "private attorneys general"[24] enables individuals to enforce their civil rights in court, advance compliance nationally, and pursue equal treatment for all.[25]

Transition and Struggle:
A Shifting Commitment to Civil Rights

During the 1970s, the nation struggled over the future direction of civil rights. The composition of the Supreme Court underwent a major change in 1969 when Warren Burger took over from the more liberal Earl Warren as Chief Justice; in 1972, the Court moved further to the right when staunch conservative William Rehnquist joined the bench.

The transformative effects of these changes are reflected in the Court's decisions. Several key decisions during this period significantly advanced civil rights. In *Griggs v. Duke Power* in 1971,[26] the Court recognized that employment practices that had the "effect" of preventing African Americans from advancing in the workplace and that could not be justified by a legitimate business purpose constituted discrimination under Title VII of the Civil Rights Act of 1964. This ruling was critical to challenging discrimination because the requirement of proving subjective "intent" to discriminate posed an increasingly high bar for most plaintiffs to reach, especially as societal changes caused discrimination to become less overt. In *Cannon v. University of Chicago* in 1979,[27] the Court recognized that individuals had the right to bring suits for the violation of rights protected under Title IX of the Education Amendments of 1972 (barring sex discrimination) and Title VI of the Civil Rights Act of 1964 (barring discrimination on the basis of race or national origin).

The Court also continued to show deference to congressional power to enforce civil rights. In *Fullilove v. Klutznick* in 1980,[28] for example, the Court acknowledged congressional power under the Fourteenth Amendment to enact remedial civil rights legislation, and respected Congress's determination of the need for affirmative action programs in federal government contracting.[29]

Other decisions during this period, however, showed that the Court had begun to limit rights that it had previously recognized, restrict broader interpretations of those rights, and narrow available remedies. In *San Antonio v. Rodriguez* in 1973, for example, the Court held that there was no fundamental right to education.[30] Thus, gross inequities in educational funding systems based on local property taxes did not violate the Constitution. Similarly, in *Milliken v. Bradley* in 1974,[31] the Court stopped school desegregation efforts at the Detroit city lines by requiring that African American children provide proof of intent to segregate by the suburban school districts before a metropolitan area-wide desegregation remedy could be imposed. By protecting "white flight" from legal challenge, this decision facilitated the entrenchment of the white suburban rings around black and brown city cen-

ters that had begun decades before with overtly discriminatory housing po-
lices, and had continued with the policies and practices of public and private officials.

The Supreme Court had previously endorsed the broad recognition of private rights of action to enforce laws adopted by Congress. That approach was
abandoned in *Cort v. Ash* in 1975.[32] In *Washington v. Davis* in 1976,[33] the Court
restricted the reach of the Equal Protection Clause of the Fourteenth Amendment by limiting its coverage to instances where plaintiffs could prove intent to
discriminate. The opinions of a fractured Court in the 1978 *Regents of the University of California v. Bakke* case[34] were widely considered to be a loss of the core
justification for affirmative action based on the nation's longstanding and well-
known history of discrimination. Only Justice Lewis Powell's endorsement of
the "diversity" justification for affirmative action saved the programs from ex-
tinction. Over the ensuing decades, Justice Powell's opinion came to be viewed
as a major civil rights victory because it provided the key rationale supporting
affirmative action programs against aggressive and unrelenting attacks. In 1980,
the Court announced in *Mobile v. Bolden*[35] that violations of the Voting Rights
Act would have to be proven by showing intent to discriminate.

Unlike the period after Reconstruction when Congress failed to legislate to
undo some of the Court's regressive decisions, Congress steadfastly exercised
its constitutionally-granted powers during the 1980s and early 1990s. Congress
enacted the Voting Rights Act Amendments of 1982, for example, rejecting the
Court's *Mobile v. Bolden* decision and establishing that violations of the Act
could be based on an "effects" test rather than proof of intent. After the 1984
Grove City College v. Bell decision that severely diminished the reach of the Civil
Rights Act of 1964,[36] Congress passed the Civil Rights Restoration Act of 1988.[37]
And in 1991, after a bitterly fought legislative battle, Congress restored the civil
rights employment laws[38] that had been virtually gutted by Court decisions in
the 1989 term.[39] When the Court found states immune from damages actions
stemming from civil rights claims in *Atascadero State Hospital v. Scanlon* in
1985,[40] Congress acted to abrogate state immunity. Congress also passed the
1988 amendments to the 1968 Fair Housing Act, strengthening its enforcement
procedures and adding protections for the disabled and families with children.[41]
Congress did not, however, attempt to fix the hostile decisions on affirmative
action such as *City of Richmond v. Croson* in 1989,[42] in which the Court adopted
strict constitutional standards for affirmative action programs.[43]

In sum, between the 1970s and the early 1990s, the Supreme Court adopted
an increasingly aggressive approach in restricting civil rights protections. Fortunately, Congress acted to reverse much of the damage and even adopted af-

firmative legislation such as the ADA in 1990. As the Court continued its attack on civil rights during the mid-to-late 1990s, however, Congress failed to respond.

Judicial Restrictions on Civil Rights in the 1990s and 2000s

By the 1990s, a solidly conservative Supreme Court under the leadership of Chief Justice Rehnquist moved further to the right in a series of 5-4 decisions, dramatically restricting the power of Congress to enact laws to remedy civil rights violations. The Court restricted civil rights either by denying a right or by hindering individuals' ability to enforce their rights by denying a remedy—the "right-remedy gap."[44]

The Supreme Court's conservative lead has been taken up by a host of extreme right wing federal judges at the appellate and trial court levels. In *Hopwood v. Texas* in 1996,[45] for example, two judges of the U.S. Court of Appeals for the Fifth Circuit struck down an affirmative action admissions program at the University of Texas School of Law, causing devastating results to black and Latino enrollments. They did this by declaring that Justice Powell's opinion in *Bakke* was no longer the law of the land, although the Court had not so ruled.[46]

The Court has used a variety of doctrinal devices to produce results that seriously threaten the long-term stability and balance of power among the three co-equal branches of government. Recent restrictions on Congress's power to legislate have been striking—so much so that even a conservative jurist, John T. Noonan, Senior Judge of the U.S. Court of Appeals for the Ninth Circuit, published a strong criticism of the Court's recent decisions.[47] A historical review of the Court's decisions captures the recent sea change in the Court's deference to Congress. From 1996 through 2001, the Court invalidated twenty-six federal laws (roughly 4.6 annually) compared with the first two hundred years after the Constitution was ratified (1787–1987), during which time the Court struck down 127 federal laws (approximately .6 annually).[48] It is evident that while power struggles have occurred, the Court's recent response has been an aggressive arrogation of power to itself at the expense of Congress, the most representative branch of our government.[49]

In the area of the free exercise of religion, the Court abandoned established precedent in *Employment Div., Dep't of Human Resources v. Smith* in 1990[50] by holding that a state law that prohibits an individual from engaging in religious practices (e.g., the sacramental use of peyote by Native Americans) does not violate the First Amendment. To counter the *Smith* decision, a broad coalition of groups from the political left, right, and center persuaded a virtually unanimous Congress to enact the Religious Freedom Restoration Act (RFRA) of 1993,[51] pursuant to the Fourteenth Amendment provision guaranteeing that no person shall be arbitrarily deprived of liberty by a state. Section 5 of the Fourteenth Amendment grants Congress the power to enforce its provisions by "appropriate legislation."

When RFRA was challenged in *City of Boerne v. Flores* in 1997,[52] however, the Court adopted a new standard of judicial review called "congruence and proportionality." Under that standard, it rejected RFRA as an unconstitutional exercise of congressional power. With the new standard, federal judges are to scrutinize the record to assess whether legislation is congruent and proportional to the wrong it is attempting to remedy—an approach that turns decades of Fourteenth Amendment jurisprudence on it head. Historically, the Court would acknowledge and generally defer to the superior fact-finding ability of Congress—a legislative body and co-equal branch of government. After *City of Boerne*, this was no longer the case.

In *United States v. Morrison* in 2000,[53] the Court struck down the Violence Against Women Act (VAWA),[54] which provided remedies to victims of gender-based civil rights discrimination. In the 5-4 decision, the Court announced that the statute could not be sustained as remedial legislation under the Fourteenth Amendment because it was aimed at the criminal conduct of private individuals (ignoring the fact that in the instances specified by the Act, the state had failed to act in the face of violence against a woman).[55] The Court also held that VAWA could not be sustained under Congress's Commerce Clause authority because it concluded that violence against women had too attenuated an effect on interstate commerce.[56]

The Court also developed an expansive notion of state immunity that is not found in the language of the Constitution itself[57]—a surprising position for justices who claimed to be strict constructionists (a position they have since been forced to abandon). By 5-4 votes in *Kimel v. Florida Bd. of Regents* in 2000[58] and *Bd. of Trs. of Univ. of Ala. v. Garrett* in 2001,[59] the Court held, respectively, that states have immunity from claims for discrimination against the aged and the disabled. Nothing in the Constitution, however, grants states this immunity; nor is there historical justification for barring these claims against states. Moreover, the argument that these protections are needed to protect state coffers would fail the Court's own strict tests. Proponents argue that these decisions adversely affect only a small portion of the workforce, but over 4.9 million state employees, not to mention the millions of people in non-employment contexts, are affected.[60]

The Court also broadly restricted access to the courts in several civil rights contexts. In *Alexander v. Sandoval* in 2001,[61] the Court ruled in a 5-4 decision that individuals had no private right of action with which to enforce the disparate impact regulations under Title VI of the Civil Rights Act of 1964. This decision effectively barred many race and national origin claims, including those in the language rights context, challenges to discriminatory educational practices, and environmental justice claims. The decision affected Title IX (gender discrimination and retaliation) claims, § 1983 claims, and may impact claims under the Age Discrimination Act of 1975. Fortunately, most of the *Sandoval* challenges to disability claims under the Rehabilitation Act and the ADA have been rebuffed on the grounds that those statutes are distinguishable from Title VI.[62] It is clear that the *Sandoval* decision was a direct attack on the private attorneys general concept essential to the enforcement of civil rights law. In her recent law review article, Stanford Law Professor Pamela Karlan describes the decision as "disarming the private attorneys general."[63] Indeed they are.

In *Buckhannon Bd. and Care Home, Inc. v. West Virginia Dept. of Health and Human Serv.* in 2001,[64] the Court addressed civil rights remedies. It ruled that attorney's fees were no longer recoverable under the Civil Rights Attorney's Fee Act where the plaintiff's claim was the "catalyst" for the defendant's changed behavior. Instead, in order to recover attorney's fees, the plaintiff must obtain an actual judgment in her favor. This ruling was a substantial departure from existing law and practice and is particularly detrimental to civil rights claimants because most lawyers simply will not take cases where they can be forced into extensive litigation only to be denied compensation. Civil rights lawyers now fear that even where the law and the facts are squarely in the plaintiff's favor, defendants will force them to litigate until the eve of trial and then correct the challenged practice to avoid the expected loss—thus barring the plaintiff's right to recover attorney's fees. As Congress and the Court recognized, most civil rights plaintiffs will be unable to obtain counsel without the ability to recover fees; their claims, therefore, will never be addressed. Thus, the *Buckhannon* decision is a serious blow to civil rights claimants seeking to change discriminatory practices.

In *Gilmer v. Interstate/Johnson Lane Corp.* in 1991[65] and *Circuit City Stores, Inc. v. Adams* in 2001,[66] the Court ruled that all employment contracts can be subject to mandatory arbitration requirements, effectively cutting out an individual's right to pursue a claim of discrimination in court. Arbitration is often conducted secretly, by non-lawyers, without a requirement that the law be followed or that procedural rights, such as the right to review evidence through discovery, are provided. Again, by denying individuals the right to sue to enforce their claims, the Court impaired the enforcement of civil rights.

Finally, in a series of decisions in 1999 and 2002 (*Toyota Motor Mfg., Ky., Ince. v. Williams,*[67] *Murphy v. United Parcel Service, Inc.,*[68] *Albertson's Inc., v. Kirkingburg,*[69] and *Chevron U.S.A. Inc. v. Echazabal*[70]), the Court limited the definition of disability, created new affirmative defenses for employers sued under the ADA, and broadly undermined the protections of the ADA.

In short, a very conservative Supreme Court has succeeded in significantly turning back the clock on many of the gains made during the Civil Rights Movement.

Charting a Successful Retreat on Civil Rights

A key question that comes to mind is how did the retreat on civil rights take hold so successfully? The answer lies, in significant part, in the appointment of right wing, ideological judges. For the past twenty years, the conservative right has understood the power of the federal judiciary and has aggressively selected and fought to confirm conservative judges willing to change the interpretation of the Constitution. As pointed out by Indiana University School of Law Professor Dawn Johnsen, the Reagan administration Department of Justice developed two publications (*Guidelines on Constitutional Litigation* and *The Constitution in the Year 2000: Choices Ahead in Constitutional Interpretation*)[71] urging the president to play a strong and independent role in interpreting the Constitution, largely through the selection of federal judges. The former publication encourages the courts to invalidate acts of Congress and recognize limits on congressional power; the latter is a guide to selecting federal judges.

Presidents Ronald Reagan and George H.W. Bush had a powerful and radical influence on current constitutional interpretation though the appointment of over five hundred federal judges. Many of these appointees were strongly influenced by the conservative ideology of organizations like the Federalist Society and the Heritage Foundation. At the Supreme Court, the conservative appointments of Justices Sandra Day O'Connor, Anthony Kennedy, Antonin Scalia, and Clarence Thomas, along with the elevation of William Rehnquist to Chief Justice, created the five-vote majority that sustains most of the decisions that are so damaging to civil rights. With the loss of liberal heavyweights like Justices Thurgood Marshall and William Brennan, the Supreme Court is now composed of Far Right and moderate jurists.

Unfortunately, the Clinton administration failed to place sufficient emphasis on the critical issue of federal judicial appointments. Unlike the conservative judges appointed by Presidents Reagan and Bush, President Clinton's appointments were generally moderates and centrists, as well as some conservatives, leaving the federal courts leaning heavily to the right.

In addition to the general focus on judicial appointments, conservative administrations have recognized the importance of the thirteen federal courts of appeals. While the Supreme Court decides less than a hundred cases annually, the federal courts of appeals decide in the range of thirty thousand cases annually. Seven of the thirteen circuits are controlled by strong right wing appointees; with the confirmation of President George W. Bush's nominees, this number could rise to as many as twelve.

Reversing the Retreat

What can we do to reverse the retreat on civil rights? First, we must educate the public about its significance, and how it can impact them. Only with sufficient public support will there be the political will required to make the needed reversal of course.

Second, we must urge Congress to assert its still considerable power against attacks on civil rights by the Supreme Court. The civil rights community has come to specialize in legislative restorations of the law. Many of the damaging decisions such as *Sandoval* can be corrected, but it will take work, careful development of the record, and no doubt a fight in Congress.

Third, we must recognize and utilize state laws. In the area of sovereign immunity, for example, states can waive the immunity that the Court has granted them. Several states are moving in that direction, and at least two have already acted.[72] Although state law can provide a meaningful substitute for protections lost under federal law, not all states will act. Many people, therefore, will be left without protection. State reform is nonetheless an important measure in the face of congressional inaction.

Fourth, aggressive but careful litigation strategies are needed to face such hostile courts.

Fifth, we must reach out to non-traditional allies. They will provide important and unique resources once they understand that their civil rights are also being adversely affected.

Sixth, it is critical that people become engaged on the issue of judicial appointments. President Bush plans to appoint more judges like Antonin Scalia and Clarence Thomas. Even if it means entering into some tough fights, it is important to defeat nominees with extreme views of the Constitution and those hostile to civil rights laws.

Finally, we must fund these activities. Developing strategies to do so is critical to the success of our campaign.

We must join together in reversing the conservative backlash against the protection of civil rights. If history repeats itself, it could be a long time before the rights that we have lost are restored. We cannot let that happen. We stand on the shoulders of the giants who came before us and who fought and won seemingly unwinnable fights. From this vantage point, we must pursue the path to justice without delay.

Endnotes

1. Norman Redlich, The Sterry R. Waterman Lectures "Out, Damned Spot; Out, I Say." The Persistence of Race in American Law, *25 Vt. L. Rev* (2001) 475, 499.

2. What remains of these statutes is codified, for example, in 42 U.S.C. §§ 1981–86, and in other sections of the U.S. Code.

3. *Slaughter-House Cases*, 83 U.S. (16 Wall.) 36 (1873).

4. See e.g., *The Civil Rights Cases*, 109 U.S. 3 (1883); *Pace v. Alabama*, 106 U.S. 583 (1883); *United States v. Cruikshank*, 92 U.S. 542 (1876); *United States v. Harris*, 106 U.S. 629 (1882); *United States v. Reese*, 92 U.S. 214 (1876).

5. *Plessy v. Ferguson*, 163 U.S. 537 (1896).

6. *Cumming v. Board of Education of Richmond County*, 175 U.S. 528 (1899).

7. *Lochner v. New York*, 198 U.S. 45 (1905) (striking a New York statute that placed a sixty-hour limit on a bakery employee's work week as an unconstitutional interference with the right to contract, despite the fact that New York had adopted the statute to protect persons where their working conditions posed a significant threat to their health).

8. *Carter v. Carter Coal Company*, 298 U.S. 238 (1936) (Congress could not constitutionally regulate the labor relations of a corporation whose business was coal mining).

9. E.g., *Missouri ex. rel Gaines v. Canada*, 305 U.S. 337 (1938); *Shelly v. Kramer*, 334 U.S. 1 (1948); *Sipuel v. Board of Regents of Univ. of Okla.*, 332 U.S. 631 (1948); *McLaurin v. Oklahoma State Regents for Higher Ed.*, 339 U.S. 637 (1950); *Sweatt v. Painter*, 339 U.S. 629 (1950).

10. *Brown v. Board of Education*, 347 U.S. 483 (1954).

11. 29 U.S.C. § 206.

12. 42 U.S.C. § 2000e.

13. 42 U.S.C. § 1973.

14. 29 U.S.C. §§ 621–34.

15. 42 U.S.C. § 3604(c).

16. 20 U.S.C. §§ 1681–88.

17. 42 U.S.C. § 2000e-5(f)(1).

18. 29 U.S.C. § 794.

19. 42 U.S.C. § 6101–07.

20. 42 U.S.C. § 1973l (e).

21. 42 U.S.C. § 1988.

22. 42 U.S.C. § 12101.

23. 42 U.S.C. § 1988.

24. *Newman v. Piggy Park Enter.*, 390 U.S. 400, 402 (1968).

25. Id.

26. *Griggs v. Duke Power Co.*, 401 U.S. 424 (1971).

27. *Cannon v. University of Chicago*, 441 U.S. 677 (1979).

28. *Fullilove v. Klutznick*, 448 U.S. 448 (1980).

29. That deference to Congress would be expressly repudiated by the Court in *Adarand v. Pena*, 515 U.S. 200 (1995).

30. *San Antonio v. Rodriguez*, 411 U.S. 1 (1973).

31. *Milliken v. Bradley*, 433 U.S. 267 (1977).

32. *Cort v. Ash*, 422 U.S. 66 (1975).

33. *Washington v. Davis*, 426 U.S. 229 (1976).

34. *Regents of the University of California v. Bakke*, 438 U.S. 265 (1978).

35. *Mobile v. Bolden*, 446 U.S. 55 (1980).

36. *Grove City College v. Bell*, 465 U.S. 555 (1984).

37. The Civil Rights Restoration Act of 1988, Pub. L. No. 100-259, 102 Stat. 28 (1988).

38. The Civil Rights Act of 1991, Pub. L. 102–66, 105 Stat. 1071 (1991).

39. See *Patterson v. McClean Credit Union*, 491 U.S. 164 (1989) (racial harassment claims were not actionable under 42 U.S.C. § 1981); *Price Waterhouse v. Hopkins*, 490 U.S. 228 (1989) (allowed employers to avoid a finding of liability for intentional discrimination where they could establish that they would have made the same employment decision regardless of the discrimination); *Lorance v. AT&T Technologies*, 490 U.S. 900 (1989) (adopted a restrictive reading of the limitations period for filing challenges to employment practices); *Martin v. Wilks*, 490 U.S. 755 (1989) (allowed collateral attacks on consent decrees in employment discrimination cases); *Wards Cove Packing Co. v. Atonio*, 490 U.S. 642 (1989) (dismantled key aspects of the disparate impact standard of proof in employment discrimination cases as established in the *Griggs v. Duke Power* decision and its progeny). The Civil Rights Act of 1991, signed into law November 21, 1991, reversed the effects of these decisions.

40. *Atascadero State Hospital v. Scanlon*, 473 U.S. 234 (1985).

41. 42 U.S.C. S 3604(f).

42. *City of Richmond v. Croson*, 488 U.S. 469 (1989).

43. These remarks preceded two Supreme Court decisions in 2003 involving affirmative action in higher education, see *Gratz v. Bollinger,* 539 U.S. 244 (2003) and *Grutter v. Bollinger,* 539 U.S. 306 (2003).

44. See John C. Jeffries, Jr., The Right-Remedy Gap in Constitutional Law, *109 Yale L.J.* (1999) 87.

45. 78 F.3d 932 (5th Cir.), *cert. denied* 518 U.S. 1033 (1996).

46. The *Hopwood* decision reflects the aggressive nature of the conservative federal bench, particularly in view of the Court's subsequent 5-4 decision in *Grutter v. Bollinger*, 539 U.S. 306 (2003), which reaffirmed Justice Powell's opinion in *Bakke,* while continuing in *Gratz v. Bollinger*, 539 U.S. 244 (2003), to restrict the means by which the goals of affirmative action can be achieved.

47. John T. Noonan, Jr., *Narrowing the Nation's Power: The Supreme Court Sides with the States* (2002).

48. See Jeffrey Rosen, "A Majority of One," *New York Times* (June 3, 2001), and Seth P. Waxman, Defending Congress, *79 N.C. L. Rev.* (2001) 1073–75.

49. *Bush v. Gore*, 531 U.S. 98 (2000), reveals the Court's willingness to assert its power even over states despite its reliance on the "states rights" mantle to retreat from civil rights.

50. *Employment Div., Dep't of Human Resources v. Smith*, 494 U.S. 872 (1990).

51. 42 U.S.C. §2000bb.

52. *City of Boerne v. Flores*, 521 U.S. 507 (1997).

53. *United States v. Morrison*, 529 U.S. 598 (2000).

54. 42 U.S.C. §13981.

55. Kerrie E. Maloney, Note, Gender Motivated Violence and the Commerce Clause, *96 Colum. L. Rev.* (1996) 1876.

56. *Morrison*, 529 U.S. at 7–19.

57. By its terms, the Eleventh Amendment bars a state from being sued by a citizen of another state.

58. *Kimel v. Florida Bd. of Regents*, 528 U.S. 62 (2000).

59. *Bd. of Trs. of Univ. of Ala. v. Garrett*, 531 U.S. 356 (2001).

60. In 2001, the states alone employed more than 4.9 million people. U.S. Dept. of Commerce, Bureau of Census, Statistical Abstract of the United States 312 (123th ed. 2003) (Table 467).

61. *Alexander v. Sandoval*, 532 U.S. 275 (2001)

62. See, e.g., *Frederick L. v. Dep't of Pub. Welfare*, 157 F. Supp. 2d 509, 536–39 (E.D. Pa. 2001) (analyzing the impact of *Sandoval* and finding a private right of action under both the ADA and Section 504 of the Rehabilitation Act of 1974 to enforce disparate impact regulations). But see *Litman v. George Mason Univ.*, 156 F. Supp. 2d 579, 587 (E.D. Va. 2001) (concluding that the *Sandoval* decision bars plaintiff's claim for retaliation under Title IX of the Education Amendments of 1972).

63. Pamela S. Karlan, Disarming the Private Attorney General, *2003 U. Ill. L. Rev.* (2003) 183.

64. *Buckhannon Bd. and Care Home, Inc. v. West Virginia Dept. of Health and Human Serv.*, 532 U.S. 598 (2001).

65. *Gilmer v. Interstate/Johnson Lane Corp.*, 500 U.S. 20 (1991).

66. *Circuit City Stores, Inc. v. Adams*, 532 U.S. 105 (2001).

67. *Toyota Motor Mfg., Ky., Inc. v. Williams*, 534 U.S. 184 (2002).

68. *Murphy v. United Parcel Service, Inc.*, 527 U.S. 516 (1999).

69. *Albertson's, Inc. v. Kirkingburg*, 527 U.S. 555 (1999).

70. *Chevron U.S.A. Inc. v. Echazabal*, 536 U.S. 73 (2002).

71. Dawn E. Johnsen, Ronald Reagan and The Rehnquist Court on Congressional Power: Presidential Influences on Constitutional Change, *78 Ind. L.Rev.* (2003) 363, 367.

72. See IL Public Act 093-0414 (Ill. 2003), at http://www.legis.state.il.us/legislation/publicacts/fulltext.asp?Name=093-0414 (waiving sovereign immunity to individual suits to enforce federal statutes, including the Age Discrimination in Employment Act, the Americans with Disabilities Act, Title VII of the Civil Rights Act of 1964, the Fair Labor Standards Act, and the Family and Medical Leave Act); M.S.A. § 1.05 (2001) (waiving the state's immunity from suit under the federal Fair Labor Standards Act, Age Discrimination in Employment Act, Americans with Disabilities Act, and the Family and Medical Leave Act).

Part II
The Impact of the
Federalism Revolution
on the Lives of Americans

CHAPTER 3

AFRICAN AMERICANS

The Rehnquist Court, the Resurrection of Plessy, and the Ever-Expanding Definition of "Societal Discrimination"

Lia B. Epperson[*]

My education cases take me to towns like Gadsden, Alabama, where echoes of the Civil War still reverberate under the mighty Coosa River's steel bridge from whose beams black men were once lynched. In Gadsden, I am litigating a school deseg- regation case, filed more than three decades ago by my predecessors at the NAACP Legal Defense and Educational Fund (LDF), which is aimed at forcing compli- ance with Brown v. Board of Education's *mandate that separate and unequal schools be eradicated.*[†]

After decades of federal court supervision, one might assume that schools in places like Gadsden would have moved further toward achieving racial equality. In 2004, however, many Gadsden children still attend a middle school named after Nathan Bedford Forrest, the uneducated, slave-owning, first Grand Wizard of the Ku Klux Klan. When my colleagues and I argued that such a name might alienate African American students, school officials resisted in a vociferous manner similar to the self-righteous resistance exhibited in most southern districts in the wake of Brown.

Our nation's history of slavery and apartheid is still reflected in symbols like a high school using a rebel gun-toting soldier as a mascot, as well as in the dispar- ities evident in the largely segregated schools. On one of my first visits to the pre- dominantly African American public high school in Gadsden, I saw broken desks

---

[*] Director of Education at the NAACP LDF. She oversees LDF's administrative and leg- islative advocacy and litigation in federal and state court in the areas of K–12 and higher education.

[†] For additional discussion of the Gadsden case, see Lia B. Epperson, Resisting Retreat: The Struggle for Educational Equity in the Post-Brown Era, *66 U. Pittsburgh L. Rev.* 131 (2005) 1.

and leaking roofs. Bathrooms lacked sufficient toilet paper and soap. The chemistry lab lacked running water and the equipment necessary to carry out the experiments listed in lesson plans. Students had fewer opportunities to take the upper level and specialized classes that were available at other schools and that make students more attractive candidates to colleges and universities.

Unfortunately, the situation facing Gadsden children is not unique. Black and brown students nation-wide experience similar patterns of segregation and inequities in facilities and curricular offerings. Few recognize, however, that educational equity has been thwarted at many turns. Fewer still understand how the Supreme Court has made it harder to achieve that ideal.

This chapter will examine how the Court has rolled back the civil rights of African Americans in the areas of educational opportunity, affirmative action, voting rights, fair employment, and disparate impact litigation.

So far as the colored people of the country are concerned, the Constitution is but a stupendous sham…keeping the promise to the eye and breaking it to the heart.…They have promised us law and abandoned us to anarchy.

Frederick Douglass

For more than sixty years, the NAACP LDF has been active in safeguarding the civil rights of African Americans and other disenfranchised groups. While LDF's early litigation strategy helped bring down Jim Crow laws, the promise of equality remains unfulfilled. I represent African American children for whom the racial equality promised in *Brown* remains a dream. They attend segregated schools in decaying buildings, where they struggle to learn the skills necessary to access the economic, political, and social networks long open to whites. Despite continuing racial disparities, recent Supreme Court decisions rolling back civil rights have made it even harder for those with the most at stake to have a voice. If allowed to continue, this Federalism Revolution—the campaign to dismantle federal protections for individual rights and upend fundamental notions of fairness and democracy—may well render the Equal Protection Clause of the Fourteenth Amendment the "stupendous sham" that Frederick Douglass deemed it at the close of the nineteenth century.

History

Over the last decade, the Supreme Court has mounted a two-pronged attack on the civil rights of African Americans, chipping away at their scope and limiting remedies available to address their violation. This rollback has been undertaken in the seemingly neutral name of federalism—restoring the balance of power between the federal and state governments, and maintaining states' rights. In reality, however, the Rehnquist Court's Federalism Revolution has enabled states to evade federal anti-discrimination laws in a manner far beyond the intent of the Constitution, has impeded Congress's ability to enact anti-discrimination laws, and has narrowed the ability of private individuals to seek remedies for discrimination.

None of this, however, is new. Rather, the Federalism Revolution is eerily reminiscent of the dark time in American history when people were fighting to preserve the "peculiar institution" of slavery. At the Constitutional Convention of 1787, delegates from southern slave-trading states fought hard to limit the federal government's power, and won concessions protecting state sovereignty to maintain the institution.[1] The same type of federalism reemerged after Reconstruction in the *Civil Rights Cases* in 1883 when, with slavery not yet cold in the grave, the Court reasserted the specious mantle of states' rights, abandoning African Americans to Klan terrorism and state-sanctioned racism. The Court held that the Thirteenth and Fourteenth Amendments did not afford Congress the authority to enact the Civil Rights Act of 1875 (prohibiting discrimination in public accommodations), because the constitution "does not invest Congress with power to legislate upon subjects which are within the domain of state legislation...."[2] Indeed, the Court almost castigated African Americans for expecting the federal government to assure them the same rights long afforded to whites. Justice Joseph Bradley stated "[w]hen a man has emerged from slavery, and by the aid of beneficent legislation has shaken off the inseparable concomitants of that state, there must be some stage in the progress of his elevation when he takes the rank of a mere citizen, and ceases to be the special favorite of the laws, and when his rights as a citizen, or a man, are to be protected in the ordinary modes by which other men's rights are protected.[3] Thirteen years later, the Court concretized this deathblow to African American civil rights in *Plessy v. Ferguson*[4] by formalizing a system of state-sanctioned apartheid that remained in place for two generations until *Brown*.[5]

Although we no longer live in a time of slavery or Jim Crow, we still live with their legacy. By the time *Brown* was decided in 1954, the systematic subjugation of African Americans was firmly entrenched in governmental policy.[6] The racial hierarchy that has resulted from decades of oppression by public and private actors continues to pervade every facet of American life. These discriminatory policies and customs are directly linked to the structural inequalities that continue to limit the educational, employment, and asset-building opportunities of African Americans.[7] Unfortunately, the rollback of civil rights threatens to make these injustices permanent.

The Federalism Revolution: The "New" Retreat from Civil Rights Enforcement

The Federalism Revolution is a chilling echo of the states' rights doctrine that prevailed at the end of the nineteenth century. Just five decades after the separate-but-equal doctrine was struck down in *Brown*, the Supreme Court has initiated a massive retreat from established civil rights protections for African Americans.

While no single case heralded this change, one central strand of the Court's reasoning stems from *City of Richmond v. Croson* in 1989, a case in which the majority of justices undermined the legal struggle against racial discrimination. In the case, a white general contractor challenged the constitutionality of a Richmond city ordinance that required city construction contractors to set aside at least thirty percent of the contract's dollar amount for minority-owned subcontractors (businesses owned or controlled by "Blacks, Spanish-speaking [people], Orientals, Indians, Eskimos, or Aleuts").[8] For the first time, the *Croson* Court rejected race-conscious remedies in favor of a color-blind approach to the law by holding that courts should subject state and local affirmative action measures to the same strict scrutiny test applied to laws designed to promote white supremacy. The strict scrutiny test is difficult to pass because it requires that the race-based measure be both justified by a "compelling government interest" and "narrowly tailored" to achieve that interest.

In language paralleling that in the *Civil Rights Cases* a century before, the Court held that detailed congressional findings of racial discrimination in the construction industry merely showed the existence of amorphous "societal discrimination," and were, therefore, insufficient to prove the lingering effects of unconstitutional race-based discrimination.[9]

> To accept Richmond's claim that past societal discrimination alone can serve as the basis for rigid racial preferences would be to open the door to competing claims for "remedial relief" for every disadvantaged group. The dream of a Nation of equal citizens in a society where race is irrelevant to personal opportunity and achievement would be lost in a mosaic of shifting preferences based on inherently unmeasurable claims of past wrongs.[10]

Noting the irony of the fact that the case arose in Richmond, VA—the former capital of the Confederacy and a city renowned for strict state-imposed segregation—Justice Thurgood Marshall could not fathom his colleagues' refusal to acknowledge that African Americans suffered discrimination in the construction industry.[11] Like in *Plessy*, the majority in *Croson* accepted the notion that racial discrimination is a social practice that neither the courts, nor Congress, nor the states have an obligation to change. This holding goes directly against the guarantees of the Fourteenth Amendment and the *Brown* decision, both of which authorized affirmative relief to overcome any continuing effects of racial apartheid. Indeed, the *Croson* opinion established an ever-expanding category of "societal discrimination" in educational opportunity, the vote, and fair employment.

School Desegregation

Nowhere is the Rehnquist Court's attack on the civil rights of African Americans more evident than in the area of school desegregation and education. Opening the doors to education means opening the doors to social, economic, and political opportunity—the very reason that LDF set about dismantling public school segregation in the early twentieth century. Yet the promise of *Brown* remains stymied by intransigent school districts, disinterested local judges, and intractable racist attitudes.

The Court's current approach to equal education differs markedly from its decisions during the twenty years following *Brown* when it expressed frustration with the sluggish pace of desegregation and required that school districts eliminate the dual school systems "root and branch."[12] In the late 1960s and early 1970s, the Court was not satisfied with merely removing the laws that required dual school systems, and instead imposed an affirmative duty on school districts to eliminate all vestiges of racial discrimination. Furthermore, the Court acknowledged that outside of racial segregation in schools, a system of residential segregation existed that was deeply tied to the country's history of racial oppression.[13] So long as substantial housing segregation persisted, therefore, a return to "neighborhood schools" would also mean a return to segregated schools.

Recent desegregation opinions by the Rehnquist Court have resurrected the question of the Court's commitment to the constitutional guarantee of equal protection for African Americans. In the 1990s, the Court began to release school districts from their obligation to desegregate public schools. In a trilogy of cases—*Board of Education v. Dowell* in 1991,[14] *Freeman v. Pitts* in 1992,[15] and *Missouri v. Jenkins* in 1995[16]— the Court concluded that school systems had achieved "unitary status," and that federal court desegregation orders were to end. These opinions subordinated the constitutional rights of the victims of racial discrimination to local interests, and restored the system of neighborhood schools and local control that had allowed segregation to flourish in the first place.

The principle of local control is inextricably linked to racial subordination. It is not mandated by the text or the tradition of the Fourteenth Amendment, and is antithetical to the aims of the Equal Protection guarantee. Many whites favor local control, however, because their children attend resource-rich suburban schools. In contrast, African American children are more likely to attend under-resourced urban schools. The Court's reliance on local control is similar to color-blindness—both standards treat blacks and whites as if they are similarly situated, ignoring the pervasive vestiges of historical segregation.

Courts have also begun to question the legality of voluntary school desegregation programs. At least one appellate court has ruled that school boards cannot consider race as they make school assignment decisions—a ruling that prevents well-meaning educators from implementing programs to desegregate schools.[17] This attack on educational diversity and the corresponding extension of the color-blind notion runs counter to thirty years of Court decisions that acknowledged the constitutionality of race-conscious public school assignments, ignores the fact that this is a multiethnic nation with serious educational and social disparities, and threatens to exacerbate the harm already inflicted upon millions of children.

The simple and awful truth is that U.S. schools remain separate and unequal. Indeed, through the 1990s, public schools became substantially more segregated.[18] While fifty years have passed since *Brown*, I see in my work that much of its guarantee remains unfulfilled. If we are to see its promise realized, we must understand that while the law no longer commands race and class apartheid, society tolerates segregation and the resulting inequities.

Affirmative Action

In 1978, the Court held that race-conscious affirmative action policies were constitutional as long as they were crafted to remedy past discrimination or promote diversity.[19] In *Adarand Constructors v. Pena* in 1995, however, a bare majority struck down a federal program designed to promote affirmative action, reiterating the color-blind position that the Court first took in *Croson* (that race-conscious programs designed for a remedial purpose must satisfy the same standard of judicial review as programs designed to subjugate minorities).[20] *Adarand* ignored the fact that Section 5 of the Fourteenth Amendment gives Congress the authority to enact legislation to combat racial discrimination against African Americans, and required strict scrutiny of *every* racial remedy, irrespective of whether it was created by federal or state legislation. Under *Adarand*, if a state university wanted to give special admissions preference to viola players, children of alumni, or athletes, it could do so without fear of judicial scrutiny. If those same state actors gave a preference to African Americans, however, the Court held that the Fourteenth Amendment would likely forbid it. As one academic noted, this doctrine of "color-blindness actually denies to racial minorities a privilege enjoyed by virtually every other minority group in the political system."[21]

The language used by Justice Clarence Thomas in his concurring opinion is hauntingly similar to that in *Plessy*. Compare Thomas's charge that "[g]overnment cannot make us equal; it can only recognize, respect, and protect us as equal before the law"[22] with *Plessy's* "[i]f the two races are to meet upon terms of social equality, it must be the result of natural affinities....Legislation is powerless to eradicate racial instincts or to abolish distinctions based upon physical differences."[23] Both opinions ignore the history of racial oppression that continues to affect educational and economic opportunities for African Americans.

More recently in the 2003 cases *Grutter v. Bollinger* and *Gratz v. Bollinger*, the Court again addressed the issue of the constitutionality of affirmative action in university admissions.[24] While the University of Michigan Law School defended its affirmative action policy by showing that racial diversity served a compelling government interest, LDF argued that the admissions policy, which included race as one of many considerations, was also necessary to remedy the continuing effects of racial segregation and discrimination. In an uncharacteristic break from its push for color-blindness, the Court upheld the use of race in admissions policies in order to further diversity.

The *Grutter* victory was due, in part, to the effort of a broad coalition of lawyers, academics, activists, community groups, businesses, and military officials. Millions of Americans expressed their support for affirmative action by submitting briefs to the Court, offering testimony, and protesting. As a result, the justices were forced to recognize the need for affirmative action in colleges and universities.

Voting Rights

In 1965, Congress enacted the Voting Rights Act, ending a century of African Americans being denied the right to vote. The next major challenge was to address the scourge of vote dilution, which requires the election of candidates at large rather than through districts (some of which are largely African American), and the drawing of district lines that splinter African

American communities and minimize their voting strength. In 1982, Congress enacted an extension to the Voting Rights Act, dispensing with the need to prove that vote dilution was intentional. Under the extension, one need only show that the challenged mechanism had the effect of diluting minority votes.

Beginning in 1993, however, the Rehnquist Court issued an opinion that, drawing on the logic of the *Croson* decision, began to chip away at the meaning of the Voting Rights Act. In *Shaw v. Reno*, white voters challenged a North Carolina reapportionment plan that, for the first time since Reconstruction, included two congressional districts in which a majority of the population was African American. Even though the plaintiffs did not claim that the plan impaired their ability to participate in the electoral process or diluted their votes, the 5-4 conservative majority upheld the white plaintiffs' Equal Protection claim. Writing for the majority, Justice Sandra Day O'-Connor invoked a new standard by declaring that race could not be the "predominant concern" in drawing district lines. Citing *Croson*, O'Connor argued that any color consciousness, regardless of its intent, was antithetical to the Constitution: "Classifications of citizens solely on the basis of race... threaten to stigmatize individuals by reason of their membership in a racial group and to incite racial hostility.... These principles apply not only to legislation that contains explicit racial distinctions, but also to those 'rare' statutes that, although race neutral, are, on their face, 'unexplainable on grounds other than race.'"[25]

The most disturbing thing about *Shaw v. Reno* was that the Court abandoned settled law and fashioned a new legal standard. In a cutting dissent, Justice Byron White stressed that it was "both a fiction and a departure from settled equal protection principles" for the majority to void a redistricting plan that allowed North Carolina to send its first African American representatives to Congress since Reconstruction.[26]

Prior to the enactment of the Voting Rights Act extension, many African American voters encountered inferior voting equipment, improper purges from the voting rolls, and voter intimidation. While the influence of minority voters has clearly increased since that time, racial inequities in voting remain. In the 2000 presidential elections, for example, many African Americans were denied the right to vote because of improper purges from the voting rolls, outdated voter equipment, and insufficient staffing at polling sites in African American precincts. It is a constant challenge to ensure that civil rights legislation is not reduced to empty words. Federal law must safeguard the voting rights of African Americans.

Fair Employment

In *Wards Cove Packing Company v. Atonio* in 1989,[27] the Court's conservative 5-4 majority undermined the 1971 *Griggs v. Duke Power Co.* decision (which had governed employment law for more than fifteen years) by extending the *Croson* color-blind rationale to fair employment. In *Griggs*, a unanimous Court held that Title VII of the Civil Rights Act of 1964 barred employment practices that adversely impact minorities or women.[28] In other words, once an employment discrimination plaintiff statistically proved that a practice adversely impacted his or her group, the employer could be required to explain its business need. Without a satisfactory explanation, the plaintiff would win—the court did not need to find that the employer intended to discriminate. *Griggs* therefore opened the doors to employment opportunities in law enforcement and white-collar occupations that had previously been shut to minority applicants because of discriminatory procedures or testing mechanisms.

In *Wards Cove*, however, the Court held that even after a plaintiff in an employment discrimination case established that a practice had an adverse impact, he or she still had the burden of persuading the Court that the practice was illegitimate. Furthermore, business necessity did not require the practice to "be 'essential' or 'indispensable' to the employer's business for it to pass muster."[29] This decision turned a blind eye to the purpose of Title VII that the Court had endorsed in *Griggs*: to prohibit employment practices that have discriminatory effects as well as those that intend to discriminate. As Justice Harry Blackmun wrote in his dissent, "[o]ne wonders whether the majority still believes that race discrimination—or, more accurately, race discrimination against nonwhites—is a problem in our society, or even remembers that it ever was."[30]

In *Patterson v. McLean Credit Union* in 1989,[31] the same 5-4 majority rejected a woman bank teller's claim that she had been verbally abused at her job because of her race, further curtailing the rights of minorities to seek redress for employment discrimination. The Court held that §1981, a post-Civil War statute that gives minorities the same rights as whites to make and enforce contracts, did not extend to her employment contract's terms and conditions. This decision ignored the fact that Congress had enacted the statute out of concern both for the employment conditions of newly-freed slaves and the continued existence of racial injustices in the workplace.

In 1991, Congress enacted new civil rights legislation that revised the *Wards Cove* and *Patterson* decisions and reversed other Supreme Court cases that had hobbled the enforcement of civil rights protections in employment (discussed in chapter 22). The 1991 Civil Rights Act demonstrates how African Americans can help garner bipartisan support for a bill; even Republican senators understood the rising power of African Americans and did not want to be viewed as opposing equal opportunity. Unfortunately, recent Federalism Revolution opinions that eviscerate Congress's ability to legislate may imperil even statutes enacted with bipartisan majorities.

Disparate Impact Litigation

In *Alexander v. Sandoval* in 2001, the Supreme Court employed the *Croson* color-blind rationale in holding that suits brought by private individuals under Title VI (a provision prohibiting discrimination by recipients of federal funding) can be brought only for *intentional* discrimination rather than institutional, structural, and systemic racism. This form of discrimination is almost impossible to prove. The decision reversed nearly thirty years of precedent—including the unanimous views of all federal circuit courts—that helped people of color gain equal access to federal programs and reinforced the constitutional fiction that continued racial inequities are the result of a private discrimination that no court is required to acknowledge or correct.

The ability of private individuals to seek justice for institutional or systemic discrimination has been essential to the enforcement of civil rights laws. For example, students wishing to challenge a public school system's discriminatory funding scheme have used this impact standard (public school funding litigation is discussed in chapter 12).[32] Likewise, African Americans have used this impact standard to contest the disproportionate placement of toxic sites in their neighborhoods (environmental justice litigation is discussed in chapter 14).[33] Now, thanks to the *Sandoval* decision, that form of remedy is lost.

The Federalism Revolution

Croson's impact has been magnified by the Federalism Revolution decisions which, although appearing to have nothing to do with racial matters, significantly affect the quality of life for many African Americans. The Court has struck down several congressional statutes that attempt to protect citizens against wrongdoing by state officials. Further, the Court has used an expanded reading of the immunity from suit accorded to states by the Eleventh Amendment, and a contracted reading of the powers conferred on Congress by the Fourteenth Amendment to invalidate suits that affect many disenfranchised groups. In many respects, this Court's activism far exceeds any of the purportedly activist opinions under Chief Justice Earl Warren.[34]

In the last decade, the Court has invalidated significant portions of the Americans with Disabilities Act,[35] the Age Discrimination in Employment

Act[36] (allowed state employees to recover damages when the state unlawfully discriminated on the basis of age or disability) (discussed in chapters 7 and 8), the Violence Against Women Act (allowed victims of gender-motivated violence to sue their attackers) (discussed in chapter 6),[37] the Brady Act (directed local law enforcement officers to do background checks for possible criminal convictions of prospective gun purchasers), and the Gun Free School Zones Act (prohibited possession of a firearm within one hundred feet of a school).[38] Indeed, between 1995 and 2001, the Court declared nearly thirty federal statutes unconstitutional in whole or in part. In the two hundred years before, the Court had struck down only 127 statutes as unconstitutional.[39]

Conclusion

As the Supreme Court continues to dismantle federal protections against racial discrimination, it becomes increasingly obvious that the federal government can no longer be looked to as a sanctuary for civil rights. Perhaps the new challenge is to look below (state and local law) and above (international human rights law) the Constitution for other remedies.

State and local law could be one venue for the enforcement of civil rights protections. State constitutions and statutes often provide civil rights protections and remedies that can be vindicated in state courts or agencies.[40] The use of federalism principles might also provide political strength to minorities when, for example, they gain control of school boards or city councils. In addition, state constitutions recognize education as a function of the state; some explicitly prohibit discrimination or the implementation of educational policies with discriminatory effects, and others guarantee a minimum level of education. Civil rights organizations are mounting grassroots campaigns to enact similar legislation in other states.[41]

We may also be able to draw support from international human rights law for domestic civil rights enforcement. Several international human rights standards relate to racial equity, including the Universal Declaration of Human Rights, the Covenant Against Discrimination in Education, the International Covenant on Economic, Social, and Cultural Rights, and the International Convention on the Elimination of All Forms of Racial Discrimination.[42] Although these standards are not binding, courts turn to them for guidance in defining rights provided under law.

Struggles over racial equality have always acted as a barometer of broader rights. For example, the Civil Rights Movement paved the way for movements promoting equal rights for women, the disabled, and gays and lesbians. The

Rehnquist Court's reversal of civil rights protections for African Americans presaged reversals we are now seeing in other areas. The Court's strength has always been that unlike elected bodies, the justices can act out of constitutional principle rather than fear in interpreting the meaning of the Constitution. Of late, however, the Rehnquist Court has abandoned the true promise of equality under the Constitution, impeding the civil rights of many who have historically been left out of educational, economic, and asset-building opportunities. African Americans are thus caught in a double bind of oppression: the racial injustice itself, and the Court's systematic denial of responsibility for that reality. If the Court continues on its current path, we will have more to fear in the coming years.

Endnotes

1. See e.g. U.S. Const. art. I, §2 (amended by U.S. Const. amend. XVI); U.S. Const. art. I, §9; U.S. Const. art. III, §1; U.S. Const. art. IV, §2 (affected by U.S. Const. amend. XIII). Southerners strongly supported federalism, hoping that it would serve as a shield against attacks on slavery by the federal government. Constitutional convention delegate Charles Cotesworth Pinckney, one of the major advocates of the southern position, provided this interpretation of the constitutional compromises to his fellow South Carolinians:

> We have a security that the general government can never emancipate [the slaves], for no such authority is granted and it is admitted, on all hands, *that the general government has no powers but which are expressly granted by the Constitution, and that all rights not expressed were reserved by the several states.* In short, considering all circumstances, we made the best terms for the security of this species of property it was in our power to make.

Joseph J. Ellis, Founding Brothers: The Revolution Generation (Knopf 2000) 95 (emphasis added, citation omitted).

2. *Civil Rights Cases*, 109 U.S. 3, 11 (1883).

3. Id. at 25.

4. 163 U.S. 537 (1896).

5. *Brown v. Bd. of Educ.*, 347 U.S. 483 (1954).

6. For example, provisions of the Social Security Act excluded domestic servants and agricultural workers more than sixty percent of whom were African American from old-age pension coverage and unemployment benefits. Robert C. Lieberman, *Shifting the Color Line: Race and the American Welfare State* (1998) 44; When Congress adopted the Fair Labor Standards Act in 1938, it incorporated these same exemptions. Marc Linder, Farm Workers and the Fair Labor Standards Act: Racial Discrimination in the New Deal, 65 *Tex. L. Rev.* (1987) 1335, 1351–53; For decades beginning in the 1930s, the Federal Housing Administration and mortgage insurance policies of federal agencies denied home loans to blacks and overlooked those devices adopted by neighborhood organizations and private citizens to maintain residential segregation. See e.g., Kenneth T. Jackson, *Crabgrass Frontier: The Suburbanization of*

the United States (1985) 196–218; Gary Orfield, Federal Policy, Local Power, and Metropolitan Segregation, *89 Pol. Sci. Q.* (1975) 777, 784–90.

7. Blacks continue to be the most residentially isolated ethnic group in this country. See e.g., John Iceland, Daniel H. Weinberg, and Erika Steinmetz, U.S. Census Bureau, *Racial and Ethnic Segregation in the United States: 1980–2000* (2002) 3–4; Douglas S. Massey and Nancy A. Denton, *American Apartheid: Segregation and the Making of the Underclass* (1993) 235; Similarly, black students are more racially isolated today than anytime in the last thirty years. Erica Frankenberg, Chungmei Lee, and Gary Orfield, A Multiracial Society with Segregated Schools: Are We Losing the Dream? Harv. Univ., *The Civil Rights Project* (Jan. 2003) 8, at http://www.civilrightsproject.harvard.edu/research/reseg03/AreWeLosingtheDream.pdf. As many as two million minority and female workers continue to face employment discrimination. Alfred W. Blumrosen and Ruth G. Blumrosen, *The Reality of Intentional Job Discrimination in Metropolitan America—1999* (1999) 230, at http://www.eeo1.com/1999_NR/Chapter17.pdf. And as of 2000, 22.1 percent of African Americans lived below the poverty line, compared with only 7.5 percent of white non-Hispanics. Joseph Dalaker, U.S. Census Bureau, *Poverty in the United States: 2000* (Sept. 2001) 4.

8. *City of Richmond v. J.A. Croson Co.*, 488 U.S. 469 (1989).

9. Id. at 531–36 (Marshall, J., dissenting) (citing congressional findings).

10. Id. at 505–6.

11. In a sharply worded dissent, Justice Marshall wrote "a majority of this Court signals that it regards racial discrimination as largely a phenomenon of the past....I, however, do not believe this Nation is anywhere close to eradicating racial discrimination or its vestiges....In constitutionalizing its wishful thinking, the majority today does a grave disservice." Id. at 552–53.

12. *Green v. County Sch. Bd.*, 391 U.S. 430, 438 (1968).

13. In 1971, the Supreme Court found that planned segregation of schools led to segregated housing, with families clustered around those schools that accepted their children. *Swann v. Charlotte-Mecklenburg Bd. of Educ.*, 402 U.S. 1 (1971). *Cf. Milliken v. Bradley*, 433 U.S. 267 (1977).

14. 498 U.S. 237 (1991). In *Dowell*, the Supreme Court held that once a "unitary" system could be established, the federal court's desegregation order should end even if it meant a resegregation of schools. Although the schools at issue remained segregated for a full seventeen years after *Brown*, the Court held that if the board "has complied in good faith" and "the vestiges of past discrimination have been eliminated to the extent practicable," the desegregation decree should be ended. Id. at 249–50. The majority held that "[l]ocal control over the education of children" is preferable. Id. at 248.

15. 503 U.S. 467 (1992). In *Freeman*, the Supreme Court held that once a portion of a desegregation order is met, the federal court should cease its efforts as to that part and remain involved only as to those aspects of the plan that have not been achieved. The majority held that "[r]eturning schools to the control of local authorities at the earliest practicable date is essential to restore their true accountability in our governmental system." Id. at 490. While extolling the benefits of local control, the Rehnquist majority was simultaneously stripping away the role of the federal government in upholding democracy and removing from the Court any responsibility or accountability for the continued existence of racial injustice.

16. 515 U.S. 70 (1995). In *Missouri v. Jenkins*, the Supreme Court ordered an end to a school desegregation order for Kansas City schools. In the opinion, Chief Justice Rehnquist reminded us that the "end purpose" of desegregation decrees "is not only 'to remedy the

violation' to the extent practicable, but also 'to restore state and local authorities to the control of a school system that is operating in compliance with the Constitution." Id. at 102 (citation omitted). Rehnquist shows that in his view, racial inequality is a social condition; the government has no responsibility to remedy that inequality absent strict proof that the government created the inequities. What is more, he appears to see racial discrimination largely as a thing of the past.

17. See *Tuttle v. Arlington County Sch. Bd.*, 195 F.3d 698 (4th Cir. 1999) (per curiam), *cert. dismissed*, 529 U.S. 1050 (2000); *Eisenberg v. Montgomery County Pub. Sch.*, 197 F.3d 123 (4th Cir. 1999), *cert. denied*, 529 U.S. 1019 (2000). It is unclear how the Supreme Court's recent decisions upholding the use of race in college and university admission policies may ultimately affect the use of race in K–12 assignment plans. See *Grutter v. Bollinger*, 539 U.S. 306 (2003); *Gratz v. Bollinger*, 539 U.S. 244 (2003) (discussed infra). Currently, there is a lower court split. See e.g., *Comfort v. Lynn Sch. Committee*, 2005 WL 1404464 (1st. Cir.); *Parents Involved in Community Sch. v. Seattle Sch. Dist.*, 377 F.3d 949 (9th Cir. 2004); *McFarland v. Jefferson County Public Sch.*, 330 F.Supp.2d 834(2004).

18. In fact, American public schools have become continually *more* segregated in the past decade. One-sixth of all black students and one-fourth of black students in the Northeast and Midwest are educated in schools with almost no white students, limited resources, and enormous poverty. Erica Frankenberg et al., *supra* note 7 at 4–5, at http://www.civilrightsproject.harvard.edu/research/reseg03/AreWeLosingtheDream.pdf. On average, such segregated schools have lower average test scores, fewer advanced courses, and less qualified teachers. Id. at 11.

19. *Regents of the Univ. of Cal. v. Bakke*, 438 U.S. 265 (1978).

20. *Adarand Constructors v. Pena*, 515 U.S. 200 (1995).

21. Jed Rubenfeld, The Anti-Antidiscrimination Agenda, *111 Yale L.J.* (2002) 1141, 1170.

22. *Pena*, 515 U.S. at 240.

23. *Plessy*, 163 U.S. at 551.

24. Members of our organization, the Legal Defense Fund, have been working to promote and defend such affirmative action policies for the better part of the last two decades. In *Gratz*, LDF represented African American and Latino students who served as interveners in the case. In *Grutter*, we authored an amicus brief to the Court. In both *Grutter* and *Gratz*, the Court upheld the use of race in admissions in order to further the compelling government interest in student body diversity. Yet the Court struck down the particular admissions policy at issue in *Gratz* on the grounds that it was not sufficiently narrowly tailored to withstand strict scrutiny.

25. *Shaw v. Reno*, 509 U.S. 630, 643 (1993).

26. *Shaw*, 509 U.S. at 659 (White, J., dissenting).

27. 490 U.S. 642 (1989).

28. *Griggs v. Duke Power Co.*, 401 U.S. 424 (1971).

29. *Atonio*, 490 U.S. at 659.

30. Id. at 662.

31. 491 U.S. 164 (1989).

32. *Powell v. Ridge*, 189 F.3d 387 (3d Cir. 1999).

33. *S. Camden Citizens in Action v. N.J. Dep't of Environmental Protection*, 274 F.3d 771 (3d Cir. 2001).

34. With respect to the Warren Court, the activism was to elevate civil liberties and civil rights over governmental abuses. In contrast, the Rehnquist Court seeks to reestablish the

failed states' rights doctrines of the past—the very doctrines that led the nation to Civil War and a system of state-sanctioned apartheid. See e.g., Brent E. Simmons, The Invincibility of Constitutional Error: The Rehnquist Court's States' Rights Assault on the Fourteenth Amendment Protections of Individual Rights, *11 Seton Hall Const. L.J.* (Spring 2001) 259, 374.

35. *Bd. of Trustees of Univ. of Alabama v. Garrett*, 531 U.S. 356 (2001).

36. *Kimel v. Fla. Bd. of Regents*, 528 U.S. 62 (2000).

37. *United States v. Morrison*, 529 U.S. 598 (2000).

38. *United States v. Lopez*, 514 U.S. 549 (1995).

39. See Seth P. Waxman, Defending Congress, *79 N. Carolina L. Rev.* (2001) 1073, 1074–75.

40. See e.g., *Sheff v. O'Neill*, 678 A.2d 1267 (Conn. 1996) (state court required that the state remedy the extreme racial and ethnic isolation in the public schools, placing affirmative responsibility on the state legislature to remedy segregation regardless of whether it was *de jure* or *de facto*); *Jackson v. Pasadena City Sch. Dist.*, 382 P.2d 878 (Cal. 1963).

41. See e.g., The Racial Justice Acts as promulgated by the NAACP, at http://www.naacp.org/.

42. Off. of the United Nations High Commissioner for Human Rights, at http://www.ohchr.org/english/law/index.htm.

CHAPTER 4

LATINOS

Un Pasito Pa'lante, Un Pasito Pa'tras:[*]
Latinos and the Rollback of Civil Rights

Sandra Del Valle[†]

When the U.S. was involved in World War I, anti-German national sentiment was virulent—many German-Americans would not speak their native language even in private, telephone operators who overheard German being spoken would disconnect the call, and state legislatures passed laws making it a crime to teach German, even in private religious schools. It was such a law that was challenged in Nebraska's state courts in 1920. In upholding the German language ban, Nebraska's Supreme Court said:

> *To allow the children of foreigners, who had emigrated here, to be taught from early childhood the language of the country of their parents was to rear them so that they must always think in that language, and as a consequence, naturally inculcate in them the ideas and sentiments foreign to the best interests of this country.*[‡]

The court clearly recognized one of the complex aspects of language—its place not only in each individual's self-identification, but also in the nation's self-conception. But instead of viewing minority languages through a lens of tolerance, as our national identity demands, the court chose to treat them as a threat to national unity.

Meyer v. Nebraska would have to make it to the U.S. Supreme Court before German bible schools would be once again allowed to use their native language. Unfortunately, by 1923, when the Court finally decided Meyer, *many schools had*

---

   * One Step Forward and One Step Back.

   † Sandra Del Valle is a civil rights lawyer who has worked at the Puerto Rican Legal Defense and Education Fund for over ten years. She specializes in language rights, especially those of immigrant children, and bilingual education.

   ‡ *Meyer v. State*, 187 N.W. 100, 102 (Neb. 1922).

closed their doors because of anti-German sentiment. Still, the Court remained unequivocal about the need to ensure constitutional protections for all: "[t]he protection of the constitution extends to all, to those who speak other languages as well as to those born with English on the tongue." *

Although the Court's words seem unambiguous and incontestable, the place of language rights within our constitutional framework is far from certain. Bilinguals and non-English speakers are still questioned about their patriotism, national identity, and moral worthiness. In 1995, for example, a Texas judge presiding over a custody dispute accused the mother of child abuse for speaking to her five-year old daughter in Spanish, claiming that such a practice would ensure that the child's future would be tied to a mop and pail. Ron Unz, the California millionaire who has waged a war on bilingual education, used the same reasoning to talk voters into abandoning bilingual education in California, Arizona, and Massachusetts. Mexican workers at a beauty products distributor in Connecticut were hounded out of their jobs when they refused to (or could not) follow an English-only workplace rule. While the latter discrimination is still being challenged in court, the protections offered to minority language speakers are precarious. The Court recently held that private parties cannot enforce the implementing regulations of Title VI of the 1964 Civil Rights Act in court, yet this very Act has been significant in ensuring a place for minority languages in our national culture because it prohibits discrimination based on ethnicity and national origin.

This chapter will compare two language rights cases both to illustrate the extent of the rollback of federal rights and explain how that rollback may foreclose the space that Latinos need in order to expand the traditional approach to civil rights to better serve their needs.

ॐ ॐ ॐ

Latinos in the U.S.

A decade ago, researchers wrote: "Latino population growth is the future."[1] According to the 2000 census, the future is now. The Latino population, predicted to make up over twenty-four percent of the U.S. population by 2050,[2] has transformed cities, towns, and rural areas. Communities that previously had virtually no Latino members have had to address linguistic and cultural issues not yet mastered by urban centers. While some welcomed the economic revitalization produced by increased immigration, others saw immigrants as

---

* *Meyer v. Neb.*, 262 U.S. 390, 401 (1923).

a threat to their homogenous communities and struck out with anger.[3] The business and political worlds have also addressed the bourgeoning Latino community by catering to presumed Latino needs and tastes and using more Spanish in campaigns.[4] Many ramifications of the Latino population growth, however, have yet to be felt.

While this is a time of great change for Latinos, one troubling reality cannot be ignored: while the Latino population is exploding, civil rights and liberties are shrinking. Latinos have always challenged the traditional construction of civil rights—which operates as though everyone is either black or white—because Latinos cross lines of race, national origin, ancestry, citizenship, and ethnicity.[5] Faced with an increasingly extremist Judiciary, however, Latinos have had to frame their civil rights struggles along classic racial lines so as to convince courts they fit into the traditional model (rather than trying to expand or even explode the model as irrelevant to their reality). The civil rights rollback endangers even that compromised position.

To illustrate the extent of the rollback and explain how it may foreclose the space needed by Latinos to expand the traditional approach to civil rights, this chapter will contrast two civil rights cases—*Katzenbach v. Morgan*,[6] a 1966 voting rights case in which the Supreme Court upheld federal legislation designed to ensure that Puerto Ricans had access to the ballot, and *Hernandez v. New York*,[7] a 1995 jury service case in which the Court found that the purposeful exclusion of bilingual people from juries did not violate the Equal Protection Clause. Both cases deal with language rights, an appropriate focus for this chapter for three reasons: Latinos comprise the single largest minority language group in the U.S.; language rights law is still in an embryonic state compared with other civil rights areas; and, because minority language usage is not specifically protected by any federal civil rights law, it is an easy target for activist judges looking for ways to limit affirmative civil rights. While the Court has come a long way in its civil rights cases, sadly it seems to be going in the wrong direction.

Katzenbach v. Morgan

Section 4(e) of the Voting Rights Act of 1965, known as the "Puerto Rico Exception," ensures that no person who has successfully completed sixth grade in a Spanish language school in Puerto Rico can be denied the right to vote because of his or her inability to read or write in English.[8] Section 4(e) was sponsored by New York congressional leaders in an effort to prevent the disenfranchisement of a large segment of the Puerto Rican population who, although literate in Spanish, might have been disqualified from voting by the state's requirement that they also be literate in English.

Shortly after Congress passed §4(e), a group of New York City voters sued to challenge its constitutionality. In the suit, *Morgan v. Katzenbach*,[9] the plaintiffs complained that their votes were diluted by those of non-English literate Puerto Ricans living in New York, and claimed that Congress did not have the power to enact §4(e) because, "[t]raditionally and historically the qualifications of voters has been invariably a matter regulated by the States."[10] The trial level federal court agreed, ruling against Puerto Rican voters.

Fortunately, the decision was appealed to the Supreme Court.[11] The main question before the Court in *Katzenbach v. Morgan* was how closely to review §4(e)—should the Court subject the legislation to judicial scrutiny, or should it presume the validity of the congressional statute? Defending its English literacy law, New York argued for a high standard of judicial review, asserting that Congress could use its Fourteenth Amendment powers to enact §4(e) only if it had found that New York's English literacy requirement violated the Equal Protection Clause. The state, however, was confident that Congress had not conducted enough of an inquiry into the purpose and effect of the English literacy law needed to constitute an Equal Protection Clause violation. To be sure, such confidence was not foolish—the Court had previously decided in *Lassiter v. Northampton County Bd. of Elections* that literacy tests were only unconstitutional if proven to be intentionally discriminatory.[12] *Lassiter* is an example of an Equal Protection analysis that relies on a showing of past wrongs perpetrated against a community by a local government, a pattern more frequently found with the treatment of African Americans than Latinos.

The federal government argued that the Court's review of §4(e) should be more limited—the Court did not need to decide that New York's English literacy requirement was unconstitutional, it had only to determine whether Congress' enacting of §4(e) was "appropriate."

The Court agreed with the federal government, rejecting New York's argument that state voting requirements conflicting with §4(e) should be evaluated on a case-by-case basis and holding that all of those voting requirements would fall if §4(e) were upheld. Accordingly, the Court decided that the only question for judicial resolution was whether §4(e) was "appropriate legislation to enforce the Equal Protection Clause."[13] The Court stated that appropriate legislation is "adapted to carry out the objects the [Equal Protection Clause has] in view, whatever tends to enforce submission to the prohibitions [that clause contains], and to secure to all persons the enjoyment of perfect equality of civil rights and the equal protection of the laws against State denial or invasion."[14] It followed that §4(e) was constitutional as long as it was enacted to enforce the Equal Protection Clause and was not "prohibited by but [was] consistent with 'the letter and spirit of the constitution.'"[15]

The Court found that, both by its language and effect, §4(e) was adapted to enforce the Equal Protection Clause because:

> [t]he practical effect of §4(e) is to prohibit New York from denying the right to vote to large segments of its Puerto Rican community. Congress has thus prohibited the State from denying to that community the right that is 'preservative of all rights'.... This enhanced political power will be helpful in gaining nondiscriminatory treatment in public services for the entire Puerto Rican community.[16]

Indeed, §4(e) ensures that Puerto Ricans will not be discriminated against either in their access to the vote or in the way government is administered (as voting rights ensure government responsiveness to their constituents).

The Court respected Congress's discretion in determining what legislation was needed to secure the guarantees afforded by the Equal Protection Clause, finding that Congress could have rejected New York's justification of its English literacy requirement: that it was necessary to force immigrants to learn English (the same rationale English-only advocates use today to justify repealing §4(e)). The Court understood that "Congress might have also questioned whether denial of a right deemed so precious and fundamental in our society was a necessary or appropriate means of encouraging persons to learn English."[17] Similarly, it held that Congress could have rejected the argument that the English literacy requirement would help ensure "intelligent exercise of the franchise" on the grounds that Spanish literacy is equally effective "for those to whom Spanish-language newspapers and Spanish-language radio and television programs are available to inform them of election issues and governmental affairs."[18] It was up to Congress, not the Court, to balance these competing interests. The Court simply had to agree that there was a basis upon which Congress could have found that New York's English literacy requirement violated the Equal Protection Clause.[19]

The Court's final inquiry was whether §4(e) itself violated the Constitution. New York argued that by not extending the provision to all non-English literate people (including those who were not educated in American flag schools), Congress perpetuated its own discrimination. This argument, however, was foolish. Because Congress can take small steps toward ameliorating social problems, "[a] statute is not invalid under the Constitution because it might have gone farther than it did."[20] Further, the Court held that Congress had a legitimate basis for recognizing the unique relationship between Puerto Rico and the U.S. through its legislation.[21]

Hernandez v. New York

In 1991, almost three decades after *Katzenbach* and in the threshold era for the rollback of civil rights, the Supreme Court heard *Hernandez v. New York.*[22] *Hernandez* was a criminal case in which both the defendant, Dionisio Hernandez, and the victims were Latinos, and much of the state's evidence consisted of recordings of conversations in Spanish. A court interpreter would translate the tapes for the judge and jury throughout the trial.

During jury selection, the state prosecutor used peremptory challenges to request the removal of Spanish-speakers because he felt that such jurors would be unlikely to accept a translated version of the testimonies. Even though the jurors said that they could accept the translator's version of what was said at trial, the prosecutor felt that "from the hesitancy in their answers and their lack of eye contact that they would not be able to do it."[23] The judge agreed, the case was tried without any bilingual jurors, and Hernandez was convicted.

On appeal to the New York Court of Appeals, Hernandez argued that since Spanish-language ability is closely related to ethnicity, the prosecutor's peremptory challenges were racially discriminatory. The Supreme Court has held that the use of peremptory challenges to exclude African Americans from a jury without a race-neutral reason violates the Sixth Amendment right to a fair jury trial and the Fourteenth Amendment Equal Protection Clause.[24]

Although the Court of Appeals upheld Hernandez's conviction,[25] Chief Judge Judith Kaye dissented, finding that the prosecutor's explanation for challenging the Latino jurors would negatively impact their ability to serve on juries because, "[t]he statistics before us indicate that, in Kings County, virtually all Latinos speak Spanish at home."[26] Excluding Spanish-speaking jurors simply because a Spanish-speaking witness will testify, said Judge Kaye, allows the prosecution to do "by indirection what can no longer be done directly."[27]

Judge Kaye reasoned that "[a]n explanation by a prosecutor that may appear facially neutral but nonetheless has a disparate impact on members of defendant's racial or ethnic group is 'inherently suspect.'"[28] To prevent the continuation of discriminatory practices, peremptory challenges must be based on more than speculation that Spanish-speaking jurors will be unfair. "[D]espite this court's repeated reference to the two jurors' initial expressed uncertainty or hesitancy," Judge Kaye said, "the fact remains that both individuals satisfied the court that they would accept the official court translation, and that they would be fair and impartial jurors."[29]

Judge Kaye's proposed solution was simple: bilingual jurors should not be stricken wholesale from juries where interpreters are used. Instead, the trial court should instruct bilingual jurors to follow the official court interpreter and to bring to the court's attention—not the other jurors—any errors in the interpretation.[30] The assumption that jurors will follow a court's instructions, whether related to the presumption of innocence or the weight to be given to certain evidence, is the lynchpin of the U.S. trial system.

Hernandez was appealed to the Supreme Court, where Judge Kaye's reasoning was given no place. The Court found that, while the prosecutor's criteria for challenging jurors would likely result in a disproportionate removal of Latinos from juries, disparate impact was insufficient to state a violation of the Equal Protection Clause (which requires proof of intentional discrimination). The Court stated that, "even if we knew that a high percentage of bilingual jurors would hesitate in answering questions like [those asked by the prosecutor] and, as a consequence, would be excluded under the prosecutor's criterion, that fact alone would not cause the criterion to fail the race-neutrality test."[31] Instead, the Court decided that the disparate impact of the challenges on prospective Latino jurors should be considered in evaluating the sincerity of the prosecutor's race-neutral rationale. In this case, the Court ruled that the trial court was right to trust the prosecutor's sincerity, and upheld that court's finding.

Hernandez also lost his claim under the Equal Protection Clause because of the Court's narrow interpretation of "race." The Court even acknowledged that the traditional understanding of race might be inappropriate when applied to discrimination against Latinos:

> [i]n holding that a race-neutral reason for a peremptory challenge means a reason other than race, we do not resolve the more difficult question of the breadth with which the concept of race should be defined for equal protection purposes. We would face a quite different case if the prosecutor had justified his peremptory challenges with the explanation that he did not want Spanish-speaking jurors. It may well be, for certain ethnic groups and in some communities, that proficiency in a particular language, like skin color, should be treated as a surrogate for race under an equal protection analysis.[32]

Despite this recognition, the Court ignored the problem. Allowing prosecutors to strike bilingual people from juries, however, will often result in their exclusion. The Court was aware of this possibility:

> [o]ur decision today does not imply that exclusion of bilinguals from jury service is wise, or even that it is constitutional in all cases. It is a harsh paradox that one may become proficient enough in English to participate in trial...only to encounter disqualification because he knows a second language as well. As the Court observed in a some-

what related context: "Mere knowledge of [a foreign] language cannot reasonably be regarded as harmful. Heretofore it has been commonly looked upon as helpful and desirable."[33]

The Court did not, however, offer guidance on how to avoid this harsh result.

How the Rollback Affects Latinos

In 1965, the *Katzenbach* Court protected a fundamental aspect of citizenship,
voting, when it could have done otherwise. To be sure, Justices John Harlan and
Potter Stewart offered a vigorous dissent that could have swayed a majority of the
justices in a more right wing court.[34] For Justices Harlan and Stewart, the negative impact of their decision on the Latino community's voting ability had no
place in their analysis—a foreshadowing of the Court's decision in *Hernandez*.

In comparison, the 1991 Court that decided *Hernandez* seems small and
bitter—even the exclusion of bilingual people from juries prompted only
some hand-wringing. Moreover, the kind of bilingualism envisioned by the
Court could not function at even a moderate level without being deemed suspicious. The Court was caught in a changing demographic situation, but was
unable to fashion new civil rights norms in response.

Bilinguals are no longer exotics. In New York, Houston, Dallas, Chicago,
Los Angeles, Hartford, and Jersey City, it is common for Spanish-speaking
bilinguals to serve on juries. Indeed, Judge Kaye's proposed measures for the
accommodation, and even the affirmative use, of bilingual jurors to ensure
accurate interpretation reflects our multilingual society. The Supreme Court,
however, refused to address the presence of bilinguals and did not attempt to
re-create racial and ethnic definitions. Instead, bilinguals were marginalized
and denied one of the fundamental rights of citizenship—jury service.

Given the Federalism Revolution's panoply of decisions curtailing federal
rights (particularly the *Sandoval* decision that took a significant step towards
eliminating disparate impact litigation, which is discussed in chapter 10), Latinos have much to fear from the current federal Judiciary. Language-based claims
will be more difficult to bring than in the past. Now that the courts are closing
the door to traditional civil rights claims, they will likely be unwilling to open
new legal avenues to address areas of particular concern to Latinos (e.g., the intersection of immigration laws and civil rights, the privileges accompanying citizenship, and the civil rights implications of increased border enforcement).

Meanwhile, other issues like education segregation (a lynchpin of the traditional civil rights struggle) must be discussed again in the context of Latino

issues. Crammed into the worst performing schools, Latinos are rapidly becoming the most segregated race in the country.[35] Latinos, however, value local schools because for bilingual education programs to be implemented, a critical mass of Spanish-dominant students must exist.

White millionaire Ron Unz, however, is targeting these bilingual programs for elimination. Unz successfully used the California initiative processes to frighten white voters into eliminating bilingual education, while Latino parents of children enrolled in the programs voted to maintain them.[36] Despite many federal court challenges, the initiative became California law. Less than three decades ago, civil rights activists were calling bilingual education a right. Today, it has become an option for some and an inconvenience for others.

Conclusion

With increased immigration and a youthful population, Latinos are poised to follow in the footsteps of previous immigrant groups who re-made communities, influenced legislation, and changed the national psyche. The reality, however, is not so promising. Latinos comprise the nation's poorest racial population, and while the group is growing, unprecedented hostility exists towards the immigrants. Whether Latinos can leverage their demographic size into economic security and political power will depend, in part, on how successfully they can reframe the traditional civil rights paradigm. Civil rights affects issues critical to the development of viable communities—language, education, employment, voting, environmental justice, immigration, and housing. Latinos cannot ignore civil rights without jeopardizing their own future.

Endnotes

1. Jorge Chapa and Richard R. Valencia, Latino Population Growth, Demographic Characteristics, and Educational Stagnation: An Examination of Recent Trends, *15 Hisp. J. Behav. Sci.* (1993) 165, 167.

2. U.S. Bureau of the Census, Current Population Reports, Series P23-194, *Population Profile of the United States: 1997* (1998) 8–9, at http://www.census.gov/prod/3/98pubs/p23-194.pdf.

3. Elizabeth Paine, Long Island Leaders Stand up to Hate Groups, *People's Weekly World* (Aug. 2001), at http://www.pww.org/; Karen Matthews, *NY: Long Island Battle Over Illegal Aliens*, at http://www.freerepublic.com/home.htm (Jul. 9, 2001).

4. Indeed, New York City's historically liberal Latino population flexed its own muscle in the 2001 mayoral race by punishing the democratic candidate Mark Green for assuming he had their vote by helping give the election to the republican Mike Bloomberg.

5. See William R. Tamayo, When the "Coloreds" Are Neither Black nor Citizens: The United States Civil Rights Movement and Global Migration, 2 Asian L.J. (1995) 1, for more on the limitations of the classic civil rights paradigm.

6. 384 U.S. 641 (1966).

7. 500 U.S. 352 (1991).

8. 42 U.S.C. § 1973b(f). Section 4(e) reads: (1) Congress hereby declares that to secure the rights under the Fourteenth Amendment of persons educated in American-flag schools in which the predominant classroom language was other than English, it is necessary to prohibit the States from conditioning the right to vote of such persons on ability to read, write, understand, or interpret any matter in the English language. (2) No person who demonstrates that he has successfully completed the sixth primary grade in a public school in, or a private school accredited by, any State or territory, the District of Columbia, or the Commonwealth of Puerto Rico in which the predominant classroom language was other than English, shall be denied the right to vote in any Federal, State, or local election because of his inability to read, write, understand, or interpret any matter in the English language, except that in States in which State law provides that a different level of education is presumptive of literacy, he shall demonstrate that he has successfully completed an equivalent level of education in a public school in, or a private school accredited by, any State of territory, the District of Columbia, or the Commonwealth of Puerto Rico in which the predominant classroom language was other than English.

9. 247 F.Supp. 196, rev'd Katzenbach, 384 U.S. 641.

10. Morgan, 247 F.Supp. at 200.

11. Also decided in 1965 was another challenge against New York's election law. In United States v. County Bd. of Elections, 248 F.Supp. 316 (W.D.N.Y. 1965), the federal government applied for a temporary restraining order for the full application of the literacy requirement and an order requiring the board of elections to register all persons who could qualify to vote under § 4(e). This time, the campaign for language rights was successful—the district court unanimously upheld the Voting Rights Act but limited its rationale to the specific situation of Puerto Ricans, citizens whose dominance in Spanish had been encouraged by the federal government. The district court detailed the historical relationship between the U.S. and Puerto Rico, and the impact of the federal acquiescence to the role of Spanish on the island, and stated, "we are confronted with American citizens of Puerto Rican birth or residence who have been encouraged by our government's Puerto Rican educational and foreign policy to use Spanish as the means of communication in both public and private life." County Bd. of Elections, 248 F.Supp. at 319. That Congress, through § 4(e), wanted to ensure that these citizens' right to vote was a judgment "Congress...was superbly suited to make." Id. at 323. Although the court was aware of the Morgan Court's different opinion on the constitutionality of § 4(e), it declined to follow that Court's reasoning. Id. Only the Morgan decision was appealed to the Supreme Court.

12. Lassiter v. Northampton County Bd. of Elections, 360 U.S. 45 (1959).

13. See Katzenbach, 384 U.S. at 650.

14. Id. (quoting Ex parte Va., 100 U.S. 339, 345–46 (1880)).

15. Id. at 651 (citations omitted).

16. Id. at 652 (citations omitted).

17. Id. at 654.

18. Id. at 655.

19. Id. at 656.

20. Roschen v. Ward, 279 U.S. 337, 339 (1929).

21. *Katzenbach*, 384 U.S. at 658. In 1965, the federal district court in *County Bd. of Elections* also acknowledged the special relationship between Puerto Rico and the U.S.

22. 500 U.S. 352.

23. Id. at 357, n.1.

24. *Batson v. Kentucky*, 476 U.S. 79 (1986).

25. *People v. Hernandez*, 75 NY.2d 350 (1990).

26. *Hernandez*, 75 NY.2d at 361.

27. Id. at 362.

28. Id.

29. Id. at 363.

30. Id. at 362.

31. *Hernandez*, 500 U.S. at 362.

32. Id. at 371.

33. Id.

34. For Harlan and Stewart, New York only had to provide a rational basis for its English literacy requirement in order to pass constitutional muster. *Katzenbach,* 384 U.S. at 663. New York's interest in having a well-informed electorate, they reasoned, could be undermined by allowing even the well-informed Spanish literate to vote because their access to information would be more limited than that of the English literate because they rely on fewer media outlets and the translation of major speeches by candidates rather than the candidate's original words.

35. Gary Orfield, Schools More Separate: Consequences of a Decade of Resegregation, Harv. Univ., *The Civil Rights Project* (Jul. 2001) 2, at http://www.civilrightsproject.harvard.edu/research/deseg/Schools_More_Separate.pdf.

36. For detailed information on Ron Unz and his campaign against bilingual education, see www.onenation.org. According to the Mauricio Gaston Institute of the University of Massachusetts, 93.2 percent of the Latinos polled voted against the anti-bilingual education initiative when it was introduced in Massachusetts. See http://www.gaston.umb.edu/ resactiv/w_papers/vote_bilingual.doc.

CHAPTER 5

ASIAN AMERICANS

Asian Americans under the Rehnquist Court:
A Protracted and Ongoing Struggle for
Justice and Recognition

Vincent A. Eng* and Julianna Lee†

When I was a child, my family took many road trips. During one Midwestern trip, as we were driving through Michigan, my dad said that we could not open the windows because an Asian American had been killed there three years before. It was summer, the air conditioner was broken, and my older sister and I could not understand why our parents would deny us fresh air—all because of an Asian man who we had never met.

Now, I understand. Vincent Chin, a Chinese American man, had been brutally murdered by two white autoworkers in the Detroit suburbs. The details of the killing were horrific enough to cause anyone to lock their doors when nearing the crime scene. It was not only the hate incident or the threat of racial violence, however, that worried my parents. It was the ensuing injustice perpetrated by the police and the judicial system—those to whom Americans entrust law enforcement and civil rights protection. My parents considered Michigan enemy territory, a dangerous place we needed to cross to get to Chicago.

In June 1982, Vincent Chin was celebrating his bachelor party in a Detroit bar. Two white men, Ronald Ebens and his stepson Michael Nitz, taunted him with racial slurs and aggressive gestures. Ebens and Nitz, both recently laid off, blamed

---

*   Vincent A. Eng is the Deputy Director of the National Asian Pacific American Legal Consortium, a national non-profit and non-partisan organization that works to advance the civil rights of Asian Americans through advocacy, public policy, public education, and litigation.
    † Julianna Lee is a third year law student at the University of Michigan, and a graduate of Wellesley College and Harvard University. In 2004, she gave a keynote address on the National Mall in Washington, DC, on the future of civil rights for the Voices of Civil Rights, a project of the Leadership Conference on Civil Rights Education Fund.

the Japanese for the downturn in the automobile industry; Chin was merely the victim of their wrath against Asians. The doorman broke up the ensuing bar fight, but Ebens and Nitz pursued the "Chinese guy" after he left the bar, then smashed his head and body with a baseball bat. Chin died four days later from brain damage and severe injuries. Before losing consciousness, he remarked, "[i]t isn't fair."

As his case went to court, the injustice escalated. Ebens and Nitz, sentenced to two years probation and a $3,700 fine, literally "got away with murder." In laying down the negligible punishment, Wayne County court Judge Charles Kauffman explained that, "[t]hese men are not going to go out and harm somebody else. I just didn't think that putting them in prison would do any good for them or society."

Asian American activists and lawyers mobilized around the injustice, forming American Citizens for Justice. The organization unsuccessfully appealed the case to two different federal district courts. Still, the efforts generated an awareness of civil rights and built a coalition within the Asian American community.

My parent's reluctance to stop the car or open the windows during our drive through Michigan shows the impact that Chin's murder had on the Asian American community. Sweating in the backseat is a memory that remains with me today, informing my understanding of the wide-spread impact of civil rights injustices.

This chapter will underscore the need to address the Rehnquist Court's rollback of civil rights and liberties. The rollback, however, is unique for Asian Americans. Rather than facing a backward movement from a progression, they instead face a continuing disregard by the Supreme Court and marginal consideration in legislation.

      ð   ð   ð

Hate crimes such as the Chin murder and the rise of anti-Asian violence following 9/11 have raised the level of discourse about minority civil rights. Many states have proposed, and some have enacted, anti-hate crime legislation. Civil rights awareness has advanced to where one can no longer rationalize the racism underlying Supreme Court decisions such as *Plessy v. Ferguson*,[1] which upheld the constitutionality of state-mandated racial segregation. Such awareness, however, particularly as it pertains to Asian Americans, has yet to penetrate the Rehnquist Court.

The Supreme Court is supposed to function as an unbiased arbiter of justice under the Constitution. The Rehnquist Court, however, has continued a tradition that began in the nineteenth century of denying Asian Americans their civil rights—examples include *Chae Chan Ping v. U.S*, the 1889 decision that upheld the legality of the Chinese Exclusion Act,[2] the Japanese American internment cases of the 1940s,[3] *Wards Cove Packing Company, Inc.*

v. Atonio, a more recent employment discrimination case that was decided against the interests of Alaska Native, Filipino, Chinese, Samoan, and Japanese workers,[4] and *Rice v. Cayetano*,[5] in which the Court struck down a state law limiting those entitled to vote for trustees of the Office of Hawaiian Affairs to people of Native Hawaiian ancestry. The legacy of those decisions remains today.

Asian Americans and the Law

Asian Americans and Latinos are the fastest growing minority groups in the U.S. According to the 2000 census, the Asian American population has increased over the past ten years by nearly forty-eight percent (to 10.2 million).[6] Although this group is growing, they are often forgotten in law and policy discussions. Worse still, the conservative right has tried to use Asian Americans as a wedge group to undermine broader civil rights—a tactic used recently by the plaintiffs in *Gratz v. Bollinger*[7] and *Grutter v. Bollinger*[8] in challenging the University of Michigan's affirmative action policies.

To understand the effects of the Court's Federalism Revolution on Asian Americans, it is necessary to examine the long and significant role that they have played in the U.S. courts (contrary to their popular characterization as recent immigrants with little political involvement). Throughout history, each of the three government branches has had a hand in setting laws and passing judgments excluding Asians from becoming citizens,[9] testifying in court,[10] owning land,[11] and receiving integrated education.[12]

The most egregious example of discriminatory treatment and racial profiling was the internment, without Due Process, of over 120,000 Japanese Americans during World War II under President Franklin D. Roosevelt's Executive Order 9066 (an Order upheld as constitutional by the Supreme Court).[13] The government then recruited Japanese American men within the barbed wire camps, pressuring them to demonstrate their patriotism to the U.S. while stigmatizing those "no-no boys" who, disillusioned by the government's duplicitous treatment, turned away from military service.[14] The enlisted troops became the segregated Japanese American 442nd Regimental Combat Team, the most highly decorated unit in military history.

The internment of Japanese Americans served as a social awakening for Asian Americans. Unfortunately, mainstream society continued to accept that constitutional rights could differ based on people's race, ethnicity, and national origin.

The Rehnquist Court and the
Civil Rights of Asian Americans

The Rehnquist Court has curtailed the civil rights of all Americans. Its decision in *Alexander v. Sandoval*[15] (discussed in chapter 10), which struck at the heart of civil rights protections for language minorities, has made it difficult for Asian Americans to enforce their rights to benefits and services under Title VI of the 1964 Civil Rights Act. While *Sandoval* has created problems for communities that contain a significant percentage of language minorities (e.g., the Asian American community), this chapter will focus on two immigrant rights cases—*Hoffman Plastic Compounds v. NLRB*[16] and *Demore v. Kim*[17]—to demonstrate the continued struggle facing all immigrants under the Rehnquist Court.

Matters concerning undocumented immigrants are often wrongly thought to affect only Latinos—a generalization that ignores demographics. The Urban Institute estimates that there are over 9.3 million undocumented immigrants, ten percent of whom are from Asian countries.[18] Moreover, undocumented people account for almost ten percent of the Asian American population.[19]

Hoffman Plastic Compounds v. NLRB

The federal National Labor Relations Act (NLRA) of 1935 remedied many significant labor issues, including ending the fourteen hour workday, improving dangerous working conditions, and disallowing the absence of benefits or health care for full-time employees. The NLRA guarantees to non-supervisory employees the right to self-organize, choose their own representatives, and negotiate for benefits. The Act also compels management to recognize worker's basic human rights by imposing financial penalties (e.g., back pay and the reinstatement of unlawfully discharged employees) on employers who interfere with those rights.

What if the working conditions in a factory today are less than ideal? Workers can explore their right to self-organize—just as José Castro did. Hoffman Plastics hired Castro in 1988 as a minimum wage employee. Shortly thereafter, Castro (along with other employees) began an organizing drive for the United Rubber, Cork, Linoleum, and Plastic Workers of America union. They distributed union authorization cards and other literature to fellow employees—activities protected under the NLRA. When Hoffman Plastics learned of the unionizing efforts, they began a "coercive and restraining" interrogation, then fired Castro and all those involved.[20]

The NLRA, which is enforced by the National Labor Relations Board (NLRB), has the authority to remedy unfair labor practices, including reinstating workers and awarding them back pay for the time they were improperly out of work. This remedy not only makes affected workers whole, but deprives employers of any competitive advantage they may have secured by acting unlawfully.

An Administrative Law Judge (ALJ) held that Hoffman had engaged in multiple unfair labor practices. The NLRB concurred, concluding that Hoffman had unlawfully interrogated employees about their union activities, and that "in order to rid itself of known union supporters, [Hoffman] discriminatorily selected union adherents for layoff" in violation of the NLRA.[21] The NLRB ordered Hoffman to cease and desist from such unfair labor practices, post a notice at the work site, and reinstate and make whole those employees it had fired.

In the compliance hearing, however, a disagreement arose over the amount of back pay that should be awarded. When Castro testified before the ALJ, Hoffman's attorney questioned him about his citizenship and his authorization to work in the U.S. The NLRB attorney objected to the question and the ALJ sustained the objection, but not before Castro had stated that he was a Mexican national and that he had borrowed the birth certificate he had used to gain employment at Hoffman from a friend. Based on his admission, the ALJ recommended neither reinstatement nor back pay.[22] The NLRB mostly complied, refusing reinstatement and limiting Castro's back pay to the period starting when he was wrongfully discharged and ending when his employer learned that he was unauthorized to work in the U.S.[23]

The case was appealed to the DC Circuit Court of Appeals where Hoffman argued that Castro was not entitled to back pay because he was an undocumented worker. The court rejected that argument, and upheld the NLRB's back pay award[24]—a decision consistent with the Supreme Court's 1984 ruling in *Sure-Tan, Inc. v. NLRB*[25] that "[i]f undocumented alien employees were excluded from participation in union activities and from protection against employer intimidation, there would be created a subclass of workers without a comparable stake in the collective goals of their legally resident co-workers, thereby eroding the unity of all employees and impeding effective collective bargaining."[26] Hoffman appealed the ruling to the Supreme Court.

In 2002, the Supreme Court ruled in *Hoffman Plastic Compounds, Inc. v. NLRB* that undocumented workers who are illegally fired for engaging in union organizing activities are not entitled to back pay (the only monetary remedy available under the NLRA). The Court held that the "legal landscape [had] now significantly changed"[27] since *Sure-Tan* with the passage of the Immigration Reform and Control Act (IRCA) of 1986,[28] an Act prohibiting employers from knowingly hiring undocumented workers. The Court maintained, however, that undocumented workers are still "employees" under the NLRA—just not with respect to the back pay remedy. The decision effectively created an incentive for non-unionized companies to hire undocumented workers, because if those workers tried to organize, the company could terminate them without fearing a financial penalty. With nearly a million undocumented Asians in the U.S. (over half unionized), the *Hoffman* decision sends a chilling message to the Asian American community.

Unsurprisingly, employers immediately attempted to extend the *Hoffman* ruling to other employment and labor laws, arguing that undocumented workers should not have the right to minimum wage and overtime protections such as those afforded by the Fair Labor Standards Act (FLSA) of 1938.[29] Retaliation claims involving undocumented workers have also been challenged.[30] Likewise, employers raised similar arguments to deny undocumented workers the right to be free from discrimination based on race, national origin, gender, sexual harassment, religion, and disability (as provided by Title VII of the Civil Rights Act of 1964 and the Americans with Disabilities Act of 1990).[31] Most troubling, employers tried to use the judicial process to determine worker's immigration status and intimidate them into dropping their claims. To date, the cases brought to expand *Hoffman* have involved South Asian, Chinese, and Latino immigrants.[32] Very few, however, reach the courts. Most undocumented workers lack the resources to bring employment litigation; moreover, the fear of deportation prevents many from even asserting their rights.

Two pieces of federal legislation still pending attempt to correct *Hoffman*— the Safe, Orderly, Legal Visas and Enforcement Act (SOLVE) of 2004,[33] and the Fairness and Individual Rights Necessary to Ensure a Stronger Society: Civil Rights Act of 2004[34] (discussed in chapter 22). Without a legislative fix, however, *Hoffman* will continue to undermine the rights of all workers to organize.

Demore v. Kim

The Due Process Clause of the Fifth Amendment requires that the government act fairly when it seeks to deprive people (not just citizens) of fundamental rights. That provision states that, "*[n]o person* shall…be deprived of life, liberty or property, without due process of law."[35] Due Process applies to all branches of government—even when Congress exercises its otherwise plenary powers over immigration, courts must act to protect citizens' constitutional guarantees of Due Process. Indeed, the Supreme Court is charged with delivering justice and laying down judgments that follow the "letter and spirit of the Constitution."[36] The Rehnquist Court has failed in this charge when it comes to civil rights.

Thirty percent of America's foreign-born population began as lawful permanent residents (green card holders). Amounting to over ten million individuals, permanent residents are a rapidly growing segment of the population.[37] As their title implies, they make the U.S. their permanent home. They are almost always treated as citizens. Many arrive when young, and build their lives in the U.S.—they invest in education, pay taxes, serve in the military, contribute skills and labor to the economy, and are the parents, siblings, and children of citizens. While their immigration status is the most favored of all, the Rehnquist Court has significantly abridged their rights.

Hyung Joon Kim's case illustrates the extent of the rollback of the civil rights of green card holders. The INS attempted to hold Kim indefinitely in a detention facility while awaiting the outcome of his removal proceedings (to determine whether he was to be deported). Kim had emigrated from South Korea in 1984 at the age of six. He and his family became lawful permanent residents two years later—a status that enabled him to live like a citizen in his neighborhood, university, and family. At eighteen, Kim was convicted of first degree burglary for breaking into a tool shed, and was sentenced to five years probation and 180 days in jail (117 of which were eventually suspended). Later, when a student at the University of California at Santa Barbara, Kim was arrested for shoplifting videotapes. He was charged and convicted of petty theft with priors, a felony carrying a maximum sentence of three years in state prison. As a lawful permanent resident, federal immigration law categorized him as a criminal immigrant, subject to deportation in addition to time served—disproportionately grave consequences that illustrate the chasm that has developed between the rights of citizens and the rights of permanent residents.

Kim was released early for good behavior, but was arrested the next day by immigration authorities and jailed under a provision of the Illegal Immigration Reform and Immigrant Responsibility Act (IIRIRA) of 1996,[38] a statute that requires mandatory detention and potential deportation of any non-citizen convicted of a crime punishable by a sentence of a year or more in prison. Kim was placed in removal proceedings, a process that has lasted thirty days for some immigrants while others have waited years to learn whether they will be deported.

Kim requested a hearing before an immigration judge to demonstrate that he was neither a flight risk nor a threat to the community and should be released from detention on bail. Although the INS conceded both, the IIRIRA forbade the immigration judge to even hear the case. When Kim contested the IIRIRA's mandatory detention provision, the Court of Appeals for the Ninth

Circuit ruled in his favor, holding the denial of an individualized bail hearing unconstitutional. Six months after he was first detained, the INS reversed course (without the immigration court bail hearing) and released him on five thousand dollars bail with minimal parole.

Kim's life began to come together again—he enrolled in business administration at San José State University, and began working as a computer technician. At the same time, however, the INS appealed the Ninth Circuit's ruling to the Supreme Court, arguing that neither the IIRIRA nor the Constitution mandated that any individual receive a bail hearing. The possibility reemerged that Kim would be indefinitely detained pending his removal hearing.

While detentions are reasonable when applied to people who might flee or who pose a danger to society, a constitutional issue arises when the government deprives an entire class of people of liberty without individualized consideration of whether they pose either risk. The Constitution does not allow the government to assume that because some criminal immigrants fail to appear at their removal hearings or pose a public threat, all immigrants will do the same. That would be the equivalent of denying all criminal suspects bail or fair hearings on the grounds that some are dangerous and/or a flight risk— a conclusion that no court would tolerate if applied to U.S. citizens. Sadly, however, the Court has made this very mistake in regarding Asian Americans and their civil rights on more than one occasion.

In the landmark civil rights case *Korematsu v. U.S.*, the Court held that military necessity justified blatant racial profiling and mandated the enforced internment of all Japanese Americans along the Western states, regardless of citizenship or suspicion of espionage.[39] *Korematsu* has since come to represent the need for judicial scrutiny when racial distinctions are made. If a law that abridges fundamental constitutional rights is not narrowly tailored to some compelling purpose (such as in Kim's case when individualized review was forsaken), it should not pass constitutional muster. Often, this requires that each person be looked at individually (the idea behind affirmative action). Rather than attempting to remedy past wrongs, however, racial profiling serves only to exacerbate them.

Unfortunately, the Rehnquist Court continues to overlook the need for individualized review and strict scrutiny. In *Demore v. Kim*, the Court held that classes of non-citizens can be detained without individualized review. To see how this constitutes a rollback, it is useful to look to two earlier cases: *Zadvydas v. Davis*[40] and *Kim Ho Ma v. Ashcroft*.[41] Like Kim, Zadvydas and Ma were lawful permanent residents who were deportable based on criminal convictions and who were held in INS custody awaiting removal. Unlike Kim, they had already received a final order of deportation. In *Zadvydas*, the statute authorizing his detention set no limit on its length, allowed no individualized hearings, and advanced no special justifications to trump the immigrant's Due Process interest. The Court ruled in favor of both Zadvydas and Ma, upholding the importance of Due Process as a fundamental constitutional right.

Two years later, many expected Kim's case to produce a similar outcome. The three cases were similar—all the detainees were lawful permanent residents, all were held in detention for similar criminal records, and all had been placed in removal proceedings. Moreover, the differences between their cases worked in Kim's favor. In *Zadvydas* and *Ma*, the immigrants had already had their removal hearings, had been determined to be deportable, and had therefore lost their legal status; Kim's removal proceedings were still pending, which meant that he remained a lawful permanent resident. He should, therefore, have been in a better position than either Zadvydas or Ma.

Despite the similarities between the cases, the Rehnquist Court justified *Kim* as "materially different"[42]; in *Zadvydas* and *Ma*, the Court held, detention no longer served a purpose as the immigrant's home countries would not accept them for repatriation. In contrast, Kim's mandatory detention could achieve its purported objective of keeping him from absconding in order to avoid deportation. Additionally, although the statute in *Kim* provided no formal upper bound for detentions, the Court accepted the generalization that most removal cases are processed within ninety days as an unambiguous termination point for his detention. This contradicted the Court's reasoning in *Zadvydas*, where detainees who were being held under a statute that set no limit on the length of their detention were released even though the vast majority were quickly deported. The Court's distinction, Justice David Souter correctly argues, "merely point[s] up that Kim's is the stronger claim."[43] Kim was placed back into INS custody and continues today to pursue post-conviction relief on the merits of his case.

The deprivation of Kim's liberty and the absence of safeguards is precisely the kind of arbitrary and capricious violation of Due Process that the Court criticized in *Zadvydas*. The government denies Due Process and violates constitutional rights when it indefinitely detains green card holders not because they pose a danger or flight risk, but because they are immigrants. While the Court purports to protect the public interest, its willingness to curb civil liberties erodes all of our rights to Due Process. While safety, crime prevention, and the deportation of dangerous criminal immigrants are public interests, freedom and liberty are fundamental constitutional rights. Due Process is a core principle of the Constitution, a protection upon which the country was founded and without which it will flounder.

Conclusion

In the civil rights stories of Asian Americans, legal matters of immigration, family, employment, health, and discrimination often result in a collective deprivation of rights similar to the loss of a "bundle of rights" when one's property is unjustly confiscated.

Consider Maslow's hierarchy of needs, the pyramid structure where basic needs (health and safety) must be achieved in order to attain the next level (love, esteem, and self-actualization).[44] Similarly, when one's fundamental constitutional rights are violated or withheld, all other aspects of life fall into chaos. Just as one cannot function without one's basic health, one cannot live as an American without rights. When Kim was detained without an individualized hearing, for example, he was left disempowered and without legal recourse. His life was put on hold, the cost of which included his liberty, freedom, Due Process, and voice.

When Asian Americans (citizens and lawful permanent residents) are deprived of basic entitlements, a rollback of civil rights occurs—the ripples of which are felt by all communities of color. When civil rights are compromised for one, they are compromised for all.

Endnotes

1. 163 U.S. 537 (1896).
2. 130 U.S. 581 (1889).
3. See *Hirabayashi v. U.S.*, 320 U.S. 81 (1943); *Yasui v. U.S.*, 320 U.S. 115 (1943); *Ex Parte Mitsuye Endo*, 323 U.S. 283 (1944); *Korematsu v. U.S.*, 323 U.S. 214 (1944).
4. 490 U.S. 642 (1989).
5. 528 U.S. 495 (2000).
6. See Jessica S. Barnes and Claudette E. Bennett, *The Asian Population: 2000*, Census 2000 Brief, C2KBR/01-16, U.S. Census Bureau, Washington, DC (Feb. 2002), at http://www.census.gov/prod/2002pubs/c2kbr01-16.pdf.
7. 539 U.S. 244 (2003).
8. 539 U.S. 306 (2003).
9. See Chinese Exclusion Act of 1882, ch. 126, 22 Stat. 58 (repealed 1943); *Ozawa v. U.S.*, 260 U.S. 178 (1922).
10. *People v. George W. Hall*, 4 Cal. 399 (Cal. 1854).
11. *Webb v. O'Brien*, 263 U.S. 313 (1923); *Terrace v. Thompson*, 263 U.S. 197 (1923).
12. *Gong Lum v. Rice*, 275 U.S. 78 (1927).
13. See *Korematsu*, 323 U.S. 214.
14. See John Okada, *No-No Boy* (1978).
15. 532 U.S. 275 (2001).
16. 535 U.S. 137 (2002).

17. 538 U.S. 510 (2003).

18. See Jeffrey S. Passel, Randy Capps, and Michael Fix, *Undocumented Immigrants: Facts And Figures* (January 12, 2004), at http://www.urban.org/UploadedPDF/1000587 _undoc_immigrants_facts.pdf.

19. Barnes and Bennett, *The Asian Population: 2000*.

20. *Hoffman Plastic Compound, Inc.*, 306 N.L.R.B. 100, 106 (1992).

21. *Hoffman Plastic*, 306 N.L.R.B. at 100.

22. *Hoffman Plastic Compounds, Inc.*, 314 N.L.R.B. 683, 685 (1994).

23. 326 NLRB 1060, 1062 (1998).

24. *Hoffman Plastic Compounds, Inc. v. NLRB*, 237 F.3d 639 (D.C. Cir 2001).

25. 467 U.S. 883 (1984).

26. Id. at 892.

27. *Hoffman Plastic*, 535 U.S. at 138.

28. Pub. L. No. 99-603, 100 Stat. 3359 (1986).

29. See, e.g., *Centeno-Bernuy v. Becker Farms*, 219 F.R.D. 59 (W.D.N.Y. 2003).

30. See, e.g., *Singh v. Julta & C.D. & R's Oil, Inc.*, 214 F.Supp.2d 1056 (N.D. Cal. 2002).

31. See, e.g., *Rivera. v. Nibco, Inc.*, 364 F.3d 1057 (9th Cir. 2004); *Lopez v. Superflex, Ltd.*, 2002 WL 1941484 (S.D.N.Y. 2002).

32. See, e.g., *Liu v. Donna Karan International, Inc.* 207 F.Supp.2d 191 (S.D.N.Y. 2002) (discovery request for disclosure of immigration status).

33. S. 2381, 108th Cong. (2004); H.R. 4262, 108th Cong. (2004). The SOLVE Act addresses three of the most important components of immigration reform. First, it would legalize undocumented immigrants who have been living, working, and paying taxes in the U.S. for five years. Second, it would keep families together by reducing backlogs in the family preference system, lowering income requirements for the affidavit of support, and repealing the three- and ten-year re-entry bars. Finally, it would channel future immigrants through legal paths by allowing 350,000 new worker visas per year, with full labor protections for immigrant and U.S. workers. The full text is at http://frwebgate.access.gpo.gov/ cgibin/getdoc.cgi?dbname=108_cong_bills&docid=f:s2381is.txt.pdf.

34. S. 2088, 108th Cong. (2004); H.R.3809, 108th Cong. (2004). The full text of the Fairness Act is at http://frwebgate.access.gpo.gov/cgi-bin/getdoc.cgi?dbname=108_cong _bills&docid=f:s2088is.txt.pdf.

35. U.S. Constitution, Fifth Amendment (emphasis added).

36. *McCulloch v. Maryland*, 17 U.S. 316, 421 (1819).

37. See Jeffrey S. Passel, Randy Capps, and Michael Fix, *Undocumented Immigrants: Facts And Figures* (January 12, 2004), Fig. 1, Legal Status of the Foreign-Born Population (2002), at http://www.urban.org/UploadedPDF/1000587_undoc_immigrants_facts.pdf.

38. Pub. L. No. 104-208, 110 Stat. 3009-546 to 3009-724. The IIRIRA provides that the attorney general shall take any alien into custody who is removable from this country because he has been convicted of one of a specified set of crimes, including an aggravated felony.

39. But see, *Korematsu v. U.S.*, 584 F.Supp. 1406 (N.D. Cal. 1984) (granting Korematsu's petition for a writ of coram nobis to vacate his 1942 conviction).

40. 533 U.S. 678 (2001).

41. Consolidated with *Zadvydas*.

42. 538 U.S. at 527–28.

43. Id. at 560–61 (Souter, J., concurring in part and dissenting in part).

44. Abraham H. Maslow, *Motivation and Personality* (1954).

CHAPTER 6

WOMEN

Making a Federal Case out of Women's Concerns: The Supreme Court's Hostility to Civil Rights for Battered Women

Emily J. Martin[*]

Twenty-four-year-old Tiffanie Alvera lived in a subsidized low-income apartment in Seaside, OR, with her husband and baby. One August night, her husband brutally assaulted her. Alvera did everything experts tell battered women to do: she fled the apartment, called the police, went to the hospital, and obtained a protective order barring her husband from their apartment as soon as she was released the next morning. Alvera then gave a copy of the order to the manager of her apartment complex so that she could help keep her husband off the premises. Instead of helping, however, the manager issued a notice for Alvera to vacate her apartment within twenty-four hours. The notice stated that, "You, someone in your control, or your pet, has seriously threatened immediately to inflict personal injury, or has inflicted substantial personal injury upon the landlord or other tenants," and specified her assault as the incident in question. The manager claimed that Alvera had violated the apartment complex's "zero tolerance for violence" policy, even though she was the victim.

The eviction notice came as Alvera was recovering; she had been forced to miss work, and had few emotional or financial resources with which to find a new home. She tried to have her husband removed from the lease, and requested that she be allowed to move to a one-bedroom apartment. The manager, however, refused both requests—that is, until Alvera found a lawyer and threatened to sue. Her attorneys were able to resolve her case. They did so, however, without any explicit state or federal protection for domestic violence victims and in the shadow

*   Staff Attorney, ACLU Women's Rights Project. I am especially grateful to Isabelle Katz Pinzler's work on the Federalism Revolution and women's rights—it was an important resource in writing this chapter.

of Supreme Court rulings that Congress has limited power to protect the civil rights of battered women.

This chapter will discuss one of the first federal statutes to be struck down in the Supreme Court's Federalism Revolution—the 1994 Violence Against Women Act (VAWA)—and will analyze the proposals for a new Act that would provide civil rights protections for domestic violence victims in housing and employment.

≈   ≈   ≈

The Violence Against Women Act (VAWA)

Congress passed VAWA in 1994.[1] The statute, in defining gender-motivated violence against women as a form of illegal discrimination, declared for the first time that women had a federal civil right to be free from such violence.[2] To enforce that right, VAWA allowed victims of gender-motivated crimes, such as rape or domestic violence, to sue their attackers in federal court.

Congress passed this Act to deal with the gender discrimination that women had long faced from police (in failing to crack down on domestic violence or sexual assault) and state courts (in depriving female victims of any redress). According to Congress, the law was "intended to respond both to the underlying attitude that...violence [against women] is somehow less serious than other crime and to the resulting failure of our criminal justice system to address such violence."[3] Its goals, therefore, were "both symbolic and practical."[4] The law was meant to address the "double victimization"—"victimization first by the attacker and, second, by society"—experienced when those to whom the victim turned for help either blamed her for the violence or minimized the crime.[5] It was also meant to correct the longstanding perception of violence against women "as a 'family' problem, as a 'private' matter, as sexual miscommunication" that hides such crimes from public view.[6]

In the four years prior to passing VAWA, Congress amassed extensive data on violence against women. Congressional hearings, testimonies, and reports indicated that up to fifty percent of homeless women and children are fleeing domestic violence. Congress found that such violence is a leading cause of injury to women, and that it causes over one million women annually to seek medical assistance. Further, health care expenses, criminal justice expenditures, and other costs such as "lost careers, decreased productivity, [and] foregone educational opportunities" amounted to between three and ten billion dollars a year.[7] Three-quarters of women refuse to go to the movies alone after dark, and half will not use public transit alone after dark, Congress found.

Moreover, half of all rape victims lose their jobs or are forced to quit, and few rapists are ever convicted of any crime.[8] These and other similar findings led Congress to conclude that gender-motivated crime impacts the economy because it deters women from traveling and working, diminishes national productivity, and increases medical and other social costs.[9]

Since the New Deal, and certainly since the Civil Rights Movement, Americans have assumed that the federal government has the authority to tackle such national problems. Whether redressing the problems of a depressed economy or a state's refusal to integrate classrooms, the federal government has served as an important agent of change. For instance, the Commerce Clause gives Congress the power to legislate to prohibit discrimination by private employers because employment discrimination affects the economy (and therefore interstate commerce).[10]

To justify VAWA as an appropriate exercise of its Commerce Clause power, Congress spent over four years gathering evidence to show that gender-motivated violence affected interstate commerce. The evidence was similar in kind to, though more extensive than, that which Congress had gathered thirty years before to support federal legislation outlawing racial discrimination in privately-owned public accommodations such as hotels and restaurants (that evidence showed that white families spent substantially more on public accommodations than black families who, deterred from traveling, were less able to produce and consume goods in interstate commerce).[11] Despite their efforts, however, VAWA's civil rights provision fell before the Supreme Court's conservative activism. In the past ten years, and by the narrowest of margins (nearly all 5-4 votes), the Court nullified or weakened a number of vital federal laws in the name of "federalism" and to protect state's rights. These rulings have diminished Congress's power to govern. Indeed, the Court's treatment of VAWA's civil rights provision provides a disturbing example of the rollback of federal power and, in particular, federal civil rights provisions.[12]

United States v. Morrison (2000)

A week after VAWA was enacted, Christy Brzonkala, an eighteen-year-old freshman at Virginia Polytechnic University, reported that she had been raped by two varsity football players, Antonio Morrison and James Crawford. Brzonkala became depressed and stopped attending class. The school held a disciplinary hearing in which Morrison confessed that he had had sex with Brzonkala after she twice told him no. The school, however, did not punish either Morrison or Crawford; to the contrary, the boys retained their full athletic scholarships. Brzonkala dropped out, losing an educational opportunity because of gender-motivated violence. She attempted, however, to sue her attackers under VAWA.

Her case reached the Supreme Court in 2000 when the Court agreed to decide whether Congress had the power to enact VAWA's civil rights provision under the Commerce Clause. Only once since the New Deal had the Court held that Congress lacked the authority to enact a law under the Commerce Clause. In 1995, the Court had found that a federal law criminalizing the possession of firearms in school zones was beyond Congress's powers.[13] In that case, the Court relied on the absence of legislative history demonstrating a connection between gun possession in school zones and interstate commerce, holding that the chain of inferences necessary to conclude that gun possession in a school zone affected interstate commerce was insufficient to justify the law's passage under the Commerce Clause.

Despite the facts that similar evidence had provided a sufficient basis for Commerce Clause legislation in 1964 (when Congress enacted the Civil Rights Act banning racial discrimination in public accommodations), and that in the following decades such evidence had been found to be a sufficient basis for other federal civil rights laws, the Court struck down VAWA's civil rights provision in *U.S. v. Morrison*.[14] The Court concluded that despite congressional findings showing the links between violence against women and interstate commerce, the legislation was unconstitutional because violent crime had always been the concern of state law. The Court reasoned that if gender-motivated violence affected interstate commerce enough to warrant Congress to exercise its Commerce Clause power, Congress would be able to justify laws addressing all violent crime or family law matters—issues that the majority of five justices reasoned are "truly local" rather than "truly national."[15] Even with evidence proving that violence against women significantly affected interstate commerce, therefore, Congress still could not regulate such activity pursuant to the Commerce Clause. Ironically, by holding that violent crime and family relationships were beyond the scope of federal law, the Court struck down a law meant to correct the longstanding misconception that violence against women was a private matter beyond the reach of law.[16]

In denying Brzonkala the right to hold her attackers accountable in federal court, the Court effectively held that gender-motivated violence did not have a significant relationship with the nation's economic and commercial interests. Like so many state and federal courts before, the Court characterized gender-motivated violence—that decreases women's employment, threatens them with homelessness, reduces their educational opportunities, increases their medical costs, reduces their freedom to travel, and otherwise directly and indirectly affects the goods and services that are produced and consumed in interstate commerce, at an annual cost of billions of dollars—as a private matter.[17]

The *Morrison* decision has concerned women's legal advocates not only for the loss of the civil rights provision, but because women's inequality continues to arise in the areas that the Court determined are beyond federal regulation—specifically, relationships and power dynamics rooted in or related to family roles and violence (or the threat of violence). Thus, the ruling casts a shadow over future efforts to use federal law to advance women's equality.

The VAWA of 2005?

Despite *Morrison*, efforts continue to use federal law to advance women's equality. In the wake of the loss of the statute that declared gender-motivated violence to be a federal civil rights violation, advocates have continued to work to protect women's civil rights and connect violence against women with gender discrimination.

Some of this work is being undertaken in the courts. While the VAWA civil rights remedy is lost, other tools remain. Women's legal advocates, for example, have recently focused on housing discrimination against domestic violence victims.[18] Public housing authorities and private landlords often respond to an incident of domestic violence by evicting both the victim and the abuser. Victims are often evicted even when their abuser lives elsewhere, and when they have used all available measures to keep their abuser from returning (e.g., cooperating with criminal prosecution and seeking a civil protection order). Some battered women are threatened with eviction if they call for police assistance in their home. Such discrimination is one reason why violence against women is a major cause of homelessness.

Landlords discriminate against domestic violence victims for various reasons. Some have adopted "zero tolerance" policies under which they evict everyone in a household when violence occurs. Some blame the victim, and evict them to keep their properties violence-free. Some believe that even when women seek help from the police or the courts, they will inevitably return to the abuser and therefore the violence will recur. Most do not understand that women are often forced to return to their abusive relationships because they lack secure housing.

Federal law also contributes to the problems facing poor victims of domestic violence; the 1988 Federal Anti-Drug Abuse Act requires public housing to, "utilize leases which provide that any criminal activity that threatens the health, safety, or right to peaceful enjoyment of the premises by other tenants... engaged in by a public housing tenant, any member of the tenant's household, or any guest or other person under the tenant's control, shall be cause for termination of tenancy."[19] Some public housing authorities rely on these lease provisions to evict victims.

While punishing victims for crimes committed against them in their homes does not on the surface discriminate between genders, such policies effectively discriminate on the basis of sex because the majority of domestic violence victims are women. According to the Department of Justice's Bureau of Justice Statistics, women were the victims in eighty-five percent of crimes committed by intimate partners in 1998.[20] Similarly, data collected by the National Institute of Justice and the Centers for Disease Control and Prevention indicate that women are significantly more likely than men to experience violence at the hand of an intimate partner, and that the disparity between women's and men's rate of assault increases with the seriousness of the assault. For example, while women were two to three times more likely to report that an intimate partner threw something or pushed, grabbed, or shoved them, they were seven to fourteen times more likely to report that an intimate partner beat them up, choked or tried to drown them, or threatened them with a weapon.[21]

Women, therefore, will be most affected by housing discrimination against domestic violence victims. Even more disturbing, because landlords most often learn about domestic violence when a tenant seeks assistance from the police or the courts, the resulting evictions send a message to battered women that they must keep quiet so as to keep their home.

Advocates have brought litigation arguing that policies that discriminate against domestic violence victims violate the federal Fair Housing Act[22] (enacted pursuant to Congress's Commerce Clause powers).[23] The Act, prohibiting housing discrimination on the basis of sex, has been consistently interpreted to forbid not only discrimination undertaken with the *intent* to harm women, but policies and practices that have the *effect* of harming women.[24] Thus with the loss of the VAWA civil rights provision, advocates have relied on the Fair Housing Act to show the link between sex discrimination and domestic violence in housing. So far, these cases have led to successful, and in some instances far-reaching, settlements.

This law, however, is no substitute for a law explicitly recognizing and protecting the civil rights of victims of gender violence. While a few states have adopted such laws, recognizing gender violence as a form of discrimination or protecting domestic violence victims' rights to fair housing and employment, most have done nothing.[25] Many battered women therefore continue to be re-victimized, losing their homes and jobs just as they are trying to separate from their abusers. For this reason (despite *Morrison*), advocates continue to push for Congress to enact a federal law that explicitly recognizes the civil rights of domestic violence victims. Such a law would, consistent with the federal government's traditional role in protecting basic civil rights, ensure that battered women do not summarily lose the material resources they need to protect themselves, and that their rights do not vary depending on the state in which they live.

A new VAWA, soon to be introduced in Congress, will likely include sections providing civil rights protection for domestic violence victims in housing and employment. Specifically, the next VAWA may:

- Prohibit landlords from evicting or otherwise restricting the tenancy of domestic violence victims because of the violence against them or because they have sought help from the police;
- Prohibit tenant screening companies from providing landlords with information such as whether a prospective tenant had ever obtained a protection order;
- Provide employment protections for victims of domestic or sexual violence—employers could be required to provide emergency unpaid leave so that victims could obtain medical or other assistance, victims who have lost their jobs will receive unemployment compensation, and discrimination by covered employers may be prohibited.

Like other federal civil rights laws passed in the last half-century, these protections would ensure consistent, nationwide protection of individuals' rights.

In striking down the first VAWA's civil rights protection, the Court objected to the law's focus on the underlying violent incident because it held that violence was a "truly local" issue and gender-motivated violence had nothing to do with commerce or economic enterprise.[26] Regardless of the difficulties in applying the Court's distinction between what is or is not economic in close cases, employment relationships and housing transactions are clearly economic under current precedent (as they take place in the public market rather than in the home). Presumably, the new VAWA's focus on these activities, rather than on the underlying violence, will assuage the Court's concern about the federal government regulating such "truly local" areas as violent crime and family law.

Unless the Court further narrows its interpretation of Congress's power under the Commerce Clause, the distinction between the type of activity regulated in the old and new VAWA will be a sufficient basis to uphold Congress's authority to pass the new law.[27] Still, this distinction's artificial formality suggests the dangerous limitations of the Court's interpretation of the Commerce Clause. While violence against women causes enormous economic and housing dislocation, the Court has deemed its effect on the economy irrelevant in justifying Congress's Commerce Clause power to regulate it because the issue is local, not national. In contrast, so long as Congress focuses on the narrow commercial context in which these injuries take place—the landlord-tenant relationship and employment—the identical impact of violence on the economy can justify Congress's exercise of its Commerce Clause power.[28]

Conclusion

Should the new VAWA become law, its protections in employment and housing will advance women's safety and equality. Nevertheless, the Court's insistence that the federal government cannot protect battered women's civil rights until they enter into market transactions is an arbitrary rule that both fails to promote sex equality and endangers women's lives. In Christy Brzonkala's case, the Court essentially ruled that federal law cannot protect victims of gender violence until they enter the public world of economic activity. Experience has shown that the notion that violence in the family is properly beyond the reach of law poses significant dangers to women.

Endnotes

1. 42 U.S.C. § 13931 *et seq.*
2. 42 U.S.C. § 13981. The statute also included other remedies and provisions addressing violence against women.
3. S. Rep. No. 103-38, at 38 (1993).
4. Id.
5. S. Rep. No. 101-545, at 33 (1990).
6. S. Rep. No. 102-97, at 37 (1991).
7. S. Rep. No. 101-545, at 33; S. Rep. No. 103-38, at 41; see also *United States v. Morrison*, 529 U.S. 598, 631–33 (2000) (Souter, J., dissenting) (citing legislative history sources).
8. S. Rep. No. 102-97, at 38, 53; S. Rep. No. 101-545, at 33 n. 30 (1990).
9. H. R. Conf. Rep. No. 103-711, at 385–86.
10. See generally *Regents v. Bakke*, 438 U.S. 265, 367 (1978) (Brennan, J. concurring in part and dissenting in part, joined by Justices White, Marshall, and Blackmun); *Great Am. Fed. Sav. & Loan Ass'n v. Novotny*, 442 U.S. 366, 395 n.20 (1979).
11. See *Morrison*, 529 U.S. at 636 (Souter, dissenting) (citing legislative history).
12. See generally Isabelle Katz Pinzler, *Toward a More Perfect Union: Understanding and Countering the Federalism Revolution* (2002).
13. See *United States v. Lopez*, 514 U.S. 549, 567–68 (1995) (striking down the Gun Free Schools Act as beyond congressional authority under the Commerce Clause).

14. See *Morrison*, 529 U.S. at 617.

15. Id. at 617–18.

16. The Court also held that Congress had no power to pass VAWA's civil rights provision under the Fourteenth Amendment, which grants Congress authority to "enforce, by appropriate legislation" the amendment's guarantee that no state shall "deprive any person of life, liberty, or property without due process of law" or "deny to any person within its jurisdiction the equal protection of the laws." U.S. Const. Amend. XIV, §§ 1, 5. It rejected arguments that this provision responded to pervasive gender bias in state justice systems, which left victims of gender-motivated violence without equal protection of the law. Congress had no power under the Fourteenth Amendment to pass the law, the Court held, because the law allowed a remedy against attackers, rather than against the state courts or local police who might have demonstrated gender bias, and the Fourteenth Amendment forbids only state-sponsored gender discrimination. *Morrison* 529 U.S. at 624–26. Thus the Court found that Congress had no power under the Constitution to authorize a civil remedy against attackers for gender-motivated violence. Id. at 627.

17. See generally, e.g., Judith Resnik, Categorical Feminism: Jurisdiction, Gender, and the Globe, *111 Yale L. J.*, (2001) 619, 629–44; Sally F. Goldfarb, Violence Against Women and the Persistence of Privacy, *61 Ohio St. L.J.* (2000) 1.

18. E.g., Lenora M. Lapidus, Doubly Victimized: Housing Discrimination Against Victims of Domestic Violence, *11 Am. U. J. Gender Soc. Pol'y & L.* (2003) 377; Wendy R. Weiser & Geoff Boehm, Housing Discrimination Against Victims of Domestic Violence, *35 Clearinghouse Rev.* (2002) 708.

19. 42 U.S.C. § 1437d(l)(6).

20. Callie Marie Rennison and Sarah Welchans, U.S. Dep't of Justice, NCJ 178247, *Intimate Partner Violence* (2000) 1, at http://www.ojp.usdoj.gov/bjs/pub/ascii/ipv.txt.

21. Patricia Tjaden and Nancy Thoennes, U.S. Dep't of Justice, NCJ 181867, *Extent, Nature and Consequences of Intimate Partner Violence: Findings from the National Violence Against Women Study* (2000) 17, at http://www.ncjrs.org/txtfiles1/nij/181867.txt.

22. 42 U.S.C. §§ 3601 *et seq.*

23. *Morgan v. HUD*, 985 F.2d 1451, 1455–56 (10th Cir. 1993). The Thirteenth Amendment is an additional source of congressional authority for the passage of the Fair Housing Act, at least in regard to race discrimination. See *United States v. Bob Lawrence Realty, Inc.*, 474 F.2d 115, 120–21 (5th Cir. 1973); *Jones v. Alfred M. Mayer Co.*, 392 U.S. 409, 437–44 (1968) (finding Congress had authority under the enforcement clause of the Thirteenth Amendment to ban racial discrimination in housing).

24. See, e.g., *Mountain Side Mobile Estates Partnership v. HUD*, 56 F.3d 1243 (10th Cir. 1995); *Keith v. Volpe*, 858 F.2d 467 (9th Cir. 1988); *Betsy v. Turtle Creek Assocs.*, 736 F.2d 983 (4th Cir. 1984).

25. In the wake of the loss of the VAWA civil rights provision, California and Illinois adopted similar provisions in state law recognizing violence against women as a form of sex discrimination and granting victims a civil cause of action against their attackers. Cal. Civ. Code § 52.4 (adopted in 2002); 740 Ill. Comp. Stat. 82/1 *et seq.* (adopted in 2003). Other states include crimes motivated by gender in broader prohibitions of bias crimes. See, e.g., Me. Rev. Stat. Ann. tit. 5 § 4684-A. In the past two years, Rhode Island and Washington have passed laws broadly prohibiting housing discrimination against domestic violence victims. RI Gen Laws § 34-37-1 *et. seq.*; Wash Rev. Code § 59.18.570. In the employment context, Illinois has adopted a law prohibiting employment discrimination against

domestic violence victims who work for employers with fifty or more employees, and requiring the employer to make reasonable accommodations related to the violence. 820 Ill. Comp. Stat. 180/1-45.

26. *Morrison*, 529 U.S. at 613.

27. It is worth noting that while an alternative holding would be radical, it is not completely impossible; Justice Thomas, often cited by President George W. Bush as his model for Supreme Court appointments, has indicated that he believes the Commerce Clause may only allow Congress to regulate the buying, selling, and transport of goods across state lines, a position that, if adopted by a majority of the Court, would invalidate almost all federal civil rights laws as well as a broad swath of other federal laws. *U.S. v. Lopez*, 514 U.S. at 584–602 (Thomas, J., concurring).

28. See *Morrison*, 529 U.S. at 657 (Souter, J., dissenting) ("[W]hy should we give critical constitutional importance to the economic, or non-economic, nature of an interstate-commerce-affecting *cause*? If chemical emanations through indirect environmental change cause identical, severe commercial harm outside a State, why should it matter whether local factories or home fireplaces release them?").

CHAPTER 7

OLDER AMERICANS

"Narrowing the Nation's Power":
The Impact on Older Americans

Simon Lazarus*

In the mid 1990s, the Florida Board of Regents agreed to implement market-based salary adjustments for professors and other personnel in the state's huge university system. When Florida State University (FSU) opted out, however, the Board failed to require them to make good on the deal. Professor Daniel J. Kimel and several of his colleagues took the Board to federal court, alleging that the state's action violated the federal Age Discrimination in Employment Act of 1967 (ADEA) because of its negative impact on senior faculty members who could command higher compensation levels in the market.

Professor Kimel's complaint is typical of the ubiquitous economic challenges that confront Americans as they age. As workers accumulate seniority, they should receive higher pay or benefits. Because their increasing health problems make them more costly to employers and insurers, however, they risk missing promotions or losing their jobs. Under these circumstances, the ADEA provides every worker with a foundation of economic security. To make real the ADEA's promise of equal opportunity, each worker must have the right to take his or her employer to court and, if successful, recover damages. It is no accident that age discrimination cases appear regularly on the dockets of state and federal courts, including the Supreme Court.

In Kimel v. Florida Board of Regents, *a 5-4 Supreme Court majority threw Professor Kimel and his colleagues out of court—not because they had no claim or because FSU and the Board of Regents were in compliance with the ADEA, but because the Court held that the several million state government employees can-*

---

  * Simon Lazarus is Public Policy Counsel to the National Senior Citizens Law Center. Mr. Lazarus received his B.A. from Harvard University *magna cum laude* and his L.L.B. from Yale Law School.

not invoke the ADEA against their employers in court, and that Congress cannot give them any such right.

The Kimel *case victims are mainstream and middle-class. It is precisely the ordinariness of their grievance that makes the Federalism Revolution such a broad and potentially historic threat. Rights secured by Congress a generation ago and taken for granted by a majority of the electorate, are targeted in this drive to turn back the constitutional clock.*

This chapter will describe how the Court's recent decisions threaten the ADEA, the Americans with Disabilities Act (ADA) of 1990, and Medicaid, and will explain why such developments jeopardize the well-being of older Americans.

ЪА   ЪА   ЪА

Beginning with the first iteration of the Social Security program in 1935, Congress enacted a vast and intricate network of laws aimed at ensuring older Americans health, economic security, and equal opportunity in employment and other areas of social life. These laws include, in addition to the Social Security Act,[1] the ADA,[2] the ADEA,[3] Medicaid,[4] Medicare,[5] the Rehabilitation Act of 1973,[6] the Nursing Home Reform Act of 1987,[7] the Family and Medical Leave Act of 1993 (FMLA),[8] the Older Americans Act of 1965,[9] and Title VI of the Civil Rights Act of 1964.[10] Every session of Congress devotes much time and energy to reviewing, reauthorizing, and revising these programs.

Congress could not have created these programs before 1935. For the first third of the twentieth century, the federal Judiciary held a restrictive view of the federal government's authority, effectively barring Congress from enacting major national social and economic regulatory programs like Medicare, Medicaid, and the ADEA. It was only after President Franklin D. Roosevelt threatened to expand the number of Supreme Court justices and then filled judicial vacancies with New Deal supporters that the Court changed its tune.[11] The new constitutional order freed Congress to devise plausible methodologies for solving domestic social or economic problems, and outlined that the role of the Court was to facilitate Congress's objectives.[12] Congress was expected to use any combination of federal agencies, state governments, and/or courts to implement and enforce its statutory objectives.[13]

Beginning in the 1970s, however, a handful of conservative academics began to repackage and expand upon the limited pre-New Deal constitutional view of national authority. In the late 1990s, a 5-4 Supreme Court majority adopted pieces of that exhumed jurisprudence. As critically described by Ninth Circuit Reagan appointee Judge John T. Noonan in *Narrowing The Nation's Power: The Supreme Court Sides with the States,* the Federalism Five (Chief Justice William Rehnquist and Justices Sandra Day O'Connor, Antonin Scalia, Anthony Kennedy, and Clarence Thomas) took aim at several building blocks of the post–New Deal Constitution in the name of the idiosyncratic concept of "federalism."[14] These decisions have curbed the ability of private individuals and organizations to enforce their federal rights in court.

This judicial assault on federal authority constitutes a new and substantial threat to older Americans. Because the elderly tend to have greater needs than the rest of the adult population, and less income with which to meet those needs, they are disproportionately dependent on government programs and protections. Moreover, the effectiveness of laws and programs aimed at senior citizens depends on the threat and reality of private court enforcement. For the most important of these programs, Medicare and Medicaid, their ability to provide beneficiaries with health guaranteed "insurance" depends on the existence of an enforceable right to benefits in accordance with federal requirements.

This chapter will summarize the implications of the Court's rollback of civil rights for older Americans, explain how the Court's recent decisions have undermined both the ADEA and the ADA (discussed in chapter 8), and discuss how those decisions could threaten the effectiveness of Medicaid (discussed in chapter 13).

The Age Discrimination in Employment Act (ADEA)

Less than two weeks after the turn of the twentieth century, the import of the contraction of federal power for older Americans became apparent. In *Kimel*, the Supreme Court took but two paragraphs to rule that the Commerce Clause did not authorize a faculty member of a state university to invoke the ADEA to recover damages in a suit challenging an age-discriminatory pay scale.[15] According to the Court, the thirty-year-old ban on age-based employment discrimination was lawful; Congress could bind state governments and extend the benefits of the ADEA to their over five million employees. Congress could not, however, use its Commerce Clause powers to ensure that those same state employees could enforce their rights under the ADEA in court.

When originally passed in 1967, the ADEA was justified as an example of Congress exercising its interstate commerce powers. However, the legislation could also have been enacted pursuant to the powers granted to Congress by the Fourteenth Amendment, which prohibits states from denying any person the "equal protection of the laws."[16] Section 5 of the Fourteenth Amendment authorizes Congress to "enforce" that equal protection provision by enacting "appropriate legislation." The main question in *Kimel* was whether this Fourteenth Amendment provision for congressional "enforcement," unlike the Commerce Clause, could trump the states' sovereign immunity. While the Supreme Court affirmed that the Fourteenth Amendment empowers Congress to abrogate state sovereign immunity and authorize private lawsuits to enforce federal rights against state governments, the Section 5 argument could not save Professor Kimel's case—the Court held that legislation based on Section 5 could overcome states' sovereign immunity against private lawsuits *only* if Congress rigorously demonstrated a *pattern* of discrimination *by state governments* (rather than discrimination in the general society) and fine-tuned a "congruent and proportionate" remedy.[17] The Court further held that when Congress passed the ADEA in the mid 1960s, its fact-finding process failed that test; states, therefore, retained their immunity from suit. Accordingly, state employees who are victims of age discrimination have no right under either the interstate Commerce Clause or the Fourteenth Amendment to recover damages from their employers. Moreover, Congress lacks the authority to grant them that right.

The Americans with Disabilities Act (ADA)

Eighteen months after barring Professor Kimel from federal court, the Supreme Court similarly dispatched the provisions of the ADA that purported to abrogate state sovereign immunity. Older Americans have a vital stake in maintaining effective guarantees against disability-related discrimination. According to the AARP's quarterly publication, *Elder Law Forum*, sixty percent of the U.S. population with disabilities is over fifty years old (the AARP is the leading nonprofit, nonpartisan membership organization for people age fifty or over).

The case *Board of Trustees of the University of Alabama v. Garrett*[18] serves to illustrate this point. The plaintiff, Patricia Garrett, originally a Director of Nursing at the University of Alabama's medical center, took leave in March 1995 after being diagnosed with breast cancer to undergo treatment. Upon returning to work two months later, Garrett was demoted to nurse manager. Her double whammy—a life-threatening disease followed by a suspiciously proximate disaster at work—haunts all aging Americans. Like the ADEA, the ADA is critical to their economic security; denying Garrett and other public employees its protection is no less an age-related threat to economic security than undermining the ADEA.

In agreeing to carve out public employees from the employment discrimination provisions (Title I) of the ADA, the Federalism Revolution majority conceded that, in contrast to the Commerce Clause, the Fourteenth Amendment does give Congress the authority to abrogate state sovereign immunity. The distinction lies in the Fourteenth Amendment's text. Section 1 forbids states from denying persons equal protection of the laws, and Section 5 authorizes Congress to "enforce" that guarantee of equal treatment with "appropriate legislation." The Court held that requiring states to pay monetary damages to discrimination victims like Patricia Garrett, however, was not "appropriate." Over the vigorous objections of four dissenting judges, the majority reasoned that in order to subject state governments to private damage suits, Congress needed to demonstrate a pattern of discrimination against the disabled. Here, the Court concluded, the legislative record failed for two reasons: the evidence provided at congressional hearings was merely "anecdotal," and because the evidence mainly (though not exclusively) involved discrimination by private sector employers, it was deemed unreasonable for Congress to equate state governmental practices with private employers.[19] Legislatures have not typically collected information in the formal or systematic manner characteristic of courts, nor have laws been struck down when based on otherwise reasonable judgments (e.g., concluding that state employers and private employers hold similar prejudices against older or disabled persons). Hence, the Court's evidentiary standard appears to be one that, inherently, Congress could not meet while continuing to function as a legislature.[20]

After the Court barred Congress from empowering disabled state employees to recover damages for employment discrimination, several lower federal courts concluded that the next logical step would be to bar private enforcement actions against states under Title II of the ADA. Title II bars discrimination by state governments in providing any service or facility to the public,[21] and prescribes the basic mandate pursuant to which state governments have, over the past fifteen years, taken a broad array of measures to ensure equal access to all state-owned, operated, and regulated facilities. Without the threat of private enforcement, it is unclear whether investment in such measures will continue at a pace commensurate with the record to date. Nevertheless, with the exception of the Sixth and Ninth Circuit Courts of Appeal, all federal appellate courts extended the bar to private suits imposed in *Garrett* to all provisions and suits against states.[22]

Three years after *Garrett*, however, the Supreme Court changed its course. More precisely, Justice Sandra Day O'Connor shifted gears. In *Tennessee v. Lane*, decided on May 17, 2004, a 5-4 majority (O'Connor plus the four erstwhile dissenters in federalism cases) upheld Congress' authority, pursuant to Title II of the ADA,[23] to require that state governments ensure disabled persons access to state court facilities, and to empower individuals to recover damages for violations of this requirement. The decision in *Lane* relaxed the restrictive boundaries drawn in *Kimel* and *Garrett* between state sovereign immunity from private lawsuits under the Eleventh Amendment and congressional authority to enforce the Fourteenth Amendment.[24] How far or how much, however, remains anything but clear.

Justice John Paul Stevens clarified that the specific holding in *Lane* covers little more than the facts of the case.

> [T]he question presented in this case is not whether Congress can validly subject the States to private suits for failing to provide reasonable access to hockey rinks, or even to voting booths, but whether Congress had the power under §5 to enforce the constitutional right of access to the courts. Because we find that Title II unquestionably is valid §5 legislation as it applies to the class of cases implicating the accessibility of judicial services, we need go no further.

Stevens' tight limitation was no doubt a key factor in Justice O'Connor's decision to join the majority. How much more than its holding does *Lane* portend? The Court's opinion gives no reliable clue. Only time and, ultimately, further rounds of judicial battles will determine whether citizens with disabilities, many of whom are elderly, will be able to look to Congress to ensure their right to contribute and participate fully as citizens.

Medicaid (Dis)entitlement?

The Critical Importance of Medicaid to Older Americans

For most senior citizens, Medicare and Medicaid are the most important federal programs. Originally, Medicare was aimed at providing health insurance-equivalent coverage for all Americans over sixty-five years old, regardless of their financial situations. In contrast, Medicaid had the purpose of providing insurance-equivalent coverage for indigent Americans of all ages.[25] In effect, however, Medicare has failed to solve the health insurance needs of many of the elderly because it does not cover all essential services, and it prices essential services too high. Medicaid has expanded to fill these gaps, and has surpassed Medicare as the nation's largest health insurance program with a total of over forty-seven million beneficiaries (who absorbed over $250 billion in combined federal and state expenditures in 2002).[26]

Twelve percent of Medicaid subscribers are elderly "dual enrollees" of both Medicare and Medicaid; this group accounts for nearly one third of all Medicaid spending, including seven billion dollars for prescription drugs and twenty-four billion dollars for nursing homes and other long-term care.[27] This is not surprising, as over one third of elderly individuals live on incomes that are less than twice the federal poverty level. For this large cohort, many of whom are retirees from long and productive working lives, Medicaid is essential to offset high Medicare deductibles, pay for pharmaceuticals not covered by Medicare, and, especially, pay for long-term institutional or home care. Indeed, Medicaid is by far the nation's main purchaser of long-term care services, accounting for forty-six percent of all nursing home spending and thirty-eight percent of all home health care spending.[28]

Even such remarkable figures understate the importance of Medicaid for those in need of long-term care. Quality-of-care standards prescribed by the Department of Health and Human Services (HHS) as prerequisites for Medicaid payments to nursing home and other long-term service providers guarantee quality for all service recipients, including those whose payments are not covered by Medicaid. In ensuring that the nation's elderly can pay for their health care needs, Medicaid (or more accurately the various expansions and programs created under the Medicaid umbrella) is no less critical than Medicare.

While Medicare is funded and administered by the federal government, Medicaid is in form a matching grant program administered by state governments. Moreover, while the Medicare statute refers to its beneficiaries as "persons entitled to benefits,"[29] similar language does not appear in the Medicaid statute.[30] Despite such differences, however, the Judiciary, Congress, the executive branch, the states, scholars, the press, and the public have considered the two equal in entitlement status.

An individual is entitled to Medicaid if he fulfills the criteria established by the state in which he lives. State Medicaid plans must comply with requirements imposed both by the Act itself and by the Secretary of HHS.[31]

Medicaid recipients are counted as having guaranteed health insurance (not an unenforceable and revocable benefit) by authoritative sources for such statistics, including the U.S. Bureau of the Census.[32]

While Medicaid has come to be seen as an individual entitlement, so too has the recognition that beneficiaries have the right to sue to enforce that entitlement. Throughout Medicaid's life, private litigation to enforce its provisions has been ubiquitous. Hundreds of cases have been brought against state health administrative authorities on behalf of beneficiaries and providers and against providers on behalf of beneficiaries. As detailed in the National Health

Law Program's authoritative review, *§1983 and Enforcement of the Medicaid Act*, federal courts have recently ordered state agencies to change the following unlawful policies and practices: elements of Due Process hearings for determining eligibility and benefit levels; compliance with mandatory administrative requirements such as consultation with medical advisory committees; providing care with "reasonable promptness"; substantive requirements concerning eligibility (e.g., the definition of "medically needy"); compliance with nursing home, home care, community-based treatment, and managed care quality of care standards; provider reimbursement issues; implementation of requirement for early and periodic screening, diagnostic, and treatment services; and other issues.[33] Certainly, Congress has felt the impact of private enforcement. Court decisions, some granting relief against state agencies and some denying it, have generated attempts at legislative reversal, some of which have been successful.[34]

For individual beneficiaries or beneficiary groups and providers, judicial enforcement (or the threat thereof) is essential to securing those rights guaranteed by Medicaid. Without such a threat, state health authorities would have little or no incentive to correct denials or circumscription of benefits in violation of federal requirements. For the same reasons, it seems clear that without private enforcement, overall compliance levels and the program's operational integrity would be degraded. Quite apart from its practical significance, the right of private enforcement is important to the status of Medicaid as an entitlement; without it, the case for continuing to characterize Medicaid as an entitlement, or classifying its beneficiaries as among the nation's "insured," is tenuous indeed.[35]

The New Judicial Threat to the Medicaid Entitlement

Despite the centrality of judicial enforcement to Medicaid's conceptual structure and operational performance, the continued existence of a private right of action for violations of Medicaid requirements is in question. Recent Supreme Court decisions have narrowed the scope of authority to enforce Spending Clause programs in court. Moreover, certain ideological lower federal court judges (drawing their inspiration from dissenting opinions by Justices Scalia and Thomas) have narrowly interpreted the scope of the Court's decisions and have generated rationales for doing away altogether with the private enforcement of Medicaid.

The 2001 decision made by an otherwise obscure Michigan district judge in *Westside Mothers v. Haveman* offers an example of this push to close courthouse doors to Medicaid beneficiaries.[36] In the case, Judge Robert Cleland implicitly put aside the law as it stood, instead treating Justice Scalia's concurring opinion in *Blessing v. Freestone*[37] as the sole relevant precedent. Justice Scalia's *Blessing* concurrence posited that conditional Spending Clause programs like Medicaid were akin to "contracts" between the federal government as grantor and the state government as recipient, with the patients relegated to the status of "third party beneficiaries." Because third party beneficiaries (arguably) could not sue to enforce contracts in the 1870s (when § 1983 was originally passed), Justice Scalia concluded that Medicaid beneficiaries could not invoke § 1983 to enforce the statutory or regulatory requirements on which states' receipt of Medicaid funds was conditioned by Congress and HHS. Judge Cleland adopted and embellished Justice Scalia's theory by adding several similarly inventive propositions:

- That federal statutes and regulations implementing the spending power are not "the supreme law of the land" because they merely authorize the federal government to enter into contracts with state governments.
- That Spending Clause requirements cannot be enforced via § 1983, because as contractual provisions they are not "rights, privileges, or immunities secured by the law of the United States."
- That sovereign immunity under the Eleventh Amendment bars Michigan's health officials from being enjoined by a federal court to comply with their Medicaid obligations to provide certain services, because the century-old exception to sovereign immunity for prospective injunctions against state officials was inapplicable for a variety of reasons—in particular, that such injunctions were unavailable to address state officials' exercise of "discretionary functions," and because the state, not the officials, was the "real party in interest."[38]

Cleland's rationale, were it to be accepted as law, would not only extinguish any private right of action to enforce Medicaid, but would compound the difficulty facing Congress in reinstating that right.[39]

To date, *Westside Mothers* has not been accepted as law. To the contrary, as detailed by Jane Perkins of the National Health Law Program in chapter 13, Judge Cleland's theory was not only unanimously reversed on appeal by the U.S. Court of Appeals for the Sixth Circuit, but was rejected by many other courts, including the right-leaning Court of Appeals for the Fourth Circuit.[40] In December 2002, the Supreme Court declined to review the Sixth Circuit's rebuff to Judge Cleland.[41]

Despite the rejection of *Westside Mothers* and the Supreme Court's recent endorsements of the private enforceability of rights delineated in Medicaid though § 1983 suits, private enforcement of Medicaid remains an open question for several reasons. First, the Court's 2002 decision in *Gonzaga University v. Doe*[42] that purported to clarify which statutory provisions are actionable under § 1983, has only added to the confusion. Without supplanting the test elaborated only five years earlier in *Blessing v. Freestone*,[43] *Gonzaga* introduced a new overlay of doctrine; the terms of which, however, are vague, and its relationship to the *Blessing* test, uncertain.[44] Some courts have read *Gonzaga* as a downgrading of *Blessing*, or at least a sharp contraction of the scope of judicially-enforceable provisions of Medicaid and similar laws. Those cases indicate that, without repudiating the principle of private Medicaid enforcement, it would be possible in practice to limit its availability to a narrow set of circumstances.

Indeed, in the spirit of Judge Cleland's *Westside Mothers* approach, some courts have read *Gonzaga* to overturn *Blessing* and the two decades of case law that it reaffirmed.[45] Given the limited number of cases the Supreme Court can review, such attempts to bypass precedent may stand as the final word. Moreover, the current trickle of such rogue decisions could swell as federal circuits become dominated by Bush appointees who act on the assumption that they have been selected expressly to advance Justice Scalia's jurisprudential agenda.[46] Jeffrey Sutton, for example, who as a private lawyer intervened in *Westside Mothers* and provided Judge Cleland with the rationale needed to declare Medicaid unenforceable, was confirmed to a Sixth Circuit seat in April 2003. Like most of the appointees, Sutton's record suggests that he will not hesitate to bend precedent to achieve desired results, such as blocking the private enforcement of Medicaid and similar social programs.[47]

To be sure, Judges Cleland and Sutton would insist that rather than intending to irreversibly bar the courthouse door to Medicaid beneficiaries, they ask only for Congress to clarify its intent to open it. If Congress intends to condition receipt of federal funds on waiving the state's sovereign immunity, they say, "it must make its intention to do so unmistakably clear in the language of the statute...."[48] In theory, therefore, Congress can preserve the enforceability of Medicaid rights simply by enacting a "clear statement" of purpose. In practice, however, what with having to face a gauntlet of unsympathetic reviewing judges, any such provision would likely prove ineffective. Some compromise, hence some ambiguity as to what is and what is not covered, is inevitable.[49]

Judges hostile to private suits against states have repeatedly seized upon minor ambiguities to justify determinations that Congress' authorization was unclear—even though Congress' awareness and acceptance of court enforcement was, as a practical matter, clear.[50] Indeed, right wing judges have proven adept at "moving the goal posts," changing the judicial rules to frustrate congressional efforts to meet newly-imposed rules.[51] The Supreme Court majority has already indicated the likelihood for this type of "Catch-22" reception to a congressional effort to endorse private Medicaid enforcement.[52] As new Bush appointees are confirmed, lower federal courts and eventually the Supreme Court may impose rules that mean, in practice and perhaps even in principle, that Congress cannot constitutionally condition receipt of Medicaid funds on waiver of a state's sovereign immunity. The seriousness of this threat was underscored when, on June 9, 2005, the Senate confirmed William Pryor to a life-time seat on the Eleventh Circuit. Barely a year earlier, Pryor insisted that, despite rejection by the Sixth Circuit and all other courts including the Supreme Court, the *Westside Mothers* District Court decision somehow remains a correct statement of the law.[53]

In sum, the incremental layering of impediments to private suits against state governments has created such dense procedural underbrush that it is easy for courts to find reasons to turn plaintiffs away. As one prominent conservative commentator enthusiastically observed, "The Supreme Court's anti-entitlement doctrines are connected, such that plaintiffs who manage to evade one obstacle are bound to stumble over another."[54]

Conclusion

The 5-4 Supreme Court majority that drove the incipient counterrevolution until June 2003 proclaimed radical new doctrinal principles. Thus far, however, results have been limited. For the most part, the Federalism Five majority stepped gingerly, making decisions that merely trimmed the edges of the post-New Deal humanitarian state. Furthermore, in two major cases in 2002 and 2003, the Federalism Five fractured and the Court upheld damage suits against states to enforce the federal FMLA[55] and Title II of the ADA.[56] In other cases decided during the 2003 term, the Court declined to follow either the logic suggested in earlier decisions or the writings of conservative academics to limit the reach of congressional power under the Commerce[57] and Spending[58] Clauses of Article I.

At the end of the 2004 term, the Court demonstrated more emphatically its reluctance to expand its late 1990's federalism jurisprudence into a comprehensive attack on post-New Deal congressional regulatory authority. In *Gonzalez v. Raich*,[59] two members of the erstwhile Federalism Five, Justice Kennedy and, in a separate concurring opinion, Justice Scalia, joined the four "liberal" dissenters to reaffirm broad congressional discretion to regulate any colorably "economic" activities that can rationally be construed to substantially affect interstate commerce. The 6-3 majority seemed intent on discouraging lower court judges from expansively interpreting its decisions in *United States v. Lopez* and *United States v. Morrison*.[60] In contrast to the approach adopted by the 5-4 *Morrison* majority, the *Raich* majority emphasized that Congress's exercise of its broad Commerce Clause power required no findings or evidence or even any indication that the rationale by which the Court justified the law was what Congress actually had in mind when it passed it.

Despite the revisionist turn, liberals have scant reason for complacency. The doctrinal logic marshaled by the Federalism Five to dismantle congressional enforcement authority under the Fourteenth Amendment remains in place. Despite the 2003 *Hibbs* decision not to apply that logic to the Family and Medical Leave Act, and the 2004 *Lane* decision not to apply it to exclusion of disabled individuals from state court proceedings, congressional authority to redress age and disability based discrimination remains tightly circumscribed. Both the *Hibbs* and *Lane* decisions reflect primarily an apparent shift of emphasis by Justice O'Connor; in light of her resignation the future is uncertain. New appointees to the lower federal courts and the Supreme Court could be dedicated to resuming in earnest the now-paused campaign to roll back federal regulatory authority. It is, as the *Washington Post* editorialized in 2004, "still too early to say that the danger of aggressive federalism jurisprudence has passed."[61]

Endnotes

1. 42 U.S.C. § 401 (2000) and its amendments.
2. 42 U.S.C. §§ 12101-89 (1994).
3. 29 U.S.C. §§ 621-34 (1994).
4. 42 U.S.C. § 1396 (2000).
5. 42 U.S.C. § 1395 (2000).
6. 29 U.S.C. §§ 701-96 (1999).
7. 42 U.S.C. §§ 1395i-3, 1396r (2000).
8. 29 U.S.C. § 2601 (1993).
9. 42 U.S.C. §§ 3001-58ee (1994).
10. 42 U.S.C. §§ 2000d-2000d-7 (1994).
11. The "switch in time that saved nine" has been described many times. A particularly interesting account is Bruce Ackerman, *We the People: Transformations* (Belknap Press, 1998), 293–348.
12. Simon Lazarus, The Most Dangerous Branch? *Atlantic Monthly* (June 2002), 24, 26, 28.
13. In late 2001, Justice Stephen G. Breyer articulated this approach in a much-noticed address at New York University Law School, in which he characterized the Constitution as primarily a "framework for the creation of democratically determined solutions." Justice Stephen G. Breyer, Address at the Fall 2001 James Madison Lecture (October 22, 2001), at http://www.supremecourtus.gov/publicinfo/speeches/sp_10-22-01.html.
14. John T. Noonan, Jr., *Narrowing the Nation's Power: The Supreme Court Sides with the States* (University of California Press, 2002).

15. *Kimel v. Fla. Bd. of Regents*, 528 U.S. 62 (2000).

16. U.S. Constitution amend. XIV, § 1 in relevant part:
No state shall make or enforce any law which shall abridge the privileges or immunities of citizens of the United States; nor shall any state deprive any person of life, liberty, or property, without due process of law; nor deny to any person within its jurisdiction the equal protection of the laws.

17. This doctrine was established in *City of Boerne v. Flores*, 521 U.S. 507, 519 (1997), in which the Court held that the Religious Freedom Restoration Act exceeds Congress' enforcement power under Section 5 of the Fourteenth Amendment.

18. *Board of Trustees of the University of Alabama v. Garrett*, 531 U.S. 356 (2001).

19. *Garrett*, 531 U.S. at 370–71.

20. See Noonan, *supra* note 14, at 111–12.

21. Title II provides that no person "shall, by reason of such disability, be excluded from participation in or be denied the benefits of the services, programs, or activities of a public entity, or be subjected to discrimination by any such entity." § 202 (codified as amended at 42 U.S.C. § 12132 (1990)). Title II supplements provisions of other statutes that imposed similar, though less comprehensive, requirements on state governments.

22. See, e.g., *Pace v. Bogalusa City School Board*, 325 F.3d 609 (5th Cir. 2003); *Garcia v. S.U.N.Y. Health Scis. Ctr.*, 280 F.3d 98 (2d Cir. 2001).

23. 42 U.S.C. §§ 12131-65.

24. 124 S. Ct. 1978 (2004).

25. Medicare and Medicaid were both established in 1965 as amendments to the Social Security Act. The two programs are codified at 42 U.S.C. § 1935 *et seq.* (Medicare) and 42 U.S.C. § 1396 *et seq.* (Medicaid).

26. Alan Weil, There's Something About Medicaid, *Health Affairs* (January–February 2003), 17.

27. Robert Pear, "Governors Resist Bush Plan to Slow Costs of Medicaid," *New York Times* (May 25, 2003), A1.

28. Andy Schneider et al., *The Medicaid Resource Book* (The Kaiser Commission on Medicaid and the Uninsured, July 2002), 32–33, 82.

29. Chapter XVIII of Title 42.

30. The phrase "persons entitled to benefits" appears over one hundred times in the Medicare statute. Timothy Jost, The Tenuous Nature of the Medicaid Entitlement, *Health Affairs,* (January–February 2003), 145.

31. *Schweiker v. Gray Panthers,* 453 U.S. 34, 36–37 (1981).

32. U.S. Census Bureau, *Health Insurance Coverage: 2001,* at http://landview.census.gov/prod/2002pubs/p60-220.pdf (2002).

33. This memorandum is authored and frequently updated by Jane Perkins and is available on the National Health Law Program website. *42 U.S.C. § 1983 and Enforcement of the Medicaid Act,* at http://nhelp.org/publications.shtml (January 26, 1999). Detailed descriptions of key cases, updated daily, along with analyses of significant developments, are produced by Herbert Semmel (a contributor to this volume), and posted on the Federal Rights Project page of the National Senior Citizens Law Center website. http://nsclc.org/issues_justice_federal.html (2000).

34. Id.

35. For a cogent exposition of this point, see Timothy Jost, *supra* note 28, at 147–48.

36. 133 F.Supp.2d 549 (E.D. Mich. 2001), rev'd, 289 F.3d 852 (6th Cir. 2002), *cert. denied*, 537 U.S. 1045 (2002).

37. *Blessing v. Freestone*, 520 U.S. 329 (1997).

38. *Westside Mothers*, 133 F.Supp.2d at 574.

39. If sovereign immunity bars injunctions against state officials exercising discretionary functions, it would appear that Congress would be powerless to authorize private individuals or groups to enforce federal law in any meaningful fashion. The consequences for maintaining the supremacy of federal law would be considerable.

40. *Antrican v. Odom*, 290 F.3d 178 (4th Cir. 2002), *cert. denied*, 537 U.S. 973 (2002).

41. *Westside Mothers*, 537 U.S. 1045. Writing for the Court in another 2002 case, Justice Scalia himself disavowed, albeit somewhat equivocally, the conclusion that Spending Clause statutes are simply contracts between equal sovereigns. *Barnes v. Gorman*, 536 U.S. 181, 186 (2002). In this case, in which the Court held that punitive damages were not permissible in suits enforcing Spending Clause requirements, Justice Scalia extensively relied upon the asserted analogy with contract principles but asserted in a footnote: "We do not imply…that suits under Spending Clause legislation are suits in contract, or that contract-law principles apply to all issues that they raise." *Gebser v. Lago Vista Indep. Sch. Dist.*, 524 U.S. 274, 287 (1998). Justices Souter (for himself and Justice O'Connor) and Stevens (for himself, Justice Breyer, and Justice Ginsburg) wrote two concurring opinions stressing that the contract analogy does not cover all aspects of Spending Clause enforcement cases.

42. 536 U.S. 273 (2002).

43. 520 U.S. 329.

44. *Gonzaga*, which involved the Family Educational Rights and Privacy Act of 1974 (FERPA), held that, where federal statutes confer neither an express nor implied private right of action (as in the case of Medicaid), authority to utilize 28 U.S.C. § 1983 to bring a private suit is triggered only when the statute in question "unambiguously" bestows "rights," not merely when it manifests an intent to "benefit" a class to which plaintiffs belong. The *Gonzaga* opinion, written by Chief Justice Rehnquist, purported to clarify, but not overrule, the test for invoking § 1983 articulated five years earlier in *Blessing*, 520 U.S. at 340–41: "Congress must have intended that the provision in question benefit the plaintiff," the right asserted must not be too "vague and amorphous" for judges to interpret, and relevant provision must be "mandatory, not precatory."

45. In an important 2004 decision, the Third Circuit Court of Appeals reversed a district court's decision that effectively precluded § 1983 enforcement of any Medicaid requirements. The court explained that *Gonzaga* did not overrule *Blessing* or the cases preceding it that authorized the private enforcement of rights-conferring Medicaid provisions. *Sabree v. Richman*, 367 F.3d 180 (3d Cir. 2004). However, Judge Samuel Alioto's curt concurring opinion offers an ominous harbinger of things to come: "While the analysis and decision of the District Court may reflect the direction that future Supreme Court cases in this area will take, currently binding precedent supports the decision of the Court. I therefore concur in the Court's decision."

46. President George W. Bush has often repeated his pledge to select judges modeled after Justices Scalia and Thomas. One of these, February 2004 recess appointee William H. Pryor, has stated that spending programs are "contracts" between the equally sovereign federal and state governments and, as such, are unenforceable by beneficiaries (e.g., the law is as it would be if the district court's *Westside Mothers* decision had been affirmed, rather than reversed, and repudiated nationwide). See *Recess Appointee Puts His Spin on Federal-*

ism, on the website of the National Senior Citizens Law Center, at http://nsclc.org/news/04/mar/pryor_advocating.htm.

47. In *Westside Mothers*, Sutton expressly urged Judge Cleland to bypass precedent.

48. 133 F.Supp. at 22 (quoting *Will v. Michigan Department of State Police*, 491 U.S. 58, 65 (1989)). Many cases reiterate this "clear statement" principle. But, as noted in the text immediately below, courts' definitions of what it takes to make a statement clear have proven highly elastic.

49. Passing a "clear statement," especially one worded tightly enough to survive the scrutiny of hostile judges, will hardly be simple given the current composition of Congress and the array of opposed lobbying forces. Moreover, since the Medicaid program is threatened with cutbacks in scope, coverage, and funding, its supporters may not be in a position to make judicial enforcement a high priority, as a matter of legislative strategy.

50. In 1975, Congress amended the Medicaid Act to require states to waive Eleventh Amendment immunity from suit as a condition for receiving Medicaid funds. See H.R. 94-1122, 94th Cong. (1975). Since then, bills to limit §1983 enforcement of Medicaid have been introduced and rejected several times. See Brief of Amici Curiae AARP et al., *Sabree v. Richman*, 367 F.3d 180 (3d Cir. 2004).

51. For example, in his opinion invalidating the Gun-Free School Zones Act in *U.S. v. Lopez*, Chief Justice Rehnquist made much of the absence of congressional findings expressly tying the law to interstate commerce. But when Congress held extensive hearings and made formal findings to address this concern, the 5-4 majority brushed them aside and struck down the laws at issue anyway. *U.S. v. Morrison*, 529 U.S. 598 (2000) (Violence Against Women Act unauthorized by the Commerce Clause despite congressional findings); *Kimel*, 528 U.S. 62 (extension of ADEA to state government employers invalid despite congressional findings that states systematically discriminate on the basis of age (as do private sector employers)).

52. In 1999, in repudiating the doctrine of constructive waiver of state immunity from suit, the majority indicated that even if Congress's "expressing unequivocally its intention" to require waiver of immunity under certain circumstances, the courts may disregard that intent if in fact the state has not "unequivocally" waived it. *Coll. Sav. Bank v. Fla. Prepaid Postsecondary Educ. Expense Bd.*, 527 U.S. 666, 680–81 (1999). "Every reasonable presumption against waiver" must be considered before determining that the waiver was voluntary. *Coll. Sav. Bank*, 527 U.S. at 682.

53. See note 46.

54. The commentator is Michael Greve, Director of the Federalism Project of the American Enterprise Institute. He explains:

> Plaintiffs who escape from restrictive statutory interpretation into §1983 will find that route, too, strewn with obstacles. They may find that their purported right was unrecognized in 1871. Or, they may find that their claims for monetary damages—which are often the only effective means of forcing state and local governments into compliance—are blocked by a slew of Supreme Court decisions granting the states sovereign immunity against such lawsuits. (Even the Americans With Disabilities Act can no longer be enforced through damage judgments.) Let plaintiffs argue that the state has waived its immunity by accepting federal funds, and they will lose. Let plaintiffs seek to obtain relief by naming a state's officers, rather than the state itself, as a defendant, and they will find that this so-called *Ex Parte Young* rule, once readily available, has become a rare exception.

Michael Greve, *Federalism Yes, Activism No*, at http://www.fed-soc.org/Publications/hottopics/august.htm (2001).

55. *Nev. Dep't of Human Res. v. Hibbs*, 538 U.S. 721 (2003).

56. *Tennessee v. Lane*, 124 S. Ct. 1978. *Tennessee v. Lane* is discussed above and on the Federal Rights Project page of the National Senior Citizens Law Center website. National Senior Citizens Law Center, *Supreme Court Upholds ADA Title II Protection of Access to Court Facilities*, at http://www.nsclc.org/news/04/may/supct_adatitle2.htm (May 27, 2004).

57. *Sabri v. United States*, 124 S. Ct. 1941 (2004).

58. *Tenn. Student Assistance Corp. v. Hood*, 124 S. Ct. 1905 (2004). *Sabri* and *Tennessee Student Assistance Corp.* are briefly noted on the National Senior Citizens Law Center website. National Senior Citizens Law Center, *Three Supreme Court Cases Upholding Congressional Power*, at http://nsclc.org/news/04/may/supct_threecases0504.htm (May 27, 2004).

59. 125 S.Ct. 2195 (2005).

60. 514 U.S. 549 (1995) and 529 U.S. 598 (2001).

61. "States' Rights Revision," *Washington Post* (July 13, 2004), A14.

CHAPTER 8

AMERICANS WITH DISABILITIES

*Judicial Revision of the Americans with
Disabilities Act of 1990: Mere Fine-Tuning?
Or Ideological Backlash?*

Caroline Palmer[*]

*The Americans with Disabilities Act (ADA) is designed to protect the rights of
people with disabilities in employment, public services, and public accommodations. The ADA's 1990 passage spurred the creation of similarly inclusive state and
local laws, and brought about a new awareness of the rights of the disabled.*

*Because discrimination still occurs, however, the ADA remains a necessary tool.
One need only look at the cases handled by the Minnesota AIDS Project Legal Services for evidence of the discrimination still facing HIV-positive people in the workplace. For example, when a package handler working for an air courier asked for
indoor duty during the winter in order to protect his HIV-weakened lungs, his request was denied. When a clerical worker at a national retailer asked that his cu-
bicle be relocated closer to a bathroom to accommodate his need to relieve himself
frequently (a side effect of his HIV medication), his request was denied and his supervisor disclosed his health status to co-workers. Similarly, a school food service
worker was forced to provide medical verification that she was not a health risk.
After she complied, she was reassigned to a crossing guard position that required
her to stand outside for hours, and her condition was disclosed to other workers.
Medical assistants, home health care attendants, and similarly situated employees
have likewise seen their workloads decrease after disclosing their medical condition
to a supervisor.*

*In the nearly fifteen years since the ADA became law, the Supreme Court has de-
cided cases that dramatically weaken its effect, limit its application, and under-*

---

 * Caroline Palmer is Pro Bono Development Director at the Minnesota State Bar Association. She was formerly a staff attorney at the Minnesota AIDS Project in Minneapolis, MN. Thanks to Erica Westin and Dan Kelly for their assistance with this chapter.

mine its key concepts. While laws commonly evolve through judicial interpretation, the ADA appears particularly vulnerable to being subverted in this manner. Despite voluminous congressional testimony gathered during the Act's development, the Court is not satisfied that sufficient evidence exists to support the law in certain situations. As a result, it has narrowed the class of people protected by the ADA, and adopted an interpretation of the law that often favors employers. Further, the Court has used the doctrine of sovereign immunity to deprive plaintiffs of legal recourse to address inarguable wrongs committed by state governments.

The ADA is too important to be dismantled in a piecemeal fashion. This chapter explores some of the most recent ADA cases, discusses how these decisions impact the law, and examines why Congressional intervention may be necessary to prevent the courts from permanently weakening the ADA.

$$\approx \quad \approx \quad \approx$$

A History of Federal Laws Prohibiting Discrimination against People with Disabilities

People with disabilities have long fought for their basic rights—access to buildings, transportation, and places of employment, equal educational opportunities, and independent living.[1] The Rehabilitation Act of 1973, prohibiting discrimination based on disability, was the first federal legislation to recognize people with disabilities as a class that faces similar barriers and discrimination.[2] Because the statute did not apply to the private sector, however, many disabled people continued to face unjust treatment without meaningful legal recourse. Still, the Act represented the first time that "exclusion and segregation of people with disabilities was viewed as discrimination. Previously, it had been assumed that the problems faced by people with disabilities, such as unemployment and lack of education, were inevitable consequences of the physical or mental limitations imposed by the disability itself."[3] The Act represented a radical shift from the previous policy of categorizing people based on their particular disability,[4] and paved the way for further legislation—including the ADA.[5]

President George H.W. Bush signed the ADA into law on July 26, 1990 after years of advocacy by the disability rights community. The federal statute has been called the most significant piece of civil rights legislation to be enacted in the last twenty-five years.[6] Created in the spirit of the Civil Rights Act of 1964,[7] the ADA filled gaps left by the Rehabilitation Act, extending legal protections against discrimination to people with disabilities in employment, public services, public accommodations, and other venues.[8] In addition, it created a national mandate to rectify the problem that "society has tended to isolate and segregate individuals with disabilities" by providing "clear, strong, consistent, enforceable standards addressing discrimination against individuals with disabilities."[9]

With the ADA's passage, disability and civil rights activists achieved an important goal: they raised public awareness about the need for inclusion and accessibility. This led to the adoption of more expansive state and local laws to protect individuals with disabilities. Discrimination still occurred—and still does—but business owners and private entities faced new accountability.[10] The success of individual lawsuits against ADA violators encouraged even greater compliance, resulting in the development of conscientious and often innovative policies to accommodate the needs of the disabled population.

Like many groundbreaking laws, the ADA has inspired much debate about the proper scope of its application, the specificity of its definitions, and even the legitimacy of the legislative process responsible for its creation. Indeed, the Supreme Court under Chief Justice William Rehnquist has questioned, circumscribed, confused, and ultimately limited the Act's application. Justice Sandra Day O'Connor provided some insight into the Court's perception of the ADA when she told an audience at the Georgetown University Law Center that the law was "an example of what happens when sponsors are so eager to get something passed that what passes hasn't been as carefully written as a group of law professors might put together. So it leaves a lot of ambiguities and gaps and things for courts to figure out."[11]

Over the past five years, the Court—led by a block of five justices—has expanded the range of acceptable defenses to ADA litigation while reducing the number of people who benefit from the law's protections. In most ADA employment discrimination cases, the Court has ruled in favor of businesses over plaintiffs.[12] While some justices have expressed admiration for the ADA, it appears that the majority of the Court is more enamored with the idea of the law than with its actual application.[13]

Some argue that the Court has so weakened the ADA that the statute can no longer be relied upon to protect against disability discrimination.[14] To be sure, recent decisions are likely to chill ADA litigation, or at least tilt settlement negotiations in defendants' favor. While the ADA is not a perfect law, its judicial evisceration dilutes important civil rights protections. Congress must buttress the ADA against further damage by the Court—the lives and livelihoods of disabled persons depend upon it.

This chapter will discuss the most recent and significant ADA cases, and some themes that run through them: the use of sovereign immunity to thwart ADA enforcement against the states, a higher burden of proof on employees for proving that they are disabled, support for paternalistic employer policies, and the continued dynamic interplay of the ADA and the Civil Rights Act of 1964. It also considers the future of the ADA, a law intended to promote accessibility for all, and the irony that the statute has been narrowed to the point where it protects only a few.

The Rehnquist Court and the ADA

The Court's aggressive re-interpretation and re-evaluation of the ADA began during its 2001 term. These decisions were preceded by the 1999 *Sutton* trilogy of ADA cases that, by holding that mitigating factors such as medications or corrective devices like eyeglasses could alter the extent to which someone is considered disabled, signaled the Court's shift toward a narrowly-focused interpretation of the ADA as well as its growing propensity for case-by-case analysis of disability claims.[15] The *Sutton* trilogy has led lower federal courts to interpret the ADA in ways that raise significant questions about the law's application and continued effectiveness.[16]

Sovereign Immunity

A survey of post-2001 ADA decisions demonstrates that the Court has adopted new—and controversial—approaches to interpreting the law. The Court has been particularly concerned that Congress extended its reach too far and interfered with state authority in enacting the ADA. This issue is central to *Board of Trustees of University of Alabama v. Garrett*,[17] in which the Court limited Congress's powers to protect the rights of individuals with disabilities from violation by states. The Court's decision set the tone for ongoing questioning of federal legislative powers in subsequent ADA decisions.[18]

Garrett involved two separate lawsuits against the state of Alabama, brought by two former employees who claimed they had been forced from their jobs.[19] Patricia Garrett was demoted after an unpaid leave of absence during which she underwent radiation and chemotherapy treatments for breast cancer, while Milton Ash, who suffered from asthma and sleep apnea, could not complete his duties because his employer refused to enforce a no-smoking rule or maintain Ash's truck so it would not emit toxic fumes.[20] The lower courts disagreed about whether the Eleventh Amendment grants states immunity from enforcement of Title I of the ADA.[21] The Supreme Court concluded that while Congress can enact "appropriate legislation" such as the ADA to protect constitutional rights, it had not demonstrated a sufficiently pervasive pattern of disability discrimination by the states to overcome the Eleventh Amendment's protection of state immunity from suit.[22] Moreover, the Court found that even if there was a pattern of unconstitutional discrimination by the states, Title I of the ADA failed the "congruence and proportionality" test because it forbids disparate impact discrimination, which is "insufficient [to state a cause of action] even where the Fourteenth Amendment subjects state action to strict scrutiny."[23] The dissenting justices argued that Congress had in fact compiled an extensive record, including testimony from thirteen hearings and some three hundred examples of discrimination by state governments. This evidence, however, was insufficient to persuade the majority of the Court that disability discrimination was so widespread as to justify interference with state autonomy.[24] The ADA, therefore, could not be used to force states to pay damages for violations of the law.[25] The *Garrett* decision dealt a significant blow to Congress's ability to address civil rights violations by state governments.

The next case involving the ADA and sovereign immunity, *Tennessee v. Lane*, benefited disabled persons while upholding the central principles of *Garrett*.[26] George Lane and Beverly Jones filed an action against the state of Tennessee claiming violations of Title II of the ADA, which provides that "no qualified individual with a disability shall, by reason of such disability, be excluded from participation or denied the benefits of services, programs or activities of a public entity...."[27] Lane had to crawl up two flights of stairs because the county courthouse where he was due to answer to criminal charges did not have an elevator.[28] When he returned to the courthouse for a hearing and refused to crawl or be carried up the stairs, he was arrested and jailed for failing to appear in court.[29] Jones, a certified court reporter, lost her job when she could not gain access to several courthouses.[30]

In an opinion authored by Justice John Paul Stevens, the Court held that in court access cases, Title II of the ADA is a "valid exercise of Congress' §5 authority to enforce the guarantees of the Fourteenth Amendment."[31] Infringements of the right of court access are subject to heightened judicial scrutiny, and the constitutionality of Title II of the ADA should be judged "with reference to the historical experience which it reflects."[32] The Court enumerated several examples of unconstitutional treatment of disabled persons by state agencies (in which discrimination persisted even after state and federal legislative action),[33] concluding that Title II was enacted "against a backdrop of pervasive unequal treatment in the administration of state services and programs, including systematic deprivations of fundamental rights."[34] The Court also cited a congressional report showing that some "76% of public services and programs housed in state-owned buildings were inaccessible to and unusable by persons with disabilities, even taking into account the possibility that the services and programs might be restructured or relocated to other parts of the buildings."[35] The Court determined that Title II's "affirmative obligation to accommodate persons with disabilities in the administration of justice cannot be said to be 'so out of proportion to a supposed remedial or preventive object that it cannot be understood as responsive to, or designed to prevent, unconstitutional behavior.'"[36] Tennessee, therefore, could not assert sovereign immunity.[37]

Chief Justice Rehnquist, Justice Antonin Scalia, and Justice Clarence Thomas all dissented from the majority opinion, asserting that Congress had failed to identify sufficient evidence to support either Title I or Title II of the ADA, and that both provisions failed the "congruent and proportional standard" requirement articulated in *Garrett*.[38]

Employment Discrimination

Most of the Court's ADA decisions since 2001 have concerned employment discrimination. These decisions, together with *Garrett* and the *Sutton* trilogy, illustrate how the Court has narrowed the application of the ADA by adopting a new legal rubric favoring employers.

In *Toyota Manufacturing, Inc. v. Williams*, for example, the Court developed a case-by-case approach for determining whether a person is disabled that places a heavy burden on claimants seeking to prove disability, and makes it harder to hold employers responsible for their discriminatory actions.[39] Ella Williams, an automobile plant worker, sued Toyota for failing to reasonably accommodate her disabilities—carpal tunnel syndrome, and some muscle, tendon, and nerve inflammation caused by the repetitive nature of her job.[40] Williams claimed that she was disabled under the ADA because her "physical impairments substantially limited her in (1) manual tasks; (2) housework; (3) gardening; (4) playing with her children; (5) lifting; and (6) working"—all of which, she argued, constituted major life activities.[41] The Court accepted the case in order to determine the proper standard for "assessing whether an individual is substantially limited in performing manual tasks,"[42] and to review the definitions of "substantial limitation" and "major life activity." The Court strictly interpreted those terms so as "to create a demanding standard for qualifying as disabled" under the ADA,[43] concluding that "substantial" "clearly precludes impairments in only a minor way with the performance of manual tasks from qualifying as disabilities," while "major life activities" are those that "are of central importance to daily life."[44]

According to the Court, Congress did not intend that "disabled" be interpreted in an overly-broad fashion because too many people would qualify for ADA protection. The Court concluded that to be considered disabled, an individual who is substantially limited in manual tasks (either inside or outside of the workplace) must also prove that she cannot perform activities central to daily life.[45] Their impairment must be at least long-term, and must be evaluated on a case-by-case basis (because symptoms vary among individuals).[46]

The Court's approach closely adhered to the ADA's definition of disability while increasing the plaintiff's burden of proof. Individual evaluations now require extensive medical evidence, analysis of mitigating factors (as determined under the *Sutton* trilogy), and a detailed assessment of the impact of the disability on the individual's daily life. While it is certainly not unreasonable to require a plaintiff to provide information to support their disability claim, the *Williams* Court sent a message that only the most severely disabled (those unable to work because of their disability) can and should reach the threshold requirements to bring suit. The decision focused on the plaintiff's burden to prove her disability rather than on the employer's alleged illegal actions, thereby placing the employee at a significant disadvantage.

Paternalistic Employer Policies

The Court has also favored employer interests by affording employers greater flexibility in accommodating the needs of disabled employees. For example, the Court has held that the ADA does not trump most seniority rules. In the 2002 *U.S. Airways v. Barnett*, the Court established that the ADA could not trump a seniority system except under "special circumstances,"[47] such as where there was evidence that other exceptions were made to the seniority system or where the employer did not strictly follow the system. In its discussion of "reasonable accommodation," the Court looked to other civil rights statutes (particularly the relationship between the Rehabilitation Act and religious accommodations such as worship schedules), and concluded that exceptions could not be made to seniority systems without sufficient evidence of flexibility in the seniority framework.[48]

In a dissent, Justice Scalia (joined by Justice Thomas) scolded the majority for holding that an employer should never be required to violate seniority rules in order to accommodate a disabled worker.[49] Justice David Souter (joined by Justice Ruth Bader Ginsburg) also dissented, arguing that a case-by-case analysis should be applied.[50] *Barnett* was a rare case in which both the right and left wings of the court dissented—albeit for different reasons—from an ADA majority opinion.

In its most recent ADA decision, *Clackamas Gastroenterology Associates, P.C. v. Wells*, the Court narrowed yet another area of employment discrimination law. Under the ADA, businesses with fewer than fifteen employees for at least twenty weeks of the year are exempt from compliance; the Act, however, does not define the term "employee."[51]

Deborah Ann Wells, a bookkeeper at a medical clinic, had a debilitating tissue disorder. She filed suit when she was fired, claiming that the clinic had violated the ADA because it had based her dismissal on her disability.[52] The clinic argued that its four physician-shareholders and Board of Directors should not be considered employees,[53] and therefore it did not have the required fifteen or more employees.[54] The Court agreed, concluding that the physicians and Board members were analogous to partners in a partnership[55] because "they apparently control the operation of the clinic, they share the profits and they are personally liable for malpractice claims."[56] Further, "[t]he answer to whether a shareholder-director is an employee or an employer cannot be decided in every case by a 'shorthand formula or magic phrase.'"[57]

Justices Stephen Breyer and Ginsburg dissented, arguing that "[t]here is nothing inherently inconsistent between the coexistence of a proprietary and an employment relationship."[58] The dissent took particular issue with an approach that would allow "a firm's coverage by the ADA...[to] sometimes turn on variations in ownership structure unrelated to the magnitude of the company's business or its capacity for complying with federal prescriptions."[59] Had just one physician-stakeholder sold his share and become an employee, they pointed out, the employer would have been subject to the ADA; yet the business would be unaltered in purpose.[60] Allowing such manipulations of job relationships deprived employees of federal protection against disability discrimination.[61]

Wells resulted in the dilution of yet another ADA protection. The Court essentially told employers how to manipulate their organizational structure in order to avoid being subject to the ADA. Fewer disabled employees, therefore, will have federal protections.

The Court has also begun to accept paternalistic "direct threat" defenses to ADA claims—in which employers argue that accommodating a disability could cause harm to the employee's health—so long as they are job-related. *Chevron v. Echazabel*, decided in 2002, echoes the strict interpretation approach adopted under *Williams*.[62] Mario Echazabel worked for independent contractors at a Chevron-owned oil refinery.[63] He twice applied for a job with Chevron, but was twice denied after the requisite physical examinations showed that he had liver damage and Hepatitis C[64]—Chevron's doctors stated conditions that would be compromised by exposure to the toxins in the refinery.[65] Chevron also requested that the independent contractor assign Echazabel to jobs where he would not be exposed to toxins.[66] The contractor laid Echazabel off. Echazabel filed suit, claiming that Chevron had violated the ADA by refusing to hire him or allow him to work in the factory because of his Hepatitis C diagnosis.[67] Chevron asserted a "direct threat" defense, claiming that Echazabel's disability represented a direct threat to his health on the job.

The Court noted that Title I of the ADA prohibits discrimination with regard to hiring and other employment actions,[68] but allows employers to require that "an individual shall not pose a direct threat to the health or safety of other individuals in the workplace."[69] The Court held that the refinery job presented a direct threat to Echazabel's health, and that the ADA did not apply because employers could screen for risks to the health of their workers and third parties.[70] So long as Chevron adhered to the ADA requirement that employee qualification standards be "job-related and consistent with business necessity," it could successfully assert the direct threat defense.[71] Further, the Court held that the EEOC's rule was not meant to be an example of workplace paternalism, but rather a means of preventing harm in specific employment situations.[72]

Echazabel has caused concern among individuals living with certain medical conditions that engender stigma and discrimination. As Rhonda Goldfein, Executive Director of the AIDS Law Project of Pennsylvania, observed, "all you need is some bad science to say there's a threat to the person and you can essentially tell them, 'you don't have enough sense to protect yourself, so we're going to do it for you.'"[73] If medical information can be manipulated to support a direct threat defense, there will likely be more cases in which employers either fail to provide appropriate accommodations or refuse employment based on overly conservative—or just plain wrong—reactions to medical findings. It is shortsighted for the Court to dismiss concerns about workplace paternalism. The direct threat defense gives the employer too much power; and the result could mean fewer opportunities for disabled employees.

The ADA and the Civil Rights Act of 1964

The Court has also begun looking to other civil rights legislation—specifically the Civil Rights Act of 1964 and the Rehabilitation Act of 1973—for guidance in interpreting the ADA. The Court seems concerned that the ADA's anti-discrimination protections extend beyond traditional civil rights standards; therefore, it is reluctant to uphold these protections without evidence of congressional intent.

In *PGA Tour, Inc. v. Martin* in 2001, the Court considered the case of Casey Martin, a golfer with Klippel-Trenaunay-Weber Syndrome (a degenerative circulatory disorder) who had been denied a request to use a golf cart in tournament play even though he supplied detailed medical justification.[74] Martin sued the Professional Golfers' Association (PGA) under the ADA's Title III requirement that entities operating "public accommodations" must make "reasonable modifications" in their policies "when...necessary to afford such... accommodations to individuals with disabilities, unless the entity can demonstrate that making such modifications would fundamentally alter the nature of such...accommodations."[75]

The Court acknowledged that Martin was disabled under the ADA's definition (possessing a "physical or mental impairment that substantially limits one or more major life activities"), and concluded that the PGA's golf tours and qualifying rounds were indeed public accommodations.[76] It determined that a "walking rule," designed to induce fatigue, did not apply because "even with the use of the cart...the fatigue [Martin] suffers from coping with his disability is 'undeniably greater' than the fatigue his able-bodied competitors endure from walking the course."[77] The Court held that Martin had been wronged by the PGA, and analogized its holding to the guarantee of, access to, and equal enjoyment of public accommodations without "discrimination or segregation on the ground of race, color, religion or national origin" in the Civil Rights Act of 1964.[78] By referencing the Civil Rights Act, the Court signaled a willingness to uphold the ADA's similarly inclusive and fundamental goals of assuring access to all, regardless of disability.

Not all comparisons of the ADA to the Civil Rights Act, however, have favored claimants. In *Barnes v. Gorman* in 2002, the Court determined that the punitive damage limitations in the Civil Rights Act should also apply to the ADA.[79] Jeffrey Gorman, a paraplegic who was arrested for trespassing after fighting with a bouncer at a Kansas City nightclub, sustained serious injuries while riding in a non-handicapped-equipped police van.[80] He sued the Kansas City Board of Police Commissioners, the Chief of Police, and the officer who had been driving. While the jury awarded him compensatory and punitive damages, the Court held that he was not entitled to punitive damages because of the interplay between the ADA, the Rehabilitation Act, the Civil Rights Act of 1964, and Congress's power under the Spending Clause (which places conditions on the granting of federal funds).[81]

The Court concluded that the relationship between the federal government and the municipality was contractual (the recipient agreed to comply with federally-imposed conditions in exchange for receiving federal funds under

Title IV of the Civil Rights Act).[82] Because punitive damages are generally unavailable for breach of contract and could exceed the amount of a federal grant, the Court held, Title IV recipients do not implicitly consent to punitive damage liability.[83] Even though the ADA and the Rehabilitation Act provide remedies, procedures, and rights for such situations, therefore, the relationship between these laws and the Civil Rights Act results in a loss of protection for an injured plaintiff. *Barnes* ultimately gives municipalities a broad defense against ADA claims using, ironically enough, the Civil Rights Act of 1964.

Protecting the Future of the ADA

What should we make of these recent Court decisions, and how are they likely to affect the future of the ADA? The Court seems to be rapidly, and perhaps dangerously, undermining the ADA by re-imagining congressional intent; with each successive decision, the Court narrows another aspect of the law and denies another plaintiff judicial recourse. Although the interpretation of a law often evolves over time, this is problematic when the interpretation prevents the law from being effective or causes it to harm those it purports to protect.

Congress should craft a legislative response to the Court's ADA decisions (see chapter 22 for proposed "legislative fixes"). To its credit, Congress has proactively encouraged businesses to comply with the ADA. Since 1990, for example, it has enacted tax credits to reward businesses that accommodate disabled employees.[84]

The most recent Court decisions send the message that employers can avoid compliance with the ADA. The Court has pulled the proverbial rug out from under Congress when it comes to encouraging equal treatment for people with disabilities. Short of major legislative reform, it seems that Congress can only respond by offering businesses more incentives for compliance (that hopefully outweigh the Court's exemptions). This response, however, is not strong enough. The many communities that joined to craft the ADA deserve a law that addresses the court-created gaps in legal protections.

Conclusion

The ADA is a visionary law. It should be accorded the same respect as other, well-established civil rights laws. Although much work remains to be done to increase public awareness, there is no doubt that the ADA has transformed the way disabled individuals are treated.[85] Social change can only come about with increased recognition of the needs of disabled Americans, and effective judicial recourse for civil rights violations.

Endnotes

1. 42 U.S.C. §12101 *et seq.* (2000 ed.). See Lisa A. Sciallo, Note, The ADA Through the Looking Glass, *68 Brook L. Rev.* (Winter 2002) 589, 595; Arlene B. Mayerson, *The History of the ADA: A Movement Perspective*, Disability Rights Education and Defense Fund, at http://www.dredf.org/articles/adahist.html (visited July 30, 2003). "Like the African-Americans who sat in at segregated lunch counters and refused to move to the back of the bus, people with disabilities sat in federal buildings, obstructed the movement of inaccessible buses, and marched through the streets to protest injustice. And like the civil rights movement before it, the disability rights movement sought justice in the courts and in the halls of Congress." Id.

2. Rehabilitation Act of 1973, 29 U.S.C. §794 (2000).

3. Mayerson, *supra* note 1.

4. Id.

5. Other ADA predecessors include: the Architectural Barriers Act of 1968, Pub. L. No. 90-480, 82 Stat. 718 (codified as amended at 42 U.S.C. §§4151 *et. seq.*) (1995); the Individuals with Disabilities Education Act Amendments of 1997, Pub. L. No. 105-17, 111 Stat. 37 (codified as amended at 42 U.S.C. §§1400 *et. seq.*) (2000); the Voting Accessibility for the Elderly and Handicapped Act of 1984, Pub. L. No. 98-435, 98 Stat. 1678 (codified as amended at 42 U.S.C. §1973ee) (2000); and the Air Carrier Access Act of 1986, Pub. L. No. 103-272, §1(e), 108 Stat. 1041 (codified as amended at 49 U.S.C. §41705) (2000).

6. Sciallo, *supra* note 1, at 595 (quoting Robert C. Mathes, Note, Civil Rights—The Status of Persons Infected with Asymptomatic HIV Under the Americans with Disabilities Act of 1990 after Bragdon—Did the Supreme Court Miss an Opportunity to Protect Disabled Americans? *Bragdon v. Abbott*, 118 S. Ct. 1196 (1998), *34 Land & Water L. Rev.* (citing Laura F. Rothstein, *Disabilities and the Law*, 1.05, 23 (2d. ed. 1997) 237, 239).

7. 42 U.S.C. §2000 *et seq.* (2000 ed.).

8. 42 U.S.C. §12101 *et seq.* Title I of the ADA covers employment, specifically: "No covered entity shall discriminate against a qualified individual with a disability because of the disability of such individual in regard to job application procedures, the hiring, advancement, or discharge of employees, employee compensation, job training, and other terms, conditions, and privileges of employment." Id. at §§12111-17. Title II relates to public services and provides that "no qualified individual with a disability shall, by reason of such disability, be excluded from participation in or be denied benefits of the services, programs, or activities of a public entity, or be subjected to discrimination by any such entity." Id. at §§12131-34. Title III, which prohibits discrimination by public accommodations, states that "[n]o individual shall be discriminated against on the basis of disability in the full and equal enjoyment of the goods, services, facilities, privileges, advantages, or accommodations of any place of public accommodation by any person who owns, leases (or leases to), or operates a place of public accommodation." Id. at §§12181-89.

9. Id. at §§12101(a)(2);12101(b)(1)–(2).

10. Mayerson, *supra* note 1. "For the first time in the history of our country, or the history of the world, businesses must stop and think about access to people with disabilities. If the ADA means anything, it means that people with disabilities will no longer be out of sight and out of mind....Accommodating a person with a disability is no longer a matter of charity but instead a basic issue of civil rights." Id.

11. William C. Smith, Drawing Boundaries, *88 A.B.A. J.* (August 2002) 49.

12. Robert F. Rich, et al. Critical Legal and Political Issues for People with Disabilities, *6 DePaul J. Healthcare L.* (Fall 2002) 1, 24.

13. See e.g., *Board of Trustees of University of Alabama v. Garrett*, 531 U.S. 356, 375 (2001) (Kennedy, J. concurring).

14. Cass R. Sunstein, A Hand in the Matter—Has the Rehnquist Court Pushed its Agenda on the Rest of the Country? *Legal Affairs* (March/April 2003), at http://www .legalaffairs.org/issues/March-April2003/feature_marapr03_sunstein.html. Sunstein interprets different aspects of judicial activism, and concludes that right wing activism within the Rehnquist Court has played a hand in invalidating laws that Congress has, or may have, the constitutional power to enact.

15. *Sutton v. United Airlines*, 527 U.S. 471 (1999); *Murphy v. United Parcel Service*, 527 U.S. 516 (1999); and *Albertson's, Inc. v. Kirkinburg*, 527 U.S. 555 (1999). Each case considers whether an individual has a disability when the impairment can be controlled by medication (for a condition such as high blood pressure) or assistive devices like eyeglasses. The *Sutton* trilogy led to some hundred lower court interpretations. See Arlene B. Mayerson and Kristan S. Mayer, Defining Disability in the Aftermath of Sutton: Where do we go from Here? Disability Rights Education and Defense Fund, *Human Rights* (Winter 2000) 27:1, and at http://www.dredf.org/articles/mayerson.html (visited July 30, 2003). According to Mayerson and Mayer, a person may still be covered by the ADA even when he or she benefits from a mitigating measure because "he or she is still substantially limited in a major life activity or because the mitigating measure itself is substantially limiting. Moreover, the mitigating measure may be effective at times but not at others, causing the person to have intermittent periods in which he or she is substantially limited." Id. For further analysis of how the terms "impairment," "major life activity," and "substantial limitation" impact an ADA determination, see *Bragdon v. Abbott*, where the Court held that a woman with asymptomatic HIV infection was limited because she could not reproduce, a major life activity as defined by the Court. 524 U.S. 624 (1998).

16. Mayerson and Mayer, *supra* note 15.

17. 531 U.S. at 363.

18. See e.g. at 365–74.

19. Id. at 362.

20. Id.

21. Id. at 362–63. The Eleventh Amendment states: "The judicial power of the United States shall not be construed to extend to any suit in law or equity, commenced or prosecuted against the United States by citizens of another state, or by citizens or subjects of any foreign state." U.S. Const. amend. XI.

22. *Garrett*, 531 U.S. at 374.

23. Id. at 373.

24. Id. at 372. In addition, fourteen states submitted amicus curie (friend of the court) briefs in support of the *Garrett* plaintiffs, suggesting a willingness by those states to be held accountable under the ADA. Id. at 356.

25. Id.

26. 124 S. Ct. 1978 (2004).

27. *Lane,* 124 S. Ct. at 1982. See 42 U.S.C. § 12132.

28. Id. at 1982–83.

29. Id. at 1983.

30. Id.

31. *Lane,* 124 S. Ct. at 1986–88 (1994).

32. Id. at 1988 (citing *South Carolina v. Katzenbach,* 383 U.S. 301, 308 (1966)).

33. Id. at 1990.

34. Id. at 1989.

35. Id. at 1990–91 (citing U.S. Civil Rights Commission, *Accommodating the Spectrum of Individual Abilities* (1983) 39).

36. Id. at 1994 citing *Boerne,* 521 U.S. at 532.

37. *Lane,* 124 S. Ct. at 1992 (1999).

38. *Lane,* 124 S. Ct. at 1997 (Renhquist, Scalia, and Thomas, Js. dissent).

39. 534 U.S. 184 (2002).

40. Id. at 187–88.

41. Id. at 192.

42. Id. at 196.

43. Id.

44. Id. at 197.

45. Id. at 198.

46. Id. at 199.

47. 535 U.S. 391 (2002).

48. Id. at 403 (referring to *Trans World Airlines v. Hardison,* 432 U.S. 63, 79–80 (1977)). "This Court has held that in the context of a Title VII religious discrimination case, an employer need not adapt to an employee's special worship schedule as a "reasonable accommodation" where doing so would conflict with the seniority rights of other employees." Id.

49. Id. at 412.

50. Id. at 420.

51. 538 U.S. 440, 444 (2003).

52. Id. at 442. See also Gina Holland, "High Court Grants Small Firms Leeway with Disability Law," *A Houston Chronical* (April 22, 2003).

53. Id. at 442.

54. 538 U.S. at 442.

55. Id. at 449 (citing EEOC Compliance Manual § 605.0009). According to the EEOC, several questions must be posed in order to determine an employer-employee relationship: "Whether the organization can hire or fire the individual or set the rules and regulations of the individual's work; Whether, and, if so, to what extent the organization supervises the individual's work; Whether the individual reports to someone higher in the organization; Whether, and, if so, to what extent the individual is able to influence the organization; Whether the parties intended that the individual be an employee, as expressed in written agreements and contracts; Whether the individual shares in the profits, losses and liabilities of the organization." Id. at 449–50 (citing EEOC Compliance Manual § 605.0009).

56. Id. at 451. "The mere fact that a person has a particular title—such as partner, director, or vice president—should not necessarily be used to determine whether he or she is an employer or a proprietor." Id. at 450 (citations omitted).

57. Id. at 450 n.10. (citing *Nationwide Mut. Ins. Co. v. Darden*, 503 U.S. 318, 324 (1992)) (quoting *NLRB v. United Ins. Co, of America*, 390 U.S. 254, 258 (1968)).

58. *Wells*, 538 U.S. at 451 (Ginsburg, J. dissent) (citing *Goldberg v. Whitaker House Coop., Inc.*, 366 U.S. 28, 32 (1961).

59. Id. at 454.

60. Id. at 454.

61. Id. at 456.

62. 536 U.S. 73 (2002).

63. Id. at 76.

64. Id.

65. Id.

66. Id.

67. *Chevron*, 536 U.S. at 76–77.

68. Id. at 78. Qualification standards used to "screen out or tend to screen out an individual with a disability" are discriminatory. Id. (citing 42 U.S.C. §12112(b)(6)).

69. Id. at 78 (citing 42 U.S.C. §12113(b))

70. Id. at 78–80. The EEOC allows the employer to screen for risks to third parties and the worker. Id. citing 29 C.F.R. §1630.15(b)(2) (2001).

71. 536 U.S. at 79 (citing 42 U.S.C. 12113(a).

72. Id. at 85.

73. Bob Adams, Is the Act Up? *HIV Plus* (June/July 2002) 19.

74. 532 U.S. 661, 668–69 (2001).

75. Id. at 669. See 42 U.S.C. §12182(b)(2)(A)(ii).

76. *Martin*, 532 U.S. at 677, 668. See also 42 U.S.C. §12102(2)(A). The Court broadened the meaning of the terms "impairment," "major life activity," and "substantial limitation" in *Bragdon v. Abbott*, 524 U.S. 624 (1998), a case involving a woman with asymptomatic HIV disease. ADA claimants must also demonstrate that their condition is widely perceived as disabling, and that they either have a record of being disabled, an actual disability, or are regarded as being disabled, whether or not the conditions associated with the disability currently exist." 42 U.S.C. §12102(2)(B)–(C).

77. *Martin*, 532 U.S. at 672 (citing *Martin v. PGA Tour, Inc.*, 994 F. Supp. 1242, 1251 (D. Or. 1998). See also 683–88 (discussion of "walking rule").

78. Id. at 681. See also 42 U.S.C. §2000a(a).

79. 536 U.S. 181 (2002).

80. Id. at 183–84.

81. Id. at 188.

82. Id. at 186–87.

83. Id.

84. Rich et al, *supra* note 12, at 52. See also United States Department of Justice, *Tax Incentives Packet on the Americans with Disabilities Act*, at www.usdoj.gov/crt/ada/tax-pack.htm (visited July 28, 2004).

85. See David M. Engle and Frank W. Munger, *Rights of Inclusion: Law and Identity in the Life Stories of Americans with Disabilities* (2003).

CHAPTER 9

SEXUAL MINORITIES

*The Federalism Revolution and the Sexual
Minority Federal Legislative Agenda*

Arthur S. Leonard[*]

John Bibby, a long-time employee at the Philadelphia Coca-Cola Bottling Company, was assaulted in the locker room by a co-worker who shook his fist in Bibby's face, grabbed him by the shirt collar, and threw him up against the lockers. Weeks later, the same co-worker used a forklift to block Bibby from leaving a platform, refused a supervisor's orders to move the forklift, and yelled "everybody knows you're gay as a three dollar bill," "everybody knows you're a faggot," and "everybody knows you take it up the ass."

When Bibby complained, the co-worker was discharged. The union filed a grievance, and the company reinstated the co-worker rather than fighting the case in arbitration. According to Bibby, he was subjected to repeated harassment when company supervisors yelled at him, ignored his reports of problems with machinery, and enforced rules against him while ignoring similar infractions by co-workers. Graffiti of a sexual nature, sometimes bearing his name, appeared on restroom walls and was allowed to remain there longer than other offensive graffiti.

When Bibby sued for sexual harassment under Title VII of the 1964 Civil Rights Act, the federal court told him that such harassment against gay people was not unlawful.[†]

This chapter will examine how the Federalism Revolution cases present significant challenges to advocates for basic federal civil rights for lesbians and gays, jeopardizing congressional authority to enact the Employee Non-Discrimination Act (ENDA), hate crimes legislation, and other expansive measures.

---

[*] Professor of Law, New York Law School. The author wishes to acknowledge research and editing assistance from Joseph Griffin, NYLS Class of 2005, and that a New York Law School faculty research grant helped support this project.

[†] *Bibby v. Philadelphia Coca-Cola Bottling Co.*, 260 F.3d 257 (3d Cir. 2001).

ಎ ಎ ಎ

Since the early 1970s, lesbian, gay, and bisexual civil rights activists have sought the enactment of federal laws to ensure their equal rights. More recently, transgendered persons have asserted the same need. While political progress has been made toward this goal, none of these sexual minorities have obtained substantive federal legislation to protect their basic civil rights. Today, Supreme Court decisions have further undermined this struggle, limiting the ability of Congress to protect individual rights against state abridgement. Whether the Federalism Revolution will prove to be a substantial barrier to attaining the goals of the sexual minority legislative agenda will depend, in part, on how expansively the courts interpret *Lawrence v. Texas*,[1] in which the Court found laws forbidding sexual intimacy between same-sex adult partners unconstitutional.

This chapter will provide a brief history of efforts made in the federal courts, Congress, and the executive branch to protect the civil rights of lesbians, gays, and bisexuals. It will then examine how the Supreme Court's rollback of federal civil rights threatens those efforts.

Efforts to Obtain Gay Rights at the Federal Level

Over the past few decades, sexual minorities have made significant progress in ending discriminatory federal policies. As early as the 1960s, sexual minorities were able to achieve some recognition of their constitutional freedoms through litigation. The first such ruling held that lesbian and gay publications were entitled to sufficient protection under the First Amendment to be distributed in the mail.[2] In the 1970s, rulings required state universities and colleges to allow lesbian and gay organizations to hold political and social events on campuses.[3] In the 1990s, the Supreme Court decided in *Romer v. Evans* that state policies enacted solely to render sexual minorities unequal (and inferior) violated the Equal Protection Clause of the Constitution.[4] These developments culminated in 2003 with the *Lawrence v. Texas*[5] decision, which held that laws forbidding consenting adults from having private, non-commercial consensual sex abridge the liberty that is protected under the Due Process Clause of the Constitution. In addition, some lower federal court decisions determined that federal statutes banning sex discrimination apply to transgendered persons and others whose conduct and/or presentation does not conform to gender stereotypes.[6]

On the legislative side, though unwilling to enact affirmative protections for sexual minorities, Congress repealed the ban on their immigration into the U.S.[7] and provided for the federal collection of data on crimes motivated by the victim's actual or perceived sexual orientation in the Hate Crimes Statistics Act (HCSA).[8]

In the executive branch, President William J. Clinton issued a historic executive order prohibiting sexual orientation discrimination in federal employment,[9] an act officially ending the ban on hiring gays and lesbians established by President Dwight D. Eisenhower.[10] Clinton also reorganized the federal security clearance system,[11] ending policies that made it difficult or impossible for sexual minorities to obtain jobs requiring security clearances in either the government or the private sector.[12]

Despite the significant progress made in ending discriminatory federal policies, sexual minorities have failed to secure affirmative legislation guaranteeing equal rights. At the same time, an anti-gay backlash has embedded measures that effectively require affirmative discrimination in federal law. In 1993, Congress codified a policy that had for generations been articulated only in regulations by banning military service by openly lesbian, gay, or bisexual individuals.[13] In 1996, Congress passed the so-called Defense of Marriage Act (DOMA),[14] forbidding the recognition of state-sanctioned same-sex marriages[15] under any federal law or policy, and purporting to relieve the states of any constitutional requirement to afford full faith and credit to such marriages.[16] In addition, Congress imposed "decency" standards on the National Endowment for the Arts (NEA), partly in response to controversies about homoerotic art produced by NEA grant recipients such as gay performance artist Tim Miller and photographer Robert Mapplethorpe. The Supreme Court upheld these standards against constitutional challenge. Depending on how these standards are implemented, they could impose serious disadvantages on sexual minority artists seeking federal funding for certain kinds of work.[17]

Congress also imposed restrictions on other expenditures, in part to avoid the "promotion" of homosexuality by legal services or public health programs.[18] Further, it overrode higher education institutions seeking to exclude anti-gay employers from campuses by hinging eligibility for federal funds on the Department of Defense (the most aggressively anti-gay employer in the federal sector) having access to recruit and interview students on campus.[19] Finally, Congress delayed the implementation of a domestic partnership benefits program for DC government employees by imposing spending restrictions in its appropriations measures.[20]

During the 1990s, however, it became conceivable to lesbian and gay advocates that they might be able to secure affirmative civil rights protection under federal law. The expansive federal gay rights bills (seeking a federal ban on sexual orientation discrimination in employment, housing, and public accommodations)[21] that had been futilely introduced in Congress for two decades, were re-drafted to focus on intentional sexual orientation discrimination in non-military public and private employment. In 1994, ENDA was introduced.[22] At the same time, gay rights advocates secured the introduction of bills intended to expand the scope of the federal definition of hate crimes to add "sexual orientation" to the categories covered by existing law.[23] Bills were also introduced to extend recognition under immigration laws to committed same-sex partners (legal spouses of U.S. citizens are entitled to certain advantages in the immigration process), and to extend spousal rights to same-sex partners under the Social Security Act.[24]

Although the lesbian and gay federal legislative agenda is now focused on passing ENDA and repealing or modifying the anti-gay policies noted above, other goals include modifying federal social and economic regulations such as the Internal Revenue Code and the Bankruptcy Code so that committed same-sex couples are provided with equal benefits. Little action is possible, however, until DOMA is repealed, amended, or judicially invalidated, as the proposed legislation requires some form of federal recognition for same-sex partners.[25]

The Federalism Revolution and the Sexual Minority Legislative Agenda

The 2000 ascendancy of a right wing political establishment meant that the lesbian and gay rights' federal legislative agenda has had to confront extraordinary political barriers. Additionally, it faces potential constitutional barriers stemming from the Supreme Court's Federalism Revolution decisions,[26] in which congressional authority to legislate on civil rights was radically curtailed, diminishing the federal government's ability both to empower state and local government employees to enforce their civil rights in court and to address social problems on a national basis through federal criminal and civil law. Those decisions jeopardize congressional authority to enact ENDA, pending hate crimes legislation, and future expansive federal civil rights measures. Clearly, the Court's view of sexual orientation discrimination under the Fourteenth Amendment will be crucial in determining whether Congress has the authority to make these laws binding on the states.

The Employment Non-Discrimination Act (ENDA)

The drafters of ENDA's most recent iteration anticipated one major Federalism Revolution objection when they limited ENDA's application to intentional discrimination.[27] The Supreme Court has held that Congress cannot authorize state employees to sue their employers for discrimination that does not independently violate the Equal Protection Clause[28] (the Court long ago held that only intentional discrimination claims could be brought under the Equal Protection Clause[29]), thereby effectively ruling out most disparate impact claims. ENDA's framers sought to avoid the argument that its adoption would require employers to extend benefits to domestic partners (the lack of which could be argued to have a disparate impact on lesbian or gay employees with same-sex partners)[30] and/or inquire into the sexual orientation of employees in order to prove their hiring practices non-discriminating.[31] By eschewing this disparate impact theory, ENDA's proponents have arguably restricted the Act to outlawing intentional discrimination—the sort that, when engaged in by government employers, could be said to violate the Fourteenth Amendment.

The Court's approach to determining the applicability to state governments of the Age Discrimination in Employment Act (ADEA), the Americans with Disabilities Act (ADA), and the Family and Medical Leave Act (FMLA), however, suggests that whether individuals will be able to sue states that violate their rights under ENDA will hinge on whether sexual orientation is considered a suspect classification—so that discrimination on the basis of sexual orientation will receive careful judicial consideration (as does racial, religious, or gender discrimination). The Court's decisions in the cases challenging the ADEA, the ADA, and the FMLA turned on whether the particular statute was aimed at protecting members of a suspect classification. Because the Court held that neither age nor disability were suspect in those cases, it concluded that states could discriminate against their employees on the basis of age or disability as long as they could provide a rational justification.[32]

Although the Court had an opportunity to address the issue of whether sexual orientation is a suspect classification in *Romer v. Evans*, its opinion instead found that the state policy being challenged was unconstitutional regardless of the level of judicial scrutiny used to evaluate it. Indeed, Justice Anthony M. Kennedy asserted that the Colorado constitutional amendment at issue in *Romer* was so broad that it defied traditional Equal Protection analysis. Consequently, the Court was able to decide the case without analyzing the factors it had considered in past decisions in order to determine what level of judicial scrutiny should be applied to a challenged governmental policy. Lower federal courts, however, have routinely cited *Romer* as holding that rationality review (rather than the more searching heightened scrutiny) is the appropriate method of analysis for sexual orientation claims under the Fourteenth Amendment.

In *Lawrence v. Texas*, the Court again avoided a direct discussion of the analytical issues raised by sexual orientation discrimination. The plaintiffs, John Lawrence and Tyron Garner, challenged the constitutionality of the Texas Homosexual Conduct Act,[33] which made it a misdemeanor for two people of the same sex to have anal or oral sex, regardless of age, consent, or the privacy of the conduct. Under Texas law, the same conduct was legal when the participants were members of opposite sexes. Lawrence and Garner were arrested for having sex in Lawrence's apartment (the arresting officers were responding to a false report filed by a grudge-bearing ex-lover of Lawrence).[34] The Texas courts denied the plaintiffs' argument that the law under which they were arrested violated their right to privacy, citing the precedent established in *Bowers v. Hardwick*,[35] the 1986 case in which the Supreme Court rejected a privacy challenge to Georgia's felony sodomy law.

In contrast, there was no precedent to direct the Court's resolution of the plaintiffs' Equal Protection Clause challenge in *Lawrence*.[36] A majority, however, choosing to decide the case on a broader ground, held that the Texas law unconstitutionally abridged a "liberty interest" protected under the Due Process Clause.

Writing for five members of the Court, Justice Kennedy conceded that an Equal Protection challenge to the Texas law presented a "tenable argument," but asserted that if the Court struck down the law on that basis, "some might question whether a prohibition would be valid if drawn differently, say, to prohibit the [sexual] conduct both between same-sex and different-sex participants."[37] Because a majority of the Court had concluded that the government cannot penalize consensual adult sexual intimacy without considering the genders of the participants, a decision on the broader Due Process ground would obviate the need to address the Equal Protection issue directly. Although an Equal Protection ruling might seem a narrower basis for striking the Texas statute (as it would directly implicate the constitutionality of only four states' laws), such a ruling might have affected all the ways in which government policies disadvantage sexual minorities, and therefore have been more far-reaching.[38]

The Federalism Revolution potentially poses another impediment to ENDA's application to private employers. It is possible, under the narrower view of the Commerce Clause power and depending on the legislative record made by Congress prior to enacting ENDA, that the Supreme Court may find inadequate support for the assertion that sexual orientation discrimination by private employers has a substantial enough effect on commerce between the states to justify federal legislation.[39] The problem lies with the lack of authoritative data. To justify using its Commerce Clause powers to enact the ADA, Congress needed to show that the number of people encountering disability-based discrimination was large enough to merit a federal response. Based on estimates, Congress concluded that forty-three million people had disabilities[40]—such a large segment of the population that nobody could doubt the commercial impact of their exclusion either from full workforce participation or the market for goods and services.

Estimates of the sexual minority population size are notoriously imprecise. The federal census has never tried to collect this data, as the outcry would likely be enormous. Even if the federal government were to try, the likelihood of obtaining an accurate number is slight. Even when promised the confidentiality of the census law (which forbids publication of information identifying individual respondents for at least seventy years), many lesbians, gays, and bisexuals are reluctant to reveal their sexual orientation in the absence of legal protection against discrimination. Even if accurate information were available, the sexual minority population would likely turn out to be a much smaller group than the disabled or the elderly. Accordingly, the question would arise as to whether sexual orientation discrimination is a significant enough factor in the national economy to justify Congress invoking its Commerce Clause power.

The best counter argument might be that ENDA, like the 1964 Civil Rights Act, is intended to protect everybody, not only members of a protected class. Heterosexuals, bisexuals, and homosexuals would all be protected against discrimination, even though few heterosexuals would likely need such protection (just as Congress probably assumed that few white people, or men, would need the protection of the Civil Rights Act). Losses sustained by private businesses from sexual orientation discrimination (due to lost investments in training and reduced productivity resulting from the discharge of experienced workers) could document its commercial impact. An attempt has been made to quantify the loss of such training investment to the Defense Department; although the amounts involved were found to be substantial, they were small relative to the overall defense budget.[41]

Nonetheless, it seems fair to say that the Federalism Revolution, if taken to the extremes hinted at by the Supreme Court, could significantly undermine the authority of Congress to enact ENDA (even in its narrow form and in the face of congressional findings that sexual orientation discrimination is a problem worthy of national attention).

Another aspect of the Federalism Revolution cases also poses a potential danger for ENDA. In the cases,[42] the Court jettisoned the normal presumption of constitutionality accorded to federal statutes, instead engaging in a non-deferential critique of the legislative history to bolster its conclusion that Congress could not subject state governments to suit because insufficient proof existed that they were violating individual rights. Substituting its own judgment for that of Congress on the issue of fact-finding underlying legislative action, the Court mandated that a substantial legislative record had to be made before Congress could overcome state immunity to suit. ENDA's drafters, whose goal was to provide the kind of record able to withstand the judicial review seen in the Federalism Revolution cases, anticipated this problem by seeking extended legislative hearings in which to present detailed testimony about discriminatory state employment practices.

Federal Hate Crimes Law

The other item on the sexual minority legislative agenda is the Federal Hate Crimes Bill,[43] also drafted with the Federalism Revolution cases in mind in the hopes that the legislation would avoid suffering the same fate as the Violence Against Women Act (VAWA) in *United States v. Morrison* (the Court invalidated VAWA's civil rights provision on the grounds that Congress did not have the authority to regulate non-economic activity unless it had compiled a legislative record showing that such activity directly impacted interstate commerce).[44] The Bill makes a wide array of factual assertions concerning the commercial impact of hate-motivated violence in an effort to establish congressional authority to legislate on the subject. Additionally, although the drafters rely primarily on the Commerce Clause, the Bill invokes the Thirteenth, Fourteenth, and Fifteenth Amendments to ground congressional authority. A substantial portion of the Bill is aimed at providing federal financial assistance to local law enforcement agencies to enhance their ability to deal with bias-motivated crimes.

The Bill also amends the federal criminal code to create a federal hate crimes offense that is narrowly defined in cases of sexual orientation, gender, and disability, applying to attempted murder, murder, attempted or actual kidnapping, and attempted or actual aggravated sexual abuse. While the Justice Department has the exclusive authority to enforce the provisions of the proposed law, it cannot initiate enforcement without first consulting state law enforcement officials. It is unlikely that courts will find that individuals have the right to bring private lawsuits to enforce their rights under the version of the Bill that was introduced in the most recent Congress.

This narrowly-drafted measure falls so far short of the more sweeping protection Congress attempted to enact in VAWA that it seems more symbolic than effectual. Under the broader view of Congress's Commerce Clause powers that existed before the Federalism Revolution, the sponsors of the hate crimes provisions would undoubtedly have felt more freedom to attack discrimination against lesbians and gays without significantly constraining the method of enforcement.

Conclusion

The gay rights movement's two main federal legislative goals, ENDA and the Federal Hate Crimes Bill, are endangered by the Federalism Revolution's narrowing of legislative power under the Commerce Clause and the Fourteenth Amendment. Gay rights advocates have therefore introduced narrowly-drafted bills on discrimination and hate crimes that may prove more symbolic than effective. If those advocates are to achieve meaningful legislative protections, they should join with other civil rights activists to restore the federal legislative authority to address social ills arising from discrimination.

Endnotes

1. 539 U.S. 558 (2003).
2. *Manual Enters., Inc. v. Day*, 370 U.S. 478 (1962).
3. *Gay Students Org. of Univ. of N.H. v. Bonner*, 509 F.2d 652 (1st Cir. 1974); *Gay Lib v. Univ. of Mo.*, 558 F.2d 848 (8th Cir. 1977), *cert. denied* sub nom. *Ratchford v. Gay Lib*, 434 U.S. 1080 (1978).
4. *Romer v. Evans*, 517 U.S. 620 (1996).
5. 539 U.S. 558 (2003).
6. See *Smith v. City of Salem*, 369 F.3d 912 (6th Cir. 2004) (discrimination against a transsexual necessarily involves gender nonconformity issues and is actionable as sex discrimination under Title VII); *Rosa v. Park W. Bank and Trust Co.*, 214 F.3d 213 (1st Cir. 2000) (federal Fair Credit Act ban on sex discrimination extends to male plaintiff denied banking services for failing to dress consistently with gender norms, in effect extending federal statutory protection to some transvestites and transsexuals who encounter discrimination because of their appearance); *Schwenk v. Hartford*, 204 F.3d 1187 (9th Cir. 2000) (Violence Against Women Act applies to violence against a transsexual motivated by the victim's gender nonconformity); *Rene v. MGM Grand Hotel, Inc.*, 305 F.3d 1061 (9th Cir. 2002) (sexual harassment motivated by perceived gender nonconformity is actionable as sex discrimination under Title VII of the 1964 Civil Rights Act); c.f. *Enriquez v. W. Jersey Health Sys.*, 777 A.2d 365 (NJ Super. Ct. App. Div. 2001) (post-operative transsexual physician who encountered employment discrimination because of transgendered status may proceed in suit under sex discrimination and disability discrimination theories).

7. The immigration ban was contained in the McCarran-Walter Immigration Act provisions dealing with medical grounds for exclusion, and was upheld against constitutional challenge in *Boutilier v. INS*, 387 U.S. 118 (1967). In 1990, Congress revised the medical exclusion grounds, omitting the terms "afflicted with psychopathic personality or sexual deviation" that had been the basis for the prior exclusion of gay people. Pub. L. No. 101-649 (1990) (codified at 8 U.S.C. §1154).

8. Pub. L. No. 101-275 (1990) (codified as amended at 28 U.S.C. §534).

9. Exec. Order No. 13,087, 63 Fed. Reg. 30,097 (May 28, 1998).

10. Exec. Order No. 10,450, 18 Fed. Reg. 2,489 (April 27, 1953).

11. Exec. Order No. 12,968, 60 Fed. Reg. 40,245 (August 2, 1995).

12. The security clearance system predating the Clinton order is described in detail, and its constitutionality is upheld, in *High Tech Gays v. Def. Indus. Sec. Clearance Office*, 895 F.2d 563 (9th Cir. 1990).

13. See 10 U.S.C. §654 (1993).

14. Defense of Marriage Act, Pub. L. No. 104-99, 110 Stat. 2419 (Sept. 21, 1996) (codified as 28 U.S.C. §1738C, 1 U.S.C. §7).

15. On November 18, 2003, the Massachusetts Supreme Judicial Court ruled in *Goodridge v. Dep't of Pub. Health*, 798 N.E.2d 941, that the state's refusal to allow same-sex couples to marry violated the Massachusetts Constitution equality requirements. The court gave the state legislature six months to adjust the law. The legislature, however, made no changes, instead initiating the process of amending the constitution to ban same-sex marriage and authorize civil unions. On May 17, 2003, same-sex couples began marrying in Massachusetts (the only state today that allows same-sex marriages). Litigation is pending in six other states seeking such marriage rights. In 1999, the Vermont Supreme Court ruled that same-sex couples were entitled to the same rights and responsibilities as opposite-sex couples under the Equal Benefits Clause of the Vermont Constitution, but left it up to the legislature to determine how such rights would be provided. *Baker v. State of Vt.*, 744 A.2d 864 (Vt. 1999). The legislature's response was to enact a Civil Union Act, 2000 Vt. Acts & Resolves 91, that creates a unique legal status for same-sex partners, encompassing almost all rights and responsibilities under state law that married couples have in Vermont. However, the legislature included a declaration that a civil union is not a marriage and same-sex couples are not authorized to marry in Vermont. Hawaii and California have passed less comprehensive legislation. In addition to Massachusetts, the DOMA ban on marriage recognition may be salient with respect to same-sex marriages contracted in the Netherlands or Canada. Belgium allows same-sex marriages only if both members of the couple are citizens of a country allowing such marriages.

16. Whether the Full Faith and Credit Clause even applies to the issue of marriage recognition is controversial; the debate about same-sex marriage spawned by the 1993 Hawaii Supreme Court decision and the subsequent passage of DOMA and over thirty state statutes banning their recognition has inspired a plethora of law journal commentary. See Michael T. Morley et al., Developments in Law and Policy: Emerging Issues in Family Law, *21 Yale Law and Pol'y Rev.* (2003), 169; Mark Strasser, Some Observations About DOMA, Marriages, Civil Unions, and Domestic Partnerships, *30 Cap. U. L. Rev.* (2002), 363; Patrick J. Shipley, Constitutionality of the Defense of Marriage Act, *11 J. Contemp, Legal Issues* (2000), 117; Scott Fruehwald, Choice of Law and Same-Sex Marriage, *51 Fla. L. Rev.* (1999), 799; Kaleen S. Hasegawa, Note, Re-Evaluating the Limits of the Full Faith and Credit Clause After *Baker v. General Motors Corporation*, *21 U. Haw. L. Rev.* (1999), 747; Deborah M. Henson, Will Same-Sex Marriages be Recognized in Sister States?: Full Faith

and Credit and Due Process Limitations on States' Choice of Law Regarding the Status and Incidents of Homosexual Marriages Following Hawaii's *Baehr v. Lewin, 32 U. Louisville J. Fam. L.* (1994), 551.

17. See *Nat'l Endowment for the Arts v. Finley*, 524 U.S. 569 (1998) (upholding 20 U.S.C. §954 against constitutional challenge). Given the legislative history of the decency requirement, it is likely that an application for funding for projects that incorporate homoerotic images or concepts would be viewed skeptically by Endowment evaluators.

18. See, e.g., *Gay Men's Health Crisis v. Sullivan*, 792 F. Supp. 278 (S.D.N.Y. 1992) (striking as unconstitutionally vague a statutory restriction on the use of federal public health money to "promote" homosexuality).

19. 10 U.S.C. §983 (1996). The Defense Department is the only federal agency with a statutory mandate to exclude individuals who engage in homosexual activity from employment. Because this mandate was enacted in 1993, thousands of lesbian, gay, and bisexual service members have been discharged, and the policy has effectively precluded openly lesbian, gay, or bisexual individuals from enlisting. See Jeffery M. Cleghorn et al., Conduct Unbecoming: The Ninth Annual Report on "Don't Ask, Don't Tell, Don't Pursue, Don't Harass", at http://www.sldn.org/binary-data/SLDN_ARTICLES/pdf_file/837.pdf (2003). The Defense Department is one of the largest employers in the U.S., with 1.4 million uniformed personnel and over 650,000 civilian personnel. See DoD 101: An Introductory Overview of the Department of Defense, at http://www.pentagon.gov/pubs/dod101/ dod101_for_2002.html.

20. See Health Care Benefits Expansion Act of 1992, DC Laws 9-114, DC Code Ann. §32-701 (amending DC Code to authorize benefits for domestic partners of municipal employees and to establish a partnership registry). The benefits were not allowed to go into effect until 2001, when a DC appropriations bill adopted during a brief period of Democratic control of the Senate was signed into law by President Bush. H.R. 2944, 107th Cong. (2001) (enacted).

21. See Civil Rights Amendments Act of 1975, H.R. 166, 94th Cong. (1975) (proposing to amend the Civil Rights Act of 1964 to prohibit discrimination based on "affectional or sexual" preferences); H.R. 2667, 94th Cong. (1975); H.R. 5452, 94th Cong. (1975); See also Civil Rights Amendments Act of 1977, H.R. 451, 95th Cong. (1977); H.R. 775, 95th Cong. (1977); H.R. 4794, 95th Cong. (1977); H.R. 5239, 95th Cong. (1977); H.R. 8268, 95th Cong. (1977); H.R. 8269, 95th Cong. (1977); Civil Rights Amendments Act of 1979, H.R. 2074, 96th Cong. (1980); Civil Rights Amendments Act of 1981, H.R. 1454, 97th Cong. (1981). Challenges have also been made in the courts, without success. See, e.g., *DeSantis v. Pac. Tel. and Tel. Co.*, 608 F.2d 327, 329–30 (9th Cir. 1979) (concluding that Title VII's prohibition of 'sex' discrimination applies only to discrimination based on gender, not sexual orientation). Accord, *Williamson v. A.G. Edwards & Sons, Inc.*, 876 F.2d 69, 70 (8th Cir. 1989); *Blum v. Gulf Oil Corp.*, 597 F.2d 936, 938 (5th Cir. 1979); *Kelley v. Vaughn*, 760 F. Supp. 161, 163 (W.D. Mo. 1991).

22. H.R. 2692, 107th Cong. (2001); S. 1284, 107th Cong. (2001).

23. Local Law Enforcement Enhancement Act, S. 625, 107th Cong. (2001), and Local Law Enforcement Hate Crimes Prevention Act, H.R. 1343, 107th Cong. (2001), are the most recent versions of this proposed legislation. The bills would make crimes of violence motivated by bias because of the victim's actual or perceived sexual orientation a federal offense. Although many states have already included "sexual orientation" in their hate crimes laws, which normally provide for an enhanced prison sentence for defendants found to have been motivated by specified categories of bias, many states—including, naturally, those where anti-gay bias is the strongest—have not done so. Securing a federal law, therefore, would fill an important gap. In June 2004, the bill was approved by the Senate as an

amendment to a defense appropriations bill, but was widely expected to be deleted in the conference committee with the House of Representatives.

24. Permanent Partners Immigration Act, H.R. 832, 108th Cong. (2003), would accord to the committed non-marital partners of U.S. citizens the same preferential rights to immigrate to the U.S. as are presently accorded to the marital partners of U.S. citizens. At present, U.S. immigration law accords no significance whatsoever to the emotional and economic interdependence of unmarried partners, regardless of gender. Equal Access to Social Security Act, H.R. 4701, 108th Cong. (2004), would provide for entitlement to dependents' and survivors' benefits under the old-age, survivors, and disability insurance program under Title II of the Social Security Act based on both permanent partnership and marriage. Both bills were principally sponsored by Rep. Jerrold Nadler (Dem-NY).

25. See Defense of Marriage Act, Pub. L. No. 104-99, 110 Stat. 2419 (Sept. 21, 1996) (codified as 28 U.S.C. §1738C, 1 U.S.C. §7).

26. See chapter 2.

27. ENDA, as drafted in 1996 and as reintroduced in each subsequent session of Congress, specifically disavows both the disparate impact theory and any interpretation requiring affirmative action, preferences, or quotas with regard to the sexual orientation of job applicants or employees. See Equal Rights and Equal Dignity for Americans Act, S. 16, 108th Cong. §701 (2003).

28. *Kimel v. Fla. Bd. of Regents*, 528 U.S. 62 (2000); *Bd. of Trs. of the Univ. of Ala. v. Garrett*, 531 U.S. 356 (2001).

29. *Washington v. Davis*, 426 U.S. 229 (1976).

30. See, e.g., *Levin v. Yeshiva Univ.*, 754 N.E.2d 1099 (NY 2001) (holding failure to accord equal rights to same-sex partners in university housing may violate municipal ordinance that bans sexual orientation discrimination using a disparate impact theory).

31. The argument, made during congressional consideration of amendments to codify the disparate impact theory under Title VII is that the disparate impact theory, in its reliance upon statistical proof of disparities between the number of women or members of racial minorities in a particular workplace as compared to the relevant labor pool from which employees are drawn, gives employers incentives to adopt preferences and quota systems so that they might achieve a workplace impervious to a disparate impact challenge.

32. See *Kimel v. Fla. Bd. of Regents*, 528 U.S. 62 (2000); *Bd. of Trs. of the Univ. of Ala. v. Garrett*, 531 U.S. 356 (2001).

33. Tex. Penal Code. Ann. §21.06 (2003).

34. *Lawrence*, 539 U.S. at 562–63. At every stage of the proceedings, the defendants preserved their arguments that their prosecution violated their rights to Equal Protection and Due Process under the Fourteenth Amendment. In petitioning for review of the lower court's decision, they asked that the Supreme Court consider whether the statute violated either the right to equal protection or the right to privacy as a violation of Due Process, and whether *Bowers v. Hardwick* should be overruled.

35. 478 U.S. 186 (1986).

36. The Court reserved the question of Equal Protection in *Bowers*, because the statute applied equally to same-sex and opposite-sex couples. In his dissent, Justice Stevens argued that homosexuals and heterosexuals had an equal interest in the protection of their liberty under the Fourteenth Amendment, and noted that the state had conceded that it could not punish adult heterosexual couples for private acts of consensual sodomy. Thus, Stevens ar-

gued that the only remaining application of the Georgia statute was to same-sex couples, raising an obvious equal protection problem. Id. at 218–19.

Lower federal courts have almost unanimously rejected the argument that sexual orientation discrimination should receive heightened or strict scrutiny under the Equal Protection Clause, but this rejection has rarely, if ever, been premised on a full, objective evaluation of the factors that the Court has articulated for performing such an analysis. Rather, the rejection has frequently been premised on *Bowers*, courts having followed a holding by the DC Circuit Court of Appeals that a classification defined by constitutionally unprotected conduct cannot be constitutionally "suspect" as a basis for discrimination. *Padula v. Webster*, 822 F.2d 97 (DC Cir. 1987). In his *Romer* dissent, Justice Scalia repeated this assertion in objecting to the Court's invalidation of Colorado's Amendment 2. *Romer*, 517 U.S. at 630.

Many lower federal court decisions have involved Equal Protection challenges to the Defense Department's treatment of lesbian and gay military service members, whether under the "Don't Ask Don't Tell" policy enacted in 1993 or under prior regulations mandating discharge of all homosexuals or bisexuals from the uniformed services. See, e.g., *Able v. United States*, 155 F.3d 628 (2d Cir. 1998). In these cases, courts have usually applied the policy of deference to military expertise in personnel matters, obviating the need for a serious analysis of the level of judicial review. There have, however, been exceptions. In *Watkins v. United States Army*, a three-judge panel of the Ninth Circuit Court of Appeals found that under the traditional indicia of "suspectness," a policy that discriminated on the basis of sexual orientation was subject to heightened scrutiny, at least to the level of scrutiny afforded policies that discriminate based on sex. 837 F.2d 1428 (1988), vacated for *en banc* review, 875 F.2d 699 (1989) (decided for plaintiff on alternative grounds). The panel majority found that the history of discrimination against gays, and the biases undermining their effective participation in the political process at the level of federal policymaking, together with the relatively fixed and significant nature of human sexual orientation as a defining personal characteristic, combined to make anti-gay discrimination by the government presumptively unconstitutional in the absence of a substantial, non-discriminatory justification. However, upon *en banc* review, a larger panel of the Circuit decided the case in Mr. Watkins' favor on grounds of estoppel, reducing the Equal Protection analysis to a concurring opinion by two members of the original three-judge panel.

37. *Lawrence*, 539 U.S. at 574–75.

38. The broader Due Process ruling, in contrast, while placing in question the constitutionality of all remaining sodomy laws (and potentially all remaining laws penalizing any aspect of private, non-commercial consensual adult sexual activity), would not necessarily decide such contentious Equal Protection issues as same-sex marriage or the treatment of same-sex partners under the immigration laws.

Justice Sandra Day O'Connor's concurring opinion, agreeing to strike down the statute on Equal Protection grounds, provides a tantalizing view of how an Equal Protection approach to *Lawrence* could have been conceived. 539 U.S. at 579–85. Justice O'Connor, who had voted with the majority in *Bowers*, would not join the Court in overruling it, but found that the differential treatment accorded same-sex and opposite-sex couples failed to survive the "more searching form of rational basis review" that she claimed the Court had developed for cases where the law "exhibits….a desire to harm a politically unpopular group." 539 U.S. at 580. Unlike Justice Kennedy, whose opinion in *Lawrence* avoids the kinds of analytical labels characteristic of an earlier generation of Fourteenth Amendment analysis, Justice O'Connor treats this as a case of sexual orientation discrimination, and posits that the appropriate analysis is a "more searching" form of rationality review. If one assumes that the majority of the Court would agree with Justice O'Connor that sexual orientation discrimination claims merit a "more searching form of rational basis review," the question remains whether this would be sufficient to satisfy the majority of the Court in *Nev. Dep't of Human Res. v. Hibbs*, 538 U.S. 721 (2003).

It would be tempting to reduce the Court's approach in *Hibbs* to a simplistic standard based on whether the kind of discrimination prohibited by a statute has been subjected to heightened scrutiny under the Fourteenth Amendment, but Chief Justice Rehnquist's opinion does not embrace such a simplistic approach. Instead, he speaks of a differential burden of justification on Congress in documenting a history of systematic state discrimination sufficient to trigger Fourteenth Amendment concerns, depending upon whether Congress is addressing the type of discrimination that the Court has previously identified as meriting heightened scrutiny. As such, it would seem that a federal civil rights law could meet the test of the Federalism Revolution cases even though it does not implicate a "suspect classification," provided sufficient proof of a pattern of discrimination by state governments has emerged and been properly documented in the legislative record. See 538 U.S. at 724–38. It is likely that such a record could be compiled in such a way as to meet the requirements set forth in *Hibbs*.

39. In considering the proposed Title VII of the Civil Rights Act of 1964, Congress relied in part on a report by the U.S. Commission on Civil Rights, *For All the People, By All the People: A Report on Equal Opportunity in State and Local Government Employment* (1969), which documented the existence of widespread discrimination against racial and ethnic minorities in state and local government employment, according to an *amicus* brief filed in *Fitzpatrick v. Bitzer*, 427 U.S. 445 (1976), a case in which the Court rejected a challenge to Title VII.

40. Americans with Disabilities Act of 1990, 42 U.S.C. §12101(a)(1).

41. "More than 9,000 Americans have been fired since 1993 because of "Don't Ask, Don't Tell," at a cost of more than a quarter billion dollars in taxpayer money." Jeffery M. Cleghorn et al., Conduct Unbecoming: The Ninth Annual Report on "Don't Ask, Don't Tell, Don't Pursue, Don't Harass", at http://www.sldn.org/binary-data/SLDN_ARTICLES/pdf_file/837.pdf (2003).

42. See e.g. *United States v. Morrison*, 529 U.S. 598 (2000); *United States v. Lopez*, 519 U.S. 879 (1996).

43. H.R. 1343, 107th Cong. (2001); S. 625, 107th Cong. (2001).

44. 529 U.S. 598 (2000).

CHAPTER 10

LANGUAGE MINORITIES

Language Rights and Loss of Judicial Remedy: The Impact of Alexander v. Sandoval *on Language Minorities*

Rose Cuison Villazor[*]

Josefa Marin brought her eight-month-old son to the emergency room of a Brooklyn public hospital after he bumped his head on his crib and developed a bruise. Ms. Marin, a Mexican immigrant who speaks only Spanish, waited twelve hours. When it became clear that her child would not receive medical attention, she decided to leave. Hospital security guards, however, blocked her path. The hospital had contacted the Administration for Children's Services (ACS) because employees who could not communicate with Ms. Marin falsely suspected her of abusing her child. ACS took her son away without anyone speaking to Ms. Marin. It took her three weeks to get him back.[†]

Ya-Chi Wu, a Mandarin-speaking Los Angeles garment worker, filed a complaint with the California State Labor Commissioner against her employer for back wages and overtime. Although she did not speak or read English, the Commissioner never provided her with translated forms or an interpreter. When her case came before an English-speaking investigating officer, she was forced to rely on her employer to interpret for her.[‡]

Eleven-year-old Ruvim Kluychits emigrated with his family from Belarus to New York. The only English-speaker in his family, he acts as interpreter whenever any of them go to the doctor. One day, his mother took him out of school to accompany her to see a dermatologist for a fingernail infection. She had been taking the

---

[*] Human Rights Fellow, Columbia Law School (2004–05).

[†] See Katie Worth, "For English Speakers Only? Emergency Room Help," *Village Voice* (May 1–7, 2002), at http://www.villagevoice.com/issues/0218/worth.php.

[‡] Rebecca Smith, Facts About the Civil Rights of Immigrant Workers to Access Department of Labor Programs and Services, Nat'l Employment Law Project (Jul. 2001), at http://www.nelp.org/docUploads/pub80%2Epdf (the story is true, but the name has been changed).

*prescribed medication for a week, but it had not worked. Ruvim translated her concerns in broken English: "She thinks she needs to take more tablets than one week as a month." After Ruvim and his mother left, the doctor confessed that he was not sure if Ruvim's mother understood his instructions.** *

These stories are just a few of many that could be told by people who are blocked access to basic services because they do not speak or read English. Generally referred to as people with limited English proficiency (LEP), these immigrants often find the doors of hospitals, schools, and government programs effectively closed. Service providers that receive federal funds, however, (e.g., hospitals, schools, housing and welfare programs, and not-for-profit organizations) are required by Title VI of the Civil Rights Act of 1964 to provide equal access to LEP people through interpreters and translators.

Many institutions fail to comply with this federal regulation. LEP patients, therefore, receive inadequate health care because they cannot communicate with their doctors. LEP students receive unequal education because linguistically appropriate classes are unavailable. LEP families who are entitled to welfare are unable to apply because application forms are not provided in their language.

Before the Supreme Court decided Alexander v. Sandoval *in 2001, those denied equal access to federal programs could at least seek relief in court. In* Sandoval, *however, the Court held that individuals lack a private right of action to enforce Title VI's regulations. Therefore, the LEP population can no longer request a judicial remedy for incidents like those described above. This chapter will explore the effect of the* Sandoval *opinion on language minority communities.*

ं ं ं

In *Lau v. Nichols* in 1974, the Supreme Court held that the San Francisco Unified School District had to provide linguistically appropriate education to students who only speak Chinese.[1] The Court concluded that by failing to provide those services, the school district had violated Title VI of the Civil Rights Act of 1964 (prohibits discrimination on the basis of race, color, or national origin in federally-funded programs and activities).[2]

> [T]here is no *equality of treatment* merely by providing students with the same facilities, textbooks, teachers and curriculum; for students who do not understand English are effectively foreclosed from any meaningful education...[it] seems obvious that the Chinese-speak-

---

* Barry Newman, "For Ill Immigrants, Doctor's Orders Get Lost in Translation," *Wall Street Journal* (Jan. 9, 2003), A1.

ing minority receive fewer benefits than the English-speaking majority from respondents' school system which denies them a meaningful
opportunity to participate in the educational program—all earmarks
of the discrimination banned by [Title VI's regulations].[3]

Lau was a landmark case for language minorities because it recognized that
language barriers effectively segregate them from English-speaking people by
blocking their access to many programs, activities, and services. By holding
that publicly-funded entities had an obligation to provide language access, the
Court reminded those entities that, "[s]imple justice requires that public
funds...not be spent in any fashion which encourages, entrenches, subsidizes,
or results in racial discrimination."[4]

Less than twenty-five years later, however, the Court significantly diminished
the language rights of LEP people in *Alexander v. Sandoval*.[5] In this case, the
State of Alabama Department of Public Safety, a federally-funded entity, refused
to allow LEP drivers license applicants to take the test in any language other than
English. Like *Lau*, *Sandoval* involved the effect of language barriers on language
minorities. Unlike *Lau*, the *Sandoval* Court held that the plaintiffs lacked the
right to bring a disparate impact claim against the Department. Plaintiffs could
only pursue a civil rights claim in federal court if they claimed that they were
intentionally discriminated against by a federally-funded program or activity.[6]
Because it is extremely difficult to prove intentional discrimination, *Sandoval*
left LEP people vulnerable to biased policies and practices and effectively sanctioned the exclusion of linguistic communities from federally-funded programs.

This chapter examines the rollback of civil rights from the perspective of
language minorities. It discusses the LEP population, the development of federal statutory language rights, and the impact of the *Sandoval* case on language minorities—particularly in the context of health care.

The LEP Population in the U.S.

Of the 262.4 million people living in the U.S. in 2000, nearly forty-seven million (eighteen percent of the population) spoke a language other than English at
home.[7] While the majority of this group reported that they also spoke English,[8]
the remaining twenty-one million people (eight percent of the population) spoke
English less than "very well."[9] It is this group that is often described as LEP.[10]

The size of the LEP population varies tremendously from state to state. The
greatest numbers of LEP people live in California (over 6.2 million), Texas (2.6
million), and New York (2.3 million).[11] In the last decade, the LEP popula-

tions in these states have grown tremendously—from nine to twenty percent in California,[12] from six to fourteen percent in Texas, and from five to thirteen percent in New York.[13] In major metropolitan areas such as Atlanta, Chicago, Miami, and New York City,[14] LEP people constitute an even higher percentage of the population. Shifting demographic patterns indicate that these numbers will likely continue to increase.

The number of people speaking particular languages is also rising. Spanish is the "non-English language most frequently spoken at home in the U.S."[15] In 2000, twenty-eight million people spoke Spanish at home—a sixty percent increase from 1990[16]—and approximately 13.8 million of these were LEP.[17] Chinese is the second non-English language most commonly spoken at home (two million people, up from 1.2 million in 1990),[18] followed by French (1.6 million), and German (1.4 million).[19] In 2000, there were approximately 1.2 million Chinese LEP, 415,038 French LEP, and 303,616 German LEP.[20]

While such numbers reflect an upsurge in the LEP population, the group represents less than ten percent of the total population. The percentage of LEP people in 2000, however, is proportionately greater than that at the end of the nineteenth century—eight percent compared to 3.6 percent in 1890.[21]

This increase has not been overlooked by those who fear that the "[r]ecord numbers of non-English speaking immigrants threaten to overwhelm the assimilative process."[22] Since 2003, three bills have been introduced in Congress aimed at restricting the ability of LEP individuals to speak their native language,[23] two of which propose that English be made the official language of the U.S.[24] Twenty-three states already have laws or policies declaring English to be their official language.[25] These state laws and proposed federal statutes reflect an increased anti-immigrant sentiment, arguably directed against LEP people of color.

The Development of Federal Statutory Language Rights

The Civil Rights Act of 1964

The right to be free from language discrimination was first protected by federal statute with the passage of the Civil Rights Act of 1964 (the cases involving constitutional language rights, *Katzenbach v. Morgan*[26] and *Hernandez v. New York*,[27] are discussed in chapter 4). §601 of Title VI of the Act ensures LEP people access to federally-funded programs and services, and prohibits the federal government from discriminating against people on the basis of race, color, or national origin.[28] Moreover, §602 empowers federal agencies to promulgate regulations in order to enforce the statute.

Subsequently, various federal agencies instituted regulations and/or issued guidelines clarifying Title VI. In 1968, for example, the Department of Health, Education and Welfare (HEW) required school systems to assure that "students of a particular race, color or national origin are not denied the opportunity to obtain the education generally obtained by other students in the system."[29]

Similarly, in 1970, HEW interpreted the right to be free from discrimination on the basis of national origin to prohibit conduct that had a disproportionate impact on language minorities. The Department guidelines clarified that "[w]here inability to speak and understand the English language excludes national origin-minority group children from effective participation in the educational program offered by a school district, the district must take affirmative steps to rectify the language deficiency in order to open its instructional program to these students."[30] It may be weaker to characterize language discrimination as a form of racial or national origin discrimination rather than as discrimination in itself because "given a general lack of understanding of bilingualism and language discrimination, judges often miss or reject the analogy [between the forms of discrimination]."[31] Nevertheless, the Title VI guidelines not only prohibited unequal treatment of LEP people, but created an affirmative obligation that federally-funded programs ensure the inclusion of language minorities.

Lau v. Nichols

In *Lau v. Nichols* in 1974, the Court affirmed that Title VI requires federally-funded programs to provide linguistically appropriate programs and services.[32] The plaintiffs—Chinese LEP students—argued that they received "unequal educational opportunities" because the San Francisco School District failed to take their language abilities into account.[33] The Court noted that the district "receives large amounts of federal financial assistance"[34] and "contractually agreed" to comply both with the Title VI regulations and the HEW guidelines.[35] By not providing bilingual courses, the Court held that the district failed to uphold its obligation to ensure that its program was open to all students.[36]

Lau was an important case because it established that racial and ethnic minorities could go to court to enforce the disparate impact regulations of Title VI.[37] In addition, *Lau* recognized the connection between language barriers and inequality. Noting that "those who do not understand English are certain to find their classroom experiences wholly incomprehensible and in no way meaningful,"[38] the Court acknowledged that language barriers (that Title VI prohibits) essentially segregate language minorities.

Second, and more importantly, the *Lau* Court recognized that government programs had an affirmative duty to provide language assistance services in order to make the term "equal access" meaningful. The Court established a statutory language *right*, the violation of which would give rise to a *judicial remedy*. Language minorities would be able to enjoin federally-funded entities from continuing their discriminatory conduct, and demand that they provide linguistically appropriate services.

Unfortunately, *Lau* did not eliminate all the language barriers preventing LEP people from accessing federally-funded programs and services. Over twenty years later, in 2000, continued inaccessibility compelled President Bill Clinton to issue Executive Order 13,166, which aimed to "improve access to federally conducted and federally assisted programs and activities" to LEP people.[39] The order did not create new obligations, but merely reminded government-funded programs that compliance with Title VI and its regulations meant that they had to provide language minorities with linguistically appropriate services. The order required government agencies to issue guidelines that would assist in providing LEP people with meaningfully access.[40] As a result, various federal agencies, including the Department of Justice (DOJ), issued "policy guidances" on how they and the entities they funded could comply with Title VI.

The Rollback of Federal Statutory Language Rights

Alexander v. Sandoval

Martha Sandoval, a Spanish-speaking housekeeper in Mobile, Alabama, walked two hours to and from work every day. While she knew how to drive, she could not get a drivers license because the written test was conducted in English only. The inability to drive, particularly in a rural area, hampers immigrants like Mrs. Sandoval from grocery shopping, taking their children to the doctor, and going to work.

From the 1970s until 1991, the State of Alabama Department of Public Safety (Department) administered its written examinations in fifteen languages.[41] In 1990, the state amended its Constitution, declaring English the official state language.[42] "The legislature and officials of the state of Alabama shall take all steps necessary to insure that the role of English as the common language of the state of Alabama is preserved and enhanced."[43] Thereafter, all state government work and business had to be conducted in English.

Mrs. Sandoval filed a suit in federal court contending that the "English-only policy [of the Department]...violated the DOJ regulation because it had the effect of subjecting non-English speakers to discrimination based on their national origin."[44] At trial, she presented evidence that the inability to "obtain a license [had] limited [LEP] individuals' job opportunities, hampered their ability to perform basic tasks such as going to work, the grocery store or the pharmacy, or taking their children to school, and has limited their ability to respond quickly in an emergency."[45] She won both the trial[46] and the appeal (the Department appealed the case to the Court of Appeals for the Eleventh Circuit),[47] both courts holding that the Department's English-only policy had a disparate effect on language minorities and therefore violated Title VI.

When the Department appealed the case to the Supreme Court, Mrs. Sandoval lost[48]—not on the merits of her case, but because the Court never addressed the validity of Alabama's English-only policy.[49] The only question before the Court was whether Mrs. Sandoval had a private right of action to enforce the disparate impact regulation of Title VI (in other words, whether she could sue to enforce her right under the statute).[50]

The Court stated that while individuals have a private right of action to enforce §601 of Title VI,[51] that section only prohibits intentional discrimination.[52] To the extent that *Lau* suggested that §601 also proscribed discrimination that has a disparate impact on language minorities, the Court held, the earlier case had been wrong.[53]

The more difficult question was whether individuals have the right to enforce the regulations promulgated under §602 that prohibit disparate impact discrimination (the Court assumed that those regulations were valid, even though they prohibited activities that were permissible under §601).[54] Based on the language in §602, the Court concluded that Congress had not intended to create any rights for individuals[55]—rather, it had given federal agencies the authority to enforce §601 by allowing them to cut off federal funds to recipients who engaged in practices that had a disparate impact.[56]

The Court held that this grant of authority to federal agencies "contradict[ed] a congressional intent to create privately enforceable rights through §602,"[57] and concluded that "[n]either as originally enacted nor as later amended does Title VI display an intent to create a freestanding private right of action to enforce regulations promulgated under §602."[58] In other words, private individuals could go to court if a federally-funded entity intentionally discriminated against them; only the federal agency providing the funds, however, could challenge disparate impact discrimination.

Sandoval's Impact on Language Minorities

Sandoval weakened the language rights established in *Lau* in at least four ways. First, given the difficulty of proving intentional discrimination in language rights cases, it was now possible that even if they showed that they received unfair treatment because of their language skills, LEP people would still be unable to prove intentional discrimination.[59]

Second, by ignoring the question of whether English-only policies constituted national origin discrimination, *Sandoval* made it harder to challenge the segregative effects of language barriers, further weakening a right that was not firmly grounded in constitutional or statutory law.

Third, the increased anti-immigrant sentiment in the U.S. post-9/11 makes the *Sandoval* case even more devastating. As noted earlier, two congressional bills have proposed that English be made the country's official language, and twenty-three states have already established English as their official language. Language minorities are facing increased hostility and discrimination in the workplace, schools, and health care facilities.

Finally, *Sandoval* weakened the affirmative obligation that federally-funded entities have to provide linguistically appropriate services. By shifting the issue in Title VI cases from whether a federally-funded entity is obligated to provide language access to whether an individual can demand such services in the first place, *Sandoval* diminished the entity's responsibility to comply with Title VI.

A Closer Examination of the Importance of Language Assistance—Health Care

To better understand the harm that *Sandoval* inflicted on language minorities, it helps to examine the impact of language barriers in health care. By depriving plaintiffs of a private right of action, that case limited the ways that LEP patients can enforce their right to equal access to health care.

The Negative Impact of Language Barriers on Health Care for LEP People

The provision of language assistance services to LEP people is critical to their ability to participate in federally-funded programs and services. Nowhere is the need for communication more important than in health care. Doctors need to be able to communicate with LEP patients in order to make effective diagnoses—poor communication often has dire consequences, ultimately affecting the mortality rates of the LEP population.[60] In addition, LEP patients experience longer delays in waiting rooms,[61] have difficulty scheduling appointments,[62] have trouble understanding English medical forms,[63] and are often confused about the types of treatment available.[64] Some even experience outright denial of health care.[65]

Studies have documented the consequences of this unequal treatment. For example, the Institute of Medicine reported that people of color, including LEP individuals, obtain lower-quality health care than whites even when they have comparable insurance, income, age, and severity of conditions.[66] The American Pediatrics Journal reported that Spanish-speaking children received medical services fraught with errors because of the lack of adequate interpreters and translators.[67] A study conducted by the Access Project of Brandeis University reported that LEP patients are susceptible to medical misdiagnosis if not provided with interpreter services.[68]

Enforcement of Language Rights in Health Care

The two options that remain available to LEP people who experience unequal access to health care services are not necessarily effective—filing a civil rights complaint with the Office for Civil Rights (OCR) of the Department of Health and Human Services (HHS), or initiating a lawsuit in state court.

1. Filing an OCR Complaint

Under § 602 of Title VI, OCR is authorized to terminate funding to a "particular program, or part thereof" if it determines that a federally-funded program violated Title VI or its regulations.[69] LEP individuals who experience linguistically inappropriate care can file a complaint with OCR within 180 days of the alleged discriminatory act.[70] OCR then determines whether the recipient of federal funds violated Title VI, and if so, can suspend or terminate funds.[71] OCR has successfully negotiated agreements that have led to equitable outcomes for language minorities through this complaint process.

OCR is severely under-funded, however, and has been criticized for ineffectively enforcing Title VI.[72] In 1999, for example, the U.S. Commission on Civil Rights released the results of its study of OCR's enforcement of Title VI, stating,

> The timid and ineffectual enforcement efforts of [OCR] have fostered, rather than combated, the discrimination that continues to infect the Nation's health care system. This is evident in the segregation, disparate treatment, and racism experienced by African Americans, His-

panic Americans, Native Americans, Asian Americans and Pacific Islanders, and members of other minority groups.[73]

Ironically, the *Sandoval* decision made OCR's role even more important in enforcing those regulations and policy guidelines that *Sandoval* itself weakened. Unfortunately, it is doubtful whether OCR, with its limited resources, can adequately enforce the rights of language minorities and other people with race- or ethnicity-based complaints.

2. Private Lawsuits under State and Local Laws

Several state and city laws either expressly require or can be interpreted to require linguistically appropriate medical care for LEP individuals.[74] For two reasons, however, these laws have rarely have been used to advance the rights of LEP people to receive interpretation services in medical settings.

First, most civil rights advocates have historically relied on federal civil rights laws (e.g., Title VI) to obtain equal access to health care. This was a logical strategy given that the laws were available and federal courts were considered receptive forums for enforcing anti-discrimination laws.[75] Moreover, succeeding in federal court meant creating precedent that could be applied across the country.

Second, civil rights advocates may not have been familiar with state laws or may have thought them less effective in fighting discrimination. Some of the state laws that require language assistance services were not enacted under the "anti-discrimination" label, but were part of public health or mental health laws.[76] Finally, state courts have not been considered receptive to claims of discrimination.[77]

There is no question, however, that individuals will now need to turn to alternative laws and legal theories to enforce their language rights. At least three factors, however, could limit the effectiveness of a state- or city-based legal strategy. First, to the extent that a state law does not include an express private right of action, a court could hold that it is privately unenforceable. New York's Public Health Law, for example, requiring that interpreters be available in hospitals,[78] lacks clear statutory language giving individuals the right to sue in court if a hospital violates the statute.[79]

Second, state laws tend to look to federal laws when examining issues of equal protection.[80] If faced with the question of whether a particular English-only policy in a medical facility violates a state constitution's Equal Protection or Anti-discrimination Clause, the state court might look to how the Supreme Court has defined language discrimination. In light of the federal language rights jurisprudence discussed earlier, reliance on state constitutional or statutory law might not yield positive results.

Finally, relying on state or local laws to advance the language rights of LEP people limits successful decisions to that particular locality—a successful campaign would have no direct effect on other jurisdictions.

Conclusion

Sandoval has limited the ability of language minorities to gain access to basic services or to privately enforce their rights, and has left them vulnerable to continued bias in the face of increased anti-immigrant sentiment. With limited alternatives available for ensuring equal treatment, however, they will continue to be effectively segregated. The rights of language minorities must be revived if we want to uphold the vision of equality upon which this country was founded.

Endnotes

1. *Lau v. Nichols*, 414 U.S. 563 (1974).
2. 42 U.S.C. § 2000d (2004).
3. *Lau,* 414 U.S. at 566–68 (emphasis added).
4. Id. at 569 (citation omitted).
5. 532 U.S. 275 (2001).
6. See *Alexander v. Sandoval*, 532 U.S. at 293.
7. See U.S. Census Bureau, *Language Use and English-Speaking Ability: 2000* (Oct. 2003) 1–2, at http://www.census.gov/prod/2003pubs/c2kbr-29.pdf ("LUESA: 2000").
8. Id. at 2–3 (stating that fifty-five percent (25.6 million people) who spoke a language other than English at home also spoke English "very well").
9. Id. at 3.
10. Limited English proficiency, or LEP, is a phrase used to describe the limited ability, or inability, of many people living in the U.S. to speak, read, or comprehend English. See Dep't of Justice, Guidance to Federal Financial Assistance Recipients Regarding Title VI Prohibition Against National Origin Discrimination Affecting Limited English Proficient Persons (Apr. 12, 2002).
11. See U.S. Census Bureau, *Language Use, English Ability, and Linguistic Isolation for the Population 18 Years and Over by State: 2000,* at http://www.census.gov/population/cen2000/phc-t20/tab03.pdf ("LUEALI 18 Years and Over") (provides state-by-state analysis of language use, English ability, and linguistic isolation).
12. See U.S. Census, *Language Use and English Ability, Persons 18 Years and Over, By State,* at http://www.census.gov/population/socdemo/language/table3.txt (provides 1990 data on how well people in the U.S. spoke English).
13. See LUEALI 18 Years and Over, *supra* note 11.
14. See LUESA: 2000, *supra* note 7, at 7.
15. See Id. at 3.
16. Id. at 4.
17. Id.

18. Id.

19. Id.

20. Id.

21. James W. Crawford, *Demographic Change and Language*, at http://ourworld .compuserve.com/homepages/JWCRAWFORD/can-pop.htm.

22. ProEnglish, *Making English Our Official Language*, at http://www.proenglish .org/issues/offeng/index.html.

23. See National Language Act, H.R. 931, 108th Cong. (2003); English Language Unity Act, H.R. 997, 108th Cong. (2003). See also To Provide That Executive Order 13166 Shall Have No Force Or Effect, And To Prohibit The Use Of Funds For Certain Purposes, H.R. 300, 108th Cong. (2003).

24. See National Language Act, H.R. 931, 108th Cong. (2003); English Language Unity Act, H.R. 997, 108th Cong. (2003).

25. ProEnglish, *Language Laws and Demographics of the Fifty States*, at http:// www.proenglish.org/issues/offeng/states.html.

26. 384 U.S. 641 (1966).

27. 500 U.S. 352 (1991).

28. See 42 U.S.C. § 2000d (2004).

29. 33 Fed. Reg. 4956 (1968).

30. 35 Fed. Reg. 11595 (1970).

31. See Juan F. Perea, Buscando America: Why Integration and Equal Protection Fail to Protect Latinos, *117 Harv. L. Rev.* (March 2004) 1420, 1434. See also Sandra Del Valle, *Un Pasito Pa'lante, Un Pasito Pa'tras: Latinos and the Rollback of Civil Rights*, Chapter 4 (criticizes the Court's juxtaposition of race with language).

32. *Lau*, 414 U.S. 563.

33. Id. at 564.

34. Id. at 566.

35. Id. at 568–69.

36. Id. at 567.

37. Id. at 566–67.

38. Id. at 566.

39. Improving Access to Services for Persons with Limited English Proficiency, Exec. Order No. 13, 166, 65 Fed. Reg. 50121 (Aug. 16, 2000).

40. Id.

41. See *Sandoval v. Hagan*, 7 F.Supp.2d 1234 (M.D. Ala. 1998).

42. Ala. Const., Amend. No. 509 (1990).

43. Id.

44. *Sandoval*, 532 U.S. at 279.

45. *Sandoval v. Hagan*, 7 F.Supp.2d at 1292.

46. Id. at 1315.

47. See *Sandoval v. Hagan*, 197 F.3d 484 (11th Cir. 1999).

48. See *Sandoval*, 532 U.S. at 293.

49. Id. at 279 ("[w]e do not inquire here…whether the courts below were correct to hold that the English-only policy had the effect of discriminating on the basis of national origin").

50. Id. at 279 (states that "we agreed to review…whether there is a private cause of action to enforce the regulation").

51. Id. at 279.

52. Id. at 280.

53. Id. at 285.

54. Id. at 281.

55. Id. at 288.

56. Id. at 289.

57. Id. at 290.

58. Id. at 293.

59. See *Hernandez v. New York*, 500 U.S. 352 (1991).

60. See Yvette Cabrera, "Crossing Border for Health Care," *Orange County Reg.* (Nov. 24, 2000) (discusses how language barriers affect the detection and treatment of breast cancer among Latinas, who die from the disease more often than non-Latinas even though its incidence among them is lower).

61. See Betsy Anne Wood, Caring for a Limited-English Proficient Patient, *AORN J.* (Feb. 2002) 305 (explaining a Latina patient's experience in obtaining emergency services).

62. See Rebeca Rodriguez, "Buena Salud," *Star-Telegram* (Aug. 5, 2001), at Metro 1 (reporting how Latinos lack access to health care because of language barriers).

63. See Id. (stating how LEP patients have complained about their inability to understand English-only consent forms).

64. See The Access Project, What A Difference an Interpreter Can Make: Health Care Experiences of Uninsured with Limited English Proficiency (Apr. 2002) 1, 7 ("Access Project Study") (reports that in a survey conducted of LEP patients, twenty-seven percent did not understand their prescribed medications because no explanation was provided in their language); Elaine Gaston, "Hispanics Must Leap Many Hurdles for Care," *The Sun News* (Mar. 1, 2001) C5 (states that immigrants have reported that the inability to understand their diagnosis and treatment was one of their biggest obstacles to medical care).

65. See Jeff Donaldson, "Language Could Be Barrier to Health Care for Immigrants," *Reno Gazette-J.* (Jan. 7, 2001) (stating that each year, "thousands of immigrants who are permanent residents or citizens are denied such services such as medical treatment because they fail to understand English").

66. See the Institute of Medicine, *Unequal Treatment: Confronting Racial and Ethnic Disparities in Health Care, Summary* (Mar. 20, 2002), at http://www.iom.edu/report.asp?id=4475.

67. See Glenn Flores, et al., Errors in Medical Interpretation and Their Potential Clinical Consequences in Pediatric Encounters, *111 Pediatrics* (2003) 6 (discusses how many errors occur in encounters between pediatricians and LEP parents).

68. See Access Project Study, *supra* note 64, at 7.

69. See 42 U.S.C. §2000d-1 (2004) (provides that federal agencies with the authority to issue federal funds have the authority to carry out the provisions of §601 of Title VI). For additional information about the Office for Civil Rights of the U.S. Department of Health and Human Services, see http://www.hhs.gov/ocr/index.html.

70. 45 C.F.R. §80.7(b) (2004).

71. 45 C.F.R. §80.8(a) (2004).

72. See Sara Rosenbaum and Joel Teitelbaum, Civil Rights Enforcement in the Modern Health Care System: Reinvigorating the Role of the Federal Government in the Aftermath of *Alexander v. Sandoval, 3 Yale J. Health Pol'y L. & Ethics* (Summer 2003) 215, 230–32 (explains OCR's ineffective enforcement of Title VI, its funding difficulties, and its inadequate complaint process).

73. Id. at 230 (quoting U.S. Comm'n on Civil Rights). See also U.S. Comm'n on Civil Rights, The Health Care Challenge: Acknowledging Disparity, Confronting Discrimination, and Ensuring Equality, Vol. I: The Role of Government and Private Health Care Programs and Initiatives (September 1999) 189–200.

74. For a comprehensive list of state laws addressing the language needs of LEP people in health care, see Jane Perkins, et al., *Ensuring Linguistic Access in Health Care Settings: Legal Rights and Responsibilities*, Appendix G, (1998) 141–50.

75. See Burt Neuborne, The Myth of Parity, *90 Harv. L. Rev.* (1977) 1105, 1115–16 (discusses litigators' preference to file constitutional claims in federal courts). But see William B. Rubenstein, The Myth of Superiority, *16 Const. Comment.* (1999) 599, 600 (states that Professor Neuborne's discussion on federal courts as more receptive to discrimination claims was inconsistent with the experience of gay and lesbian plaintiffs who fared better in state courts).

76. See e.g. 10 NY Comp. Codes R. & Regs. §405.7 (2004) (states that under New York's Public Health law and regulations, hospitals must provide language assistance to LEP people); Cal. Health & Saf. Code § 1259 (2004) (requiring acute care hospitals to provide language assistance to LEP patients); 25 Tex. Admin. Code §415.154 (West 2003) (provides that facilities for people with mental retardation must make necessary provisions to assess non-English-speaking individuals).

77. See Id.

78. See 10 NY Comp. Codes R. & Regs. §405.7(a)(7)(i)–(ii) (2004) (provides LEP patients and families with the right to an interpreter, but does not set forth private enforcements). See also NY Pub. Health §2801-c (2004) (explains that a court can issue injunctions upon the filing of an affidavit, but does not specifically identify an individual right of action).

79. See NY Pub. Health §2801-c (2004) (explains that a court can issue injunctions upon the filing of an affidavit).

80. See Jeffrey M. Shaman, The Evolution of Equality in State Constitutional Law, *34 Rutgers L. J.* (2003) 1013, 1018–19 (discusses the influence of federal constitutional interpretation on jurisprudential conception of equality under state law).

CHAPTER 11

Immigrant Workers

The Rollback of Immigrant Workers' Civil Rights

Marielena Hincapié[*] and Ana Avendaño-Denier[†]

In 2003, a group of fifteen immigrant workers sued the landscape company that employed them for failing to pay the minimum wage and overtime. The workers claimed that they were illegally housed in a warehouse surrounded by barbed wire that had no windows and was not zoned for human habitation. In response to the suit, the employer locked the workers in the warehouse at night and sued the workers' lawyers for abuse of process, seeking three million dollars in damages. The employer's agents traveled to Mexico and paid some of the workers to sign statements saying that they disavowed the suit, and that their lawyers had paid them to take part. The employer also threatened to bring federal criminal charges of "harboring illegal aliens" against the workers' lawyers.[‡]

When one young immigrant worker was deposed by the employer's lawyers, he was asked whether he was authorized to work in the U.S. At the insistence of his attorney, he asserted his Fifth Amendment privilege and refused to answer. During a break, opposing counsel called the police. Three police officers arrived and asked him whether he was a "legal citizen." When his lawyer refused to allow him to answer, the police called the Department of Homeland Security's Bureau of Citizenship and Immigration Services.

Although the employer's tactics seem extreme, they are all too often the reality for immigrant workers who attempt to enforce their labor rights.

This chapter explains the importance of attending to the rollback of immigrant workers' civil rights given the profound demographic changes that have occurred

---

[*] Marielena Hincapié is the Program Director of the National Immigration Law Center (NILC), where she also heads NILC's labor and employment program on behalf of low-wage immigrant workers.

[†] Ana Avendaño-Denier is Associate General Counsel and Director of the Immigrant Worker Program at the AFL-CIO.

[‡] Conversations with the plaintiff's attorney (notes on file with author).

over the last decade. It then discusses the tensions between the enforcement of immigration laws and labor laws. Finally, it analyzes how the Rehnquist Court has stripped low-wage immigrant workers of their civil rights, thereby limiting their access to the judicial system.

                                     🙡 🙡 🙡

Give me your tired, your poor, your huddled masses yearning to breathe free, the wretched refuse of your teeming shore, send these, the homeless, tempest-tossed, to me: I lift my lamp beside the golden door.

                                       Emma Lazarus

For centuries, immigrants have come to the U.S. seeking refuge from social, political, and religious oppression, and searching for economic opportunity. Indeed, immigrants, toiling in difficult conditions for minimum or substandard wages, have helped build the U.S. into the economic power it is today. This was true of the immigrants from Germany, Great Britain, Ireland, China, and Japan at the turn of the twentieth century (the last great wave of immigration),[1] as it is today of immigrants from countries including Mexico, China, India, Korea, the Philippines, Vietnam, Cuba, the Dominican Republic, El Salvador, and Canada.[2]

Providing non-citizens with meaningful access to the judicial system is an important measure of a just society. Millions of low-income immigrants, however, face racial, ethnic, cultural, and linguistic obstacles in accessing the courts. To make matters worse, the Rehnquist Court's 2002 decision to deny undocumented workers the right to sue for back pay under the National Labor Relations Act (NLRA)[3] in *Hoffman Plastic Compounds, Inc v. NLRB*[4] provides employers with added incentive to exploit already vulnerable workers. Keeping in mind the economic contributions made by low-wage immigrant workers, the demographic shifts that have occurred over the last decade, and the changing face of this country in the context of globalization, it is important to analyze this situation. Our failure to address this rollback of immigrant workers' civil rights will harm all low-wage workers at a time when the gap between the working poor and the wealthy is growing rapidly.[5]

Immigrant Workers in the U.S.

According to the 2000 census, twenty-nine million foreign-born individuals live in the U.S., accounting for roughly eleven percent of the population[6] and 12.4 percent of the labor force.[7] In the 1990s, half of all new entrants into the labor market (including those who are working or looking for work) were immigrants, accounting for much of the growth in the civilian labor force.[8] Indeed, new immigrants accounted for the entire labor growth in the Northeast and mid-Atlantic regions, and seventy-two percent of the growth in the Pacific region.[9]

Many unskilled immigrants work under exploitative conditions and often earn less than minimum wage.[10] As a result, immigrants head one out of five low-wage families.[11] The barriers that immigrants confront are exacerbated by the fact that forty percent of the estimated 8.6 million low-wage immigrant workers lack legal citizenship/immigration status. Despite having a labor force participation rate similar to that of native-born Americans,[12] forty-four percent of immigrants who work full-time earn incomes under twice the poverty level (compared with only twenty-two percent of native-born workers).[13] Immigrants are disproportionately represented in dangerous industries (e.g., construction, manufacturing, and agriculture), and in hazardous occupations within those industries.[14] The number of work fatalities among immigrant workers far exceeds that of native-born workers—in 2002, immigrant workers made up fifteen percent of the workforce but accounted for sixty-nine percent of workplace fatalities,[15] and Mexican workers were eighty percent more likely to die in a workplace accident than native-born workers.[16] According to a recent investigation conducted by the *Associated Press*, one Mexican immigrant worker dies on the job every day.[17] Factors including their limited English proficiency, their lack of formal education, and their immigration status make immigrants vulnerable to workplace exploitation.

Enforcement of Immigration Laws and Labor Law

Enforcement of immigration laws in the workplace is a recent phenomenon. Until 1986, when Congress passed the Immigration Reform and Control Act (IRCA),[18] workers were not required to provide their employers with proof that they were authorized to work in the U.S.[19] Congress adopted the IRCA "to reduce illegal immigration by eliminating employers' economic incentive to hire undocumented aliens."[20] IRCA set up an employment verification system (I-9 Form), which requires that the employer check the worker's identity and work eligibility.[21] In addition, IRCA imposed civil and criminal penalties on employers who knowingly hired, or continued to employ, illegal workers.[22] By this scheme, "the IRCA, in effect, deputizes every U.S. employer to the understaffed [Department of Homeland Security],"[23] and legitimized employers' union-busting practices.

Long before IRCA, employers attempted to use workers' immigration status to defeat collective action,[24] a tactic consistently rejected[25] by the National Labor Relations Board (NLRB).[26] Prior to the Supreme Court's *Hoffman* decision[27] (held that undocumented workers who were fired in violation of the NLRA were not entitled to the remedy of back pay), courts had been careful to ensure that all workers, regardless of status, were protected by workplace laws. In fact, Justice Anthony Kennedy recognized that "if the NLRA were inapplicable to workers who are illegal aliens, we would leave helpless the very persons who most need protection."[28]

Advocates were also particularly concerned with protecting workers' rights to back pay because back pay is critical to the enforcement of labor and employment laws. In enforcing the NLRA, therefore, the NLRB usually awarded a two-pronged remedy: reinstatement and back pay.[29] Reinstatement puts the wronged worker back to work.[30] Back pay is a "make-whole" remedy, based on the principle that but for the employer's unlawful conduct, the employee would have continued to work and receive all the benefits of his employment.[31] That remedy is critical to enforcing compliance with labor laws; it "has the twofold purpose of reimbursing employees for actual losses suffered as a result of a discriminatory discharge and of furthering the public interest in deterring such discharges."[32] Indeed, if "employers faced only the prospect of an injunctive order, they would have little incentive to shun practices of dubious legality."[33] Further, because the NLRA is not a "punitive" statute, back pay is the only economic liability facing employers.[34] Back pay also serves the important purpose of "dissipating the deeply coercive effects upon other employees who may desire self-organization, but have been discouraged therefrom by the threat to them implicit in the discrimination."[35]

The Court first struggled with the issue of workplace protection for undocumented workers in *Sure-Tan, Inc. v. NLRB* in 1984,[36] concluding that undocumented workers were "employees" within the meaning of the NLRA.[37] This meant that all workers, regardless of their citizenship status, were entitled to protections under the law; further, they could join a labor union, bargain collectively, and vote in union elections.[38]

In *Sure-Tan,* the Immigration and Naturalization Service (INS) arrested five workers involved in a union organizing campaign in a Chicago tannery after their employer called in a tip.[39] Rather than face incarceration and lengthy legal proceedings, the workers chose to leave the country.[40] The NLRB, finding that the employer had violated the NLRA by reporting the workers to the INS, ordered a remedy that the Court was eventually called on to review.

In an opinion written by Justice Sandra Day O'Connor, the Court rejected the employer's argument that the undocumented workers were not entitled to the protection of the NLRA.[41] "The Board's categorization of undocumented aliens as protected employees furthers the purposes of the NLRA, [and]...enforcement of the NLRA with respect to undocumented alien employees is compatible with the policies of the INA."[42] The Court approved the remedy, which conditioned reinstatement on the employees' legal reentry into the U.S. and "deemed the employees unavailable for work (and the accrual of back pay therefore tolled) during any period when they were not lawfully entitled to be present and employed in the United States."[43]

Following the passage of IRCA, the NLRB adopted a remedial scheme that was based on the premise that "IRCA and the NLRA can and must be read in harmony as complementary elements of a legislative scheme explicitly intended, in both cases, to protect the rights of employees in the American workplace."[44] The NLRB determined that:

> the most effective way for the Board to accommodate—and indeed to further—the immigration policies IRCA embodies is, to the extent possible, to provide the protections and remedies of the NLRA to undocumented workers in the same manner as to other employees. To do otherwise would increase the incentives for some unscrupulous employers to play the provisions of the NLRA and IRCA against each other to defeat the fundamental objectives of each, while profiting from their own wrongdoing with relative impunity.[45]

Accordingly, the NLRB crafted a limited remedy that conditioned reinstatement on the worker proving that he had obtained authorization to work, and in some cases limiting back pay to the date that the employer had learned that the worker lacked employment authorization.[46]

Hoffman: Deterioration of the Rights of Undocumented Workers

The Rehnquist Court issued its decision in *Hoffman* against the backdrop of the post-9/11 anti-immigrant sentiment.[47] The decision has had a profound impact on low-wage immigrant workers and their families, and has made employing undocumented workers more attractive to unscrupulous employers. Indeed, *Hoffman* has acted as a catalyst, eroding non-citizens' civil rights in the workplace.

Hoffman *Assaults Low-Wage Immigrant Workers and Serves as a Union-Buster*

In *Hoffman*, the Court ruled that the NLRB could not "award back pay to an illegal alien....for wages that could not lawfully have been earned, and for a job obtained in the first instance by a criminal fraud."[48] The Court focused on the worker's "wrongdoing," ignoring the employer's labor violations.

The case involved a Mexican immigrant, Jose Castro, who worked as a machine operator in the Hoffman Plastic Compounds chemical factory. In 1988, he and several co-workers were fired after getting involved in a union organizing campaign.[49] Three years later, the NLRB found that Hoffman had unlawfully selected employees, including Mr. Castro, for layoff "in order to rid itself of known union supporters."[50] To remedy the violations, the NLRB ordered that Hoffman offer to reinstate Mr. Castro and compensate him with back pay equivalent to what he would have earned absent the employer's unlawful conduct (minus any earnings from other sources after he was fired).[51]

During the hearing to determining the amount of back pay owed, Mr. Castro admitted that he did not have authorization to work in the U.S., and that he had used a friend's Texas birth certificate to gain employment.[52] Because of his admission, and based on precedent, the NLRB limited Mr. Castro's back pay to 4.5 years—from the date he was wrongfully fired to the date Hoffman first learned that he lacked work authorization.[53] Mr. Castro was awarded $66,951 plus interest. Hoffman appealed the case, and in a 5-4 decision, the Supreme Court reversed the NLRB's back pay order, focusing on Mr. Castro's "serious illegal conduct" in obtaining his job.

The *Hoffman* Court framed its analysis on the notion that the "legal landscape [had] now significantly changed" with IRCA,[54] and concluded that allowing Mr. Castro to be awarded back pay "not only trivializes the immigration laws, it also condones and encourages future violations."[55] In other words, the Court believed that the possibility of being discriminated against and then winning monetary damages in a labor claim was luring undocumented workers to the U.S. This rationale is disrespectful of the conditions under which undocumented workers are employed, and the fact that they and other low-wage workers often work multiple jobs to make ends meet.[56] Even under normal circumstances, for a worker to collect back pay, she would have to be involved in collective action, get fired, and go through lengthy legal proceedings.[57]

This position was a reversal from *Sure-Tan* ten years earlier, where the Court recognized that "if an employer realizes that there will be no advantage under the NLRB in preferring illegal aliens to legal resident workers, any incentive to hire such illegal aliens is correspondingly lessened," and "if the demand for undocumented aliens declines, there may then be fewer incentives for aliens themselves to enter in violation of federal immigration laws."[58] The dissenting justices in *Hoffman* similarly recognized that denying back pay—the only monetary remedy available under the NLRA—would result in employers concluding "that they can violate the labor laws at least once with impunity."[59] Denying back pay "lowers the cost to the employer of an initial labor law violation (provided, of course, that the only victims are illegal aliens). It thereby increases the employer's incentive to find and to hire illegal-alien employees."[60] This, in turn, provides employers with a "legal" union-busting weapon because many union organizing drives involve immigrant workers.[61] By placing a worker's immigration status at issue, the Rehnquist Court has greatly diminished low-wage workers' ability to counter unfair labor practices through the NLRB process.

Hoffman *Limits Access to the Courts and to Administrative Agencies Charged with Enforcing Civil Rights*

Prior to *Hoffman,* the NLRB awarded back pay up to the date that the employer discovered the worker's undocumented status,[62] and even greater back pay in those cases where the employer knew the employee was undocumented at the time of hiring.[63] *Hoffman,* however, wiped out even those modest remedies.

In light of the decision, the NLRB issued guidance to its regional and field offices on how to handle cases involving workers who may be undocumented, reaffirming that all workers "enjoy protections from unfair labor practices and the right to vote in NLRB elections without regard to their immigration status" and that investigations into alleged violations of the NLRA should begin with the "presum[ption] that employees are lawfully authorized to work."[64] Since then, however, regional offices have been inconsistent in processing unfair labor practices charges by workers assumed to be undocumented.

The U.S. Equal Employment Opportunity Commission (EEOC) and the Department of Labor (DOL) also issued guidances. On June 28, 2002, EEOC announced its unanimous decision to rescind its 1999 guidance called "Remedies Available to Undocumented Workers Under Federal Employment Discrimination Laws."[65] However, it also reaffirmed its commitment to protecting undocumented workers, reiterating that *Hoffman* did not call into question the principle that undocumented workers are covered by federal statutes prohibiting unlawful employment discrimination (e.g., Title VII of the Civil Rights Act, which prohibits national origin discrimination and sexual harassment).[66] While EEOC has been silent regarding the impact of *Hoffman* on the monetary remedies available to undocumented workers under federal employment discrimination statutes, at least one regional office has stated that it will not represent or seek remedies on behalf of any worker found to have used false documents to obtain employment.[67] Recent EEOC litigation indicates, however, that they might be taking a more proactive approach to protecting immigrant workers' rights.[68]

DOL stated that it would continue to enforce the rights of all workers, regardless of immigration status, under the Fair Labor Standards Act (FLSA).[69] DOL distinguished the back pay remedy in *Hoffman* from the wages owed for work already performed, and stated that *Hoffman* did not affect the rights of undocumented workers under the Migrant and Seasonal Agricultural Worker Protection Act (AWPA) (which requires employers and farm labor contractors to pay wages owed to migrant or seasonal agricultural workers). DOL has, however, remained silent on how *Hoffman* affects other laws, such as the anti-retaliation provisions of the FLSA in which the back pay remedy is arguably more analogous to the issue in *Hoffman*.

Employers have attempted to extend *Hoffman* to curtail undocumented workers' rights to workers' compensation (widely recognized as a state law issue). In less than two years, courts and state agencies in ten states (Arizona, Florida, Oklahoma, Massachusetts, Minnesota, Michigan, Nebraska, Pennsylvania, Tennessee, and Texas) issued opinions about *Hoffman's* effect on workers' compensation.[70] While most courts ruled that injured undocumented workers are entitled to workers' compensation, workers often exposed themselves during those proceedings by needlessly disclosing their immigration status.[71] Cases are currently pending in Maryland, Massachusetts, and Nebraska.[72] In each, employers argued that undocumented workers, especially those who used false documents in order to get a job, are either not entitled to workers' compensation or are not entitled to certain benefits (e.g., lost wages).

Since *Hoffman*, at least one state court has placed limitations on the availability of time loss recovery for injured workers based on immigration status. The Michigan Court of Appeals held that, under a state law that allows suspension of wage loss benefits if a worker commits a "crime" that prevents him or her from working or obtaining work, wage loss compensation could be suspended from the date that the employer "discovered" (in the context of his workers' compensation claim) that the worker lacked work authorization.[73] Although the Pennsylvania Supreme Court held that an injured undocumented worker was entitled to medical benefits, it found that his immigration status might justify terminating benefits for temporary total disability.[74]

Hoffman: *A License to Abuse?*

Employers' reaction to the *Hoffman* decision was swift: they sought to extend the ruling to other workers' rights. In one absurd case just a few days after the decision, an employer's attorney warned a community group who had planned to protest unpaid wages that *Hoffman* had outlawed any such demonstrations, and threatened legal action if the group went forward.[75] Employers began to threaten to call immigration authorities against immigrant workers pursuing claims, and requested that courts considering employment cases order an inquiry into the employees' immigration status.[76]

The dissenting justices were right: *Hoffman* is proving to be an incentive for employers to violate both labor and immigration law. The perverse effects of the decision are clear in a case currently before the general counsel of the NLRB, where the employer is relying on its own admitted violation of immigration laws to absolve itself of back pay liability.[77] In the case, ten bakery employees complained to the general manager that a night-shift supervisor had failed to provide adequate lunch and bathroom breaks, and had made abusive remarks, including "fucking Hispanics, you can't do anything," and "they work for nothing, whatever I decide to pay them, stupid Hispanics."[78] He also made sexual remarks, and threatened one worker with death. The workers were fired. They filed a charge with the NLRB.

Upon learning of the charge, the employer asked that the workers provide proof of work authorization and, more importantly, convinced the Board agent investigating the case to require that the workers provide her with proof of their immigration status. The employer argued that it was required to ask for work authorization because it had never completed I-9 forms—in other words, the employer argued that *Hoffman's* ban on back pay should be triggered because it had violated immigration law by hiring undocumented workers.[79] The NLRB accepted the employer's logic, and refused to seek back pay for the workers.[80] Following an outcry from the workers' lawyer and the AFL-CIO, the Board decided to seek back pay, but stated that if the employer could show that the workers were undocumented, it would be allowed to use that status as a defense to back pay liability.

This approach is equally destructive of workers' rights. A worker who knows that her immigration status is likely to be investigated if she complains about workplace conditions—whether that investigation is in the form of direct questions or through third parties—is unlikely to seek to enforce her rights.[81]

In another case before the NLRB, a Michigan employer is using a more subtle but equally destructive tactic to avoid back pay liability. In that case, a group of immigrant workers filed charges after they were fired from a produce factory. The employer obtained a "chart" from the Social Security Administration outlining which of the workers' social security numbers were invalid,[82] and obtained "verification" from immigration authorities that some of the workers lack work authorization. When the employer admitted that it had no reason to suspect that the workers were undocumented until they filed the charge, the workers filed a second charge alleging that the investigation itself was a violation of the NLRA because it was triggered by the filing of the charge. The NLRB dismissed that charge, citing *Hoffman*.[83]

As a result of the government's post-*Hoffman* policies, undocumented workers are left with little recourse under exploitive conditions. Congress has given the NLRB wide discretion in determining what cases it prosecutes and what remedies it seeks.[84] Instead of using that discretion to ensure that all workers' rights are protected, the Bush-appointed general counsel has unfortunately restricted access to the NLRB's processes.

Conclusion

For a country that prides itself on equal protection under the law and the notion of "inalienable" rights, we have created a sub-class of workers who have no meaningful way of protecting their civil rights. The system harms workers and undermines immigration law and enforcement. Congress should act to clarify that all workers, regardless of immigration status, are entitled to the same legal protections and remedies as citizens. At the same time, Congress must amend the immigration policy in such a way that it recognizes the valuable contributions that undocumented workers made to our society.

Endnotes

1. In 1890, thirty percent of the foreign-born were from Germany. Dianne Schmidley, *Profile of the Foreign-Born Population in the United States: 2000*, Current Population Reports-Special Studies, U.S. Census Bureau, Series P23-206 (December 2001) 13, at http://usa.usembassy.de/etexts/soc/cprforeignborn2000.pdf.

2. According to the census, these are the top ten sending countries in 2000. Id. at 19.

3. The NLRA sets out the basic labor-management relations policy, which is "to eliminate the causes of certain substantial obstructions to the free flow of commerce and to mitigate and eliminate these obstructions when they have occurred by encouraging the practice and procedure of collective bargaining and by protecting the exercise by workers of full freedom of association, self-organization, and designation of representatives of their own choosing, for the purpose of negotiating the terms and conditions of their employment or other mutual aid or protection." 29 U.S.C. §151 (1976).

4. 535 U.S. 137 (2002).

5. See Jared Bernstein, Heather Boushey, Elizabeth McNichol, and Robert Zahradnik, *Pulling Apart: A State-by-State Analysis of Income Trends* at vii, Center on Budget and Policy Priorities and the Economic Policy Institute (April 2002) ("Income disparities between the top fifth of families and families at the bottom of the income distribution grew in all but five states over the past two decades. The gap between high-income and low-income families grew in over half the states during the 1990s and declined in only 6 states"), at http://www.cbpp.org/4-23-02sfp.pdf.

6. Schmidley, *Profile of the Foreign-Born Population,* at 9, at http://www.census.gov/prod/2002pubs/p23–206.pdf.

7. Id. at 12.

8. Sum, Fogg, Harrington, et al. *Immigrant Workers and the Great American Job Machine: The Contributions of New Foreign Immigration to National and Regional Labor Force in the 1990s,* National Business Roundtable (August 2002) 17–18.

9. Id. at 21.

10. Randolph Capps, Michael E. Fix, Jeffrey S. Passel, et al., *A Profile of the Low-Wage Immigrant Workforce,* Urban Institute (Oct. 27, 2003), at http://www.urban.org/url.cfm?ID=310880.

11. Fix, Michael, Urban Institute Tabulations of Current Population Survey (November 2001).

12. In March 2002, the foreign-born participation was 66.6 percent, and the native-born participation was 67.3 percent. *Profile of the Foreign-Born Population in the United States: 2000,* Current Population reports, U.S. Census Bureau (December 2001) 38.

13. Michael E. Fix and Jeffrey S. Passel, *Lessons of Welfare Reform for Immigrant Integration,* Urban Institute (March 8, 2002), at http://www.urban.org/url.cfm?ID=900497.

14. *Improving Health and Safety Conditions for California's Immigrant Workers,* The Working Immigrant Safety and Health Coalition (November 2002).

15. *National Census of Fatal Occupational Injuries,* U.S. Department of Labor, Bureau of Labor Statistics (2002).

16. Justin Pritchard, "Mexican Worker Deaths Rise Sharply," *Associated Press* (March 12, 2004).

17. Id.

18. Pub L. No. 99-603, 100 Stat. 3359 (1986).

19. Although it was a crime to harbor an unauthorized alien, the INA stated that employing an unauthorized alien did not constitute harboring. 8 U.S.C. §1324(a)(2). Employers of unauthorized workers faced no penalty under the INA, but unauthorized workers were subject to deportation. 8 U.S.C. §1251(a)(2).

20. *Patel v. Quality Inn South,* 846 F.2d 700, 704 (11th Cir. 1988), *cert. denied,* 489 U.S. 1011 (1989).

21. 8 U.S.C. §1324a(b). Nothing in the IRCA makes it unlawful for an alien to work in the U.S. without proper documentation. Employers who violate the work authorization provisions of IRCA are subject to escalating civil penalties, as well as potential criminal penalties in cases where the employer is found to have engaged in a pattern or practice of unlawful hiring violations. 8 U.S.C. §1324a(f)(1). IRCA does not impose any civil or criminal liability directly upon the alien worker who accepts or continues employment without proper work authorization, unless that worker has engaged in document fraud with respect to the I-9 process. 8 U.S.C. §1324c(a); 18 U.S.C. §1546(b)(1986).

22. See 8 U.S.C. § 1324a(a)(1)-(2).

23. Robert C. Divine, *Immigration Practice* (2004–05 ed.) § 19-3.

24. The NLRA grants workers "the right to self-organization, to form, join, or assist labor organizations, to bargain collectively through representatives of their own choosing, and to engage in other concerted activities for the purpose of collective bargaining or other mutual aid or protection." 29 U.S.C. § 157. These rights are commonly known as "Section 7" rights.

25. The NLRB administers the NLRA. 29 U.S.C. § 153. The agency is a quasi-judicial body, and has two separate components. The Board has five members, who are appointed by the president to five-year terms, and primarily acts as a quasi-judicial body in deciding cases on the basis of formal records in administrative proceedings. The general counsel, appointed by the president to a four-year term, is independent from the Board and is responsible for the investigation and prosecution of unfair labor practice cases and for the general supervision of the NLRB field offices in the processing of cases. http://www.nlrb.gov/nlrb/about.

26. In each of the following cases, the Board found that the employer had committed an unfair labor practice, in violation of the NLRA: *John Dory Boat Works, Inc.,* 229 NLRB 844 (1977) (the employer subpoenaed employees' passports, green cards, and work authorization cards); *Del Rey Tortilleria, Inc.,* 272 NLRB 1106 (1984) enf'd 787 F.2d 1118 (7th Cir. 1986) (two days after the representation election, the employer required workers to produce social security cards and green cards to receive their pay); *County Window Cleaning,* 328 NLRB No. 26 (April 30, 1999) (the employer, who knew that the employee had been working for five years with an invalid social security number, requested that the employee provide a "real" security number only after the employee expressed support for the union); *Regal Recycling,* 329 NLRB No. 38 (Sept. 30, 1999) (the employer asked select workers to produce proof of immigration status during an organizing campaign); *Nortech Waste,* 336 NLRB No. 79 (Sept. 28, 2001) (following a representation election, the employer began an unprecedented review of I-9s); *Met Food,* 337 NLRB No. 14 (Dec. 20, 2001) (the employer requested proof of work authorization in an offer of reinstatement); *Domsey Trading Corp.,* 310 NLRB 777 (1993) (the employer required reinstated strikers to provide proof of work authorization); *Impressive Textiles, Inc.,* 317 NLRB 8 (1995) (employer threatened to report workers to INS before union election, and told workers that because they had voted for unionization, they would be required to show immigration documents).

27. 535 U.S. 137 (2002).

28. *NLRB v. Apollo Tire Co., Inc.,* 604 F.2d 1180 (9th Cir. 1979) (Kennedy concurring).

29. See *Albemarle Paper Co. v. Moody,* 422 U.S. 405, 420 n. 12 (1975) (internal quotations omitted) ("in all but a few cases involving discriminatory discharges…in violation of [the NLRA], the Board has ordered the employer to offer reinstatement to the employee discriminated against and to make whole such employee for any loss of pay that he has suffered by reason of the discrimination.").

30. See NLRB Compliance Manual, § 105271 (Reinstatement), at www.nlrb.gov.

31. See *NLRB v. Mastro Plastics Corp.,* 354 F.2d 170, 178 (2d Cir. 1965).

32. Id. at 175.

33. *Albemarle Paper,* 422 U.S. at 417 (1975).

34. *Republic Steel Corp. v. NLRB,* 311 U.S. 7, 9–12 (1940).

35. *Ford Motor Co.,* 31 NLRB 994, 1099–1100 (1941).

36. 467 U.S. 883 (1984).

37. Id. at 891–92 ("Since undocumented aliens are not among the few groups of workers expressly exempted by Congress, they plainly come within the broad statutory definition of 'employee'").

38. See e.g., *NLRB v. Kolkka*, 170 F.3d 937, 941 (9th Cir. 1999) (rejecting the employer's contention that undocumented workers should be excluded from a bargaining unit).

39. *NLRB v. Sure-Tan Inc.* 672 F.2d 592, 599 (7th Cir. 1982).

40. The workers signed "voluntary departure" forms, the use of which has been criticized by advocates because of the coercive nature of the INS's practices around those forms. In a well known case involving Salvadorans who had been detained and who may have been eligible for asylum, *Orantes-Hernandez v. Meese*, 685 F. Supp. 1488 (C.D. Cal. 1988), *aff'd*, 919 F.2d 549 (9th Cir. 1990), the Court found that "INS agents directed, intimidated, or otherwise coerced Salvadorans within their custody, who had not expressed a desire to return to El Salvador, to sign form I-274A for voluntary departure. INS agents used a variety of techniques to procure voluntary departure, ranging from subtle persuasion to outright threats and misrepresentations. Many class members were intimidated or coerced to accept voluntary departure even when they had unequivocally expressed a fear of returning to El Salvador." Id. at 1494. The Court further found that "INS as a practice did not permit many class members to read form I-274A nor were its contents otherwise communicated to them before signing." Id. The practices challenged in *Orantes-Hernandez* were in place at the time that the *Sure-Tan* workers "voluntarily" departed. That aspect of the case, however, was never pursued.

41. Chief Justice William Rehnquist, along with Justice Lewis Powell, dissented from that holding and found it "unlikely" that Congress meant to protect "persons wanted by the United States for the violations of our criminal laws." *Sure-Tan*, 467 U.S. at 913 (Powell, J., dissenting). Those justices believed that "the illegal alien workers are not entitled to any remedy." Id.

42. Id. at 892–93.

43. Id. at 902–3.

44. *A.P.R.A. Fuel Oil Buyers Group, Inc.*, 320 NLRB 408 (1995), enforced, *A.P.R.A. Fuel Oil Buyers Group v. NLRB*, 159 F.3d 1345 (2d. Cir. 1998).

45. Id. at 415.

46. Id; NLRB Office of the General Counsel, Memorandum GC98-15 (December 4, 1998) (superceded); See *Regal Recycling*, 329 NLRB 355 (1999); *Met Food*, 337 NLRB No. 14, *7 (2001).

47. 535 U.S. 137 (2002).

48. Id at 149.

49. *Hoffman Plastic Compounds, Inc.*, 306 NLRB 100, 104 (1992).

50. Id at 100.

51. Id. at 107–8.

52. Id.

53. *Hoffman Plastic Compounds, Inc.*, 326 NLRB 1060, 1062 (1998).

54. *Hoffman*, 535 U.S. at 147.

55. Id. at 150.

56. See, e.g., Capps, Fix, Passel, et al., *supra* n. 10.

57. *Hoffman* is a good example of the cumbersome NLRB process: Jose Castro was fired in 1988, but it was not until late March 2002 — fourteen years later — that his case reached the end of the judicial process.

58. *Sure-Tan*, 467 U.S. at 893.

59. *Hoffman*, 535 U.S. 153 (Bryer, dissenting).

60. Id. at 155.

61. See e.g., Katia Hetter, "Ballot Item Deepens Union-Immigrant Ties; Non-Citizens are Key to Labor's New Base," *San Francisco Chronicle* (Aug. 22, 2004) B1.

62. *Hoffman Plastic Compounds, Inc*, 326 NLRB 1060, 1061 (1998). The NLRB would order conditional reinstatement providing undocumented workers with the opportunity to be reinstated if they could present valid work authorization within a reasonable time. *A.P.R.A. Fuel Oil Buyers Group, Inc.*, 320 NLRB 408 (1995) enforced, 134 F.3d 50 (2d Cir. 1997).

63. *A.P.R.A.*, 320 NLRB at 414–17 (back pay continued until the employer reinstated the employee or the employee was unable, after a reasonable period, to provide the documents required to complete a new I-9 form).

64. "Procedures and Remedies for Discriminatees Who May Be Undocumented Aliens after *Hoffman Plastic Compounds, Inc.*," GC-02-06 (July 19, 2002), at http://www.nlrb.gov/nlrb/shared_files/gcmemo/gcmemo/gc02-06.asp?useShared=/nlrb/legal/ gcmemo/gcmemo/default.asp#foot2.

65. See U.S. Equal Employment Opportunity Commission, *Rescission of Enforcement Guidance on Remedies Available to Undocumented Workers Under Federal Employment Discrimination Laws* (Jun. 27, 2002), at http://www.eeoc.gov/policy/docs/undoc-rescind.html.

66. 42 U.S.C. §2000e *et seq.*; the Ninth Circuit has recently called into question whether *Hoffman* applies to claims brought under Title VII. See *Rivera v. Nibco*, 364 F.3d 1057, 1067 (9th Cir. 2004) ("We seriously doubt that *Hoffman* is as broadly applicable as [the employer]contends, and specifically believe it unlikely that it applies in Title VII cases").

67. See Section 3, infra. Correspondence from Robert Alvarez, Esq., to Gail Cober, August 12, 2004, on file with author.

68. *EEOC Obtains Protective Order Limiting Discovery That Could Adversely Affect Immigrant Workers*, Immigrants' Rights Update, Vol. 18, No. 4 (June 18, 2004), at http://www.nilc.org/immsemplymnt/emprights/emprights078.htm.

69. See U.S. Department of Labor, *Fact Sheet #48: Application of U.S. Labor Laws to Immigrant Workers: Effect of* Hoffman Plastics *decision on laws enforced by the Wage and Hour Division*, at http://www.dol.gov/esa/regs/compliance/whd/whdfs48.htm.

70. See, e.g., *Trejo v. Manpower of Muskegon*, 02-0405, MI Workers' Compensation Appellate Commission, 2003 ACO #76, 2003 MIWCLR (LRP) LEXIS 80 (dismissing undocumented worker's claim for benefits); *Ortiz v. Chief Ind., Inc.*, DOC: 201 No. 1725, NE Workers' Compensation Court, 2002 NE Wrk. Comp. LEXIS 1200 (March 26, 2003) (finding that *Hoffman* does not bar benefits).

71. E.g., *Correa v. Waymouth Farms, Inc.*, 664 N.W.2d 324, 2003 Minn. LEXIS 394, 7 No. 27 Minn. Lawyer 7 (2003); *Cherokee Indus. v. Alvarez* (2004), Okla. Civ. App. 15, 84 P.3d 798 (2003), Okla. Civ. App. LEXIS 119, 75 Okla. B.J. 645 (Okla. Ct. App. (2003)).

72. *Medillin v. Cashman*, Docket 040-05-0017 (Mass. App. 2004); *Design Kitchen and Baths, et. al. v. Lagos*, No. 00624 is pending before the Maryland Court of Special Appeals, and *Ortiz v. Chief Ind., Inc.*, supra, n. 70 is pending before the Nebraska Court of Appeals.

73. *Sanchez v. Eagle Alloy*, 658 N.W.2d 510 (Ct. Apps. Mich. (2003)), *appeal granted*, 671 N.W.2d 874 (Mich. 2003), *vacated*, 2004 Mich. LEXIS 1557 (July 23, 2004).

74. *The Reinforced Earth Company v. Workers' Compensation Appeal Board*, 810 A. 2d 99 (Pa. 2002).

75. Nancy Cleeland, "Employers Test Ruling on Immigrants," *Los Angeles Times* (Apr. 22 2002).

76. Mexican American Legal Defense and Educational Fund (MALDEF) and National

Employment Law Project (NELP), *Used and Abused: The Treatment of Undocumented Victims of Labor Law Violations Since* Hoffman Plastic Compounds v. NLRB, at www.nelp.org.

77. *Mezonos Maven Bakery*, 29-CA-25476.

78. Statement of X, employee who wishes to remain anonymous. On file with author.

79. See Answer of Respondent, filed May 6, 2003.

80. See correspondence from Alvin Blyer, Regional Director, Region 29, NLRB, to Ana Avendaño Denier, dated July 28, 2003 (on file with author).

81. The *in terrorem* effect of the threat of disclosure of immigration status has been recognized by the courts, even post-*Hoffman*. See e.g., *Zeng Liu v. Donna Karan Int'l, Inc.*, 207 F. Supp. 2d 191, 193 (2002) (finding that even if the defendants agreed to a confidentiality agreement, questioning the plaintiffs about their immigration status would still have the "'danger of intimidation, the danger of destroying the cause of action' and would inhibit plaintiffs in pursuing their rights").

82. The workers' attorney has filed litigation against SSA for this action, which may violate the Privacy Act. Conversation with Robert Alvarez, Michigan Migrant Legal Assistance, notes on file with author.

83. Correspondence from Stephen Glasser, Regional Director, NLRB to Robert Alvarez, June 19, 2004, on file with author. The workers are now trying to file charges with the EEOC, but have been told by a regional office that the agency will not seek remedies in cases such as this one. See note lxi, *supra*. Advocates are working with the regional and national offices of the EEOC to clarify that policy, but, even if the regional office's policy is based on a misunderstanding of the EEOC's national policy, the effect on workers and their advocates is a negative one.

84. See *Vaca v. Sipes*, 386 U.S. 171, 182 (1967).

Part III
The Impact of the Federalism Revolution on Access to Courts to Protect Essential Services and Fundamental Rights

CHAPTER 12

PUBLIC EDUCATION

Reneging on the Promise of Brown: *The Rehnquist Court and Education Rights*

Denise C. Morgan[*]

In 1999, when Rasheda Daniel was a seventeen-year-old senior at Inglewood High School in Los Angeles, CA, no Advanced Placement (AP) history classes were offered. Jorge Guiterez, a ninth-grader at the same school, wanted to be a veterinarian, but no AP biology classes were offered. At the time, the nearby and mostly white Beverly Hills High School had fourteen AP classes. Inglewood, which was mostly black, had only three.

Rasheda, Jorge, and other Inglewood students faced two problems—their high school's curriculum was not diverse enough to satisfy their interests, and, more importantly, it did not offer the range of AP classes necessary for them to get a first-rate education. AP courses give qualified and motivated high school students the opportunity to tackle more challenging studies, enabling them to earn more than a perfect 4.0 in a class and be more competitive when applying to colleges. Moreover, achieving a score of three or higher on an AP exam earns students college credit, allowing them to opt out of certain introductory classes and reduce their college tuition costs. In 1998, U.C. Berkeley rejected eight thousand applicants whose GPAs were 4.0 in favor of students with higher GPAs due to their enrollment in AP courses.

It was not until the ACLU of Southern California filed suit on behalf of Rasheda, Jorge, and other African American, Latino, and low-income high school students

---

[*] Professor of Law, New York Law School. Professor Morgan has been involved in the *CFE* case since it was filed in 1993—first as an associate at Cleary Gottlieb Steen & Hamilton representing (on a pro bono basis) New York City and the New York City Board of Education in a companion case (dismissed in 1995). Since joining the faculty at NYLS she has represented the Black, Puerto Rican, and Hispanic Legislative Caucus of the New York state legislature in the *CFE* case, and has written and submitted several amicus briefs on their behalf.

that California agreed to provide more equal access to AP courses in its public schools. Unfortunately, Title VI, the federal law used to challenge the unfair distribution of AP classes,* has since been eviscerated by the Rehnquist Court's Federalism Revolution.

This chapter will discuss the Supreme Court's rollback of education rights that began in the 1970s. It will then focus on the recent New York state public school finance case and explain how the Court's decisions are tying the hands of education rights advocates and lawyers.

ès   ès   ès

It is no accident that public education reform was the centerpiece of the NAACP Legal Defense Fund (LDF) litigation strategy in the early 1930s.[1] LDF's goal was to bring an end to the Jim Crow Era, a period during which U.S. laws and customs crippled the life chances of African Americans by depriving them access to most societal opportunities and benefits.[2] Many of LDF's early cases dealt with public education because LDF lawyers recognized that equal educational opportunity was necessary to gain and maintain full citizenship. Education's revolutionary potential was clear: because free public schools can sever the link binding the social, political, and economic circumstances of one generation and the next, they have the power to erode entrenched racial caste systems.[3] Moreover, equal educational opportunity is essential to democracy because no society in which social, political, and economic power are concentrated in one group can call itself democratic. In *Brown v. Board of Education*, the 1954 case in which the Supreme Court declared racially segregated public schools unequal (the crowning achievement of LDF's early litigation strategy), the Court acknowledged the wisdom of LDF's approach:

> Today, education is perhaps the most important function of state and local governments. Compulsory school attendance laws and the great expenditures for education both demonstrate our recognition of the importance of education to our democratic society. It is required in the performance of our most basic public responsibilities, even service in the armed forces. It is the very foundation of good citizenship. Today it is a principal instrument in awakening the child to cultural values, in preparing him for later professional training, and in helping him to adjust normally to his environment. In these days, it is

---

* The students also brought suit under California state law.

doubtful that any child may reasonably be expected to succeed in life if he is denied the opportunity of an education.[4]

Brown's promise was equal educational opportunity—and the full citizenship that it implies.

Given the importance of public schools, it is unfortunate that the Court has not championed educational rights in recent years. Since the mid-1970s, the Court has gradually reneged on the promise of *Brown*. Worse still, the Rehnquist Court's Federalism Revolution has exacerbated the problems caused by the defeats of the 1970s. Today, many public schools are as segregated as they were in the 1960s, and the fiscal inequities between rich and poor school districts are growing. At the same time, it has become increasingly difficult to sue to remedy those civil rights violations. If allowed to continue, this roll-back will allow the dominant societal group (white and wealthy), to concentrate power in future generations—an act that would fundamentally threaten democracy.

The first section of this chapter will discuss the Court's rejection of civil rights claims in three of the most important desegregation and school finance cases of the 1970s. The second section will focus on how the Rehnquist Court's rollback of civil rights has had a devastating impact on the education rights of children.

The Early Roadblocks to Equal Educational Opportunity

It would be understandable if, after reading *Brown*, one believed that the Constitution guarantees educational equality for all. Such an assumption, however, would be wrong. In the 1970s, the Supreme Court decided three cases undermining its holding in *Brown*: *Keyes v. School District No. 1*,[5] *San Antonio Independent School District v. Rodriguez*,[6] and *Milliken v. Bradley*.[7] Today, we are living with the consequences of those decisions.

Only Intentional Segregation is Illegal: Keyes

The Court signaled the beginning of the end of desegregation with its 1973 decision in *Keyes v. School District No. 1*. Although the plaintiffs won, the Court's rejection of the position that "[p]ublic schools are creatures of the State, and whether the segregation is state-created or state-assisted or merely state-perpetuated should be irrelevant to constitutional principle"[8] made it more difficult for plaintiffs to prevail in future desegregation suits. The Court backed away from its pronouncement in *Brown* that separate schooling was inherently unequal, and held that plaintiffs had to prove intentional racial discrimination in order to be entitled to a remedy. Intentional discrimination, however, is easy to conceal and hard to prove. As a result, *Keyes* made it much more difficult for desegregation cases to succeed in states outside of the former Jim Crow South.

Education is not a Fundamental Right: Rodriguez

Although most people associate *Brown* with racial segregation, the case was primarily about access to quality education. Unfortunately, because the *Keyes* Court interpreted the Constitution to require proof of intentional race-based segregation, no guarantee of equal education exists for children who live where segregation was never mandated by law and whose lawyers cannot prove that their schools were intentionally made segregated by racist school officials. Education advocates, therefore, were forced to turn to school finance litigation to promote equal educational opportunity.

San Antonio School District v. Rodriguez, decided in 1973, was the first (and last) school finance litigation to reach the Supreme Court. Demetrio Rodriguez, a Navy and Air Force veteran and father of four, argued that his rights under the Equal Protection Clause were violated by the large disparity in education aid awarded by the state of Texas to poor versus wealthy school districts.[9] For example, the state contributed less aid in Edgewood, which had a median family income of $4,686 and whose population was ninety percent Mexican American, than it did in Alamo Heights, which had a median family income of $8,001 and whose population was eighty percent white.[10] As a result, Edgewood public schools could only spend $356 annually on each student while Alamo Heights schools could spend $594 annually (even though the property tax rates were higher in Edgewood than in Alamo Heights).[11]

Rodriguez lost his case. The Court held that discrimination against the poor should not receive the same strict scrutiny as racial or religious discrimination, and that education was not a fundamental constitutional right—the inequitable distribution of public education funding, therefore, does not violate any federal constitutional rights.[12] The case allowed parents in property-rich school districts to continue to fund their local schools at levels that parents in property-poor districts could not achieve no matter how much they taxed themselves. Money might not buy everything, but it can buy smaller class sizes, qualified teachers, and state-of-the-art equipment—all of which promote better educational outcomes.[13]

Desegregation Does Not Extend to the Suburbs: Milliken

Rodriguez may not have had such a tremendous racial impact if desegregation litigation had successfully integrated children of color from property-poor school districts and white children from property-rich school districts into the same public schools. The 1974 *Milliken v. Bradley* decision, however, crippled desegregation litigation. Since then, it has been difficult for courts to order remedies that have a realistic chance of dismantling racial isolation.

It is common knowledge that U.S. cities are marked by the de facto segregation of poorer colored students in urban centers and wealthier white students in the suburbs.[14] Most often, school district lines are drawn along these same boundaries. The *Milliken* Court, however, constitutionalized those demographic facts by holding that federal courts cannot order desegregation across those geographic boundaries.[15] The holding made court-ordered school desegregation virtually impossible, as anything short of inter-district remedies seldom achieves meaningful integration. Perhaps more importantly, the decision concentrated poverty, the factor most closely associated with educational failure, in urban schools.[16] This is not to say that poor public schools cannot be academically successful—such a phenomenon is difficult to achieve, however, and even more difficult to replicate.[17] Accordingly, *Milliken* magnified and gave a racial cast to the educational inequality previously sanctioned by *Rodriguez*.

The Fallout

By the early 1990s, the Supreme Court had moved from discussing how to properly litigate equal education lawsuits to discussing how to terminate those cases.[18] At the same time, lower federal courts began rejecting parent, school, and state-initiated desegregation and affirmative action plans.[19] The result of this judicial hostility has been a rapid increase in segregation and educational inequality.

Today, children nation-wide are increasingly racially isolated in public schools. The Harvard Civil Rights Project's 1999 report, *Resegregation in American Schools*, found that:

> [t]he percent of black students in majority white schools peaked in the early 1980s and declined to the levels of the 1960s by the 1996–97 school year. In terms of intense segregation, this number has turned up only in the more recent past and the increase has been modest. Latino segregation by both measures has grown steadily throughout the past 28 years, surpassing the black level in predom-

inantly non-white schools by 1980 and slightly exceeding the proportion in intensely segregated schools (90–100% minority) in the 1990s.[20]

Although Asian American students are less likely than black or Latino students to be affected by racial isolation, the report stated that they are more likely than their white counterparts to attend public schools with a high poverty rate, and their segregation is growing rapidly.[21] Indeed, white students are becoming more and more isolated from an increasingly diverse citizenry.[22]

A significant link exists between the lack of racial integration in public schools and racial disparities in educational opportunity. Schools that serve predominantly minority student bodies tend to have more poor students.[23] And, "[h]igh poverty schools have been shown to increase educational inequality for students in these schools because of problems such as a lack of resources, a dearth of experienced and credentialed teachers, lower parental involvement, and high teacher turnover."[24] As a result, school integration is one of the most effective ways of equalizing school resources and dispersing those concentrations of poverty that are so detrimental to learning.[25]

Reducing segregation and concentrations of poverty in public schools can significantly increase student educational outcomes.[26] It is unsurprising, therefore, that as segregation increased in the 1990s, the performance gap on standardized tests between whites and Asian Americans on one hand, and blacks and Latinos on the other, also increased[27]—the same gap that had decreased steadily between the 1960s and 1980s.[28] National Assessment of Educational Progress test results from that earlier period show that "scores for all racial-ethnic groups rose in reading and mathematics for all age groups. [But, while]...whites' scores rose by smaller amounts,...scores for [Latinos] and blacks rose dramatically."[29]

The Rehnquist Court's Rollback of Education Rights

Even in the wake of the Supreme Court decisions that seemed to deny the importance of equal educational opportunity, parents, children's rights advocates, and education lawyers did not give up their struggle. Indeed, they worked to devise new strategies to ensure that all children have access to quality education.

One of the most promising of these strategies relied on Title VI of the 1964 Civil Rights Act, a federal law prohibiting discrimination in federally-funded programs or activities. Different education rights suits have been brought to enforce that statute—for example, cases challenging the shunting of children into special education classes,[30] the fact that qualified students lack access to AP classes,[31] the failure of school districts to provide appropriate programs for children whose first language is not English,[32] and the unfair distribution of public school dollars.[33] These lawsuits share the goal of promoting equal educational opportunity and full citizenship; the Rehnquist Court's rollback of civil rights, however, threatens their future.

The Rollback in Civil Rights Law

The 1964 Civil Rights Act, arguably the most influential federal civil rights statute, promoted equal citizenship by prohibiting racial discrimination in a broad spectrum of areas (e.g., public accommodations, private employment, and programs or activities receiving federal funds). Congress enacted Title VI of that Act "to make sure that the funds of the United States [were] not used to support racial discrimination."[34] To match that far-reaching goal, Congress used inclusive language: "[n]o person in the United States shall, on grounds of race, color, or national origin, be excluded from participation in, be denied the benefits of, or be subjected to discrimination under any program or activity receiving Federal financial assistance."[35]

To establish a violation of Title VI, the Supreme Court requires proof that a federally-funded program *intentionally* discriminates on the basis of race.[36] Every federal agency's regulations to implement Title VI, however, state that recipients of federal funds may not engage in activity that have the *effect* of discriminating on the basis of race. For the last quarter century, courts have allowed citizens to bring suit to enforce those Title VI regulations.[37] The Rehnquist Court, however, eliminated this right in *Alexander v. Sandoval*[38] in 2001, and curtailed individuals' ability to sue states and state officials for violating those Title VI regulations through § 1983 suits in *Gonzaga University v. Doe*[39] in 2002. Sadly, rights without remedies are no rights at all.[40]

The Rollback: Reneging on the Promise of Brown

This recent rollback of civil rights law has had a devastating impact on the education rights of children. The *Campaign for Fiscal Equity (CFE)* litigation provides an example of the impact of the Rehnquist Court's rollback on the promise of equal educational opportunity. The case involved a Title VI disparate impact claim that, given the rollback, is now difficult to argue successfully. While the plaintiffs won their state law claims, the New York Court of Appeals, the state's highest court, was forced to reject their federal claims.

Since the turn of the twentieth century, it has been obvious that New York's school funding formula is unfair. Despite ongoing reform efforts,[41] however, the inequities have resisted change. As a result, thousands of New York City students are forced to attend underfunded, overcrowded schools with inadequate supplies and uncertified teachers (at the time of the *CFE* suit teacher salaries were twenty-eight percent lower than in the surrounding suburbs). Those resource shortfalls profoundly affect the quality of learning in public schools. For example, the Board of Regents' most recent 655 Report documented,

> a dismaying alignment of disadvantaged students (disproportionately children of color), schools with the poorest educational resources (fiscal and human), and substandard achievement....Perhaps the sharpest contrasts exist between public schools in New York City and those in districts (most suburban) with low percentages of students in poverty and high levels of income and property wealth.[42]

The *CFE* plaintiffs brought suit to challenge these injustices. They argued that, in violation of their state constitutional rights, New York City public school students do not receive a sound basic education. In addition, they asserted that the funding shortfall resulting from New York's school aid formula hits black and Latino students particularly hard, violating the Department of Education's implementing regulations for Title VI.

The Title VI implementing regulations require that there be some educational justification for policies that disproportionately hurt minority students. The *CFE* plaintiffs argued that New York's public school funding formula violates those regulations because it treats minority students worse than their white counterparts. In recent years, New York City has educated thirty-seven percent of students in the state, but has only received thirty-five percent of New York's aid for education. While a two percent difference may seem small, it equates to $400 million annually. This shortfall, then, disproportionately impacts minority children because the City educates seventy-three percent of the state's minority students and its public school population is composed of eighty-four percent minorities. Indeed, a regression analysis showed that instead of ensuring that similarly needy students were receiving the same amount of aid, the New York school funding formula gives "minority students...less State aid as their over-all concentration increases in a particular district."[43]

To make matters worse, New York could not justify this racially disparate impact because the plaintiffs submitted proof that the funding formula was the result of a political compromise. For fifteen years, New York City received 38.86 percent of all annual increases in aid from the state. As the state's funding formula fluctuated over time (depending on student need, the City's wealth, student attendance, and student enrollment), that percentage remained constant. The trial court judge, Leland DeGrasse, found those facts convincing and held "that New York City does not receive State aid commensurate with the needs of its students and that it in fact receives less State aid than districts with similar student need."[44] He also understood that the funding shortfall mattered—"money is a crucial determinant of educational quality, and that receipt of less educational funding by minority students is an adverse disparate impact within the purview of…Title VI…."[45]

Why, therefore, did the New York Court of Appeals reject the seemingly basic civil rights claim that the state cannot treat people of color worse than it treats similarly situated whites?[46] Because of the Rehnquist Court's rollback of civil rights.

One way the Court has diminished our ability to enforce federal rights is by asserting that a difference exists between having a right and having a private right of action (the right to sue to enforce that right). Under current case law, unless Congress states its intent that individuals should be able to sue to enforce a federal law, individuals will be denied that right.[47] The consequences of this interpretation are all too clear. When individuals have a private right of action to enforce their federal rights, potential violators are more likely to follow the law. Without this deterrent, these same people may feel able to violate the federal rights of others.

When Congress enacts statutes, however, it is not always explicit about its intent to confer a private right of action.[48] Historically, the Court usually implied a private right of action in order to fulfill Congress's objectives.[49] In the last twenty-five years, however, the Court has required much more explicit proof of congressional intent.[50] Once the Court revised its test to determine whether or not a private right of action exists, Congress should have understood that it had to be explicit in stating its intent with all new legislation. Older statutes like Title VI that were passed before the Court ratcheted up the standard, however, cannot now be made more explicit.

This issue came to a head in *Sandoval*, in which non-English speaking Alabama residents argued that offering the state driver's license test only in English violated their rights under the Title VI implementing regulations.[51] The plaintiffs lost because the Court held that no private right of action exists under those regulations.[52] Although the plaintiffs had the right not to be discriminated against, they had no means by which to enforce that right.[53]

The Court has similarly rolled back the protections historically provided by other civil rights laws. For example, plaintiffs have used 42 U.S.C. §1983, a Reconstruction Era civil rights statute, to enforce federal statutes that do not contain private rights of action.[54] Under § 1983, plaintiffs have the right to sue state officials in federal court for violations of "any rights, privileges, or immunities secured by the Constitution and laws [of the United States]." The Court, however, has curtailed the ability to enforce civil rights against states and state officials through these types of suits. In recent cases, the Court has narrowly construed both who can be sued under § 1983,[55] and what constitutes a federal right for the purposes of that statute.[56]

In *Gonzaga University v. Doe* in 2002, the Court reversed prior case law that had distinguished between the rigorous test for inferring a private right of action under a federal statute and the more lenient one for determining whether a statute confers a federal right that is enforceable through § 1983.[57] Now, § 1983 suits are virtually superfluous because they are available only when a private right of action would exist anyway.

After *Sandoval* and *Gonzaga*, although both Title VI and its implementing regulations remain valid federal laws, it is difficult to sue to enforce them. While the facts of the *CFE* plaintiffs' Title VI claim remain true, therefore, it has become increasingly difficult to remedy the injustice.

But why does it matter if *CFE* was won on state or federal grounds? For two reasons—one immediate and practical, the other longer-term and theoretical. The immediate problem is one of strategy. The rejection of the *CFE* plaintiffs' Title VI argument signals the demise of one of the more promising new strategies to ensure children access to quality education. Particularly for children living in states where the state constitution has not protected educational rights as much as it has in New York, the loss of that federal claim will be disastrous.

More importantly, something significant is lost when the law fails to recognize the type of *race-based* injury that the *CFE* plaintiffs proved at trial. The plaintiffs' federal claim, and only their federal claim, takes into account the injuries caused by the unjustified misdistribution of government resources by race—the harm to communities of color and to our democratic society.[58] State aid formulas that systematically apportion less money to children of color than to their white peers reinforce the notion that people of color are somehow less deserving, less equal. Moreover, a state funding scheme that deprives communities of color of necessary educational resources, thereby ill-preparing children to exercise their citizenship rights, will likely create an enduring underclass. If equal citizenship is truly important to our national identity, it is important both to acknowledge when we fail to live up to that ideal and to correct lasting patterns of injustice.

Conclusion

This country experienced the horror of a two-tiered education system marked by race—and rejected it as un-American. That was what *Brown* was about. Sadly, by reneging on the promise of *Brown*, the Rehnquist Court has condemned America to repeat that historical mistake.

Endnotes

1. See Richard Kluger, *Simple Justice* (1975) 132–37, (describes LDF's development of a litigation strategy centered around ending racial segregation in public education).

2. See C. Vann Woodward, *The Strange Career of Jim Crow* (1974); Glenda E. Gilmore, *Gender and Jim Crow: Women and the Politics of White Supremacy in North Carolina, 1896–1920* (1996). Other people of color were also relegated to second class citizenship by force of law during this period. See, e.g., *Terrace v. Thompson*, 263 U.S. 197 (1923); *Gong Lum v. Rice*, 275 U.S. 78 (1927).

3. See generally Denise C. Morgan, The Less Polite Questions: Race, Place, Poverty and Public Education, *1998 Ann. Surv. Am. L.* (1998) 267.

4. *Brown v. Bd. of Educ.*, 347 U.S. 483, 493 (1954).

5. 413 U.S. 189 (1973).

6. 411 U.S. 1 (1973).

7. 418 U.S. 717 (1974).

8. 413 U.S. at 227 (Powell, J., concurring and dissenting).

9. See Peter Irons, *The Courage of their Convictions* (1990) 283–85.

10. *Rodriguez*, 411 U.S. at 11–13. Although the stated goal of Texas' school aid formula was to compensate for inequalities in the amounts of money that could be raised locally for education, the formula had the opposite effect.....The state added $222 to the $26 per student that was raised annually through Edgewood local property taxes, but added $225 to the $333 per student that Alamo Heights raised annually. The remaining aid came from federal sources. Id.

11. Id.

12. See Id. at 54–55.

13. See Morgan, The Less Polite Questions, *1998 Ann. Surv. Am. L.* at 268–74 (arguing that there is a causal link between school funding and educational opportunity).

14. See generally Douglas S. Massey and Nancy A. Denton, *American Apartheid: Segregation and the Making of the Underclass* (1993).

15. See 418 U.S. at 745–47.

16. See Gary Orfield and John T. Yun, *Resegregation in American Schools* (Harv. Univ., The Civil Rights Project, June 1999) 3, at http://www.civilrightsproject.harvard.edu/research/deseg/Resegregation_American_ Schools99.pdf ("School level poverty is related to many variables that effect a school's overall chance at successfully educating students, including parent education levels, availability of advanced courses, teachers with credentials in the subject they are teaching, instability of enrollment, dropouts, untreated health problems, lower college-going rates and many other important factors."). See also Gary

Orfield and Susan E. Eaton, *Dismantling Desegregation: The Quiet Reversal of* Brown v. Board of Education (1996) 53 ("One of the most consistent findings in research on education has been the powerful relationship between concentrated poverty and virtually every measure of school-level academic results").

17. See Richard Rothstein, "Lessons; Poverty, Achievement, and Great Misconceptions," *New York Times* (Jan. 3, 2001) B8.

18. See *Bd. of Educ. v. Dowell*, 498 U.S. 237 (1991); *Freeman v. Pitts*, 503 U.S. 467 (1992); *Missouri v. Jenkins*, 515 U.S. 70 (1995).

19. See Phillip O'Connor and Lynn Horsley, "Court Ends Desegregation Case; Loss of Accreditation Stands; Relief, Dismay Follow Decision," *Kansas City Star* (Nov. 18, 1999) A1 (twenty-two-year-old desegregation case dismissed in Kansas City, MO, despite increasing numbers of racially isolated schools); Richard Lee Colvin, "Ruling Ends Historic Forced Busing Program; Desegregation: Judge Nullifies N. Carolina Decision That Led to Efforts Nationwide to Achieve Racial Balance in Schools," *LA Times* (Sept. 11, 1999) A1 (thirty-year-old desegregation case dismissed in Charlotte, NC); James Heaney, "School Desegregation Case is Over," *Buffalo News* (Oct 18, 1995) 1A (twenty-three-year-old desegregation case dismissed in Buffalo, NY); "Many Cities Targeting Busing, '70s Desegregation Plans," *Dallas Morning News* (Sept. 26, 1995) 4A (describing challenges to desegregation in Denver, CO, Minneapolis, MN, Wilmington, DE, Norfolk, VA, and Oklahoma City, OK). See also *Johnson v. Bd. of Regents of Univ. of Ga.*, 263 F.3d 1234, 1254 (11th Cir. 2001) (striking down the University of Georgia's race-based affirmative action program); *Eisenberg v. Montgomery County Pub. Sch.*, 197 F.3d 123, 133 (4th Cir. 1999) (prohibiting consideration of race in transfers to public magnet school for purpose of promoting racial diversity); *Wessmann v. Gittens*, 160 F.3d 790, 792 (1st Cir. 1998) (prohibiting use of race and ethnicity as admissions criteria at Boston Latin public school); *Hopwood v. Texas*, 78 F.3d 932, 934 (5th Cir. 1996) (striking down affirmative action program at University of Texas School of Law). But see *Grutter v. Bollinger*, 539 U.S. 306 (2003).

20. Orfield and Yun, *supra* note 15, at 13–14.

> The West, where Latinos are the dominant minority group has a substantial increase in segregation and now has 77% of Latino children in predominantly minority schools. A very substantial share of Latinos are now attending intensely segregated (90–100% non-white) schools—46% in the Northeast, 38% in the South, and 33% in the West, where this level of segregation was uncommon two decades ago.

Id. at 22. See also Gary Orfield, *Schools More Separate: Consequences of a Decade of Resegregation* (Harv. Univ., The Civil Rights Project, Jul. 2001), at http://www.civilrights project.harvard.edu/research/deseg/Schools_More_Separate.pdf (stating that new data from the 1998–99 school year shows that school segregation has intensified throughout the 1990s); Erica Frankenberg, Chungmei Lee and Gary Orfield, *A Multiracial Society with Segregated Schools: Are We Losing the Dream?* (Harv. Univ., The Civil Rights Project, Jan. 2003), at http://www.civilrightsproject.harvard.edu/research/reseg03/AreWeLosingtheDream.pdf.

21. The average white student attends a school in which 18.7 percent of students qualify for free or reduced price lunches. Orfield and Yun, *supra* note 15, at 16. In comparison, the average Asian American student attends a school in which 29.3 percent of the students so qualify. Id. The statistics for Native American, African American, and Latino students are 30.9 percent, 42.7 percent, and 46 percent respectively. Id.

22. "[B]ased on the national average, the average white student is in a school with 8.6%

black students, 6.6% Latinos, 2.8% Asians, and 1% American Indians. Whites are the only racial group that attend schools where the overwhelming majority of students are from their own race." Id. at 15.

23. See House Comm. on Educ. & Labor, 101st Cong., *A Report on Shortchanging Children: The Impact of Fiscal Inequity on the Education of Students at Risk* (Comm. Print 1990) ("[I]n many states the principal victims of fiscal inequity are members of racial and ethnic minorities and the poor").

24. Frankenberg, Lee, and Orfield, *supra* note 20, at 35.

25. Orfield and Yun explain that

[w]hen African-American and Latino students are segregated into schools where the majority of students are non-white, they are very likely to find themselves in schools where poverty is concentrated. This is of course not the case with segregated white students, whose majority-white schools almost always enroll high proportions of students from the middle class. This is a crucial difference, because concentrated poverty is linked to lower educational achievement.

Orfield and Yun, *supra* note 16, at 3.

26. Jens Ludwig, Helen F. Ladd, and Greg J. Duncan, Urban Poverty and Educational Outcomes, *Brookings-Wharton Papers of Urban Affairs* (William G. Gale and Janet Rothenberg Pack, eds., 2001), at http://muse.jhu.edu/journals/brookings-wharton_papers_on _urban_affairs/v2001/2001.1ludwig01.html. See also Leonard S. Rubinowitz and James E. Rosenbaum, *Crossing the Class and Color Lines: From Public Housing to White Suburbia* (2000) 189 (finding positive effects of decreasing concentrations of poverty on educational achievement in the Gautreaux program in Chicago, IL).

27. See Kate Zernike, "Gap Widens Again on Tests Given to Blacks and Whites," *NY Times* (Aug. 25, 2000) A14 (reporting that the gap between the test scores of black and white students narrowed in the 1980s but widened in the 1990s).

28. See Larry V. Hedges and Amy Nowell, Black-White Test Score Convergence Since 1965, *The Black-White Test Score Gap,* Christopher Jencks and Meredith Phillips, eds. (1998), 155 ("The racial gap narrows for all tests administered as part of NAEP during the 1980s").

29. David Grissmer, Ann Flanagan, and Stephanie Williamson, Does Money Matter for Minority and Disadvantaged Students? Assessing the New Empirical Evidence, *Developments in School Finance 1997,* William J. Fowler, Jr. ed. (1998), 15–16.

30. See *Larry P. v. Riles,* 793 F.2d 969 (9th Cir. 1984).

31. See *Daniel v. California,* at http://www.aclu-sc.org/Courts/.

32. See *Serna v. Portales Mun. Sch.,* 499 F.2d 1147 (10th Cir. 1974); *Flores v. Arizona,* 48 F.Supp.2d 937 (D. Ariz 1999).

33. See *Powell v. Ridge,* 189 F.3d 387 (3d Cir. 1999), *cert. denied* 528 U.S. 1046 (1999); *Robinson v. Kansas,* 117 F. Supp. 2d 1124 (D. Kan. 2000); *Ceasar v. Pataki,* 2000 WL 1154318 (S.D.N.Y. Aug. 14, 2000); *Kasayulie v. State,* No. 3AN-97-3782 CIV, slip op. at 11 (Alaska Super. Ct. Sept. 1, 1999); *Campaign for Fiscal Equity v. State,* 744 N.Y.S.2d 130 (1st Dep't 2002); *Williams v. California,* No. 312236 (Cal. Super. Ct. filed May 2000, settled Aug. 2004).

34. 110 Cong. Rec. 6544 (1964) (Statement of Sen. Humphrey).

35. 42 U.S.C. §2000d.

36. *Guardians Ass'n v. Civil Serv. Comm'n,* 463 U.S. 582 (1983).

37. At the time the Supreme Court decided *Alexander v. Sandoval,* ten of the thirteen Courts of Appeals had either explicitly or implicitly held that a private right of action existed to enforce the Title VI disparate impact regulation. No Court of Appeal had ever

reached a contrary conclusion. See *Alexander v. Sandoval*, 532 U.S. 275, 295 n.1 (2001) (Stevens, J., dissenting) (citing cases).

38. 532 U.S. 275.

39. 536 U.S. 273 (2002).

40. For a more complete discussion of the impact of the Rehnquist Court's Federalism Revolution on Congress's ability to protect civil rights and to make them enforceable, see Denise C. Morgan and Rebecca E. Zietlow, The New Parity Debate: Congress and Rights of Belonging, *73 Cincinnati L.Rev.* (2005) 1347.

41. See Edwin Margolis and Stanley Moses, *The Elusive Quest: The Struggle for Educational Opportunity* (1992) 28, 30, 35–38 (discussing the state's first equalization efforts in 1902, the 1921 educational Finance Inquiry Commission, the 1972 Fleischmann Commission, the 1982 Rubin Task Force, and other studies). See also *Funding for Fairness*, The NY State Temporary State Commission on the Distribution of State Aid to Local School Districts (Salerno Commission Report, Dec. 1988); *Putting Children First*, NY State Special Commission on Educational Structure, Policies and Practices (Moreland Act Commission Report, Dec. 1993).

42. *New York, The State of Learning: A Report to the Governor and the Legislature on the Educational Status of the State's Schools* vi (The Univ. of the State of NY/The State Educ. Dep't, July 2003), at http://www.emsc.nysed.gov/irts/655report/2003/volume1-2003/655 report-volume1.pdf.

43. *Campaign for Fiscal Equity v. State*, 719 NYS 2d 475, 546 (NY Sup. Ct. 2001). The plaintiffs' regression analysis held constant factors that should affect school funding—like district wealth, the number of English language learners, local tax effort, student enrollment, and student attendance.

44. *Campaign for Fiscal Equity*, 719 NYS 2d at 547. The plaintiffs' regression analysis held constant factors that should affect school funding—district wealth, the number of English language learners, local tax effort, student enrollment, and student attendance.

45. Id. at 541.

46. *Campaign for Fiscal Equity, Inc. v. State*, 100 NY 2d 893 (NY 2003).

47. See *Touche Ross & Co. v. Redington*, 442 U.S. 560, 578 (1979).

48. See *Cannon v. Univ. of Chicago*, 441 U.S. 677, 717–18 (1979) (Rehnquist, J., concurring).

49. See *J.I. Case Co. v. Borak*, 377 U.S. 426, 433–35 (1964).

50. See *Karahalios v. Nat'l Fed'n of Fed. Employees*, 489 U.S. 527, 536 (1989); *Redington*, 442 U.S. at 568.

51. 532 U.S. 275 (2001).

52. Id. at 293.

53. See id.

54. See *Wright v. Roanoke Redev. & Hous. Auth.*, 479 U.S. 418, 429 (1987) (permitting private §1983 action by tenants for violation of the Brooke Amendment to the Housing Act of 1937).

55. See *Will v. Mich. Dept. of State Police*, 491 U.S. 58, 71 (1989).

56. See *Gonzaga Univ. v. Doe*, 536 U.S. 273 (2002).

57. Id. at 283 ("[A] plaintiff suing under an implied right of action still must show that the statute manifests an intent to create not just a private right but also a private remedy").

58. See generally Denise C. Morgan, The New School Finance Litigation: Acknowledging that Race Discrimination in Public Education is More Than Just a Tort, *96 NW U. L. Rev.* (Fall 2001) 99.

CHAPTER 13

HEALTH CARE

The Civil Rights Rollback: It's Bad for Your Health

Jane Perkins[*]

The federal Medicaid program, administered through the states, provides millions of people who would otherwise be uninsured with access to quality health care. Federal law includes specific consumer protections to ensure that states offer Medicaid beneficiaries appropriate care in a timely manner. Without those protections and the ability to enforce them in court, beneficiaries' access to health care would be jeopardized. The following examples come from the National Health Law Program, a public interest law firm working to improve health care for low-income people, minorities, children, the elderly, and the disabled.

> *Arlo,[†] a six-year-old boy, lives with his grandparents in the mountains of North Carolina. Although both adults work full time, Arlo qualifies for Medicaid because they cannot afford private health insurance. When Arlo fell and chipped several front teeth, his grandparents contacted dentists in the surrounding three counties. They refused to accept Medicaid, saying that their payments would not cover their costs. The family finally located a dentist who accepted Medicaid, but they had to drive three and a half hours each way.*

The federal Medicaid Act requires states to establish payment scales so that medical services are available to Medicaid beneficiaries at least to the extent that such services are available to the general population in the area. When states fail to live up to their obligations, children like Arlo suffer.

> *Lizbeth is a fifty-seven-year-old woman with cerebral palsy and other developmental disabilities. When her mother (and caregiver) had a*

---

* Jane Perkins is Legal Director at the National Health Law Program, a public interest law firm working to improve health care for low-income people, minorities, children, the elderly, and people with disabilities.

† The stories are true, but the names have been changed.

stroke six years ago, Lizbeth was placed in a nursing home, paid for by Medicaid. She remains there today, with limited access to the community—not because of her condition, but because she has few opportunities to leave. She has little, if any, choice in what or when she eats. She does not receive active treatment or habilitation services. She has little privacy, sharing her room with up to five strangers.

The Medicaid Act requires states to assure that participating nursing homes provide residents with active treatment tailored to their individual needs, participation in social, religious, and community activities, and privacy of accommodations and treatment. When states and nursing homes fail to comply with these requirements, an informal administrative hearing is usually insufficient to address the problems facing people like Lizbeth, because the hearing officers are not empowered to order the needed system-wide relief.

Thirty-two-year-old Carlos has a traumatic brain injury. With Medicaid-approved home health and personal care, he is able to live in his own apartment rather than in a long-term care facility. Although his condition demands consistency and a focus on social modeling, he experiences frequent interruption in care. Individuals who provide him services are often untrained and exhibit inappropriate behavior. On one occasion, Carlos' mother was called to his apartment only to find the care provider passed out drunk on the sofa, naked from the waist down.

Christa is a nine-year-old Medicaid beneficiary with cerebral palsy, mental retardation, and developmental delay. Although her doctor determined that she needs physical and speech therapy, the state Medicaid agency would not cover such services. An administrative appeal was filed, and the hearing officer ordered the agency to provide Christa therapy within thirty days. Years passed, however, and Christa continued to go without services.

The Medicaid Act requires that states provide services with reasonable promptness and a certain quality of care. Often, however, it is not until a federal court case is filed that people like Carlos and Christa receive the care they need.

While these stories differ, they share common threads. Each involves someone who depends on Medicaid for health care. In each case, the federal Medicaid Act should ensure that the individual gets appropriate health care in a timely manner. In each case, however, the beneficiary had to turn to the courts to ensure that that federal law was enforced.

Unfortunately for these individuals and others like them, the right to privately enforce the Medicaid Act in court has come under fire. Medicaid has never *shaken its stigma as a "welfare" program, and so continues to be a target for the increasingly conservative Judiciary. The current effort to eliminate private enforcement of the Medicaid Act fits squarely into the states' rights movement that seeks to curtail the authority of Congress over the states, insulate states from private lawsuits, and roll back public benefits.*

This chapter will describe the Medicaid program and discuss how the current civil rights rollback effort is affecting the fifty million elderly, disabled, and low-income Americans who depend on Medicaid for health care.

☙   ☙   ☙

Medicaid: Health Care for Over Fifty Million Americans

Since its enactment as part of the 1965 Social Security Act, Medicaid has guaranteed every eligible citizen the legal right to receive necessary health care benefits.[1] In other words, Medicaid is an "entitlement." As such, Medicaid cannot refuse new enrollees or cap its expenditures mid-year; rather, the program responds to the population's changing needs—growth in numbers, aging, rising unemployment, loss of private health care coverage, natural disasters, and increasing disability rates.[2]

For the past four decades, Medicaid has provided coverage to millions who would otherwise be uninsured because they could not afford private insurance, because their employers did not provide insurance, or because commercial insurers denied them coverage due to chronic health conditions. Medicaid, insuring more people than any other public or private insurer in the country,[3] is often the only coverage for more than fifty million people—forty million children and their caretakers, and twelve million with disabilities.[4] Every state participates in Medicaid, and every state is legally entitled to matching federal funds for their Medicaid expenditures.[5] Federal funding pays for at least half the Medicaid services provided.

An individual is not eligible for Medicaid simply because he or she is poor. Rather, individuals must pass several screens before being awarded a Medicaid card.[6] First, recipients must fit into one of the eligibility categories—children and their caretakers, pregnant women, the elderly, and people with disabilities. In most states, for example, individuals receiving Supplemental Security Income because of a disability automatically qualify.[7] Second, recipients must have limited income and resources.[8] Third, they must have the appropriate immigration status—in most cases, U.S. citizenship (legal immigrants are temporarily excluded from the Medicaid program).[9] Finally, they must reside in the state in which they are applying for benefits.[10]

Medicaid is a linchpin for four distinct groups:

1. The elderly and the disabled. Medicaid is *the* largest single purchaser of long-term care services for the elderly and the disabled.[11] In 2002, Medicaid funded half of the country's total nursing home expenditures and forty-three percent of total long-term care expenditures.[12] Almost three-quarters of the projected increase in federal Medicaid spending from 2001 to 2006 is associated with the provision of health care to these beneficiaries.[13]

2. Medicare beneficiaries with incomes below the federal poverty level. Medicaid provides financial support for beneficiaries who are unable to pay Medicare costs. In 2004, for example, a patient had to pay an $876 deductible before Medicare would begin covering a hospital stay, as well as a $100 annual deductible and a $66.60 monthly premium for other medical care.[14] Medicaid's supplemental insurance program requires states to pay the premiums and cost-sharing amounts for this group.[15] By 1997, over half of such beneficiaries relied on Medicaid for supplemental health insurance coverage.[16]

3. Children under twenty-one. In 2002, twenty-five million children and youth (one in every four) accounted for over half of Medicaid's beneficiaries.[17] Adult caretakers represented another thirteen million beneficiaries.[18] Although children and their caretakers represent about three-quarters of the Medicaid population, they account for only thirty percent of Medicaid spending (the elderly and disabled make up the remaining seventy percent).[19]

4. A wide range of health care providers. In 1998, Medicaid participants included over five thousand public hospitals, fifteen thousand nursing homes, seven thousand group homes and institutions for the mentally retarded, seven hundred community health centers, and 585 managed health care plans.[20]

By facilitating access to health care, Medicaid has improved the health of its enrollees.[21] Compared with the uninsured, Medicaid children are more likely to receive well-child care and immunizations, and are seventy percent more likely to receive care for conditions such as asthma, recurring ear infections, and sore throats.[22] By providing routine medical care, Medicaid has reduced avoidable hospital stays for conditions such as diabetes and malignant hypertension.[23] Further, state Medicaid programs have been innovators in providing beneficiaries with home and community-based services.

The Medicaid Act requires that states establish reasonable standards for determining the extent of medical assistance required,[24] and provide services sufficient in amount, duration, and scope.[25] States must provide coverage for certain services, including inpatient and outpatient hospital services,[26] physician services,[27] nursing facility services for individuals over twenty-one,[28] and periodic screening, diagnosis, and treatment for children under twenty-one.[29] States can then choose whether or not to cover twenty-three optional services, including prescription drugs,[30] dental services,[31] physical and related therapies,[32] and intermediate care facility services for the mentally retarded.[33]

Over its forty year history, Medicaid has been expanded, restricted, and modified—all too often as part of eleventh-hour compromises in Congress.[34] As a result, the program has evolved into a complex and at times confounding entity. In the words of a judge, "[Medicaid is] almost unintelligible to the uninitiated."[35] Variation exists between states in the administration, eligibility, benefits, and provider payments available.

Congress is, however, able to set basic rules.[36] Congress enacted the Medicaid Act pursuant to its authority under the Spending Clause of the Constitution[37] (which allows Congress to condition the grant of federal funds to the states on the states agreeing to take certain steps). For instance, Congress has conditioned federal Medicaid funding on the states' ensuring that all individuals wishing to apply can do so quickly, and will receive state assistance promptly after meeting eligibility requirements.[38]

Unfortunately, it is not uncommon for states to ignore the federal coverage rules. Medicaid beneficiaries have therefore come to depend on the courts to ensure that states adhere to federal requirements and cover such needs as intermediate care facility services for the mentally retarded,[39] Clozaril to treat schizophrenia,[40] AZT to treat AIDS,[41] medically necessary eyeglasses,[42] and augmentative communication devices for individuals with speech disabilities.[43]

Challenges to Medicaid

Despite Medicaid's unquestioned successes, the program faces serious challenges. In addition to the usual political pressures and budgetary problems,[44] of particular concern is whether beneficiaries will retain their legal right to make states comply with the Medicaid Act—in other words, whether Medicaid will remain an entitlement.

When it was enacted in 1965, the Medicaid Act did not expressly provide its beneficiaries with the right to enforce their rights in court. The courts have long recognized, however, that § 1983 of Title 42 of the U.S. Code allows individuals to take legal action against state officials who deprive them of rights, privileges, or immunities guaranteed by the Constitution or federal laws. A person can use § 1983 to remedy violations of any federal law unless that law does not create enforceable rights within the meaning of § 1983, or unless Congress has indicated in the law itself that § 1983 may not be used to enforce it.[45]

In the past, states have not been able to claim "sovereign immunity" (immunity from being sued because they are sovereign states) to avoid private lawsuits aimed at enforcing the Medicaid Act. Although the Eleventh Amendment has been interpreted to prevent a citizen from suing his or her own state for almost a century,[46] an exception to that rule created in the 1908 *Ex Parte Young* case prevents state officials from benefiting from sovereign immunity when they disobey federal law.[47]

Two cases, *Sabree v. Houston*,[48] decided in 2003, and *Westside Mothers v. Haveman*,[49] decided in 2001, illustrate how the the proponents of a civil rights roll back are challenging these precedents, thereby jeopardizing the ability of Medicaid beneficiaries to go to court. *Sabree* was a § 1983 suit filed by Pennsylvania Medicaid beneficiaries who had been waiting months—in some cases, years—for placement in intermediate-care facilities for the mentally retarded. Although the state was required to cover this service under the state Medicaid plan, individuals were told to wait.

The beneficiaries filed suit in federal court to get the state to provide the needed services. Rather than contest whether the claims were true, the attorneys representing Pennsylvania argued that the beneficiaries had no right to be heard in court. In January 2003, the district court judge agreed.

To support its ruling, the court relied almost exclusively on a 2002 Supreme Court case, *Gonzaga University v. Doe*,[50] in which the Court did three important things. First, it noted that, since 1981, the Court had only twice found that Spending Clause legislation confers federal rights that are enforceable through § 1983. Second, it clarified the test for deciding when Spending Clause legislation can be enforced under § 1983—federal law must contain rights-creating language stating that Congress intends for private individuals to be able to enforce the law. Third, applying this standard, the Court refused to allow individuals to sue the states to enforce the Spending Clause legislation at issue—the Family Educational Rights and Privacy Act (FERPA).[51] The *Sabree* District Court assumed that if individuals could not sue to enforce their federal rights under FERPA, neither could they sue under Medicaid to enforce their right to appropriate placement in intermediate-care facilities for the mentally retarded. Going further, the court said that beneficiaries could never privately enforce the Medicaid Act.

The beneficiaries appealed to the Third Circuit Court of Appeals, all the while needing the intermediate care services. The Third Circuit found flaws in the lower court's reasoning and reversed the decision. *Gonzaga* concerned FERPA, the Third Circuit pointed out, not the Medicaid Act. Although both statutes were enacted pursuant to Congress's power under the Spending Clause, the two acts have different structures, texts, purposes, and legislative histories. According to the Third Circuit, while the FERPA provisions at issue in *Gonzaga* were directed at the federal government, the Medicaid Act provisions at issue in *Sabree* unambiguously conferred an enforceable right on Medicaid beneficiaries.

The *Sabree* Circuit Court decision is good news for Medicaid beneficiaries. Unfortunately, the Pennsylvania Attorney General's decision to contest the beneficiaries' right to sue and the district court's holding are representative of the roadblocks now confronting individuals who seek to halt states' ongoing violations of the Medicaid Act. In the past two years, state attorneys have urged courts to adopt the *Sabree* District Court's reasoning in over fifty Medicaid cases.[52] The arguments are aimed at Medicaid more than any other Spending Clause enactment—not surprising, given that conservative policy-makers and jurists see Medicaid as the "mother of all spending programs." Unfortunately, some judges, most appointed by Presidents Ronald Reagan, George H. W. Bush, and George W. Bush, have agreed with the *Sabree* District Court in refusing to allow beneficiaries to enforce the Medicaid Act. The plaintiffs in these cases obtained no remedy. Even in cases that are ultimately successful, plaintiffs have sometimes had to wait years without needed services while attorneys argued about court access. Ultimately, the Supreme Court may decide to enter the debate.

In *Westside Mothers v. Haveman*,[53] another federal district court announced a radical and expansive view of state sovereign immunity that would have affected all legislation enacted by Congress pursuant to its Spending Clause authority.[54] In the case, a group of children eligible for Medicaid filed suit under § 1983 against the Michigan Medicaid officials, claiming that the state had not provided the early periodic screening, diagnostic, and treatment (EPSDT) services required by the Medicaid Act. Some children, for example, had not received mandatory check-ups, lead blood testing, or dental exams, and others had not even been informed of the existence of EPSDT.

The district court in *Westside Mothers* acknowledged that the suit's objective was "commendable," but held that it could not provide the children any relief.[55] In a detailed opinion, the court found that the state's sovereign immunity prevented citizens from suing to force Michigan to obey federal law, reasoning that Spending Clause legislation such as Medicaid was not "the supreme law of the land."[56] According to the court, therefore, Spending Clause enactments could not take precedence over state policies.[57]

Central to the district court's reasoning was the ability of the state to decide whether to participate in Medicaid. Because Michigan's participation was voluntary, the court held that Medicaid was merely a contract between the federal government and the participating state—not an entitlement.[58]

From this finding, the district court reached a number of conclusions that provided a basis for barring private enforcement of the Medicaid Act. First, if private suits to enforce Spending Clause legislation against the state were to be allowed, they had to be a clear part of the contract. Just because states agree to participate in the Medicaid program and accept federal funds does not mean that they agree to waive their sovereign immunity.[59] Second, the court concluded that *Ex Parte Young* did not apply because the case was merely a breach of contract action, while the exception only concerns allegations of noncompliance with federal laws. Therefore, the Eleventh Amendment, which gives states immunity from suits by their citizens, bars the suit. The court also found *Ex Parte Young* inapplicable because the Medicaid Act includes a remedial scheme allowing the Secretary of Health and Human Services to terminate federal funding to states not complying with federal requirements.[60] Third, the court held that Medicaid is not a "right secured by federal law," but a contract between the state and federal governments that cannot be enforced by someone not a party to that contract.[61] The *Westside Mothers* court found that because third-party beneficiaries could not enforce contracts when § 1983 was enacted in 1871, that statute could not be used to allow Medicaid beneficiaries (who the court characterized as third-party beneficiaries) to sue the states to enforce the contract with the federal government.[62] Finally, the court discounted the Supreme Court and lower court cases that recognized that under the Supremacy Clause, Spending Clause enactments such as Medicaid *do* take precedence over conflicting state actions,[63] and that individuals can bring *Ex Parte Young* actions to enforce those federal laws.[64]

On appeal, the Sixth Circuit Court of Appeals reversed the district court's decision.[65] The court's reasoning, however, continues to generate controversy because of the new legal ground it attempted to plow;[66] state attorneys continue to press its reasoning in Medicaid cases. Some district court judges have adopted parts of that reasoning,[67] and some recently-appointed federal Circuit Court of Appeals judges have supported the *Westside Mothers* decision (including Eleventh Circuit Judge William Pryor, who called the reasoning "brilliant" and "sublime," and Sixth Circuit Judge Jeffrey Sutton who, when he was an attorney, wrote an amicus brief that formed the basis for much of the district court's decision).

Equally troubling, the Court's most conservative justices agree with at least some of the district court's reasoning, and appear to be intent on eradicating the private enforcement of Medicaid (and other Spending Clause programs). In a 2003 Medicaid case, for example, Justice Clarence Thomas wrote a separate opinion to state that the health care providers who filed the case were merely third party beneficiaries of the Medicaid contract, and therefore should not be able to enforce the Act in court.[68] As with § 1983 cases, the Court may decide to examine these sovereign immunity issues in future cases.

Conclusion

The federal Medicaid program will face significant challenges in the coming years. Without universal health insurance coverage, the aging population will increasingly depend on Medicaid. At the same time, conservative policymakers and justices are seeking to "reform" Medicaid by blocking individual enforcement suits and ending the program's guarantee of legal rights. Individuals who depend on Medicare for themselves or a family member should watch these developments carefully, lobby to improve Medicaid benefits, and work to protect their rights to enforce that federal law.[69]

Endnotes

1. See 42 U.S.C. §§ 1396a(a)(10), 1396a(a)(8) (2000); *Schweiker v. Gray Panthers*, 453 U.S. 34, 36–37 (1981) ("An individual is entitled to Medicaid if he fulfills the criteria established by the State in which he lives."). See also, e.g., *Antrican v. Odom*, 290 F.3d 178, 191 (4th Cir. 2002) ("[T]he Medicaid Act clearly mandates that a State provide a certain level and quality of…care").

2. See *Faces of Medicaid*, The Kaiser Commission on Medicaid and the Uninsured (Apr. 2004), at http://www.kff.org/about/kcmu.cfm.

3. See Andy Schneider et al., *The Medicaid Resource Book*, The Kaiser Commission on Medicaid and the Uninsured (Jul. 2002) 1, at http://www.kff.org/about/kcmu.cfm.

4. See *Faces of Medicaid*, *supra* note 2.

5. Federal matching payments to states for Medicaid services can vary from fifty percent to eighty-three percent of total expenditures, with poorer per capita income states receiving higher federal payments. See 42 U.S.C.A. §§ 1396d(a), 1396d(b) (2001). Federal funding averaged fifty-seven percent in 1998. See *Medicaid: A Primer*, The Kaiser Commission on Medicaid and the Uninsured (Apr. 2001) 1, at http://www.kff.org/about/kcmu.cfm.

6. For an explanation of the eligibility rules, see *An Advocate's Guide to Medicaid*, National Health Law Program (June 2001) 3.3–3.6 (available from National Health Law Program, Los Angeles, CA). Given the strict eligibility requirements, it is not surprising that not all poor people qualify for Medicaid. In 1999, Medicaid covered only thirty-seven per-

cent of non-elderly Americans with incomes below the federal poverty level. See *The Kaiser Commission on Medicaid and the Uninsured, Health Insurance Coverage in America: 1999 Data Update*, Catherine Hoffman and Mary Pohl, eds., (Dec. 2000) 6, at http://www.kff .org/about/kcmu.cfm.

7. See 42 U.S.C.A. § 1396a(a)(10)(A)(i)(II) (2003). To be disabled, a person must have a "medically determinable physical or mental impairment which results in marked and severe functional limitation, and which can be expected to result in death or which has lasted or can be expected to last for a continuous period of not less than 12 months." 42 U.S.C.A. § 1382c(a) (2000).

8. See Id. at § 1396a(a)(17) (2000). For example, possession of a car with an equity value of $1500, or less at state option, makes an applicant ineligible for Medicaid. See, e.g., *Hazard v. Shalala*, 44 F.3d 399 (6th Cir. 1995) (upholding the $1500 limit on automobile exclusion).

9. Most immigrants who arrive legally in the U.S. after August 22, 1996 are barred from receiving full Medicaid benefits for at least five years. Medicaid will cover treatment of emergency medical conditions for these persons. See 8 U.S.C.A. § 1601 *et seq.* (2000); 42 U.S.C.A. §§ 1320b-7, 1396b(v) (2003).

10. See 42 C.F.R. § 435.403 (2000).

11. Medicare, the federally funded and administered program for the elderly and disabled, limits nursing home coverage. Commercial insurers have generally avoided the long-term care market and, while coverage is growing, quality policies are often affordable only to middle and upper income persons who do not qualify for Medicaid. See *Long-Term Care: Medicaid's Role and Challenges*, The Kaiser Commission on Medicaid and the Uninsured (Nov. 1999) 9–10, at http://www.kff.org/about/kcmu.cfm.

12. See *The Kaiser Commission on Medicaid and the Uninsured, Medicaid and Long-term Care*, Ellen O'Brien and Risa Elias, eds. (May 2004) 2–3, at http://www.kff.org/about/ kcmu.cfm.

13. See Leighton Ku and Jocelyn Guyer, *Medicaid Spending: Rising Again, but not to Crisis Level, Ctr. on Budget & Policy Priorities* (Apr. 20, 2001) 2, at http://www.cbpp.org (hereinafter "*Medicaid Spending: Rising Again*").

14. See *Medicare and You 2005*, U.S. Dep't of Health & Human Servs. Ctrs. for Medicare & Medicaid Servs., at http://www.medicare.gov.

15. See 42 U.S.C.A. §§ 1396a(a)(10)(E)(iii), 1396d(p) (2003).

16. *Medicaid Overview: Briefing Charts*, The Kaiser Commission on Medicaid and the Uninsured (Apr. 2001) 11, Figure 22, at http://www.kff.org/about/kcmu.cfm.

17. See *The Medicaid Program at a Glance*, The Kaiser Commission on Medicaid and the Uninsured (Jan. 2004) 1, at http://www.kff.org/about/kcmu.cfm.

18. Id.

19. Id. In 2002, Medicaid spending averaged $1,475 per child, compared to $12,764 for each elderly beneficiary and $11,468 for each disabled beneficiary. Id.

20. See *Medicaid: A Primer, supra* note 3, at 2.

21. See *The Kaiser Commission on Medicaid and the Uninsured, Uninsured in America*, Catherine Hoffman and Alan Schlobohm, eds., 2d Ed. (May 2000) 67, at http://www .kff.org/about/kcmu.cfm.

22. See Id. at 68–70.

23. See Id. at 71.

24. See 42 U.S.C.A. §§ 1396a(a)(10)(B), 1396a(a)(17) (2003).

25. See 42 C.F.R. § 440.230(b) (2000).

26. See 42 U.S.C.A. § 1396d(a)(1) (2003); 42 C.F.R. § 440.10(a) (2000).

27. See 42 U.S.C.A. § 1396d(a)(5)(A) (2003); 42 C.F.R. § 440.50 (2000).

28. See 42 U.S.C.A. §§ 1396a(a)(10)(A), 1396a(a)(43), 1396d(a)(4)(B), 1396d(r) (2003).

29. See 42 U.S.C.A. §§ 1396a(a)(10)(A), 1396d(a)(4)(A) (2003).

30. See 42 U.S.C.A. § 1396d(a)(12) (2003); 42 C.F.R. § 440.120 (2000).

31. See 42 U.S.C.A. § 1396d(a)(10) (2003); 42 C.F.R. § 440.100 (2000).

32. See 42 U.S.C.A. § 1396d(a)(11) (2003); 42 C.F.R. § 440.110 (2000).

33. See 42 U.S.C.A. § 1396d(a)(15) (2003); 42 C.F.R. § 483.400 (2000).

34. In fact, Medicaid was the product of a last-minute political compromise when the Medicare program was enacted. See Rand E. Rosenblatt, et al., *Law and the American Health Care System* (1997) 415–21.

35. *Friedman v. Berger*, 547 F.2d 724, 727 n. 7 (2d Cir. 1976) (J. Friendly).

36. See, e.g., *Wilder v. Va. Hosp. Ass'n*, 496 U.S. 498, 502 (1990) ("Although participation in the program is voluntary, participating States must comply with certain requirements imposed by the Medicaid Act (Act) and regulations promulgated by the Secretary of Health and Human Services"); *Schweiker*, 453 U.S. at 36–37 ("An individual is entitled to Medicaid if he fulfills the criteria established by the State in which he lives. State Medicaid plans must comply with requirements imposed both by the Act itself and by the Secretary of Health and Human Services").

37. U.S. Const. art. I, § 8, cl. 1. Numerous programs have been created pursuant to the Spending Clause, including public housing, food support, transportation, and disabilities education programs. These programs "are a pervasive feature of modern American governance and play an especially pivotal role in the lives of Americans who face limited opportunities and access to the levers of power." *Brief of Amici Curiae Catholic Charities*, AARP, et al., at 1, *Westside Mothers v. Havemen*, 289 F.3d 852 (6th Cir. 2002) (No. 01-1494) (on file with author).

38. See 42 U.S.C.A. § 1396a(a)(8) (Supp. 2003); 42 C.F.R. § 435.906 (2000).

39. See, e.g., *Parry v. Crawford*, 990 F. Supp. 1250 (D. Nev. 1998).

40. See, e.g., *Visser v. Taylor*, 756 F. Supp. 501 (D. Kan. 1990).

41. See, e.g., *Weaver v. Reagen*, 886 F.2d 194 (8th Cir. 1989).

42. See, e.g., *White v. Beal*, 555 F.2d 1146 (3d Cir. 1977).

43. See, e.g., *Hunter v. Chiles*, 944 F. Supp. 914 (S.D. Fla. 1996).

44. Congress has repeatedly considered removing the private right of enforcement and transforming Medicaid into a block grant program, which would provide an annual allocation to the states on which Congress puts a ceiling or cap. These efforts have, to date, failed. For an in depth discussion of these legislative efforts, see *Brief of Amici Curiae AARP*, SEIU, et al., *Clayworth v. Bonta*, 295 F. Supp.2d 1110 (E.D. Cal. 2003) (Nos. 04-15498, 04-15532) (on file with author). The Bush administration has repeatedly proposed this "reform" in the budgets it sends to Congress. Updates on the federal Medicaid budget process are available at www.healthlaw.org, the website of the National Health Law Program. At any given time, there is a real danger that proposals could pass. Although Medicaid is a relatively small portion of the total federal budget, it is a prime target of budget cutting because it must compete with larger but more politically popular entitlement programs such as Social Security, Medicare, and military and civilian retirement programs.

45. See *Wright v. Roanoke Redev. & Hous. Auth.*, 479 U.S. 418, 423 (1987). In *Wilder*, 496 U.S. at 522, the Supreme Court held that Medicaid does not include a sufficiently comprehensive remedial scheme to preclude enforcement of the Medicaid Act under § 1983. Whether a person may use § 1983 to enforce a particular federal right has historically turned

on three factors: first, whether the federal law clearly confers a right on the person initiating legal action; second, whether the statute identifies the person's rights well enough for the courts to enforce them; and third, whether the provision imposes binding obligations on the state. See, e.g., *Blessing v. Freestone*, 520 U.S. 329 (1997); *Wilder*, 496 U.S. at 509–10; *Wright*, 479 U.S. 418.

46. See *Hans v. Louisiana*, 134 U.S. 1 (1890). The Eleventh Amendment provides: "The Judicial power of the United States shall not be construed to extend to any suit in law or equity, commenced or prosecuted against one of the United States by Citizens of another State, or by Citizens or Subjects of any Foreign State." See also, e.g., *Green v. Mansour*, 474 U.S. 64, 68 (1985) ("[T]he availability of prospective relief of the sort awarded in *Ex Parte Young* gives life to the Supremacy Clause. Remedies designed to end a continuing violation of federal law are necessary to vindicate the federal interest in assuring the supremacy of that law"). The principle that government officials can be sued for injunctive relief can be traced to old English law. See, e.g., Louis L. Jaffe, Suits Against Governments and Officers: Sovereign Immunity, *77 Harv. L. Rev.* (1963) 1, 9 (discussing thirteenth century principles that the King's officers could be sued).

47. See *Ex parte Young*, 209 U.S. 123 (1908).

48. 245 F. Supp.2d 653 (E.D. Penn. 2003), *rev'd* sub nom. *Sabree v. Richman*, 367 F.3d 180 (3d Cir. 2004).

49. 133 F. Supp.2d 549 (E.D. Mich. 2001), rev'd, 289 F.3d 852 (6th Cir. 2002), *cert. denied*, 537 U.S. 1045 (2002).

50. 536 U.S. 273 (2002). For discussion of *Gonzaga's* effect on enforcement of a range of federal laws, see Jane Perkins, Using Section 1983 to Enforce Federal Laws, 39 *Clearinghouse Rev.* (Mar.–April 2005) 720.

51. The Supreme Court was also persuaded in part by the existence of an alternative scheme for seeking enforcement that had been written into the FERPA legislation.

52. For more information about these cases, please contact the author.

53. See 133 F. Supp.2d 549, *rev'd*, 289 F.3d 852, *cert. denied*, 537 U.S. 1045.

54. Many of Judge Cleland's ideas were taken from a friend of the court brief he requested from Jeffrey Sutton (now a Sixth Circuit judge) on behalf of the Michigan Municipal League Legal Defense Fund.

55. *Westside Mothers*, 133 F. Supp.2d at 552.

56. See U.S. Const. art. VI, §2.

57. *Westside Mothers*, 133 F. Supp.2d at 561–62.

58. Id. at 557–58, 561, 581–82. The court relied, in particular, on language from *Pennhurst State Sch. & Hosp. v. Halderman*, 451 U.S. 1, 17 (1981) ("Legislation enacted pursuant to the spending power is much in the nature of a contract; in return for federal funds, the States agree to comply with federally imposed conditions"). Notably, however, *Pennhurst* went on to apply the second and third prongs of the traditional enforcement test, finding that the provisions at issue were "precatory" and lacked sufficient clarity to be mandatory on the state. Id. Moreover, the district court's reasoning fails to acknowledge there are two choices for the state to make—first, whether to participate in the program, and second, whether to adhere to the federal requirements of the program.

59. Compare, e.g., 42 U.S.C. §1320a-2 (2000) (re-establishing private rights of action to enforce the Social Security Act as they existed prior to *Suter v. Artist M.*, 503 U.S. 347 (1992)).

60. In *Wilder*, the Court held that Medicaid does not contain an enforcement scheme sufficient to foreclose enforcement of the statute through § 1983. See *Wilder*, 496 U.S. at 522. Moreover, the Secretary has rarely—if ever—exercised this enforcement authority.

61. *Westside Mothers*, 133 F. Supp.2d at 557–59.

62. Id. at 577. Contra *Will v. Mich. Dep't of State Police*, 491 U.S. 58, 71 n. 10 (1989) (stating "official-capacity actions for prospective relief are not treated as actions against the State. This distinction is commonplace in sovereign immunity doctrine and would not have been foreign to the 19th century Congress that enacted § 1983").

63. See, e.g., *Townsend v. Swank*, 404 U.S. 282, 285 (1971) (holding in an *Ex parte Young* action that policies in the State of Illinois violated the Social Security Act and were therefore "invalid under the Supremacy Clause"); *Dalton v. Little Rock Family Planning Servs.*, 516 U.S. 474, 476 (1996) (per curium) (In a pre-emption case such as this, state law is displaced as inconsistent with the Medicaid statute "only to the extent that it actually conflicts with federal law.") (Internal quotation marks omitted); *Bennett v. Ky. Dep't of Educ.*, 470 U.S. 656, 669 (1985) ("Although we agree with the State that Title I grant agreements had a contractual aspect, the program cannot be viewed in the same manner as a bilateral contract governing a discrete transaction. Unlike normal contractual undertakings, federal grant programs originate in and remain governed by statutory provisions expressing the judgment of Congress concerning desirable public policy"); *Carleson v. Remillard*, 406 U.S. 598, 600 (1972). The *Westside Mothers* district court said this line of cases was called into question by *Alden v. Maine*, 527 U.S. 706 (1999). *Westside Mothers*, 133 F. Supp.2d at 561. However, *Alden*'s discussion is irrelevant to the question of whether Spending Clause enactments are supreme and, since *Alden*, the Supreme Court has held that they are. See *Norfolk S. Ry. Co. v. Shanklin*, 529 U.S. 344 (2000).

64. See, e.g., *Golden State Transit Corp. v. Los Angeles*, 493 U.S. 103 (1989); *Wilder*, 496 U.S. 498; *Wright*, 479 U.S. 418; *Me. v. Thiboutot*, 448 U.S. 1 (1980); *Edelman v. Jordan*, 415 U.S. 651 (1974); *Rosado v. Wyman*, 397 U.S. 397 (1970). See also 42 U.S.C.A. § 1320a-2 (2000) (re-establishing private rights of action to enforce the Social Security Act as they existed prior to *Suter*, 503 U.S. 347).

65. 289 F.3d 852, *cert. denied*, 537 U.S. 1045. See also *Antrican v. Buell*, 158 F. Supp.2d 663, *aff'd sub nom.*, *Antrican*, 290 F.3d 178, *cert denied*, 537 U.S. 973 (2002) (rejecting arguments that Medicaid is not the supreme law of the land because it is a Spending Clause enactment).

66. Six amici curiae briefs were filed asking the Sixth Circuit to reverse the district court decision. These briefs were filed by the Department of Justice, the City of Detroit, a number of health care provider associations (including the American Academy of Pediatrics, the National Association of Public Hospitals and Health Systems, the American Hospital Association, and the National Association of Community Health Centers), over seventy law professors, community based groups (including Catholic Charities USA, AARP, National Mental Heath Association, the ARC of the U.S., National Alliance for the Mentally Ill, and Older Women's League of Michigan), and a group of congressmen. Two briefs asked the Sixth Circuit to uphold the decision. These briefs were filed by then-Governor John Engler, the Michigan Municipal League, and the Texas Justice Foundation, a nonprofit foundation established to litigate and educate in cases involving private property rights, limited government, and free enterprise.

67. See, e.g., *Sanders v. Kan. Dep't of Soc. & Rehab. Servs.*, 317 F. Supp.2d 1233 (D. Kan. 2004) (on appeal to the Tenth Circuit Court of Appeals).

68. See *Pharm. Research & Mfrs. of Am. v. Walsh*, 538 U.S. 644, 682–83 (2003) (Thomas, J., concurring).

69. For information about congressional and court developments, see National Health Law Program, at www.healthlaw.org (court watch folder and alerts).

CHAPTER 14

THE ENVIRONMENT

Permitted to Pollute: The Rollback of Environmental Justice

Olga Pomar[*] and Rachel D. Godsil[†]

On a hazy August 2003 afternoon, children slide and swing at a playground in the Waterfront South neighborhood of Camden, NJ. In most places, such a picture would be a happy one. Immediately beside the playground, however, are the St. Lawrence Cement factory's smoke stacks. Behind the playground is the county sewage treatment plant. On a "clear" day, the county waste incinerator is visible across the street. The grass around the playground is covered with broken glass. And all the children are African American.

Camden residents have struggled against environmental racism for decades. Despite their resistance, however, officials continue to allow waste facilities and heavy industry to locate in Camden's low-income communities of color. In 2001, residents filed a civil rights lawsuit, claiming that the issuance of a yet another permit violated the Environmental Protection Agency's (EPA) Title VI regulations. In an historic decision, the district court issued an injunction, halting the operation of a cement grinding facility in Waterfront South. Five days later, in Alexander v. Sandoval,[‡] *the Supreme Court held that private citizens could not bring suit to enforce the Title VI regulations, and the injunction was lifted.*

The Waterfront South story illustrates the impact of the Court's rollback of civil rights on communities of color in their fight against environmental racism. In a single decision, the Court deprived a politically powerless low-income community of a crucial legal tool in its battle against a corporate giant and a state bureaucracy. Despite continued organizing and legal resistance, the cement company now spews toxins into Waterfront South.

---

[*] Attorney, South Jersey Legal Services. Lead counsel in *South Camden Citizens in Action v. NJ Dept. of Environmental Protection and St. Lawrence Cement.*

[†] Professor of Law, Seton Hall Law School.

[‡] *Alexander v. Sandoval,* 532 U.S. 275 (2001).

೨ል   ೨ል   ೨ል

Environmental Racism

The pollution experienced by Camden's mainly African American and Latino residents is not uncommon—researchers have found that the more African American and Latino residents there are in a community, the more likely the community is to be polluted.[1] Further, people of color live mainly in urban areas, which are more likely to suffer chronic air quality problems.[2] Air pollution, including ozone and particulate matter,[3] causes short-term adverse health effects (particularly for children and the elderly) and aggravates chronic conditions such as asthma, bronchitis, and cardiovascular disease.[4] According to the EPA, repeated exposure to ozone can cause lung inflammation and "damage children's developing lungs, which may lead to permanent reductions in lung function."[5]

Since the specter of "environmental racism" was first recognized in the 1980s, communities of color have organized for a healthier environment.[6] Activists have challenged industrial polluters, officials who have failed to respond to lead paint contamination and air and water pollution, and agribusinesses that use pesticides.[7] These battles have often been waged at the grassroots level, and have resulted in some stunning victories.[8]

Political battles, however, are not always winnable. In such cases, communities have been forced into litigation. Some states, including California and New York, have enacted environmental review laws.[9] Others, including New Jersey, have either failed to enact environmental review laws or have enacted laws that provide little protection.[10]

Prior to the Court's recent rollback, residents in states with weak environmental laws could turn to federal civil rights laws. This chapter tells the story of Waterfront South, in which residents' civil rights were rendered meaningless when the Court held that that some federal rights are unenforceable in court.

Camden and Waterfront South: Studies in Environmental Racism

A former industrial city, Camden houses close to eighty thousand people, most of whom are African American or Latino.[11] Residents struggle to create a sense of community despite severe poverty and the noxious environment (polluted land and abandoned factories that were left over from the city's manufacturing base). Camden is the poorest city in New Jersey, and one of the poorest in the nation; per capita income is approximately ten thousand dollars (less than half of the county and state income levels),[12] the poverty rate is over thirty percent,[13] infant mortality rates equal those of developing nations,[14] and both the murder rate and the school drop-out rates are the highest in the state. The city is filled with vacant lots and abandoned houses.

Waterfront South, a neighborhood less than one square mile long at the southern tip of the city, is particularly devastated and environmentally degraded. Sandwiched between the interstate highway and the Delaware River, the neighborhood encompasses most of the South Jersey Port (the former base for a major shipbuilding company), a historic residential core, and a deteriorated commercial corridor. Industrial sites are interspersed between schools, homes, and churches.

Waterfront South is beset with environment hazards that have been largely ignored by the government. It contains two Superfund sites (a federal program established in 1980 and administered by the EPA in cooperation with individual states and tribal governments to locate, investigate, and clean up uncontrolled and/or abandoned hazardous waste sites)—the General Gas Mantle site and the Martin Aaron Drum site.

The General Gas Mantle site contains radioactive thorium, the by-product of a gas lantern mantle manufacturer. After the company closed in 1940, the property was used as a warehouse. Workers were exposed to radon gas and tracked radioactive materials through surrounding neighborhoods. The New Jersey Department of Environmental Protection (NJDEP) discovered the radioactivity in 1981, but did not tear down the building until 2002. The radioactive soil at the site and in nearby backyards and basements has yet to be removed. Families living beside the Superfund site were only relocated in 2002. The site's long-term damage to residents is as yet unknown. The EPA, however, has estimated that the long-term exposure to low-level radiation has increased their cancer risk by 1.8 percent.[15]

The second Superfund site was created by a hazardous drum "recycler" who flushed out the toxic contents of drums into drainage basins. The area became contaminated with carcinogens, volatile organic compounds, PCB's, arsenic, and barium. This site, too, is still awaiting an EPA clean-up. In light of the limited funding available for Superfund clean-ups under the Bush administration, the wait is likely to be long.

Waterfront South contains thirteen other sites that are contaminated with lead, mercury, tetracholoroethylene, trichchoroethylene, and other dangerous contaminants. The active industries in the area are equally troubling—four junkyards, two scrap metal recyclers, several auto body shops, a paint and varnish company, a chemical company, three food processing plants, a hazardous waste container recycler and, just north of the neighborhood, the large and dusty G.P. Gypsum plant—which contaminate the soil, pollute the air and by relying on diesel trucks to transport materials, cause additional damage to the environment.

County and state officials continue to permit dangerous facilities to be built in Waterfront South. In the early 1980s, the county chose a Waterfront South sewage plant to process the sewage from thirty-five mostly affluent and white municipalities, constructed an open-air sewage-sludge composting facility beside the plant, and permitted the construction of a regional trash-to-steam incinerator (one of the largest in the state) less than a mile away. In the early 1990s, Waterfront South was chosen as the site for a power plant. Despite strong community opposition, NJDEP freely granted permits for all of these facilities.

Waterfront South was once a reasonably livable neighborhood. Long-time resident and community leader Phyllis Holmes was the first African American to move onto her block thirty years ago. She recalls enjoying her neighbors and the friendly community atmosphere. The quality of life dramatically changed with the arrival of the sewage plant, the incinerator, and other polluters. For decades, residents have endured toxic fumes, dust, horrific odors, and noise. Truck drivers have violated traffic codes and endangered children by taking shortcuts down residential streets.

Waterfront South has one of the state's highest readings for inhalable particulate pollution, which are known to cause lung cancer, aggravate respiratory illnesses such as asthma, emphysema, and bronchitis, trigger cardiovascular symptoms, and bring on premature death.[16] In addition, the ozone levels exceed federal health-based air quality standards.[17] In the last decade, the air pollution has caused a dramatic increase in the rates of respiratory problems. One study showed that sixty-one percent of residents experienced some type of respiratory symptoms compared to thirty-five percent in another Camden neighborhood.[18] At a local elementary school, almost a quarter of students have asthma.

The quality of daily life has been most affected by the sewage treatment plant. The plant reeks of raw sewage. According to the school principal, children consider recess a punishment. Many people have found their senses of smell impaired.[19] Residents stay indoors on summer days, leaving backyards and stoops vacant. Moreover, the community became stigmatized as families felt too embarrassed to invite friends and relatives to visit.

Between 1970 and 1990, Camden suffered from increasing blight; and Waterfront South was especially devastated. Many residents and businesses relocated to more desirable areas in the city and suburbs. City services decreased.

Housing values dropped. Waterfront South now has fewer than two thousand residents, half of whom are children.[20]

Standing Up for the Community

Camden has long benefited from community activism—a labor movement in the early twentieth century, civil rights activists during the 1960s and 1970s (who challenged housing discrimination and urban renewal policies), and community members organizing in the 1980s and 1990s against the construction of a prison and an incinerator.

Camden's recent environmental justice struggle was initiated by a group of Waterfront South residents known as South Camden Citizens in Action (SCCIA). Formed in 1997 when a local nonprofit organization sponsored a grassroots neighborhood planning project to explore how living conditions could be improved, SCCIA's leaders were mostly very low-income African American women, some in poor health, who had lived in Camden a long time and who shared a commitment to improving the community. Until her death from cancer in February 2004, SCCIA President Bonnie Sanders, a long-time resident and leader in community environmental struggles, was raising a granddaughter and a foster child (both of whom suffered from respiratory ailments) in a row house in the city's residential core.

SCCIA found itself focused on environmental problems. At the first community meeting, residents decided to tackle the odor from the sewage plant. SCCIA developed a record of odor violations, and recruited the support of local officials. When NJDEP failed to address the complaints, SCCIA hired a public interest lawyer to bring a citizen lawsuit to enforce the odor regulations,[21] and won a settlement requiring the facility to upgrade its odor controls. While the litigation was still pending, an EPA representative informed residents about one of the Superfund sites; residents learned that their neighborhood had been contaminated by low-level radiation for over eighty years. SCCIA members evaluated the EPA's remediation plans, and the EPA accepted their recommendation that all contaminated materials be removed.

SCCIA began to make strong demands, and soon acquired a formidable reputation. Soon after its initial successes, however, SCCIA lost the support of its sponsoring nonprofit and began to function as a volunteer organization. Leaders met in one another's living rooms and donated their own money for refreshments and supplies.

In 1999, then, this fragile group confronted a major environmental justice struggle: the St. Lawrence Cement Company (SLC) decided to locate its new cement-grinding facility in Waterfront South.

The Fight against St. Lawrence Cement

SLC is one of the world's largest cement manufacturers. In March 1999, SLC negotiated a lease with the South Jersey Port Corporation to construct a cement-grinding facility on twelve acres in Waterfront South. SLC would ship Italian blast furnace slag to a dock in Camden, truck it three miles to the Waterfront South facility, and grind it into fine powder for use as a cement additive. Trucks would then distribute the product throughout the northeastern U.S. Operations would generate over seventy-seven thousand diesel truck trips through the neighborhood and would emit a hundred tons of pollutants annually—almost sixty tons of inhalable particulates (PM-10),[22] and a significant amount of the smallest and therefore most dangerous particulates (PM-2.5).[23]

The facility, like most industries that locate in poor and minority communities, would offer the community no benefits. Because it would be located on state land, SLC would pay Camden no property taxes. The mechanized cement-grinding operations would produce only fifteen jobs. Worse still, the facility would discourage more desirable and labor-intensive businesses from locating nearby. Indeed, the proliferation of waste disposal and recycling facilities, transfer stations, and heavy industry in Waterfront South has not alleviated Camden's high unemployment and poverty rates, which continue to rise along with pollution levels.

SLC sought to secure all kinds of support—community, political, and governmental—for their construction plans. The company hired a public relations consultant, and paid for lobbyists in Trenton (the state capital) and DC. After signing the lease, SLC began discussing its plans with NJDEP. Significantly, because port land was exempt from zoning and planning, the company did not need local board approvals. In August 1999, SLC submitted its permit application to the Department and conducted an aggressive public relations campaign to win the support of local churches, nonprofit organizations, and community groups. It held community meetings, organized a community advisory panel, and even paid for experts to review the permit application.

From the start, SCCIA members were suspicious of the company's tactics. Eventually, SCCIA members saw that SLC was trying to use neighborhood organizations to demonstrate that it had community support, and opposed the company with petitions, letters, neighborhood speak-outs, and independent meetings with NJDEP officials.

The NJDEP evaluation of SLC's permit was troubling. NJDEP applied the 1987 PM-10 standard then in effect, even though the standard was inadequate to protect human health.[24] NJDEP did not investigate the SLC's more dangerous PM-2.5 emissions, or the effects of the diesel truck fumes on air quality (NJDEP was under no legal obligation to do so because the Clean Air Act does not include such "mobile source emissions" in permitting review). Nor did NJDEP consider the local conditions, the potential cumulative and synergistic effects of the pollution, the poor health of the residents, or whether its permitting decisions disproportionately burdened African American and Latino residents with environmental hazards.

SLC took full advantage of the New Jersey state law that allows companies to construct facilities at their own risk prior to the final issuance of permits.[25] By the time NJDEP issued a draft permit and scheduled the first and only public hearing in 2000, construction of the $50 million facility was over half complete. Some residents were lulled into submission by the early construction, reasonably viewing SCCIA's campaign as futile and the public hearing process as meaningless. Still, over 120 people attended the public hearing, most opposing the plant based on civil rights and health concerns. The opposition had no effect. As SCCIA President Sanders later told an NJDEP official, "There was a public hearing, but no one got heard."

In October 2000, SCCIA filed administrative civil rights complaints with both NJDEP and the EPA, contending that the facility would have a discriminatory impact on African American and Latino residents. Neither agency responded. On October 31, 2000, NJDEP issued the final permits, and litigation became the only option for continuing the struggle.

On February 13, 2001, SCCIA filed a lawsuit in a district court to prevent SLC from starting operations. SCCIA did not raise any environmental claims, but rather argued that residents' civil rights had been violated—a strategic decision that came about when the group saw that it would be impossible to prove a technical violation of the Clean Air Act. SCCIA hoped to prove that NJDEP had violated federal civil rights regulations (enacted under Title VI of the Civil Rights Act of 1964)[26] because NJDEP had ignored the permit's discriminatory *effects*, and had therefore perpetuated environmental racism. SCCIA also alleged violation of the Fair Housing Act,[27] and intentional discrimination in violation of Title VI and the Equal Protection Clause of the Constitution.

On April 19, 2001, Judge Stephen Orlofsky issued his first ruling. Along with a detailed description of the siting and applicable environmental regulations, the 140-page opinion described the already dire circumstances in Waterfront South, noting the excessive number of noxious facilities, the truck traffic, and the high rates of respiratory ailments. The court considered the question of "whether a recipient of EPA funding has an obligation under Title VI to consider racially discriminatory disparate impacts when determining whether to issue a permit, in addition to compliance with applicable environmental standards."[28] Judge Orlofsky found that NJDEP did have such an obligation, relying on the EPA regulations to Title VI that prohibit recipients such as NJDEP from "utilizing 'criteria and methods' which have the 'purpose or effect' of discrimination."[29] He found that these regulations necessarily impose a burden on recipients "to consider the potential adverse, disparate impacts of their permitting decisions."[30]

Judge Orlofsky ordered NJDEP to conduct such an analysis within thirty days. Based on the area's environmental and health conditions and the harm likely to result from SLC's operations, he concluded that SCCIA would likely prevail on the merits of the case. Most importantly, he enjoined operation of the cement-grinding facility.[31]

Judge Orlofsky's decision drew national attention. Not only was it a major victory for environmental justice advocacy, but it marked the first time in U.S. history that a court found a permitting agency, like NJDEP, to have violated plaintiffs' civil rights. The victory, however, was short-lived. Only five days later, the Supreme Court decided *Alexander v. Sandoval*, holding that Congress did not intend to provide citizens with the right to enforce the Title VI regulations—the heart of SCCIA's case.[32]

Despite *Sandoval*, Judge Orlofsky kept the injunction in place and allowed SCCIA to amend its complaint to include a claim under § 1983 (the Supreme Court had previously held that § 1983 provides a remedy for the deprivation of any "rights secured by the Constitution and the laws").[33] SCCIA therefore argued that § 1983 provided them with a private right of action to enforce the Title VI regulations. Judge Orlofsky agreed, issuing a second decision.[34] This was the first decision to interpret *Sandoval*, and it offered a hopeful roadmap for civil rights litigants nationally.[35]

SLC and NJDEP appealed both trial court decisions. In June 2001, the Third Circuit Court of Appeals lifted Judge Orlofsky's injunction and allowed the cement company to begin operations. In December of that year, the Court reversed the trial court's decision to allow SCCIA to proceed on their § 1983 claim. The circuit court acknowledged that rights created by federal statutes are often enforceable through § 1983 suits, but held that the Title VI regulations fell within an exception to this rule.[36] Specifically, the right SCCIA sought to enforce—the right to be free from practices that had a disparate racial impact—were created by federal regulations, not by Title VI itself. Based on this distinction, the Third Circuit held that the EPA's Title VI regulations were not enforceable through § 1983.[37]

As a result of *Sandoval* and the Third Circuit's decision, federal courts lack the power to enforce Title VI regulations. Although NJDEP's permitting practices violate those regulations by having a disparate impact on African Americans and Latinos, New Jersey residents cannot sue to challenge those practices.

EPA Enforcement of Environmental Justice?

The Title VI regulations prohibiting federally-funded agencies from engaging in discriminatory practices are still in force.[38] Now, however, after rulings in cases such as *Sandoval* and *South Camden*, individuals and communities are forced to rely upon federal agencies to enforce these protections.[39] The EPA has the authority to refuse, delay, or discontinue EPA funding to any program that has the "effect of subjecting a person to discrimination because of race, color, or national origin."[40] Sadly, the EPA's enforcement record has been abysmal; communities like Waterfront South, therefore, have little reason to expect that the EPA will protect them against discrimination.

Although the Title VI regulations were promulgated in 1972, they were ignored until political pressure from communities and activists led President Clinton to issue Executive Order 12,898, "Federal Actions to Address Environmental Justice in Minority Populations and Low-Income Populations," in 1994.[41] The order did not contain a private right of enforcement, but instead directed agencies to develop environmental justice strategies. Nonetheless, many were hopeful that it would result in meaningful change.[42]

This hope has not been realized under either the Clinton or Bush administrations. According to the National Academy of Public Administration (NAPA) and the EPA's own inspector general, few substantive changes in environmental policy have occurred. The Bush administration has not included environmental justice as "part of EPA's core mission,"[43] and has even supported environmental policies harming low-income communities and communities of color.[44]

In light of the Bush administration's track record on environmental justice, it is not surprising that EPA's enforcement of Title VI regulations has not favored communities experiencing unfair environmental burdens. EPA has not yet issued a final Title VI guidance, lending uncertainty to its complaint processing. Still, eighty-six communities filed complaints between 1993 and 2003, claiming that their state or local environmental permitting process was discriminatory.[45] Most were rejected without any investigation, and thirteen were accepted for investigation, a few of which were informally resolved. None resulted in a finding of agency discrimination, much less an agency losing federal funding.

Conclusion

The ultimate resolution of the South Camden lawsuit remains unknown. SCCIA's intentional discrimination claim remains, and SCCIA's counsel has added a state law nuisance claim against SLC[46]—both are expected to proceed to trial in 2005. Meanwhile, SLC's plant spews invisible but dangerous particulates into the air. On most days, dust from slag piles blows about the streets. Diesel trucks rumble through the neighborhood, and children breathe unhealthy air.

Endnotes

1. See, e.g. Luke Cole and Sheila Foster, *From the Ground Up: Environmental Racism and the Rise of the Environmental Justice Movement* (2001) 167–84 (describing studies).

2. See *Environmental Protection Agency's Draft Report on the Environment 2003*, 1–5, 4–7.

3. Id.

4. Id. at 1–4, 1–13, 1–15.

5. Id. at 4–15.

6. See generally Robert D. Bullard, Anatomy of Environmental Racism and the Environmental Justice Movement, *Confronting Environmental Racism: Voices from the Grass Roots* (1993).

7. Id.

8. Id.

9. See, e.g., Luke Cole, Environmental Justice Litigation: Another Stone in David's Sling, *21 Fordham Urb. L. J.* (1994) 523; New York State Environmental Quality Review Act, *N.Y. Envtl. Conserv. Law* §§ 8-0101 to 8-0117 (McKinney 1984 and Supp. 1994).

10. See, e.g. Rachel D. Godsil, Viewing the Cathedral from Behind the Color Line: Property Rules, Liability Rules and Environmental Racism, *53 Emory L. J.* (2005) 1807.

11. Only 7.1 percent of Camden city residents are non-Hispanic whites, compared to almost seventy percent of Camden county's residents. See U.S. 2000 Census Data.

12. U.S. 2000 Census Data.

13. See Id.

14. See Ctr. for Health Statistics, NJ Dep't of Health & Senior Servs., New Jersey Health Statistics 1998: Table M43. Infant and Fetal Mortality in Selected Municipalities. Http://www.state.nj.us/health/chs/stats98/m43.htm.

15. The EPA considers one in ten thousand to one in a million an "acceptable" cancer risk. The elevated risk found here of 1.8 in one hundred grossly exceeds this standard.

16. New Jersey DEP 2000 Air Quality Report, *Environmental Protection Agency's Draft Report on the Environment 2003.*

17. Id. Camden is ranked as being in "severe non-attainment" for ozone pollution. Ozone pollution, like particulates, causes and aggravates respiratory ailments.

18. Pamela Dalton, *Monell Chem. Senses Ctr., Odor, Annoyance, and Health Symptoms in a Residential Community Exposed to Industrial Odors* (Nov. 1997) (unpublished manuscript on file with author).

19. See Dalton study, cited above, endnote 6.

20. See, e.g. Godsil, Viewing the Cathedral from Behind the Color Line.

21. The lawsuit was brought on behalf of SCCIA by Jerome Balter, Esq. of the Public Interest Law Center of Philadelphia.

22. PM-10 is particulate matter sized ten microns or smaller.

23. PM-2.5 is particulate matter sized 2.5 microns or smaller.

24. In 1997, after studying extensive scientific research, the EPA issued a more stringent PM-2.5 standard that was immediately challenged by industry groups. Although the Supreme Court upheld its validity, it has not yet been put into effect. *American Trucking Assn. v. EPA,* 175 F.3d 1027 (D.C. Cir. 1999), modified on reh'g, 195 F.3d 4 (DC Cir. 1999), aff'd in part, rev'd in part sub nom. *Whitman v. American Trucking Assn,* 531 U.S. 457 (2001).

25. New Jersey law allows the company to construct but not operate the facility once the application is deemed administratively complete but before the Department of Environmental Protection issues a "permit to construct." NJ Stat. Ann. § 26:2C-9.2(j) (West 2001); NJ Admin. Code § 7:27–8.24 (2001). Because the developer may not hold the department liable for any losses if the department ultimately denies the permit, the construction is "at risk" to the business. Id.

26. Title VI of the Civil Rights Act of 1964, 42 U.S.C. § 2000d *et seq.*; EPA Title VI regulations, 40 C.F.R. Part 7.

27. 42 U.S.C. § 3601 *et seq.*

28. *S. Camden Citizens in Action v. NJ Dep't of Env. Protection,* 145 F. Supp. 2d 446, 474 (D. NJ 2001).

29. Id. at 476.

30. Id. at 480.

31. Id. at 497–505.

32. See generally *Alexander v. Sandoval,* 532 U.S. 275 (2001)

33. *Monroe v. Pape,* 365 U.S. 167 (1961) (holding that § 1983 provides individuals a right to bring suit to enforce their constitutional rights).

34. *South Camden Citizens in Action v. NJ Dep't of Env. Protection,* 145 F. Supp. 2d 505 (D. NJ 2001)

35. The precedential value of the decision is reflected in the number of amicus curiae briefs submitted on appeal for both sides. Major civil rights groups (e.g., the NAACP, the Puerto Rican Legal Defense Fund, and the ACLU) and major environmental organizations (e.g., the Natural Resources Defense Council, Environmental Defense, and the Sierra Club) supported SCCIA, while industry groups (e.g., the Chamber of Commerce, the National Association of Manufacturers, and the Washington Legal Fund) filed briefs on behalf of the appellants. A total of thirteen amicus briefs, signed by forty-nine organizations and individuals, were filed.

36. South Camden Citizens in Action, 274 F.3d 771, 779 (3d Cir. 2001).

37. Id.

38. See 40 C.F.R. 7.35(b)(2002).

39. 532 U.S. at 293, see also U.S. Commission on Civil Rights, Redefining Rights in America: The Civil Rights Record of the George W. Bush Administration, 2001–2004 (Draft Report for Commissioners' Review (Sept. 2004) 73.

40. Nondiscrimination in Programs Receiving Federal Assistance from the Environmental Protection Agency—Effectuation of Title VI of the Civil Rights Act of 1964, 38 Fed. Reg. 17,968, 17,969 (1973).

41. Id. at 74.

42. See U.S. Commission on Civil Rights: Not in My Backyard: Executive Order 12,898 and Title VI as Tools for Achieving Environmental Justice (Oct. 2003) 4.

43. Redefining Rights at 75.

44. Examples include the "Clean Skies Act" which despite its propitious title allows more air pollution in some regions and repeals the current requirement that old polluting facilities that were never regulated by the Clean Air Act update their pollution control equipment if they wish to expand their production. Id at 78. These older facilities are disproportionately in communities of color.

45. Not in My Backyard at 58.

46. *South Camden Citizens in Action v. NJ Dep't of Env. Protection*, 254 F. Supp.2d 486 (D. NJ 2003).

CHAPTER 15

OUR CRIMINAL JUSTICE SYSTEM

Federalism, Race, and Criminal Justice

Michelle Alexander[*]

"This is a case about federalism."[†] *That is the opening line of a 1991 Supreme Court decision denying Roger Keith Coleman the right to appeal his death sentence because his lawyers filed his appeal three days late. Those six words extinguished any lingering doubt about whether federalism—the division of power between the states and the federal government—is the friend of criminal defendants. Emboldened by its slim 5-4 majority, the right wing justices have since deferred to the states by refusing to intervene in, or even review, criminal cases involving alleged constitutional violations by state or local officials. This brash display of states' rights has obliterated the rights of criminal defendants, particularly those facing execution. As Justice Harry Blackmun noted in despair in 1993, the Court has displayed an "obvious eagerness to do away with any restriction on the States' power to execute whomever and however they please."*[‡]

The public views federalism as a technical, abstract concept that does not impact their daily lives. Because the media and mainstream political discourse portrays criminal defendants as dangerous, morally bankrupt individuals, it is difficult to cultivate public interest in, much less outrage over, the evisceration of defendants' constitutional protections in the Court's opaque federalism decisions. And yet, I believe, the hard work must be done.

Today, federalism and criminal justice concerns are expressed primarily in scholarly journals, outside the earshot of the public and most members of the judicial branch. While communities of color may bemoan rising incarceration rates, their

---

[*] Associate Professor of Law and Director of the Civil Rights Clinic at Stanford Law School. This chapter is adapted from a speech given at the Equal Justice Society Conference at Harvard Law School on April 5, 2002. At that time, I was Director of the Racial Justice Project for the ACLU of Northern California.

[†] *Coleman v. Thompson*, 501 U.S. 722, 726 (1991).

[‡] *Herrera v. Collins*, 506 U.S. 390, 446 (1993) (Blackmun, J., dissenting).

complaints about the criminal justice system are often diffuse, ranging from griev-ances over discriminatory police practices and biased juries to the insufficient re-sources that are devoted to fighting crime in poor communities. In the absence of a coherent critique of our criminal justice system — one that explains the system's role in preserving racial inequality — the work of civil rights advocates holds lit-tle chance of long-term success.

This chapter will begin a dialogue about federalism, race, and criminal justice that situates the status of criminal defendants, as well as the concept of federal-ism itself, in the relevant social, historical, and political context. Hopefully this will help lay the foundation for strategic political action to challenge both racial bias in the criminal justice system and the phenomenon of mass incarceration.

Contextualizing Federalism

I first became interested in placing federalism in a historical context when I was invited to speak on a panel at a Harvard Law School conference cele-brating the birth of the Equal Justice Society.[1] I must confess that I was initially puzzled by the panel's title: "Federalism's Emerging Threat to Civil Rights." Hadn't federalism always threatened civil rights? As an African American woman lawyer, I had always thought so. Federalism — at least as articulated by the Federalist Society — consistently privileges the rights of states, localities, and their officials over the rights of people traditionally lacking political power and suffering discrimination. In fact, it seems fair to say that the history of fed-eralism has in fact been the history of propertied white men attempting to con-trol black and brown people for economic and political benefit, while seeking a deregulated economic and political environment for themselves.

Supporters of modern federalism would argue that such a definition is a gross over-simplification and that federalism offers a more principled and nu-anced approach to the relationship between the federal government and the states, one rooted in the belief that freedom, liberty, and individual auton-omy can only be maximized with a limited federal government.[2] They would argue that federalism was conceived of not as a tool for oppression, but as an instrument of liberation. A majority of the Supreme Court has embraced this sentiment, justifying its Federalism Revolution as a way of enhancing liberty.[3] In the words of Chief Justice William Rehnquist: "This constitutionally man-dated division of authority 'was adopted by the Framers to ensure protection of our fundamental liberties.'"[4]

The Federalist Society insists that its version of federalism is consistent with the intentions of the Founding Fathers.[5] To be sure, the Founding Fathers adopted a Constitution explicitly designed to maintain an extraordinary form of social control of black and brown people—slavery—while at the same time granting propertied white men freedom of speech, freedom of religion, and a host of other rights.

The Fourteenth Amendment was designed to correct this flaw by granting racial minorities equal treatment under the law. During the Reconstruction Era, this promise was nearly realized. After some progress, however, the crude federalist argument reemerged and a new system of coercion and control was imposed on blacks—Jim Crow segregation.[6] Jim Crow was justified not only on the grounds of white supremacy, but also on the grounds that states and localities should be free to oppress African Americans without federal interference.

What is the New Threat to Civil Rights?

Most Americans today can look back and see slavery and Jim Crow laws for what they were—extraordinary and immoral forms of social control used to oppress black and brown people. However, few believe that a similar form of social control exists today. What I have come to recognize is that, contrary to popular belief, a new form of social control does exist, as disastrous and morally indefensible as Jim Crow—the mass incarceration of people of color.

There is an important story to be told that helps explain the role of the criminal justice system in resurrecting, in a new guise, the same policies of racial segregation, political disenfranchisement, and social stigmatization that have long oppressed and controlled all people of color, particularly African Americans. The story begins with federalism and its evolving methods of maintaining white supremacy. A recent twist has been added; one that the civil rights community has failed to explain to those who do not read reports issued by the Bureau of Justice Statistics or Supreme Court decisions.

In 1980, 330,000 people were incarcerated in federal and state prisons[7]—the vast majority of whom were people of color.[8] Since then, the number has more than quadrupled to over 1.3 million.[9] When prison and jail populations are combined, the number jumps to over two million.[10] Although African American men comprise less than seven percent of the population, they comprise half of the prison and jail population.[11] Today, one out of three African American men is either in prison, on probation, or on parole.[12] Latinos are not far behind. They are the fastest growing racial group being imprisoned, comprising 10.9 percent of all state and federal inmates in 1985, and nineteen percent in 2003.[13]

We know how this happened. In 1980, the Reagan administration ushered in the War on Drugs, another major backlash against civil rights. Although we typically think of the Reagan era backlash as attacking affirmative action and civil rights laws, the War on Drugs is perhaps the most sweeping and damaging manifestation of deliberate indifference—or downright hostility—to communities of color. This war, which continues today, has nothing to do with solving drug abuse, and everything to do with creating a political environment in which communities of color can be lawfully targeted for mass incarceration.[14]

Not unlike slavery and Jim Crow, mass incarceration provides the white elite with social benefits. By segregating, incarcerating, and rendering unemployable huge segments of the black and brown population, the racial hierarchy remains intact. By denying blacks an equal and adequate education, barring them from certain forms of employment, and relegating them to the worst neighborhoods, the white elite has ensured that whites will never occupy the bottom rung of that hierarchy. Today, slavery and Jim Crow laws no longer exist, and affirmative action has opened doors to some, upsetting the racial caste system. Mass incarceration, however, has emerged as a new, and arguably more durable, form of social control.[15]

In addition to protecting their social position, mass incarceration provides white elites with clear economic and political benefits. The prison industry is hugely profitable. Marc Mauer's excellent book *Race to Incarcerate* documents the unprecedented expansion of our criminal justice system and the ways that the race to incarcerate has devastated communities of color.[16] He cites promotional literature from the prison industry, one piece of which stated: "While arrests and convictions are steadily on the rise, profits are to be made—profits from crime. Get in on the ground floor of this booming industry now."[17] Prisons have become central to the development of many small, predominately white, rural communities, not unlike the economic base formerly provided by plantations in the rural South.[18] Moreover, the Thirteenth Amendment, which bars slavery, provides an exception for forced labor in prisons.[19] Corporations like Victoria's Secret, therefore, commonly use prison labor, paying prisoners sweatshop wages.[20]

On the political front, felon disenfranchisement laws in many states, especially those with large black populations, have tilted the scales of power in favor of the white electorate.[21] In fourteen states, a felon permanently loses the right to vote; in seven states, one in four black men has been permanently disenfranchised.[22] A total of 1.4 million black men, or thirteen percent of the black male adult population, are either temporarily or permanently disenfranchised.[23] The 2000 presidential election illustrated the dramatic effects of felon disenfranchisement. Florida disenfranchises the most, including six hundred thousand who have served their sentences and have been discharged from the criminal justice system. Had those people been allowed to vote, Al Gore could have won Florida by more than thirty-one thousand votes.[24]

To make matters worse, mass incarceration results in fewer legislative seats for communities of color.[25] Because the Census Bureau counts inmates as living where they are incarcerated, rural communities that house large prisons gain a disproportionate number of elected officials representing them in their state legislature and Congress.[26] Meanwhile, no one is representing the people of color behind bars, and the communities from which they came lose representatives because their population has declined.[27]

Quickly, quietly, and with virtually no political opposition, this new form of social control has become entrenched in the social, political, and economic structure. Like slavery and Jim Crow, mass incarceration is predicated on the inferiority of a certain class of people, defined largely by race. The genius of the new system is that it successfully blames the victim; black and brown people are segregated, stripped of political rights, and used for the economic benefit of propertied whites because they *chose* to engage in criminal behavior. That the overwhelming majority of inmates lack a basic education and only ever earned monthly incomes of less than one thousand dollars goes unreported.[28] Similarly, scant attention is given to the recent resegregation of schools, and how staggering proportions of black youth graduating from their segregated, under-funded schools can barely read (discussed in chapters 3 and 12).[29] The school-to-prison track for black and brown youth reflects no racial bias, we are told; rather, these kids have chosen a life of crime.

We should not be confused or distracted by such rhetoric. While the strategies and mechanisms of control have changed, the goals and beneficiaries remain the same. The backlash against the Civil Rights Movement has produced a new method of control on a scale that was unimaginable just twenty years ago. And this system is built to last.

Federalism's Role in Maintaining Racial Bias in Criminal Justice

How does federalism fit into this picture? In keeping with its historical pattern, the Supreme Court has moved swiftly to immunize mass incarceration from judicial scrutiny and federal intervention.[30] The crude federalist impulse to protect the rights of states and localities to control people of color has emerged yet again, without any greater moral justification than in earlier eras. State and local governments have been granted nearly unbridled discretion to implement mass incarceration, even when its effects are plainly discriminatory. The rules of the game are as follows: so long as no state or local actor admits to acting with a conscious intent to discriminate, they can control black and brown communities as they see fit.

With little fanfare, the Supreme Court has closed off every stage of the criminal justice process to judicial scrutiny for racial bias, except the point of entry.[31] The Court's decisions do not constitute mere restrictions on court access, or the chipping away of constitutional rights—rather, they amount to a near complete denial of access to the court system to challenge any form of racism in the criminal justice system.

Sentencing

In *McCleskey v. Kemp* in 1987, the Court held that severe racial disparities in sentencing, even if shown through statistical evidence, could not be challenged under the Fourteenth Amendment in the absence of clear evidence of discriminatory intent, because to allow such challenges would call into question the integrity of the entire criminal justice system. [32]

Jury Selection

In *Batson v. Kentucky* in 1986, the Court held that prosecutors cannot discriminate on the basis of race when selecting a jury, a decision hailed as an important safeguard against all-white juries locking up blacks.[33] In recent years, however, courts have imposed an unreasonably high discriminatory intent standard and have looked the other way in the face of clear evidence of systemic discrimination.[34] Indeed, challenges to racial bias in jury selection have become all but impossible to win in the absence of some sort of admission by the prosecution.[35]

Prosecutorial Discretion

In *United States v. Armstrong* in 1996, the Court barred challenges to racial bias in the exercise of prosecutorial discretion.[36] In that case, African American defendants challenged the failure of the U.S. Attorney for the Central District of California to charge white people with crimes related to the use, sale, or possession of crack cocaine. According to an affidavit submitted by the Office of the Federal Public Defender, only African Americans were prosecuted for possession or sale of crack in 1991, despite the fact that the majority of users were white.[37]

The Court did not question the accuracy of the Federal Public Defender's evidence, but deferred to the exercise of prosecutorial discretion and held that unless whites who had not been charged under circumstances similar to those in which blacks had been charged could be brought before the court, the defendants were out of luck.[38] Imagine being a public defender, with little time or resources, charged with such an unrealistic task. Because of *Armstrong*, access to the courts has been denied to those who would challenge racial bias in prosecutorial discretion.

The Decision to Detain and Arrest

Finally, the courthouse doors have been nearly closed to those challenging racial bias at the point of entry. It remains possible to challenge racial bias in the exercise of police discretion, although it might not remain this way for long. The Court has yet to decide whether, and to what extent, race can be used as a factor in deciding who to stop and search. Unfortunately, early indications have been discouraging.[39]

In *United States v. Brignoni-Ponce* in 1975, the Court indicated that the police could take a person's Mexican appearance into account when developing reasonable suspicion that a vehicle may contain undocumented aliens. The Court said that "the likelihood that any person of Mexican ancestry is an alien is high enough to make Mexican appearance a relevant factor."[40]

Notwithstanding *Brignoni-Ponce*, it remains possible to challenge racial profiling and the discriminatory exercise of police discretion—under narrow circumstances.[41] If the Court continues down its chosen path, however, the current litigation challenging racial profiling may be the last wave of litigation challenging racial bias in the criminal justice system for a long, long time.[42]

Planting the Seeds of a Movement

Mass incarceration has, therefore, emerged as the white elite's new form of extraordinary social control over black and brown people. Federalism, as articulated by states' rights advocates, has been used to avoid the federal scrutiny of slavery, Jim Crow segregation, and now mass incarceration. Throughout history, the crude federalist argument that states, localities, and government officials should be free to oppress and control people of color has played a key role in immunizing some of society's most racist and destructive institutions, beginning with slavery. Consistent with its historical pattern, the Supreme Court has made it virtually impossible to challenge mass incarceration on the grounds of racial bias at all stages of the criminal justice process except the point of entry.

Viewed in this way, it is an act of defiance when civil rights advocates file litigation challenging racial bias in the criminal justice system. When we make it into the courtroom, it is only because we slipped in quietly through a back door, defying the sign that reads: Access to the Judicial System Denied.

We should ignore that sign. Too often, I hear fellow civil rights advocates say, "There is nothing that we can do to challenge mass incarceration or racial bias in the criminal justice system, particularly given cases like *McCleskey v. Kemp.*" Imagine if Thurgood Marshall had said, "There is nothing that we can do to challenge racial segregation, given *Plessy v. Ferguson.*" We cannot be so easily deterred.

At the same time, however, we must begin to plant the seeds for a broader movement. If we, as advocates, are to be anything more than a flea on the elephant's back, we must describe the criminal justice system in language that makes clear our interest in challenging more than isolated criminal justice policies or discrete violations of individuals' constitutional rights. We must build a movement that seeks the eradication of the latest manifestation of a fundamentally racist ideology, an ideology rooted in American history and adaptable to changing times.

The necessity of a movement-building approach becomes clear once the emergence of the mass incarceration policy, and the Court's role in protecting it, is put in its proper historical and political context. Looking back, it is clear that piecemeal policy reform or litigation alone would have been a futile approach to dismantling Jim Crow segregation. While those strategies certainly have their place, the Civil Rights Act of 1964 and the concomitant cultural shift would never have occurred without the cultivation of political consciousness in the African American community and the resulting widespread activism.

We have defeated enemies of racial justice before, and we can do it again. It will take persistence, creativity, and the courage to reinvent ourselves as advocates. The freedom fighters who came before us would expect no less.

Endnotes

1. EJS' mission is the unification and organization of those committed to the development of legal strategies to eliminate the prevailing conservative bias of our legal system.

For more information regarding EJS, visit www.equaljusticesociety.org. EJS is intended to be the antidote to the Federalist Society, an influential, right wing legal organization (see chapter 20).

2. See, e.g., Martin A. Feigenbaum, The Preservation of Individual Liberty Through the Separation of Powers and Federalism: Reflections on the Shaping of Constitutional Immorality, *37 Emory L. J.* (Summer 1998) 613.

3. See *United States v. Lopez*, 514 U.S. 549 (1995). See also *Printz v. United States*, 521 U.S. 898, 921 (1997) ("This separation of the two spheres is one of the Constitution's structural protections of liberty"); *Gregory v. Ashcroft*, 501 U.S. 452, 458 (1991) ("Just as the separation and independence of the coordinate branches of the Federal Government serve to prevent the accumulation of excessive power in any one branch, a healthy balance of power between the States and the Federal Government will reduce the risk of tyranny and abuse from either front").

4. *United States v. Lopez*, 514 U.S. 552 citing *Gregory v. Ashcroft*, 501 U.S. 458.

5. For more about the views of the Federalist Society, visit www.fed-soc.org.

6. See, e.g., Robert C. Post and Reva B. Siegel, Equal Protection by Law: Federal Antidiscrimination Legislation After Morrison and Kimel, *110 Yale L. J.* (2000) 441. As Post and Siegel describe, during the Civil Rights Movement of the 1960s, protestors staged sit-ins designed to challenge the freedom of whites to segregate African Americans in ordinary social transactions. Id. at 492. Business owners turned to federalism and invoked their right to segregate commercial establishments. "The ensuing conflicts posed deep questions about whether national power should intervene to uproot this racialized conception of property and liberty, or whether it should instead turn a blind eye, as it had since the end of Reconstruction." Id.

7. Crime Policy Report, *Prisoner Reentry in Perspective* (September 2001) 4. Also at http://www.urban.org/pdfs/410213_reentry.pdf.

8. Two-thirds of federal prisoners are racial and ethnic minorities (thirty-nine percent African American, twenty-nine percent Latino). The Sentencing Project, Briefing Sheets, *The Expanding Federal Prison Population* (Washington DC), at www.sentencingproject.or/ pubs_02.cfm. In 2003, forty-four percent of state and federal prison inmates were African American, and nineteen percent were Latino; The Sentencing Project, Briefing Sheets, *Facts About Prisons and Prisoners*, *supra*. African Americans are admitted to state prisons on drug charges at a rate that is 13.4 times greater than whites; Human Rights Watch, *Punishment and Prejudice: Racial Disparities in the War on Drugs* (May 2000). In seven states, blacks make up between eighty and ninety percent of drug prisoners, and in fifteen states, blacks are admitted to prison on drug charges twenty to fifty-seven times more frequently than whites. Id.

9. Id.

10. Bureau of Justice Statistics, U.S. Department of Justice, Bulletin, *Prisoners and Jail Inmates at Midyear 2002* (April 2003). There are now 6.7 million Americans incarcerated or on probation or parole, an increase of more than 258 percent since 1980; Bureau of Justice Statistics, U.S. Department of Justice, Bulletin, *Probation and Parole in the United States 2002* (August 2003). In 2003, the U.S. rate of incarceration of 714 inmates per 100,000 population is the highest reported in the world, ahead of Russia's rate of 584 per 100,000; The Sentencing Project, Briefing Sheets, *Facts About Prisons and Prisoners* (August 2003), at http://www.sentencingproject.org/pubs_02.cfm.

11. David Cole, No Equal Justice: Race and Class in the American Criminal Justice System, *The New Press* (1999) 4.

12. Marc Mauer, Race to Incarcerate, *The New Press* (1999) 125.

13. The Sentencing Project, Briefing Sheets, *Hispanic Prisoners in the United States* (February 2003), at http://www.sentencingproject.org/pubs_02.cfm.

14. The United States is incarcerating African American men at a rate approximately four times the rate of incarceration of black men in South Africa under apartheid. C. Haney and P. Zimbardo, The Past and Future of U.S. Prison Policy, *American Psychologist* (July 1998) Vol. 53, No. 7. Already, the number of African American men in prison equals or surpasses the number of men enslaved in 1820, and if current trends continue, less than fifteen years remain before the U.S. incarcerates as many African American men as were in bondage at slavery's peak in 1860. Graham Boyd, The Drug War is the New Jim Crow, *NACLA Report on the Americas* (July/August 2001). Notably, the mass incarceration of people of color in the War on Drugs has not solved the problem of drug abuse.

15. Although this new form of social control—mass incarceration—is intended to protect the interests of the white elite, many whites, particularly poor whites, suffer terribly as a result of the new regime. The real targets of the War on Drugs are black and brown, but there is significant collateral damage in poor white communities. One of the most important challenges for civil rights advocates today is to help poor whites and communities of color see that they share a common destiny and a common interest in eradicating the racism that makes mass incarceration possible.

16. Mauer, *supra* note 18.

17. Id. at 10.

18. Id. at 16.

19. U.S. Const. XIII.

20. Joel Dyer, The Perpetual Prisoner Machine: How America Profits from Crime, *Westview Press* (2000) 19.

21. See Jamie Fellner and Marc Mauer, *Losing the Vote: The Impact of Felony Disenfranchisement Laws in the United States* (1998), at http://www.hrw.org/reports98/vote.

22. Id.

23. Fellner and Mauer, *supra* note 27.

24. Christopher Uggen and Jeff Manza, Democratic Contraction? The Political Consequences of Felon Disenfranchisement in the United States, *67 Am. Soc. Rev.* (2002) 777. This estimate is based on the assumption that 68.9 percent of ex-felons would have voted for Gore and that they would have had a turnout rate of 13.6 percent. Id at 792.

25. See, e.g., Jonathan Tilove, Minority Prison Inmates Skew Local Populations as States Redistrict, *Newhouse News Service* (March 11, 2002); Peter Wagner, *Census Quirk Sustains New York's Love Affair with Prisons* (Aug. 2002), at http://www.prisonpolicy.org/articles/clj0802.shtml.

26. Id.

27. The parallels between modern felon disenfranchisement laws and the strategies used in the post-Civil War era to diminish black voting strength are striking. After passage of the Fifteenth Amendment, white Southerners began adopting seemingly race-neutral voting restrictions in an effort to undermine their Reconstruction-era political gains. Fellner and Mauer, *supra* note 27, at 3; See also J. Morgan Kousser, *The Shaping of Southern Politics: Suffrage Restriction and the Establishment of the One-Party South, 1880–1910* (1974) 45–72. In fact, between 1890 and 1910, in addition to adopting poll taxes and literacy tests, Southern states drafted their criminal disenfranchisement laws to target blacks by including crimes that blacks were deemed likely to commit. Fellner and Mauer, *supra* note 27, at 3; The disqualifying crimes included adultery, thievery, arson, wife-beating, housebreak-

ing, and attempted rape. Andrew L. Shapiro, Challenging Criminal Disenfranchisement Under the Voting Rights Act: A New Strategy, *103 Yale L.J.* (1993) 537, 541. The impact of these disenfranchisement laws on black political power was immediate and severe. Id. at 538. Although many of these laws were repealed or invalidated during the Civil Rights era, we are now witnessing the rise of felon disenfranchisement laws to accomplish the same goals pursued by segregationists at the turn of the century.

28. Sixty-eight percent of prison inmates in 1997 had not completed high school, and sixty-four percent had monthly incomes of under one thousand dollars in the month before their arrest. The Sentencing Project, Briefing Sheets, *Facts About Prisons and Prisoners, supra* note 8.

29. The Harvard Civil Rights Project reported that, in the 1990s, the proportion of African Americans attending majority white schools declined dramatically, reaching the lowest level since 1968. Erika Frankenberg and Chungmei Lee, Race in American Public Schools: Rapidly Resegregating School Districts, *Harvard Civil Rights Project* (August 2002). Rather than decreasing, racial segregation has also been steadily increasing for Latinos since the 1960s. Id at 2. The trend toward increased racial segregation is due, in significant part, to the Court's 1990s desegregation decisions which relaxed the judicial standards that school districts had to meet in order to be released from court oversight. Therefore, many school districts are no longer under desegregation plans. Id at 22.

30. This trend has arguably been most blatant in the Court's refusal to entertain even potentially meritorious habeas petitions by prisoners. Federal courts are required to entertain petitions from state prisoners who allege they are held "in violation of the Constitution or laws or treaties of the United States." 28 U.S.C. 2254(a). In recent years, however, the Supreme Court has erected numerous barriers to the federal Judiciary's review of constitutional claims of criminal defendants. See, e.g., *Herrera v. Collins,* 506 U.S. 390 (1993) (claim of actual innocence based on new evidence is not ground for federal habeas relief); *Coleman v. Thompson, supra* (federal habeas relief is not available where defendant procedurally defaulted on appeal in state court, regardless of the existence of legitimate federal constitutional claims); *McCleskey v. Zant,* 499 U.S. 467 (1991) (even if new evidence or misconduct is discovered, defendant must show cause or actual prejudice for failure to raise in original habeas petition in order for second or subsequent writ to proceed); *Keeney v. Tamayo-Reyes,* 504 U.S. 1 (1992) (overruling *Townsend v. Sain,* 372 U.S. 293 (1963) in part) (defendant must show cause and prejudice for failing to raise claim in state court, rather than the more lenient standard that defendant did not deliberately bypass claim in state court); *Teague v. Lane,* 489 U.S. 288 (1989) (limits retroactivity of new constitutional rights of criminal procedure in collateral review); *Butler v. McKellar,* 494 U.S. 407 (1990) (good faith effort of state court to follow current established law that is later overruled is not cause to make new rule retroactive on collateral review); *Terry Williams v. Taylor,* 120 S. Ct. 1495 (2000) (habeas review limited to state court decisions that are objectively unreasonable, not just incorrect).

31. There will be those who argue that some of the cases described above are not "federalism" cases per se, because they do not squarely address the proper relationship between the federal government and states or localities (*Armstrong v. United States*, for example, dealt with alleged discrimination by a federal prosecutor, not a state government actor). In addition, critics may note that the cases turn largely on the Court's interpretation of the Equal Protection Clause of the Fourteenth Amendment—which has been interpreted to prohibit intentional race discrimination—rather than principles of federalism that arguably can be found in the Tenth or Eleventh Amendments, or the structure of the Constitution

as a whole. What this critique overlooks, however, is that *Plessy v. Ferguson*—the infamous Supreme Court case that upheld Jim Crow segregation and the "separate but equal" doctrine—was also a Fourteenth Amendment case, but was clearly driven by the crude federalist impulse to defer to states and localities regarding their decisions about how to deal with communities of color following emancipation. It is precisely that impulse—to defer to government officials in their implementation of racialized social control—that drives much of the Court's Fourteenth Amendment jurisprudence today. *Armstrong v. United States* is, therefore, an excellent example of the crude federalist impulse to look the other way when the tactics of mass incarceration are challenged as racially discriminatory.

32. *McKleskey v. Kemp*, 481 U. S. 279 (1987). Warren McKleskey argued that the Georgia capital sentencing scheme was administered in a racially discriminatory manner in violation of the Eighth and Fourteenth Amendments. McKleskey was an African American who had been sentenced to death for the killing of a white police officer during the course of an armed robbery. Id. at 283. In support of his claim, he proffered a highly reliable statistical study, known as the Baldus study. See David Baldus et al., *Equal Justice and the Death Penalty: A Legal and Empirical Analysis* (1990). The study revealed that the Georgia death penalty scheme was infected by racial bias, and that the determination of who received the death penalty was based, in significant part, on the races of the defendant and the victim. The study demonstrated that the death penalty was imposed in twenty-two percent of the cases involving black defendants and white victims, eight percent of cases involving white defendants and white victims, three percent of cases involving white defendants and black victims, and one percent of cases involving black defendants and black victims. Id. at 286–89. As Justice William Brennan noted in dissent, "After taking into account some 230 nonracial factors that might legitimately influence a sentencer, [the study demonstrates that] the jury *more likely than not* would have spared McCleskey's life had his victim been black." Id. at 325 (emphasis in original) (Brennan, J., dissenting).

The McCleskey majority, for the purposes of its analysis, assumed that the empirical evidence was correct. The Court nonetheless ruled that Georgia's death penalty was constitutional. Justice Lewis Powell wrote that, "taken to its logical conclusion, [McCleskey's proposal to eliminate capital punishment in Georgia because it is administered in a discriminatory manner] throws into serious question the principles that underlie our entire criminal justice system." Id. at 314–15. The Court was clearly concerned that if the death penalty was deemed unconstitutional because of discriminatory enforcement, it would create precedent that would require the elimination of many other kinds of punishment that may be imposed in a discriminatory manner.

33. *Batson v. Kentucky*, 476 U.S. 79 (1986) (holding that, in cases with black defendants, the Equal Protection Clause prohibited peremptory challenges of African American jurors solely on account of their race). See also *Powers v. Ohio*, 499 U.S. 400 (1991) (extending *Batson* to any race-based peremptory challenge, regardless of the race of the defendant or the excluded jurors).

34. See e.g. *Purkett v. Elem*, 514 U.S. 765 (1995) (holding that the "neutral explanation" required by *Batson* to rebut a challenge need not be persuasive or plausible). In *Purkett*, the Supreme Court found that the prosecutor's rationale for the challenge—that the juror had long hair, a beard, and a moustache—was race-neutral. The Court did not require a finding that the rationale was plausible. Id. But see *Miller-El v. Dretke*, 2005 WL 1383365 (June 13, 2005) (reversing the Fifth Circuit's refusal to review the district court's denial of a habeas challenge to racial bias by a prosecutor who excluded ten of eleven black potential jurors).

35. Bryan Stevenson and Ruth Friedman have documented appalling cases of racial bias in jury selection in Alabama. For example:

"In a 1986 case out of Emanuel County, Georgia, the prosecutor used all ten of his peremptory strikes to remove all ten African Americans from the venire. When called upon to explain his reasons, he opined that he needed to strike one venire member because he looked 'dumb as a fencepost' and another because he resembled the defendant. The judge accepted these as valid reasons for removing the jurors, and the case proceeded to trial....

At one Dallas County Batson hearing held in 1991—in which twenty-three of twenty-eight strikes were used against African Americans—the district attorney stated that he struck a Ms. Johnson because she was related to various persons named Johnson whom he had previously prosecuted. When given the opportunity on voir dire, he declined to ask the venire member if she was indeed related to those who shared her common surname. Ms. Johnson then took the stand to say that she had never heard of these alleged relatives. Despite the fact that the asserted reason easily was proved false, the trial court denied the challenge....

A trial court found no proof of racial taint when the prosecution eliminated every black person from three different juries in a single case (one each to determine competency, guilt, and punishment), even when it was disclosed that the state had segregated the potential jurors into four lists denominated "strong," "medium," "weak," and "black" prior to trial and had struck every black individual in order from the list."

Bryan A. Stevenson and Ruth E. Friedman, Deliberate Indifference: Judicial Tolerance of Racial Bias in Criminal Justice, 51 *Wash. & Lee L. Rev.* (1994) 509, 522–23. After reviewing numerous cases involving blatant—yet unremedied—racial bias in jury selection, Stevenson and Friedman concluded: "No evidence of bias has been too blatant for state courts to ignore." Id. at 523.

36. *U.S. v. Armstrong*, 517 U.S. 456 (1996)

37. Id. at 459. The defendants sought discovery of the prosecutor's files in their effort to prove that whites suspected of crack-related offenses were prosecuted in state court, rather than federal court, because the penalties in state court were much less severe. In support of their request for discovery, the defendants submitted an affidavit from the Office of the Federal Public Defender stating that, during 1991, the office had closed twenty-four cases involving prosecutions for crack offenses. Id. In each of those cases, the defendant was black. Id. The defendants also offered an affidavit from an intake coordinator from a drug treatment center explaining that there are "an equal number of Caucasian users and dealers to minority users and dealers." Id at 460. Another affidavit was submitted from a criminal defense attorney alleging that, in his experience, many whites are routinely prosecuted for crack offenses in state court, where they can avoid harsh penalties. Finally, defendants offered a *Los Angeles Times* article reporting that blacks suspected of crack offenses were being prosecuted in federal court, where they faced extremely harsh penalties, while whites were being prosecuted in state court or were having their charges dismissed. Id. at 465. This evidence, the defendants argued, should be enough to get discovery of the prosecutor's charging practices, particularly in light of the fact that whites constitute the majority of crack users. Id. at 479–80 (J. Stevens, dissenting) ("[W]hile 65% of the persons who had used crack were white, in 1993, they represented only 4% of the federal offenders convicted of trafficking in crack.....Eighty percent of such defendants were black.") See also United States Sentencing Commission, *Special Report to Congress: Cocaine and Federal Sentencing Policy* (Feb. 1995) 39, 161.

38. *Armstrong*, 517 U.S. at 458, 470.

39. See *U.S. v. Brignoni-Ponce,* 422 U.S. 873 (1975); *United States v. Martinez-Fuerte,* 428 U.S. 543 (1976).

40. *Brignoni-Ponce,* 422 U.S. 886–87.

41. It is extraordinarily difficult to prove that officials acted with discriminatory intent, as required to prevail in a claim under the Equal Protection Clause of the Fourteenth Amendment. See Michael Selmi, Proving Intentional Discrimination: The Reality of Supreme Court Rhetoric, *86 Geo L. J.* (1997) 279. Nonetheless, it has remained possible to challenge racial profiling by law enforcement thanks to the regulations promulgated pursuant to Title VI of the Civil Rights Act of 1964. Title VI regulations prohibit federally-funded programs or activities from having an unnecessary racially disparate impact. Accordingly, plaintiffs have pursued racial profiling litigation under the theory that the drug interdiction programs violate Title VI regulations because they have a disparate impact on African American and Latino motorists, an impact that is demonstrably unnecessary because so few drugs are successfully recovered through these operations. See *Rodriguez, et al. v. California Highway Patrol,* 89 F. Supp. 2d. 1131 (N.D. Cal. 2000). Moreover, available data often indicates that people of color are no more likely to be carrying drugs or other contraband in their vehicles than whites, making racial profiling unwise as well as unnecessary. Id. Two years ago, this strategy was dealt a near fatal blow when the Supreme Court ruled that Title VI regulations did not afford a private right of action. *Alexander v. Sandoval,* 532 U.S. 275 (2001). Some courts have held that it remains possible to enforce Title VI regulations by invoking 42 USC § 1983. See *Rodriguez, et al., supra.* However, the Court's decision in *Gonzaga v. Doe,* 536 U.S. 273 (2002), which held that Title VI's implementing regulations were not enforceable through § 1983 suits, may well have foreclosed this option.

42. It bears emphasis that, even if you bring a racial profiling case and attempt to slide through the loopholes, you will face numerous procedural barriers which operate to deny standing to plaintiffs, afford immunity to law enforcement, deny damages to class members, and deny attorney's fees—even if you win. See Michael Avery, David Rudofsky, and Karen Blum, *Police Misconduct Law and Litigation* (2001).

CHAPTER 16

OUR CIVIL LIBERTIES

Who's Watching the Home Front?

Barbara J. Olshansky[*]

Imagine that you are a Middle Easterner and have come to the U.S. seeking political asylum. You are now a legal permanent resident (a green card holder). You live in New York City with your American wife and American-born children. Imagine next that you are stopped by the police because your car has a broken taillight, and that when the officer pulls up your name on the law enforcement computer, he finds that you have failed to register your recent change of address with the immigration authorities. You are arrested and placed in immigration detention in a federal correctional facility. What happens next? Even though you are here legally, have a family here, and sought political asylum to escape the abuses of your country, you will likely be deported.

This chapter will place the civil rights rollback within the larger political context of the ongoing "war on terror," and will examine the ramifications of this new assault on civil liberties.

❧   ❧   ❧

Justice, Equality, and Fairness on Trial

For over a decade, the political spirit of the American people has been under siege. The enemy, however, is not *at* the gate—rather, the attack comes from those whom we have trusted to guard it.

More than lives and buildings were destroyed on 9/11. Our constitutional rights were also gravely wounded. Within a day of the tragedy, the Bush ad-

---

[*] Director Counsel, Global Justice Initiative, Center for Constitutional Rights. Her docket includes class action lawsuits concerning international human rights, immigrant rights, racial justice in employment, education, public health, prisoner rights, and Native American rights.

ministration began to institute policies that chip away at our hard-won civil liberties. At stake are some of our most fundamental constitutional rights: due process, equal protection of the laws, fair trial, the right to counsel, and the right to be free from unlawful seizures and coerced self-incrimination. Who will safeguard these fundamental freedoms? Given that the current assault by the executive branch comes in the wake of a serious rollback of civil rights by the Supreme Court, only the people—individually, collectively, and through their elected representatives—can reclaim these rights.

After 9/11, the U.S. moved into a period of operation by executive fiat. The executive branch's usurpation of authority is evident in law enforcement actions, executive orders, and pressure to enact sweeping legislation aimed at eroding civil liberties. This power grab threatens a cornerstone of American democracy, the separation of powers between the executive, the legislature, and the judicial branches of government.

This chapter surveys the landscape of the civil rights rollback, places that rollback within the larger political context of the ongoing "war on terror," and examines the ramifications for all committed to creating a just society.

The Tilting Scales of Justice

To grasp the seriousness of this assault on our civil rights and liberties, we need to consider the health of our system of checks and balances as it existed the day before 9/11. By that time a series of tremors had already cracked the foundation of our democracy, particularly the separation of powers cornerstone. These tremors, however, barely registered on our constitutional seismograph.

What caused these tremors? How did the magnitude and scope of the tremors rolling back our civil rights go unnoticed? One reason is that the changes were incremental and steeped in formulaic legal analysis. The series of Supreme Court decisions (described in Part II) commenced an assault on civil rights while merely hinting at the true nature of the changes being wrought.

To be sure, organizations and individuals committed to social justice were already aware that right wing activists, cloaked in the robes of law and using rhetoric sweetened by the guise of civility, were systematically disassembling constitutional and statutory civil rights protections. Anti-discrimination laws were being undermined by the innocuous-sounding forces of "federalism" and "states' rights," such that people's ability to speak through their representatives regarding discrimination on the basis of race, gender, disability, age, and immigration status was already significantly shut down. The Fourteenth Amendment's Equal Protection Clause, once considered the essence of a just society, was so eviscerated that only the most blatant constitutional violations could be corrected. The Supreme Court had moved far beyond its role of interpreting what the law is to dictating what it ought to be.[1] Packed with judges belonging to the elitist Federalist Society, the Court had stripped the citizenry of its right to enforce federal laws protecting workers, women, the disabled, the elderly, and the environment, effectively transferring those powers to a president and an attorney general who disregarded and refused to enforce those laws.

The Rule of Law Hanging in the Balance

The Bush administration's response to 9/11 widened the cracks in the foundation of democracy, threatening its entire structure. Today, the executive branch continues to expand its powers at the expense of both Congress and the courts.

When the Justice Department requested new law enforcement tools with which to fight terrorism, Congress passed the USA PATRIOT Act.[2] The executive branch, however, then claimed even greater powers by issuing executive orders and interim regulations (that are beyond congressional review and that change how federal agencies operate and what rules they enforce), by abusing existing laws and regulations, and by announcing new policies and practices that override or bypass congressional and judicial authority.

Executive Orders: The Creation of an Unauthorized Military Commission System

One of the administration's most unsettling acts was President Bush's November 13, 2001 Executive Order creating a new form of military commission to try accused terrorists.[3] This act is clearly beyond his constitutional authority; only Congress has the power under Article III of the Constitution to create federal courts. The Order concentrates power in the hands of the executive—the president defines the offenses to be tried (and can change those crimes at any time), who will be tried, and creates the rules under which the commissions operate. Further, the president appoints the judges, prosecutors, and defense attorneys, sets the penalties (including execution), and decides all appeals. No federal court can review the decisions—not even the imposition of the death penalty. Because the press was severely restricted in its access, the American public will likely never know the outcome of these commission proceedings.

The Abuse of Existing Laws and Regulations: Unlawful Detentions of Visitors and Immigrants

Another disconcerting example of the aggrandizement of executive power in the wake of 9/11 is the Justice Department's use of basic immigration law violations (e.g., simple tourist visa overstays) as a basis for investigative detention (holding people until they are cleared of connections to terrorism or are determined to have no further value to intelligence gathering). Investigative detention is calculated to evade the constitutional safeguards provided under criminal law—probable cause to arrest, the right to be brought before a judge within forty-eight hours of arrest to test the existence of probable cause, the right to court-appointed counsel, and the right to a speedy and public trial.

In the past, people accused of overstaying their visas or working while on a tourist visa were released while their immigration cases proceeded. After 9/11, however, the Justice Department kept "special interest" detainees confined without evidence that they were dangerous or a flight risk. Many were held in solitary confinement for months even after judges issued orders permitting them to return home. Despite the fact that they were never charged with any crime or any connection to terrorism, the mere fact that they were held in American prisons has been sufficient to besmirch their character.

In the weeks following 9/11, the federal government arrested hundreds of Middle Easterners, South Asians, and Muslims, relying on one of two legal justifications: immigration violations (even though immigration laws do not provide for criminal penalties for overstaying a visa) and the federal material witness statute (federal prosecutors can hold people who may have information relevant to a case in order to ensure their appearance before a grand jury, provided that they demonstrate the witness's value to a specific case and show that he or she may be unavailable to the court if released).[4]

In an attempt to locate people whose families were searching for them, civil and human rights groups used the federal Freedom of Information Act[5] to demand that then-Attorney General John Ashcroft disclose how many people had been detained and upon what basis, their nationality and/or ethnicity, their access to counsel and consulates, the length of time that material witnesses who testified before a grand jury would be held, and the basis for the government's request to hold secret proceedings and place attorneys under gag orders. Even though two lower federal courts required Ashcroft to produce the information,[6] he refused. The Supreme Court eventually upheld the government's failure to comply with the Freedom of Information Act.[7]

What do we know about what happened to these immigration detainees? Initially, when civil and human rights groups inquired about them, they were told that there were no court records showing where or why the people were being held, or the status of their cases. However, a report released by the Justice Department's Inspector General on June 2, 2003, entitled "The September 11 Detainees: A Review of the Treatment of Aliens Held on Immigration Charges in Connection with the Investigation of the September 11 Attacks,"[8] provides a wealth of details regarding the mistreatment of Arab and Muslim nationals. People designated as individuals "of interest" to the government's investigation of the attacks were wrongfully arrested, detained, and subjected to an array of unconstitutional practices.

The government kept these detainees in custody for extended periods of time not for any legitimate immigration law enforcement purpose, but to incarcerate them without probable cause pursuant to a "hold until cleared policy" while authorities determined whether they had any ties to terrorism. Individuals were deemed "of interest" so long as the FBI could not immediately rule out any connection to terrorism.[9] Instead of being presumed innocent until proven guilty, detainees were presumed guilty until proven innocent—a violation of their Fourth and Fifth Amendment rights.[10]

Individuals were singled out for arrest and detention simply because the FBI received uncorroborated tips based on religious or ethnic identity, such as a tip stating that "too many" Muslim men were working in a convenience store.[11] Those arrested were detained without charge for months. Beyond the minor civil immigration violations, however, those detained were never charged with or accused of any crime. Strict constitutional limits regulate the length of time that an individual may be detained before being afforded both notice of the charges against him and a judicial determination as to whether the arrest was supported by probable cause.[12] Yet the government kept people in legal limbo for periods stretching from several months to nearly two years.

What were conditions like for the detainees? Many, if not all, were held in solitary confinement in overcrowded and unsanitary federal prison and county jail facilities.[13] In New York, people were placed in tiny cells for over twenty-three hours a day, then strip-searched, manacled, and shackled when taken out. Many suffered physical and verbal abuse by guards, were subjected to coercive, involuntary interrogations, and were denied contact with their families or lawyers for weeks.

Soon after the detentions began, the Justice Department announced a wave of interrogations for five thousand men of Middle Eastern descent between the ages of eighteen and thirty-three who had legally entered the U.S. after January 1, 2000 on passports from countries with "known links to terrorism, Al Qaeda or Osama bin Laden." While the order was purportedly part of the Justice Department's effort to investigate Al Qaeda, the questionnaire sought general information about political associations. Although the Justice Department admits that its actions constituted racial/ethnic profiling, it nevertheless insists that such measures were necessary to the criminal investigation.[14]

Usurping Congressional and Judicial Power

The third wave of the Bush administration's power grab took the form of new policies and practices aimed at overriding or bypassing the authority of Congress and the judicial branch. Soon after 9/11, Ashcroft announced that the Freedom of Information Act was not applicable during the "war on terror."[15] Moreover, the administration argued that the federal courts lack the authority to review actions that the executive branch undertakes as part of the "war on terror"—a stance that directly undermines the principle of separation of powers.

Perhaps one of the most visible examples of the executive branch running roughshod over Congress was President Bush's detention of American citizens as "enemy combatants." On May 8, 2002, Jose Padilla was arrested upon his arrival at O'Hare International Airport. Padilla, who had traveled to Chicago to visit his son, was arrested on the authority of a material witness warrant issued by a federal district court commanding his appearance before a grand jury.[16] On June 9, 2002, two days before the initial court hearing on Padilla's motion to be released from police custody until his grand jury appearance, President Bush filed a declaration with the court designating Padilla an "enemy combatant" and ordering the Secretary of Defense to take him into custody. Padilla was flown to the Consolidated Naval Brig in Charleston, SC, where he remains in solitary confinement.

The government's justification for this unprecedented action poses a grave threat to the constitutional rights of all Americans. Under the guise of President Bush's power to act as Commander-in-Chief of the Armed Forces, the government seeks to strip the protections afforded to all citizens from those it labels "enemy combatants." The government's argument here is no different from the "sweeping proposition" criticized by the Fourth Circuit Court of Appeals in *Hamdi v. Rumsfeld*, another "enemy combatant" case in which the court said "that, with no meaningful judicial review, any American citizen alleged to be an enemy combatant could be detained indefinitely without charges or counsel on the government's say-so."[17]

The president's assertion that he has the power to declare citizens "enemy combatants" violates the principal of separation of powers. The president's constitutional powers do not authorize the indefinite detention without Due Process of U.S. citizens. No allegations have been made that Padilla participated in 9/11 or any other terrorist or criminal acts against the U.S. Rather, the government intends to keep Padilla in solitary confinement for the duration of the "war on terror"—admittedly an indefinite period of time—for investigatory purposes. Even more chilling is the government's justification for Padilla's detention: that providing him with access to family or counsel may "threaten the perceived dependency and trust between [Padilla] and [the] interrogator."[18]

Congress has expressly prohibited this type of investigative or preventative detention through the enactment of the Anti-Detention Act. That law provides that "no citizen shall be imprisoned or otherwise detained by the United States except pursuant to an Act of Congress."[19] With this legislation, Congress intended to prevent the recurrence of incidents like the internment of Japanese-Americans during World War II by depriving the executive of the authority to detain citizens—even during wartime—without explicit statutory authorization and Due Process protections. In a case addressing the Act's applicability, the Court declared that "the plain language of §4001(a) proscrib[es] detention *of any kind* by the United States, absent a congressional grant of authority to detain."[20] Congress has not granted the president the authority to detain indefinitely, without trial or judicial review, citizens seized in the U.S. and not charged with any crime. Yet President Bush has disregarded Congress' wishes and has exercised this power over Padilla.

Chief Justice William Rehnquist, writing the majority opinion for five justices (Justices Antonin Scalia, Sandra Day O'Connor, Anthony Kennedy, Clarence Thomas, and himself) in *Rumsfeld v. Padilla* (2004),[21] declined to address the merits of Padilla's claim that he had been unlawfully detained and instead focused on the technical issue of who was the proper party to be named in Padilla's habeas petition. According to the majority, the papers filed on Padilla's behalf should have named as the respondent Commander Melanie Marr, the commander of the South Carolina naval brig where Padilla is being held, rather than Secretary of Defense Donald Rumsfeld, because she is his "immediate custodian."[22] The Court held that the wrong person had been sued and that the case had been filed in the wrong federal district; Padilla's petition should have been filed in the federal district in which he was confined, not where Secretary Rumsfeld can be served.[23] By focusing on this issue, the majority was able to delay its consideration of the legality of the use of the term "enemy combatant" to hold Padilla without charge or trial.

What does all of this mean? At the least, it means that we must understand that the real threat to democracy is coming from within our own borders. We cannot stand by while the executive branch arrogates so much power to itself that the country is ruled only by the president and the military.

Conclusion: A Call for a Government Accountable to the People

Our federal courts, especially the Supreme Court, have played an extraordinary role in times of political and social crisis—for good and bad. At times, the Court has successfully tackled an issue that other social and political institutions were incapable of addressing, let alone resolving—the brightest example being *Brown v. Board of Education*, which held that racial segregation in public education was unconstitutional.[24] And there are others: *Griswold v. Connecticut*,[25] which recognized the right of married couples to information about birth control, struck an important blow for the right of privacy and got the state out of citizens' bedrooms; *Roe v. Wade*,[26] which recognized the constitutional right to abortion; *Baker v. Carr*,[27] which constitutionalized the principle of one person one vote; and *Engel v. Vitale*,[28] which prohibited mandatory prayer in public schools.

On the other hand, there are many examples of situations in which the Court has played an unethical and immoral role. One of the most egregious examples is the *Dred Scott v. Sandford* decision, which declared that all blacks—slaves as well as free—were not and could never become U.S. citizens.[29] Others include: *Plessy v. Ferguson*,[30] which upheld state-mandated racial segregation; *The Civil Rights Cases*,[31] which struck down the Civil Rights Act of 1875 that prohibited racial discrimination in places of public accommodation; *Dennis v. United States*,[32] which upheld the convictions of Communist Party leaders for the mere teaching of communist philosophies; and *Korematsu v. United States*,[33] which upheld the internment of American citizens of Japanese descent during World War II. These are but a few examples of the Court's failure to stand up to the popular demagoguery of the day.

Unfortunately, recent Court decisions—in the name of federalism and states' rights—have eroded citizen's rights to remedy discrimination in all areas of life. We must all watch closely to see how the Court addresses the current crisis of civil liberties, and act now to put an immediate halt to the erosion of the hard-won rights that have made this country a decent place in which to learn, work, and live. In real terms, this means that everyone who cares about social justice, equality, and individual dignity must work together to confront the rollback of civil rights. If the Court and the executive branch are permitted to tie the hands of our elected representatives, the people will no longer have a say in how this country is run or what it stands for. It is up to each of us to take back the power of government for the people—the true meaning of democracy.

Endnotes

1. Article I, § 1 of the Constitution vests the power to make laws in Congress. *Myers v. United States*, 272 U.S. 52 (1926). Congress may not delegate its inherent lawmaking power to another branch, and no other branch may assert this power. See e.g., *Loving v. United States*, 517 U.S. 748, 758 (1996) ("[T]he lawmaking function belongs to Congress... and may not be conveyed to another branch or entity").

2. Uniting and Strengthening America by Providing Appropriate Tools Required to Intercept and Obstruct Terrorism (USA Patriot Act) Act of 2001, Pub. L. No. 107-56, 115 Stat. 272.

3. *President Issues Military Order: Detention, Treatment, and Trial of Certain Non-Citizens in the War Against Terrorism* (Nov. 13, 2001), at http://www.whitehouse.gov/news/releases/2001/11/20011113-27.html.

4. The law says that people may be held for a "reasonable period of time." Plainly, this language was not intended to mean that people could be held for indefinite detentions. This is clear from the purpose of the material witness law, which was intended to allow the government to hold people so that it could get them before a grand jury.

5. 5 U.S.C. § 552 (1996).

6. See *Center For Nat. Sec. Studies v. Dept. of Justice*, 215 F.Supp.2d 94 (D.D.C. 2002); *Center for Nat. Sec. Studies v. Dept. of Justice,* 331 F.3d 918 (D.C. Cir. 2003).

7. See *Center for National Security Studies v. Department of Justice*, 124 S.Ct. 1041 (2004).

8. Office of the Inspector General (OIG) (Jun. 2, 2003), at http://www.usdoj.gov/oig/special/0306/index.htm.

9. OIG, *supra* note 6, 18.

10. See OIG, *supra* note 6, 78–80.

11. OIG, *supra* note 6, 16–17.

12. See *County of Riverside v. McLaughlin*, 500 U.S. 44, 56 (1991).

13. See OIG, *supra* note 6, at 40–80.

14. See statement of John Bell, special agent in charge of the Detroit FBI office, recounted in Federal Plans Concern Arab Leaders, *AP* (Nov. 16, 2001).

15. Office of Information & Privacy, U.S. Dep't of Justice, FOIA Post: New Attorney General FOIA Memorandum Issued (Oct. 12, 2001), at http://www.usdoj.gov/oip/foiapost/2001foiapost19.htm.

16. *Padilla v. Bush*, 233 F.Supp.2d 564, 568 (S.D.N.Y. 2002).

17. *Hamdi v. Rumsfeld*, 296 F.3d 278, 283 (4th Cir. 2002). Although in *Hamdi* the government claimed that it developed a set of criteria governing its determination of "enemy combatant" status, no such guidelines have been made available to counsel for Petitioner Hamdi or counsel for Petitioner Padilla. As a result, it is impossible to know who in the executive branch participates in the decision to designate an individual an "enemy combatant," what factors are considered when this assessment is made, what standard of proof

is required for the evidence submitted when the assessment is made, who reviews the assessment and under what standard, and how the decision is made either to prosecute the individual in the criminal justice system or transfer him to military custody for indefinite executive detention.

18. These conditions are permitted only for those who commit serious crimes while already incarcerated.

19. See 18 U.S.C. §4001(a) (2000).

20. *Howe v. Smith*, 452 U.S. 473, 479 n.3 (1981) (emphasis in original).

21. 124 S. Ct. 2711 (2004).

22. Id. at 2721–22.

23. Id. at 2722–23.

24. *Brown v. Bd. of Educ.*, 347 U.S. 483 (1954).

25. 381 U.S. 479 (1965).

26. *Roe v. Wade*, 410 U.S. 113 (1973).

27. 369 U.S. 186 (1962).

28. *Engel v. Vitale*, 370 U.S. 421 (1962).

29. *Dred Scott v. Sandford*, 60 U.S. 393 (1857).

30. 163 U.S. 537 (1896).

31. 109 U.S. 3 (1883).

32. 341 U.S. 494 (1951).

33. 323 U.S. 214 (1944).

CHAPTER 17

IMMIGRATION

*Abuse of (Plenary) Power? Judicial Deference
and the Post-9/11 War on Immigrants*

Lori A. Nessel[*] and Anjum Gupta[†]

*In October 2002, when twenty-year-old David Joseph's family was attacked and
their home destroyed, he joined about two hundred others and boarded a boat
that carried them from the politically motivated violence in Haiti to Florida.
Rather than finding the safety and freedom that David dreamed of, however, he
was labeled a "national security threat," placed in mandatory detention for over
two years, and then sent back to Haiti.*

*Both the immigration judge and the Board of Immigration Appeals found that
David posed no threat to public safety—he had no criminal record and had an
uncle in New York willing to support him during his asylum proceedings—and
ordered his release on bond pending a full hearing on his asylum claim. However,
then-Attorney General John Ashcroft intervened, mandating David's ongoing detention for reasons of "national security." Ashcroft insisted that releasing David
would encourage a mass migration from Haiti, and would allow Haiti to be used
as a terrorist staging ground. When Senator Arlen Specter suggested that the Department of Justice (DOJ) uphold David's Due Process right to an individualized
determination as to whether he posed a security threat, Ashcroft responded,
"sometimes individual treatment is important. Sometimes it's important to make
a statement about groups of people that come."[‡]*

*This chapter explores the threat to civil rights posed by changes in the U.S. im-
migration regime since the terrorist attacks on September 11, 2001. While these
changes originated in the Bush administration and Congress, the Supreme Court*

---

[*] Associate Professor of Law and Director, Immigration & Human Rights Clinic, Center for Social Justice, Seton Hall University School of Law.

[†] Clinical Fellow, Center for Social Justice, Seton Hall University School of Law.

[‡] Bob Herbert, "Ashcroft's Quiet Prisoner," *New York Times* (August 13, 2004) A21.

is complicit because it has deferred regulation of immigration matters to the legislative and executive branches. This deference stands in stark contrast to the Court's willingness to overrule Congress in many Federalism Revolution cases.

We urge the Court to send the message that any constitutionally problematic acts, even in times of war or national crisis, will come under rigorous judicial scrutiny. We fear, however, that this Court will not heed our call.

ঌ   ঌ   ঌ

Our nation's immigration laws have often been constricted in times of political or economic uncertainty. It is therefore not surprising that the tragic events of 9/11 prompted major immigration reforms. Immigration laws offer "a window into our national psyche,"[1] which at the time was enveloped by fear. While the initiatives and laws were ostensibly aimed at preventing terrorists from entering or remaining in the country, they have severely curtailed noncitizens' civil rights. If unchecked by the Judiciary, this rollback could lead to the restriction of citizens' civil rights.

The Plenary Power Doctrine: Judicial Deference to Congress and the Executive

It has been stated of immigration law that "no other area of American law has been so radically insulated and divergent from those fundamental norms of constitutional right, administrative procedure, and judicial role that animate the rest of our legal system."[2] This disjuncture is the result of the plenary power doctrine, which provides that the authority to regulate immigration is allocated to Congress (and to the Executive, if acting under authority delegated by Congress), with limited judicial review.[3]

Although the plenary power doctrine is implied, not explicitly enumerated in the Constitution, the Court has used strong language to justify its deference to the legislative and executive branches when dealing with immigration regulation. It has stated, for example, that the doctrine is necessary to allow the federal government to control our identity as a nation, to regulate foreign policy, and to ensure that the country stands on equal footing with other sovereign nations.[4]

The Court first defined the contours of this doctrine in the *Chinese Exclusion Case* of 1889.[5] While Chinese laborers had been welcomed in order to build the transcontinental railroad, xenophobic concerns arose once the work was completed.[6] The Chinese were viewed as dishonest, insular, and different. Congress responded by passing the Chinese Exclusion Act, prohibiting Chinese laborers from entering the U.S.

The Court upheld the Act, stating that Congress's decisions are conclusive on the Judiciary when immigration regulation is at issue,[7] and reasoning that the power to exclude noncitizens was tantamount to the power of a sovereign state to control its own territory. According to the Court, "[i]f…the government of the United States, through its legislative department, considers the presence of foreigners of a different race in this country, who will not assimilate with us, to be dangerous to its peace and security, their exclusion is not to be stayed because at the time there are no actual hostilities with the nation of which the foreigners are subjects."[8] The Act remained in effect until 1943, when China and the U.S. became allies in World War II.

The absence of constitutional language regulating immigration has contributed to the notion that ordinary constitutional principles do not apply to that area of the law. The Court has reinforced its deferential role in immigration matters by stating that, at least regarding noncitizens seeking initial admission to the U.S., Due Process is whatever Congress defines it to be.[9] The Court has also repeatedly recognized Congress's power to enact immigration rules that would be unacceptable if applied to citizens (whose Due Process rights are explicitly protected by the Constitution).[10]

Not surprisingly, the plenary power doctrine has been applied most rigidly when national security is at issue. For example, in the *Mezei* case in 1953,[11] a man who had been a lawful permanent resident in the U.S. for over twenty-five years left the country to visit his ailing mother in Romania, and was denied readmission upon his return. Set against the context of the red scare, then-Attorney General J. Howard McGrath relied on secret evidence to allege that Mr. Mezei posed a threat to national security, justifying the man's detention on Ellis Island without formal charges or hearings. When Mr. Mezei challenged the lack of Due Process, the majority of the Court found that he had not been deprived of constitutional or statutory rights. The Court stated, "[w]hatever our individual estimate of that policy and the fears on which it rests, respondent's right to enter the United States depends on the congressional will, and courts cannot substitute their judgment for the legislative mandate."[12]

Given this history of judicial deference in immigration matters, particularly in times of war or national crisis, it remains to be seen whether the Court will take an active role in stemming current legislative and executive actions that violate immigrants' civil rights.

Recent Immigration Initiatives

In the wake of 9/11, Congress and the Executive instituted a series of constitutionally questionable initiatives that may go unchecked by our courts. Days after the attacks, the Uniting and Strengthening America by Providing Appropriate Tools Required to Intercept and Obstruct Terrorism Act of 2001 (USA PATRIOT Act) was introduced in Congress (discussed in chapter 16).[13] The Act, in addition to arguably violating the civil liberties of citizens, includes several provisions aimed at immigrants and other noncitizens. For example, the Act requires the mandatory detention of noncitizens certified by the attorney general as having committed a criminal offense or immigration violation or as being "engaged in any other activity that endangers the national security of the United States."[14] Noncitizens are not offered any hearing.[15] In addition, the Act expands the government's authority to designate terrorist groups and its surveillance powers.[16]

Subsequent executive initiatives further restricted the civil liberties of noncitizens, particularly those of Middle Eastern or South Asian descent. In early 2002, DOJ announced its "Absconder Apprehension Initiative."[17] As part of a larger effort to apprehend 314,000 alien absconders (noncitizens who had ignored deportation or removal orders), DOJ announced that it would prioritize the apprehension of six thousand individuals who hailed from "countries in which there has been Al Qaeda terrorist presence or activity."[18] These individuals were the first entered into the National Crime Information Center (NCIC) database, a database used by local law enforcement officials to identify criminals.[19] The American-Arab Antidiscrimination Committee has publicly condemned this and other similar initiatives (e.g., DOJ's plan to interview over five thousand Muslim and Arab men who entered the U.S. after January 1, 2000), calling them "unconscionable" as they are "based on a hierarchy of concern that is ethnically defined."[20]

Further singling out Arab and Muslim men, the attorney general then announced the implementation of the National Security Entry Exit Registration System (NSEERS). NSEERS, or "Special Registration," required nationals of certain countries (predominantly Muslims, Arabs, and South Asians) to be photographed and fingerprinted by immigration officials.[21] Under "Port-of-Entry Registration," noncitizens were registered upon arrival in the U.S., and were required to report to an immigration office for a follow-up interview within forty days of their registration, and again within ten days of the anniversary of their registration. NSEERS also required "Special Call-In Registration" for those noncitizens already in the U.S.[22] Initially, DOJ said that this program would apply to nationals of Iran, Iraq, Libya, Sudan, and

Syria. While the government later extended Port-of-Entry Registration to nationals of more than 150 counties, it has never specified which countries. It is widely believed, however, that the program was applied overwhelmingly to noncitizens from Muslim, Arab, and South Asian countries.

The Special Registration requirements resulted in the deportation of hundreds of noncitizens. Because of confusion about the registration requirements (even on the part of immigration attorneys), hundreds of noncitizens failed to comply. Individuals who registered late, failed to register, or failed to show up for their follow-up interviews were placed in removal proceedings (to be deported).[23] Those who registered in time were sometimes shackled and detained, humiliated, questioned about their religious or political beliefs, and placed in removal proceedings without access to attorneys or interpreters.[24] Between September 11, 2002 and September 30, 2003, over 177,000 individuals registered through NSEERS. Of these, 14,000 were put into removal proceedings and 3,000 were detained.[25] None were charged with crimes related to terrorism.[26]

While the post-9/11 immigration initiatives initially focused on Muslims and Arabs, the government then targeted an increasingly broader group of noncitizens. As a result, noncitizens such as the Haitian asylum seeker David Joseph, have been profoundly impacted by the war on terrorism. In 2003, Ashcroft stayed the Board of Immigration Appeals' order in Joseph's case, and ordered that he be detained without bond, citing the "national security implication of encouraging future mass migrations by sea from Haiti."[27] This decision came after Florida immigration authorities began summarily detaining all Haitian asylum seekers, citing similar concerns about terrorism.[28]

The Supreme Court Must Check Post-9/11 Immigration Initiatives

Given the Court's historical reluctance to curtail congressional and executive actions taken in the name of immigration regulation, it is reasonable to fear that the government's post-9/11 initiatives may similarly go unchecked. The plenary power doctrine has resulted in the Court's application of the lowest level of constitutional scrutiny when examining challenges to immigration regulation. However, a trilogy of cases decided shortly before 9/11 raised hopes that the Court would take a more active role in reviewing immigration laws. While those cases greatly limited access to courts in immigration matters by upholding congressional legislation that largely stripped federal courts of jurisdiction, they also reaffirmed the essential constitutional protections that had been threatened by the executive and legislative branches.

In *Zadvydas v. Davis*, for example, the majority of the Court curtailed the government's practice of indefinite detention[29] and rejected the government's claim that Congress had authorized the indefinite detention of noncitizens with final removal orders whose native countries would not accept them.[30] The Court noted that the statutory provision at issue was not limited to "a small segment of particularly dangerous individuals" such as suspected terrorists, but was applied to a broad group of noncitizens with final removal orders, including those who had overstayed visas.[31] The Court therefore interpreted the statute to authorize only a reasonable period of detention.

In two related cases, *INS v. St Cyr*[32] and *Calcano-Martinez v. INS*,[33] the Court was called upon to review the constitutionality of immigration and anti-terrorism legislation, including provisions in the Illegal Immigration Reform and Immigrant Responsibility Act of 1996 that stripped courts of jurisdiction in most immigration cases. While the Court upheld the congressional restriction of judicial review in cases involving "criminal aliens," it stopped short of revoking access to the courts via habeas corpus, a form of relief under the Constitution to challenge the legality of detention. In each case, a 5-4 majority concluded that the Court retained jurisdiction in cases involving a claim of habeas corpus because Congress had not expressed an unambiguous intent to repeal habeas corpus review of the legality of detention by the executive branch.[34]

Just months after 9/11 in *Demore v. Hyung Joon Kim*[35] (discussed in chapter 5), however, the Court was faced with assessing the constitutionality of a statutory provision that required the mandatory detention, without possibility of release on bond, of criminal noncitizens during removal proceedings. Notwithstanding its earlier decision curtailing such indefinite detention after the completion of removal proceedings, the Court overruled the decisions of four courts of appeals and upheld the constitutionality of mandatory detention during removal proceedings, relying on the "terrorist exception" hinted at in *Zadvydas*.

The Court showed similar deference to the executive branch in refusing to address the First Amendment implications of the post-9/11 closed immigration hearings. Ten days after 9/11, Chief Immigration Judge Michael Creppy issued a directive informing immigration judges of their duty to hold closed hearings for certain cases. The memorandum instructed immigration judges to "avoid discussing the case or avoid disclosing any information about the case to anyone outside the Immigration Court."[36] These "special interest" hearings were assigned to judges who held secret clearance and were closed to the public, including family members and the press. Even the detainee's attorney received only the unclassified portions of the record of proceeding.[37] DOJ later disclosed that over six hundred individuals had been classified as special interest detainees,[38] the vast majority of whom were found to have no connection to terrorism and were eventually released or removed for minor immigration violations.[39] The government continues to withhold information about these secret detentions.[40]

In two different jurisdictions, members of the press sued the government, alleging that the secret proceedings violated the First Amendment. In *Detroit Free Press v. Ashcroft*, the Sixth Circuit Court of Appeals ruled in favor of the plaintiff newspapers, stating, "[d]emocracies die behind closed doors."[41] The Sixth Circuit noted that the public provides a meaningful safeguard against the government's otherwise unchecked power to protect our borders, and that by holding secret removal proceedings, the Executive sought to "take this safeguard away from the public by placing its actions beyond public scrutiny."[42]

In contrast, in *North Jersey Media Group v. Ashcroft*, the Third Circuit Court of Appeals ruled in favor of the government, noting, "[t]he era that dawned on September 11th, and the war against terrorism that has pervaded the sinews of our national life since that day, are reflected in thousands of ways in legislative and national policy" and "the primary national policy must be self-preservation."[43] Though the plaintiff newspapers petitioned for the Supreme Court to hear the case, the Court declined to resolve the circuit-split.[44] The Court's post 9/11 silence serves as a disturbing reminder of its past silence when immigrants' civil liberties were curtailed in the name of national security.

Conclusion

The Supreme Court has historically deferred to the other branches of government regarding immigration regulation, particularly in times of war or national crisis. The legislative and executive branches have often relied on this deference in enacting and enforcing constitutionally suspect immigration rules. Since 9/11, the U.S. government has instituted a series of initiatives targeting noncitizens, especially those of Middle Eastern or South Asian descent. A few recent cases have offered some hope that the Court will not allow Congress and the Executive unchecked power to regulate immigration law at the expense of the civil rights of noncitizens. It is too early to tell, however, whether the Court will take a more active role in curtailing the rollback of immigrants' civil rights—a rollback that can quickly expand to citizens as well.[45]

Endnotes

1. Michael C. LeMay, *Anatomy of a Public Policy: The Reform Of Contemporary American Immigration Law* (1994) 4 (quoting 9 In Defense of the Alien ix (Lydio Tomasi ed., 1987).

2. Peter H. Schuck, The Transformation of Immigration Law, *84 Colum. L. Rev.* (1984) 1,1.

3. *Chae Chan Ping v. United States* ("*The Chinese Exclusion Case*"), 130 U.S. 581 (1889); *Kleindienst v. Mandel*, 408 U.S. 753 (1972).

4. See e.g., *Nishimura Ekiu v. The United States*, 142 US 651, 659 (1892).

5. *The Chinese Exclusion Case*, 130 U.S. 581.

6. Stephen H. Legomsky, *Immigration and Refugee Law and Policy* (2002) 14 (citing Frank F. Chuman, *The Bamboo People* (1976) 3–4).

7. *The Chinese Exclusion Case*, 130 U.S. 581, 606.

8. Id.

9. See *Nishimura Ekiu*, 142 U.S. 651 (1892); *Knauff v. Shaughnessy*, 338 U.S. 537 (1950).

10. *Zadvydas v. Davis*, 533 U.S. 678, 692–95 (2001); *Fiallo v. Bell*, 430 U.S. 787, 792 (1977); *Mathews v. Diaz*, 426 U.S. 67, 79–80 (1976); *United States v. Verdugo-Urquidez*, 494 U.S. 259, 273–75 (1990).

11. *Shaughnessy v. United States ex rel. Mezei*, 345 U.S. 206 (1953).

12. Id. at 216.

13. Pub. L. No. 107-56, 115 Stat. 272 (2001).

14. Pub. L. No. 107-56, 115 Stat. 412 (2001) (codified as amended at 8 U.S.C. §1226a(a)(3)(B) (2004)).

15. John L. Pinnix, Civil Liberties in America During Times of War: From the Alien and Seditions Acts to the USA PATRIOT Act, *Immigration Law Today* (Sept/Oct 2004).

16. See e.g., USA PATRIOT Act §§101, 102, 106, 107, 126; Pinnix, *supra* note 19.

17. Memorandum from the Deputy Attorney General to the INS Commissioner, FBI Director, U.S. Marshals Service Director and U.S. Attorneys (January 25, 2002), at http://news.findlaw.com/hdocs/docs/doj/abscndr012502mem.pdf.

18. Id.; Dan Eggen and Cheryl W. Thompson, "U.S. Seeks Thousands of Fugitive Deportees; Middle Eastern Men are Focus of Search," *Washington Post* (Jan. 8, 2002) AO1. "DOJ Focusing on Removal of 6,000 Men from Al-Qaeda Haven Countries," *79 Interpreter Releases* (Jan. 21, 2002) 115, 155 [hereinafter "Al-Qaeda Haven Countries"].

19. Eggen and Thompson, *supra* note 29; "Al-Qaeda Haven Countries," *supra* note 155.

20. Id.

21. John Ashcroft, Attorney General Prepared Remarks on the National Security Entry-Exit Registration System (June 6, 2002), at http://www.usdoj.gov/ag/speeches/2002/060502agpreparedremarks.htm.

22. Call-In Registration applied to noncitizens, including students and tourists, from twenty-five nations—twenty-four Muslim countries and North Korea—who had arrived in the U.S. during or before September 2002. These individuals were similarly required to report to an immigration office for a follow-up interview within ten days of the one-year anniversary of their registration. Amer. Immigration Law Foundation, Immigration Policy Ctr., "Targets of Suspicion: The Impact of Post-9/11 Policies on Muslims, Arabs and South Asians in the United States," *Immigration Policy In Focus*, Vol. 3, Issue 2 (May 2004), at www.ailf.org/ipc/ipf050104.asp [hereinafter AILF, "Targets of Suspicion"].

23. AILF, "Targets of Suspicion," *supra* note 33.

24. The New York Immigration Coalition, NSEERS Special Registration, Issue Backgrounder (March 31, 2004), at http://www.thenyic.org/templates/documentFinder.asp?did=86.

25. AILF, "Targets of Suspicion," *supra* note 33.

26. Rachel L. Swarns, "Program's Value in Dispute as a Tool to Fight Terrorism," *New York Times* (December 21, 2004), A26.

27. Matter of D-J-, 23 I. & N. Dec. 572 (Att'y Gen. 2003).

28. *Jeanty v. Bulger*, 204 F.Supp.2d 1366, 1379 (S.D. Fla. 2002).

29. *Zadvydas*, 533 U.S. 678.

30. The Court recently extended this "reasonable period" requirement to even those noncitizens, such as Mariel Cubans, who were deemed inadmissible to the United States. *Clark v. Martinez*, 543 U.S. __ (2005).

31. Id. at 691.

32. 533 U.S. 289 (2001).

33. 533 U.S. 348 (2001).

34. In *St Cyr*, the Court held that Congress had not clearly stated an intention to *retroactively* repeal the availability of discretionary relief from deportation for "criminal aliens" who had pled guilty to crimes in reliance on the availability of such relief from deportation.

35. 538 U.S. 510 (2003).

36. Memorandum from Michael Creppy to All Immigration Judges; Court Administrators (Sept. 19, 2001), at http://news.findlaw.com/hdocs/docs/aclu/creppy092101 memo.pdf.

37. Patricia Medige, "Immigration Issues in a Security Minded America," *Colorado Lawyer* (Mar. 2004) 11.

38. Id.

39. Id.

40. Dan Christensen, "Freedom of Information Comes at a $372,799 Cost," *Daily Business Review* (Jan. 31, 2005), at http://www.law.com/jsp/article.jsp?id=1106573749323.

41. *Detroit Free Press v. Ashcroft*, 303 F.3d 681, 683 (6th Cir. 2002).

42. Id.

43. *North Jersey Media Group v. Ashcroft*, 308 F.3d 198, 202 (3d Cir. 2002).

44. *North Jersey Media Group v. Ashcroft*, 538 U.S. 1056 (May 27, 2003).

45. For example, in 1798, Congress enacted the Enemy Alien Act, authorizing the president to detain, deport, or otherwise restrict the liberties of any citizen over fourteen years of age from a country with which we are at war, without an individualized showing of disloyalty, criminal conduct, or suspicion. That law remains in place today. Similarly, the targeting of immigrants for "subversive" political associations laid the foundation for the McCarthy-era red hunt on citizens. David Cole, Enemy Aliens, *54 Stan. L.Rev.* (May 2002) 953, 957–59.

Part IV
The Federalism Revolution:
Principle or Politics?

CHAPTER 18

IT'S NOT ABOUT STATES' RIGHTS

Double-Talk by the Activist Supreme Court Majority

Herbert Semmel*

Ruby Calad underwent a hysterectomy. Although her doctor recommended that she be allowed an extended hospital stay, she was discharged the day after the surgery when her HMO refused to pay for it. The next day, Ms. Calad experienced complications that required her to return to the emergency room.

Ms. Calad brought suit under the Texas Health Care Liability Act (which allows suits to be filed against HMOs that fail "to exercise ordinary care when making health care treatment decisions and [holds them] liable for [harm to an insured or enrollee]"), arguing that her HMO had failed to exercise ordinary care. The Supreme Court refused to allow Ms. Calad's suit on the grounds that the Texas law was trumped—or preempted—by the Employee Retirement Income Security Act of 1974 (ERISA), the federal law that governs employee benefits.†

Is the Court's Federalism Revolution really motivated by concerns about state sovereignty? If so, why have the Court's right wing Justices repeatedly held that federal law preempts state law?

This chapter will expose the hypocrisy of the Court's right wing voting block. While the justices hold themselves out as champions of states' rights by denying individuals the right to sue states for violating federal civil rights laws, they consistently preempt state law in order to further their anti-civil rights agenda.

ða ða ða

Since 1991, when President George H.W. Bush appointed Justice Clarence Thomas, the Supreme Court has been dominated by a five-justice voting block that has zealously pursued an anti-civil rights agenda despite the fact

---

* Herb Semmel died on February 5, 2004. Director of the National Senior Citizen Law Center's Federal Rights Project, he was an essential resource for the civil rights, poverty law, and elder law communities. He is missed.

† *Aetna Health Inc. v. Davila*, 124 S. Ct. 2488, 2497 (2004).

that judicial activism—when unelected judges overturn settled precedents or refuse to defer to the considered judgments of legislative bodies—runs contrary to conservative philosophies regarding the proper role of courts.[1] While holding themselves out as champions of states' rights, and denying individuals the right to sue states for violating federal civil rights laws, the right wing justices have preempted state law in order to further their anti-civil rights agenda. Simply put, the Court has engaged in double-talk.

If a state violates a federal civil rights law by discriminating against a citizen, for example, the activist justices have held that the citizen cannot recover damages from the state unless the state consents to be sued.[2] Similarly, if a state does not pay its employees overtime as required by federal law, the Court has held that the employee cannot recover damages.[3] These denials of justice are perpetrated in the name of sovereign immunity. "[T]he doctrine's central purpose is to accord the States the respect owed them as joint sovereigns [with the federal government]" by preventing individuals from suing state governments for money damages.[4] According to the five activist justices, sovereign immunity is based on respect for the state's dignity—a principle they supposedly hold in great esteem.

These justices, however, regularly affront states' dignity when they use federal preemption to substitute federal laws for state laws. Preemption is accomplished in two ways: expressly and by implication. Congress can act under its constitutional powers to override state laws, and sometimes does so explicitly.[5] Federal copyright laws are an example of "express preemption." In those statutes, Congress explicitly preempts state copyright law, leaving the federal government with the sole authority to issue and regulate copyright.[6]

In "implied preemption," judges decide whether a federal law overrides a state law even if Congress has not expressly provided for preemption.[7] *Geier v. American Honda Motor Co.* in 2000 illustrates how implied preemption works against the dignity and authority of the states.[8] The case involved an auto accident, which traditionally gives rise to claims under state common law. The injured plaintiff sued Honda under state law for failing to install an air bag (she did not sue under federal law because, at the time, federal regulations did not require all cars to have air bags). The Court, however, held that the claim was preempted by the safety standards in the National Traffic and Motor Vehicle Safety Act—despite the statute's savings clause that provided that "[c]ompliance with a motor vehicle safety standard prescribed under this chapter does not exempt a person from liability at common law."[9] Four of the five activist justices determined that allowing states to require greater safety standards than Congress required would conflict with federal law (despite the explicit language preserving the authority of states in state common law actions), and struck down the state law on the grounds of federal preemption.

Egelhoff v. Egelhoff provides another example of the Court overriding state law.[10] That case involved divorce law, a matter so embedded in state law that the Court created an exception to federal court jurisdiction for cases involving divorce, alimony, and child custody in which the parties live in different states.[11] A Washington state statute said that when parties filed for divorce, the designation of the former spouse as the beneficiary of certain assets was automatically revoked. All five activist justices held that ERISA, the federal law governing employee benefit plans, preempted the state law as it applied to life insurance policies. The rationale for the decision was partly that it would be too burdensome to require that large interstate corporations learn the law regarding who gets the proceeds of life insurance policies in every state in which they operate (although it is reasonable to assume that many large corporations are already familiar with this body of law).

To see how the Court is not applying neutral principles in its sovereign immunity cases, one need only examine the vast difference between the standard the activist justices apply in determining whether Congress intended to preempt state law and the standard they apply in determining whether Congress intended to eliminate state sovereign immunity. When it comes to sovereign immunity, the justices require that Congress includes specific language allowing individuals to sue states for damages in a federal statute. A general authorization for suit in federal court to enforce a federal law is insufficient to abrogate state sovereign immunity.[12] The Court has also imposed a strict test to determine whether Congress intended to create a private right of action to allow individuals to sue to enforce federal laws, including provisions of the Civil Rights Acts.[13] When it comes to state laws waiving a state's sovereign immunity, the Court's requirement for specificity goes one step further. Even if a state statute authorizes suit against the state *in a state court*, the activist majority requires a clear statement of consent to suit *in federal court*.[14]

Preemption cases, on the other hand, require no specific congressional language, and preemption can be found even if Congress never mentions the subject in the law in question (supposedly because that is what Congress intended). Similarly, the Court never asks whether Congress intended to allow the regulated business to sue to enforce federal law. Clearly, the activist Court is imposing a political agenda to benefit state governments and large businesses (e.g., tobacco companies, railroads, and telephone companies). Their double-talk is a cover for unjust results.

A true conservative, Judge John T. Noonan of the federal Ninth Circuit Court of Appeals exposed the politicization of Court decisions in *Narrowing the Nation's Power.*

> A doctrine that has swelled beyond bounds, a doctrine that cannot be consistently applied or reconciled with the federal system, state immunity from suit suffers from one further, final difficulty for a doctrine of the law. It is unjust. Why should a state not pay its just debts, why should it be saved from compensating for the harm it tortiously causes? Why should it be subject to federal patent law, federal copyright law, and federal prohibitions of discrimination in employment and not be accountable for the patent or copyright it invades, not accountable for its discriminatory acts as an employer? No reason in the constitution or in the nature of things or in the acts of Congress supplies an answer. The states are permitted to act unjustly only because the highest court in the land has, by its own will, moved the middle ground and narrowed the nation's power.[15]

This chapter discusses a few of the many cases in which the activist justices have voted to override state law (in addition to preemption cases, the list includes cases decided on other constitutional grounds). The decisions begin in 1992, when the appointment of Justice Thomas gave the activists a five-member majority. While the activists sometimes join the majority opinion and sometimes dissent, in these cases at least three of the five voted against state interests while at least one Supreme Court Justice ruled for the state.

The Double-Talk Cases, 1992–2003

Abortion

Madsen v. Women's Health Ctr., Inc., 512 U.S. 753 (1994). A Florida state court granted injunctive relief to a health clinic that performed abortions in order to prevent petitioners from engaging in protest activities near the facility, reasoning that the First Amendment right to free speech must yield if its protection substantially interferes with public operations. The Supreme Court majority upheld the prohibition of protestors from a thirty-six-foot zone surrounding the clinic entrance. Justices Antonin Scalia, Thomas, and Anthony Kennedy argued in dissent that the injunction violated the petitioners' First Amendment rights.

Hill v. Colorado, 530 U.S. 703 (2000). The Court considered the constitutionality of a Colorado statute intended to protect women's safe access to abortion facilities. The law prohibited a person from "knowingly approach-ing" another, without that person's consent, to distribute handbills, display signs, or engage in oral protest within a hundred feet of a health care facil-ity. The Court majority upheld the law, reasoning that the unwilling listener's right to be let alone outweighed the protestor's First Amendment right to free speech. The dissenting opinions of Justices Kennedy and Scalia, joined by Justice Thomas, argued that the state law's content-based prohibition of speech in a public forum violated the First Amendment and could not with-stand strict scrutiny.

Business Practices

Quill Corp. v. North Dakota, 504 U.S. 298 (1992). The Court considered whether North Dakota had the power to require out-of-state mail-order busi-nesses to collect and pay a use tax pursuant to a state law applying to anyone who does "regular or systematic solicitation" (three or more advertisements within a twelve month period) in that state. Quill, the mail-order company, claimed that the tax violated both the Due Process Clause and the Dormant Commerce Clause. All five activist justices agreed that the state could enforce its use tax because this case satisfied the "minimum contacts" requirement of the Due Process Clause, but Chief Justice William Rehnquist and Justice San-dra Day O'Connor joined the majority in striking down the state use tax law as an impermissible burden on interstate commerce. Justices Scalia, Kennedy, and Thomas concurred.

Morales v. Trans World Airlines, 504 U.S. 374 (1992). The Court considered whether the Airline Deregulation Act of 1978 (ADA) preempted state decep-tive practices laws that prohibit misleading airline fare advertisements (as de-fined by the National Association of Attorneys General (NAAG) guidelines). Justice Scalia, Kennedy, and Thomas delivered the majority opinion, holding that the ADA preempts § 2.5 of the NAAG guidelines—state enforcement ac-tions connected to airline rates, routes, or services were therefore prohibited. Chief Justice Rehnquist joined Justice John Paul Stevens' dissenting opinion, criticizing the majority's failure to determine whether Congress intended the ADA to preempt the NAAG guidelines.

Pharmaceuticals Research & Mfrs. of Am. v. Walsh, 538 U.S. 644 (2003). At issue was whether the federal Medicaid Act preempted a Maine statute regarding a prescription drug rebate program, and whether the state's statute violated the Commerce Clause by requiring Medicaid beneficiaries to receive drugs from particular manufacturers. The Court plurality ruled that Maine's

drug program did not impose a disparate impact on out-of-state drug manufacturers in such a way as to violate the Commerce Clause, and agreed that
the drug manufacturers had been unable to prove that Maine's statute was
preempted by the Medicaid Act. Justice Scalia, concurring in judgment,
thought the preemption claim should be dismissed because the manufacturers should seek relief under the Medicaid Act by appealing to the Secretary of Health and Human Services. Justice Thomas, also concurring, concluded that not only was Maine's law free from preemption, but the federal
statute provided states with broad discretion to impose certain requirements
within their own Medicaid programs. Chief Justice Rehnquist and Justice
Kennedy joined Justice O'Connor's opinion, concurring in part and dissenting in part—while they agreed that the state could not place burdens
on Medicaid beneficiaries without legitimate reason, they contended that
the Medicaid Act should preempt Maine's statute unless Maine could show
that its requirements of prior authorization were linked to a Medicaid purpose.

Beneficial Nat'l Bank v. Anderson, 539 U.S. 1 (2003). The Court considered whether the National Bank Act preempted the Alabama state usury law
and therefore could determine the interest rate, what remedies were available for charging excessive rates, and the availability to remove cases to federal court for all national banks. Chief Justice Rehnquist, Justice O'Connor,
and Justice Kennedy joined Justice Stevens' majority opinion, holding that
the federal law preempts state law and provides the exclusive cause of action
for claims of usury against a national bank; therefore, the respondent's
claims could be removed to federal court. Justice Scalia issued a dissenting
opinion, joined by Justice Thomas, criticizing the holding with respect to
removal.

Campaign Contributions

Nixon v. Shrink Mo. Gov't PAC, 528 U.S. 377 (2000). The Court considered
the legality of Missouri's campaign finance law that limited the amount of
contributions to candidates. The majority applied *Buckley v. Valeo*, 424 U.S.
1 (1976), holding that state campaign contribution restrictions do not violate
the First Amendment. Justice Scalia joined Justice Thomas' dissenting opinion, and Justice Kennedy filed a separate dissenting opinion, that *Buckley*
should be overruled on the grounds that campaign contributions are constitutionally protected political speech, and Missouri's contribution limits should
be struck down.

Environmental Protection

Chem. Waste Mgmt., Inc. v. Hunt, 504 U.S. 334 (1992). The Court considered the constitutionality of an Alabama state law that charged higher taxes for the disposal of waste generated out-of-state than that generated in-state. The Court, including Justices Scalia, O'Connor, Kennedy, and Thomas, held that the state law's economic protectionism violated the Dormant Commerce Clause. Chief Justice Rehnquist's dissent argued that the Alabama law was legitimately directed at preserving the state's resources.

Fort Gratiot Sanitary Landfill, Inc. v. Mich. Dep't of Natural Res., 504 U.S. 353 (1992). The Court considered whether Michigan's Solid Waste Management Act, which forbids privately-owned landfills from accepting out-of-state solid waste, violated the Dormant Commerce Clause. Four of the five activist justices (excepting Chief Justice Rehnquist) joined the majority opinion, holding that the state law was unconstitutional in the absence of proof that the state's health and safety concerns could not be satisfied by nondiscriminatory alternatives. The Chief Justice argued that the state law was a good faith effort to address legitimate local concerns rather than unlawful economic protectionism.

Gade v. Nat'l Solid Wastes Mgmt. Ass'n, 505 U.S. 88 (1992). The Court considered whether the 1970 Occupational Safety and Health Act preempted an Illinois state law that required occupational training, testing, and licensing for hazardous waste workers. Justice O'Connor delivered the majority opinion, joined by Chief Justice Rehnquist and Justice Scalia, holding that the federal law implicitly preempted the state law. Justice Kennedy concurred in part and dissented in part, finding that the federal law expressly preempted the state law. Justice Thomas joined the dissenting opinion, arguing that insufficient evidence existed to show that Congress intended to preempt state law.

Family Law

Troxel v. Granville, 530 U.S. 57 (2000). The Court considered the constitutionality of a Washington state law that allowed a court to overrule a custodial parent's decisions regarding a third party's ability to have visitation with their child. The Court struck down the law, reasoning that it violated the Due Process Clause by infringing on a parent's right to make decisions regarding the rearing of his/her child. Justice O'Connor, joined by Chief Justice Rehnquist, wrote the majority decision; Justice Thomas filed a concurring opinion. Justices Scalia and Kennedy filed dissenting opinions.

Egelhoff v. Egelhoff, 532 U.S. 141 (2001). The Court considered whether ERISA, the 1974 federal law governing employee benefit plans, preempted a Washington state law providing that when parties divorce, the designation of the former spouse as beneficiary of non-probate assets is automatically revoked. All five activists joined in the majority, holding that ERISA preempted the state law as it applied to life insurance policies. The majority argued that while most family issues were left to the states, federal law clearly preempted in this instance.

Gay Rights

Boy Scouts of Am. v. Dale, 530 U.S. 640 (2000). The Court considered whether the New Jersey public accommodation law, which prohibits discrimination on the basis of sexual orientation, violated the Boy Scout's First Amendment right of expressive association. All five activist judges joined in the majority, striking down the state law.

Health Insurance

District of Columbia v. Greater Wash. Bd. of Trade, 506 U.S. 125 (1992). The Court considered whether ERISA preempted the District of Columbia Workers' Compensation Equity Amendment Act, requiring employers who provide health insurance for employees to provide equivalent coverage for injured employees who are eligible for workers compensation. Justice Thomas issued a majority opinion (that was joined by the other four activist justices), holding that ERISA preempted the state law. Justice Stevens dissented.

Rush Prudential HMO, Inc. v. Moran, 536 U.S. 355 (2002). The Court considered whether ERISA preempted an Illinois state law requiring an independent review of an HMO's denial of benefits. The majority opinion, joined by Justice O'Connor, held that ERISA did not preempt state laws that regulate health insurance. Justice Thomas filed a dissenting opinion, joined by Chief Justice Rehnquist, Justice Scalia, and Justice Kennedy, contending that ERISA preempted Illinois state law.

Land Use

Lucas v. S.C. Coastal Council, 505 U.S. 1003 (1994). The Court considered whether the South Carolina Beachfront Management Act, pursuant to which the petitioner was denied a permit to build houses on his beachfront property, violated the Fifth Amendment Takings Clause. Justice Scalia authored the majority opinion, and was joined by Chief Justice Rehnquist, Justice O'Connor, and Justice Thomas in holding that regulations depriving property owners of all "economically viable use" of their land were unconstitutional if not accompanied by just compensation. Justice Kennedy filed a concurring opinion.

Dolan v. City of Tigard, 512 U.S. 374 (1994). The Court considered the constitutionality of an Oregon Land Use Board of Appeals' decision to place specific conditions on the petitioner's application to expand her business property. Chief Justice Rehnquist delivered the majority opinion, ruling that such conditions were an unjust taking of petitioner's land in violation of the Fifth Amendment. The four other activist judges joined in the majority opinion.

Tahoe-Sierra Pres. Council, Inc. v. Tahoe Reg'l Planning Agency, 535 U.S. 302 (2002). The Court considered whether the Tahoe Regional Planning Agency's thirty-two month moratorium on land development in the Lake Tahoe area violated the Fifth Amendment Takings Clause. The majority opinion, written by Justice Stevens and joined by Justices Kennedy and O'Connor, held that a moratorium that caused a temporary decrease in property value did not violate the Takings Clause because the property would recover its value when the moratorium was lifted. Chief Justice Rehnquist filed a dissenting opinion, which Justices Scalia and Thomas joined, arguing that the moratorium was for six years rather than thirty-two months, and there was no difference between a temporary taking and a permanent taking; in both instances the government deprived property owners of all economic benefit of the land. Justice Thomas also filed a dissenting opinion, which Justice Scalia joined, taking issue with the majority's distinction between a temporary and a permanent taking.

Medical Marijuana

United States v. Oakland Cannabis Buyers Coop., 532 U.S. 483 (2001). The Court considered whether a California initiative allowing the distribution of marijuana for medical purposes violated the Controlled Substance Act, which prohibits the distribution, manufacturing, or possession of marijuana. The Court ruled that the federal statute clearly prohibits the distribution of marijuana under any circumstances, and did not recognize a medical necessity defense as a valid exception. Justice Thomas submitted the majority opinion, and was joined by the other four activist justices.

State Tort Law

City of Cincinnati v. Discovery Network, Inc., 507 U.S. 410 (1993). Discovery Networks sued Cincinnati when the city revoked Discovery's permit to place news racks on public property in order to distribute free magazines that consisted mostly of advertisements. Justices O'Connor, Scalia, and Kennedy joined the majority's opinion, holding that the city's action was inconsistent with the First Amendment because it had failed to show a reasonable correlation between its legitimate interests in safety and esthetics and its revocation of Discovery's permits. Chief Justice Rehnquist submitted a dissenting opinion, joined by Justice Thomas, arguing that commercial speech was entitled to less protection under the First Amendment than other forms of speech.

CSX Transp., Inc. v. Easterwood, 507 U.S. 658 (1993). The Court considered whether the Federal Railroad Safety Act (FRSA) preempted a widow's state common law wrongful death suit. In a decision delivered by Justice Byron White, the Court unanimously held that the widow's claim regarding the petitioner's failure to maintain adequate warning devices was not preempted. Only Chief Justice Rehnquist and Justices O'Connor, Kennedy, and Scalia, however, joined the portion of Justice White's opinion that held that the widow's negligence claim for a train operating at excessive speed was preempted by the FRSA. Justice Thomas dissented from the latter portion of the opinion.

Honda Motor Co. v. Oberg, 512 U.S. 415 (1994). The Court considered whether an amendment to the Oregon Constitution that prohibited judicial review of the amount of punitive damages awarded by jury "unless the court can affirmatively say there is no evidence to support the verdict" violated the Due Process Clause of the Fifth Amendment, which prevents guilty defendants from being unjustly punished. Writing for the majority, Justice Stevens held that Oregon's denial of review did indeed violate the Due Process Clause. Justices Kennedy, O'Connor, Scalia, and Thomas joined in the majority's decision. Justice Scalia submitted a concurring opinion, recognizing that the amendment did not prohibit a court from finding a jury award to be excessive, but prevented a court from acting upon its finding. Chief Justice Rehnquist joined Justice Ruth Bader Ginsberg's dissenting opinion, stating that Oregon's procedures ensure adequate judicial guidance when a case is tried before a jury, and therefore afford defendants Due Process.

ATT v. Cent. Office Tel., Inc., 524 U.S. 214 (1998). The Court considered whether the Federal Communications Act's (FCA) requirements that the petitioner file all its tariffs or charges for interstate services with the Federal Communication Commission (FCC) preempted the respondent's state law claims. Justice Scalia wrote the majority decision, which Chief Justice Rehnquist, Justice Kennedy, and Justice Thomas joined, holding that the FCA preempted the state law. Justice O'Connor played no role in the review of this case.

Norfolk Southern Railway Company. v. Shanklin, 529 U.S. 344 (2000). The Court considered whether the Federal Railroad Safety Act (FRSA) and the regulations promulgated by the Federal Highway Administration preempted the respondent's state tort law claim. The majority decision, written by Justice O'Connor and joined by the four other activist justices, held that the FRSA and its regulations preempted state law, stating that because Tennessee used federal funds to install safety devices on the railroads, federal regulations governed the selection and installation of those devices, leaving states and railroad companies free from accountability for defective devices under state tort law.

Geier v. Am. Honda Motor Co., 529 U.S. 861 (2000). The petitioner filed a product liability action under District of Columbia law after being involved in a car accident while wearing a manual shoulder and lap seat belt, claiming that the respondent had negligently designed the car by not including an airbag. The Court held that the Federal Motor Vehicle Safety Act preempted the petitioner's claim, reasoning that the claim conflicted with the federal Act's goal to gradually phase in airbags over a number of years while in the meantime allowing car manufacturers to choose from a number of passive restraint systems. Chief Justice Rehnquist and Justices O'Connor, Scalia, and Kennedy joined in the majority opinion. Justice Stevens wrote a dissenting opinion, joined by Justice Thomas, arguing that the Court had expanded the doctrine of preemption to such a degree that it violated the principles of federalism.

Tobacco Products

Lorillard Tobacco Co. v. Reilly, 533 U.S. 525 (2001). After the Massachusetts Attorney General passed a number of regulations restricting the sale, promotion, and labeling of tobacco products, cigarette and tobacco manufacturers and sellers filed suit alleging that the Federal Cigarette Labeling and Advertising Act (FCLAA) preempted the restrictions, and that the restrictions violated the First Amendment. All five activist justices agreed that the FCLAA preempted the attorney general's regulations, and the regulations violated the petitioner's First Amendment rights because they were broader than necessary to serve the interests of the state. Justice Kennedy (joined by Justice Scalia) and Justice Thomas filed separate concurring opinions, agreeing with the Court's judgment but disagreeing with the standard used to reach that judgment.

Endnotes

1. The five justices are Chief Justice William Rehnquist, Justices Sandra Day O'Connor, Antonin Scalia, Anthony Kennedy, and Clarence Thomas. For an analysis reaching a similar conclusion, see Jed Rubenfeld, The Anti-Discrimination Agenda, *111 Yale L.J.* (2002) 1141.

2. See *Bd. of Trs. of the Univ. of Ala. v. Garrett,* 531 U.S. 356 (2001).

3. See *Alden v. Maine,* 527 U.S. 706 (1999).

4. *F.M.C. v. S.C. State Ports Auth.,* 535 U.S. 743, 765 (2002) (citations omitted); But see *Ex Parte Young,* 209 U.S. 123 (1908).

5. See *Pacific Gas & Elec. Co. v. State Energy Res. Conservation & Dev. Comm'n,* 461 U.S. 190, 203 (1983).

6. 17 U.S.C. § 301(a) (2004).

7. See *Pacific Gas,* 461 U.S. at 203–4.

8. *Geier v. Am. Honda Motor Co.,* 529 U.S. 861 (2000).

9. National Traffic and Motor Vehicle Safety Act of 1966, 15 U.S.C. § 1397(k) (repealed 1994) (codified as amended at 15 U.S.C. § 30103(e) (1994)).

10. 532 U.S. 141 (2001).

11. See *Barber v. Barber,* 62 U.S. 582, 584 (1859); *Ankenbrandt v. Richards,* 504 U.S. 689 (1992).

12. See *Seminole Tribe v. Fla.,* 517 U.S. 44, 55–56 (1996).

13. See *Alexander v. Sandoval,* 532 U.S. 275 (2001).

14. See *Coll. Sav. Bank v. Fla. Prepaid Postsecondary Educ. Expense Bd.,* 527 U.S. 666, 675–76 (1999).

15. John T. Noonan, Jr., *Narrowing the Nation's Power: The Supreme Court Sides with the States* (2002).

CHAPTER 19

WORKERS' RIGHTS

Federalist Hypocrisy and the Preemption of State Labor Laws

Nathan Newman[*]

Union organizers have rarely considered courts their friends. The New Deal and the Warren Court provided short reprieves from the long history of conspiracy prosecutions against union leaders and injunctions to stop strikes. Courts are not much friendlier to workers today; federal and state judges strike down laws protecting the right to unionize or guarding workers against unfair treatment. Examples include:

Gould, Inc., a manufacturing firm, was found to have repeatedly violated federal labor laws, including firing workers for striking. Wisconsin passed a law barring companies that repeatedly violated federal labor law from doing business with the state. The Supreme Court struck down that law, declaring it preempted by federal law.[†]

When union organizers hand billed employees in the parking lot of a Connecticut Lechmere retail store, managers ordered them off the property—an act that the National Labor Relations Board (NLRB) deemed illegal under federal law. The Supreme Court overruled the NLRB and declared that the state trespass law overrode the federal labor laws that gave employees the right to be informed about the union campaign.[‡]

Saint Clair Adams, a Circuit City salesperson, was forced to leave her job because of sexual harassment. When she filed suit under California's state civil rights laws, her former employer asked the court to bar her suit, claiming that she had signed an agreement requiring her to submit any claim to an arbitra-

---

[*] Director, Agenda for Justice.

[†] *Wisc. Dep't of Indus., Labor & Human Rels. v. Gould, Inc.*, 475 U.S. 282 (1986).

[‡] *Lechmere, Inc. v. NLRB*, 502 U.S. 527 (1992).

tor, whose costs she would be required to help pay. Despite the fact that such agreements had been declared illegal under California contract law, the Supreme Court held that the Federal Arbitration Act overrode Adams' right to pursue her state law claim in court.*

Sometimes federal laws are struck down, sometimes state laws are struck down—but in most cases, laws favoring workers' rights lose out. This chapter will highlight how conservatives' theoretical commitment to states' rights inevitably yields to their substantive agenda of promoting employer power at the expense of labor rights.

ɞ ɞ ɞ

Do conservatives have a states' rights vision of labor law? Despite rhetoric about restraining federal judicial power, conservatives have only deferred to state governments on labor law to undermine workers' rights. Early in the twentieth century, for example, conservative jurists used the federal courts to overturn state laws mandating a minimum wage for workers.[1] In this period—called the *Lochner* era after a Supreme Court decision that struck down a state law limiting the working hours of bakers—protection of property and corporate power consistently won out over any theoretical commitment to states' rights.

In the era following the New Deal, the Court started to exercise deference when state legislatures and Congress enacted labor laws.[2] In recent years, however, conservative federal judges and politicians have returned to an anti-labor stance that is indifferent to states' rights. Their decisions about whether centralized regulation should trump local control of the employment relationship have been based on which level of government best protects corporate profits. Where local law favors employer property rights over worker organizing rights, for example, the courts have found that federal law must defer to local power. When local governments have sought to ban the use of tax money to support anti-union companies, however, conservative courts have struck down local law. For workers claiming unpaid wages or discrimination, the Rehnquist Court has declared that national rules override state employment laws, allowing employers to impose mandatory arbitration—using employer-selected judges—for labor complaints.

This chapter will trace the Court's treatment of labor and employment—the right of union organizers to access employer property, whether federal law can compel state governments to fund anti-labor businesses, and whether federal courts can overturn state laws barring arbitration of employment con-

---

* *Circuit City Stores v. Adams*, 532 U.S. 105 (2001).

tracts—and will highlight how conservatives have betrayed the principle of states' rights in pursuing their anti-labor agenda.

Property Rights and Federal Preemption in Labor Law

The Assumption of Preemption in Federal Labor Law

In the post-New Deal era, the courts and Congress embraced the presumption that the federal government had monopoly authority in the area of labor relations. A desire for consistency across national corporations led to the 1935 enactment of the National Labor Relations Act (NLRA) and the development of the National Labor Relations Board (NLRB) to oversee the Act's implementation. For the first time, workers had federally-recognized labor rights (e.g., the right to unionize and be paid the minimum wage). Conservatives in Congress immediately fought back by passing legislation undermining those rights. In the past few decades, federal courts have joined in the assault.

The anti-union Taft-Hartley Act of 1947 weakened workers' rights under federal labor laws, but its expansive regulatory framework also strengthened the presumption that federal labor law would trump state law. Subsequently, in *San Diego Building Trades Council v. Garmon* in 1959[3] and *Machinists v. Wisconsin Employment Relations Comm'n* in 1976,[4] the Supreme Court decided that states would have little role in regulating how unions or employers engaged in organizing campaigns or what economic weapons they could use during strikes and related activity. As the Court stated in *Garmon*, whenever any union or employer conduct "is arguably subject to §7 or §8 of the [National Labor Relations] Act, the States as well as the federal courts must defer to the exclusive competence of the National Labor Relations Board if the danger of state interference with national policy is to be averted."[5] Even a potential conflict with federal law would preempt state law unless a "compelling state interest…in the maintenance of domestic peace" (e.g., preventing physical violence) was at stake.[6] Regardless of whether a state law helped or hurt workers, therefore, it would be struck down.

Similarly, in *Machinists*, the Court declared that Congress meant to leave "self-help" economic weapons in labor conflict largely unregulated.[7] For example, state laws could not ban union members from refusing to work overtime.[8] Labor conflict was to be "controlled by the free play of economic forces."[9] The message to the federal courts and the states was to leave labor regulation to the NLRB. The courts, however, have increasingly ignored that message in recent years.

The Property Rights Exception to Garmon *Preemption*

To assure the right to unionize, unions must have access to employees to inform them of their rights (employers have daily access to employees to campaign against the union). While federal labor law clearly protects the right of employees to talk to one another on company property,[10] the disputed legal issue has been the extent to which *non-employee* union organizers and picketers could encroach on employer property to inform employees about their rights to unionize.[11] For decades, the NLRB curtailed employer property rights to ensure that a real debate over unionization could occur on the shop floor. For example, in 1968 the Court held that under the First Amendment, unions could not be barred from picketing in shopping centers open "generally to the public."[12]

As the Court became more conservative in the 1970s, however, it reversed its position. In *Hudgens v. N.L.R.B.* in 1976,[13] the Court ruled that there was no First Amendment right of access to shopping malls,[14] but left open the issue of whether the picketing might be protected under the NLRA (because the picketers were employees of the company being picketed even though they were not employees of the mall owner).[15] The NLRB subsequently found that while the picketing was indeed trespassing, it was protected under Section 7 of the Act.[16]

The Court went even further in *Sears, Roebuck & Co. v. San Diego County Dist. Council of Carpenters* in 1978.[17] In *Sears*, a union picketed in a department store parking lot to protest the store's failure to hire workers from the union hiring hall. While the Court noted that this situation clearly fell within the *Garmon* preemption doctrine, it upheld the state court's enforcement of a state trespass law against the picketers, relying primarily on deference to property rights.

> [P]ermitting state courts to evaluate the merits of an argument that certain trespassory activity is protected does not create an unacceptable risk of interference with conduct which the Board, and a court reviewing the Board's decision, would find protected.[18]

This statement contradicts the *Garmon* standard of preempting state law whenever the possibility exists that it will conflict with NLRB policy. Moreover, given that the NLRB found that labor law protected worker trespassing in *Hudgens*, the *Sears* majority decision seemed even stranger. As Justice William Brennan emphasized in dissent, "[b]y holding that the arguably protected character of union activity will no longer be sufficient to pre-empt state-court jurisdiction, the Court creates an exception of indeterminate dimensions to a principle of labor law preemption that has been followed for at least two decades."[19] Justice Brennan also condemned the majority decision for fatally undermining uniform national labor law because the result left state courts to interpret federal labor law.[20]

The Rehnquist Court Tightens the Noose on Organizing Rights

The neutering of *Garmon* preemption was the Court's first step in undermining the NLRA in favor of employers' property rights. In the 1980s, the Republican-appointed NLRB fleshed out where the Act trumped the property rights of employers by giving non-employee organizers the right to communicate with employees. This series of decisions culminated in the 1988 ruling in *NLRB v. Jean Country*,[21] which balanced the right to organize with property rights: "[O]ur ultimate concern…is the extent of impairment of the Section 7 right if access should be denied, in balance with the extent of impairment of the private property right if access should be granted."[22] *Jean Country* allowed union organizers to engage in informational picketing inside a shopping mall, and area-standards picketing on the premises of a two-store shopping center.[23]

Under the conservative Rehnquist Court, however, even that balancing test fell. In *Lechmere Inc. v. NLRB* in 1992,[24] Justice Clarence Thomas' majority decision declared that local property rights trumped the NLRA unless non-employee organizers had "no reasonable alternative [way]" to communicate with employees.[25] Because the union could picket at a distance or advertise in local newspapers, the Court held that it had the NLRA-required access to workers.[26]

The dissenting justices, including Justices Harry Blackmun, Byron White, and John Paul Stevens (all of whom had joined the anti-union majority opinions in *Sears* and *Hudgens*), castigated Justice Thomas' decision, claiming that it violated the principle of deference to administrative agency interpretation of statutes and twisted the Court's own precedents into a "narrow, ironclad rule."[27]

> If employees are entitled to learn from others the advantages of self-organization…it is singularly unpersuasive to suggest that the union has sufficient access for this purpose by being able to hold up signs from a public grassy strip adjacent to the highway leading to the parking lot.[28]

Not only had unions lost their First Amendment right to communicate with employees, but the NLRB's fifty-five-year-old statutory authority to override state trespass laws in favor of federally-protected union rights had been eliminated.

The principle that state trespass laws trump federal labor law still left open the possibility that union communication with employees could be accommodated by having states modify their trespass laws.[29] In direct response to the Court decisions in *Hudgens* and *Sears,* West Virginia passed a statute that state trespass law and local police could not be used to interfere with a labor dispute.[30] Yet a federal appeals court struck down this law in 1991, explaining "[t]he Trespass Statute appears, however, to infringe on an area preempted by federal law, namely, the Company's ability to withstand a strike."[31] The Court later approved this logic, stating, "[a state] may not, consistently with the NLRA, withhold protections of state anti-trespass law from [an] employer involved in labor dispute."[32]

Unions today, therefore, may face a Catch-22: under *Lechmere*, state trespass law trumps NLRB federal protection for union access to employer property during labor disputes, while federal law preempts any state modification of trespass law to accommodate those labor rights. As a result, labor rights almost always lose out to property rights.[33]

States Lose Control of Their Spending Power

Nothing makes the hypocrisy of conservative proponents of states' rights clearer than their efforts to block state governments from controlling their own spending. In the last twenty years, states have increasingly used private contractors to provide public services, but the law has limited when states can subject those contractors' receipt of public funds to the condition that they satisfy broad social goals (e.g., protect labor rights or promote local employment). Foreign policy and trade concerns have motivated some of these limitations—such as the striking down of Massachusetts' "Burma law," which banned the state government from purchasing from firms doing business with the Burmese dictatorship.[34] Another Supreme Court decision, however, struck down a requirement that local government contractors hire local urban residents.[35]

Under federal labor law, state and local governments have increasingly found themselves unable to prevent labor lawbreakers from being awarded public contracts.[36] As a result, employees are being increasingly subjected to whatever labor abuse the "lowest cost bidder" dishes out—even if the abuse allows these companies to underbid their competition. Public funds, therefore, are subsidizing competition against law-abiding firms. While public outrage might lead a corporation to discontinue hiring a sweatshop labor lawbreaker, a local government is unable to make that same choice.

Limits on state government procurement requirements derive largely from the 1986 *Wisconsin Department of Industry, Labor & Human Relations v. Gould, Inc.* decision,[37] in which the Court struck down a Wisconsin law barring companies with three labor law violations in a five-year span from bidding to provide services to the state government. Even though the Court had previously explained that "[t]here is no indication of a constitutional plan to limit the ability of the States themselves to operate freely in the free market,"[38] the *Gould* Court declared that unlike private employers, state governments could not ensure that public funds were not going to labor lawbreakers.[39] Because the Wisconsin law was deemed to impose penalties on a labor law violator beyond those mandated by the NLRA, the Court preempted the law under the *Garmon* doctrine. "The manifest purpose and inevitable effect of the debarment rule is to enforce the requirements of the NLRA. That goal may be laudable, but it assumes for the State of Wisconsin a role Congress reserved exclusively for the Board."[40]

For liberals on the Court, that statement reflected their decades-old support for expanding the preemption policy. For conservatives supposedly wedded to states' rights and restricting the NLRB's power to enforce labor rights,[41] however, the decision was a hypocritical twist. Conservatives insisted that property rights were so fundamental to state authority that Congress could not give the Board the power to abridge state property laws, but that the NLRA could override state governments' power to decide how to direct their own funds—the only consistent feature in *Lechmere* and *Gould* is that labor rights lost in both. In 1996, the DC Circuit Court of Appeals extended the *Gould* rationale to apply to federal procurement policies, striking down an executive order from the Clinton administration barring companies that had hired striker replacements from bidding on federal contracts.[42]

Boston Harbor: *Upholding Project Labor Agreements*

In 1993, the Court muddied the principles established in *Gould*. In *Building & Construction Trades Council v. Associated Builders and Contractors* ("*Boston Harbor*"),[43] the Court upheld a Boston Project Labor Agreement (PLA) that required contractor unionization on a large public works project in exchange for a promise of no strikes by participating unions. Why the inconsistency with *Gould*'s prohibition of state government procurement requirements? The Court gave several answers. First, the NLRA specifically legalized PLAs for private contractors in the building industry.[44] Second, the policy in question applied to a single project and was not a sweeping regulation-like policy.[45] Finally, there were clear economic advantages for Boston in signing the PLA.[46]

If all these conditions were necessary to uphold a government purchasing rule affecting labor rights, then *Boston Harbor* would be a narrow, but important, exception to *Gould*. The *Boston Harbor* Court, however, indicated that a broader principle was at work when it hinted that it would strike down laws penalizing companies for labor law violations against their workers not employed on government projects, but would uphold laws that penalized companies for labor law violations against only those employees doing government work.[47] This interpretation would make the *Boston Harbor* decision a much larger exception to *Gould* (and would be consistent with a number of circuit court decisions decided both before and after that case).[48] The Court has not yet resolved the confusion over its *Gould-Boston Harbor* doctrine; indeed, the issue is still contested at the circuit court level.[49]

In 2001, however, President George W. Bush issued an executive order banning local governments that receive federal funds from requiring PLAs.[50] This policy—itself an attack on local government freedom—made the *Boston Harbor* exception to *Gould* less important for unions, given the pervasiveness of federal funding for public works.[51]

The hypocrisy of the Bush administration in issuing this executive order was multifold. Most obviously, the administration, which claims to support states' rights, had removed local discretion to manage most public works projects. Moreover, the administration could hardly argue that all PLAs were bad policy for contracting authorities, given that it advocated a PLA in its oil drilling plan in the Alaska National Wildlife Refuge (in order to secure the Teamster and construction unions' support for its energy plan).[52]

The DC Circuit Court upheld the executive order in *Building and Construction Trades Department, AFL-CIO v. Allbaugh*,[53] adopting a broad interpretation of *Boston Harbor*. The court upheld procurement policies on government projects so long as they did not restrict labor policies on non-government work. It is ironic that state and local governments gained the legal right to adopt pro-union policies in a case upholding an anti-union executive order that largely stripped those governments of the practical option to require pro-union PLAs in public works projects.

Even more hypocritically, the Bush administration then supported a narrow interpretation of *Boston Harbor* in order to challenge a California law that banned contractors for all state services from using state funds to "subsidize efforts…to assist, promote, or deter union organizing."[54] With an eye on *Gould* and *Boston Harbor*, California lawmakers had placed no restrictions on the use of non-state funds by contractors to oppose unions. Yet Bush's Republican appointees to the NLRB urged that the Ninth Circuit strike the law down as preempted by federal law.[55] The Bush-appointed NLRB general counsel argued that *Boston Harbor* was merely an exception for the construction industry,[56] while any broad policy over public spending such as the California statute was illegal, even if it had no effect on the labor policies governing employees not funded by the state.[57] The Ninth Circuit endorsed the Bush administration's position.[58]

Here is the absurdity of this position. Employees funded under government contracts are not allowed to use their work time to campaign for or against a union, but instead must spend their work time on activities as instructed by the employer. Any union campaigning must be conducted during their free time. Yet Bush's NLRB counsel argued that employers receiving public contracts should be able to hijack public money and their employees' time for campaigns *against* unionization.

The only consistencies between the Bush administration's position in its executive order banning PLAs and the NLRB's position in California were the anti-union sentiment and the opposition to states having the right to control how their funds were spent locally. For an administration that has repeatedly claimed that states should have more flexibility in managing government programs, the hypocrisy of its selective federalist arguments is overwhelming.

A Note on Living Wage Preemption in the States

A core tenet of the Federalism Revolution is that the government closest to the people should control public funds. Whatever its merit, conservatives have repeatedly proven their disdain for the principle. To see evidence of this hypocrisy, one must only look at the politics around living wage laws.

Since Baltimore enacted its living wage law in 1994, over one hundred cities and counties have adopted ordinances requiring employers that receive city or county contracts to pay wages higher than the federal minimum wage.[59] But conservative state legislators and governors have been organizing to overturn these local laws through state preemption statutes. The Florida state legislature, for example, overturned a provision in the Miami-Dade ordinance ensuring that airport security personnel were paid enough to attract qualified employees.[60] Other states (e.g., Utah and Georgia) passed similar laws preempting local communities from requiring that local contractors boost wages as a condition of receiving public funds. Many states followed "model language" promoted by the conservative American Legislative Exchange Council, which advocates for "local control" and "states' rights," but lobbies for national and state laws that hobble local government.[61] Whether in the courts or the legislature, conservatives preach about letting local governments control their own funds, but attack that right whenever labor stands to benefit.

The Supreme Court Undermines
Individual Labor Rights

The Supreme Court has engaged in a wholesale obliteration of individual labor rights. In the name of state "sovereign immunity," the Court has broadly denied state government employees the right to sue to enforce their rights when state governments violate federal wage and discrimination laws. Starting with *Alden v. Maine* in 1999,[62] where the Court held that state employees could not sue for overtime violations under the Fair Labor Standards Act, subsequent decisions have similarly eliminated the right of state employees to collect monetary damages for age[63] and disability[64] discrimination (the *Kimel* and *Garrett* decisions are discussed in chapters 7 and 8). While the liberals on the Court managed to preserve the right of state employees to family leave under the Family and Medical Leave Act,[65] the decisions comprise a core part of the Court's federalism jurisprudence. What makes it all the more ironic is that this same Court has used the doctrine of federal supremacy to undermine the right of private employees to sue when an employment right *protected by state law* is violated.

No case shows the Court's willingness to abandon its professed states' rights ideals more than *Circuit City Stores v. Adams* in 2001.[66] In that decision, the 5-4 majority threw out a discrimination lawsuit filed under California state law against Circuit City, declaring that the 1925 Federal Arbitration Act (FAA) (designed to promote arbitration between businesses in commercial transactions) meant that the arbitration clause signed by the employee superseded any statutory right to a day in court. In making this decision, the Court overruled state statutes specifically barring arbitration in employment contracts (a fact that twenty-two state attorneys general raised in *amici* petitions). The ruling "pre-empts those state employment laws which restrict or limit the ability of employees and employers to enter into arbitration agreements."[67]

The Court imposed this radical restriction on state power and individual labor rights despite a clear exception for employment contracts in the FAA, which stated that no arbitration would apply "to contracts of employment of seamen, railroad employees, or any other class of workers engaged in foreign or interstate commerce."[68] This clause was enacted because organized labor only withdrew its opposition to the Act when it was assured that Congress did not intend to apply arbitration to individual employment contracts. How did the Court majority arrive at its ruling despite the clear legislative history?[69] As Justice Stevens explained in dissent, they ignored it, "[p]laying ostrich to the substantial history behind the amendment."[70]

The fears of labor advocates concerning arbitration of individual disputes were well-founded. Unlike the arbitration used on union contracts, where each side is well-funded and experienced, individuals thrown into arbitration are forced into a David-versus-Goliath contest without courtroom protections. As David S. Schwartz, senior staff attorney at the ACLU of Southern California, argued:

> Corporate defendants, with some empirical justification, may believe that they are likely to get more sympathy from arbitrators, if not downright bias in their favor. There is a historical tendency to draw arbitrators from the business community.... [I]ndividual arbitrators have an economic stake in being selected again, and their judgment may well be shaded by a desire to build a "track record" of decisions that corporate repeat-users will view approvingly. Even the independent arbitration companies have an economic interest in being looked on kindly by large institutional corporate defendants who can bring repeat business. [Where] [a]n individual plaintiff is likely to have one arbitration in his or her entire life.... A large company, however, will not only have numerous arbitrations, but can also refer arbitration business in a variety of legal fields where business disputes arise. Unsurprisingly, at least one study has detected that corporate defendants have a repeat-player advantage in arbitration.[71]

While the secrecy of most arbitrations makes the collection of accurate data nearly impossible, it is thought that arbitrators give smaller awards than juries because they are more jaded, particularly in egregious cases where punitive damages are available.[72]

The *Circuit City* decision left open the extent to which an arbitration agreement in an employment contract can be one-sided before it violates employees' rights. *Circuit City* followed the *Gilmer v. Interstate/Johnson Lane Corp* decision,[73] which, while not directly addressing the question of whether the FAA covered employment contracts, indicated that the Court was ready to reverse the presumption (from the 1974 *Alexander v. Gardner-Denver Co.* decision[74]) that individual statutory claims could not be waived through arbitration without unfair bias against a plaintiff. The *Gilmer* Court indicated that: "[m]ere inequality in bargaining power ... is not a sufficient reason to hold that arbitration agreements are never enforceable in the employment context."[75] While some lower courts have struck down arbitration agreements for creating inherent bias against the employee[76] or for forcing employees to pay costs that would deter the review of statutory claims,[77] other courts have upheld burdensome conditions on employees (e.g., forcing individuals to split arbitration fees with the corporations that employ them).[78] It is unclear where the Court will go when it revisits the issue; signs from *Gilmer*, however, are discouraging.

Conclusion

The common thread running through conservatives' approach to labor rights and federalism is a deep cynicism—cynicism in their disregard of legislative intent, cynicism in twisting precedent, and cynicism in opportunistically citing states rights or federal power. Supreme Court decisions on property rights and the NLRA threaten to cut off options at the state and federal level to protect fair access for unions to communicate with employees about labor rights. Despite their odes to "state sovereignty," conservatives have stripped state governments of the ability to control who they do business with when they contract out services. Moreover, the Bush administration has blocked the use of pro-union PLAs by local governments receiving federal funds while hypocritically promoting a PLA in Alaska oil drilling to secure votes in Congress. The *Circuit City* decision (vacating state laws banning arbitration clauses in employment contracts despite legislative history indicating that no such preemption was intended) only reinforces the conclusion that the conservatives' vision of federalism in regards to labor rights is merely rhetorical.

Endnotes

1. See *Lochner v. New York*, 198 U.S. 45 (1905). See also *Coppage v. Kansas*, 236 U.S. 1 (1915) (striking down a state law prohibiting employers from requiring employees to agree not to become or remain a member of any labor organization during the time of their employment); *Adkins v. Children's Hosp.*, 261 U.S. 525 (1923) (striking down the minimum wage for female workers in DC); *Chas. Wolff Packing Co. v. Court of Indust. Rels.*, 262 U.S. 522 (1923) (striking down a Kansas Industrial Court Act that set wages in the meatpacking industry).

2. See *West Coast Hotel Co. v. Parrish*, 300 U.S. 379 (1937) (upholding Wagner Act); *United States v. Darby*, 312 U.S. 100 (1941) (upholding the Federal Fair Labor Standards Act); *Ky. Whip & Collar Co. v. Ill. C. R. Co.*, 299 U.S. 334 (1937) (upholding a federal law preventing interstate commerce using convict labor); *Olsen v. Nebraska*, 313 U.S. 236 (1941) (upholding a Nebraska statute limiting employment agency charges for employees).

3. *San Diego Bldg. Trades Council v. Garmon*, 359 U.S. 236, 244 (1959).

4. *Int'l Ass'n of Machinists & Aerospace Workers v. Wisc. Employment Rels. Comm'n*, 427 U.S. 132, 140 (1976).

5. *Garmon*, 359 U.S. at 245.

6. Id. at 247. While labor activity containing elements of violence may violate Section 8(b)(1)(A), it might seem to come under *Garmon* preemption, see Id. at 247–48, but the Court has allowed state courts to stop violent or threatening actions by unions. See *Milk Wagon Drivers Union v. Meadowmoor Dairies, Inc.*, 312 U.S. 287 (1941) (upholding the prohibition of picketing due to extreme violence); *United Constr. Workers v. Laburnum Con-*

str. Corp., 347 U.S. 656 (1954) (damages allowed in state court due to the violence of the threats involved). *Garmon* emphasized that these kinds of state actions were allowed only because of the "'type of conduct' involved (e.g., 'intimidation and threats of violence')." *Garmon*, 359 U.S. at 248.

7. *Machinists*, 427 U.S. at 140.

8. This was the state law involved in the *Machinists* decision.

9. *Machinists*, at 140 (quoting *NLRB v. Nash-Finch Co.*, 404 U.S. 138, 144 (1971)).

10. *Republic Aviation Corp. v. NLRB*, 324 U.S. 793 (1945) (affirmed that pro-union employees could promote unionization on company property so long as they did so on their own time).

11. In *NLRB v. Babcock & Wilcox Co.*, 351 U.S. 105, 112 (1956), the Court held that "an employer may validly post his property against nonemployee distribution of union literature."

12. *Amalgamated Food Employees Union v. Logan Valley Plaza*, 391 U.S. 308, 313, 319 (1968).

13. 424 U.S. 507 (1976).

14. *Hudgens v. NLRB*, 424 U.S. 507, 518–21 (1976).

15. Id. at 521–22.

16. See Scott Hudgens, 230 NLRB (1977) 414.

17. *Sears, Roebuck & Co. v. San Diego County Dist. Council of Carpenters*, 436 U.S. 180 (1978).

18. *Sears*, 436 U.S. at 205.

19. Id. at 215.

20. Id. at 231–32.

21. *NLRB v. Jean Country*, 291 NLRB (1988) 11.

22. Id. at 19.

23. See Giant Food Mkts., Inc., 241 NLRB (1979) 727.

24. 502 U.S. 527 (1992).

25. *Lechmere, Inc. v. NLRB*, 502 U.S. 527, 537–38 (1992).

26. Id. at 540.

27. Id. at 544.

28. Id. at 543 (citation omitted).

29. One indication of this principle was highlighted by a 1999 Ninth Circuit decision, *NLRB v. Calkins*, 187 F.3d 1080 (9th Cir. 1999), giving unions the ability to distribute leaflets in malls, because state law gave general protection to free expression in quasi-public property. The case cited to dicta in *Thunder Basin Coal Co. v. Reich*, 510 U.S. 200, 217 n. 21 (1994), which argued, "[t]he right of employers to exclude union organizers from their private property emanates from state common law, and while this right is not superseded by the NLRA, nothing in the NLRA expressly protects it." *Calkins*, 187 F.3d at 1088.

30. W. Va. Code §61-3B-3 (1991).

31. *Rum Creek Coal Sales, Inc. v. Caperton*, 926 F.2d 353, 365 (4th Cir. 1991).

32. *Livadas v. Bradshaw*, 512 U.S. 107, 119 n. 13 (1994). This case cited to the *Rum Creek Coal Sales, Inc. v. Caperton*, 971 F.2d 1148 (4th Cir. 1992) decision involving the Neutrality Statute, but the argument seems parallel.

33. There is the possibility that *Rum Creek* will be confined to the facts of the case, an especially violent disruptive mining strike, where the Fourth Circuit cited the "violent and illegal means" used by the strikers as making the law vulnerable. In 1980, the California Supreme Court in *Sears, Roebuck & Co. v. San Diego County Dist. Council of Carpenters*,

599 P.2d 676 (Cal. 1979) ("*Sears II*"), upheld trespassing during a union strike as authorized by state statutory law, and the Supreme Court denied cert, *Sears II*, 447 U.S. 935 (1980). One indication of a more positive approach is dicta in *Reich*, 510 U.S. at 217 n.21, where the Court stated, "The right of employers to exclude union organizers from their private property emanates from state common law, and while this right is not superseded by the NLRA, nothing in the NLRA expressly protects it." It is possible, therefore, that states could retain the ability to allow generic trespass during labor conflict while only being required to prevent "violent and illegal means" beyond that basic trespass activity. However, the conservative Rehnquist Court could, especially with the addition of an additional conservative justice or two, support a more expansive anti-union interpretation of its *Lechmere* decision following *Rum Creek*'s example.

34. See *Crosby v. Nat'l Foreign Trade Council*, 530 U.S. 363 (2000) (national legislation imposing sanctions on Burma preempted additional sanctions or actions by state governments).

35. See *United Bldg. & Constr. Trades Council v. Camden*, 465 U.S. 208 (1984) (citing the "privileges or immunities clause").

36. See *Wisc. Dep't of Indus., Labor & Human Rels. v. Gould, Inc.*, 475 U.S. 282 (1986). See also *CF & I Steel, L.P. v. Bay Area Rapid Transit Dist.*, 2000 WL 1375277, 142 Lab. Cas. P 59,131 (N.D. Cal. Sep 19, 2000).

37. *Gould, Inc.*, 475 U.S. 282.

38. *Reeves, Inc. v. Stake*, 447 U.S. 429, 437 (1980) (state could choose to give preference to in-state buyers from state-run cement factory); *White v. Mass. Council of Constr. Emplrs., Inc.*, 460 U.S. 204 (1983) (city contractor requirements that only residents of the city be hired was deemed constitutional under the Commerce Clause through the market-participant doctrine; the clause was later struck down under the Privileges or Immunities Clause in *Camden*, 465 U.S. 208).

39. *Gould, Inc.*, 475 U.S. at 290 ("Nothing in the NLRA, of course, prevents private purchasers from boycotting labor law violators. But government occupies a unique position of power in our society, and its conduct, regardless of form, is rightly subject to special restraints.").

40. Id. at 291.

41. The Supreme Court has repeatedly overruled NLRB decisions favorable to labor rights. Examples include *Textile Workers Union v. Darlington Mfg. Co.*, 380 U.S. 263 (1965) (employers could shut down operations without negotiating with unions); *NLRB v. Yeshiva Univ.*, 444 U.S. 672 (1980) (overturned NLRB, declaring that the university faculty could not unionize); *First Nat'l Maint. Corp. v. NLRB*, 452 U.S. 666 (1981) (overruled NLRB and determined that employers had no obligation to bargain with unions before closing part of their operations); *NLRB v. Ky. River Cmty. Care, Inc.*, 532 U.S. 706 (2001) (overturned the NLRB definition of supervisor and declared certain registered nurses unprotected by federal labor law).

42. See *Chamber of Commerce of the U.S. v. Reich*, 74 F.3d 1322 (DC Cir. 1996).

43. *Bldg. & Constr. Trades Council v. Associated Builders and Contrs.*, 507 U.S. 218 (1993) ("*Boston Harbor*").

44. "Permitting the States to participate freely in the market-place is not only consistent with NLRA preemption principles generally but also, in these cases, promotes the legislative goals that animated the passage of the §§8(e) and (f) exceptions for the construction industry." *Boston Harbor*, 507 U.S. at 230.

45. "The challenged action in this litigation was specifically tailored to one particular job." Id. at 232.

46. "MWRA was attempting to ensure an efficient project that would be completed as quickly and effectively as possible at the lowest cost." Id. at 232.

47. The Court explained that preemption had occurred in *Gould* because the "statute at issue in *Gould* addressed employer conduct unrelated to the employer's performance of contractual obligations to the state. Id. at 228–29.

48. See *Image Carrier Corp. v. Beame*, 567 F.2d 1197 (2d Cir. 1977) (upholding the New York City law requiring that all flat form printing for the city be done by union shops); *Hoke Co. v. Tenn. Valley Authority*, 854 F.2d 820 (6th Cir. 1988) (upholding the rejection by the Tennessee Valley Authority of a bid by a non-union contractor to supply coal); *Alameda Newspapers v. City of Oakland*, 95 F.3d 1406 (9th Cir. 1996) (upholding Oakland's refusal to buy paper from a striking newspaper company).

49. *Bldg. & Constr. Trades Dep't v. Allbaugh*, 295 F.3d 28 (DC Cir. 2002), *cert. denied* 537 U.S. 1171 (2003).

50. Preservation of Open Competition and Government Neutrality Towards Government Contractors' Labor Relations on Federal and Federally Funded Construction Projects, Exec. Order No. 13,202, 66 Fed. Reg. 11,225 (Feb. 17, 2001). Section 1(a) provides that, "[t]o the extent permitted by law," no federal agency or construction manager acting on the agency's behalf shall "in its bid specifications, project agreements, or other controlling documents [for a construction project] [r]equire or prohibit bidders, offerors, contractors, or subcontractors to enter into or adhere to agreements with one or more labor organizations, on the same or other related project(s)." This was similar to an executive order issued by President George H.W. Bush in 1992. See Exec. Order No. 12,818, 57 Fed. Reg. 48,713 (Oct. 23, 1992).

51. See Assoc. of Washington Business, Labor Agreements Risk Federal Earthquake Aid, *Washington Business* (Apr. 2001).

52. Arctic Coastal Plain Oil and Gas Leasing: Testimony of Gerald L. Hood, Secretary-Treasurer of Teamster Local 959, Before the Senate Comm. on Energy and Natural Resources, 106th Cong. (April 5, 2000), at http://www.akteamsters.com/media_coverage.cfm.

53. 295 F.3d 28 (DC Cir. 2002).

54. 2000 Cal. Stat. Ch. 872, § 1 (codified at Cal. Gov't Cod § 16645 (2000)).

55. "NLRB 3-2 Authorizes General Counsel To Oppose California Labor Neutrality Law." *BNA Daily Labor Report* (June 2, 2003). The two Democratic appointees on the NLRB dissented.

56. NLRB's Ninth Circuit *Amicus* Brief: "[T]he Court found [in *Boston Harbor*] that the Authority did no more than restrict participation in the particular project in the same manner as is permitted for private construction industry employers under NLRA Sections 8(e) and (f). [*Boston Harbor*, 507 U.S.]…at 229–233."

57. *Amicus* Brief for NLRB, *Chamber of Commerce of the U.S. v. Lockyer*, 364 F.3d 1154 (9th Cir. 2004).

58. *Chamber of Commerce of the U.S. v. Lockyer*, 364 F.3d 1154 (9th Cir. 2004). A petition for Panel Rehearing was granted on May 13, 2005, so the initial decision may be overturned on rehearing.

59. See ACORN Living Wage Resource Center, at http://www.livingwagecampaign.org/.

60. Lesley Clark, "Penelas Critical of New Pay Law: Bush Signs Bill but Shares Fears," *Miami Herald* (Jun. 05, 2003).

61. See American Legislative Exchange Council's mission statement supporting "federalism" at http://www.alec.org/viewpage.cfm?pgname=1.1d. See also American Legislative Exchange Council, Testimony of California State Senator Ray Haynes Before the House Ju-

diciary Subcommittee on Commercial and Administrative Law on Behalf of the American Legislative Exchange Council, at http://www.alec.org/viewpage.cfm?pgname=5.07a2, arguing for limits on state government control of Internet taxation.

62. *Alden v. Maine,* 527 U.S. 706 (1999).

63. *Kimel v. Fla. Bd. of Regents,* 528 U.S. 62 (2000).

64. *Bd. of Trs. of the Univ. of Ala. v. Garrett,* 531 U.S. 356 (2001).

65. *Nev. Dep't of Human Res. v. Hibbs,* 538 U.S. 721 (2003).

66. *Circuit City Stores v. Adams,* 532 U.S. 105 (2001).

67. *Adams,* 532 U.S. at 121–22.

68. Id. at 127 (citation omitted).

69. Justice Stevens' dissent observed that

> ... [T]he original bill was opposed by representatives of organized labor, most notably the president of the International Seamen's Union of America, because of their concern that the legislation might authorize federal judicial enforcement of arbitration clauses in employment contracts and collective-bargaining agreements. In response to those objections, the chairman of the ABA committee that drafted the legislation emphasized at a Senate Judiciary Subcommittee hearing that "it is not intended that this shall be an act referring to labor disputes at all," but he also observed that "if your honorable committee should feel that there is any danger of that, they should add to the bill the following language, 'but nothing herein contained shall apply to seamen or any class of workers in interstate and foreign commerce.'" (citation omitted) Similarly, another supporter of the bill, then Secretary of Commerce Herbert Hoover, suggested that "if objection appears to the inclusion of workers' contracts in the law's scheme, it might be well amended by stating 'but nothing herein contained shall apply to contracts of employment of seamen, railroad employees, or any other class of workers engaged in interstate or foreign commerce.'" (citation omitted) The legislation was reintroduced in the next session of Congress with Secretary Hoover's exclusionary language added to § 1, n7 and the amendment eliminated organized labor's opposition to the proposed law.

Id. at 116–27 (Stevens, J., dissenting).

70. Id. at 128.

71. David S. Schwartz, Enforcing Small Print to Protect Big Business: Employee and Consumer Rights Claims in an Age of Compelled Arbitration, *1997 Wis. L. Rev.* (1997) 33, 60–61.

72. Id.

73. *Gilmer v. Interstate/Johnson Lane Corp.,* 500 U.S. 20 (1991).

74. 415 U.S. 36, 56–57 (1974)

75. *Gilmer,* 500 U.S. at 33.

76. See *Penn v. Ryan's Family Steak Houses, Inc.,* 269 F.3d 753 (7th Cir. 2001); *Floss v. Ryan's Family Steak Houses, Inc.,* 211 F.3d 306 (6th Cir. 2000); *Geiger v. Ryan's Family Steak Houses, Inc.,* 134 F.Supp.2d 985 (S.D. Ind. 2001)—all involving referrals of arbitration to a single arbitral company that receives most of its funding from employers.

77. *Cole v. Burns Int'l Sec. Servs.,* 105 F.3d 1465, 1468 (DC Cir. 1997) ("The only way that an arbitration agreement of the sort at issue here can be lawful is if the employer assumes responsibility for the payment of the arbitrator's compensation.").

78. *Bradford v. Rockwell Semiconductor Sys., Inc.,* 238 F.3d 549 (4th Cir. 2001) (upholding a fee-splitting provision requiring the employee to pay half of an arbitrator's fees and costs).

Part V
Strategies for Reversing the Civil Rights Rollback

CHAPTER 20

LESSONS FROM THE RIGHT

Fighting the Civil Rights Rollback:
Lessons from the Right

Lee Cokorinos[*] and Alfred F. Ross[†]

"I joined the Republican National Committee during the 2002 mid-term election season as a legal analyst in the opposition research shop," Christopher Jennings explains on the "Find a Republican Lawyer" website. "Now I am a political appointee to the U.S. Commission on Civil Rights, where I advise Commissioner Peter N. Kirsanow on a host of civil rights issues, including affirmative action, voting rights, religious freedom, education choice, and other emerging civil rights issues." His practice areas: Civil Rights, Constitutional Law, and the Fourteenth Amendment.[‡]

One doesn't often hear the words "opposition research" and "civil rights" together. Kirsanow, however, one of the most conservative members of the Civil Rights Commission (appointed in 2001 by President George W. Bush) and former head of the conservative Center for New Black Leadership, has learned one of the right wing lessons well: Know Your Opposition.

The goal of this chapter is to help progressives committed to a fair and diverse society to learn that same lesson. To better understand those leading the comprehensive assault on the Civil Rights Movement's hard-won gains, we outline the history and structure of the conservative movement, and offer ten lessons to learn from the Right.

---

   * Lee Cokorinos is Executive Director of the Capacity Development Group, and author of *The Assault on Diversity: An Organized Challenge to Racial and Gender Justice*, Rowman & Littlefield/Institute for Democracy Studies (2003).

   † Alfred F. Ross is Founder and President of the Institute for Democracy Studies.

   ‡ "Mr. Christopher A. Jennings" web page on the Republican National Lawyers Association "Find a Republican Lawyer" site, at http://www.rnla.org/bio/BioDetail.asp?MemberID=2223.

"This country is going so far to the right you won't recognize it."

John Mitchell, Attorney General to Richard Nixon[1]

More than thirty years ago, after decades of bloodshed and strife, the Civil Rights Movement forced leading American institutions to accept racial integration. To rectify past and present injustices, many states and the federal government required agencies and independent contractors to assemble workforces that better reflected our increasingly diverse society. Businesses began to adopt non-discriminatory staff recruitment and management selection processes, and educational institutions developed admissions and staffing policies more sensitive to gender and race, including programs falling under the rubric of affirmative action.

Federal and state court judges also recognized the importance of changes in race relations, and began to acknowledge their own disgraceful role in sanctioning racial segregation. Building upon the Supreme Court's landmark 1954 ruling in *Brown v. Board of Education*,[2] that racial segregation in public education was unconstitutional, federal and state judiciaries punished those who discriminated and sanctioned affirmative action policies, thereby creating the legal space for the success of a movement toward a racially inclusive society. With widespread public support, and vigorous social justice movements supporting the judicial decisions, these changes seemed permanent.

They were not.

Conservatives have long been working to weaken or eliminate civil rights laws and government-sanctioned affirmative action. Since the 1970s, the context within which the battle for equality and justice has been fought has fundamentally changed; the corpus of progressive public policy measures adopted in the last century, including progressive taxation and social security, are now under threat. The Right's efforts have resulted in the emergence of conservative funding institutions, strategic umbrella organizations, think tanks, media capacities, and networking structures that have fundamentally altered the discussion of social justice.[3] This chapter will outline the history and structure of the conservative movement, and offer progressives ten lessons they can use in their campaign to stop the rollback of civil rights.

The Rise of the Conservative
Legal Infrastructure

The conservative movement must be placed in its proper historical context in order to be understood. Neither its rise nor its attacks on civil rights and diversity programs occurred in a political vacuum. One of the most dramatic shifts in twentieth century racial politics occurred in *Brown*, when the Court overturned the doctrine of separate-but-equal in public schools.[4] Though largely forgotten, *Brown* was the result of decades of strategic litigation by the NAACP Legal Defense Fund (LDF), a model that the right wing went on to emulate.[5]

Brown ushered in a period of political action and civil protest that culminated in the 1963 March on Washington. The multi-ethnic crowd that converged on the national mall to hear Martin Luther King Jr. deliver his famous "I Have a Dream" speech contributed greatly to the political atmosphere necessary to pass the Civil Rights Act of 1964.[6] The legislation officially ended the Jim Crow era by prohibiting segregation in public places such as hotels, restaurants, and movie theaters, and by outlawing educational inequities, employment discrimination, and discrimination in federally-funded programs.

The Modern Conservative Movement

During the 1960s, the conservative movement coalesced around the presidential candidacy of Barry Goldwater, who favored radical cutbacks in federal power and spending, opposed increases in government social programs, voted against the 1964 Civil Rights Act, and supported restrictive amendments to earlier civil rights legislation.[7] While Goldwater lost to incumbent President Lyndon Johnson (garnering only thirty-six percent of the popular vote), his supporters continued their quest to rollback the recent civil rights gains. Movement conservatives who had cut their teeth in the Goldwater campaign focused on building national and regional think tanks (e.g., the Heritage Foundation, the Manhattan Institute, and the Claremont Institute), gaining grassroots allies from the religious right, the legal community, and college campuses, and developing a media machine to spread their message.[8]

The Reagan Era

In 1964, when Ronald Reagan was the chair of California Citizens for Goldwater, he delivered a nationally-televised speech entitled "A Time for Choosing" that galvanized the right wing of the Republican Party and established him as its future standard bearer.[9] During that same election, Reagan was a leading supporter of a ballot initiative that sought to repeal California's Fair Housing Act on the grounds that citizens had the right to segregate their own neighborhoods. Elected governor of California in 1966, Reagan served two terms before becoming president.

Swept into power with the Reagan presidency, a core of right wing ideological hardliners appointed their allies to key posts in the bureaucracy and the federal courts in order to upend the federal commitment to civil rights enforcement. Reagan's first attorney general, William French Smith, inaugurated a sweeping transformation in civil rights policy, focusing on busing and affirmative action. Edwin Meese III, Reagan's chief of staff during his tenure as governor of California, succeeded Smith. After working for years with Heritage Foundation officials on a new strategy for the legal right wing, Meese headed up the Reagan transition team in 1981, which promptly received a blueprint from a Heritage Foundation taskforce urging the administration to uproot affirmative action.

A few of the principal players linking the Reagan Justice Department to the broader legal Right included William Bradford Reynolds (assistant attorney general for civil rights, 1981–87), T. Kenneth Cribb, Jr. (Meese's counselor), and Bruce Fein (associate deputy attorney general, 1981–82).

William Bradford Reynolds was one of the key figures to nurture the assault on diversity. In 1985, the Senate Judiciary Committee rejected his nomination to become associate attorney general. Senators claimed that Reynolds had been less than candid, and had placed himself above the law by refusing to accept court interpretations of civil rights statutes. To get around this issue, Meese named Reynolds as his counselor, from which position Reynolds acted as a key contact to the White House and ran the Justice Department's agenda-setting Strategic Planning Board.

T. Kenneth Cribb, Jr., a classic New Right activist in the Reagan Department of Justice, now sits on the Federalist Society Board of Directors (whose civil rights practice group plays an important networking role in the assault on diversity policies). Cribb is also listed under "advisors and contributors" on the masthead of *Southern Partisan*, a neo-confederate magazine. A member of President Reagan's 1980 transition team, he was the unofficial liaison between the new administration and the Heritage Foundation, whose *Mandate for Leadership* became the playbook for the Reagan revolution.[10] He was known for his role in personnel development (assigning movement activists staff positions) as well as for his ideological influence in staking out the Far Right edge of Reagan's domestic policy agenda.

Bruce Fein also exerted great influence on the Meese Justice Department, having worked for Attorney General William French Smith and the Federal Communications Commission. In the 1980s, from his perch at the American Enterprise Institute, Fein was one of the most public opponents of affirmative action.

Rolling Back Civil Rights in the 1990s

Encouraged by the gains made during the Reagan and George H.W. Bush administrations, right wing activists spent the 1990s strategizing on how to overturn the gains of the Civil Rights Movement. Activists published a "litigation blueprint" entitled *Unfinished Business: A Civil Rights Strategy for America's Third Century* for those organizations fighting to eliminate affirmative action.[11] While the book was penned by Clint Bolick, a conservative activist who has spent over twenty years challenging diversity programs, it was the product of a task force that included many prominent members of the Reagan and both Bush administrations. The foreword was written by Charles Murray, author of the controversial *The Bell Curve*[12] (which argued that intelligence is predetermined by genetic factors correlating with race, and that social policy—particularly in the area of education—should be formulated accordingly).

At the heart of *Unfinished Business* was the new strategy of using think tanks and litigating organizations to roll back race and gender inclusiveness in American institutions. Urging his colleagues to overcome their preoccupation with judicial restraint, Bolick called for aggressive judicial activism, rejecting the national consensus that practical steps were needed to redress racial imbalances. According to Bolick, the idea that "the judiciary must always defer to the popular will" was an "intellectual bogeyman." To advance a radical conception of "natural rights principles," Bolick sketched out a legal agenda that included overturning longstanding Supreme Court decisions.

Around the time of the book's publication, many of the major anti-diversity organizations were established: The Center for Individual Rights (1989), the Institute for Justice (1991), Campaign for a Color Blind America (1993), and the Center for Equal Opportunity (1994).

Many conservatives were disappointed when the Bush administration let stand a Clinton-era friend of the court brief that defended a race-based federal highway contracting program. Such tensions, however, existed long before George W. Bush took office. For instance, Bolick accused President George H.W. Bush of having lost his nerve in the fight to roll back civil rights protections, and "the administration's loyal allies were left to lick the wounds of betrayal."

However, these fears were exaggerated. The Bush administration argued against affirmative action in higher education in the landmark University of

Michigan cases of 2003, *Grutter v. Bollinger* and *Gratz v. Bollinger*.[13] Then-Solicitor General Ted Olson, a veteran activist who had argued *Hopwood v. Texas*[14] (outlawing affirmative action in Texas and surrounding states), argued on the federal government's behalf. Bush also appointed a raft of right wing judges (see chapter 21) who will be able to use their enforcement powers against diversity for the duration of their lifetime appointments.

With Bush's 2004 victory, the stage is set for a number of Supreme Court appointments that could radically change constitutional law for generations to come.

The Organizational Structure of the Conservative Movement

In order to understand how the conservative movement operates, one must be aware of the underlying structures that have enabled the movement to grow in power and influence—think tanks, funding networks, legal organizations, law schools, and law reviews.

Think Tanks

Conservatives first established a number of think tanks in the 1970s. These organizations develop, disseminate, and "spin" social science research that supports the right wing agenda. The most prominent think tanks include the American Enterprise Institute (founded in 1943 and rejuvenated in the 1970s, this organization provides a base for leading conservatives including Charles Murray and former Supreme Court nominee Robert Bork), the Heritage Foundation (founded in 1973), the Manhattan Institute (founded in 1978), and the Claremont Institute (founded in 1979).

Legal and Advocacy Organizations

The power of the conservative movement is concentrated in the legal and professional organizations that influence federal policies and develop the arguments to undermine civil rights laws. Such organizations include the Federalist Society, the Center for Individual Rights (CIR), the Institute for Justice (IJ), the American Civil Rights Institute (ACRI), and the Center for Equal Opportunity (CEO).

The Federalist Society. Formed in 1982, the Federalist Society has become the Right's preeminent legal networking organization with some twenty-five thousand members, a growing faculty division, and chapters at over 150 law schools.[15] Backed by millions of dollars from leading conservative foundations, the Federalist Society's fifteen practice groups successfully shape jurisprudence by targeting the courts, law schools, and the American Bar Association. It also played a key role in the selection of both Bush administrations' judicial nominees and in the staffing of the Justice Department. Its leadership includes some of the most influential figures on the Right, including Edwin Meese III, Robert Bork, and former Christian Coalition President Donald Paul Hodel.

The Federalist Society's Civil Rights Practice Group is a virtual who's who of the anti-diversity movement. Although the group has no official agenda, its *Civil Rights News* bulletin reflects a determined opposition to governmental intervention to prevent or remedy civil rights discrimination. In 1998, Bolick reported on the struggle to defeat the nomination of Bill Lann Lee as assistant attorney general for civil rights,[16] describing how he organized "two dozen anti-preference groups" to voice their opposition to Senate Judiciary Committee Chairman Orrin G. Hatch (the national co-chair of the Federalist Society Board of Visitors). After heading off Lee's confirmation, Bolick concluded that the battle was "an example of how teamwork and principled advocacy can carry the day—even in the most cynical of environments."

The Center for Individual Rights (CIR). Founded in 1988 by Michael McDonald and Michael Greve (who later spearheaded the Federalism Project at the American Enterprise Institute), CIR blazed onto the national litigation stage when it won *Hopwood v. Texas*,[17] in which the Fifth Circuit held that the University of Texas' use of race or gender as a criterion for admissions was unconstitutional. Theodore Olson, former head of the DC lawyer's chapter of the Federalist Society and former U.S. solicitor general, aided in the case. "This was some rinky-dink discrimination case," said Greve. "It's not so natural that someone of Ted's stature would commit that much energy and time to it...it took a lot of political courage."

CIR recently fought the most important "reverse discrimination" cases in years (*Gratz* and *Grutter*), in which they sought to have the Court eliminate affirmative action in higher education. The effort was ultimately unsuccessful. CIR won *Gratz*, in which the Court held that the University of Michigan's undergraduate admissions plan was unconstitutional. However, in *Grutter*, the Court upheld Michigan Law School's plan, finding that diversity in higher education constitutes a compelling government interest.

According to Greve, "The only legalized discrimination in this country is against whites and males."[18] Referring to universities practicing affirmative action, he declared, "We'll sue you for punitive damages. We will attack your integrity. We will nail you to the wall."[19] CIR is continuing this battle by challenging university minority scholarship programs and other practices intended to support students of color upon their admission to college and graduate programs.

CIR is well funded. In 2000, CIR received $150,000 from the Olin Foundation,[20] $150,000 from the Bradley Foundation (with another $50,000 earmarked),[21] and $150,000 from the Sarah Scaife Foundation.[22] CIR's 1999 budget was $1.6 million, and its 2000 budget was $1.4 million.[23] Corporate donors include Archer Daniels Midland, ARCO Foundation, Chevron USA, Adolph Coors Foundation, Pfizer Inc., Philip Morris Cos. and Philip Morris USA, Texaco, USX Corp., and the Xerox Foundation.[24]

The Institute for Justice (IJ). IJ was founded in September 1991 by Clint Bolick and Chip Mellor, former director of the conservative Pacific Research Institute. Although IJ has recently focused its efforts on trying to privatize the public school system, the organization—especially its leader, Bolick—remains an important player in the national attack on diversity policies.

IJ's history is steeped in the affirmative action wars. Bolick previously worked at Mountain States Legal Foundation, founded by beer baron Joseph Coors, which challenged the constitutionality of diversity initiatives in minority contracting in *Adarand Constructors, Inc. v. Mineta* in 2001.[25] Bolick was the driving force behind the devastating assault on Lani Guinier, President Clinton's 1993 nominee to head the Civil Rights Division of the Justice Department. In 1995, he worked with Newt Gingrich to cut off funding for 160 affirmative action provisions in federal law.[26] Finally, he was a legal advisor to the sponsors of California's Proposition 209, which eliminated affirmative action programs in that state.

IJ was established and maintained by grants from the Koch family, a mainstay of right wing libertarian causes. In 1992, the family contributed $700,000—seventy percent of IJ's 1993 budget. In 1996, IJ received $100,000 from the William H. Donner Foundation. In 1999–2000, the David H. Koch Charitable Foundation gave $500,000. IJ also raises much of its $5.2 million annual budget from right wing foundations such as Bradley ($240,000 in 2000), Olin ($225,000 in 2000), and Sarah Scaife ($100,000 in 2000). Along with Bolick and Mellor, IJ's board includes Abigail Thernstrom, a leading anti-diversity academic, and its chair is Earhart Foundation President David B. Kennedy.

American Civil Rights Institute (ACRI). ACRI, born out of the campaign to pass Proposition 209, was founded by Ward Connerly, an African American contractor who was appointed to the California Board of Regents by then-Governor Pete Wilson. Its ties to the Right, however, cover a broader agenda than race politics. Thomas L. "Dusty" Rhodes, currently ACRI's co-chair with Connerly, is president of *National Review* magazine (one of the leading Right publications) and sits on the Board of Directors of the Bradley Foundation.

ACRI has received substantial funding from the Bradley, Donner, Olin, and Sarah Scaife foundations.

In October 2000, ACRI acquired Edward Blum's Texas-based Campaign for a Color Blind America, creating a new division called American Civil Rights Institute, Legal Defense Fund. Blum, a former Paine Webber trader who resigned in 1997 after being asked by the company to stop publishing anti-affirmative action views,[27] launched the so-called "racial privacy initiative" that became Proposition 54 in California. The ballot measure, which was ultimately defeated, would have prevented the state from collecting statistics based on race.

Connerly has also spearheaded efforts to ban affirmative action through ballot initiatives, and is waging a campaign to overturn the Court's upholding of affirmative action in *Grutter* through the so-called Michigan Civil Rights Initiative. The initiative has drawn intense opposition from Michigan-based and national civil rights organizations. Although it failed to get a spot on the November 2004 ballot, its proponents are aiming for 2006. According to Michigan campaign finance records, the bulk of the financial support for that initiative came from Connerly's American Civil Rights Coalition.[28]

Center for Equal Opportunity (CEO). Linda Chavez founded the CEO in 1985 to "counter the divisive impact of race conscious public policies."[29] Despite her statement that, "I have been a beneficiary of affirmative action.... [y]ou can't be a minority woman today without being a beneficiary,"[30] she has led CEO to become one of the country's most virulently anti-affirmative action organizations. Once a Young Socialist, Chavez's background is as a conservative columnist who went on to become the Reagan-appointed staff director of the U.S. Commission on Civil Rights.[31]

In the late 1980s, Chavez headed the controversial organization U.S. English, which came under a torrent of criticism for racism. In the 1990s, she advised conservative millionaire Ron Unz on his successful campaign to bar bilingual education in California's public schools (Proposition 227).[32] Though nominated by President George W. Bush to be Labor Secretary, she was never confirmed because it got out that she might have broken the law in hiring a domestic worker. She has since rededicated herself to CEO, speaking out against affirmative action. She is also is a contributing editor at *Crisis*, the conservative Catholic magazine, and a former fellow at the Manhattan Institute.

CEO has declared itself "the first think tank in Washington devoted exclusively to race, ethnicity, immigration, and public policy."[33] CEO works with like-minded academics to produce ideologically-driven "research," then pushes the findings into public debate through seminars, congressional testimony, and a network of media contacts. Occasionally, CEO participates in litigation, such as when it joined ACRI and the Pacific Legal Foundation to file an amicus brief supporting the plaintiff in *Adarand v. Mineta.*

Through its parent group, the Equal Opportunity Foundation, CEO receives money from the leading foundations underwriting the conservative movement, including the Olin, Bradley, and Sarah Scaife foundations. The Claude R. Lambe Foundation, with right wing libertarian Charles G. Koch on its Board, granted $100,000 to CEO in 1998.[34]

Law Schools and Law Reviews

Radical right wing law schools are training thousands of legal activists, and are generating extreme legal theories in every practice area. These schools include Pat Robertson's Regent University School of Law (Virginia), Jerry Falwell's Liberty University School of Law (Virginia), the University of St. Thomas School of Law (Minnesota), and Ave Maria School of Law (Michigan). Thomas S. Monaghan, former owner of Domino's Pizza and a major supporter of anti-choice campaigns, funds Ave Maria; and its faculty includes Robert Bork.[35] These new schools have added to the wave of conservative law reviews, such as *Regent University Law Review*, the Federalist Society-linked *Harvard Journal of Law and Public Policy*, *Ave Maria Law Review*, and *Texas Review of Law and Politics*.

Strategies to Counteract the Right's Agenda

The Right is on the verge of succeeding in rolling back the civil rights revolution. Bruce Fein, associate deputy attorney general under the Reagan administration, has all but declared victory. "Reagan's meticulously devised and brilliantly executed plan to populate the federal bench with trenchant thinkers and writers scornful of Great Society enthusiasms proved a stupendous success."[36] Bragging that right wing doctrines "dominate the constitutional landscape in the Supreme Court....in the fields of racial or ethnic preferences, church-state relations, federalism, and powers of the police and prosecutors," Fein assures Republican senators that they "have nothing to fear" by throwing "even 10–20 percent of the next fifty judicial vacancies" to previous Clinton judicial nominees to buy off the Democrats and short-circuit Senate filibuster battles over a handful of extreme right wing nominees.[37]

If Fein is right, what lessons can be drawn from this political and legal shift to the Right?

1. Patience and Persistence Pay Off. It took the Right over three decades to become a force in national politics. While efforts to restore civil rights will take time and planning, they can succeed.

2. Think Long Term. Considering the successes of the Right, and the weaknesses of the social justice movement, some may conclude that only incremental progress is possible. If we are drawing lessons from the Right, however, the anti-rollback movement should scale up its objectives and incorporate strategic planning into its thinking and practices. There is a critical difference between focusing tactically on winnable victories and thinking small.

The Right recognized that regaining the strategic initiative was impossible so long as they were locked in a mindset governed by daily "spin wars," election cycles, and "magic bullet" issues. Critically important as these battles were, they were considered a means to an end. The Right focused its efforts on a long-term strategy for building the movement and changing the balance of forces. They also learned that the favorite shibboleth of American politicians, "all politics is local," is somewhat overrated—local issues are often driven by the national media "echo chamber," which is in turn rooted in the organizational infrastructure of the Right. Ward Connerly's anti-affirmative action Prop 209, for example, succeeded because of outside talent and money.

3. Study the Opposition. For a generation, the Right has studied its opposition. In 1965, in the wake of the passage of the Civil Rights Act and the Voting Rights Act, M. Stanton Evans published *The Liberal Establishment*.[38] The book, a survey of the main pillars of the Great Society that the Right wanted to destroy or marginalize, began the long process of preparing the intellectual ground for building up structures of permanent political warfare in order to oust social justice concerns from their rightful place at the table of American democracy.

In the years that followed, the Right continued to study the literature of the Civil Rights Movement, the means by which the Movement brought pressure to bear on politicians, and the NAACP LDF's model of strategic litigation.[39] They used this research to transform the Republican Party so that it would support the Far Right's programs.

Progressives concerned with the rollback of civil rights should study the conservative movement's history and structures. Reading this chapter is a good start, but a more thorough analysis is necessary. Such research, properly funded, timely, rigorous, and focused on the Right's organizations and strategies, is indispensable for formulating short- and long-term strategies.

4. Don't Underestimate Your Opponent. Even if there is widespread public support for your cause, do not take your opposition lightly. Public support does not automatically yield success in policy or law.

There is, for example, widespread public support for the provisions of the 1964 Civil Rights Act. While some advocates may have concluded that it was safe from attack, conservatives have proven this notion wrong by significantly reducing civil rights protections. Anti-rollback activists should base their long-term goals on the premise that conservatives can destroy federal civil rights protections and programs.

5. Messaging and Framing is Important. By the mid-1990s, right wing leadership was spin-doctoring the bitter anti-civil rights politics of the 1970s and 1980s with anti-discrimination language. For example, they gained new converts by preaching a simplistic message depicting white males as victims of racism, reverse discrimination, and unfair affirmative action policies. Advocates fighting the rollback must consider both the messaging behind their movement, and how they frame the debate. Furthermore, advocates must counteract the Right's messages by refuting their claims through sound research and by "flipping" their messages (e.g., using themes such as individual liberty to support civil rights measures).

6. Consider Non-Legal Strategies. Right wing litigating organizations have played a critical role in the assault on diversity and social justice. This legal attack, however, was but an extension of a more comprehensive effort. To fight the legal battle, anti-rollback activists must create the political context, and therefore the necessary infrastructure, to support progressive litigation. This context can be created through the strategic use of the media for messaging, and the development of supportive research in think tanks, colleges, and universities.

7. Maximize the Effectiveness of Organizational Structures. The conservative movement has strategically developed strong and effective organizations and coalitions such as the Heritage Foundation and the Federalist Society, and have mastered the art of dividing labor among coalition members. The anti-rollback movement must continue dividing up the necessary labor and developing effective umbrella structures to coordinate their efforts.

8. Develop and Train Determined Leadership. The Heritage Foundation likes to say that "people are policy." Experienced members of the Goldwater campaign, the Reagan administration, and the Bush administrations invested time to train new leaders to carry on the movement. Young activists were taught to be firm and determined in their beliefs, and to develop the organizational skills needed to give their beliefs political relevance. Progressives must likewise develop methods for attracting and training young advocates.

9. Money is Important. Money has played a crucial role in the Right's success— not only because of its scale, but because of how it was used. The foundations and individuals that fund the Heritage Foundation, the Federalist Society, CIR, and CEO, are equally or even more committed to displacing their opposition as the people whose work they support. They understand that pursuing their social goals requires both this commitment and a varied and skilled infrastructure. As researchers from the Center for Responsive Philanthropy have pointed out, mainstream and progressive funders still have far to go in this regard.[40]

10. The Proper Mindset is Crucial. Right wing advocates understood they would have to work hard to achieve their goals. Advocates must develop clear goals and be willing to take risks.

Conclusion

Society's democratic institutions and traditions are in danger of succumbing to the sustained attack from the Right. In the years following the 2000 and 2004 elections, conservatives captured both houses of Congress, the Supreme Court, and most of the appellate courts, and made major inroads in key media and communications outlets, universities, and policymaking. Indeed, the Right's enduring infrastructure has permanently altered the political and social landscape.

In spite of the Right's central position in American life, its members' backgrounds, beliefs, strategies, and leadership are not widely understood. This lack of scrutiny has served their efforts. The defenders of diversity and social programs now face a political chessboard on which the Right occupies the most strategic squares. However, the anti-rollback movement can still win if we study the game and develop our own strategies. Many lessons can be learned from researching the Right's history and structures. Provided that we are determined and willing to work hard, we can ensure that this country remains committed to justice, equality, and fairness.

Endnotes

1. "John N. Mitchell Dies at 75; Major Figure in Watergate," *New York Times* (November 10, 1988) A1.

2. 347 U.S. 483 (1954).

3. A more extensive treatment of this process can be found in Lee Cokorinos, *The Assault on Diversity: An Organized Challenge to Racial and Gender Justice* (2003).

4. 347 U.S. 483 (1954).

5. Eva Paterson, Lee Cokorinos, Susan Kiyomi Serrano, and William C. Kidder, Breathing Life into *Brown* at Fifty: Lessons About Equal Justice, *The Black Scholar*, Vol. 34, No. 2 (Summer 2004) 2–13.

6. 42 U.S.C. §2000e.

7. Bart Barnes, "Barry Goldwater, GOP Hero, Dies," *The Washington Post* (May 30, 1998) A01.

8. On the creation and early days of the right wing media machine, see John S. Saloma III, *Ominous Politics: The New Conservative Labyrinth* (1984) chapter 9.

9. Sidney Blumenthal, *Rise of the Counter-Establishment: From Conservative Ideology to Political Power* (1986) 40.

10. See the Heritage Foundation website, http://www.heritage.org/Research/Features/Mandate.

11. Clint Bolick, *Unfinished Business: A Civil Rights Strategy for America's Third Century* (1990).

12. Richard J. Herrnstein and Charles Murray, *The Bell Curve: Intelligence and Class Structure in American Life* (1994).

13. *Grutter v. Bollinger*, 539 U.S. 306 (2003) and *Gratz v. Bollinger*, 539 U.S. 244 (2003).

14. 78 F.3d 932 (5th Cir. 1996).

15. For more on the Federalist Society, see Lee Cokorinos and Julie R. F. Gerchik, *The Federalist Society and the Challenge to a Democratic Jurisprudence*, Institute for Democracy Studies (2000).

16. Clint Bolick, Fighting a Left Turn on Rights: The Battle against the Bill Lann Lee Nomination, *Civil Rights News*, Vol. 2, Issue 1 (Spring 1998).

17. 78 F.3d 932 (5th Cir. 1996).

18. Rochelle L. Stanfield, The Wedge Issue, *National Journal* (April 1, 1995) 790.

19. Anne Kornhauser, "The Right Versus the Correct: Free-Market Firm Sees Campuses as Fertile Battleground," *Legal Times* (April 29, 1991) 1; Paul Feldman, "Group's Funding Of Immigration Measure Assailed," *Los Angeles Times* (September 10, 1994) B3.

20. Olin Foundation, 2000 IRS Form 990.

21. Lynde and Harry Bradley Foundation 2000 Annual Report.

22. Sarah Scaife Foundation, 2000 IRS Form 990.

23. CIR, 2000 IRS Form 990. See also Stephen Goode, Conservative Legal Eagles Fight for Individual Rights, *Insight on the News* (January 11, 1999).

24. Terry Carter, On a Roll(Back), *ABA Journal* (February 1998).

25. 534 U.S. 103 (2001).

26. Jean Stefancic and Richard Delgado, *No Mercy: How Conservative Think Tanks Changed America's Social Agenda* (1996) 46.

27. Julie Mason, "Prop. A Leader Leaves Job, Says City Official Interfered; Blum Claims Attempt Made To Silence Him," *Houston Chronicle* (July 10, 1998) A1.

28. Michigan Dept. of State, Bureau of Elections, "Non-Qualification CS Statement," Michigan Civil Rights Initiative Committee (August 8, 2004); Chad Selweski, "California Group Bankrolls Bulk of Anti-Affirmative Action Drive," *Macomb Daily News* (September 2, 2004).

29. CEO website, http://www.ceousa.org/general.html.

30. Robert Pear, "Rights Aide Asserts the Right to Speak Her Mind," *New York Times* (June 11, 1984) A24.

31. CEO biographical profiles. CEO promotional packet, distributed January 28, 1999, Washington DC. See also Don Kowet, "She Would Bring Back Melting Pot; Multicultural Gurus Can't Abide Lessons Life Taught Linda Chavez," *Washington Times* (January 9, 1992) E1.

32. Macarena Hernandez, "Conservative and Hispanic, Linda Chavez Carves Out Leadership Niche," *New York Times* (August 19, 1998) A28.

33. "Linda Chavez Founds Think Tank on Race and Ethnicity," *PR Newswire* (February 21, 1995).

34. Claude R. Lambe Charitable Foundation 1998 IRS Form 990.

35. See Ave Maria Law School website, http://www.avemarialaw.edu/prospective/faculty/ fac1.cfm.

36. Bruce Fein, "Strategy to Break the Bench Logjam," *The Washington Times* (May 13, 2003).

37. Id.

38. M. Stanton Evans, *The Liberal Establishment: Who Runs America...and How* (1965).

39. These themes are woven through the bible of the anti-affirmative action movement. See Clint Bolick, *The Affirmative Action Fraud: Can We Restore the American Civil Rights Vision?* (1996).

40. See David Callahan, *$1 Billion for Ideas: Conservative Think Tanks in the 1990s*, National Committee for Responsive Philanthropy (March 1999); and Sally Covington, *Moving a Public Policy Agenda: The Strategic Philanthropy of Conservative Foundations*, National Committee for Responsive Philanthropy (July 1997).

CHAPTER 21

RESTORING THE BALANCE OF
POWER IN THE FEDERAL COURTS

Saving the Courts

Susan Lerner[*]

In June 2001, President George W. Bush nominated Los Angeles Superior Court Judge and Federalist Society member Carolyn Kuhl to the Ninth Circuit Court of Appeals. The Justice For All Project—a California coalition composed of civil rights activists, feminists, labor, disability rights activists, environmental activists, workers and employment rights activists, Asian Americans, African Americans, Latinos, consumers, taxpayers, and religious groups that supports the appointment of fair and open-minded federal judges—looked into Kuhl's record only to find evidence of her extremist ideology. While working in the Department of Justice during the Reagan administration, Kuhl had urged the government to argue that Roe v. Wade (the *Supreme Court case establishing the right to safe legal abortion) should be overturned or ignored; that Bob Jones University and other racially discriminatory schools should be exempt from paying federal taxes; and that groups such as labor unions and environmental rights organizations should not have the right to sue on behalf of their members. Further, when Kuhl was a California state trial court judge, she had ruled to restrict the ability of people to protect their basic individual rights in court.[†]*

The Justice For All Project alerted its members about Kuhl's nomination and urged the half million Californians represented by its membership organizations to write to Senator Barbara Boxer expressing their opposition. As a result, Sena-

---

[*] Founder and chair of the Committee for Judicial Independence, a grassroots organization dedicated to educating Americans about the importance of an independent and open-minded federal judiciary, and about the threat posed by the extreme Right's concerted effort to take over the federal courts. This chapter was funded by the Equal Justice Society.

[†] See *Independent Judiciary's Report on Carolyn Kuhl*, at http://independentjudiciary .org/nominees/nominee.cfm?NomineeID=18.

283

tor Boxer came out against Kuhl's appointment, and led the Democratic caucus in a filibuster against the nomination.

Senator Dianne Feinstein was harder to convince. Over the next two years, the coalition worked to ensure that all progressive Californians were aware of Kuhl's record. Coalition members contacted colleagues in Oregon, Nevada, and Washington, three of the other Ninth Circuit states. As a result, groups and individuals throughout the Ninth Circuit wrote to Senator Feinstein expressing their opposition. In addition, the coalition circulated an opposition letter on law school campuses that was signed by over a hundred law professors in the Ninth Circuit states, and an additional hundred law professors across the country. Op-ed pieces by coalition members appeared in west coast papers, many leading papers editorialized against the nomination after receiving information from the coalition, and coalition press conferences received print and broadcast media coverage. Although early signs pointed to Senator Feinstein supporting Kuhl's confirmation, she voted against Kuhl after receiving over twenty-one thousand calls, faxes, and letters.

In January 2005, newly re-elected President Bush indicated that he would nominate Kuhl again to the Ninth Circuit. Aware that her nomination faced continuing opposition in the Senate, Kuhl chose to withdraw.

This chapter will explain how the extreme Right has taken over the federal judiciary in the past quarter century, and how the resulting dominance of conservative federal judges is largely responsible for the nation's rollback of civil rights.

There are few factors that are more critical to determining the course of the Nation, and yet are more often overlooked, than the values and philosophies of the men and women who populate the third co-equal branch of the national government—the federal judiciary.

> Office of Legal Policy, Department of Justice, The Constitution in the Year 2000: Choices Ahead in Constitutional Interpretation (October 11, 1988).

How Did We Get Here?

The selection of federal judges has always been political. The Constitution outlines the procedure for appointing judges—the president nominates judges and the Senate must confirm or reject those nominees.[1] As a result, political considerations are often involved, and judicial confirmation battles can be contentious. The Senate refused George Washington's nomination of John Rutledge to be Chief Justice in 1795 because Rutledge had criticized the Jay Treaty.[2] Since then, many federal nominees have been similarly rejected on political grounds.

Presidents have ascribed varying levels of importance to their judicial nominations.[3] Some have regarded their power of appointment as a way to further their party's position by rewarding friends and supporters, while others have viewed judicial appointments more as a means to further their legal agendas. Of course, even the latter were not always successful in selecting judges who would reliably act in line with the party's goals. Conservative Republican President Dwight Eisenhower, for example, appointed Earl Warren, who proved to be one of the most liberal Supreme Court justices.[4]

The Reagan Administration

More than any administration since President Roosevelt, the Reagan administration sought to—and succeeded in—remaking the federal judiciary in its political image. During the 1980 presidential election, the Republican party platform promised to appoint judges whose conservative legal philosophy would undo advances in civil liberties and civil rights by having "the highest regard for protecting the rights of law-abiding citizens…[through a] belief in the decentralization of the federal government…[and by] return[ing] decision-making power to state and local elected officials."[5]

By the 1980s, the extreme Right understood that they would be unable to successfully lobby Congress to roll back popular advances in civil liberties, civil rights, environmental protections, and women's rights. Even conservative members of Congress recognized that an attempt to repeal the Voting Rights Act or the Clean Water Act would be political suicide. The extreme Right also realized, however, that any legislation that Congress could not directly repeal could be undermined or struck down by hostile federal judges. In 1985, Associate Deputy Attorney General Bruce Fein defended using judicial appointments to change the law. "It became evident after [Reagan's] first term that there was no way to make legislative gains in many areas of social and civil rights. *The president has to do it by changing the jurisprudence.*"[6]

The Reagan administration made good on its promises, appointing 368 judges to lower federal courts and three justices to the Supreme Court, including arch-conservative Federalist Society member Antonin Scalia.[7] With the appointment of Edwin Meese III as attorney general, judicial selection became even more focused on nominees whose legal philosophy matched that of the extreme Right. Meese brought lawyers from the Federalist Society, a relatively new ultra-conservative legal network (described in chapter 20),[8] into the Justice Department to reform law and assist in the selection of federal judges.

Contemporaneous press reports discuss the rigorous ideological examination that nominees were subjected to by those Federalist Society gatekeepers.[9]

In addition, the Reagan Justice Department issued a virtual roadmap for the legal changes they expected from their judicial appointees.[10] The two reports, described as "a list of targets,"[11] clearly presage the attack on civil rights and liberties detailed in Part II, setting forth specific legal theories that could affect the rollback and identifying Court precedents that would have to be overturned or modified.

The First Bush Administration

President George H. W. Bush continued the strategy of nominating ideologues with rigid conservative convictions to the bench. He appointed two Supreme Court justices, including ultra-rightist Clarence Thomas,[12] and by the end of his presidency, the majority of appointees in eleven of the thirteen circuit courts had been nominated by Republicans.[13] Federalist Society members boasted that *every* Bush judicial nominee was a member,[14] and Lee Liberman Otis, a Federalist Society founder and assistant counsel to Bush, vetted all judicial candidates for "ideological purity."[15] The effect of the concerted strategy to appoint only judges who espoused an extreme Right ideology was evident in decisions that retreated from advances in civil rights and liberties at all levels of the federal court system.

The Clinton Administration

Unfortunately, President Clinton did not make judicial appointments a priority. When faced with disciplined Republican opposition, including deliberate delays and refusals to confirm even moderate judicial nominees, the Clinton administration gave in and appointed moderate to conservative, sometimes Republican, judges. Clinton's two Supreme Court appointments, Justices Ruth Bader Ginsburg and Stephen Breyer, are both considered moderates. More progressive candidates would not have been confirmed by the Republican-controlled Senate (during Clinton's second term); moreover, Far Right senators such as Orrin Hatch (R-UT), Chairman of the Senate Judiciary Committee, were willing to use whatever means necessary to block Clinton's nominees so as to ensure that a future Republican president could fill the largest possible number of judicial vacancies.

To be sure, this Republican intransigence was effective. Between 1995 and 2000, the Senate blocked forty-five percent of Clinton's circuit court nominees. Fifty-five Clinton judicial nominees never got a confirmation hearing before the Senate Judiciary Committee, and ten more got a hearing but no vote. By the end of the Clinton presidency, there was a crisis number of vacancies in the federal courts—over one hundred federal judgeships (out of 875)—some having remained empty for five years.

The Current Situation

President George W. Bush campaigned on the promise that he would appoint judges like Supreme Court Justices Scalia and Thomas. He has been true to his word, populating his administration (including the Office of White House Counsel and a special committee of Justice Department lawyers, both of which are responsible for selecting judicial nominees)[16] with Federalist Society members whose influence is apparent in nominations to the federal Judiciary. Early in the Bush administration, the Office of White House Counsel announced that it was ending a near fifty year tradition—started by President Dwight Eisenhower—of having the American Bar Association's (ABA) bipartisan and non-ideological panel evaluate judicial nominees for professionalism and legal qualifications. In its place, the Federalist Society and the Heritage Foundation began performing ideological vettings.

As a result, most of Bush's judicial nominees have impeccable radical Right credentials; many even seem to have been chosen by the principles set forth in Ed R. Haden's 2001 law review article *Judicial Selection: A Pragmatic Approach*[17] in which Haden argues that "[t]o increase the likelihood that his legislation will be upheld by the courts, the new President should select nominees that share his judicial, or legal, philosophy."[18] The article is an astonishingly candid review of how to select judicial nominees whose primary virtue will be an adherence to a radical Right legal philosophy.

Haden argues that an in-depth review of a candidate's career is essential, and sets forth three factors that should guide the selection process:

1. *Proven record of legal philosophy.* It is essential to "assess whether each candidate has a proven record of applying consistent legal philosophy in practice, in academia, or even better, on the bench." Most important is "[a] thorough examination of the candidate's record," which "should be the determinative factor in assessing whether a candidate possesses, and will retain, a consistent legal philosophy post confirmation."[19] Haden also advocates evaluating "how a candidate analyzes constitutional and statutory questions of law," avoiding those with "a propensity to employ a nontextualist judicial philosophy." Haden notes that "[w]ithout a developed legal philosophy, the nominee's future voting patterns are less predictable."[20]

2. *"Where his ego is, there will his vote be also."* Haden asserts that "[h]istory has shown the best predictor of how a candidate will vote once confirmed is not merely loyalty to the President, home-state Senators, or a political party, but a proven record of consistent application of a legal philosophy in which the candidate's ego is vested."[21] Nominees whose identities are invested in conservative ideologies are more likely to remain true to their extreme Right base. Therefore, "the new President's staff should determine if the candidate's ego is vested in his application of textualist philosophy."[22] Haden also advocates asking whether "this person [is] strongly convinced of his own philosophy," seeking to avoid those who "[w]ill...likely be unduly swayed by academic, media, peer or other pressures" and looking for those who have "held to [their] legal philosophy under fire."[23]

3. *The ability to groom a coalition on the Court.* "In addition to a proven track record and a vested personal interest in a legal philosophy that will predict their own votes, candidates for appellate courts will also be able to influence other judges' votes by the force of their arguments and their interpersonal demeanors. Thus, the new President should assess Supreme Court and circuit court candidates for their abilities to wield majorities on the court for which they are being considered—i.e., their ability to command the respect of the other Justices and judges—and their interpersonal skills that could persuade the other Justices or judges to join opinions."[24]

Haden concedes that "[a] candidate's personal and professional integrity, technical qualifications, temperament, ability to handle a work load, and age and health" must be examined so as to avoid "politically costly embarrassment to the new President in the confirmations process."[25] However, his approach to judicial selection is chilling in its goals: it seeks the adherence to a radical Right legal philosophy over all other measures of qualification, including moderation, open-mindedness, and fairness.

Of the federal judges nominated by the second Bush administration, the selection of the following could easily have been guided by Haden's factors:

- Claude Allen, nominated to the Fourth Circuit Court of Appeals[26]
- Janice Rogers Brown, confirmed to the District of Columbia Court of Appeals[27]
- Jay Bybee, confirmed to the Ninth Circuit Court of Appeals[28]
- Paul Cassell, confirmed to the Utah District Court[29]
- Deborah Cook, nominated to the Sixth Circuit Court of Appeals[30]
- William Haynes, nominated to the Fourth Circuit Court of Appeals[31]

- Brett Kavanaugh, nominated to the District of Columbia Circuit Court of Appeals[32]
- Carolyn B. Kuhl, nominated to the Ninth Circuit Court of Appeals[33]
- Michael McConnell, confirmed to the Tenth Circuit Court of Appeals[34]
- David W. McKeague, confirmed to the Sixth Circuit Court of Appeals[35]
- William Myers, nominated to the Ninth Circuit Court of Appeals[36]
- Priscilla R. Owen, confirmed to the Fifth Circuit Court of Appeals[37]
- William H. Pryor, Jr., recess appointment to the Eleventh Circuit Court of Appeals[38]
- John G. Roberts, confirmed to the District of Columbia Circuit Court of Appeals[39]
- Henry Saad, nominated to the Sixth Circuit Court of Appeals[40]
- D. Brooks Smith, confirmed to the Third Circuit Court of Appeals[41]
- Jeffrey Sutton, confirmed to the Sixth Circuit Court of Appeals[42]
- Diana Sykes, confirmed to the Seventh Circuit Court of Appeals[43]

During the first Bush term, more than two hundred federal nominees were confirmed, resulting in the lowest vacancy rate in the federal courts in many years. Only ten extremist nominees have had their confirmations blocked by filibuster in the Senate. Moreover, the lack of effective Senate opposition to the confirmation of extremists encouraged the administration to nominate more extreme ideological nominees to circuit courts—for example, Alabama State Attorney General William Pryor, a states' rights zealot who is anti-choice and anti-gay, and William Haynes, a Defense Department lawyer with little courtroom experience but impeccable Right credentials.

The re-election of George W. Bush, accompanied by renewed promises to appoint more Justices like Scalia and Thomas, appears to have emboldened the administration to be even more radical in ensuring a radical Right takeover of the federal courts. Contrary to expectations, the administration re-nominated all ten nominees who were filibustered by the Senate (even Thomas Griffith, who has been practicing law without a license for the last seven years—a disqualifying factor in any normal process of judicial selection). Two vacancies on the Supreme Court in mid-2005, caused by Justice O'Connor's retirement and Chief Justice Rehnquist's death, give the Bush administration the opportunity to nominate similarly radical candidates to populate the highest court of the land.

The impact of the resulting Republican dominance of the federal judiciary is deep and likely long-lasting. Research by Professors Cass R. Sunstein of the University of Chicago Law School and David A. Schkade of the University of Texas at Austin showed that judges appointed by Republican presidents vote more con-servatively than those appointed by Democratic presidents. Circuit court pan-els made up of three Republican appointees will only find in favor of female plaintiffs alleging sexual discrimination thirty-one percent of the time, while panels made up of three Democratic appointees will find for the female plain-tiff seventy-five percent of the time. Moreover, companies facing Republican-appointee panels successfully challenge environmental regulations nearly sev-enty-five percent of the time, but only twenty-five percent of the time before Democratic-appointee panels. Finally, white plaintiffs win two out of three chal-lenges to affirmative action programs before Republican-appointee panels, but only one out of six before Democratic-appointee panels.[44]

People for the American Way has performed a similar study in which it compared Michigan Supreme Court rulings when the bench was composed mostly of moderate judges to rulings when the majority belonged to the Fed-eralist Society. The study found that when individuals sued insurance com-panies or large corporations before a moderate court, the plaintiffs won twenty-two out of forty-five cases; when the majority turned conservative, however, plaintiffs lost nineteen out of twenty cases.[45]

A review of the decisions handed down by Bush's more extreme nominees reveals that they have, indeed, brought an ideological agenda with them onto the bench. Individuals whose confirmations were opposed because of their ex-treme Right views in a particular area of the law have issued draconian deci-sions in other areas where their views were unknown. Many, for example, op-posed the appointment of Paul Cassells to the Utah District Court because of his vehement attack on defendants' *Miranda* rights. Once on the bench, Cas-sell issued a series of decisions in environmental cases that favored the Bush administration, and took a straight Federalist Society line in an immigration case, holding that an undocumented immigrant is not protected by the Fourth Amendment.[46]

What We Can Do

The extreme Right's strategy is working. Americans, however, do not want an extremist, politicized federal judiciary. It may not be too late to save the federal courts. A few things everyone can do to help: stay informed and in-form others; focus on circuit courts, not only the Supreme Court; tell the sto-ries of those who have been harmed by the federal court's rightward swing; and encourage senators to oppose the confirmation of extremist judicial nom-inees and demand the appointment of moderate nominees.

Stay Informed and Inform Others

The radical Right's judicial appointment strategy has succeeded over the last quarter century because it has stayed below the radar of average Americans. Without the weight of public opinion, Republican senators have blocked the confirmations of qualified moderate judges, and Democratic senators have avoided fighting the confirmation of extremist nominees.

Disseminating information is the first step in defeating the extreme Right's strategy. The public must increase their awareness of the nomination process for the federal bench by staying informed about judicial nominees and their progress toward confirmation (see Appendix B for a list of websites that contain updated information).

Focus on Circuit Courts, not only the Supreme Court

The extreme Right's strategy is based on the assumption that Americans only know and care about the Supreme Court. Lower federal courts, however, are increasingly important. Since the 1960s, the number of cases decided annually by the Supreme Court has fallen from approximately 150 to between seventy and eighty.[47] In contrast, the thirteen circuit courts resolve approximately 67,000 cases annually, and publish between 5,200 and 6,000 of those decisions.[48]

In virtually every instance, therefore, circuit courts function like mini-Supreme Courts in interpreting constitutional rights and enforcing federal statutes that protect the rights of individuals, consumers, people with disabilities, people of color, women, workers, and the environment. Indeed, the radical Right's campaign to takeover the Judiciary has recently been directed primarily towards the circuit courts — the Bush administration has nominated more ideological extremists to the circuit courts than the district courts.

Tell the Stories of those who have been Harmed by the Federal Court's Rightward Swing

For too long, Americans have thought that the legal system is either too complicated to understand or does not touch their lives. Nothing could be further from the truth, as shown in Part II by the stories of people to whom justice was denied, who were hurt with no way to protect themselves or to be made whole under the law. It is time for activists and lawyers to allow such powerful stories to speak for themselves. Discussions should no longer center on abstract principles such as "original intent," "federalism," or "separation of powers."

Encourage Senators to Oppose the Confirmation of Extremist Judicial Nominees

As the president's partner in the appointment of federal judges, the Senate is the natural place to resist the radical Right's takeover of the federal courts. Senators, however, tend to give judicial nominees the benefit of the doubt (e.g., Clarence Thomas) and, until recently, shy away from confirmation fights. As a leading ultra-conservative observed, "many senators hate judicial confirmation fights and they may tend, having voted against a president, to be with him the next time even if the two nominees are not all that different."[49]

As increasing numbers of Americans have become aware of the alarming Federalism Revolution, unprecedented numbers have contacted their senators to oppose the confirmation of radical Right nominees to the federal bench. In one instance, Senator Feinstein received over 3,300 calls in *one day* opposing the confirmation of a Bush nominee.[50] On another occasion, she received over twenty-one thousand letters, faxes, and calls opposing an ultra-conservative nominee to the circuit court.[51] Senator Feinstein voted against both nominees.

As a result of the public's increased attention, more senators are now willing to examine the legal ideology of judicial nominees and challenge those with extremist views and records. The Constitution anticipates that the Senate will be an equal partner to the president in the confirmation of judges. To be sure, the Founding Fathers feared precisely what is happening today, the takeover of the federal Judiciary by followers of one party or president.

Given that there will soon be at least one Supreme Court vacancy, there is much discussion about the Senate's handling of judicial nominees. In the event of a Court vacancy, the radical Right will work to widen and solidify its five-four majority. Such an effort will be met by strong resistance from Senate Democrats and progressives throughout the country.

Senate Democrats have requested more consultation and cooperation by the White House in making judicial nominations—requests that have been summarily rebuffed. The Senate has, therefore, been using the filibuster to stop the confirmation of radical Right judicial nominees. Such a strong measure seems the only tool available with which to force the administration to adopt a more moderate nomination policy. Senate Republicans are threatening to use a procedural maneuver to eliminate filibusters for judicial nominees. Public opinion must be marshaled in order to ensure that the Senate continues to vigorously perform its constitutional obligation of advising on all judicial nominees.

While Senate Democrats have begun to show the resolve and the unified strategy needed to end the radical Rights' takeover of the federal courts, they need continued support from their constituents. Public participation in the discussion on judicial appointments—through letters to the editor and contact with senators—will reinforce the fact that we expect senators to protect the federal courts. Strengthening the resolve of Senate Democrats will help restore a federal bench that is populated with judges with diverse ideological viewpoints, including moderates chosen for their intellectual excellence. The future of civil rights hangs in the balance.

Endnotes

1. U.S. Const. Art. II, §2.

2. See Richard Barry, *Mr. Rutledge of South Carolina* (Ayer 1993) 355–58; Learning About the Senate, Series of "Historical Minutes," 1790–1850, U.S. Senate, December 15, 1795: A Chief Justice Rejected, at http://permanent.access.gpo.gov/lps12426/www.senate.gov/learning/min_2aza.html.

3. This historical and theoretical summary of judicial selection is loosely based on Sheldon Goldman's excellent book, *Picking Federal Judges: Lower Court Selection From Roosevelt Through Reagan* (1997). If I have mischaracterized his arguments or failed to restate them clearly, the error is mine.

4. An interesting discussion of instances where presidents were surprised by their appointees can be found in Ed R. Haden, Judicial Selection: A Pragmatic Approach, *24 Harv. J.L. & Pub. Pol'y* (2001) 531, 537–38.

5. As quoted by Goldman, *supra* note 3, at 297.

6. Quoted in Nadine Strossen, A Constitutional Litmus Test, *Am. Prospect* (Jun. 23, 1993), at http://www.prospect.org/print/V4/14/strossen-n.html.

7. President Reagan also elevated Justices Sandra Day O'Connor and Anthony Kennedy to the Supreme Court.

8. Jeffrey Toobin, Advice and Dissent: The Fight Over the President's Judicial Nominations, *New Yorker* (May 26, 2003), at http://www.newyorker.com/fact/content/ ?030526fa _fact (describing the Federalist Society as "an organization of conservative lawyers that has served as an essential networking tool on the right").

9. As cited by Strossen, *supra* note 7.

10. Office of Pol'y Planning, U.S. Dep't of Justice, *Guidelines on Constitutional Litigation* (Feb. 19. 1988); Office of Legal Pol'y, U.S. Dep't of Justice, *The Constitution in the Year 2000: Choices Ahead in Constitutional Interpretation* (October 11, 1988).

11. Dawn Johnsen, Tipping the Scale, *Wash. Monthly* (Jul/Aug. 2002) 15.

12. President George H. W. Bush also elevated Justice David Souter to the Supreme Court.

13. Alliance for Justice, *14th Annual Report on the State of the Judiciary 2000*, at ii.

14. Lawrence Walsh, *Firewall: The Iran-Contra Conspiracy and Cover Up* (1997) 248.

15. Hon. Roger J. Miner, Remark: Advice and Consent in Theory and Practice, *41 Am. U.L. Rev.* (1992) 1075, 1081.

16. People for the American Way Foundation, *The Federalist Society: From Obscurity to Power, The Lawyers Who are Shaping the Bush Administration's Decisions on Legal Policies*

and Judicial Nominations (Aug. 2001, updated Jan. 2003), at http://www.pfaw.org/pfaw/
dfiles/file_148.pdf; Anthony Lewis, "An Injudicious Trend," *Los Angeles Times* (Jun. 23, 2003).

17. Haden is identified as "Chief Counsel, Subcommittee on Administrative Oversight
and the Courts for the Committee on the Judiciary of the United States Senate and former
Counsel, Committee on the Judiciary (Nominations Unit)" in the article, Judicial Selection: A Pragmatic Approach, *24 Harv. J.L. & Pub. Pol'y* (2001) 531, n.1.

18. Id. at 537.

19. Id. at 539.

20. Id. at 540–41.

21. Id. at 537.

22. Id. at 541.

23. Id.

24. Id. at 545–46.

25. Id. at 548.

26. Former aide to Jesse Helms and Deputy Secretary in Bush's Health and Human Services Dept., has been on the ultra-conservative side of political battles regarding abortion
and child care, abstinence and sexual education, health care and welfare, Medicaid and the
mentally disabled, cloning, stem-cell research, and the "right to die." He has limited courtroom experience.

27. Arch-conservative/libertarian California Supreme Court Justice nominated to the
DC Circuit. She has extreme hostility to government regulation—in some circumstances,
she regards it as "theft." Brown is anti-choice and anti-gay, exhibits a consistent pro-cor-
porate/anti-consumer/anti-worker bias in her decisions, and is known for her sharp and
acerbic dissents.

28. Federalist Society member, served in the Reagan Department of Justice, law professor
at Louisiana State University and then at the newly founded University of Nevada Law School.
Assistant Attorney General for the Office of Legal Counsel under Attorney General John
Ashcroft, attributed author of one of the infamous "torture memos." Does not believe that the
Establishment Clause protects individuals' free exercise of religion, but simply prohibits Congress from interfering with the states' regulation of religion. He is anti-gay rights, and advocates the repeal of the Eighteenth Amendment providing for the direct election of senators.

29. Spent a decade advocating that *Miranda* be reversed, culminating in a case before
the Supreme Court. The Court rejected all of his arguments. Also led a movement to amend
the Constitution to provide for victim's rights and is a fierce defender of capital punishment.

30. Most conservative member of the Ohio Supreme Court, Federalist Society member, received more money in campaign contributions from manufacturing and other business interests than any other justice. She is anti-choice and her rulings are generally pro-
big business, anti-plaintiff, and anti-civil rights.

31. He has little courtroom experience—the bulk of his legal career has been as a lawyer
in the Department of Defense. Most recently, he was the Department's principle author
and defender of the administration's designation and handling of "enemy combatants" and
the denial of the Geneva Convention protections to persons captured on the battlefield.

32. A thirty-nine-year-old Federalist Society member, he worked for Kenneth Starr in
the Office of the Independent Counsel, investigating Vince Foster's suicide and drafting
many sections of the Starr Report. In the Bush administration he was in the Office of White
House Counsel vetting potential judicial nominees, and is now the White House staff secretary in charge of paper flow to and from the Oval Office.

33. Los Angeles Superior Court Judge, former Reagan Department of Justice attorney, private litigator, Federalist Society member. While in the Reagan Department of Justice, she persuaded the attorney general to file briefs arguing that *Roe v. Wade* should be overturned or ignored, defended Bob Jones University's tax exempt status even though it racially discriminated against its students, and sought to overturn the concept of associational standing which allows unions and other associations to sue on behalf of its members. As LA Superior Court Judge, she ruled that the presence of male drug salesman during a breast cancer patient's breast exam did not violate the patient's privacy.

34. Law professor, member of the Federalist Society Board, the Christian Legal Society, and the Becket Fund (all right wing extremist groups). He is consistently anti-choice, anti-gay, and anti-separation of church and state. In a law review article, he praised a federal judge who had, in defiance of a clearly stated law, acquitted two protestors after they were arrested for blocking the doors to a women's medical clinic.

35. Federalist Society member appointed by President George H.W. Bush to the U.S. District Court. His record suggests a bias against some plaintiffs and a predisposition to grant summary judgment in favor of civil defendants.

36. Lobbyist for beef and mining industries, solicitor general of the Interior Department, where he was instrumental in rolling back several Clinton-era environmental protections by using result-oriented legal reasoning and deliberate misconstruction of statutory terms. Described by the *Idaho Statesman* as having "a reputation for being pro-ranching, pro-grazing and being shaky on the environment." Accused of violating ethical rules by meeting with former employers and companies he lobbied for while he was solicitor general. His nomination was opposed by the National Congress of American Indians because of the deleterious effect his anti-environment, pro-mining positions have had on Native American sacred grounds.

37. Texas Supreme Court Associate Justice and Federalist Society member. She is anti-choice, and has been accused of judicial activism by Alberto Gonzales for her ruling in a parental notification case. She is hostile to jury verdicts and favors corporate interests.

38. Alabama attorney general, member of Federalist Society and Washington Legal Foundation. Extremely hostile to a woman's constitutional right to reproductive choice, leads proponents of reviving states' rights at the expense of federal civil rights protections, is hostile to the rights of gays and lesbians, has demonstrated a lack of respect for the constitutional separation of church and state, and is a vocal opponent of the rights of criminal defendants.

39. Confirmed as Chief Justice of the Supreme Court in 2005.

40. Federalist Society member on the Michigan Court of Appeals, he was originally nominated by President George H.W. Bush, but the nomination lapsed. He is a judicial activist who summarily asserts his views, shaping facts and law—or omitting them entirely—to justify a result, particularly in the areas of workers rights and personal injury.

41. Former district attorney, state court judge, and Reagan-appointed federal district court judge. Holds a radically constrained view of federal powers and the Commerce Clause, embraces a pro-business stance that would invalidate environmental regulations solely on economic grounds, and failed to recuse himself from a case involving the bank that employs his wife and that impacted his financial affairs.

42. Former law clerk for Justice Scalia, former Ohio State Solicitor. Chief lawyer in cases arguing that individuals have no right to enforce the civil rights protections that Congress has given them. Officer of the Separation of Powers practice group of the Federalist Society, he has not only acted as an advocate for his clients, but has admitted that he "loves this

Federalism stuff," is often "on the lookout" for cases that support his hostility towards federal civil rights protections, and has advocated radical restrictions on Congress's power to protect civil rights.

43. Holds a constrained view of individual rights and constitutional protections for the underrepresented, is hostile to reproductive freedom, and has consistently ruled against individuals in favor of corporations, insurance, and big business.

44. Cass R. Sunstein and David A. Schkade, "Judging By Where You Sit," *New York Times* (Jun. 11, 2003) A31.

45. People for the American Way Foundation, *supra* note 17, 30.

46. *Utah Envtl. Cong. v. Bosworth (I)*, No. 2:01-CV-00316PGC (D. Utah Mar. 27, 2003); *Utah Envtl. Cong. v. Bosworth (II)*, 285 F.Supp.2d 1257 (D. Utah Sept. 25, 2003); *U.S. v. Esparza-Mendoza*, 265 F.Supp.2d 1254 (D. Utah May 29, 2003) (finding that the Fourth Amendment's protection of the "[t]he *right of the people* to be secure in their persons, houses, papers, and effects, against unreasonable searches and seizures...." does not apply to previously removed aliens).

47. Private communication with Prof. Erwin Chemerinsky.

48. Id.

49. Steven G. Calabresi, Advice to the Next Conservative President of the United States, 24 *Harv. J.L. & Pub. Pol'y* (2001) 369, 377–78.

50. Hearings on Miguel Estrada Before the Senate Comm. on the Judiciary, 108th Cong. (Jan. 30, 2003).

51. Hearings on Carolyn Kuhl Before the Senate Comm. on the Judiciary, 108th Cong. (May 8, 2003).

CHAPTER 22

REVITALIZING FEDERAL CIVIL RIGHTS LEGISLATION

Protecting Ideals of Equality and Justice for All:
Progressive Legislation in a Conservative Era

Joy Moses[*]

I do know one thing—I want my civil rights. I worked for them. I earned them. I am a human being and I think that's the whole issue. These are human rights.[†]

Patricia Garrett, breast cancer survivor

After taking a four-month leave from the University of Alabama hospital to undergo treatment for cancer, Ms. Garrett returned to work able to assume the duties she had performed for seventeen years. When her supervisor informed her that she could no longer serve as Director of Nursing, however, she was forced to take a lower paying, less prestigious position.

Ms. Garrett turned to the courts and federal civil rights laws. The Supreme Court, however, denied her claim. The justices did not conclude that she had not been discriminated against—in fact, they did not even examine her complaint. Rather, a five-justice majority held that Ms. Garrett had no right to sue her employer because she worked for a state. Alabama was therefore free to discriminate against its disabled employees without fear of federal civil rights law suits.

Ms. Garrett did not stop fighting for her rights. She took her case to Congress and the court of public opinion. Today, federal civil rights laws—and society's progress towards equality and fairness for all—are under attack. This chapter will explore how Congress can help fight back.

---

[*] Staff attorney with the Education Project at the National Law Center on Homelessness and Poverty.

[†] *Take Back the Courts*, Firelight Media (2003), available at the National Campaign to Restore Civil Rights' website, www.rollbackcampaign.org.

ॐ   ॐ   ॐ

The Conservative Courts have
Undercut Federal Civil Rights Laws

It seems like every move we make, everywhere we turn…[our nation's courts are] violating us. They're taking away something that people battled for back there in the '60s.

Bonnie Sanders, President of South Camden Citizens in Action[1]

Federal courts have moved increasingly to the Right over the last three decades. Judges appointed by Presidents Ronald Reagan, George H.W. Bush, and George W. Bush have weakened laws protecting racial minorities, women, senior citizens, individuals with disabilities, working people, and low-income families. Their decisions have undermined the hard-won victories of the Civil Rights era when the Jim Crow system of legally-mandated segregation was dismantled and replaced with a vision of fairness and justice for all. Instead of directly attacking the civil rights victories, however, the activist judiciary has undercut them by limiting the enforceability of federal civil rights laws in court.

For members of South Camden Citizens In Action, the Supreme Court's decision that citizens could not seek the enforcement of federal civil rights regulations in order to challenge New Jersey environmental policies that disproportionately harmed the people of South Camden meant that community members would continue living with environmental health hazards that had caused unusually high rates of asthma and cancer among children and the elderly (the case is discussed in chapter 14). In closing their doors to people like Ms. Sanders, the courts have not only ignored the needs of civil rights plaintiffs, but have thwarted the will of Congress by limiting the effectiveness and enforceability of civil rights laws.

Fortunately, Congress can rewrite legislation when the courts misinterpret its legislative intent. Advocates have already turned to Congress, asking for new civil rights legislation to repair the damage done. The most comprehensive of these proposed statutes is the Fairness and Individual Rights Necessary to Ensure a Stronger Society Act (the Fairness Act).[2]

The Fairness Act

Introduced in February 2004, the Fairness Act seeks to reinstate the right of individuals such as Bonnie Sanders to have their discrimination claims heard in court and considered on the basis of merit. According to the bill's authors, the legislation will "restore, reaffirm, and reconcile legal rights and remedies under civil rights statutes"[3] for women, racial minorities, working people, military personnel, senior citizens, people with disabilities, and low-income Americans. The bill was originally co-sponsored by over a hundred Democrats, including Senators Barbara Boxer, Edward Kennedy, Hillary Clinton, and Christopher Dodd, Representatives Nancy Pelosi, John Conyers Jr., and Charles Rangel, and by 2004 presidential and vice-presidential contenders John Kerry and John Edwards. The key provisions of the Fairness Act are as follows:

Provision	Reasoning
Assure court access to victims of race, national origin, age, or sex discrimination	Before the Federalism Revolution, plaintiffs were able to bring discrimination lawsuits by presenting evidence of the disproportionate harmful effect of policies or practices. The Court's ruling in *Alexander v. Sandoval* (discussed in chapter 10) eliminated these "disparate impact" claims under Title VI of the Civil Rights Act of 1964.[4] Moreover, following the logic of that case, disparate impact claims under Title IX of the Education Amendments of 1972 and the Age Discrimination Act of 1967 are in jeopardy (discussed in chapters 6 and 7). The Fairness Act would restore the vitality of discrimination claims based on race, national origin, sex, and age.
Protect people who have been discriminated against from retaliation	Employers and educational institutions sometimes retaliate against victims of discrimination who try to enforce their civil rights. Acts of retaliation include firing, demoting, cutting salaries, denying promotion, or denying graduation. The Fairness Act would solidify existing anti-retaliation protections that have been called into question by the Court's ruling in *Sandoval*.[5]
Institute financial punishments for intentional discrimination	The Fairness Act would allow judges and juries in intentional discrimination cases to award punitive damages—monetary payments that defendants make to plaintiffs to punish them for their egregious conduct and to deter other similar bad behavior.
Provide greater protections for victims of harassment	The Fairness Act would respond to the Court's decision in *Gebser v. Lago Vista Independent School District* by requiring recipients of federal funds to take reasonable care in preventing and responding to harassment.[6] It would also allow harassed individuals to collect monetary damages (including punitive damages). Recipients of federal funds could demonstrate reasonable care by proving that they have anti-

harassment policies in place, and that they diligently respond to complaints.

Allow military service members to sue state employers for damages

The Fairness Act would close a loophole in the Uniformed Services Employment and Reemployment Act (USERRA) caused by *Seminole Tribe of Florida v. Florida*[7] and *Alden v. Maine*[8] (discussed in chapter 19). USERRA requires employers to rehire former active duty troops to the civilian jobs they abandoned when deployed (except under limited circumstances). The Act also protects members of the military from discrimination based on their status as reservists. The Court's decisions in *Seminole* and *Alden* could prevent service members from collecting damages from state government employers who violate the law.

Make legal services available to low-income clients

The Attorney's Fees Act allows winning attorneys to collect fees from losing defendants. Those fees are important to low-income clients because litigation expenses (e.g., support staff salaries, filing fees, expert witness expenses, travel costs, copy charges, and postage) can be high. Attorneys cannot afford to take on new cases if their clients are unable to pay these costs and the courts do not force losing defendants to pick up the bill for their wrong-doings. Recent decisions such as *West Virginia University Hospitals Inc. v. Casey*[9] and *Buckhannon Bd. & Care Home, Inc. v. West Virginia Department of Health and Human Resources*[10] limit the ability of attorneys to collect such fees. The Fairness Act would once again allow attorneys to collect fees when their work results in substantial positive change (even if they settle the case).

Ensure court access to employees who have signed mandatory arbitration agreements

Mandatory arbitration provisions, which people often unknowingly sign as part of their work orientation packages, limit employee rights by preventing them from suing their employers. Instead, employees must bring their complaints to a third party arbitrator who is hired by the employer to resolve disputes. Employees are sometimes asked to contribute to the arbitrator's costs, which may prevent low-income workers from even filing a complaint. The Fairness Act would address the Court's decision in *Circuit City Stores, Inc. v. Adams*[11] (discussed in chapter 19) by allowing employees to bring their cases to court even if they have signed mandatory arbitration agreements.

Promote equal pay for equal work

The Fairness Act would bolster the provisions of the Fair Labor Standards Act that require pay equity for women. It would require the Department of Labor to research lingering pay disparities and publish its findings along with a list of best practices for businesses. The proposed legislation would also encourage the Secretary of Labor to award medals of honor to businesses that have promoted pay equity.

Ensure that undocumented workers receive rightful pay while helping citizens to compete in the job market

Under the National Labor Relations Act (NLRA), employees cannot be fired or demoted for participating in union organizing activities. If a court finds that an employer has acted unlawfully in this manner, employees are eligible for back pay to compensate them for the time they were out of work or earning less than they would otherwise have been. The Court's decision in *Hoffman Plastics*[12] (discussed in chapters 5 and 11) excludes undocumented workers from many of these provisions—they can still sue to be rehired, but cannot be awarded back pay. *Hoffman* is likely to deter undocumented workers from unionizing or engaging in collective bargaining agreements, causing them to experience greater exploitation and providing a disincentive for employers to hire American workers who cannot be similarly exploited. The Fairness Act would allow undocumented workers to collect back pay for violations of the NLRA.

The provisions of the Fairness Act enhance individual rights to sue for discrimination, promote equal pay for equal work, provide additional protection against harassment, increase the availability of legal services to low-income clients, and protect the right to unionize. The Act's road to passage will likely be lengthy, requiring patience, determination, political skill, and strategy. Its proponents will have to learn from the past in determining how to move forward. Helpful historical references include the Civil Rights Act of 1964, which ended legal racial segregation, and the Civil Rights Act of 1991, a "legislative fix" in response to Court decisions diminishing civil rights.

The Civil Rights Act of 1964

When Lyndon Johnson signed the Civil Rights Act on July 2, 1964, America was forever changed. That legislation officially ended the Jim Crow era by outlawing discrimination in public accommodations and employment. Many lessons can be learned from studying its road to passage, which was hard-fought by Democrats, Republicans, two presidents, and a coalition of civil rights groups working under the umbrella of the Leadership Conference on Civil Rights (LCCR).

For years, civil rights activists tried to convince Congress to pass comprehensive legislation that would help African Americans realize the promise of equal citizenship. While their movement picked up steam with the 1954 Supreme Court decision in *Brown v. Board of Education*,[13] the legislative and executive branches had not yet undertaken any meaningful action to promote civil rights by the early 1960s. Although Congress passed civil rights legislation in 1957 and 1960, neither statute changed the conditions facing African Americans.[14]

Joseph Rauh was LCCR's primary lobbyist for civil rights in the early 1960s. Soon after the Civil Rights Act's passage, he wrote an article documenting the efforts of the civil rights coalition[15]—below is a summary of that article, which may help advocates today develop strategies to secure passage of the Fairness Act.

Joseph Rauh's History of the Civil Rights Act of 1964

Rauh's story begins in February 1963 when President John F. Kennedy proposed a new civil rights bill that LCCR believed would have only a limited impact on segregation. Feeling the momentum of the unprecedented Civil Rights Movement that had encompassed massive protests such as the Montgomery Bus Boycott and the Freedom Rides, the group was poised to ask for a stronger bill when they received unexpected assistance from Bull Connor, a Birmingham police commissioner. Television news cameras captured images of Connor's officers using dogs, fire hoses, and electric cattle prods to attack unarmed African Americans during a peaceful protest. The nation and the world watched in horror. President Kennedy quickly summoned the civil rights leadership to the White House, where they mobilized behind his civil rights bill. The president remarked, "'Bull' Connor has done more for civil rights than anyone in this room."[16] By all accounts, his assessment was correct—work on the bill began in earnest.

From the outset, the bill's proponents studied their opposition and identified three congressional roadblocks: the conservative makeup of the House Judiciary Committee, which would be the first congressional group to consider, draft, and recommend the bill for a vote by the entire House of Representatives; the Dixicrat-Republican-controlled House Rules Committee, which would determine when and if the House would actually vote on the bill; and the threat of a Senate filibuster, which could prevent the bill from being voted on in the Senate.

LCCR representatives, believing that the best defense is a good offense, were determined to ask that key provisions exceeding those proposed be inserted into the act. When the administration failed to recommend LCCR's suggested improvements to the House Judiciary Committee, the advocates approached the Committee directly. Committee Chairman Emanuel Celler became an ally, agreeing to some ideas and remaining open to others.

The bill's proponents also began a mass mobilization campaign designed to pressure members of Congress. LCCR's Roy Wilkins proposed enlarging the Leadership Conference so as to build upon an existing network of grassroots advocates, while Dr. King suggested a March on Washington. LCCR aggressively pursued both suggestions in order to demonstrate public support and ensure the legislation's passage. The March on Washington took place while the bill was being considered by the House Judiciary Committee. Many members of Congress came to the Lincoln Memorial and heard the crowd chant, "pass the bill, pass the bill." The day affected both the representatives and the nation.

Shortly after, the Judiciary Committee completed its version of the bill and recommended that it be considered by the rest of the House. Before reaching the floor, however, the bill would have to go through the Rules Committee, which decides whether a bill will be considered and then develops the rules to guide its passage. LCCR had identified the Rules Committee's southern Dixiecrat leadership as a potential problem. While advocates worked to overcome this hurdle, the nation suffered a terrible tragedy—the assassination of President Kennedy. As the nation mourned, the fate of African Americans seemed unclear. Shortly after taking office, however, President Lyndon Johnson informed Congress that he would see President Kennedy's bill through to passage. When grassroots advocates pressured House members to vote to bypass the Rules Committee, the Committee, fearing the embarrassment of having its power usurped, gave in and allowed the bill to be considered by the House.

LCCR mobilized volunteers to call each representative daily to encourage "no votes" on proposed negative amendments to the legislation. They also packed the public viewing galleries of the Capitol building to observe and report back to constituents how the representatives voted (there were no transcripts of votes at the time). The House passed the civil rights bill.

LCCR next turned its attention to the Senate. Senate consideration of the bill led to the expected filibuster, a device that allows senators to delay or prevent the enactment of legislation by engaging in prolonged debate on the Senate floor. The only way to stop the speeches is through cloture, or garnering enough votes from senators to close the discussion.[17] Public pressure proved useful in stopping the filibuster—two conservative senators, for example, bowed to the religious lobby. When the Leadership Conference distributed several hundred thousand question-and-answer booklets in the various states to refute the misstatements of a conservative group, the senators received even more calls from their constituents demanding passage of the bill without dilution. Ultimately, enough conservative senators agreed to a compromise that ended the filibuster. The bill cleared the Senate, and President Johnson signed the Civil Rights Act into law one year after President Kennedy first sent his original package to Capitol Hill.

Lessons Learned from LCCR Strategies

LCCR's victory relied on a strong, forceful, and consistent approach. Advocates studied the opposition and were prepared to counteract their actions; they expanded their coalition, which helped mobilize constituencies and supporters in Congress; they countered negative messages with positive ones; and they accomplished all of this through the careful organization of their members and volunteers. Their efforts paved the way for the passage of several other pieces of progressive legislation, including the 1965 Voting Rights Act,[18] the 1968 Fair Housing Act,[19] and Title IX of the Education Amendments of 1972.[20]

The Civil Rights Act of 1991

Congress has long responded to right wing judicial opinions by enacting corrective civil rights legislation. Such legislation includes the 1982 amendments to the Voting Rights Act of 1965[21] that extended some provisions of the Act for an additional twenty-five years, the Handicapped Children's Protection Act of 1986 that expanded the Education for All Handicapped Children Act,[22] and the Civil Rights Restoration Act of 1987[23] that addressed regressive Court interpretations of various civil rights statutes. There is hope, therefore, that Congress will act once again.

The Civil Rights Act of 1991, the most recent major civil rights bill, provides one of the best historical references for the current effort to pass the Fairness Act. The fight for its passage took a couple of years because right wing conservatives in Congress and the George H.W. Bush administration presented significant opposition—including the first presidential veto of civil rights legislation since Reconstruction. The White House, however, eventually signed into law a version of the bill largely championed by civil rights lobbyists.

Many on the Right regarded the Act's passage as a setback that warranted the development of a new game plan. Because this plan will likely come into play during considerations of the Fairness Act, it requires thorough analysis, including thinking about possible counter-strategies. An example of such right wing thinking can be found in the writings of Roger Clegg, a former member of the Reagan administration who opposed the 1991 Act and published an article discussing the legislative process leading up to its passage.[24] The following is an analysis of Clegg's critique of the Bush administration's strategy to defeat the 1991 Civil Rights Act:

Clegg's Critique	Implication for Future Right Wing Strategy	Potential Counter-Strategy of Fairness Act Supporters
Failure to present a unified front. George H.W. Bush put up a "tentative defense" to the civil rights groups' outrage towards court decisions involving employment discrimination.[27] Clegg argues that Bush should have presented a stronger united front with the right wing courts. Undoubtedly, Clegg would also find fault with moderate Republicans who supported the 1991 legislation—their demands, after all, were key in the White House's eventual decision to sign the Act.[28]	The Right will likely place intense pressure on moderates to remain silent in future political battles over civil rights. Such a notion is consistent with the silencing of moderate Republicans like Senator Arlen Specter, who voiced support for *Roe v. Wade*, and the tension-filled service of moderate Republican Colin Powell as Secretary of State.[29]	Advocates must counter-pressure moderates by building grassroots support in their home states and by refuting anti-civil rights arguments made by the Right.
Making concessions. When civil rights groups and their congressional allies first introduced the bill, the Bush camp responded by proposing its own version. In doing so, Clegg believes that President Bush conceded the need for civil rights legislation. He argues that the administration's early concession made later negotiations more difficult.[30] Clegg was not the only commentator to criticize Bush for his compromises—many on the Right had little tolerance for either moderate Republicans or civil rights legislation.[31] Bush's decision to first veto and then sign a civil rights bill was considered part of a larger pattern of flip-flopping, aimed at garnering the support of both moderates and conservatives.[32] His efforts to placate both sides may well have contributed to his lost re-election bid in 1992.	Right wing politicians are likely to oppose the bill from the outset, and then refuse to compromise.	Advocates must leverage grassroots support to force a conversation about civil rights, and must criticize this right wing strategy as hindering democratic dialogue.

Clegg's Critique	Implication for Future Right Wing Strategy	Potential Counter-Strategy of Fairness Act Supporters
Inconsistent messaging. The Right successfully coined the term "quota bill" to refer to the Civil Rights Act of 1991.[33] An informal survey of *Washington Post* coverage revealed that this phrase appeared in over a hundred articles while the legislation was making its way through Congress, often in statements made by members of the administration. This catchy language cast the Act in a negative light and reduced complicated issues to a sound bite: "Are you for or against the quota bill." The right wing messaging undoubtedly bolstered public support for their position.	The Right will likely employ similar messaging techniques in any battle over the Fairness Act.	Advocates must define the case for the Fairness Act in clear language, and vigorously promote that definition in order to set the terms of the debate. They must also be ready to refute counter-assertions by the Right.
Failure to propose alternatives to anti-discrimination laws. Clegg argues that racial discrimination is no longer a relevant problem for disadvantaged minorities,[34] and chided civil rights groups for lobbying for civil rights legislation that did not address what he considered to be the real issue: individuals' failure to take responsibility for their own lives.[35] He suggests that the Bush administration should have countered demands for an anti-discrimination law by proposing alternative legislation to "empower' the disadvantaged— of all races and ethnicities—to run their own schools, own their own homes, start their own businesses, and cut through the layers of bureaucratic red tape that might keep them from doing so."[36]	The Right will likely cite alternative legislation that they have supported (e.g., school voucher bills and the No Child Left Behind Act) in order to avoid discussing the need for anti-discrimination laws. For instance, while on the campaign trail in 2004, President Bush highlighted his efforts to increase minority home ownership and support small businesses.[37]	Advocates must force civil rights issues into the public debate, encourage constituents to ask their representatives questions about civil rights, and document the need for civil rights laws.

Clegg's Critique	Implication for Future Right Wing Strategy	Potential Counter-Strategy of Fairness Act Supporters
Failure to use and publicize anti-civil rights studies. The Bush administration commissioned two studies while the 1991 legislation was pending—one arguing that the legislation was unnecessary, and another supporting an alternative approach.[38] According to Clegg, the administration failed to promote the studies.[39] In the 1970s, the Right began to build regional and national think tanks and develop a reliable media machine to disseminate their messages (the Right's strategy is discussed in chapter 20).[40]	The Right will promote studies supporting their positions. They may look to right wing think tanks such as the Heritage Foundation, the Manhattan Institute, and the Claremont Institute as well as right wing media outlets.	Advocates must develop accurate and reliable research studies, be prepared to distribute that research to media outlets, and secure the assistance of experts to examine and critique the research of right wing ideologues.

Based on Clegg's analysis, it appears likely that those opposing the Fairness Act will use research, creative media messaging, pressure directed towards moderates, a firm stance, and avoidance of the issue of civil rights to oppose the Fairness Act. Advocates for the Act must be prepared to counteract these strategies by establishing the need for the legislation, effectively communicating their views, and using grassroots connections to exert pressure on Congress.

Obstacles on the Road to Fairness for All

The Fairness Act faces formidable obstacles. The White House and both houses of Congress are currently under Republican control, not even one Republican member of Congress has endorsed the legislation, and many Democratic and Independent members of Congress have failed to vigorously support legislation designed to increase access to the courts for victims of discrimination. Understanding the primary obstacles facing the Fairness Act will help civil rights advocates in strategizing to overcome them.

Obstacle #1: Opposition from Right Wing Republicans

The extreme Right—which will likely present the greatest opposition to the Fairness Act—has become increasingly dominant in the Republican Party. Its views tend to reject traditional notions of civil rights while favoring alternative theories. The following are rationales given for right wing opposition to civil rights legislation:

Right Wing Argument	Reasoning
Civil rights laws do not prevent discrimination or compensate for it; rather, they confer benefits on some groups at the expense of others.	Right wing Republicans argue that taking into account race or sex-based disparities will lead to the use of quotas and preferences. Indeed, some radical right wingers assert that civil rights laws discriminate against white men.[39] These same individuals will almost certainly oppose legislation to revitalize disparate impact claims for discrimination cases involving racial minorities, women, people with disabilities, and the elderly.
Civil rights laws divide us.	Right wing Republicans suggest that civil rights laws—which they associate with preferences, quotas, and set asides—divide Americans and create questions about minority and female accomplishments. They ignore the fact that civil rights laws prevent discrimination and tear down traditional barriers for minority groups. Rather than divid-

ing us, those laws have brought the races and sexes together in the workplace and in higher education to the betterment of society.

Civil rights laws are unnecessary and undesirable. Right wing Republicans have expressed concern about the use of the disparate impact standard in traditional anti-discrimination laws.[40] Rather than suggesting a better way to remedy unfair disparities, however, they have advocated symbolic and narrow remedies.[41] President Bush, for example, has assembled a diverse cabinet, but has limited his anti-discrimination legislative efforts to his under-funded and largely ineffective education program.

The federal government should not interfere with business in the interest of promoting civil rights. Right wing Republicans favor protecting businesses from government regulation over protecting individuals from discrimination and other unfair treatment by corporations.[42] This issue was often raised in the testimony of congressional witnesses and by representatives during debates about employment discrimination under the Civil Rights Act of 1991.[43] The radical Right will likely argue against the provisions of the Fairness Act that affect employers (e.g., Equal Work for Equal Pay and modifying mandatory arbitration clauses).

State sovereignty is more important than civil rights. The Supreme Court has limited the ability of individuals to sue states. Likewise, right wing Republicans in Congress have given state governments increased control over federal programs in areas such as education and poverty assistance.[44] Accordingly, they are likely to oppose the provisions of the Fairness Act that increase individuals' access to courts for suits against state governments.

President George W. Bush, who is favored by the Right, generally avoids discussions about civil rights issues—he used the words "civil rights," "diversity," and "discrimination" only 153 times between January 2001 and December 2003 (mostly when he was discussing historical events or how the unavailability of government funding for faith-based programs was a form of discrimination).[45] To decipher the president's views on traditional civil rights, therefore, one must examine his actions. According to a U.S. Commission on Civil Rights report, President Bush has, for example, appointed anti-civil rights judges, decreased the spending power of federal civil rights enforcement agencies, opposed higher education affirmative action in the Supreme Court, delayed implementation of the Help America Vote Act, failed to protect poor and minority communities from environmental hazards, refused to meet with civil rights groups such as the NAACP and the

National Council of La Raza, closed or tried to close women's programs in the White House and the Department of Labor, ended the distribution of information about the workplace rights of women, removed sexual harassment guidance from the Department of Education website, attempted to weaken female sports programs, questioned the concept of "hate crimes," opposed employment discrimination and hate crimes legislation designed to protect gays and lesbians, and supported a constitutional amendment banning same-sex marriages.[46]

Although the Republican Party is currently dominated by the right wing, it has refused to formally adopt views or positions opposed to traditional civil rights. Rather, its 2004 platform uses wording designed to appeal to party moderates:

> Our nation is a land of opportunity for all, and our communities must represent the ideal of equality and justice for every citizen. The Republican Party favors aggressive, proactive measures to ensure that no individual is discriminated against on the basis of race, national origin, gender, or other characteristics covered by our civil rights laws. We also favor recruitment and outreach policies that cast the widest possible net so that the best qualified individuals are encouraged to apply for jobs, contracts, and university admissions.[47]

The party's moderate official position is likely the product of several factors: internal disagreement about the party's proper place on the political spectrum; a fear that right wing positions are contrary to public opinion; and a concern about alienating moderate and swing voters. The reluctance of some on the Right to publicly express their views and the Republican Party's decision not to fully embrace right wing ideology in its platform present an opening that civil rights activists must exploit. If the Right is afraid of alienating moderate Republicans, for example, any advocacy plan must take those moderates into consideration. Fairness Act advocates must also present a comprehensive argument for civil rights laws that addresses and refutes those issues raised by the extreme Right. Advocates must highlight both the limits of the Right's approach and the benefits of civil rights.

Obstacle #2: Lack of Overwhelming Democratic Support

A number of Democratic members of Congress have co-sponsored the Fairness Act. Further, the Democratic Party's 2004 platform embraces traditional civil rights laws:

> Our commitment to civil rights is ironclad. We will restore vigorous federal enforcement of our civil rights laws for all our people, from fair housing to equal employment opportunity, from Title IX to the Americans with Disabilities Act. We support affirmative action to redress discrimination and to achieve the diversity from which all Americans benefit. We believe a day's work is worth a day's pay, and at a time when women still earn 77 cents for every dollar earned by men, we need stronger equal pay laws and stronger enforcement of them. We will enact the bipartisan legislation barring workplace discrimination based on sexual orientation. We are committed to equal treatment of all service members and believe all patriotic Americans should be allowed to serve our country without discrimination, persecution, or violence. We support the appointment of judges who will uphold our laws and constitutional rights, not their own narrow agendas.[48]

Accordingly, it is likely that the bill's sponsors and others who agree with the Democratic Party platform will continue to support the Fairness Act. However, the results of the 2004 election might affect the vigor of their advocacy. Republicans won both the presidency and large majorities in both the House and the Senate. As a result, Democrats will spend some time reviewing their goals and methods. Advocates must ensure that a firm commitment to civil rights is not lost in this process.

Of particular concern are statistics released by one pollster who found post-Civil Rights Act of 1991 hostility towards the Democratic Party among white working-class suburbanites who associated that party with favoring blacks (who they viewed as an obstacle to their personal achievement).[49] Although the Fairness Act seeks to address the discrimination faced by a broad spectrum of Americans (e.g., women, people with disabilities, senior citizens, the poor, and various racial groups), advocates must better communicate that the benefits of effective civil rights laws extend to every segment of American society.

Finally, congressional supporters of the bill must learn from those who have stood up for civil rights despite the political consequences. As historians Zachary Karabell and Jonathan Rosenberg explain, "[i]n an era when we think of politics as all calculation, what Kennedy and Johnson did on civil rights is a reminder that every now and then, politicians sacrifice what is expedient for what is right. And every now and then, they get rewarded at the polls."[50] Both men were determined to pass viable civil rights legislation in the face of opposition from their southern constituencies.[51] Despite the risk he took, Johnson was overwhelmingly elected to the presidency in 1968.[52]

Conclusion

For progressives concerned with the preservation of anti-discrimination laws, much work lies ahead. With time and an effective strategy, however, legislation can be passed that will preserve access to the courts for discrimination plaintiffs, and reverse the civil rights rollback.

Victory will depend on developing creative strategies informed by the political history of civil rights legislation. Any advocacy plan should include ideas about media messaging and counteracting misinformation disseminated by the right wing, and must rely on well-developed research, effective coalition work, and grassroots advocacy targeting Democratic supporters and moderate Republicans.

One last look to the past might be both helpful and inspirational. The writings of Martin Luther King Jr. reveal a sense of certainty, despite unimaginable obstacles, that one day African Americans would achieve their dream of equality.[53] It was this faith that carried the Civil Rights Movement to heights deemed impossible. Progressives today must move forward with the same certainty to reverse the rollback of civil rights and reawaken the dream of enduring equality for all Americans.

Endnotes

1. *Take Back the Courts*, Firelight Media (2003), at the National Campaign to Restore Civil Rights' website, www.rollbackcampaign.org.

2. The Fairness Act (S 2088, H.R. 3809) seeks to make amendments to Title VI of the Civil Rights Act of 1964, Title IX of the Education Amendments of 1973, the Age Discrimination Act of 1975, the Age Discrimination in Employment Act of 1974, Section 504 of the Rehabilitation Act of 1973, the Air Carrier Access Act of 1986, the Uniformed Services Employment and Reemployment Rights Act of 1994, the Fair Labor Standards Act of 1938, the Voting Rights Act of 1965, the Fair Housing Act of 1968, the Individuals with Disabilities Education Act, the Equal Credit Opportunity Act, the Fair Credit Reporting Act, the Freedom of Information Act, the Privacy Act, the Truth in Lending Act, the Fair Labor Standards Act, the National Labor Relations Act, and the Immigration and Nationality Act.

3. See S. 2088, 108th Cong. (2004); H.R.3809, 108th Cong. (2004). The full text of the Fairness Act is at http://frwebgate.access.gpo.gov/cgi-bin/getdoc.cgi?dbname=108_cong_bills&docid=f:s2088is.txt.pdf.

4. 532 U.S. 275 (2001).

5. 532 U.S. 275 (2001).

6. 524 U.S. 274 (1998).

7. 517 U.S. 44 (1996).

8. 527 U.S. 706 (1999).

9. 499 U.S. 83 (1991).

10. 532 U.S. 598 (2001).

11. 532 U.S. 105 (2001).

12. 535 U.S. 137 (2002).

13. 347 U.S. 483 (1954).

14. The Civil Rights Act of 1957, 71 Stat. 637, created the Commission on Civil Rights and increased the ability of the U.S. Department of Justice to fight for the civil rights of African Americans. While the Civil Rights Act of 1960, 74 Stat. 90, was aimed at activities that prevented African Americans from voting, it had weak enforcement mechanisms.

15. The summary in this section is drawn from Joseph L. Rauh, "The Role of the Leadership Conference on Civil Rights in the Civil Rights Struggle of 1963–1964," *The Civil Rights Act of 1964: The Passage of the Law that Ended Racial Segregation*, Robert D. Loevy, ed. (1997).

16. Id. at 53.

17. In 1964, cloture required the agreement of two-thirds of the senators. Today, only a three-fifths vote is required.

18. Pub. L. No. 89-110, 79 Stat. 437 (1965) (codified at 42 U.S.C. § 1973, *et. seq.*).

19. Pub. L. No. 90-284, 82 Stat. 81 (1968) (codified at 42 U.S.C. § 3601, *et. seq.*).

20. Pub. L. No. 92-318, 86 Stat. 373 (codified at 20 U.S.C. § 1681, *et. seq.*).

21. Pub. L. No. 97-205, 96 Stat. 134 (1982) (codified as amended at 42 U.S.C. § 1973, *et. seq.*).

22. Pub. L. No. 99-372, 100 Stat. 796 (1986) (codified as amended at 20 U.S.C. § 1400, *et. seq.*).

23. Pub. L. No. 100-259, 102 Stat. 28 (1987).

24. Roger Clegg, A Brief Legislative History of the Civil Rights Act of 1991, *54 La. L. Rev.* (July 1994) 1459.

25. Id. at 1463.

26. See David Lauter, "Rush of Events Broke Rights Bill Impasse," *Los Angeles Times* (Oct. 26, 1991) 1.

27. See Gebe Martinez, "GOP Moderates in Congress Get Cold Shoulder/Conservatives Show They Are Ready to Wield Power," *Houston Chronicle* (November 22, 2004); "Sonni Efron, Great Promise, Muted Results," *Los Angeles Times* (November 16, 2004) A1.

28. Clegg, *supra* at 1466.

29. See e.g., National Review, "Means Over Ends," v. 43, n. 12 (July 8, 1991) 14; The New Republic, "Uncivil Rites," v. 205, n. 25 (Dec. 16, 1991) 9.

30. Dan Goodgame, "White House Nervous and Nasty Bush's Feckless Efforts to Have It Both Ways on Civil Rights and the Economy Have Plunged His Administration into Disarray," *Time*, v. 138, n. 22 (Dec. 2, 1991) 18.

31. Clegg, *supra* at 1466.

32. Id. at 1467.

33. Id.

34. Id.

35. Republican National Committee, *2004 Republican Party Platform: A Safer World and a More Helpful America* (August 26, 2004), at http://www.gop.com/media/2004platform.pdf.

36. Id. at 1466.

37. Id.

38. Lee Cokorinos, *The Assault on Diversity*, Institute for Democracy Studies (2003) 19.

39. James Forman, Jr., Victory by Surrender: The Voting Rights Amendments of 1982 and the Civil Rights Act of 1991, *10 Yale L. & Pol'y Rev.* (1992) 133.

40. Id.

41. Id.

42. Id.

43. Id.

44. Republican National Committee, *supra*, note 35.

45. Redefining Rights in America: The Civil Rights Record of the George W. Bush Administration, 2001–2004, U.S. Commission on Civil Rights, Office of Civil Rights Evaluation September (2004) 9, at http://www.usccr.gov/pubs/bush/bush04.pdf.

46. Id.

47. Republican National Committee, *supra*, note 35.

48. Democratic National Convention Committee, Inc., Strong at Home, Respected in the World: The 2004 Democratic National Platform for America (July 27, 2004), at http://a9.g.akamai.net/7/9/8082/v002/www.democrats.org/pdfs/2004platform.pdf.

49. Forman, *supra*, note 39 at 163.

50. Zachary Karabell and Jonathan Rosenberg, "The Turing Point for a Reluctant White House," *The Washington Post* (Aug. 24, 2003).

51. Id.

52. Id.

53. Martin Luther King Jr., Letter from Birmingham Jail (April 16, 1963).

CHAPTER 23

STATE REFORM STRATEGIES

State Strategies to Reverse the Civil Rights Rollback

Dennis D. Parker[*]

The signing of the Americans with Disabilities Act (ADA) on July 26, 1990 was the culmination of years of effort by members of the disability rights movement who fought to raise awareness about the pervasiveness of discrimination against people with disabilities. ADA advocates marshaled overwhelming evidence of inaccessibility and discrimination by gathering "discrimination diaries" and public testimony from disabled individuals nation-wide. They then presented Congress with hundreds of hours of testimony and thousands of pages of documents conveying the need for disability rights legislation. Congress approved the ADA, recognizing people with disabilities as full members of the community.

Eleven years later, in Board of Trustees v. Garrett, *the Supreme Court cited the alleged absence of evidence of state discrimination against people with disabilities when it narrowed the ADA's application to state employers. In this way, the disabled were added to the growing roster of people whose civil rights have been compromised by the Federalism Revolution.*

In response to the Court's decision in Garrett, *however, Minnesota, North Carolina, and Illinois have enacted state legislation that waives state sovereign immunity and expands anti-discrimination coverage under the ADA. Other states are considering similar laws to protect their disabled citizens.*

This chapter considers how state-focused strategies can fill at least some of the void that the Federalism Revolution has created in federal civil rights enforcement. The chapter discusses three strategies in particular: state enforcement of federal civil rights laws; state opposition to "states' rights" cases that do not pro-

---

[*] Bureau Chief for the Civil Rights Bureau of the Office of the New York State Attorney General. Any opinions expressed are those of the author and do not necessarily reflect the views of the office of the attorney general.

mote the best interests of their citizens; and legislative waiver of state sovereign immunity in federal civil rights actions.

❦ ❦ ❦

In recent years, the Supreme Court's Federalism Revolution has harmed civil rights enforcement both by limiting individuals' ability to sue in federal court to redress civil rights violations and by diminishing the power of the federal government relative to that of the states. To make matters worse, federal agencies have also failed to aggressively enforce civil rights. Certainly, not every recent legal development has been negative. For the most part, however, the legal changes in the last few decades have been detrimental to those looking to the federal courts for relief from discrimination.

One way to mitigate this negative trend is for civil rights activists to rely more on resources provided by the states. This is a radical shift in strategy. Historically, states' rights has been synonymous with hostility towards civil rights. While true in the days of state resistance to civil rights enforcement, however, this is no longer necessarily the case. Today, elevating federal interests over states' rights has complicated effects on civil rights enforcement. It is crucial, therefore, that we rethink the role of states in the federal scheme.

The Federalism Revolution has Rolled Back the Enforcement of Federal Civil Rights Laws

Parts one though three of this volume explain the many ways that the Supreme Court has recently undermined federal civil rights laws. Some of the problems caused by the rollback of civil rights can be addressed, at least in part, by taking action at the state level. Such measures include restoring the ability of individuals to prosecute civil rights matters, and providing protection for individuals left relatively unprotected by the expansion of state sovereign immunity.

Weakening the Private Attorney General

One of the greatest casualties of the federal court's retrenchment of civil rights is the ability of individual litigants to serve as private attorneys general in federal civil rights cases. This long-standing concept is based upon the recognition that enforcement of civil rights statutes is difficult and necessarily dependent upon private litigation "as a means of securing broad compliance with the law."[1] As such, the interests served by private lawsuits are broader than the results usually sought by individuals. "When a plaintiff brings an action under… [a federal civil rights statute]…he does so not for himself alone but also as a 'private attorney general', vindicating a policy that Congress considered of the highest priority."[2]

Two decisions stand out in hindering the ability of individuals to serve as private attorneys generals. The first, *Buckhannon Bd. and Care Home, Inc. v. West Virginia Dep't of Health and Human Resources*,[3] erected a barrier for individual civil rights litigants by circumscribing their ability to recover attorney's fees under provisions of the Fair Housing Amendments Act[4] (FHAA) and the ADA.[5] Under the Civil Rights Attorney's Fees Awards Act of 1976, prevailing parties in civil rights litigation are permitted to recover counsel fees.[6] In *Buckhannon*, however, the Court denied the plaintiffs' fee application even though the contested state rule was repealed as a direct result of the lawsuit. The Court did not deny the fees because the plaintiffs had been unsuccessful—to the contrary, the litigation's goal was to repeal the state rule—but rather because that goal had been achieved without the issuance of a court order. By denying the attorney's fees application, the Court effectively punished the plaintiffs for their resounding success.

In so holding, the *Buckhannon* Court repudiated the "catalyst rule," subscribed to by all federal Courts of Appeal,[7] which provides that a party prevails for purposes of collecting attorney's fees when its suit spurred the change sought even in the absence of a court-ordered decree. The ruling, therefore, made it possible that a plaintiff could invest time and money, achieve the goals sought in litigation, and then be denied reimbursement for the fees to which he would otherwise have been entitled if the defendant ceased engaging in illegal practices during the course of the lawsuit. Such a result undercuts one of the purposes of fee-shifting statutes: "Congress prescribed fee-shifting provisions like those included in the FHAA and ADA to encourage private enforcement of laws designed to advance civil rights. Fidelity to that purpose calls for court-awarded fees when a private party's lawsuit, whether or not its settlement is registered in court, vindicates rights Congress sought to secure."[8]

While *Buckhannon* created potential disincentives for private litigants to bring individual actions, *Alexander v. Sandoval*[9] produced a more dramatic result: no private right of action at all. *Sandoval* addressed the question of whether individuals could avail themselves of causes of action under regulations promulgated under Title VI of the Civil Rights Act of 1964,[10] which prohibits discrimination on the basis of race, ethnicity, or national origin by recipients of federal funds. By holding that they could not, the Court denied plaintiffs the opportunity to bring an action alleging that defendants violated Title VI's regulations by implementing policies that had a disparate impact on a member of one or more of those protected classes. Unlike the agencies responsible for promulgating and enforcing the disparate impact regulations, private plaintiffs were required to satisfy the more stringent requirement of demonstrating intentional discrimination. As was true in *Buckhannon* with regards to an attorney fees award, the dissent in *Sandoval* (along with civil rights advocates) viewed the decision as being fundamentally at odds with Congress' intent in drafting the statute:

> The "effects" regulations at issue in this case represent the considered judgment of the relevant agencies that discrimination on the basis of race, ethnicity, and national origin by federal contractees are significant social problems that might be remedied, or at least ameliorated, by the application of a broad prophylactic rule. Given the judgment underlying them, the regulations are inspired by, at the service of, and inseparably intertwined with... [the] antidiscrimination mandate.[11]

The effect of these and similar decisions would be less harsh if the federal government were more aggressive in exercising its authority to enforce civil rights. However, in *Redefining Rights in America: The Civil Rights Record of the George W. Bush Administration, 2001–2004*, the U.S. Commission on Civil Rights concluded that President Bush has failed to advocate for civil rights[12] — civil rights issues are absent from presidential public statements, the president makes meager requests for funding such efforts,[13] and the administration's policies retreat from previous anti-discrimination efforts.[14]

The Bush administration's lack of effort in the area of environmental justice exemplifies its regressive treatment of areas of law that impact communities of color and low-income communities.[15] Under prior administrations, the federal Environmental Protection Agency (EPA) took steps to protect environmentally vulnerable communities, beginning in 1972 with the promulgation of regulations under Title VI to ensure non-discrimination by recipients of federal funding and including efforts in 1995 to bolster environmental justice enforcement under President Bill Clinton's Executive Order 12,898.[16] Following that order's mandate for agencies to ensure environmental justice, the EPA encouraged regional offices to develop effective environmental justice plans,[17] and launched the Environmental Justice Collaborative Problem Solving Grant Program to assist communities in finding solutions to environmental justice problems.[18]

More recently, however, the EPA has failed to adopt aggressive methods to promote environmental justice by failing to establish measures of agency progress,[19] by dismissing or rejecting complaints notwithstanding the absence of guidelines defining disparate impact, and by choosing not to issue guidelines outlining when complaints can be filed, how long they should take to be processed, how communities can participate,[20] and how to balance industry with community interests.[21] Further, in a 2001 memorandum, former head of the EPA Christine Todd Whitman de-emphasized the greater implications of environmental pollutants upon minority and low-income populations.[22] Taken together, these actions suggest a disregard for the environmental interests of vulnerable communities.

Striking Down Federal Civil Rights Laws

The Supreme Court has rendered a number of decisions that have thwarted congressional attempts to expand federal civil rights through the creation of causes of action and remedies. Perhaps the most striking example is *United States v. Morrison*[23] in which the Court struck down the civil rights provision of the Violence Against Women Act (VAWA), a statute designed to address the increasing gender-related violence. The statute represented a comprehensive approach to the nation-wide problems of domestic violence and violence against women that called for, among other things, coordination among federal, state, and local law enforcement. Most significant among VAWA's provisions was one that made gender-motivated violence a federal civil rights violation and that created an individual cause of action under which a successful plaintiff could recover compensatory and punitive damages, injunctive and declaratory relief, attorney's fees, and other relief deemed appropriate by a court.[24]

The Court struck down VAWA on the grounds that it believed that neither the Commerce Clause nor Section 5 of the Fourteenth Amendment gave Congress the authority to enact the statute. Ultimately, the decision was based on a finding that VAWA represented an incursion by the federal government into an area of state law.

Strengthening State Sovereign Immunity

In addition to the limitations imposed by *Buckhannon* and *Sandoval*, the Court has held that states are not susceptible to many lawsuits brought by individuals. A number of cases are particularly illustrative of this trend. In *Kimel v. Florida Board of Regents*,[25] the Court held that Congress lacked the necessary constitutional authority to subject states to individual lawsuits for damages and back pay under the Age Discrimination in Employment Act (ADEA). Similarly, in *Bd. Of Trustees v. Garrett*,[26] the Court found that Congress could not abrogate state sovereign immunity and subject states to lawsuits by individuals seeking monetary damages for alleged employment discrimination on the basis of disability pursuant to the ADA. Taken together, the decisions rendered the federal courts out of reach for state employees seeking to challenge discrimination by states.

Despite the negative effects of *Garrett* and *Kimel*, not all of the news regarding the ability of individuals to sue in federal court has been bad. Unlike *Garrett*, which involved employment claims brought under Title I of the ADA, *Tennessee v. Lane*[27] was brought under Title II, which prohibits the exclusion of people with disabilities from, or being denied the benefits of, services, programs, or activities. In contrast with the employment issue at stake in *Garrett*, the *Lane* Court found that Congress operated within its constitutional authority in crafting legislation to address the question of court access. Notwithstanding this one area in which individuals may sue states, however, the overall ability of individuals to assert their federal rights against states has substantially diminished over the past decade.

State Responses to Federal Civil Rights Retrenchment

States, individuals, and advocacy groups have undertaken a variety of measures to soften the impact of the trends noted above. The efficacy of these state-level measures is uncertain, particularly given the wide range of responses by states to the civil rights rollback (some states have tried to restore federal rights, while others have fought the abrogation of their state sovereign immunity). Still, given the unlikelihood of substantial change occurring in civil rights enforcement in the federal courts, Congress, and the current administration, any steps to protect individual civil rights must include state governments and courts.

State Support for Federal Civil Rights Enforcement

State attorneys generals have stepped into the void left by the decreased federal enforcement of civil rights laws and the increased difficulty of asserting private federal civil rights claims by bringing claims under federal civil rights actions themselves. Such claims can be brought based upon *parens patriae* standing. *Parens patriae* means "parent of the country," and provides states with the ability to sue in any case in which there is a "quasi-sovereign" interest in the health of its citizens.[28] Although the requirements for bringing cases as *parens patriae* differ slightly from circuit to circuit, states must generally demonstrate an interest apart from those of an individual party, an injury to a substantial segment of the population, and a showing that individuals could not otherwise obtain complete relief.[29]

Parens patriae cases are ideally suited to taking up the slack left by private individuals or the federal government in civil rights cases. In *Puerto Rico ex rel. Quiros v. Bramkamp*,[30] the Court upheld the standing of the Commonwealth of Puerto Rico to bring an employment discrimination action on behalf of migrant Puerto Rican farm workers under the Wagner-Peyser Act of 1933[31] and the Immigration and Nationality Act of 1952.[32] In that case, the Court outlined the unique qualifications of the Commonwealth:

> In this case, it is unlikely that the individual Puerto Ricans who were injured by the alleged discrimination in 1978 will achieve the complete relief sought by the Commonwealth.... There is no assurance that the individual workers could bear the cost of a lawsuit that would achieve complete relief... [E]ven if the workers could marshall the resources to institute and effectively prosecute actions or a class action in their own behalf, there is no assurance that all named defendants herein should be sued or that relief against widespread and future discrimination would be actively pursued.[33]

Relying on their *parens patriae* standing, states have brought a wide range of civil rights cases, including those alleging discrimination in housing,[34] public accommodations,[35] access to health care,[36] and employment,[37] as well as some alleging police misconduct.[38]

Although *parens patriae* cases brought by state attorneys general will continue to be used to address the federal rollback in civil rights enforcement, individuals barred from seeking redress in federal courts because they cannot satisfy the intentional discrimination requirement under Title VI are still constrained by states' immunity from suit in certain types of cases as a result of the *Garrett* and *Kimel* decisions.

State Opposition to the Civil Rights Rollback

One dramatic example of state opposition to the rollback of civil rights can be seen in state responses to the Supreme Court's decision to strike down VAWA's civil rights provision. Although the Court undoubtedly viewed its decision as an assertion of states' rights, a group consisting of state attorneys general (fervent supporters of states' rights) defended that statute when it was pending re-authorization in Congress and, later, when it was under attack in the courts. This group recognized that the best interests of the states are not always protected by jealously guarding state authority against federal incursion. In a letter from the National Association of Attorneys General to Senator Orrin Hatch and Representative Henry Hyde, Chairs of their respective Committees on the Judiciary, fifty-four state or territorial attorneys general urged the approval of VAWA, stating that it "would foster the essential role of the states in protecting its women and children."

Likewise, thirty-seven attorneys general joined in an *amicus* brief to urge the Court to uphold VAWA, arguing that gender-motivated violence affects interstate commerce by impacting employment and raising costs for medical and governmental services, and that state efforts to eliminate gender-motivated violence, while substantial, are inadequate.[39] Although ultimately unsuccessful in moving the Court, the state attorneys general's support for VAWA recognized that the needs of the states and its citizens can be best served by encouraging the sharing of authority between states and the federal government. Similarly, although some states took the position that sovereign immunity protected them from lawsuits for damages under the ADA, a number of state attorneys general joined in *amicus* briefs urging the Court to uphold the ADA as a reasonable and constitutionally permissible remedy for disability discrimination by the states in the circumstances presented in *Lane* and *Garrett*.[40]

It is difficult to determine what position each state will take in any given civil rights rollback case because those decisions are driven by a complex set of factors. It is clear, however, that civil rights advocacy groups should understand the positions of state attorneys general, as this group might lend them crucial support.

Waiver of State Sovereign Immunity

State legislation waiving sovereign immunity has been most successful in addressing the consequences of the rollback. To date, three states have adopted laws waiving their sovereign immunity. In 2001, Minnesota and North Carolina became the first two states to pass such legislation. Illinois followed suit in 2003.[41] A number of other states have considered similar bills that either waive sovereign immunity or expand anti-discrimination coverage.[42] The scope of the waiver, including who may sue the state, under which laws, and what recovery might be available, differs between states.

Minnesota's sovereign immunity waiver statute permits state employees (past, present, or prospective) to sue the state for damages for violations of the ADEA, the Fair Labor Standards Act (FLSA), the Family Medical Leave

Act (FMLA), and Title I of the ADA.[43] Because of the statute's lack of specificity regarding whether it waived sovereign immunity for lawsuits in federal court, the Eighth Circuit Court of Appeals held in *Faibisch v. University of Minnesota*[44] that Minnesota did not waive its sovereign immunity in such cases. Under the State Employee Federal Remedy Restoration Act,[45] North Carolina state employees (except those in policy-making positions) can bring civil cases under the same federal statutes available to Minnesota state employees. North Carolina's statute, however, clearly states that lawsuits may be brought in both state and federal courts, and contains an explicit damages cap of $500,000. Illinois' waiver statute allows state employees to bring actions for damages in state or federal court under the ADA, the ADEA, Title VII of the Civil Rights Act of 1964, the FMLA, and the FLSA.[46] Additional sovereign immunity waiver statutes are likely to be approved in the future.

Unfortunately, state legislative action can just as easily hinder civil rights enforcement. One example of this is the proliferation of referenda intended to limit the use of affirmative action programs in individual states. Anti-affirmative action bills have also been introduced in the Massachusetts, New Jersey, New York, Texas, and Utah state legislatures.[47] Ironically, these referenda stake out a more conservative position than that taken by the Supreme Court. The first of these, California's Proposition 209, essentially eliminated race-based affirmative action programs in the state. Ward Connerly, one of its chief proponents, responded to the Court decision in *Grutter v. Bollinger*[48] (holding that considerations of race are lawful in university admissions) by launching an initiative to amend the Michigan Constitution to outlaw the use of race in university admissions and state hiring and contracting.[49] Connerly has announced his intention to launch similar ballot initiatives in Arizona, Colorado, Missouri, and New Hampshire.

Conclusion

Although state responses to the federal rollback of civil rights are subject to the vagaries of the laws in each state, they provide a means of addressing many concerns. Given the current federal climate, states have no choice but to become leaders in the enforcement of civil rights until such a time when they can once again enter into a partnership with the federal government to assure that civil rights are vigorously protected.

Endnotes

1. *Newman v. Piggie Park Enter. Inc.*, 390 U.S. 400, 402 (1968).

2. Id.

3. 532 U.S. 598 (2001).

4. 42 U.S.C.A. §3613(c)(2)(2003).

5. 42 U.S.C.A. §12205.

6. 42 U.S.C.A. §1988 (2003).

7. Except for the Fourth Circuit, which changed its position in 1994. See, *S-1 and S-2 v. State Bd. of Educ. of North Carolina*, 21 F.3d 49 (Fourth Cir. 1994) (*en banc*).

8. *Buckhannon*, 532 U.S. at 644 (Ginsburg, J. dissenting).

9. 532 U.S. 275 (2001).

10. 42 U.S.C.A. §§2000d to 200d-7.

11. *Sandoval*, 532 U.S. at 307 (J. Stevens, dissenting).

12. U. S. Commission on Civil Rights, Office of Civil Rights Evaluation, *Redefining Rights in America: The Civil Rights Record of the George W. Bush Administration, 2001–2004*, (Draft Report for Commissioners' Review) (September 2004) vii, at http://www.truthout .org/mm_01/4.CRCReport0904.pdf.

13. Id.

14. Id. at viii–x.

15. The EPA defines environmental justice as the "fair treatment and meaningful involvement of all people" so that "no group of people, including a racial, ethnic or socioeconomic group should bear a disproportionate share of the negative environmental consequences resulting from industrial, municipal, and commercial operations or the execution of federal, state, local, and tribal programs and policies." U.S. Envtl. Protection Agency, *Environmental Justice*, at http://www.eh.doe.gov/oepa/guidance/justice/eo12898.pdf.

16. "Federal Actions to Address Environmental Justice in Minority Populations and Low-Income Populations," Exec. Order No. 12,898, 59 F.R. 7629 (1995).

17. Office of Civil Rights Evaluation, U.S. Comm'n on Civil Rights, *Redefining Rights in America*, 74.

18. Office of Environmental Justice, EPA, "EPA's Commitment to Environmental Justice" (May 2003) at http://epa.gov/compliance/resources/publications/ej/ej_fact_ sheet _commitment.pdf.

19. U.S. Comm'n on Civil Rights, *Not in My Backyard*, 145 (citing Nat'l Academy of Pub. Admin., *Environmental Justice in EPA Permitting*, 2) at http://www.usccr.gov/pubs/ envjust/ej0104.pdf.

20. Office of Civil Rights Evaluation, U.S. Comm'n on Civil Rights, *Redefining Rights in America*, 76.

21. Id.

22. Id. at 75.

23. 529 U.S. 598 (2000).

24. 42 U.S.C.A. 1988, 13981(c).

25. 528 U.S. 62 (2000).

26. 531 U.S. 356 (2001).

27. 124 S. Ct. 1978 (2004).

28. *Alfred L. Snapp & Sons, Inc. v. Puerto Rico ex rel. Barez*, 458 U.S. 592, 602–3 (1972).

29. See, e.g., *People by Abrams v. 11 Cornwell Co.*, 695 F.2d 34, 38–40 (2d Cir. 1982), vacated in part on other grounds, 718 F.2d 22 (2d Cir. 1983) (*en banc*).

30. 654 F.2d 212 (2d Cir. 1981).

31. 29 U.S.C.A. §§ 49–49k.

32. 8 U.S.C.A. §§ 1101–1524.

33. *Bramkamp*, 654 F.2d at 217. See also, *Massachusetts v. Bull HN Information Sys.*, 16 F. Supp 2d 90, 98 (D. Mass. 1998) (barring the Massachusetts Attorney General from bringing an ADEA case might make potential defendants feel immunized from suit; public rights should not be subject to pressures of private litigation where victims may not have resources, tenacity, or sufficient damages to pursue litigation).

34. See, e.g., *Puerto Rico Public Hous. Admin. v. United States Dep't of Housing & Urban Dev.*, 59 F. Supp. 2d 310 (D. P.R. 1999); *Support Ministries for Persons with AIDS, Inc. v. Village of Waterford*, 799 F. Supp. 272 (N.D.N.Y. 1992) (zoning discrimination against residence home for persons with AIDS).

35. See, e.g., *People v. Peter & John's Pump House, Inc.*, 914 F. Supp. 809 (N.D.N.Y. 1996) (racial discrimination in a nightclub).

36. See, e.g., *People by Vacco v. Mid Hudson Medical Group, P.C.*, 877 F. Supp. 143 (S.D.N.Y. 1995) (disability discrimination suit against hospital for failure to provide sign language interpreting).

37. See, e.g., *Puerto Rico v. Bramkamp*, 654 F.2d 212 (2d Cir. 1981); *Equal Employment Opportunity Commission v. Federal Express Corp.*, 268 F. Supp. 2d 192 (E.D.N.Y. 2003); *Pennsylvania v. Flaherty*, 404 F. Supp. 1022 (W.D. Pa. 1975) (gender and race discrimination in police department); *Pennsylvania v. Glickman*, 370 F.Supp. 724 (W.D. Pa. 1974) (racial discrimination in employment of firefighters).

38. *Pennsylvania v. Porter*, 659 F.2d 306 (3d Cir. 1981).

39. See Brief of the States of Arizona, Alaska, Arkansas, California, Colorado, Connecticut, Delaware, Georgia, Hawaii, Illinois, Iowa, Kansas, Kentucky, Louisiana, Maine, Maryland, Minnesota, Mississippi, Missouri, Montana, Nevada, New Hampshire, New Mexico, New York, North Carolina, North Dakota, Oklahoma, Oregon, Rhode Island, Tennessee, Utah, Vermont, Washington, West Virginia, and Wisconsin, and the Commonwealths of Massachusetts and Puerto Rico, as *amici curiae* in Support of Petitioner's Brief on the Merits, *United States v. Morrison* and *Brzonkala v. Morrison*, 1999 WL 1032809 (1999).

40. Fourteen state attorneys general signed on to the *amicus* brief supporting the abrogation of sovereign immunity in *Garrett*, and eight took a similar position in *Lane*.

41. Since 1972, Montana's Constitution has contained a provision waiving immunity. Pursuant to Art. II, Section 18, the state "shall have no immunity from suit for injury to a person or property." Despite the apparent breadth of the statute, it is unclear whether that waiver was intended to apply to immunity in both state and federal courts.

42. In the past three years, these states have included California, Connecticut, Maryland, Missouri, Rhode Island, and New York.

43. Minn. Stat. § 1.05 (2001).

44. 304 F. 3d 797 (Eighth Cir. 2002).

45. N.C. Gen. Stat. § 143-300.35 (2001).

46. 745 Ill. Comp. Stat. 5/1.5 (2003).

47. See website for People for the American Way, at http://www.pfaw.org/pfaw/general/default.aspx?oid=14826.

48. 539 U.S. 306 (2003).

49. See Karen W. Arenson, "Ballot Measures Seen in Wake of Court Ruling," *New York Times* (July 10, 2003) A17.

CHAPTER 24

ACTIVIST STRATEGIES

We Shall Be Moved: Community Activism
as a Tool for Reversing the Rollback

Andrew Friedman[*]
Robert García & Erica Flores Baltodano[†]
Julie Hyman, Brad Williams & Tracie Crandell[‡]

Local community organizing has always been the driving force behind social change. From the tumultuous Civil Rights Movement of the 1950s and 60s to the current battle against the Rehnquist Court's Federalism Revolution, community activists have been invaluable in increasing public awareness and empowering people to redress injustices. Grassroots campaigns provide the foot soldiers that play a critical role in bringing about positive and lasting change by marching,

[*] Andrew Friedman is the Co-Founder and Co-Director of Make the Road by Walking, a membership-led organization based in the Bushwick section of Brooklyn, NY, that promotes economic justice and participatory democracy by increasing residents' power to achieve self-determination through collective action. See www.maketheroad.org. Friedman currently works as an attorney and organizer in that organization's Economic Justice and Democracy Project.

[†] Robert García is a civil rights attorney and Executive Director of the Center for Law in the Public Interest. See www.clipi.org. The mission of the City Project at the Center is to achieve equal justice, democracy, and livability for all. The Center is spearheading a diverse coalition that is helping to create urban parks and schools in underserved communities. Erica Flores Baltodano is Assistant Director and an attorney at the Center.

[‡] Julie Hyman is the senior policy analyst at the Center for Independence of the Disabled in New York, a disability advocacy organization that pursues a local and state policy agenda that focuses on the interests of people with disabilities. See www.cidny.org. Brad Williams is the Executive Director of the New York Independent Living Council, which provides technical assistance and training, looks to increase public awareness about independent living, and pursues a public policy agenda that results in systematic change for people with disabilities. See www.nysilc.org. Tracie Crandell is a member of NYS ADAPT and a policy analyst at the Center for Disability Rights, an organization that works for the integration, independence, and civil rights of people with disabilities. See www.rochestercdr.org.

protesting, boycotting, phoning, letter writing, and e-mailing. In order to successfully stop the rollback of civil rights, advocates must recognize that it is not a series of attacks on individual communities but rather an attack on us all, identify the commonalities between different causes, and organize into larger more powerful communities.

The frontline advocates and authors of this chapter have joined to share their knowledge about building and sustaining successful activist campaigns. They work on a broad range of issues: Andrew Friedman dedicates his time to economic justice in New York City; Robert García and Erica Flores Baltodano spearhead efforts to ensure equal access to parks, recreation, and schools in Los Angeles; and Julie Hyman, Brad Williams, and Tracie Crandell are disability advocates in New York. Although their work differs, they share one goal—reversing the rollback of civil rights. This chapter will provide their blueprints for achieving this important aim.

ᔕ   ᔕ   ᔕ

Friedman: Economic Justice for Low-Income Immigrant Communities

When my marriage broke up, I was left by myself to care for my daughters. Then it turned out that they both had a variety of bronchial problems and asthma. As a result of these circumstances, I had no alternative but to seek support from the government to be able to be available to help my daughter comply with her medication regimen. I had to hook Gabriela up to a machine to clean her lungs every six hours. When I went to the Welfare Center to apply for Medicaid, it was very difficult for me to communicate with the social workers because they only spoke English and I speak Spanish. I was unable to apply for benefits. These difficulties affected my little daughter even more than they affected me.

Irania Sanchez[1]

Civil rights advocates must use community-based strategies to raise awareness about unlawful discriminatory practices, empower communities as they struggle to shape their collective destinies, encourage individuals to comply with civil rights laws, and pressure public officials to enforce compliance with those laws.[2] Community-based strategies include: participatory action research, leadership development through legal and organizing training, media work, accountability meetings with administrators and legislators, direct action, and coalition-building. These strategies are not new—to the contrary, they were all used in the Civil Rights Movement—but they are increasingly important in facing the renewed attacks on civil rights.

To be sure, community-based approaches have their limitations.[3] Perpe-trators of discrimination may be unwilling to change their behavior unless forced. Because organizing is a gradual approach to building power, it takes time to generate enough coercive force to change behavior. Nevertheless, grassroots organizing can promote civil rights by creating political power for marginalized communities.

Community-Based Lawyering at Work

Members of my organization, Make the Road By Walking, have used com-munity-based lawyering to advocate for change in New York City. We spear-headed a four year direct action and coalition organizing effort to reverse the rollback of and expand language rights for the growing population of Limited English Proficient (LEP) immigrants. Our effort led to the enactment of the Equal Access to Health and Human Services Act, which will ensure equality of services for hundreds of thousands of LEP applicants or recipients of sub-sistence government benefits (e.g., Medicaid, food stamps, and public assis-tance).

Our strategy was timely because of the growing anti-immigrant, English-only movement, and because *Alexander v. Sandoval* (discussed in Chapter 10)[4] made it more difficult for victims of language discrimination to find justice in federal courts. Currently, twenty-seven states have declared English to be their official language.[5] While English-only policies do not override the responsi-bilities of federally-funded entities (e.g., medical facilities) to ensure equal ac-cess to their services and programs as required by Title VI of the Civil Rights Act of 1964, *Sandoval* has made it so that individuals can no longer sue such entities for adopting English-only policies and practices; their only option is to seek enforcement of Title VI before an administrative agency. Advocates have worked to pass language access laws to dismantle the English-only poli-cies that often deprive LEP people of their basic civil rights.

In April 2001, after two years of grassroots participatory action research, intensive leadership development work, direct action organizing, and only nominally successful civil rights complaints and litigation, our organization began working with other language rights advocates to lobby the New York City Council to pass the Equal Access to Health and Human Services Act. The legislation requires the Human Resources Administration (HRA) to provide comprehensive language assistance services (interpretation and translation) to LEP people, and requires HRA and three other agencies—the Department of Health and Mental Health, the Administration for Children's Services, and the Department of Homeless Services—to track and report the need for language assistance services along with their capacity to meet the need.[6] The Act helps fill the void caused by the *Sandoval* opinion.

The movement to pass the Act grew out of concern among Brooklyn's Latino community about the inadequacy of interpretation and translation services at local welfare offices. Community residents described the lack of such services as alienating, confusing, and, more important, a threat to their ability to access government benefits.

Residents decided to research the extent of the problem for other low-income, immigrant New Yorkers. They spent hours at welfare centers surveying hundreds of other applicants for, and recipients of, government benefits, then held a press conference/protest to announce the results. Indeed, their surveys demonstrated that significant percentages of LEP welfare claimants had experienced problems resulting from a lack of adequate translation and interpretation services at their local welfare centers.[7] At the same time, they announced that they had filed a complaint with the U.S. Department of Health and Human Services Office for Civil Rights (OCR). Their protest and subsequent demonstrations were designed to pressure OCR to conduct a fast and comprehensive investigation of the complaint (when a similar complaint was filed in the early 1970s, OCR took over three years to complete their investigation). This grassroots community organizing garnered a firestorm of attention in the Spanish-language daily newspapers and transformed stigmatized immigrant welfare mothers into dynamic spokespersons for the civil rights of immigrants.

In October 1999, just five months after the survey results were announced, this active community engagement and public pressure began to pay off. OCR issued a Letter of Findings that supported the immigrant community's allegations of national origin discrimination within HRA because of the inadequacy of interpretation and translation services at welfare offices. OCR demanded a corrective action plan from then-Mayor Rudolph Giuliani within thirty days. The Republican executive, however, employed an effective strategy of delay and noncompliance; OCR has not yet taken action to compel New York City to comply with federal civil rights laws or respect the rights of LEP welfare claimants.

Months later, the immigrant community reached out to progressive members of the New York City Council, as well as to immigrant's rights, advocacy, and labor organizations, to spark interest in creating local civil rights legislation to protect the growing LEP population. The broad coalition of politicians and organizations that drafted the Equal Access to Health and Human Services Act brought together considerable public policy experience and expertise, and attached political power to the immigrants' initiative. Our strategies eventually proved successful—over ninety percent of the New York City

Council, as well as its black, Latino, and Asian caucus, agreed to sponsor the legislation, and Republican Mayor Michael Bloomberg signed the bill into law on December 22, 2003.

The Act requires HRA to provide interpretation services to every LEP New Yorker in need. Additionally, it requires HRA to translate documents (e.g., application forms and informational notices regarding benefits levels) into Spanish, Arabic, Chinese, Russian, Creole, and Korean. The Act imposes strict record-keeping and public reporting requirements to ensure compliance, and requires three other city agencies to track the need for language assistance services and to report annually whether the need is being met.

The One-Two Punch of Lawyering and Community Activism

Working together, lawyers and community organizers present a potent force in campaigns to win or protect civil rights. Because of their educational status, societal privilege, and capacity to create legal accountability, lawyers command the attention and respect of the institutional or governmental target. For the same reasons, the media tend to accept the statements of "expert" attorneys more than those of low-income immigrant community activists. Lawyers can also help build a coalition by ensuring that immigrant activists feel protected during the initial phases of the campaign. Attorney activists, however, are often labeled "outside agitators" or "opportunists." A strong alliance between community members and attorneys is necessary to effectively counteract this prejudice.

Community involvement brings grassroots political power and an indispensable perspective to civil rights struggles. Low-income immigrant community members can speak to the precise nature of the civil rights problems "on the ground," put a human face on the dire consequences of civil rights violations, educate peers about community problems, recruit participants, and address the fears of retaliation often experienced by new activists. Moreover, an organizing agenda that involves community members in identifying problems and crafting public policy solutions serves to develop grassroots leadership that in turn better positions immigrant communities to defend themselves in future civil rights struggles.

Grassroots community support is also essential when seeking the support of local politicians. Because politicians often supply government resources to local hospitals or city agencies, they have enormous leverage in demanding reforms. Furthermore, community institutions, dependent on local use, are sensitive to campaigns that may affect their bottom line.

Summary

Both legal work and grassroots organizing are important in campaigns to win or protect civil rights. Given the current aggressive rollback of civil rights, the judicial and political landscape looks bleak. Nonetheless, by thinking creatively about how we can exercise our political power as attorneys, community members, organizers, and workers, and how we can build on this power through civic engagement, coalition-building, and organizing, we can enforce state civil rights laws, pass local legislation to fill the space once occupied by a federal Judiciary committed to equality and civil rights, and nurture new participants and leaders in the ongoing movement to reverse the rollback of our civil rights.

García and Baltodano: The Urban Park Movement

The California beach is the latest front in the struggle for equal justice. Beaches are not a luxury. Rather, they are a democratic commons that provide a place for children and parents to wade, swim, "people-watch," surf, lounge under an umbrella, jump between tide pools, or gaze at the sunset. Public access to the beach is integral to democracy and equality.

The urban park movement seeks equal access to recreation areas such as beaches, parks, school yards, and forests. People of color and low-income communities face societal structures that limit access to such recreation, leisure, and improved human health. To ensure equal access to public resources, the urban park movement is creating parks in neglected neighborhoods, advocating for the fair distribution of environmental benefits (e.g., parks and beaches), and improving human health and the environment. In light of the ongoing civil rights rollback, the movement has developed strategies for addressing inequalities that focus on the planning, administrative, and political processes.

A strategic campaign must begin with a collective vision. The next step is the building of broad-based, multi-cultural alliances. Multidisciplinary research and analyses are essential to pinpoint racial and ethnic inequalities, determine who benefits from the investment of public resources and who gets left behind, investigate how society arrived at its current situation, and suggest improvements. The urban park movement has successfully used strategic media and education campaigns to increase public awareness and political pressure.

The Vision: Access to Parks and Beaches in the Fight for Equal Justice

In 1930, Olmsted Brothers (the firm started by the sons of the landscape architect Frederick Law Olmsted) and Bartholomew and Associates presented a plan for developing parks, schools, beaches, forests, and transportation that would have made LA one of the most beautiful and livable cities. According to the Olmsted Report:

> Continued prosperity [in LA] will depend on providing needed parks, because, with the growth of a great metropolis here, the absence of parks will make living conditions less and less attractive, less and less wholesome....In so far, therefore, as the people fail to show the understanding, courage, and organizing ability necessary at this crisis, the growth of the Region will tend to strangle itself.[8]

Those words remain true. Unfortunately, civic leaders and private interests ignored the report, leaving LA with less than one acre of park per thousand residents (less than any other major U.S. city) compared to the six to ten acres that is the National Recreation and Park Association standard.

There are also vast disparities in access to parks and recreation—0.3 acres of parks per thousand residents in the inner city (where low-income communities of color live disproportionately) compared to 1.7 acres per thousand residents in relatively white and wealthy areas.[9] These inner city communities do not contain adequate parks or green space, nor do their inhabitants have fair access to the parks, beaches, and open spaces in areas like Malibu.

Today, the urban park movement seeks to restore part of the Olmsted vision and the beauty of LA. The Center for Law in the Public Interest has led coalitions to create a thirty-two-acre state park in the Chinatown Cornfield, a forty-acre state park in Taylor Yard as part of a planned hundred-acre park along the LA River, and a two-square-mile park in the Baldwin Hills, the historic heart of African American LA.

Wealthy beachfront homeowners in areas like Malibu, however, are attempting to block equal access to beaches, parks, and other recreation. Keeping the beach free for all, therefore, is the urban park movement's next battle.

From the Mountains to the Sea: A History
of Discrimination at Los Angeles Beaches

The history of beach and park access in the LA area is plagued with racial discrimination. The inequities today did not develop because of unplanned growth or a free market in beachfront properties, but rather because of years of discriminatory land use planning and park funding policies, restrictive housing covenants, and federal mortgage subsidies restricted to racially homogenous neighborhoods.[10]

Historically, beaches in the mountains were off limits to people of color. From the 1920s on, for example, racially restrictive covenants prevented people of color from occupying or using Lake Arrowhead (the major mountain lake near LA) property.[11] Today, Arrowhead is known as "the Beverly Hills of the Mountains," with private mansions and businesses ringing the lake. There is no public beach access. [12]

The history of Malibu also includes racial discrimination. At the turn of the century, Malibu was owned by Frederick H. Rindge, and consisted of the Topanga Malibu Sequit, a 13,316-acre rancho comprising a twenty-five-mile stretch of beaches, mountains, and canyons.[13] After Rindge's death, his widow May began leasing and selling off land parcels to celebrities in order to pay her taxes.[14] Beach parcels like those now owned by entertainment mogul David Geffen originally carried racially restrictive covenants that were intended to run with the land in perpetuity. These covenants read, in part:

> [S]aid land or any part thereof shall not be used or occupied or permitted to be used or occupied by any person not of the white or Caucasian race, except such persons not of the white or Caucasian race as are engaged on said property in the bona fide domestic employment of the owner of said land or those holding under said owner and said employee shall not be permitted upon the beach part of said lands for bathing, fishing or recreational purposes.[15]

Today, the white and wealthy enclave of Malibu is 88.5 percent non-Hispanic white, six percent Hispanic, 2.6 percent Asian or Pacific Islander, 0.9 percent black, and 0.2 percent Native American. According to 2000 census data, twenty-five percent of Malibu households have an annual income over $200,000, and the median household annual income is $102,031. In contrast, LA County is only thirty-one percent non-Hispanic white, the median household income is $42,189, and only 3.5 percent of households have an annual income of $200,000 or more.[16]

In many parts of Malibu, wealthy beachfront homeowners have exclusive access to the public beach. Although there should be a public access path every thousand feet, only twelve paths are open in the twenty-seven miles of coast-line; one three-mile stretch provides no access at all. Many property owners do what they can to prevent public access to the beach—phony "private beach" signs deter beachgoers from "trespassing" on public land, private se-curity guards intimidate those who dare walk the coast, and residents dis-cretely pass keys around to locked gates that block access to strips of "private" beaches.

Malibu has largely succeeded in deterring the public. While the California Coastal Commission issued cease and desist orders to force Malibu to remove boulders that were blocking public beach parking (the first time the Com-mission ever issued such orders against a city), people generally think the beach is private. To ensure fair and equal enjoyment of natural resources, this must change.

In response to the advocacy of the Center for Law in the Public Interest, the California Coastal Commission is taking steps to maximize Malibu pub-lic beach access. The Commission has ordered an end to phony "no trespass-ing" and "private beach" signs on Broad Beach, and to security guards who harass the public. The sheriff's department has agreed to protect the public's right to use the beach. Further, the Commission has published a guide with maps showing public access to Broad Beach. Hopefully, a similar guide will be published for the entire California coast.[17]

Putting Strategies to Work to Protect Coastal Access

The following strategies, successfully used in other aspects of the urban park movement, can be used to secure equal access to California's beaches despite the rollback. These strategies include coalition-building, interdisciplinary research and analysis, public education, strategic media campaigns, legislative and ad-ministrative advocacy, and, as a last resort, litigation.

1. Coalition-Building

Alliances are necessary in creating a broad movement. The broader and more diverse the coalition, the more likely it will influence public opinion and political leadership. Natural allies of the beach access movement include or-ganizations whose members have traditionally been excluded from using the beach and, more generally, from the "good life." While communities of color and low-income communities are disproportionately impacted by the loss of beach access, for example, they were the biggest supporters of California's recent Proposition 40, the largest resource bond in U.S. history with $2.6 billion for parks, clean water, and clean air.

Passed in March 2002 with the support of seventy-seven percent of blacks, seventy-four percent of Latinos, sixty percent of Asians, and fifty-six percent of non-Hispanic whites, Prop 40 demolished the myth that communities of color and low-income communities do not care about or are not willing to pay for a healthy environment. Seventy-five percent of voters with an annual family income below twenty thousand dollars and sixty-one percent with a high school diploma or less supported Prop 40—the highest among any income or education levels.[18] Despite their support, however, these communities are disproportionately denied access to parks and recreation. They are, therefore, likely allies in the beach access movement.

It is also important to engage the business community that would benefit financially from increased beach access. Because beach access is part of the larger struggle for social equality, proponents should find common ground with the broader civil rights and environmental justice movements.

2. Interdisciplinary Research and Analyses

Hard data is essential to influence public opinion and affect policy changes. A financial analysis determines who benefits and who gets left behind with the investment of public resources, census data analysis provides demographic information, geographic information systems (GIS) mapping reveals where inequities exist, and historical research helps explain why things are the way they are and how they could improve.

Historical information regarding racially restrictive covenants on beach access helps to explain how white homeowners came to dominate Southern California beachfront areas. The history highlights the inequities, and inspires thought about possible remedies. The legal right to beach access, even if not enforced with litigation, can support policy arguments and persuade the unwilling to comply.

3. Public Education

Public education should begin after detailed data has been assembled. The public must be informed that they own the coastline and therefore have a right to use the beach. Possible channels for education include: "Your Rights at the Beach" pamphlets, public displays, signs, artwork, a photographic history, mass e-mail, a website, schools, and children's books. Regional access guides and maps, including public transportation routes, should clearly mark beach access paths. Law enforcement must be educated about enforcing public rights rather than siding with beachfront homeowners who unlawfully seek to deny beach access.

4. Strategic Media Campaigns

Along with public education, a strategic media campaign can help inform the public and increase pressure on those who seek to block public beach access. Doonesbury artist Gary Trudeau has used irony and wit to expose the hypocrisy inherent in closing off public beaches for private use.[19] Such creative media strategies can be supplemented by radio and television appearances and newspaper articles.

5. Legislative and Administrative Advocacy

Political advocacy can also be a powerful tool in amassing the resources necessary to protect public beach access. Strategies should include: ballot measures like Prop 40 to fund urban parks and beach access; legislative advocacy and lobbying; informing elected officials and community leadership about the issues; advocacy through administrative and planning processes; developing policy agendas with an overarching vision, mission, and plan; and strengthening public involvement in the decision-making process through voter registration and get-out-the-vote drives.

Advocates supported California Senate Bill 1962 (SB 1962), for example, which provides a legislative safety net for public beach access. Hundreds of coastal access paths could expire because they have not yet been enforced by the state.[20] SB 1962 mandates that a minimum of three such access ways be opened every year, and requires the Coastal Conservancy to report annually on its progress. Former Governor Grey Davis signed SB 1962 into law on September 12, 2002, proclaiming that "California's coast line belongs to the people."

Also in 2002, a coalition consisting of the Center for Law in the Public Interest, the Advancement Project, Latino Issues Forum, Latino Urban Forum, the Mexican American Legal Defense and Education Fund, Mothers of East LA, Santa Isabel, Planning and Conservation League, the William C. Velazquez Institute, and the Sierra Club persuaded the Coastal Commission to adopt a plan in which Malibu would maximize coastal public access and recreational opportunities while ensuring the fair treatment of people of all races, cultures, and incomes.[21]

Finally, political advocacy has been used to address remarks made by California politicians. Newport Beach City Councilman Richard Nichols stated that he opposes improvements to Corona Del Mar State Beach because "with grass we usually get Mexicans coming in there early in the morning and they claim it as theirs and it becomes their personal, private grounds all day."[22] The statement prompted *Los Angeles Times* columnist Steve Lopez to write "[i]f not for the likes of Nichols letting loose now and then, we'd have to constantly remind ourselves why we have civil rights attorneys."[23] The statement presented yet another opportunity to seek equal justice through political advocacy.

Newport Beach is overwhelmingly white and wealthy (eighty-nine percent non-Hispanic white compared to just fifty-one percent in surrounding Orange County). 25.8 percent of Newport Beach households gross over $150,000 annually compared to the 9.6 percent in Orange County.[24] Newport Beach, like Malibu, must maximize public coastal access and recreational opportunities while ensuring the fair treatment of people of all races, cultures, and incomes—and local governing bodies must make this commitment public.

6. Litigation

While the Federalism Revolution cases have made it more difficult to enforce civil rights in court, federal and state laws prohibit both intentional discrimination and policies with unjustified disparate racial impacts. Indeed, recipients of federal funds remain obligated to prohibit both types of discrimination. The Equal Protection Clause of the Fourteenth Amendment (prohibiting intentional discrimination) and § 1983 (allowing for the enforcement of laws prohibiting discrimination) remain viable options for bringing federal litigation.

Advocates searching for new ways to enforce civil rights protections should also look to state law to make up for diminishing federal protections. In California, Government Code § 11135 prohibits recipients of state funds from intentionally discriminating or creating unjustified discriminatory impacts on the basis of national origin, ethnic group, religion, age, sex, color, or disability.[25] Although this law remains largely untested, it provides a potentially powerful tool for fighting discrimination. Similarly, a new California law defines environmental justice as "the fair treatment of people of all races, cultures, and incomes with respect to the development, adoption, implementation, and enforcement of environmental laws, regulations, and policies."[26]

Summary

The complexities of equal justice require far-reaching strategic campaigns. The urban park movement has shown that success can be achieved through creatively engaging opponents to find common ground. This provides an opportunity to build multicultural alliances, influence public opinion through education and strategic media campaigns, and use planning, administrative, and political processes to address discriminatory impact issues. The urban park movement is overcoming the Court's rollback of civil rights while making California a better place to live, work, and play.

Hyman, Williams, and Crandell: Organizing in the Disability Community

The New York Statewide Systems Advocacy Network (SSAN) provides an excellent model of coordinated advocacy. The SSAN consists of thirty-six independent living centers. Its activities, coordinated by the New York State Independent Living Council (NYSILC), include: sponsoring a statewide disability caucus; developing a disability legislative agenda; organizing participation at hearings, rallies, and press conferences; issuing action alerts; distributing news releases; providing ongoing training; meeting and negotiating with state and national leaders; and developing broad coalition support. The model is a hybrid of similar networks in Pennsylvania, California, and Kansas.

At each independent living center, a part- or full-time systems advocate recruits and trains volunteers, responds to action alerts and communications, establishes local media relationships, disseminates news releases, tracks local media coverage, and encourages voter education and registration. To recruit volunteers, advocates use public forums, monthly meetings, and training. The NYSILC works with three regional coordinators who support and maximize the potential of the SSAN. Each coordinator supports approximately twelve advocates to coordinate activities, sustain volunteer recruitment and training, encourage voter registration, and promote media relations.

Over the past three years, the SSAN has grown into a group of lay and professional advocates (approximately 2,181 individuals) coordinated under a unified statewide agenda. The SSAN has functioned well for several reasons. First, its advocates work with a local focus while keeping with a statewide agenda. Second, people directly impacted by the issues become involved, bringing commitment and passion to the cause. Advocates are trained to increase their level of involvement based on skill and opportunity. Third, the SSAN's leadership has brokered its resources with several other statewide groups. Frequent coalition partners include the New York Association of Psychiatric Rehabilitation Services (mental health community), Housing Works (HIV/AIDS community), the Brain Injury Association of New York State, and the United

Spinal Association (formerly the Eastern Paralyzed Veterans Association). To facilitate state implementation of the Supreme Court's 1999 *Olmstead* decision,[27] which requires that services for the disabled be provided in the most integrated setting possible the SSAN established two crucial alliances with the New York Statewide Senior Action Council (StateWide) and New York ADAPT (specifically, the SSAN collaborated with the umbrella group ADAPT had created around the issue, the Committee To Implement *Olmstead* in New York (CTIONY)).

StateWide is a New York grassroots organization made up of senior citizens and senior citizen clubs. StateWide was organized in 1972 from War on Poverty funds with the goal of developing a statewide organization of older New Yorkers who could advocate for their needs.

Founded in 1983, ADAPT originally stood for American Disabled for Access to Public Transit, was changed to Americans with Disabilities for Attendant Programs in 1990. It now exists as an acronym without specific reference to an issue because ADAPT has earned national name recognition for its work on a variety of disability rights issues. ADAPT is known for a several "pronged" advocacy approach that ranges from professional policy development to public protest and civil disobedience. The relationship represented the first time the state council had recognized and valued the work of a grassroots advocacy organization. The linkages between the disabled and senior communities offered a rare opportunity to coordinate efforts toward a common goal—and the partnership had a lasting impact.

These relationships set the stage for an intense nine-month advocacy campaign to get the Most-Integrated Setting (MIS) bill signed into law. The bill looked to establish a policy-making state council with the power to develop and implement a comprehensive plan to enforce *Olmstead*.[28] When state agency officials stalled progress in February 2002, the disability and senior communities united for a massive protest at the New York State Department of Health. After the state retaliated, advocates provided training and centralized support so that over seventy-five federal Office of Civil Rights (OCR) complaints could be filed.

On the last day of the state legislative session, ADAPT staged a protest at the Capitol building. The Senate majority leader kept his word and introduced the bill on the floor for a vote. It passed unanimously. Advocacy strategy then shifted to the executive. Advocates met Governor George Pataki to ask that he "do the right thing" and sign the bill into law, and people wrote to the editors of local newspapers. On the last day, a team of ADAPT and CTIONY advocates shuttled between the governor's office and the Assembly to demand passage of the bill. Others lit up the phone lines. A final agreement was reached and announced to the over seventy-five advocates who were perched in the second floor foyer of the Capitol building.

Imagine if other issue-centered networks developed coalitions around common concerns. Much could be gained if disability advocates, for example, entered into a coalition with women's rights advocates and racial equality advocates with the common goal of defeating a states' rights agenda. Such coalitions would demonstrate the commonality of such civil rights issues for a diverse group of Americans. In addition, a network would provide more opportunities to raise funds, share resources, identify supportive judges, groups, elected officials, businesses, and individuals, and urge these players to get involved financially or politically.

The SSAN offers the following suggestions to ensure effective coalition building.

- Reach out to new coalition partners. A good faith approach would be to offer contact information and an agenda to each potential member, who would hopefully reciprocate. With this exchange, common interests would become clear.

- Take advantage of opportunities to coalesce around common issues. Each group should evaluate their level of participation based on the issue's priority level.

- Develop a broad coalition, communication, and meeting structure in which members receive information, provide input, and help devise a shared strategy. If each network makes their internal meeting structure available only to members, positions and strategies can be debated without being influenced by outside stakeholders.

- Allow coalition members to participate in major leadership activities. Examples include speaking at press conferences, being quoted in press releases, and taking part in negotiations.

- Realize that there are potential negatives associated with coalition-building in a political environment. For example, a group might trade information for its own benefit. If someone from another network asks you to do something, and you feel uncomfortable, simply tell them that you will find out and get back to them. Relay the request to the appropriate person in your network.

Working in a coalition is one way to advance a legislative agenda. However, three additional factors have a profound influence on public policy: money, votes, and the media. All three can be used to build support to adopt or amend legislation, as well as to prevent harmful policies from being enacted.

1. Money

Money influences public policy. While grassroots organizations may not be able to create a Political Action Committee to raise money or buy public policy favors, they should exploit other avenues for fundraising.

Individuals should purchase tickets to political fundraisers. This promotes the visual inclusion of certain groups (e.g. the disabled) at such events, which, in turn, can communicate the importance of disability issues to elected officials and community leaders. Further, because more than forty percent of the businesses and individuals who give political and campaign contributions also give charitable contributions, these events can offer an opportunity to make contact with possible donors.

Advocates should determine which individuals and corporations are donating money to candidates and elected officials that support states' rights at the expense of groups like people with disabilities (see www.opensecrets.org). Those individuals and companies can then be targeted with direct action (e.g., boycotts of their products and picket lines) in order to discourage others from patronizing their businesses.

2. The Vote

The 2000 presidential election reinforced the importance of the vote in determining public policy. Unless constituencies impacted by the rollback of civil rights are active at the polls, they will be seen as paper tigers. Fortunately, the disability community rose to the occasion in 2000—over half a million registered to vote (many because of an aggressive campaign led by the National Organization on Disability), and fourteen million voted (forty-one percent of the disabled population), up dramatically from 11.3 million (thirty percent) in 1996.[29]

This advocacy taught some important lessons. Advocates, especially those with responsibilities under the National Voter Registration Act, should conduct proactive year-round voter registration and ensure that the voting process is accessible to all.

In its first two years, the SSAN registered 6,393 new voters. It is looking to expand upon its current "voter pledge" model, which asks registered voters to sign a pledge to vote in all elections, encourages others to register and vote, and provides education about issues important to people with disabilities.

In the fall of 2002, advocates sponsored or co-sponsored non-partisan candidate forums in Albany, Buffalo, Corning, Plattsburgh, Rochester, Staten Island, Watertown, and Yonkers, designed to educate political leaders and the public about disability issues. More than fifty candidates participated, from those seeking the governorship to those running for town council. Candidates were given between five and ten minutes to make a statement, then took questions. Every event received media coverage. Advocates replicated the process at the local level. Both activities prompted incumbents and candidates to make public commitments on disability issues.

The 2000 Harris Poll concluded that citizens with disabilities constitute a cohesive voting bloc. Indeed, fifty percent of disabled people consider disability issues a major concern when they vote, and twenty-three percent consider it the highest priority. Voting patterns are therefore determined by more than party affiliation.

If we can convince our groups to register and vote, we will have political clout, we will be able to hold elected officials accountable, and we will be better able to help campaign staff develop platforms that prioritize reversing the rollback of civil rights.

3. Media

While the media influences public policy, it can be a doubled-edged sword. If the coverage supports your point of view, it can advance your issue or block an opposing effort. An aggressive group of disability advocates used the press during their two-year campaign to get New York to approve a Medicaid Buy-In program (the program made Medicaid available to the low-income working disabled population). After the advocates made the press corps aware of the issue, reporters hounded the press secretaries for the governor and Senate majority leader until they declared their support. The affiliate of one major television station, a weekly public television show, a public radio station, and four newspapers covered the press conference and rally on the Capitol steps.

On the other hand, if a reporter puts a "spin" on your issue, the media's influence can be detrimental. When advocates held a press conference to emphasize the need to pass the Medicaid Buy-In program, for example, several reporters encouraged advocates to make negative comments about a misleading campaign ad put out by Rick Lazio's U.S. Senate campaign. Maria Dibble, a skilled disability rights advocate, was able to redirect reporters to the issue at hand. Had she not, the papers may have claimed that advocates had come to the Capitol to protest Lazio's ad.

Advocates can learn from the disability community's experiences. First, advocates should develop a universal message, talking points, and pointed questions for the media. Without such a coordinated effort, advocates may not have been as successful in their campaign to focus reporters on the Medicaid Buy-In issue. Second, media savvy and training are essential. Were it not for the skill of one of the disability advocates, a valuable opportunity to get the group's message across would have been lost. Finally, advocates should consider investing resources in public relations personnel.

Summary

The call to battle has been issued; civil rights advocates must organize, strategize, and respond in a unified and aggressive manner. Lawyers, interest groups, and others involved in opposing the civil rights rollback must develop a comprehensive and coordinated advocacy plan. Grassroots advocates must coordinate their efforts into the larger national network, because a broad coalition can be a powerful tool in reversing the civil rights rollback.

Conclusion

Lessons from language rights advocacy, the urban parks movement, and the disability network all suggest that successful community activism requires coalitions and networks, media campaigns, and getting-out-the-vote. Together, these elements provide advocates with powerful tools in the war to protect civil rights. Great things happen when diverse communities join with a unified purpose.

Endnotes

1. In the past five years, Irenia Sanchez has joined with hundreds of New York City low-income immigrant women, community organizers, and civil rights attorneys not only to defend the civil rights of LEP applicants and recipients of government benefits, but to expand those rights.

2. Litigation-centered advocacy models have been criticized on the grounds that they perpetuate the sense of powerlessness felt by poor and marginalized clients. See Jennifer Gordon, We Make the Road by Walking: Immigrant Workers, the Workplace Project, and the Struggle for Social Change, *30 Harv. C.R.-C.L. L. Rev.* (1995) 407, 438–39 (contending that litigation promotes a reliance on lawyers, which undermines the development of community empowerment); Lucie E. White, Mobilization on the Margins of the Lawsuit: Making Space for Clients to Speak, *16 N.Y.U Rev. L. & Soc. Change* (1987–88) 535, 543–44 (commenting that litigation silenced poor people).

3. In addition, lawyers who engage in "community-lawyering" may also face certain practical and ethical challenges such as potential conflicts of interest, violation of confidentiality rules, and the establishment of attorney-client relationships. See Scott L. Cummings and Ingrid V. Eagly, A Critical Reflection on Law and Organizing, *48 U.C.L.A. L. Rev.* (2001) 443, 502–16 (discussing some of the constraints of law and organizing).

4. In fact, the *Sandoval* case was brought to court as a result of the Alabama Department of Public Safety's implementation of an English-only policy after the state amended its Constitution to declare English its official language. See *Alexander v. Sandoval*, 121 S. Ct. 1511, 1515 (2001).

5. These states are Alabama, Alaska, Arkansas, California, Colorado, Florida, Georgia, Hawaii, Illinois, Indiana, Iowa, Kentucky, Louisiana, Massachusetts, Mississippi, Missouri, Montana, Nebraska, New Hampshire, North Carolina, North Dakota, South Carolina, South Dakota, Tennessee, Utah, Virginia, and Wyoming. See U.S. English, States with Official English Language Laws, at http://www.us-english.org/inc/official/states.asp. We strongly disagree with English-only laws because we view them as overt acts of racism.

6. At least two other cities have language access laws that apply to the provision of city-government services. See Oakland Municipal Code §2.30 *et seq.* (2003) ("Equal Access to Services Ordinance"); San Francisco Admin. Code §91.1-91.14. ("Equal Access to Services Ordinance").

7. See Make the Road by Walking, System Failure, at http://www.maketheroad .org/transrept1.htm (1999).

8. Olmsted Brothers & Bartholomew and Associates, *Parks, Playgrounds and Beaches for the Los Angeles Region* (1930) ("the Olmsted Report") at 1, reprinted in Greg Hise and William Deverell, *Eden by Design* (2000).

9. Jocelyn Stewart, "Officials Resort to Creativity in Trying to Meet Need for Parks," *Los Angeles Times* (June 15, 1998) (based on 1990 census data).

10. The Center for Law in the Public Interest has published extensively on equal justice, democracy, and livability through the urban park movement. See generally Robert García et al., "Anatomy of the Urban Parks Movement: Equal Justice, Democracy and Livability in Los Angeles," chapter in book by Robert Bullard, ed., *Wasting Away: Environmental Justice, Human Rights, and the Politics of Pollution*, Sierra Club (2005); "Cross Road Blues: Transportation Justice and the MTA Consent Decree," chapter in book by Karen Lucas, ed., *Running on Empty: Transport, Social Exclusion and Environmental Justice* (2004); Robert García et al., Healthy Children, Healthy Communities: Parks, Schools, and Sustainable Regional Planning, *31 Fordham Urban Law Journal* (2004) 101; Robert García et al., *The Cornfield and the Flow of History: People, Place, and Culture*, Center for Law in the Public Interest (2004), at http://www.clipi.org/images/CornfieldFlowofHistory.pdf; Robert García et al., *Dreams of Fields: Soccer, Community, and Equal Justice*, Center for Law in the Public Interest (2002), at http://www.clipi.org/images/Dreams_of_Fields.pdf; Robert García, *Equal Access to California's Beaches*, in the Proceedings of the Second National People of Color Environmental Leadership Summit - Summit II, at www.ejrc.cau.edu/summit2/Beach.pdf. See also Josh Sides, *LA City Limits: African American Los Angeles from the Great Depression to the Present* (2004) 21–22; Mike Davis, "How Eden Lost Its Garden," chapter in book by Mike Davis, *Ecology of Fear: Los Angeles and the Imagination of Disaster* (1998) 57–91; "The Case for Letting Malibu Burn," chapter in book by Mike Davis, *The Ecology of Fear: Los Angeles and the Imagination of Disaster* (1999); and Mike Davis, *City of Quartz: Excavating the Future in Los Angeles* (1990).

11. Stan Bellamy, *My Mountain, My People Vol. I: Arrowhead!* (2000) 188.

12. John W. Robinson, *The San Bernardinos* (1989) 127–32.

13. Leonard Pitt and Dale Pitt, *Los Angeles A to Z: An Encyclopedia of the City and County* (1997) 313.

14. Id. at 313–14.

15. Malibu property restrictions recorded 1945 (on file with the Center for Law in the Public Interest).

16. 2000 U.S. census data.

17. The Commission's guide to Broad Beach is available on the Center's website at http://www.clipi.org/images/BeachAccessPolicyPaper.pdf.

18. *Los Angeles Times* statewide exit poll, March 7, 2002. For a discussion, see Paul Rogers, "Latinos Taking Lead on Environmental Issues," *San Jose Mercury News* (March 16, 2002).

19. Doonesbury on coastal access is at www.doonesbury.com.

20. To comply with the Coastal Act's public access requirements, the California Coastal Commission—the agency charged with implementing the California Coastal Act—can require a developer or property owner to provide a public access easement (also called an Offer to Dedicate (OTD) a public easement) as a way of mitigating the effects of the development project on public access. California Coastal Commission, *Public Access Action Plan*, at 13, at http://www.coastal.ca.gov/access/accesspl.pdf. Until the offer is accepted by a government agency or nonprofit organization, the interest belongs to the property owner. Id. at 14. See also Cal. Public Resources Code §30212(a).

21. The Coastal Commission mandated that one of the overriding goals of Malibu's Local Coastal Program (LCP) shall be to "[m]aximize public access to and along the coast and maximize public recreational opportunities in the coastal zone" and that "[i]n addition, a goal of the LCP is to promote the fair treatment of people of all races, cultures, and incomes with respect to the the development, adoption, implementation, and enforcement of environmental laws, regulations and policies." *City of Malibu Local Coastal Program Land Use Plan*, adopted by the California Coastal Commission on September 13, 2002, at http://www.coastal.ca.gov/ventura/malibu-lup-final.pdf. The Commission was responsible for drafting the plan after Malibu failed for years to create a local coastal plan that was acceptable to the state. Malibu has informed the Commission that it deems the LCP to be "suspended and not in effect" because of a pending referendum. See http://www.coastal.ca.gov/ ventura/malibu-lcp-letter-10-17-mm2.pdf.

22. Stanley Allison, "Nichols Urged Again to Leave City Council," *Los Angeles Times* (June 25, 2003) 3.

23. Steve Lopez, "Councilman Visits Archie Bunker Dimension to Justify Comments," *Los Angeles Times* (June 20, 2003).

24. 2000 U.S. census data: GreenInfo Network.

25. See Cal. Gov't Code §11135 *et seq* and 22 CCR §9810.

26. Cal. Gov't Code §65040.12. The Governor's Office of Planning and Research is to implement this code section.

27. *Olmstead v. L.C.*, 527 U.S. 581 (1999).

28. 527 U.S. 581 (1999).

29. Data from the NOD/Harris Poll.

CHAPTER 25

STUDENT ADVOCACY

Building a Student Movement: Lessons Learned and Suggestions for the Future

Lisa Zeidner[*] and Luke Blocher[**]

For 384 consecutive hours students stood outside and read aloud from biographies of judicial nominees, poetry, the Constitution, the phonebook, children's books and other sources.[†] When one student tired, another took her place. When it rained, the demonstrators held umbrellas but they did not stop talking. They were college students protesting the proposed elimination of the judicial filibuster in the Senate by staging their own mock filibuster on campus, and they attracted the attention of national media outlets, US Senators, and the American public. What began as a small group of students, organizing on a single campus, soon became a movement. After two weeks, the Princeton students who organized the "Filibuster for Democracy" brought their protest to Washington DC, where they were joined by students from around the country in their fight for an independent and balanced judiciary.

Two years earlier, thousands of students descended on the nation's capitol to support affirmative action as the Supreme Court heard oral arguments in the cases that would help decide the future of diversity programs in higher education. Two thousand students marched from Howard University carrying blankets and extra coats, and slept on the pavement in front of the Court. Over a thousand Detroit high school students held fundraisers and chartered buses to take them to DC. Still other students arrived by car and train from around the country to lend their voices to the cause.[‡]

---

* Lisa Zeidner is a student at Columbia Law School. She is an active member of the Columbia Coalition to Restore Civil Rights.

** Luke Blocher is a student at Columbia Law School. He is President of the Columbia American Constitution Society chapter.

† The Filibuster for Democracy began at 11:00 am on April 28, 2005. See www .filibusterfrist.com.

‡ See "Thousands of Students Gather Outside Court in Support of Admission Policies,"

The filibuster and affirmative action demonstrators used organizing tactics similar to those used by the United Students Against Sweatshops (USAS), a group that spearheaded the ambitious fight for sweatshop-free labor conditions and workers' rights by targeting the $2.5 billion collegiate licensing industry. USAS conducted sit-ins, e-mail drives, knit-ins, and even mock fashion shows to call attention to inhumane labor conditions, and to discourage colleges and universities from doing business with the perpetrators of those conditions. They organized, they demanded, and school administrators took notice; many colleges and universities have changed their policies and raised their standards.*

These examples of student activism illustrate how students united behind a common cause have the power to bring about social change. Young people today have the potential to create a new social justice movement aimed at reversing the rollback of civil rights. To be successful, they must design an effective agenda, make use of existing resources, and motivate progressive action.

This chapter will discuss how university campuses can be mobilized to fight the rollback of civil rights and will explain why the larger social justice movement should invest in the mobilization of students.

ᏜᏜ ᏜᏜ ᏜᏜ

On April 2, 2003, the University of Pennsylvania's campus newspaper, the *Daily Pennsylvanian*, headlined: "University Students Protest Affirmative Action."[1] The day before, students from over 250 schools had headed to Washington, DC to protest while the Supreme Court heard oral arguments in the University of Michigan affirmative action cases, *Grutter v. Bollinger* and *Gratz v. Bollinger*.[2] Approximately sixty thousand people, including many students, had showed up to make their voices heard.[3]

That protest was not an isolated event. While some of the students had never been involved in social activism, many had been working to address civil rights issues on their campuses and belonged to campus organizations such as the Campaign for Civil Rights at Georgetown University and the Civil Rights Society at Columbia Law School. Others had joined national organizations like the American Constitution Society, an organization for progressive law students that had grown to include over fifty chapters on law school campuses in its first four years.[4]

Students and student organizations must be similarly mobilized in the national movement to restore civil rights because they can offer a fresh perspec-

---

New York Times (April 2, 2003) A14.

    * See "Students Urge Colleges to Join A New Anti-Sweatshop Group," *New York Times* (Oct. 20, 1999) A23; United Students Against Sweatshops, www.studentsagainstsweatshops.org.

tive and will play a crucial role in sustaining social justice efforts. To this end, graduate, undergraduate, and high school students should be targeted, recruited, supported, and encouraged to participate in—and lead—the campaign to restore the federal civil rights rolled back by the nation's conservative Judiciary and political leaders in the past few decades.

This chapter seeks to answer—or at least begin to answer—two questions: how can isolated campuses be mobilized to fight, and why should the movement invest in the mobilization of students? It is our aim, in answering the former question, to prove the latter. Social movement theory will provide our inquiry with a conceptual framework, and the anti-sweatshop movement's successful beginnings will serve as our organizational template. Finally, the chapter will lay the groundwork for a national student movement to restore civil rights, and will offer suggestions about message framing, organizing, and next steps.

Social Movement Theory

Social movement theory is guided by one question: Why do people act collectively in protest? Scholars have asked this question for as long as people have rebelled against authority—Alexis De Tocqueville's *The Old Regime and the French Revolution*, originally published in 1856, could be described as a work of social movement theory. The field, however, has evolved rapidly in the past thirty years due to the success of social movements in the 1960s.

Much scholarly opinion has coalesced around the basic tenets of social movement theory, outlined in Doug McAdam's *Political Process and the Development of Black Insurgency*.[5] His political process model—one that we will employ in this chapter—explains how social movements emerge and grow in three stages: recognizing political opportunities, applying indigenous organizational resources, and cognitively mobilizing members of the excluded group.

Recognizing Political Opportunities

Assuming that power is concentrated within certain groups, or "elites," social movement theory is first concerned with helping excluded people realize that they can change the status quo and claim a share of the power. According to the political process model, the critical variable that sparks social movements is, "any event or broad social process that serves to undermine the calculations and assumptions on which the political establishment is structured."[6] The result is a shift in an existing power relationship; challengers assume a position of greater leverage. For example, when a student sit-in garners media and alumni attention, activists create leverage and political opportunity. Invigorated protesters, emboldened by success, then organize more aggressively and make stronger demands. Of course, political opportunities do not require such breakthrough events—if a new student group attracts thirty people to a meeting, they might feel that success is possible and plan more ambitious events.

The actions of one excluded group can also create political opportunities for other non-elites. One group's radical claim, for example, may allow a more moderate group to seize support. Alternatively, collective action places issues in the public sphere that might attract other groups. The effect of this type of political opportunity is magnified during times that social movement theorist Sydney Tarrow calls "cycles of contention,"[7] when the claims of multiple groups encourage others who might otherwise have felt powerless to make claims of their own. The process repeats itself until the sheer volume of protests tips the balance of power so that almost any challenger has a political opportunity.[8]

The main goal of a mass student rollback movement is to increase the amount of student advocacy targeting modern civil rights issues, in turn creating political opportunities that will mobilize more people.

Applying Indigenous Organizational Resources

The importance of organization to a social movement is twofold. First, for social movement to be possible, the group making a claim must possess the organizational resources to take advantage of a political opportunity. Second, for a movement to be sustainable, the right decisions must be made about how to use those resources.

Community groups can provide indigenous organizational resources. McAdam lays out four specific resources typically offered by these organizations:

- Membership. The established lines of interaction between like-minded community group members facilitates recruitment, while the membership itself provides movement organizers with a bloc of participants from which to recruit.
- Incentives to motivate participation. If incentives can be transferred from participation in one organization to participation in a movement, entire organizations can be recruited.
- A network of communication. This allows information to be dissemi-

nated in a coordinated fashion to large groups of people.

- Leaders. Individual leaders, often the first to join movements, bring with them prestige and organizational skills.[9]

As predicted by McAdam's model, the most successful student movements of the past thirty years (including USAS) have mobilized existing campus groups. Likewise, the rollback movement should make use of existing student groups.

Decisions about how indigenous resources should be used in organizing the new movement are critical. As Tarrow points out, the central dilemma facing organizers is how to organize a mass movement while preserving local autonomy within existing community organizations. To err toward either end is to invite failure. A movement based on the rules of a centralized organization risks becoming more concerned with the organization's survival than with promoting the movement's goals.[10] On the other hand, without a central organizing force, the organization risks being unable to coordinate.

The trick is to build a new movement that can coordinate its members without institutionalizing them and sapping their zeal for change. A new movement must have what Tarrow calls "connective tissue"—strong but loose bonds, often through groups that remain formally unaffiliated with the movement (e.g., religious organizations), that can be used to recruit members and coordinate efforts.[11]

Cognitively Mobilizing Members

While the expansion of political opportunities and the wise use of organizational resources can set the stage for the emergence of a social movement, an excluded group must desire change for anything to happen. This transformation occurs through "cognitive mobilization," a process that attempts to replace a "dominant belief system that legitimizes the status quo with an alternative mobilizing belief system that supports collective action for change."[12] A simple version of the process goes something like this:

> First, "the system"—or those aspects of the system that people experience and perceive—loses legitimacy. Large numbers of men and women who ordinarily accept the authority of their rulers and the legitimacy of institutional arrangements come to believe in some measure that these rulers and these arrangements are unjust and wrong. Second, people who are ordinarily fatalistic, who believe that existing arrangements are inevitable, begin to assert "rights" that imply demands for change. Third, there is new sense of efficacy; people who

ordinarily consider themselves helpless come to believe that they have some capacity to alter their lot.[13]

Cognitive mobilization works to convince social movement participants that they *can* and *should* change the status quo. Moreover, in defining the reasons for the change, cognitive mobilization justifies the movement to elites, at times earning their support. A masterful example was the original use of "rights" rhetoric by civil rights leaders. While the idea of citizen's rights had always been present in the U.S., the Civil Rights Movement injected new life into the notion by pointing out the discrepancies between the constitutional status of southern blacks and their reality. Initially proclaiming their goals to be full citizenship for blacks, movement leaders were able to inspire blacks to rededicate themselves to fighting the oppression of the Jim Crow system, and garner the support of many whites interested in upholding the Constitution.[14]

The cognitive mobilization of students for a modern rollback movement requires that the dominant belief system (e.g., that students have no opportunity to influence courts' treatment of civil rights) be replaced by a collective action frame (e.g., that students can and should participate in lobbying for the selection of fair judges, and that students with interest in the outcome of civil rights cases can and should petition as friends of the court).

An Example of Organizational Success: United Students Against Sweatshops (USAS)

The anti-sweatshop movement that swept college campuses in the late 1990s serves to demonstrate social movement theory. Since 1996, AFL-CIO president John Sweeney has focused on student outreach. To this end, the AFL-CIO created the "Union Summer" program, which recruited and placed students in organizing internships with local unions across the country. In the summer of 1997, eleven college students interned at the New York office of the Union of Needle and Industrial and Textile Employees (UNITE), and took part in the campaign to discredit the Apparel Industry Partnership.[15]

In their search for a collective action frame that would motivate their peers, these interns (and their co-workers) came upon the $2.5 billion collegiate licensing industry in which apparel companies pay royalties—resulting in multi-million dollar payouts to many schools—for the right to put college and university logos on items such as clothes and hats. The students decided that the universities should be held morally responsible for the conditions under which the apparel brandishing their names was produced. Given the size of the collegiate licensing industry, student organizers knew that a victory would impact the entire apparel industry. Armed with this new collective action frame, the eleven interns returned to their respective campuses.[16]

The first protest activity took place at Duke University in the fall of 1997 when UNITE intern Tico Almeida, his friend Ben Au, and seventeen of their classmates formed the first Students Against Sweatshops (SAS) chapter. The group chose a non-radical tactic that required minimal student mobilization — a mass e-mail drive directed at the university president. The university bowed to their pressure; by March 1998, it had adopted a comprehensive code of conduct to be applied to all school licensees.

This breakthrough was made with relative ease because the students made modest demands, including a moderate factory location disclosure provision that did not mandate, or even require, the public disclosure of information about who would monitor future practices. The terms left open the possibility that university disclosures could go to a corporate monitoring firm that would be unfriendly to workers. As the first group to negotiate such an agreement, the Duke SAS chapter treaded lightly.[17]

Nonetheless, the success (and the seeming ease with which it was accomplished) sparked a political opportunity for this nascent student labor movement. The UNITE interns began to start new groups on campuses nation-wide. Using e-mail, Duke students counseled student leaders on other campuses. The results were impressive. Yale students staged a "knit-in," while Holy Cross and U.C. Santa Barbara students held mock fashion shows announcing the labor conditions under which the clothes being modeled were made. By the end of the school year, students were organizing against sweatshops at thirty colleges and universities.[18] Media attention aided this rapid spread of awareness — ESPN, for example, aired a special investigation highlighting the production of Nike shoes in Vietnamese sweatshops, and discussed the University of North Carolina anti-sweatshop activity focusing on Nike.[19]

The leaders of the various campus campaigns, already linked through the internet, held a conference in July 1998 to coordinate their efforts more formally. Representatives from thirty campuses gathered in New York for the founding of USAS. UNITE and the National Labor Committee (NLC), seeking to promote this new activism, were heavily involved in the planning and funding. UNITE sponsored a trip to a New York sweatshop, NLC founder Charles Kernaghan lectured on the importance of codes of conduct,[20] and NLC sponsored a trip to an El Salvador sweatshop late that summer.[21]

While the new organization would govern itself through committees, its real medium of organization would be the internet. The most important result of the 1998 conference, therefore, was the creation of the USAS listserv—a discussion board that became the primary means of disseminating information and coordinating activity among chapters. Indeed, the listserv enabled activists to swap tactics, and offered young students a forum in which to get technical advice from experienced unionists or sympathetic professors.[22]

In the fall of 1998, as existing chapters sought to expand and new chapters fought to become established, a larger, more powerful student sweatshop movement emerged. To gain the widest possible support, each chapter employed the collective action frame of calling for humane working conditions, which student groups then modified to appeal to local interests. Student groups then modified the collective action frame to appeal to local interests. Catholic school students, for example, stressed the contradictions between exploitative sweatshop conditions and Catholic teachings. As a Georgetown activist said, "We can't walk around in these sweatshirts that stand for Jesuit and Catholic identity when we know the conditions they are produced in."[23]

When sweatshop movements began on campuses lacking indigenous networks, activists tried to cast as wide a net as possible with their collective action frame while maintaining the same central goal—the elimination of sweatshops. To reach out to students who were not part of activist networks, organization leaders tried to connect students to abused sweatshop workers on a personal level. As Princeton activist David Tannenbaum observed, this collective action frame was powerful. "This [sweatshops] was an issue that really moved people because, while the workers are making our clothes thousands of miles away, in other ways we're close to it—we're wearing these clothes everyday."[24]

The flexibility of the sweatshop as a collective action frame combined the political opportunities, indigenous resources, and cognitive mobilization necessary for social movements. Moreover, the frame allowed for the consolidation of indigenous resources that is usually necessary to challenge an existing social problem (an effective coalition of activist networks) while creating the political opportunities needed to momentarily tip the balance in favor of a challenger (student labor activists).

This flexibility was the key to the student sweatshop movement's early success. Between January and April 1999, long sit-ins and public demonstrations produced codes of conduct with both tighter disclosure and monitoring provisions at six universities: Duke, Georgetown, Wisconsin (also achieved a living wage stipulation), Michigan, North Carolina, and Arizona.[25] Many schools were able to win tough codes of conduct with the mere threat of direct action. As the NLC student action web page noted, "each sit-in has built upon the victories of the last—in this way, our bargaining power grew as administrations realized that this was in fact a national movement."[26] And national it was. Less than a year after the 1998 founding conference, the ranks of USAS chapters had grown from the thirty attendees to over one hundred. By the end of April 1999, fifteen schools had agreed to mandate disclosure of factory locations, while seventeen had conceded to some version of a living wage requirement.[27]

Preparing for a Student Movement to Reverse the Rollback of Civil Rights

Social movement theory and the USAS example should inform the creation of a student movement to reverse the rollback of civil rights. Plans must begin with a clearly defined mission, framed to fit student interests. Participants must then consider how they will organize. Finally, they must develop a set of initial action items.

Framing the Mission of the Rollback Movement

The mission of the rollback movement is to prevent the dismantling of civil rights established by legislatures and the Judiciary during the past century. A necessary corollary to that mission is the need to educate the public about the role of the courts in protecting civil rights and the potential influence of student advocacy.

Most importantly, the rollback movement must frame the issue in a way that is palpable and compelling to student activists. While the movement's broad array of issues (e.g., criminal justice, environmental justice, immigration issues, and gay rights) may help attract students who are passionate about different causes, they can also seem overwhelming. Worse yet, the movement could be prone to in-fighting as students jockey to have their cause take priority.

USAS focused on the collegiate licensing industry within the larger international labor and trade movement because the issue was closer to student experiences and more within their control. Even without the technical expertise of established labor leaders, students were able to contribute. The recent protests, focused on affirmative action in higher education, provide the rollback movement with an example. Students related to the subject matter because it concerned their campuses. All students had either recently been or could be affected by admissions policies. Further, the issue was one for which students could provide a unique contribution. Students, therefore, were the only group the courts allowed to intervene as friends of the court in the *Grut-*

ter and *Gratz* affirmative action cases; some became parties in the proceedings that served as a prelude to the Supreme Court ruling. The rollback movement can and must align with more such issues in order to engage student activists.

Organizing

When the issues are properly framed, the rollback movement could dovetail with current campus organizing efforts. The first step is to identify and target student leaders of existing student organizations so as to create an umbrella organization. A call to the student government or dean of students is a good start, as these individuals often keep lists of contact information for recognized campus groups. Many campuses also have centers for public interest or community service, which keep lists of active student leaders. The best time to contact student leaders is at the beginning of the school year or during the summer, when they are planning for the year.

Although campus organization presidents may be busy running their clubs, they can identify younger members who might appreciate the opportunity to act as the campus liaison for the rollback movement, and unaffiliated students with the time and energy to get involved. Alternatively, the rollback movement could lure the presidents of campus organizations to join their effort by offering resources, contacts, and an exciting agenda of activities.

Columbia Law School students were able to form an umbrella organization for campus groups concerned about the rollback of civil rights; their story highlights both the positive and negative aspects of using this method to create a movement. In 2001, a group of fifteen students led by Sarah Alvarez organized a student coalition as part of the national rollback movement. Lacking a model to emulate, the group focused on (and spent a significant amount of time determining) administrative details like choosing a name (the Columbia Coalition to Restore Civil Rights (CCRCR)), structuring the organization, and selecting officers.

CCRCR fashioned itself as an umbrella organization and solicited representatives from existing student clubs including the Civil Rights Law Society, the Black Law Students Association, the Columbia Law Women's Association, the Environmental Law Association, and the American Constitution Society. Non-affiliated students were encouraged to get involved, although the focus, at least initially, was to ensure the representation of each pertinent student organization. CCRCR recruited students through e-mail and word of mouth, and its membership began to grow.

CCRCR's umbrella organizational structure allowed it to benefit from, in McAdam's words, Columbia Law School's indigenous resources. Representatives of the various organizations provided legitimacy, diverse viewpoints, experience, and numbers. Each representative gave updates (including upcoming CCRCR events and ways to become involved) to his or her "home organization." This ability to disperse information was one of the major strengths of the CCRCR model.

The drawback of the umbrella structure was that at times, interests diverged because each student group had different priorities within the civil rights agenda. While the Black Students Association prioritized affirmative action, for example, the Environmental Law Society focused on environmental justice issues. Such differing interests presents a problem to the formation of a coalition; student leaders must balance their interests in order to achieve the benefits that a coalition can offer. One of CCRCR's initial obstacles, for example, was identifying a focus within the overwhelming array of civil rights issues perceived by the students to be vulnerable to rollback.

The group also became bogged down with administrative details like securing a charter from the Student Senate. While the group had to spend time on administrative details in order to exist, they risked spending too much time and losing sight of their purpose. Had other groups been able to serve as an organizational template, CCRCR might have initially been able to spend less time on such issues. It is our hope that CCRCR's experience can serve as a template for students at other schools.

To overcome administrative challenges, the coalition leaders formed sub-committees and delegated responsibility to members. One student was assigned the task of drawing up a club charter to fulfill the Student Senate requirements. Sub-committees on affirmative action and judicial nominations reflected the organizing priorities of the coalition members. CCRCR was able to be more active by focusing its members' energy. The affirmative action sub-committee, for example, worked to educate the campus about the *Grutter* and *Gratz* cases, then sponsored a bus to take 125 students to protest in DC on the day of the Court's oral arguments. CCRCR also organized students to meet with their senators to lobby for more progressive judicial nominations.

Action Items: Suggestions for Future Organizing

CCRCR can be used as a blueprint for starting umbrella groups on campuses and nation-wide. Student leaders should consider the following list of "lessons learned."

- Be compelling. The rollback coalition and student leaders must continue to frame legal and civil rights issues in ways that will engage students on law school and college campuses.
- Start small. As seen in the USAS example, a group's initial achievement, no matter how minor, is critical to kick-starting a movement because it serves as a political opportunity and cognitive mobilizer. This is not to say that the student rollback movement should shy away from big issues. Rather, the movement should target attainable goals that can serve as a base for more ambitious aspirations.
- Compile a university directory (U-directory) of key student leaders and organizations in high schools, colleges, graduate schools, and law schools across the country. A directory would help students communicate with each other, and would identify indigenous resources that could be tapped for membership.
- Work with existing organizations like ACS. The rollback movement should use those existing student groups and networks that are discovered while creating the U-directory to create an umbrella organization.
- Develop web resources. The USAS listserv kept nation-wide campus activists apprised of each other's activities, and the website provided organizational resources like model codes of conduct and even songs to sing at rallies.[28] This kind of loose coordination combined the best of bureaucratization (organizational continuity and strong lines of communication) with the best of decentralization (the freedom to innovate). Among the information that should be accessible are talking points regarding key Supreme Court decisions and related legal issues.
- Seek support for a summer training program. Like Union Summer, a "Rollback Summer" would provide students with training, resources, and motivation; students, then, could return to their campuses to organize. Students should work with national organizations involved in the rollback movement in order to create valuable summer training experiences.

Conclusion

Students can and should play a major role in the national rollback movement. National leaders should allow students a role in forming the movement's agenda in order to ensure that issues are framed in such a way that they compel student activism. Students have many indigenous resources to contribute, including large numbers, active related organizations, time, creativity, and enthusiasm. They have proven their value as labor and affirmative action activists. Given the same opportunity, a student rollback movement could significantly contribute to the larger movement.

Endnotes

1. Laura Sullivan and Spencer Willig, "University Students Protest for Affirmative Action in DC," *Daily Pennsylvanian* (April 2, 2003), at http://www.dailypennsylvanian.com/vnews/display.v/ART/2003/04/02/3e8ac64984be4?in_archive=1.

2. March on Washington Organizing Page, Civil Rights March to the Supreme Court, Coalition to Defend Affirmative Action, Integration and Immigration Rights and Fight for Equality By Any Means Necessary (April 1, 2003), at http://www.bamn.com/wdc/campuses.asp.

3. Sullivan and Willig, *supra* note 1.

4. The stated purpose of the American Constitution Society is "to ensure that the fundamental principles of human dignity, individual rights and liberties, genuine equality, and access to justice are in their rightful, central place in American law." Goals of the American Constitution Society for Law & Policy, at http://www.acslaw.org/about/index. shtml#Goals.

5. Our paper assumes the basic tenets of McAdam's theories. Its limited length prevents a more detailed description. For those readers interested in the sociological theories, we encourage a full reading of Doug McAdam, *Political Process and the Development of Black Insurgency, 1930–1970* (1982). See also Sidney Tarrow's synthesis of social movement theory, *Power in Movement: Social Movements and Contentious Politics,* Cambridge Univ. Press, 2d ed. (1998).

6. McAdam, *supra* note 5, at 41.

7. Tarrow, *supra* note 5, at 142.

8. Id.

9. McAdam, *supra* note 5, at 46–48.

10. Frances Fox Piven and Richard A. Cloward, *Poor People's Movements: Why They Succeed, How They Fail* (1978) 5.

11. Tarrow, *supra* note 5, at 128–29, 137.

12. Tarrow, *supra* note 5, at 106.

13. Piven and Cloward, *supra* note 10, at 3–4.

14. Id. at 118.

15. The success of the USAS was immediately predated by the long national campaign against sweatshops by a group called the National Labor Committee (NLC). In a little over a decade, NLC and some of its fellow travelers like the Union of Needle and Textile and Industrial Employees (UNITE) had publicized the plight of the sweatshop worker to the point that a December 1996 *U.S. News & World Report* public opinion poll reported that six out of ten Americans were "concerned" about sweatshop conditions in the U.S., and nine out of ten were concerned about sweatshop conditions in Asia or Latin America. William J. Holstein, Brian Palmer, Shahid Ur-Rehman, and Timothy M. Ito, Santa's Sweatshop, *U.S. News & World Report* (Dec. 16, 1996) 50. The Apparel Industry Partnership is a "monitoring" apparatus established by the apparel industry in response to this negative publicity. Labor Educ. & Action Project at Ga. State Univ., at http://members.aol.com/LEAPGSU/.

16. Richard Appelbaum and Peter Dreier, The Campus Anti-Sweatshop Movement, *Am. Prospect* (Sept./Oct. 1999) 71; Kathleen Welborn, Students Against Sweatshops—

United States Against Sweatshops, *Dollars & Sense* (Sept./Oct. 1998) 6–7.

17. Appelbaum and Dreier, *supra* note 16.

18. Id.

19. Labor Educ. & Action Project at Ga. State Univ., at http://members.aol.com/LEAPGSU/.

20. Welborn, *supra* note 16.

21. Charles Kernaghan, Sweatshop Blues: Companies Love Misery, *Dollars & Sense* (Mar./Apr. 1999) 18–21.

22. Appelbaum and Dreier, *supra* note 16.

23. Robert A. Senser, High-Priced Shoes, Low-Cost Labor, *America* (Oct. 24, 1998).

24. Steven Greenhouse, "Activism Surges at Campuses Nationwide, and Labor is at Issue," *New York Times* (Mar. 29, 1999).

25. Students Team Up to Shed Light on Sweatshops (information gathered by the NLC), at http://www.adaction.org/sweatshopinfo.html.

26. Id.

27. Id.

28. United Students Against Sweatshops, at http://www.studentsagainstsweatshops.org/.

CHAPTER 26

LITIGATION STRATEGIES

Lawyering and Litigation during the Rollback:
Legal Strategies to Pursue Social Justice

Marianne Engelman Lado[*]

What legal strategies are available when civil rights are no longer enforceable in federal court? In the aftermath of the 1974 Milliken v. Bradley *decision,[†] a Supreme Court ruling that shielded northern school districts from desegregation orders, community-based activists, and lawyers, the NAACP Legal Defense & Educational Fund (LDF), the American Civil Liberties Union, and the Puerto Rican Legal Defense & Education Fund (PRLDF) adopted a new strategy: they turned to state law and state courts.*

Hartford, a small city surrounded by suburbs, occupies only 18.4 square miles. In the late 1980s, twenty-four thousand children attended its dilapidated public schools. At one elementary school, there were no sports fields—only a rusted metal climbing set with no safety mats. The school's roof had caved in, and hundreds of dead pigeons had fallen into the classrooms with the debris. Nearby, another elementary school was built for seven to eight hundred students, but contained eleven hundred. The school offered no counselor to advise students on academic issues; its two social workers, however, were overwhelmed dealing with suicides and other such issues.

Lawyers representing the children of Hartford made three novel arguments. First, they argued that the Connecticut Constitution barred the segregation of children by race and ethnicity in schools—even if that segregation was unintentional. Sec-

---

  * General Counsel, New York Lawyers for the Public Interest. Portions of this chapter were originally written with Chris Malone as part of a background paper for a 1998 conference convened by the Aspen Institute's Roundtable on Comprehensive Community Initiatives. Special thanks to the members of the CUNY Faculty Publications Program and the Reading Group at Baruch College's School of Public Affairs, as well as privatization activists Peg Graham and Georgianna Deas, for their comments on that earlier paper.
  † 418 U.S. 717 (1974).

ond, they argued that the combined effects of racial, ethnic, and economic isolation, along with inadequate resources, deprived children in Hartford of equal educational opportunity. Third, they argued that the state had failed to provide those children with an adequate education. While each of these claims was grounded in community concerns and had a solid foundation in state law, each required the lawyers to expand the boundaries of their expertise.

In its 1996 decision in Sheff v. O'Neill, the Connecticut Supreme Court stated, "The public elementary and high school students in Hartford suffer daily from the devastating effects that racial and ethnic isolation, as well as poverty, have had on their education."* The Court then ordered the state to take action to address the isolation. This decision, and the leverage it gave to community residents in their efforts to press for educational equity, was the result of legal innovation in the face of adversity.

The rollback of civil rights in the federal courts limits the tools available to lawyers challenging discriminatory policies and practices. Following in the footsteps of generations of civil rights lawyers who persevered despite hostility to their claims, lawyers today are pursuing multiple strategies to redress injustice, vindicate the rights of their clients, and, in partnership with communities, shift the balance of power on local, state, and national levels.

This chapter will touch on historical antecedents to today's challenges, and examine new strategies for pursuing justice. The overriding theme is that we can take heart: lawyers are pursuing a number of fruitful strategies to balance the scales of justice.

While this chapter focuses on lawyering and litigation, it does not assume that lawyers are or should be the central players in the struggle for equality. The law continues to play a role, however, in bringing about social change. As Martin Luther King said in December 1956, explaining why it was important to continue the legal struggle for equality, "I quite agree that it is impossible to change a man's internal feelings merely through law. But that really is not the intention of the law. The law does not seek to change one's internal feelings; it seeks rather to control the external effects of those internal feelings."† Moreover, law "is a form of education.... The words of the Supreme Court, of Congress, and of the Constitution are eloquent instructors."‡

---

* *Sheff v. O'Neill*, 238 Conn. 1, 3 (Conn. 1996).

† James M. Washington, ed., *A Testament of Hope: The Essential Writings and Speeches of Martin Luther King, Jr.*, HarperCollins (1991) 142 (address before the First Annual Institute on Non-Violence and Social Change, Montgomery, Alabama, 1956).

‡ Martin Luther King, Jr., *Stride Toward Freedom*, Harper & Row (1958) 199.

ɞ ɞ ɞ

Creativity in the Face of Adversity

Over the course of American history, the courts have played a crucial, albeit inconsistent, role in protecting civil rights and advancing the vision of a more just society. Despite hostile conditions, people have always found ways to assert their claims for freedom and justice in court. Even before the American Revolution, enslaved African Americans won claims in colonial courts that their masters had betrayed promises to release them or were holding a defective slave title.[1] By the mid-1770s, slaves used the rhetoric of the revolution to petition colonial legislatures for freedom.[2] In 1773, four slaves filed a collective petition in Massachusetts, stating: "As the people of this province seem to be actuated by the principles of equity and justice, we cannot but expect your house will again take our deplorable case into serious consideration, and give us that ample relief which, as men, we have a natural right to."[3] Indeed, Massachusetts slaves tested the legality of slavery itself in court, and, according to some historians, a court order abolished slavery in that state.[4] Our forbearers understood that while the courts might be the least democratic branch of government, court access is a necessary predicate to real democracy.[5]

Phoenix-Like: Everett Waring, Charles Hamilton Houston, and Thurgood Marshall

In the period following the Civil War and the passage of the Thirteenth, Fourteenth, and Fifteenth Amendments (which were intended to nationalize the rights of freedom and citizenship), the Supreme Court played an active role in sanctioning a retrenchment in civil rights.[6] In *Hall v. DeCuir* in 1878, the Court invalidated a Louisiana statute prohibiting segregation in transportation on the grounds that it burdened interstate commerce[7]—an interpretation of federal powers that effectively limited what states could do to prohibit segregation. In an almost perfect Catch-22, then, the Court invalidated the Civil Rights Act of 1875 (which prohibited discrimination and segregation in places of public accommodation, including railroads) and, in the 1883 *Civil Rights Cases*, found that the federal government lacked the power to regulate such conduct.[8] The Court also ruled that the Fourteenth Amendment's Equal Protection Clause did not empower Congress to regulate the behavior of private individuals; rather, private individuals were governed only by state civil rights laws (that the Court had invalidated in *Hall v. DeCuir*).[9] The Court seemed to have all but shut the courthouse doors on claims for racial justice.

The Court's rulings were controversial, particularly within African American communities.[10] In 1883, an assembly of more than two thousand people in DC passed a resolution calling for the adoption of state laws to protect civil rights and the creation of civil rights organizations to agitate for the cause.[11] North Carolinian James O'Hara, one of the two African Americans remaining in Congress at the time, proposed a constitutional amendment to restore what had been lost in the *Civil Rights Cases*.[12] In addition, an African American lawyer named Everett James Waring formed the Brotherhood of Liberty,[13] and outlined the role he envisioned for the Brotherhood in challenging oppression based on race.

> We should organize the country over. Raise funds and employ counsel. Then, if an individual is denied some right or privilege, let the race make his wrong their wrong and test the cause in law....Some may say that this is futile—that we shall fail. Suppose we do at first, do we not know that in the end, phoenix-like, there will emerge from a sea of failures glorious success.[14]

The Brotherhood intended to test infringements of the civil rights of African Americans in court. Waring's goal was to bring test cases to disclose "the transparent veils of legal fiction under cover of which the civil rights of all races are being slowly undermined."[15]

Waring's efforts started a tradition of lawyering that culminated in Charles Hamilton Houston and Thurgood Marshall's legal campaign to overturn the Court's 1896 ruling in *Plessy v. Ferguson* (which upheld the constitutionality of segregation). The Brotherhood's work presaged that of modern organizations dedicated to pursuing social justice through law, such as the NAACP, the NAACP LDF, the PRLDF, the Asian American Legal Defense Fund, Legal Momentum, and Earth Justice. The Brotherhood also offers a lesson for lawyers today. In response to a legal system that systematically denied the privileges of citizenship on the basis of race, those African American lawyers pioneered a different model of lawyering—they were deliberate in selecting cases, representing clients whose claims would reveal injustice or establish precedent that would lead to the transformation of inequitable legal principles.

Houston and Marshall took Waring's approach one step further. Under their leadership, the NAACP, and later the NAACP LDF, refined the idea of using litigation to bring about social change by selecting their docket of cases with an eye toward their long-range strategy.[16] According to the 1934 NAACP

Annual Report, Houston and Marshall's campaign was intended to secure decisions, rulings, and public opinion on broad principles.[17]

LDF had unparalleled success in the 1940s and 1950s; and today, a range of organizations seeking to transform the law follow its approach. Ironically, conservative legal organizations such as the Center for Individual Rights, which has attacked affirmative action in the courts, have also begun to follow its approach (discussed in chapter 20).[18] As Professors David Schultz and Stephen Gottlieb wrote,

> Since *Brown v. Board of Education*...Americans have turned as never before to the courts for assistance in reforming society. Citizens have attempted to reform institutions such as schools, prisons, mental hospitals, and malapportioned legislatures through filing suit. Some laud these efforts as necessary to protect minority rights, ensure continued access to the political process, or otherwise to remedy legal wrongs. Others complain that such judicial activity is countermajoritarian, that it undermines confidence in local legislatures, or that it allots to the judiciary a task which it is ill-equipped to undertake. Despite their differences, however, both critic and reformer alike seem to share the functionalist faith in which modern legal thought seems so firmly grounded, the faith that courts can, for better or worse, change society.[19]

Out of the ashes of a post-Reconstruction retrenchment in the courts, Waring, Houston, and Marshall shaped the contours of public interest lawyering and set an example for how generations of civil rights lawyers would address barriers to social justice.

A Myriad Strategies

The lessons of previous generations are evident in the creative strategies employed by lawyers in this latest period of civil rights retrenchment. Some advocates are challenging discriminatory practices in state court based on state law theories. Others are providing technical assistance and information on legal processes to community groups so that those groups can better assert their rights. Still others are following in the spirit of Waring, Houston, and Marshall, developing and testing long-term strategies to ensure that rights are enforceable in federal courts.

Other chapters discuss legal strategies, from the use of administrative forums (e.g., Offices for Civil Rights) or local and state human rights commissions to ensuring that state law enforcement officials (e.g., the state attorney general) enforce civil rights laws (see chapters 10, 14, and 23). Lawyers for social justice are like weary boxers who refuse to give up, but instead look for their next opportunity to fell their opponent. The remainder of this chapter will touch on a few examples of such countermoves.

Going Back to Basics: Looking to State Law

In 1995, New York City Mayor Rudolph Giuliani announced his decision to privatize three hospitals in Queens and Brooklyn. The future of the New York City Health and Hospitals Corporation (HHC), a public system established by state law to provide comprehensive care to all residents regardless of their ability to pay, was uncertain, and Giuliani's plan raised a number of concerns. Despite the abundance of private hospital beds and doctors in New York City, many low-income communities relied on HHC services. In fact, HHC provided fifty percent of the City's outpatient visits. In many areas, uninsured patients had virtually nowhere else to go for non-emergent care.[20] Community groups were concerned that the sale or lease of HHC facilities would affect both access to care and the range of services available to patients.

Statistics on HHC health care services offer a sense of the stakes involved. In 1994, HHC facilities admitted more than two hundred thousand individuals for inpatient services (sixty-five hundred patients were treated daily), received one million emergency room visits and 4.7 million clinic visits, and served forty percent of TB patients and thirty-seven percent of AIDS patients in the City.[21]

Although the privatization of New York's public hospitals was a local issue, the loss of accessible health care in poor communities of color followed a long-term national trend; the outcome of the struggle, therefore, had national implications. In 1980, Congress heard testimony that physicians in private practice were leaving neighborhoods with large populations of color—a development that undermined the viability of inner city health care facilities.[22] More recently, the conversion of public and non-profit facilities to for-profit status diminished the accessibility of care to poor communities.[23] The result of this process was, in the words of the author of a study of the role of African American and Latino physicians in providing health care for under-served populations, that "[c]ommunities with high proportions of black and Hispanic residents [are] four times as likely as others to have a shortage of physicians, regardless of community income."[24]

Indeed, in the 1970s and early 1980s, LDF and the Center for Law and Social Policy worked with community residents and activists to challenge the clo-
sure of hospitals in a number of cities. Residents argued that the relocation of
hospitals to the suburbs would have a harmful effect on their health, in violation of Title VI of the Civil Rights of 1964 (which prohibits discrimination
the basis of race and ethnicity). While those cases were rarely successful, they
were important to community efforts to retain accessible services.[25] Although
the plaintiffs in the 1980 case *Bryan v. Koch* lost their suit, for example, community pressure helped to save one of the two public hospitals that then
Mayor Ed Koch had planned to close.[26]

It was not surprising, therefore, when community groups and labor unions
asked LDF to initiate a challenge under Title VI and its regulations.[27] After analyzing the probable negative outcome—including the past cases and the legal
attacks on Title VI that culminated in *Alexander v. Sandoval*[28]—LDF convened
a legal strategy session. Attorneys (including solo practitioners, lawyers from
private law firms working *pro bono*, and lawyers at the Center for Constitutional Rights, PRLDF, Queens Legal Services, and labor organizations) and
community representatives gathered and brainstormed monthly for two years
about procedural flaws in Mayor Giuliani's approach to the hospital sale.
While the meetings were open to community representatives, the agendas were
focused on legal theories and tactics and were not intended to supplant the
strategizing and organizing efforts taking place among community groups.

The legal team researched issues of conflict of interest, corporate law, and
municipal procurement law. Private attorneys conducted a title search, and
the team investigated whether there were any restrictions on the use of the
land on which the facilities were located. The effort generated multiple viable
legal theories (most of which were outside the lawyers' traditional areas of expertise), and spawned a number of state court challenges.

The first case, *Queens Hospital Center v. HHC*,[29] involved allegations by the
Queens Community Advisory Board (CAB) that HHC had violated its obligations under state law by failing to consult with the CAB. The judge granted
a temporary restraining order, but then ruled that the CAB did not have authority to bring a lawsuit. The case was appealed unsuccessfully. The second
case, *Campaign to Save Our Public Hospitals v. Giuliani*,[30] made procedural
and substantive arguments under both a local land use law and the state law
that established the public hospitals. The trial judge agreed with arguments
made by both the Campaign to Save Our Public Hospitals and the City Council that state law precluded dismantling the HHC system and, in particular,
prohibited the transfer of control envisioned by the mayor, and that any lease
of an HHC facility had to be approved pursuant to the local land use law and

by the City Council. The plaintiffs' victory in this second case was ultimately affirmed on appeal, and put a halt to the mayor's plan to privatize the public hospitals.[31] The success of *Campaign to Save Our Public Hospitals* and its companion case *City Council v. Giuliani* slowed the privatization process and carved out additional time for community input.[32] Indeed, although the state legislature had the power to amend state law so as to allow privatization, the mayor never pursued the issue after receiving the court ruling. The joint effort by the lawyers and community groups no doubt affected the prospect of legislative action in favor of privatization.

The effort to challenge the privatization of New York City's public hospitals exemplifies how civil rights lawyers at organizations such as LDF, the Center for Constitutional Rights, and PRLDF are creatively responding to community calls for representation on civil rights issues. The lawyers looked beyond their traditional federal statutory grounds in mounting a legitimate legal challenge.

Community Lawyering: Providing Technical Assistance to Communities Seeking Justice

Some activists and scholars have argued that national legal reform models will never result in true societal change. According to this view, creative lawyering employed in response to the absence of federal enforcement of civil rights is more likely to serve communities. Gerald Lopez, a critic of national reform efforts, has written about "rebellious lawyering," which grounds advocacy "in the lives and in the communities of the subordinated themselves," collaborating with others in strategic planning, joining coalitions, and developing "the sensibilities and skills compatible with a collective fight for social change."[33] Lopez argues that lawyers must know how to work with—not merely on behalf of—women, low-income communities, people of color, gays and lesbians, people with disabilities, the elderly, and others. Lawyers "must open themselves up to being educated by those with whom they come in contact, particularly about the traditions and experiences of life on the bottom and at the margins."[34] In contrast to the public interest lawyers of earlier days, he argues, "rebellious lawyers" are deeply involved in the communities in which they live and work, educate community members about their rights, and work directly with clients and service agencies. These lawyers can indeed play a role in community struggles for empowerment and justice.

Those engaged in the Environmental Justice Movement have pioneered various forms of "rebellious" community lawyering, working with grassroots groups striving for social and economic justice.[35] The SouthWest Organizing Project has described the problem.

> Working class people of color have paid the historical price of disproportionate and adverse affects of toxic chemicals in and around the communities *where we live, work and play.* The Environmental Justice Movement is the response by working class people all over the world who have been affected by this form of racism.[36]

In response, lawyers at local, regional, and national groups have provided technical assistance to grassroots groups as they battle polluters and plan for the future of their communities. At New York Lawyers for the Public Interest (NYLPI), "community lawyers, organizers and advocates work with community activists and stakeholders to provide the tools and support they request in their bid for self-empowerment."[37] The legal tools used include research, support for coalition building and citywide networking, advocacy in the policy arena, and litigation.[38] In 2002, NYLPI and its partner, the Organization of Waterfront Neighborhoods (OWN), won a tremendous victory using this multi-faceted advocacy. While the victory included state court litigation,[39] it was actually achieved in the policy arena. After six years of organized effort, New York Mayor Michael Bloomberg adopted OWN's plan for the equitable distribution of waste transfer facilities, including the retrofit of the city's marine transfer stations to compact, containerize, and export residential waste.[40]

Impact Litigation and Long-Term Planning Toward a Vision of Social Justice

Creative legal efforts also continue in federal court; litigators have both staved off further erosion of civil rights, and have achieved some victories. Perhaps the most exciting recent moment occurred in June 2003 when the Supreme Court ruled on the Michigan University affirmative action cases. In *Grutter v. Bollinger*, the Court upheld the School of Law's admissions program, rejecting arguments that race is irrelevant to school admissions and that, outside of providing a remedy for unconstitutional discrimination, educational institutions have no interest in racial diversity. The majority opinion stated, "[t]he Law School's educational judgment that diversity is essential to its educational mission is one to which we defer."[41]

The Michigan decisions, which no doubt benefited from a high level of public discussion, indicated that at least a holding pattern had been attained in the Court's affirmative action jurisprudence. The positive outcome was, at least in part, due to the creative efforts made by the litigators involved, including shining the public spotlight on the debate. Civil rights advocates engaged people from across society—the Court received briefs in support of Michigan's admissions policies from General Motors and other corporations, as well as from ex-officials from the military, and current college students. In its discussion of the benefits of diversity, the Court stated:

> These benefits are not theoretical but real, as major American businesses have made clear that the skills needed in today's increasingly global marketplace can only be developed through exposure to widely diverse people, cultures, ideas, and viewpoints. Brief for 3M et al. as *Amicus Curiae* 5, brief for General Motors Corp. as *Amicus Curiae* 3-4. What is more, high-ranking retired officers and civilian leaders in the United States military assert that '[b]ased on [their] decades of experience,' a 'highly qualified racially diverse officer corps...is essential to the military's ability to fulfill its principle mission to provide national security.' Brief for Julius W. Becton, Jr. et al. as *Amicus Curiae* 27.

Indeed, efforts are very much alive to develop legal campaigns to secure court decisions and influence public opinion on broad principles of social justice. Groups such as the Equal Justice Society (EJS), a national organization of scholars and advocates, are working to implement innovative legal theories. "As heirs of the innovative legal and political strategists of *Brown v. Board of Education*, EJS will marshal our forces to defeat the right wing assault on social and racial justice."[42]

Finally, litigators considering actions in federal court may be concerned about the current climate of skepticism, if not hostility, toward their claims. They may worry that defendants will benefit from the willingness of the courts to question the authority of Congress to pass or enforce civil rights laws. However, civil rights lawyers continue to bring and even win cases. For example, the National Lawyers Guild/Maurice and Jane Sugar Law Center for Economic Justice (the Guild Law Center) and the Mexican-American Legal Defense and Educational Fund (MALDEF) successfully challenged the construction of an elementary school on a Detroit site that housed contaminated industrial waste.[43] The Guild Law Center's mission states, in part, "We provide legal advocacy, representation, education and technical support to empower community groups, workers' rights groups and individuals seeking systemic change toward economic and social justice."[44] In this case, lawyers argued in federal court that the regulations implementing Title VI of the Civil Rights Act of 1964 were enforceable—despite the Court's *Sandoval* ruling (discussed in chapter 10). The

Michigan federal district court issued a preliminary injunction, stating that "the facility would likely cause a significant adverse impact on the minority community in violation of Title VI,"[45] and adopted the community's argument that, while the Court had ruled in *Sandoval* that Title VI's regulations were not in themselves enforceable, private parties could nonetheless enforce their rights under §1983, which allows for general enforcement of federal rights.[46] The district court stood by its decision, even after a federal appellate court held that Title VI was not enforceable through §1983.[47] The district court wrote that "[t]he right not be subjected to discrimination based upon race, color or national origin is not vague and Congress has imposed a binding obligation on the states of mandatory compliance."[48] The case was allowed to go forward and, ultimately, the parents whose children attended the school negotiated a settlement requiring the construction of a barrier to prevent the children's exposure to contaminants, regular inspection, and necessary reporting.[49]

Impact litigation continues to have a number of interrelated purposes.[50] First, and perhaps most importantly, lawsuits challenge discriminatory, exclusionary, or otherwise harmful practices, and can bring relief to plaintiffs, such as the families concerned about having the school located on a toxic site. Such cases may have precedential value, and may act as a deterrent to other policymakers or wrongdoers. Second, impact litigation builds a record regarding undesirable practices that can be used by community members and advocates to educate others and support legislative and administrative change. In this vein, Cornel West argued that legal work can play a significant role in educating the public on the fundamental principles and workings of our political arrangements. Such legal work constitutes "one of few buffers against cultural conservatism that recasts the law in its own racist…image," it "helps keep alive memory traces left by past progressive movements of resistance," and it serves "as a basis for the next wave of radical action."[51] Finally, impact litigation can be a front against the direct assault on harmful, unjust, or otherwise inequitable laws, policies, or practices.[52]

Observations and Conclusions: Hope

Lawyers play a continuing role in the struggle for social justice. In *Sheff v. O'Neill*, the hospital privatization cases, and the environmental justice efforts, legal assistance and litigation helped create leverage and room for dialogue and political action. For example, in Hartford, plaintiffs and independent Latino, African American, white, and multi-ethnic organizations held teach-ins, debates, conferences, and forums on *Sheff*, educational inequality, and racial issues. Lawyers often take a back seat at such events, except to provide a review or an update on legal developments. Similarly, during the *Campaign to Save Our Public Hospitals*, litigation encouraged increased levels of community participation. In his comprehensive study of the relationship between litigation regarding bilingual education and Latino community transformation, Luis Antonio Baez writes "[a]dherence to a standard of inclusion of parents, students, and other community members in the litigation process can turn the process itself into a learning and community building experience, something vitally important if we hope to prepare communities to sustain and fine tune the reforms which successful litigation may help to create."[53] Even an unsuccessful lawsuit can have transformative value in creating leverage.

While lawyers are facing challenges in the current civil rights rollback era, they can take heart from the experiences of our forbearers and from the creative approaches being adopted by their colleagues.

Endnotes

1. Arthur Zilversmit, *The First Emancipation: The Abolition of Slavery in the North*, Univ. of Chicago Press (1967) 103.

2. Id.

3. Herbert Aptheker, ed., *A Documentary History of the Negro People in the United States*, Carol Publishing Group (1990) 8 (petition by Peter Bestes, Sambo Freeman, Felix Holbrook, and Chester Joie, 1773).

4. Zilversmit, at 103–4.

5. See generally, John Hart Ely, *Democracy and Distrust: A Theory of Judicial Review*, Harvard Univ. Press (1980). See, e.g., Richard Kluger, *Simple Justice: The History of* Brown v. Board of Education *and Black America's Struggle for Equality*, Vintage Books (1977) 53–83 (the Court's role in the post-Reconstruction era), and 126–54 (the early development of legal strategies to attack discrimination); see also Rayford W. Logan, *The Betrayal of the Negro*, Collier Books (1965).

6. See Eric Foner, *Reconstruction: America's Unfinished Revolution, 1863–1877* (1988).

7. *Hall v. DeCuir*, 95 U.S. 485 (1878).

8. *The Civil Rights Cases*, 109 U.S. 3 (1883), *United States v. Stanley* (hotel accommodations), *United States v. Ryan* (theater privileges), *United States v. Nichols* (hotel accommodations), and *United States v. Singleton* (theatre privileges).

9. Id. at 11.

10. See Marianne L. Engelman Lado, A Question of Justice: African American Legal Perspectives on the 1883 *Civil Rights Cases*, 70 *Chicago-Kent L. Rev.* (1995) 1123, 1172–73.

11. Id. at 1135.

12. Id. at 1141.

13. Id. at 1172.

14. Id. at 1173.

15. Id. at 1173–74.

16. Mark Tushnet, *The NAACP Strategy Against Segregated Education: 1925–1950*, Univ. of NC Press (1987) 33.

17. Derrick Bell, Serving Two Masters: Integration Ideals and Client Interests in School Desegregation Litigation, in *Critical Race Theory: The Cutting Edge* (Richard Delgado, ed 1995) 229.

18. The Center for Individual Rights (CIR) asserts that its litigation is based on a principle of strict state neutrality: "The state must not advantage some or disadvantage others because of their race." http://www.cir-usa.org/civil_rights_theme.html. CIR fashions litigation to advance its view of "the anti-discrimination principle," challenging affirmative action in employment, student admissions, contracting, and other government benefits. Id. CIR's mission extends beyond the vision of a race-neutral government, however, and includes advocacy to "preserve private citizens' right to deal or not to deal with other private citizens." Id.

19. David Schultz and Stephen E. Gottlieb, Legal Functionalism and Social Change: A Reassessment of Rosenberg's *The Hollow Hope: Can Courts Bring About Social Change? 12 J. L. & Policy* (1995) 63–65.

20. All hospitals that receive money from the federal government are required to provide *emergency care* without regard to source of payment or ability to pay, in accordance with 42 U.S.C. 1395dd ("Examination and Treatment for Emergency Medical Conditions and Women in Labor Act").

21. Elisabeth Rosenthal, "A Mayoral Panel Urges Dismantling of City Hospitals," *New York Times* (August 16, 1995) A1; see also Charles Brecher and Sheila Spiezio, *Privatization and Public Hospitals: Choosing Wisely for New York City*, Twentieth Century Fund (1995) 7–24 ("Profile of the New York City Health and Hospitals Corporation").

22. Alan Sagar, "Urban Hospital Closings in the Face of Racial Change," Testimony on Hospital Financing Problems Before the Subcomm. on Health of the House Comm. on Ways and Means (March 14, 1980).

23. See, e.g., Jones and Clifford, The Privatization of Treatment Services for Alcohol Abusers: Effect on the Black Community, *82 J.N.M.A.* (1990) 337.

24. Komaromy, The Role of Black and Hispanic Physicians in Providing Health Care for Underserved Populations, *334 New England J. of Med.* (1996) 1305.

25. See, e.g., *Heath v. Charlotte-Mecklenburg Hosp. Auth.*, 681 F.2d 814 (4th Cir. 1982); *Hatcher v. Methodist Hospital,* N.D. Ind. Civil Action No. H77-154 (1977).

26. *Bryan v. Koch*, 627 F.2d 612 (2d Cir. 1980).

27. 42 U.S.C. 2000d, 45 C.F.R. Part 80 (regulations promulgated by the U.S. Department of Health and Human Services).

28. 532 U.S. 275 (2001).

29. *Queens Hospital Center v. HHC*, No. 123734/95 (NY Sup. Ct. filed September 27, 1995).

30. *Campaign to Save Our Public Hospitals v. Giuliani*, No. 97-01339 (NY Sup. Ct. filed May 15, 1996).

31. *Campaign to Save Our Public Hospitals v. Giuliani,* 93 N.Y.2d 60, 710 N.E.2d 255, 687 N.Y.S.2d 609, 1999 NY Slip op. 02634 (Court of Appeals, March 30, 1999).

32. Two additional suits, also based on novel legal theories for civil rights lawyers, were filed but held in abeyance given the ruling in *Campaign to Save Our Public Hospitals*, and ultimately dismissed as moot. The first was brought on behalf of a number of HHC Board members, among others, arguing that they had received insufficient information about the

sale to make decisions consistent with their fiduciary responsibilities. This case also alleged that the transaction violated applicable laws governing the procurement of services. The second alleged a violation of the State Environmental Quality Review Act.

33. Gerald P. López, *Rebellious Lawyering: One Chicano's Vision of Progressive Law Practice* (1992) 38.

34. Id. at 37.

35. See, e.g., http://www.swop.net (11/28/2004) ("Since 1980 SouthWest Organizing Project has worked from the grassroots to 'empower our communities to realize racial and gender equality and social and economic justice'").

36. http://www.swop.net/envirojust.htm (11/28/2004) (emphasis in original).

37. http://nylpi.org/communitylawyering.html.

38. Id.

39. See *Neighbors Against Garbage (NAG) et al. v. Doherty*, Index. No. 109023/96 (Sup. Ct. NY Co., March 16, 1997), aff'd *NAG et al. v. Doherty*, 245 A.D. 81, 665 N.Y.S.2d 640 (1st Dep't 1997); *OWN v. Carpinello*, Index. No. 103661/99 (Sup. Ct. NY Co., Oct. 18, 2001) (actions to enforce Local Law 40, NYC Code 16-130 et seq.).

40. http://nylpi.org/area_4_waste.html (11/28/2004).

41. *Grutter v. Bollinger,* 539 U.S. 306, 328 (2003).

42. http://www.equaljusticesociety.org/about.html.

43. *Lucero v. Detroit Public Schools*, 160 F.Supp.2d 767 (E.D. Mich., 2001).

44. http://www.sugarlaw.org/us/mission.shtml.

45. *Lucero*, 160 F.Supp.2d at 781.

46. Id. at 784; see 42 U.S.C. 1983.

47. *South Camden Citizens in Action v. New Jersey Department of Environmental Protection*, 274 F.3d 771 (3d Cir. 2001), *cert denied* 536 U. S. 939 (2002).

48. *Lucero*, 160 F.Supp.2d at 784.

49. "GLC Successfully Settles Landmark EJ Case at 'New Beard School.'" Newsletter, The NLG/Maurice and Jane Sugar Law Center for Economic & Social Justice (Summer 2004) 1. http://www.sugarlaw.org/pubs/news_summer2004.pdf.

50. Perhaps the critique of public interest lawyers and the focus on community lawyering belies doubt in the utility of national legal campaigns, a position shared by current scholarship arguing that *Brown* and its progeny had minimal impact. See Gerald Rosenberg, *The Hollow Hope: Can Courts Bring About Social Change?* Univ. of Chicago (1991) 155–56; see also Michal Belknap, *Federal Law and Southern Order: Racial Violence and Constitutional Conflict in the Post-Brown South*, Univ. of Georgia Press (1987) (arguing that civil rights prosecutions and laws were less significant in decreasing racial violence than restraints imposed by southern political culture); Michael J. Klarman, A Brown, Racial Change, and the Civil Rights Movement, *80 Va. L. Rev.* (1994) 7 (arguing that racial change would have come regardless of *Brown*, though contending that federal legislative intervention was necessary); but see David Schultz and Stephen E. Gottlieb, Legal Functionalism and Social Change: A Reassessment of Rosenberg's *The Hollow Hope: Can Courts Bring About Social Change? 12 J. L. & Policy* (1996) 63 (noting that Rosenberg's evaluation of the effectiveness of law reform fails to inquire whether social change would occur if courts did not seek to effect change, without regard to whether court mandates are effectively implemented).

51. Cornel West, The Role of Law in Progressive Politics, *43 Vand. L. Rev.* (1990) 1797, 1799–1800. As has been noted elsewhere, the role of an attorney in rendering grievances and words into legal narrative is necessarily fraught with danger. See Clark D. Cunning-

ham, The Lawyer as Translator, Representation as Text: Towards an Ethnography of Legal Discourse, 77 *Cornell L. Rev.* (1992) 1298; James B. White, Translation as a Mode of Thought, 77 *Cornell L. Rev.* (1992) 1388, 1397.

52. Indeed, recent scholarship downplaying the significance of *Brown* advances and relies upon an overly simplified measure of the impact of court action, ignores the subtle ways in which litigation and judicial mandates inspire and complement activism, and affect social mores and, ultimately, behavior. For example, in *The Hollow Hope*, Gerald Rosenberg argues that there is "no evidence" that civil rights litigation inspired student organization and bravery. Rosenberg at 142. He notes, "The SCLC was founded in the winter of 1957," but then discounts any possible influence by *Brown* or civil rights litigation: "The moving force behind it was not the inspiration of *Brown* but an attempt to capitalize on the success of the Montgomery bus boycott." Id. at 143. In Martin Luther King, Jr.'s own account of the Montgomery bus boycott, however, King wrote about the influence of *Brown* and the work of the NAACP lawyers on the movement in Montgomery. King suggested that the Supreme Court's decision on desegregation "might help to explain why the protest occurred when it did," although it could not explain why it took place in Montgomery. Martin Luther King, Jr., *Stride Toward Freedom: The Montgomery Story*, Harper & Row (1958) 64. In fact, in the course of the protest, King and other community members filed suit in federal district court, "asking for an end of bus segregation on the grounds that it was contrary to the Fourteenth Amendment." Id. at 151. Robert Carter, of the NAACP's legal staff, represented the Montgomery residents, arguing that local segregation laws were inconsistent with *Brown*: "This injustice and inconsistency in the segregation laws was the object of Bob Carter's brilliant attack," King wrote. Id. at 152. The widespread impact of *Brown* is poignantly illustrated in Patricia Williams' recent recounting of how the case affected her father's thinking. She quotes her father:

> [A]fter *Brown* I remember it dawning on me that I *could* have gone to the University of Georgia....And people began to talk to you a little differently; I remember [the white doctor who treated Williams' family in Boston, where she grew up] used to treat us in such a completely offhand way.....But after *Brown*,] he wanted to discuss it with us, he asked questions, what I thought....He wanted my opinion and I suddenly realized that no white person had ever asked what I thought about anything.

Patricia Williams, *The Rooster's Egg: On the Persistence of Prejudice*, Harvard Univ. Press (1995) 23 (parentheticals modified).

53. Luis Antonio Baez, *From Transformative School Goals to Assimilationist and Remedial Bilingual Education: A Critical Review of Key Precedent-Setting Hispanic Bilingual Litigation Decided by Federal Courts Between 1974 and 1983*, Univ. of Wisconsin (1995) 299.

GLOSSARY OF TERMS

Abrogate
To abolish, do away with, or annul. Congress can abrogate state sovereign immunity and allow individuals to sue states that violate federal law only under limited circumstances. See *Sovereign Immunity*.

Administrative Hearing
A legal proceeding before a government agency. Administrative hearings are similar to hearings in courts (parties are each permitted to tell their sides of the story) however procedural rules, like those applying to the admission of evidence, tend to be more relaxed. In some instances, the rulings of the agency can be appealed to a court.

Affirmative Action
Policies which give special consideration to certain groups—including women, racial and ethnic minorities, and people with disabilities—in hiring, promotion, or admissions decisions. Most often, affirmative action policies are adopted to compensate for ongoing discrimination, make up for past discrimination, and/or achieve diversity.

Amicus Curiae
Latin term meaning "friend of the court." An individual or organization that is not a party to a lawsuit, but has a strong interest in the case, may file an amicus brief presenting arguments.

Arbitration
A legal proceeding in which an arbitrator, instead of a judge, resolves the dispute. These proceedings resolve disputes in a less formal, less expensive, and faster manner than in federal or state court, but without the same procedural protections. Some statutes and private contracts require mandatory arbitration, rather than litigation, in the case of disputes.

Catalyst Theory
The catalyst theory holds that a plaintiff is a "prevailing party" and is therefore entitled to collect fees under the attorney's fees provisions of various civil
rights statutes when their litigation is a catalyst to create a desired policy
change. The catalyst theory encourages attorneys to resolve litigation in the
most expeditious manner (often by settlement) rather than forcing them to
litigate to final judgment in order to be entitled to collect fees.

Circuit Courts
Also known as Courts of Appeals. The federal court system divides the country into thirteen regions that include multiple states. Each region, or "circuit,"
has a panel of judges who hear cases on appeal from the district or trial courts
in that same region. See *District Court.*

Commerce Clause
Article I, Section 8, Clause 3 of the U.S. Constitution. This provision gives
Congress exclusive authority to regulate commerce between or among the
states (interstate commerce). Congress has used its Commerce Clause powers
to enact civil rights legislation.

Compelling State Interest
See *Strict Scrutiny.*

Concurrence
An opinion written by a judge who agrees with the holding of the majority
opinion, but does not agree with its reasoning.

Consent Decree
A consent decree ends a lawsuit before it is resolved by a judge or jury. The
parties to the suit agree to end the suit in exchange for some form of relief,
and the judge formalizes their agreement in a court order. The judge then
monitors the consent decree to ensure that both sides comply with their agreement. See *Settlement Agreement.*

Court of Appeals
See *Circuit Court.*

Damages
Damages, usually monetary, are awarded by a court to the winning side in a law-
suit as compensation for their loss or injury. Damages are paid by the losing side.
See *Injunction.*

De Facto
Latin term meaning "in fact." The term is used to refer to a circumstance that
has developed without government regulation. See *De Jure.* Example: In 2005,

the Detroit public school that Malcolm attends is ninety percent minority even though neither the state nor the school board has taken any affirmative steps to promote racially isolated facilities. Malcolm's public school is operating under a system of de facto segregation.

Defendant

The person or group accused of wrongdoing in a lawsuit. See *Plaintiff*.

De Jure

Latin term meaning "by right." Refers to a circumstance that has developed as a result of legal requirement. See *De Facto*. Example: In 1953, the Topeka public school that Martin attends is one hundred percent minority. The Topeka Board of Education requires that white children and children of color be educated in separate facilities. Martin's public school is operating under a system of de jure segregation.

Department of Justice (DOJ)

An executive branch department, established by Congress in 1870, that is charged with enforcing federal laws, including federal civil rights laws. The U.S. Attorney General is the head of the Department of Justice.

Disparate Impact

When a non-discriminatory policy or practice has a disproportionately large negative impact on a group of people. See *Intentional Discrimination*. Example: A company requires its employees to have a high school diploma in order to be promoted from all but the lowest paying positions. Although the requirement is the same for all employees, it has a disparate impact on any racial group that has lower high school graduation rates.

Dissent

An opinion written by a judge who disagrees with the majority opinion. Unlike a majority opinion, a dissent does not have the power of law.

District Courts

The federal trial courts. Article III of the U.S. Constitution enumerates the circumstances under which a case may be heard by a federal district court rather than by a state court. Cases may be heard in federal court if, for example, the U.S. is either the plaintiff or the defendant, a federal law is involved, or the person suing and the person being sued are citizens of different states and the dispute between them is worth more than $75,000.

Dormant Commerce Clause

The Supreme Court has interpreted the Commerce Clause, which gives Congress the power to regulate interstate commerce, to create the negative inference that states do not have the authority to do so. When Congress chooses not to exercise its Commerce Clause powers, its exclusive authority is dormant and states still cannot regulate.

Due Process Clause
There are two Due Process Clauses in the U.S. Constitution. The first, found in the Fifth Amendment, creates rights that are enforceable against the federal government; the second, found in Section 1 of the Fourteenth Amendment, creates rights that are enforceable against state governments. Both Due Process Clauses guarantee fair procedures and protect property from unfair government interference. Example: A government official deprives Goldberg of his government entitlement without holding a hearing prior to the termination of that entitlement to allow him to rebut the evidence against him and explain why he is qualified to receive it. Goldberg has been denied Due Process.

Effects Test
A test used by courts to determine whether discrimination has occurred. The test requires the court to examine the actual effect of a practice rather than the purpose stated to justify the practice. See *Intentional Discrimination*.

Eleventh Amendment
The Eleventh Amendment, ratified in 1795, provides that "The Judicial power of the United States shall not be construed to extend to any suit in law or equity, commenced or prosecuted against one of the United States by Citizens of another State, or by Citizens or Subjects of any Foreign State." The Supreme Court has interpreted the Eleventh Amendment to prevent individuals from suing states for damages. However, Congress has the power to make exceptions to or abrogate state sovereign immunity, individuals can sue state officials for injunctive relief, and states can consent to being sued. See *Sovereign Immunity*.

Environmental Justice
The fair and equitable treatment of all people, regardless of race, class, or culture, in the enforcement of environmental laws and the distribution of environmental hazards. No group should bare a disproportionately large share of the negative health and economic impacts of pollution.

Equal Employment Opportunity Commission (EEOC)
A federal agency, established by Title VII of the Civil Rights Act of 1964, that is authorized to investigate and resolve employment discrimination claims based on race, color, religion, age, sex, national origin, and disability.

The Equal Protection Clause
The Equal Protection Clause, found in Section 1 of the Fourteenth Amendment, prohibits states from depriving people of equal treatment under the law.

The Supreme Court has held the federal government similarly accountable for equal protection through the Due Process Clause of the Fifth Amendment. See *Strict Scrutiny*, *Intermediate Scrutiny*, and *Rational Basis Scrutiny*.

Executive Order
A declaration by the president, a governor, or a local executive that has the force of law as long as it does not conflict either with a law enacted by the legislative branch or a court decision.

Federal Judiciary
The judges of the U.S. government. Includes judges of the district courts and courts of appeals, U.S. Supreme Court justices, and other federal judicial officers (such as magistrate judges).

Federalism
The division of power between the states and the federal government. Scholars have proposed a wide spectrum of ideas about what model of federalism is embodied in the U.S. Constitution: from almost complete state autonomy and states' rights on one end, to the unlimited ability of the federal government to regulate state governance on the other.

The Fifteenth Amendment
The Fifteenth Amendment, ratified in 1870, provides that "The right of citizens of the United States to vote shall not be denied or abridged by the United States or by any State on account of race, color, or previous condition of servitude." The amendment empowers Congress to enforce its provisions with appropriate legislation. For decades after its adoption southern states continued to deny African Americans and other people of color the right to vote by enacting Jim Crow laws. Congress exercised its power to enforce the amendment's guarantees when it enacted the Voting Rights Act of 1965. See *Jim Crow*.

Fifth Amendment Privilege against Self-Incrimination
The Fifth Amendment provides, in part, that "[no person] shall be compelled in any criminal case to be a witness against himself." The privilege gives individuals the right to refuse to answer any questions or make any statements, when to do so would help establish that they had committed a crime or were connected to criminal activity.

The First Amendment
The First Amendment, ratified in 1791, provides that "Congress shall make no law respecting an establishment of religion, or prohibiting the free exercise thereof; or abridging the freedom of speech, or of the press; or the right of the people peaceably to assemble, and to petition the Government for a re-

dress of grievances." The Supreme Court has interpreted the amendment to apply to both the state and federal governments.

The Fourteenth Amendment
The Fourteenth Amendment was ratified in 1868 to protect the civil rights of formerly enslaved black people and all others in the United States. The first section of the Fourteenth Amendment provides that "All persons born or naturalized in the United States, and subject to the jurisdiction thereof, are citizens of the United States and of the State wherein they reside. No State shall make or enforce any law which shall abridge the privileges or immunities of citizens of the United States; nor shall any State deprive any person of life, liberty, or property, without due process of law; nor deny to any person within its jurisdiction the equal protection of the laws." Section 5 of the Fourteenth Amendment empowers Congress to enforce the amendment's provisions with appropriate legislation. Like the Fifteenth Amendment, the Fourteenth Amendment was ignored by Southern states, which continued to discriminate against African Americans and other people of color by enforcing Jim Crow laws through the 1960s. See *Jim Crow.*

Fundamental Constitutional Right
Rights that are either expressly written or implied in the U.S. Constitution. Examples of expressly written fundamental rights include the right to free speech and the right to vote. An example of an implied fundamental right is the right to privacy.

Gender-Based Violence
Violence directed at a person because of his or her sex, such as sexual harassment, domestic violence, and rape. Most victims of gender-based violence are women.

Grand Jury
Unlike trial juries, which decide a defendant's guilt or innocence, grand juries decide whether probable cause exists to prosecute someone for committing a crime.

Green Card
An immigration registration card showing that someone is a lawful permanent resident in the U.S. See *Lawful Permanent Resident.*

Habeas Corpus
Latin term meaning "you have the body." The right of an imprisoned person to challenge the legality of his or her confinement by seeking a writ of habeas corpus from a court is protected by Article I, Section 9 of the Constitution, which provides that: "The privilege of the Writ of Habeas Corpus shall not be

suspended, unless when in Cases of Rebellion or Invasion the public Safety may require it."

Holding
A court's conclusion of law regarding the legal significance of the facts presented in a case.

Implementing Regulation
A regulation issued by a federal agency to implement a congressional statute. Example: The Department of Justice and most federal agencies have issued implementing regulations for Title VI of the Civil Rights Act of 1964 that prohibit practices that have the effect of discriminating on the basis of race, color, or national origin.

Implied Right of Action
The ability of an individual to bring suit to enforce a constitutional or statutory right, even though the law they are suing under does not explicitly state that individuals have a right to do so. Courts will imply rights of action only under limited circumstances. See *Private Right of Action.*

Injunction
Also known as injunctive relief. A court order requiring one side in a lawsuit to do something or to refrain from doing something. There are two kinds of injunctions: temporary and permanent. Temporary injunctions are granted only until a court can make a final decision at trial. Permanent injunctions are granted after the conclusion of a trial, and remain in effect as long as ordered by the court. Example: A federal court can enter an injunction to prevent a state agency from enforcing a racially discriminatory regulation. See *Damages.*

Injunctive Relief
See *Injunction.*

Intentional Discrimination
When one person purposefully discriminates against another; discrimination that is motivated by animus. Proving intentional discrimination can be difficult because it requires evidence of the motivation behind the allegedly discriminatory action, as opposed to an examination of the actual effects of the practice. See *Disparate Impact.* Example: State laws mandating racial segregation.

Intermediate Scrutiny
A standard applied by courts to determine whether discrimination is unlawful under the Equal Protection Clause. Under this standard, a law is considered unconstitutional if it is not substantially related to an important govern-

ment interest. Courts usually apply intermediate scrutiny in cases involving sex or gender discrimination. See *Rational Basis Scrutiny* and *Strict Scrutiny*.

Jim Crow Laws

Laws enacted throughout the southern states beginning in the 1880s that denied African Americans political, economic, and social power. Jim Crow laws legalized racial segregation in all areas of life, disenfranchised African American voters, and prohibited mixed race marriages. The Supreme Court upheld the constitutionality of legislation requiring racial segregation in *Plessy v. Ferguson* (1896). The Court later repudiated Jim Crow and the doctrine of "separate but equal" in *Brown v. Board of Education* (1954).

Judicial Activist

A judge who interprets laws according to his or her political convictions, rather than following precedent.

Judicial Appointment

When there is a vacancy on a federal court, the president nominates a candidate and the Senate decides whether to confirm the nominee. Upon confirmation, the nominee has a lifetime appointment.

Lawful Permanent Resident (LPR)

An immigrant who has legal authority to remain permanently in the U.S. Upon obtaining permanent residency, LPRs receive green cards as proof of their legal status. After a few years, an LPR may apply to become a naturalized U.S. citizen. See *Green Card*.

Legislative History

The events leading up to the enactment of a statute, including hearings and debates. Legislative history is sometimes used to interpret the meaning of ambiguous language in a statute. See *Statute*.

Liability

Legal responsibility or obligation.

Limited English Proficiency (LEP)

LEP people do not speak, understand, or read English well. Example: Most people in the U.S. who speak a language other than English at home also speak English. The LEP population, twenty-one million people (eight percent of the U.S. population), speaks English less than very well.

Living Wage

The salary that a full-time worker would need to earn in order to live above the federal and state poverty levels. This amount varies depending on the cost of living in a geographical area. Some advocates have calculated the living wage to be more than twice the federal minimum wage (even higher in expensive cities).

Major Life Activity
For an impairment to qualify as a "disability" under the Americans with Disabilities Act of 1990 or the Rehabilitation Act of 1973, the Supreme Court has held that it must substantially limit one or more major life activities. Major life activities are those that are of central importance to daily life, such as caring for one's self, performing manual tasks, walking, seeing, hearing, speaking, and breathing.

Medicaid
A national health insurance program that is jointly funded by the federal and state governments. Medicaid provides health care coverage for low-income people who cannot otherwise afford to pay for their medical care.

Medicare
A national health insurance program that provides health care coverage to the elderly and the disabled.

National Labor Relations Board (NLRB)
A federal agency, established by the National Labor Relations Act of 1935, authorized to prevent and remedy unfair labor practices by private sector employers and labor organizations.

Peremptory Challenge
The right of a party to dismiss a juror before trial without stating a reason. The Supreme Court has held that parties may not use peremptory challenges to systematically exclude jurors on the basis of race or sex.

Plaintiff
The person or group that brings a lawsuit. See *Defendant*.

Plenary Power
Complete control. When Congress has plenary power over an area of law, its authority to enact statutes or decide policy in that area is unlikely to be questioned by another branch of government. Example: Because Congress has plenary power over immigration law, Congress's enactments in that area almost always receive deferential judicial review.

Precedent
A judicial opinion establishing legal principles that are to be followed in subsequent similar cases. Example: Federal district courts in Ohio are bound by precedent established by the Sixth Circuit Court of Appeals.

Preemption
Federal legislation will usually preempt—or trump—any state law that conflicts with it. Preemption can be accomplished in two ways: expressly or by implication. Congress can act under its constitutional powers to override state laws, and sometimes does so explicitly. In implied preemption, judges decide whether a federal law overrides a state law even if Congress has not expressly provided for preemption. Example: Federal copyright laws are an example of express preemption. In those statutes, Congress explicitly preempts state copyright law, leaving the federal government with sole authority to issue and regulate copyright.

Private Right of Action
The right of an individual to bring suit to enforce a constitutional or statutory right. Some laws explicitly provide that individuals can enforce the rights they create by filing a lawsuit in court. Other laws do not contain such a provision and only the government or an administrative agency has the authority to bring suit when the law is violated. See *Implied Right of Action*. Example: The Supreme Court has interpreted Title VI of the Civil Rights Act of 1964 to contain a private right of action that allows individuals to bring suit in court when their rights under that statute are violated. However, the Court has held that there is no private right of action to enforce the implementing regulations of Title VI, so only a government agency can bring suit to challenge a violation of those regulations.

Privileges or Immunities Clause
Section 1 of the Fourteenth Amendment provides, in part, that: "No State shall make or enforce any law which shall abridge the privileges or immunities of citizens of the United States." The Supreme Court has declined to interpret the Privileges or Immunities Clause to create substantive federal citizenship rights that are enforceable against the states, but instead in the *Slaughter-House Cases* in 1873 read the clause so narrowly as to render it practically irrelevant. Article I, Section 2, Clause 1 of the Constitution contains a Privileges *and* Immunities Clause: "The Citizens of each State shall be entitled to all Privileges and Immunities of Citizens in the several States." The Court has interpreted the Privileges and Immunities Clause to prohibit states from placing unreasonable burdens on out-of-state residents.

Probable Cause
Reasonable ground to believe that something is likely to be true. Example: The Fourth Amendment, which protects people against unreasonable searches and seizures, requires judges to have probable cause to believe that the person to be searched has committed a crime in order to issue a search warrant.

Punitive Damages
Monetary damages that are awarded by a court—in addition to compensatory damages which cover the actual cost of the injury to the plaintiff—to penalize the wrongdoer and deter future wrongful conduct. Punitive damages cannot be recovered unless the defendant engaged in intentional, malicious, or egregious behavior.

Rational Basis Scrutiny
A standard applied by courts to determine whether discrimination is unlawful under the Equal Protection Clause. Under this standard, a law is unconstitutional only if the government did not have a rational reason for enacting it. Rational basis scrutiny, the least demanding of the Equal Protection Clause tests, is used to determine the legality of most economic legislation and any laws that do not impact a fundamental right or involve a classification on the basis of race, religion, color, or national origin. See *Intermediate Scrutiny* and *Strict Scrutiny*.

Reapportionment
The process of allocating the 435 seats in the House of Representatives to accurately reflect the most recent U.S. Census data on the population of the states. Reapportionment is important in presidential elections because the number of electoral votes allocated to each state is calculated based on the number of seats the state holds in Congress (the number of House representatives plus each state's two senatorial seats). See *Redistricting*.

Reconstruction Era (1865-77)
The period after the Civil War during which the federal government readmitted the eleven Confederate states that had seceded before the war into the Union, and tried to integrate newly emancipated African Americans into U.S. citizenship. The Thirteenth Amendment, which abolished slavery, the Fourteenth Amendment, which expanded the guarantees of citizenship, and the Fifteenth Amendment, which prohibited race-based voting restrictions, were enacted during the Reconstruction Era. The first federal civil rights legislation was also passed during this era. Reconstruction was followed by a period during which the civil rights of people of color were eviscerated by Jim Crow laws and state-sanctioned violence. See *Jim Crow Laws*.

Redistricting
The process of redrawing state legislative district boundaries to reflect population shifts. In *Baker v. Carr* (1962), the Supreme Court held that federal

courts could hear cases alleging unfair redistricting practices that resulted in the arbitrary appointment of state and federal representatives. In subsequent cases, the Court established the principle of equal representation: "one man, one vote." See *Reapportionment*.

Rehnquist Court

The Supreme Court under the leadership of Chief Justice William Rehnquist. Justice Rehnquist was appointed to the Supreme Court by President Richard Nixon in 1972, and has been Chief Justice since 1986. See *Supreme Court*.

Remand

An appellate court remands a lawsuit when it sends the case back to a lower court for further action. Example: A federal circuit court can reverse a district court's judgment and remand the case back to the district court for a new trial.

Section 5 of the Fourteenth Amendment

Section 5 of the Fourteenth Amendment provides that: "The Congress shall have power to enforce, by appropriate legislation, the provisions of this article." This provision authorizes Congress to pass civil rights legislation that can be enforced against the states.

Settlement Agreement

An agreement between the parties to a lawsuit to end the suit in exchange for some form of compensation. Courts do not monitor settlement agreements. See *Consent Decree*.

Sovereign Immunity

The right of the government—state or federal—not to have to answer to suit. See *Abrogate, Eleventh Amendment,* and *State Waiver of Sovereign Immunity*. Example: Patricia's employer violates her federal rights. However, because Patricia works for a state university hospital or other state institution, she cannot sue her employer in state or federal court.

Spending Clause

Article I, Section 8, Clause 1 of the Constitution provides that: "The Congress shall have Power To lay and collect Taxes, Duties, Imposts and Excises, to pay the Debts and provide for the common Defense and general Welfare of the United States." The Supreme Court has interpreted the clause to authorize Congress to solicit a state's agreement to comply with conditions as a condition of accepting federal monies. Congress has used its Spending Clause powers to enact civil rights legislation.

States' Rights

Proponents of states' rights assert that the power of the federal government should be limited so as not to encroach on the sovereignty of the states. Although the doctrine is most closely associated with opponents of civil rights who used states' rights to support their argument that southern states should be entitled to maintain racial segregation in the 1950s and 60s, both sides of the debate over slavery prior to the Civil War pressed states' rights arguments when that furthered their substantive political goals. See *Federalism*. Example: Officials in northern states asserted state sovereignty in opposing federal fugitive slave laws that required the return of escaped slaves to their southern masters; and southern leaders often raised states' rights arguments in opposition to the federal government's unwillingness to extend slavery into the federal territories.

State Waiver of Sovereign Immunity

One of two ways that a state can lose its sovereign immunity and expose itself to suits by private individuals for damages. Either the state can pass legislation voluntarily relinquishing, or waiving, this immunity, or Congress can abrogate state sovereign immunity. See *Sovereign Immunity*.

Statute

A law passed by Congress or a state legislature.

Strict Scrutiny

A standard applied by courts to determine whether discrimination is unlawful under the Equal Protection and Due Process Clauses. Under this standard, a law is considered unconstitutional unless it is necessary to further a compelling government interest and is, in addition, narrowly tailored to achieve that end. Courts apply strict scrutiny in cases involving discrimination on the basis of race, religion, color, or national origin, and for laws affecting fundamental rights. Very few legislative acts are upheld when reviewed under this standard. See *Rational Basis Scrutiny* and *Intermediate Scrutiny*.

Supremacy Clause

Article VI of the Constitution provides, in part, that: "This Constitution, and the Laws of the United States which shall be made in Pursuance thereof; and all Treaties made, or which shall be made, under the Authority of the United States, shall be the supreme Law of the Land; and the Judges in every State shall be bound thereby, any Thing in the Constitution or Laws of any State to the Contrary notwithstanding." The clause provides that the Constitution, federal statutes, and U.S. treaties are the highest form of law in the U.S. legal system, and requires state judges to uphold them, even if they conflict with state law.

The Supreme Court
The highest court in the U.S. The Supreme Court has the power to interpret the Constitution and to decide whether laws passed by Congress are consistent with the Constitution. There are nine justices on the Court: Chief Justice William Rehnquist (1972–2005), John Paul Stevens (1975), Sandra Day O'Connor (1981–2005), Antonin Scalia (1986), Anthony Kennedy (1988), David Souter (1990), Clarence Thomas (1991), Ruth Bader Ginsberg (1993), and Steven Breyer (1994). A majority of at least five justices must agree to make a decision that is law.

Takings Clause
The Takings Clause of the Fifth Amendment states that: "Nor shall private property be taken for public use, without just compensation." Both the federal and state governments have the power, through eminent domain, to take a person's private property; the Takings Clause requires the government to pay just compensation if they do so. The government does not necessarily have to pay just compensation when it enacts regulations that merely diminish the value of private property.

Third Party Beneficiary
A person who, while not a party to a contract, has enforceable rights under that contract because it was entered into for their benefit. Example: Holly owes $300 to Lawrence. Holly loans $300 to Fox in exchange for Fox's promise to pay the $300 to Lawrence. If Fox fails to pay, Lawrence—the third party beneficiary—can sue to enforce Fox's promise to Holly.

Thirteenth Amendment
The Thirteenth Amendment, ratified in 1865, abolished slavery in the U.S. The amendment provides that: "Neither slavery nor involuntary servitude, except as a punishment for crime whereof the party shall have been duly convicted, shall exist within the United States, or any place subject to their jurisdiction." It also empowers Congress to enforce its provisions with appropriate legislation. See *Reconstruction Era.*

Undocumented Immigrant
A person who does not have the legal documents or immigration authority to reside in the U.S.

Waiver of Sovereign Immunity
See *State Waiver of Sovereign Immunity.*

APPENDIX B

Websites with Information about Federal Judicial Nominations

Supporting Judicial Independence

- Alliance for Justice: www.independentjudiciary.org
- Brennan Center for Justice at NYU: www.brennancenter.org
- Committee for Judicial Independence email sign-up: info@ extremistcourts.org
- Community Rights Counsel: www.communityrights.org (the environment)
- Court Selection Project: www.afj.org
- EarthJustice: http://www.earthjustice.org/policy/judicial/nominees/ (the environment)
- Leadership Conference on Civil Rights: www.saveourcourts.org
- NARAL: www.naral.org (reproductive rights)
- National Organization for Women: http://www.now.org/issues/ legislat/nominees/
- People for the American Way: www.pfaw.org (reports: *Courting Disaster* and *The Federalist Society*)

Government Websites about the Courts and Judicial Nominations

- Senate Judiciary Committee: http://judiciary.senate.gov (lists members, schedule for hearings, transcripts)
- U.S. Dept. of Justice, Office of Legal Policy: http://www .usdoj.gov/olp(list of judicial nominees and status of nominations)
- U.S. Federal Judiciary: www.uscourts.gov (judicial vacancies: http://www.uscourts.gov/vacancies/judgevacancy.htm)

APPENDIX C

THE CONSTITUTION OF THE UNITED STATES

We the People of the United States, in Order to form a more perfect Union, establish Justice, insure domestic Tranquility, provide for the common defence, promote the general Welfare, and secure the Blessings of Liberty to ourselves and our Posterity, do ordain and establish this Constitution for the United States of America.

Article I

Section 1
All legislative Powers herein granted shall be vested in a Congress of the United States, which shall consist of a Senate and House of Representatives.

Section 2, Clause 1
The House of Representatives shall be composed of Members chosen every second Year by the People of the several States, and the Electors in each State shall have the Qualifications requisite for Electors of the most numerous Branch of the State Legislature.

Section 2, Clause 2
No Person shall be a Representative who shall not have attained to the Age of twenty five Years, and been seven Years a Citizen of the United States, and who shall not, when elected, be an Inhabitant of that State in which he shall be chosen.

Section 2, Clause 3
Representatives and direct Taxes shall be apportioned among the several States which may be included within this Union, according to their respective Num-

bers, which shall be determined by adding to the whole Number of free Persons, including those bound to Service for a Term of Years, and excluding Indians not taxed, three fifths of all other Persons.

The actual Enumeration shall be made within three Years after the first Meeting of the Congress of the United States, and within every subsequent Term of ten Years, in such Manner as they shall by Law direct. The Number of Representatives shall not exceed one for every thirty Thousand, but each State shall have at Least one Representative; and until such enumeration shall be made, the State of New Hampshire shall be entitled to chuse three, Massachusetts eight, Rhode Island and Providence Plantations one, Connecticut five, New York six, New Jersey four, Pennsylvania eight, Delaware one, Maryland six, Virginia ten, North Carolina five, South Carolina five and Georgia three.

Section 2, Clause 4
When vacancies happen in the Representation from any State, the Executive Authority thereof shall issue Writs of Election to fill such Vacancies.

Section 2, Clause 5
The House of Representatives shall chuse their Speaker and other Officers; and shall have the sole Power of Impeachment.

Section 3, Clause 1
The Senate of the United States shall be composed of two Senators from each State, chosen by the Legislature thereof, for six Years; and each Senator shall have one Vote.

Section 3, Clause 2
Immediately after they shall be assembled in Consequence of the first Election, they shall be divided as equally as may be into three Classes. The Seats of the Senators of the first Class shall be vacated at the Expiration of the second Year, of the second Class at the Expiration of the fourth Year, and of the third Class at the Expiration of the sixth Year, so that one third may be chosen every second Year; and if Vacancies happen by Resignation, or otherwise, during the Recess of the Legislature of any State, the Executive thereof may make temporary Appointments until the next Meeting of the Legislature, which shall then fill such Vacancies.

Section 3, Clause 3

No person shall be a Senator who shall not have attained to the Age of thirty Years, and been nine Years a Citizen of the United States, and who shall not, when elected, be an Inhabitant of that State for which he shall be chosen.

Section 3, Clause 4

The Vice President of the United States shall be President of the Senate, but shall have no Vote, unless they be equally divided.

Section 3, Clause 5

The Senate shall chuse their other Officers, and also a President pro tempore, in the absence of the Vice President, or when he shall exercise the Office of President of the United States.

Section 3, Clause 6

The Senate shall have the sole Power to try all Impeachments. When sitting for that Purpose, they shall be on Oath or Affirmation. When the President of the United States is tried, the Chief Justice shall preside: And no Person shall be convicted without the Concurrence of two thirds of the Members present.

Section 3, Clause 7

Judgment in Cases of Impeachment shall not extend further than to removal from Office, and disqualification to hold and enjoy any Office of honor, Trust or Profit under the United States: but the Party convicted shall nevertheless be liable and subject to Indictment, Trial, Judgment and Punishment, according to Law.

Section 4, Clause 1

The Times, Places and Manner of holding Elections for Senators and Representatives, shall be prescribed in each State by the Legislature thereof; but the Congress may at any time by Law make or alter such Regulations, except as to the Place of Chusing Senators.

Section 4, Clause 2

The Congress shall assemble at least once in every Year, and such Meeting shall be on the first Monday in December, unless they shall by Law appoint a different Day.

Section 5, Clause 1
Each House shall be the Judge of the Elections, Returns and Qualifications of its own Members, and a Majority of each shall constitute a Quorum to do Business; but a smaller number may adjourn from day to day, and may be authorized to compel the Attendance of absent Members, in such Manner, and under such Penalties as each House may provide.

Section 5, Clause 2
Each House may determine the Rules of its Proceedings, punish its Members for disorderly Behavior, and, with the Concurrence of two-thirds, expel a Member.

Section 5, Clause 3
Each House shall keep a Journal of its Proceedings, and from time to time publish the same, excepting such Parts as may in their Judgment require Secrecy; and the Yeas and Nays of the Members of either House on any question shall, at the Desire of one fifth of those Present, be entered on the Journal.

Section 5, Clause 4
Neither House, during the Session of Congress, shall, without the Consent of the other, adjourn for more than three days, nor to any other Place than that in which the two Houses shall be sitting.

Section 6, Clause 1
The Senators and Representatives shall receive a Compensation for their Services, to be ascertained by Law, and paid out of the Treasury of the United States. They shall in all Cases, except Treason, Felony and Breach of the Peace, be privileged from Arrest during their Attendance at the Session of their respective Houses, and in going to and returning from the same; and for any Speech or Debate in either House, they shall not be questioned in any other Place.

Section 6, Clause 2
No Senator or Representative shall, during the Time for which he was elected, be appointed to any civil Office under the Authority of the United States which shall have been created, or the Emoluments whereof shall have been increased during such time; and no Person holding any Office under the United States, shall be a Member of either House during his Continuance in Office.

Section 7, Clause 1

All bills for raising Revenue shall originate in the House of Representatives; but the Senate may propose or concur with Amendments as on other Bills.

Section 7, Clause 2

Every Bill which shall have passed the House of Representatives and the Senate, shall, before it become a Law, be presented to the President of the United States; If he approve he shall sign it, but if not he shall return it, with his Objections to that House in which it shall have originated, who shall enter the Objections at large on their Journal, and proceed to reconsider it. If after such Reconsideration two thirds of that House shall agree to pass the Bill, it shall be sent, together with the Objections, to the other House, by which it shall likewise be reconsidered, and if approved by two thirds of that House, it shall become a Law. But in all such Cases the Votes of both Houses shall be determined by Yeas and Nays, and the Names of the Persons voting for and against the Bill shall be entered on the Journal of each House respectively. If any Bill shall not be returned by the President within ten Days (Sundays excepted) after it shall have been presented to him, the Same shall be a Law, in like Manner as if he had signed it, unless the Congress by their Adjournment prevent its Return, in which Case it shall not be a Law.

Section 7, Clause 3

Every Order, Resolution, or Vote to which the Concurrence of the Senate and House of Representatives may be necessary (except on a question of Adjournment) shall be presented to the President of the United States; and before the Same shall take Effect, shall be approved by him, or being disapproved by him, shall be repassed by two thirds of the Senate and House of Representatives, according to the Rules and Limitations prescribed in the Case of a Bill.

Section 8, Clause 1

The Congress shall have Power To lay and collect Taxes, Duties, Imposts and Excises, to pay the Debts and provide for the common Defence and general Welfare of the United States; but all Duties, Imposts and Excises shall be uniform throughout the United States;

Section 8, Clause 2

To borrow money on the credit of the United States;

Section 8, Clause 3
To regulate Commerce with foreign Nations, and among the several States, and with the Indian Tribes;

Section 8, Clause 4
To establish an uniform Rule of Naturalization, and uniform Laws on the subject of Bankruptcies throughout the United States;

Section 8, Clause 5
To coin Money, regulate the Value thereof, and of foreign Coin, and fix the Standard of Weights and Measures;

Section 8, Clause 6
To provide for the Punishment of counterfeiting the Securities and current Coin of the United States;

Section 8, Clause 7
To establish Post Offices and Post Roads;

Section 8, Clause 8
To promote the Progress of Science and useful Arts, by securing for limited Times to Authors and Inventors the exclusive Right to their respective Writings and Discoveries;

Section 8, Clause 9
To constitute Tribunals inferior to the supreme Court;

Section 8, Clause 10
To define and punish Piracies and Felonies committed on the high Seas, and Offenses against the Law of Nations;

Section 8, Clause 11
To declare War, grant Letters of Marque and Reprisal, and make Rules concerning Captures on Land and Water;

Section 8, Clause 12
To raise and support Armies, but no Appropriation of Money to that Use shall be for a longer Term than two Years;

Section 8, Clause 13
To provide and maintain a Navy;

Section 8, Clause 14
To make Rules for the Government and Regulation of the land and naval Forces;

Section 8, Clause 15
To provide for calling forth the Militia to execute the Laws of the Union, suppress Insurrections and repel Invasions;

Section 8, Clause 16
To provide for organizing, arming, and disciplining the Militia, and for governing such Part of them as may be employed in the Service of the United States, reserving to the States respectively, the Appointment of the Officers, and the Authority of training the Militia according to the discipline prescribed by Congress;

Section 8, Clause 17
To exercise exclusive Legislation in all Cases whatsoever, over such District (not exceeding ten Miles square) as may, by Cession of particular States, and the acceptance of Congress, become the Seat of the Government of the United States, and to exercise like Authority over all Places purchased by the Consent of the Legislature of the State in which the Same shall be, for the Erection of Forts, Magazines, Arsenals, dock-Yards, and other needful Buildings; And

Section 8, Clause 18
To make all Laws which shall be necessary and proper for carrying into Execution the foregoing Powers, and all other Powers vested by this Constitution in the Government of the United States, or in any Department or Officer thereof.

Section 9, Clause 1
The Migration or Importation of such Persons as any of the States now existing shall think proper to admit, shall not be prohibited by the Congress prior to the Year one thousand eight hundred and eight, but a tax or duty may be imposed on such Importation, not exceeding ten dollars for each Person.

Section 9, Clause 2

The privilege of the Writ of Habeas Corpus shall not be suspended, unless when in Cases of Rebellion or Invasion the public Safety may require it.

Section 9, Clause 3

No Bill of Attainder or ex post facto Law shall be passed.

Section 9, Clause 4

No capitation, or other direct, Tax shall be laid, unless in Proportion to the Census or Enumeration herein before directed to be taken.

Section 9, Clause 5

No Tax or Duty shall be laid on Articles exported from any State.

Section 9, Clause 6

No Preference shall be given by any Regulation of Commerce or Revenue to the Ports of one State over those of another: nor shall Vessels bound to, or from, one State, be obliged to enter, clear, or pay Duties in another.

Section 9, Clause 7

No Money shall be drawn from the Treasury, but in Consequence of Appropriations made by Law; and a regular Statement and Account of the Receipts and Expenditures of all public Money shall be published from time to time.

Section 9, Clause 8

No Title of Nobility shall be granted by the United States: And no Person holding any Office of Profit or Trust under them, shall, without the Consent of the Congress, accept of any present, Emolument, Office, or Title, of any kind whatever, from any King, Prince or foreign State.

Section 10, Clause 1

No State shall enter into any Treaty, Alliance, or Confederation; grant Letters of Marque and Reprisal; coin Money; emit Bills of Credit; make any Thing but gold and silver Coin a Tender in Payment of Debts; pass any Bill of Attainder, ex post facto Law, or Law impairing the Obligation of Contracts, or grant any Title of Nobility.

Section 10, Clause 2

No State shall, without the Consent of the Congress, lay any Imposts or Duties on Imports or Exports, except what may be absolutely necessary for executing it's inspection Laws: and the net Produce of all Duties and Imposts, laid by any State on Imports or Exports, shall be for the Use of the Treasury of the United States; and all such Laws shall be subject to the Revision and Controul of the Congress.

Section 10, Clause 3
No State shall, without the Consent of Congress, lay any duty of Tonnage, keep Troops, or Ships of War in time of Peace, enter into any Agreement or Compact with another State, or with a foreign Power, or engage in War, unless actually invaded, or in such imminent Danger as will not admit of delay.

Article II

Section 1, Clause 1
The executive Power shall be vested in a President of the United States of America. He shall hold his Office during the Term of four Years, and, together with the Vice-President chosen for the same Term, be elected, as follows:

Section 1, Clause 2
Each State shall appoint, in such Manner as the Legislature thereof may direct, a Number of Electors, equal to the whole Number of Senators and Representatives to which the State may be entitled in the Congress: but no Senator or Representative, or Person holding an Office of Trust or Profit under the United States, shall be appointed an Elector.

Section 1, Clause 3
The Electors shall meet in their respective States, and vote by Ballot for two persons, of whom one at least shall not lie an Inhabitant of the same State with themselves. And they shall make a List of all the Persons voted for, and of the Number of Votes for each; which List they shall sign and certify, and transmit sealed to the Seat of the Government of the United States, directed to the President of the Senate. The President of the Senate shall, in the Presence of the Senate and House of Representatives, open all the Certificates, and the Votes shall then be counted. The Person having the greatest Number of Votes shall be the President, if such Number be a Majority of the whole Number of Electors appointed; and if there be more than one who have such Majority, and have an equal Number of Votes, then the House of Representatives shall immediately chuse by Ballot one of them for President; and if no Person have a Majority, then from the five highest on the List the said House shall in like Manner chuse the President. But in chusing the President, the Votes shall

be taken by States, the Representation from each State having one Vote; a quorum for this Purpose shall consist of a Member or Members from two-thirds of the States, and a Majority of all the States shall be necessary to a Choice. In every Case, after the Choice of the President, the Person having the greatest Number of Votes of the Electors shall be the Vice President. But if there should remain two or more who have equal Votes, the Senate shall chuse from them by Ballot the Vice-President.

Section 1, Clause 4
The Congress may determine the Time of chusing the Electors, and the Day on which they shall give their Votes; which Day shall be the same throughout the United States.

Section 1, Clause 5
No person except a natural born Citizen, or a Citizen of the United States, at the time of the Adoption of this Constitution, shall be eligible to the Office of President; neither shall any Person be eligible to that Office who shall not have attained to the Age of thirty-five Years, and been fourteen Years a Resident within the United States.

Section 1, Clause 6
In Case of the Removal of the President from Office, or of his Death, Resignation, or Inability to discharge the Powers and Duties of the said Office, the same shall devolve on the Vice President, and the Congress may by Law provide for the Case of Removal, Death, Resignation or Inability, both of the President and Vice President, declaring what Officer shall then act as President, and such Officer shall act accordingly, until the Disability be removed, or a President shall be elected.

Section 1, Clause 7
The President shall, at stated Times, receive for his Services, a Compensation, which shall neither be increased nor diminished during the Period for which he shall have been elected, and he shall not receive within that Period any other Emolument from the United States, or any of them.

Section 1, Clause 8
Before he enter on the Execution of his Office, he shall take the following Oath or Affirmation: "I do solemnly swear (or affirm) that I will faithfully execute the Office of President of the United States, and will to the best of my Ability, preserve, protect and defend the Constitution of the United States."

Section 2, Clause 1

The President shall be Commander in Chief of the Army and Navy of the United States, and of the Militia of the several States, when called into the actual Service of the United States; he may require the Opinion, in writing, of the principal Officer in each of the executive Departments, upon any subject relating to the Duties of their respective Offices, and he shall have Power to Grant Reprieves and Pardons for Offenses against the United States, except in Cases of Impeachment.

Section 2, Clause 2

He shall have Power, by and with the Advice and Consent of the Senate, to make Treaties, provided two thirds of the Senators present concur; and he shall nominate, and by and with the Advice and Consent of the Senate, shall appoint Ambassadors, other public Ministers and Consuls, Judges of the supreme Court, and all other Officers of the United States, whose Appointments are not herein otherwise provided for, and which shall be established by Law: but the Congress may by Law vest the Appointment of such inferior Officers, as they think proper, in the President alone, in the Courts of Law, or in the Heads of Departments.

Section 2, Clause 3

The President shall have Power to fill up all Vacancies that may happen during the Recess of the Senate, by granting Commissions which shall expire at the End of their next Session.

Section 3

He shall from time to time give to the Congress Information of the State of the Union, and recommend to their Consideration such Measures as he shall judge necessary and expedient; he may, on extraordinary Occasions, convene both Houses, or either of them, and in Case of Disagreement between them, with Respect to the Time of Adjournment, he may adjourn them to such Time as he shall think proper; he shall receive Ambassadors and other public Ministers; he shall take Care that the Laws be faithfully executed, and shall Commission all the Officers of the United States.

Section 4

The President, Vice President and all civil Officers of the United States, shall be removed from Office on Impeachment for, and Conviction of, Treason, Bribery, or other high Crimes and Misdemeanors.

Article III

Section 1
The judicial Power of the United States, shall be vested in one supreme Court, and in such inferior Courts as the Congress may from time to time ordain and establish. The Judges, both of the supreme and inferior Courts, shall hold their Offices during good Behavior, and shall, at stated Times, receive for their Services a Compensation which shall not be diminished during their Continuance in Office.

Section 2, Clause 1
The judicial Power shall extend to all Cases, in Law and Equity, arising under this Constitution, the Laws of the United States, and Treaties made, or which shall be made, under their Authority; to all Cases affecting Ambassadors, other public Ministers and Consuls; to all Cases of admiralty and maritime Jurisdiction; to Controversies to which the United States shall be a Party; to Controversies between two or more States; between a State and Citizens of another State; between Citizens of different States; between Citizens of the same State claiming Lands under Grants of different States, and between a State, or the Citizens thereof, and foreign States, Citizens or Subjects.

Section 2, Clause 2
In all Cases affecting Ambassadors, other public Ministers and Consuls, and those in which a State shall be Party, the supreme Court shall have original Jurisdiction. In all the other Cases before mentioned, the supreme Court shall have appellate Jurisdiction, both as to Law and Fact, with such Exceptions, and under such Regulations as the Congress shall make.

Section 2, Clause 3
The Trial of all Crimes, except in Cases of Impeachment, shall be by Jury; and such Trial shall be held in the State where the said Crimes shall have been committed; but when not committed within any State, the Trial shall be at such Place or Places as the Congress may by Law have directed.

Section 3, Clause 1
Treason against the United States, shall consist only in levying War against them, or in adhering to their Enemies, giving them Aid and Comfort. No Person shall be convicted of Treason unless on the Testimony of two Witnesses to the same overt Act, or on Confession in open Court.

Section 3, Clause 2

The Congress shall have power to declare the Punishment of Treason, but no Attainder of Treason shall work Corruption of Blood, or Forfeiture except during the Life of the Person attainted.

Article IV

Section 1

Full Faith and Credit shall be given in each State to the public Acts, Records, and judicial Proceedings of every other State. And the Congress may by general Laws prescribe the Manner in which such Acts, Records and Proceedings shall be proved, and the Effect thereof.

Section 2, Clause 1

The Citizens of each State shall be entitled to all Privileges and Immunities of Citizens in the several States.

Section 2, Clause 2

A Person charged in any State with Treason, Felony, or other Crime, who shall flee from Justice, and be found in another State, shall on demand of the executive Authority of the State from which he fled, be delivered up, to be removed to the State having Jurisdiction of the Crime.

Section 2, Clause 3

No Person held to Service or Labour in one State, under the Laws thereof, escaping into another, shall, in Consequence of any Law or Regulation therein, be discharged from such Service or Labour, But shall be delivered up on Claim of the Party to whom such Service or Labour may be due.

Section 3, Clause 1

New States may be admitted by the Congress into this Union; but no new States shall be formed or erected within the Jurisdiction of any other State; nor any State be formed by the Junction of two or more States, or parts of States, without the Consent of the Legislatures of the States concerned as well as of the Congress.

Section 3, Clause 2

The Congress shall have Power to dispose of and make all needful Rules and Regulations respecting the Territory or other Property belonging to the United

States; and nothing in this Constitution shall be so construed as to Prejudice any Claims of the United States, or of any particular State.

Section 4

The United States shall guarantee to every State in this Union a Republican Form of Government, and shall protect each of them against Invasion; and on Application of the Legislature, or of the Executive (when the Legislature cannot be convened) against domestic Violence.

Article V

The Congress, whenever two thirds of both Houses shall deem it necessary, shall propose Amendments to this Constitution, or, on the Application of the Legislatures of two thirds of the several States, shall call a Convention for proposing Amendments, which, in either Case, shall be valid to all Intents and Purposes, as part of this Constitution, when ratified by the Legislatures of three fourths of the several States, or by Conventions in three fourths thereof, as the one or the other Mode of Ratification may be proposed by the Congress; Provided that no Amendment which may be made prior to the Year One thousand eight hundred and eight shall in any Manner affect the first and fourth Clauses in the Ninth Section of the first Article; and that no State, without its Consent, shall be deprived of its equal Suffrage in the Senate.

Article VI

Section 1, Clause 1

All Debts contracted and Engagements entered into, before the Adoption of this Constitution, shall be as valid against the United States under this Constitution, as under the Confederation.

Section 1, Clause 2

This Constitution, and the Laws of the United States which shall be made in Pursuance thereof; and all Treaties made, or which shall be made, under the Authority of the United States, shall be the supreme Law of the Land; and the Judges in every State shall be bound thereby, any Thing in the Constitution or Laws of any State to the Contrary notwithstanding.

Section 1, Clause 3

The Senators and Representatives before mentioned, and the Members of the several State Legislatures, and all executive and judicial Officers, both of the

United States and of the several States, shall be bound by Oath or Affirmation, to support this Constitution; but no religious Test shall ever be required as a Qualification to any Office or public Trust under the United States.

Article VII

The Ratification of the Conventions of nine States, shall be sufficient for the Establishment of this Constitution between the States so ratifying the Same.

Amendment I

Congress shall make no law respecting an establishment of religion, or prohibiting the free exercise thereof; or abridging the freedom of speech, or of the press; or the right of the people peaceably to assemble, and to petition the Government for a redress of grievances.

Amendment II

A well regulated Militia, being necessary to the security of a free State, the right of the people to keep and bear Arms, shall not be infringed.

Amendment III

No Soldier shall, in time of peace be quartered in any house, without the consent of the Owner, nor in time of war, but in a manner to be prescribed by law.

Amendment IV

The right of the people to be secure in their persons, houses, papers, and effects, against unreasonable searches and seizures, shall not be violated, and no Warrants shall issue, but upon probable cause, supported by Oath or affirmation, and particularly describing the place to be searched, and the persons or things to be seized.

Amendment V

No person shall be held to answer for a capital, or otherwise infamous crime, unless on a presentment or indictment of a Grand Jury, except in cases arising in the land or naval forces, or in the Militia, when in actual service in time of War or public danger; nor shall any person be subject for the same offense to be twice put in jeopardy of life or limb; nor shall be compelled in any criminal case to be a witness against himself, nor be deprived of life, liberty, or property, without due process of law; nor shall private property be taken for public use, without just compensation.

Amendment VI

In all criminal prosecutions, the accused shall enjoy the right to a speedy and public trial, by an impartial jury of the State and district wherein the crime shall have been committed, which district shall have been previously ascertained by law, and to be informed of the nature and cause of the accusation; to be confronted with the witnesses against him; to have compulsory process for obtaining witnesses in his favor, and to have the Assistance of Counsel for his defence.

Amendment VII

In Suits at common law, where the value in controversy shall exceed twenty dollars, the right of trial by jury shall be preserved, and no fact tried by a jury, shall be otherwise re-examined in any Court of the United States, than according to the rules of the common law.

Amendment VIII

Excessive bail shall not be required, nor excessive fines imposed, nor cruel and unusual punishments inflicted.

Amendment IX

The enumeration in the Constitution, of certain rights, shall not be construed to deny or disparage others retained by the people.

Amendment X

The powers not delegated to the United States by the Constitution, nor prohibited by it to the States, are reserved to the States respectively, or to the people.

Amendment XI

The Judicial power of the United States shall not be construed to extend to any suit in law or equity, commenced or prosecuted against one of the United States by Citizens of another State, or by Citizens or Subjects of any Foreign State.

Amendment XII

The Electors shall meet in their respective states, and vote by ballot for President and Vice-President, one of whom, at least, shall not be an inhabitant of the same state with themselves; they shall name in their ballots the person voted for as President, and in distinct ballots the person voted for as Vice-President, and they shall make distinct lists of all persons voted for as President, and of all persons voted for as Vice-President and of the number of votes for each, which lists they shall sign and certify, and transmit sealed to the seat of the government of the United States, directed to the President of the Senate;

The President of the Senate shall, in the presence of the Senate and House of Representatives, open all the certificates and the votes shall then be counted;

The person having the greatest Number of votes for President, shall be the President, if such number be a majority of the whole number of Electors appointed; and if no person have such majority, then from the persons having the highest numbers not exceeding three on the list of those voted for as President, the House of Representatives shall choose immediately, by ballot, the President. But in choosing the President, the votes shall be taken by states, the representation from each state having one vote; a quorum for this purpose shall consist of a member or members from two-thirds of the states, and a majority of all the states shall be necessary to a choice. And if the House of Representatives shall not choose a President whenever the right of choice shall devolve upon them, before the fourth day of March next following, then the Vice-President shall act as President, as in the case of the death or other constitutional disability of the President.

The person having the greatest number of votes as Vice-President, shall be the Vice-President, if such number be a majority of the whole number of Electors appointed, and if no person have a majority, then from the two highest numbers on the list, the Senate shall choose the Vice-President; a quorum for the purpose shall consist of two-thirds of the whole number of Senators, and a majority of the whole number shall be necessary to a choice. But no person constitutionally ineligible to the office of President shall be eligible to that of Vice-President of the United States.

Amendment XIII

1. Neither slavery nor involuntary servitude, except as a punishment for crime whereof the party shall have been duly convicted, shall exist within the United States, or any place subject to their jurisdiction.

2. Congress shall have power to enforce this article by appropriate legislation.

Amendment XIV

1. All persons born or naturalized in the United States, and subject to the jurisdiction thereof, are citizens of the United States and of the State wherein

they reside. No State shall make or enforce any law which shall abridge the privileges or immunities of citizens of the United States; nor shall any State deprive any person of life, liberty, or property, without due process of law; nor deny to any person within its jurisdiction the equal protection of the laws.

2. Representatives shall be apportioned among the several States according to their respective numbers, counting the whole number of persons in each State, excluding Indians not taxed. But when the right to vote at any election for the choice of electors for President and Vice-President of the United States, Representatives in Congress, the Executive and Judicial officers of a State, or the members of the Legislature thereof, is denied to any of the male inhabitants of such State, being twenty-one years of age, and citizens of the United States, or in any way abridged, except for participation in rebellion,
or other crime, the basis of representation therein shall be reduced in the proportion which the number of such male citizens shall bear to the whole number of male citizens twenty-one years of age in such State.

3. No person shall be a Senator or Representative in Congress, or elector of President and Vice-President, or hold any office, civil or military, under the United States, or under any State, who, having previously taken an oath, as a member of Congress, or as an officer of the United States, or as a member of any State legislature, or as an executive or judicial officer of any State, to support the Constitution of the United States, shall have engaged in insurrection or rebellion against the same, or given aid or comfort to the enemies thereof. But Congress may by a vote of two-thirds of each House, remove such disability.

4. The validity of the public debt of the United States, authorized by law, including debts incurred for payment of pensions and bounties for services in suppressing insurrection or rebellion, shall not be questioned. But neither the United States nor any State shall assume or pay any debt or obligation incurred in aid of insurrection or rebellion against the United States, or any claim for the loss or emancipation of any slave; but all such debts, obligations and claims shall be held illegal and void.

5. The Congress shall have power to enforce, by appropriate legislation, the provisions of this article.

Amendment XV

1. The right of citizens of the United States to vote shall not be denied or abridged by the United States or by any State on account of race, color, or previous condition of servitude.

2. The Congress shall have power to enforce this article by appropriate legislation.

Amendment XVI

The Congress shall have power to lay and collect taxes on incomes, from whatever source derived, without apportionment among the several States, and without regard to any census or enumeration.

Amendment XVII

The Senate of the United States shall be composed of two Senators from each State, elected by the people thereof, for six years; and each Senator shall have one vote. The electors in each State shall have the qualifications requisite for electors of the most numerous branch of the State legislatures.

When vacancies happen in the representation of any State in the Senate, the executive authority of such State shall issue writs of election to fill such vacancies: Provided, That the legislature of any State may empower the executive thereof to make temporary appointments until the people fill the vacancies by election as the legislature may direct.

This amendment shall not be so construed as to affect the election or term of any Senator chosen before it becomes valid as part of the Constitution.

Amendment XVIII

1. After one year from the ratification of this article the manufacture, sale, or transportation of intoxicating liquors within, the importation thereof into, or the exportation thereof from the United States and all territory subject to the jurisdiction thereof for beverage purposes is hereby prohibited.

2. The Congress and the several States shall have concurrent power to enforce this article by appropriate legislation.

3. This article shall be inoperative unless it shall have been ratified as an amendment to the Constitution by the legislatures of the several States, as pro-

vided in the Constitution, within seven years from the date of the submission hereof to the States by the Congress.

Amendment XIX

The right of citizens of the United States to vote shall not be denied or abridged by the United States or by any State on account of sex.

Congress shall have power to enforce this article by appropriate legislation.

Amendment XX

1. The terms of the President and Vice President shall end at noon on the 20th day of January, and the terms of Senators and Representatives at noon on the 3d day of January, of the years in which such terms would have ended if this article had not been ratified; and the terms of their successors shall then begin.

2. The Congress shall assemble at least once in every year, and such meeting shall begin at noon on the 3d day of January, unless they shall by law appoint a different day.

3. If, at the time fixed for the beginning of the term of the President, the President elect shall have died, the Vice President elect shall become President. If a President shall not have been chosen before the time fixed for the beginning of his term, or if the President elect shall have failed to qualify, then the Vice President elect shall act as President until a President shall have qualified; and the Congress may by law provide for the case wherein neither a President elect nor a Vice President elect shall have qualified, declaring who shall then act as President, or the manner in which one who is to act shall be selected, and such person shall act accordingly until a President or Vice President shall have qualified.

4. The Congress may by law provide for the case of the death of any of the persons from whom the House of Representatives may choose a President whenever the right of choice shall have devolved upon them, and for the case of the death of any of the persons from whom the Senate may choose a Vice President whenever the right of choice shall have devolved upon them.

5. Sections 1 and 2 shall take effect on the 15th day of October following the ratification of this article.

6. This article shall be inoperative unless it shall have been ratified as an amendment to the Constitution by the legislatures of three-fourths of the several States within seven years from the date of its submission.

Amendment XXI

1. The eighteenth article of amendment to the Constitution of the United States is hereby repealed.

2. The transportation or importation into any State, Territory, or possession of the United States for delivery or use therein of intoxicating liquors, in violation of the laws thereof, is hereby prohibited.

3. The article shall be inoperative unless it shall have been ratified as an amendment to the Constitution by conventions in the several States, as provided in the Constitution, within seven years from the date of the submission hereof to the States by the Congress.

Amendment XXII

1. No person shall be elected to the office of the President more than twice, and no person who has held the office of President, or acted as President, for more than two years of a term to which some other person was elected President shall be elected to the office of the President more than once. But this Article shall not apply to any person holding the office of President, when this Article was proposed by the Congress, and shall not prevent any person who may be holding the office of President, or acting as President, during the term within which this Article becomes operative from holding the office of President or acting as President during the remainder of such term.

2. This article shall be inoperative unless it shall have been ratified as an amendment to the Constitution by the legislatures of three-fourths of the several States within seven years from the date of its submission to the States by the Congress.

Amendment XXIII

1. The District constituting the seat of Government of the United States shall appoint in such manner as the Congress may direct: A number of electors of President and Vice President equal to the whole number of Senators and Representatives in Congress to which the District would be entitled if it were a State, but in no event more than the least populous State; they shall be in ad-

dition to those appointed by the States, but they shall be considered, for the purposes of the election of President and Vice President, to be electors appointed by a State; and they shall meet in the District and perform such duties as provided by the twelfth article of amendment.

2. The Congress shall have power to enforce this article by appropriate legislation.

Amendment XXIV

1. The right of citizens of the United States to vote in any primary or other election for President or Vice President, for electors for President or Vice President, or for Senator or Representative in Congress, shall not be denied or abridged by the United States or any State by reason of failure to pay any poll tax or other tax.

2. The Congress shall have power to enforce this article by appropriate legislation.

Amendment XXV

1. In case of the removal of the President from office or of his death or resignation, the Vice President shall become President.

2. Whenever there is a vacancy in the office of the Vice President, the President shall nominate a Vice President who shall take office upon confirmation by a majority vote of both Houses of Congress.

3. Whenever the President transmits to the President pro tempore of the Senate and the Speaker of the House of Representatives his written declaration that he is unable to discharge the powers and duties of his office, and until he transmits to them a written declaration to the contrary, such powers and duties shall be discharged by the Vice President as Acting President.

4. Whenever the Vice President and a majority of either the principal officers of the executive departments or of such other body as Congress may by law provide, transmit to the President pro tempore of the Senate and the Speaker of the House of Representatives their written declaration that the President is unable to discharge the powers and duties of his office, the Vice President shall immediately assume the powers and duties of the office as Acting President.

Thereafter, when the President transmits to the President pro tempore of the Senate and the Speaker of the House of Representatives his written declaration that no inability exists, he shall resume the powers and duties of his office unless the Vice President and a majority of either the principal officers of the executive department or of such other body as Congress may by law provide, transmit within four days to the President pro tempore of the Senate and the Speaker of the House of Representatives their written declaration that the President is unable to discharge the powers and duties of his office. Thereupon
Congress shall decide the issue, assembling within forty eight hours for that purpose if not in session. If the Congress, within twenty one days after receipt of the latter written declaration, or, if Congress is not in session, within twenty one days after Congress is required to assemble, determines by two thirds vote of both Houses that the President is unable to discharge the powers and duties of his office, the Vice President shall continue to discharge the same as Acting President; otherwise, the President shall resume the powers and duties of his office.

Amendment XXVI

1. The right of citizens of the United States, who are eighteen years of age or older, to vote shall not be denied or abridged by the United States or by any State on account of age.

2. The Congress shall have power to enforce this article by appropriate legislation.

Amendment XXVII

No law, varying the compensation for the services of the Senators and Representatives, shall take effect, until an election of Representatives shall have intervened.

About the Contributors

Michelle Alexander is an Associate Professor of Law and the Director of Civil Rights Clinics at Stanford Law School. Prior to joining the Stanford Law School faculty in 2002, she was the Director of the Racial Justice Project of the American Civil Liberties Union of Northern California, and a litigator at Saperstein, Goldstein, Demchak & Baller, a law firm specializing in class action suits alleging race and gender discrimination in employment, and at Hogan & Hartson. She also taught as an adjunct professor at Boalt Hall School of Law. Prof. Alexander clerked for Supreme Court Justice Harry A. Blackmun and Chief Judge Abner Mikva of the U.S. Court of Appeals for the DC Circuit. She received her B.A. from Vanderbilt University in 1989 and her J.D. as a member of the *Order of the Coif* from Stanford Law School in 1992.

Penny Austen (copyeditor) has a decade of professional writing and editing experience. Prior to becoming a freelance editor, she spent eight years in the corporate world at KPMG Peat Marwick LLP, Angoss Software, and most recently SAS Institute. During this time, she honed her marketing skills, was a frequent public speaker, and published analytical and technical papers. As a freelance editor, she has worked with numerous authors on a variety of works, both academic and literary. Mrs. Austen graduated with a B.A. from McGill University and an M.B.A. from Duke University's Fuqua School of Business.

Ana Avendaño-Denier is Assistant General Counsel of the AFL-CIO, and was recently appointed as director of the AFL-CIO's Immigrant Worker Program. Ms. Avendaño-Denier previously served as a consultant with the National Immigration Law Center, where she assisted in the development of strategies to protect immigrant workers following the Supreme Court's decision in *Hoffman Plastic Compounds v. NLRB*. Ms. Avendaño-Denier also served as Assistant General Counsel of the 1.4 million-member United Food and Commercial Workers International Union, where she was a front-line advocate in campaigns for immigrant workers' rights. Ms. Avendaño-Denier also served in the Appellate Court Branch of the National Labor Relations Board, and worked in private practice in Washington, DC, and San Francisco, California. She is a graduate of Georgetown University Law School and the University of California at Berkeley.

Erica Flores Baltodano is Assistant Director and an attorney at the Center for Law in the Public Interest in Los Angeles. Ms. Baltodano received her J.D. from the University of California at Berkeley, Boalt Hall, where she earned the Francine Diaz Memorial Award for her commitment to public interest work. She graduated *magna cum laude* from UCLA with a B.A. in Sociology and a minor in Public Policy.

Luke Blocher attends Columbia Law School, where he is a former president of the American Constitution Society chapter. Prior to law school, he worked as a field director of a congressional campaign in Ohio's 1st District, on the Cincinnati City Council, and at the Hamilton County Office of the Public Defender. He has interned at the Democratic National Committee and the Offices of U.S. Senators Evan Bayh and Mike DeWine. Mr. Blocher is a *magna cum laude* graduate of Amherst College, where in his senior thesis he used social movement theory to compare the evolution of two successful student movements: the Student Nonviolent Coordinating Committee and United Students Against Sweatshops.

Janell Byrd-Chichester is an attorney with The Cochran Firm in Washington, DC, where she practices civil rights law. Ms. Byrd-Chichester litigates in the areas of sexual harassment, police misconduct, public accommodations, and education discrimination, and consults on civil rights legislative and policy matters. Ms. Byrd-Chichester is a graduate of Boalt Hall School of Law at the University of California, Berkeley, where she was an Associate Editor of the *California Law Review*. After law school, Ms. Byrd-Chichester clerked for the Honorable Cecil F. Poole on the US Court of Appeals for the Ninth Circuit in San Francisco, then practiced securities law at Wilmer, Cutler & Pickering in Washington, DC. In 1987, Ms. Byrd-Chichester joined the NAACP LDF where she litigated many school desegregation and affirmative action cases, including *Johnson v. Board of Regents of the University of Georgia* (appealing the district court ruling that struck down the affirmative action admissions program at the University of Georgia), *Podberesky v. Kirwan* (defending the minority scholarship program at the University of Maryland at College Park), and *Hopwood v. Texas* (defending the admissions program at the University of Texas School of Law). In 2003, she prepared the Supreme Court amicus brief for Howard University in the *Gratz* and *Grutter* cases (defending affirmative action at the University of Michigan). Ms. Byrd-Chichester has taught on affirmative action, education, civil procedure, and environmental justice at the University of Maryland School of Law and Florida State University School of Law. She has made television appearances on the *Today Show*, *CBS Nightly News*, *MacNeil-Lehrer Newshour*, *CNN*, and *Washington Journal*.

Erwin Chemerinsky is the Alston & Bird Professor of Law at the Duke Law School. Between 1983 and 2004, he was the Sydney M. Irmas Professor of Public Interest Law, Legal Ethics, and Political Science at the University of Southern California Law School. He graduated with honors from Northwestern University (B.S., 1975), and Harvard Law School (J.D., 1978). He was a trial attorney at the U.S. Department of Justice in Washington, DC, and an attorney at Dobrovir, Oakes & Gebhardt. He has taught at DePaul, Duke, Loyola, and UCLA Law Schools. He is the author of four books: *Federal Jurisdiction*, Aspen Law & Business, 4th ed. (2003) (a one volume treatise on federal courts); *Constitutional Law: Principles and Policies*, Aspen Law & Business, 2d ed. (2002) (a one volume treatise on constitutional law); *Constitutional Law*, Aspen Law & Business (2001) (a casebook); and *Interpreting the Constitution*, Praeger (1987). He is also the author of over one hundred law review articles that have appeared in journals such as the *Harvard Law Review, Michigan Law Review, Northwestern Law Review, University of Pennsylvania Law Review, Stanford Law Review*, and *Yale Law Journal*. Recent articles include, The Constitution and Punishment, *56 Stanford Law Review* (2004) 1049; Entrenchment of Ordinary Legislation: A Response to Professors Posner and Vermeule, *91 California Law Review* (2003) 1773 (with John Roberts); The Rhetoric of Constitutional Law, *100 Michigan Law Review* (2002) 2008; and Against Sovereign Immunity, *53 Stanford Law Review* (2001) 1201. He also writes a regular column on the Supreme Court for *California Lawyer, Los Angeles Daily Journal*, and *Trial Magazine*. He frequently argues appellate cases in the U.S. Supreme Court and Courts of Appeals. He has testified many times before committees of Congress, the California Legislature, and the Los Angeles City Council.

Lee Cokorinos is Executive Director of the Capacity Development Group. Previously, he was Research Director with the Institute for Democracy Studies (IDS) in New York, where he coordinated research programs in law, reproductive rights, and religion. He is a former research consultant with the Public Policy Institute of Planned Parenthood Federation of America, and directed the Southern African Literature Society in Botswana. Mr. Cokorinos is the author of a recent landmark study on the right wing organizations that have waged the legal and political campaign against affirmative action, *The Assault on Diversity: An Organized Challenge to Racial and Gender Justice*, Rowman &

Littlefield (2003). Mr. Cokorinos has also edited and contributed to the IDS investigative newsletter, *IDS Insights*, is the author of the IDS report *Antifeminist Organizations: Institutionalizing the Backlash*, and co-authored the IDS briefing papers *The Federalist Society and the Challenge to a Democratic Jurisprudence*; *Priests for Life: A New Era in Antiabortion Activism*; *The American Life League Enters Mexico: Recruiting Anti-Choice Activists for U.S. Right-Wing Goals*; and *The Global Assault on Reproductive Rights: A Crucial Turning Point*. Mr. Cokorinos has published ground-breaking research on the Promise Keepers men's movement, and edited *PK Watch* for the Nation Institute's Center for Democracy Studies. Mr. Cokorinos has years of experience in conducting and managing political and organizational research, developing collaborative partnerships among NGOs, and assisting organizations to better understand the wider policy and strategic environments in which they operate. He is a graduate of the Columbia University Graduate School of Arts and Sciences, and has been a lecturer in International Political Economy at Fordham University.

Tracie Crandell is the policy analyst for the Center for Disability Rights (CDR), a Center for Independent Living in Rochester, New York. Ms. Crandell has also been involved with the New York chapter of ADAPT, a nationwide grassroots disability rights organization focused on using direct action to end the institutional bias of long-term care so that seniors and people with disabilities have a choice in where they live and receive services. At CDR, Ms. Crandell is responsible for developing policy and legislative recommendations that uphold the rights of the disabled. Ms. Crandell's main interest is ending the institutional bias of the Medicaid-funded long-term care system. Ms. Crandell has been the lead staff on the development of numerous policy papers, including a position paper on accessible housing in New York, the implementation of *Olmstead* in New York, and the opposition to a proposal to create a "mega-waiver" for long-term care. Ms. Crandell developed and carried out advanced training on nursing facility transition and the Supreme Court *Olmstead* decision. Prior to joining CDR, Ms. Crandell worked as a Medicaid examiner at a Department of Social Services and as a hospital discharge planner. Ms. Crandell is a graduate of Binghamton University, where she received her B.A. in Political Science.

Sandra Del Valle is a civil rights lawyer who has worked at the Puerto Rican Legal Defense and Education Fund for over ten years. During her time there, she has specialized in language rights, especially those of immigrant children and bilingual education. She has written for U.S. and Puerto Rican journals on the struggle for bilingual education for Latinos. She recently published a book on language rights, *Law and Language Rights in the U.S.: Finding Our*

Voices, Multilingual Matters, Ltd. (2003). She graduated from Columbia University School of Law in 1988.

Vincent A. Eng is the Deputy Director of the National Asian Pacific American Legal Consortium (NAPALC). Mr. Eng is a graduate of Brandeis University, where he received his B.A. in Politics. He received his J.D., M.S. in Criminal Justice from the American University, and worked toward his M.B.A. Mr. Eng serves as Chair of the Leadership Conference on Civil Rights Committee on Language Rights. Before joining NAPALC, Mr. Eng was the Managing Editor of Bernan Press. Prior to that position, he was an attorney-advisor at the U.S. Department of Justice. Currently, Mr. Eng is an adjunct associate professor of law at the American University, Washington College of Law, and Columbia Law School, where he has lectured on Asian Americans and the Law, Criminal Sentencing, and Legal Research and Writing. He is also the faculty advisor for the National Security and the Law Society at the Washington College of Law. He has written and edited over ten books on various legal and political matters, and has served as the editor-in-chief of the *Almanac of the Executive Branch*. His latest major law school casebook, *Sentencing, Sanctions, and Corrections*, was published by Foundation Press, a division of West Publishing.

Lia Epperson is the Director of Education at the NAACP Legal Defense and Educational Fund, Inc. (LDF). She oversees LDF's administrative and legislative advocacy and litigation in federal and state court in the areas of K-12 and higher education. Ms. Epperson has worked in LDF's national office in New York, and currently works in its Washington, DC office. She has co-authored a number of *amicus* briefs to the U.S. Supreme Court, including one on behalf of LDF in support of the University of Michigan Law School in *Grutter v. Bollinger*. Ms. Epperson also serves as the Co-Chair of the Education Task Force of the Leadership Conference on Civil Rights. In December 2001, Ms. Epperson was listed as one of Ebony Magazine's "30 Leaders of the Future." Before joining LDF, Ms. Epperson was a litigation associate at Morrison & Foerster in Palo Alto, California, where she worked on commercial and civil rights litigation. Prior to her work at Morrison & Foerster, she served as a law clerk to the Honorable Timothy K. Lewis of the U.S. Court of Appeals for the Third Circuit. Ms. Epperson received her law degree from Stanford University, where she served as an editor of the *Stanford Law Review*. Ms. Epperson also holds a B.A. in Sociology, *magna cum laude*, from Harvard University.

Paul Finkelman is the Chapman Distinguished Professor of Law at the University of Tulsa College of Law. Prior to joining the faculty in 1999, Prof. Finkelman was the John F. Seiberling Professor of Law at the University of Akron Law School. In addition, he previously taught at Cleveland Marshall,

Hamline, the University of Miami, Chicago-Kent, Brooklyn Law, and the University of Texas-Austin. A specialist in American legal history, race and the law, and First Amendment issues, Finkelman is the author or editor of numerous articles and books, including *A March of Liberty: A Constitutional History of the United States*, *Slavery and the Founders: Race and Liberty in the Age of Jefferson*, *Baseball and the American Legal Mind*, and *American Legal History: Cases and Materials*. He was a fellow in Law and the Humanities at Harvard Law School, and received his Ph.D. and M.A. from the University of Chicago. Prof. Finkelman teaches constitutional law and American legal history.

Andrew Friedman co-founded Make the Road by Walking with Oona Chatterjee in March 1997. Mr. Friedman has worked with the Latino Workers' Center, the Neighborhood Defender Service of Harlem, the Center for Urban Community Services' Transitional Living Community for mentally ill homeless women, the Government Benefits Unit at Brooklyn Legal Services Corporation A, MFY Legal Services Mental Health Law Project, and REACH. He was awarded the 1999 Union Square Award of the Fund for the City of New York for his work at Make the Road by Walking. Mr. Friedman was a Skadden Public Interest Fellow and is currently a Senior Fellow at the Drum Major Institute for Public Policy and a Wasserstein Fellow at Harvard Law School. He is a magna cum laude graduate of Columbia College and a cum laude graduate of the New York University School of Law.

Robert García is Executive Director of the Center for Law in the Public Interest, a Los Angeles non-profit law and policy organization that seeks justice for under-represented people and organizations, and engages in advocacy and litigation on broad range of public interest issues. Mr. García has extensive experience in public policy and legal advocacy, mediation, and litigation involving complex civil rights, environmental, and criminal justice matters. He has influenced the investment of $20 billion in underserved communities. Mr. García graduated from Stanford University and Stanford Law School, where he served on the Board of Editors of the *Stanford Law Review*. His publications include: "Anatomy of the Urban Parks Movement: Equal Justice, Democracy and Livability in Los Angeles," chapter in book by Robert Bullard, ed., *Wasting Away: Environmental Justice, Human Rights, and the Politics of Pollution*, Sierra Club (2005); "Cross Road Blues: Transportation Justice and the MTA Consent Decree," chapter in book by Karen Lucas, ed., *Running on Empty: Transport, Social Exclusion and Environmental Justice* (2004); Healthy Children, Healthy Communities: Parks, Schools, and Sustainable Regional Planning, *31 Fordham Urban Law Journal* (2004) 101. He served as Assistant U.S. Attorney in the Southern District of New York, and as Western Regional

Counsel for the NAACP LDF. He has taught at Stanford and UCLA Law Schools.

Rachel D. Godsil teaches Equality under American Law, Property, and Zoning and Land Use Policy at Seton Hall University School of Law. Prof. Godsil has been involved in environmental justice law and policy, and has recently been working with attorneys representing the South Camden Citizens in Action. Prof. Godsil has written extensively on the convergence of race, poverty, and the environment. Her publications include: Viewing the Cathedral from Behind the Color Line: Property Rules, Liability Rules, and Environmental Racism, 53 *Emory L. Rev.* (2004) 1807; Environmental Justice and the Integration Ideal, 59 *New York L. Rev.* (2004–2005) 1109; Expressivism, Empathy and Equality, 36 *Mich. J. L. Ref.* (2003) 247; Jobs, Trees, and Autonomy: The Convergence of the Environmental Justice Movement and Community Economic Development, co-author with James Freeman, 5 *U. Maryland J. of Contemp. Legal Issues* (1993-94) 25; The Question of Risk: Incorporating Community Perceptions into Environmental Risk Assessments, co-author with James Freeman, 21 *Fordham Urban L.J.* (1994) 547; and Note, Remedying Environmental Racism, 90 *Mich. L. Rev.* (1991) 394. Prior to joining the Seton Hall School of Law faculty in 2000, Prof. Godsil was an Assistant U.S. Attorney for the Southern District of New York, an associate counsel at the NAACP LDF, an associate with Berle, Kass & Case and Arnold & Porter in New York City, and a law clerk for the Honorable John M. Walker, Jr., U.S. Court of Appeals for the Second Circuit. She received her B.A. from the University of Wisconsin, Madison, and her J.D., *magna cum laude,* from the University of Michigan Law School. At Michigan, Prof. Godsil served as the executive article editor of the *Michigan Law Review*, was awarded the Henry M. Bates Memorial Award, and was elected to the *Order of the Coif.*

Anjum Gupta serves as a Clinical Fellow at the Center for Social Justice at Seton Hall University School of Law where she teaches in the Immigration and Human Rights Clinic and the Civil Litigation Clinic. She earned her B.A. in Psychology and Women's Studies from the University of Michigan, with high honors in Psychology. She received her J.D. from Yale Law School. Her clinical experience includes work at Yale Law School's Jerome N. Frank Legal Services Organization in the Immigration Legal Services Clinic (where she served as a student director and supervisor) and in the Advocacy for Parents and Children Clinic. She has also worked at the American Civil Liberties Union Immigrants' Rights Project, the New Haven Legal Assistance Association, the National Coalition Against Domestic Violence, the Domestic Violence Project SAFEhouse, and the National Science Foundation. During law school, she had an active public interest focus, including serving as Director of the Rebellious Lawyering Conference as well as Co-Founder and Director of the Temporary Restraining Order Project's Domestic Violence Clinic. She also served as Vice-President of the Initiative for Public Interest Law at Yale, Chair of the South Asian Law Students Association, and as student director of the Chile portion of the Yale Law School Linkage program, an academic exchange program between the law school and several Latin American countries.

Wade Henderson is the Executive Director of the Leadership Conference on Civil Rights (the Leadership Conference) and counsel to the Leadership Conference Education Fund. The Leadership Conference is the nation's premiere civil and human rights coalition. Since taking the helm in June 1996, Mr. Henderson has worked to address emerging policy issues of concern to the civil rights community and to strengthen the effectiveness of the coalition. Prior to his role with the Leadership Conference, Mr. Henderson was the Washington Bureau Director of the NAACP. In that capacity, he directed government affairs and the national legislative program. He was also the Director of the NAACP's Voter Empowerment Program. He was the NAACP's advocate on the Civil Rights Act of 1991, the National Voter Registration Act ("Motor-Voter" Law), the Brady Handgun Prevention Act, and the Family and Medical Leave Act. A tireless civil rights leader and advocate, Mr. Henderson has received countless awards and honors. He currently serves as the Joseph L. Rauh, Jr. Professor of Public Interest Law at the David A. Clarke School of Law at the University of the District of Columbia. He is the author of numerous articles on civil rights and public policy issues. Mr. Henderson is a graduate of Howard University and the Rutgers University School of Law.

Marielena Hincapié is the Program Director of the National Immigration Law Center (NILC), and heads NILC's labor and employment program on behalf of low-wage immigrant workers. Ms. Hincapié also specializes in advancing the rights of immigrant workers. She writes articles and policy analyses, provides technical assistance, and trains legal and social service providers, labor unions, and community-based organizations. In addition, she litigates law reform and impact cases dealing with the intersection of immigration and employment/labor law. Before joining NILC, she worked for the Legal Aid Society of San Francisco's Employment Law Center, where she founded the center's Immigrant Workers' Rights Project. Ms. Hincapié holds a J.D. from the Northeastern University School of Law.

Julie Hyman is the Senior Policy Analyst at the Center for Independence of the Disabled in New York (CIDNY), a disability advocacy organization that pursues a local and state policy agenda focusing on the interests of people with disabilities. Prior to joining CIDNY, Ms. Hyman served as a policy analyst for

Manhattan Borough President C. Virginia Fields, focusing on child and family policy. She holds a Master's Degree in Social Work from the Wurzweiler School of Social Work at Yeshiva University.

Marianne Engelman Lado is General Counsel for New York Lawyers for the Public Interest (NYLPI), where she administers the litigation program with a docket that encompasses cases and advocacy on issues of disability rights, environmental justice, and access to health care. Prior to joining NYLPI in 1999, she was an assistant professor at Baruch College, and a staff attorney for the NAACP LDF. Ms. Engelman Lado is the author of a number of articles on civil rights law including, Unfinished Agenda: The Need for Civil Rights Litigation to Address Race Discrimination and Inequalities in Health Care Delivery, *6 Tex. F. on C.L. & C.R.* (2001) 1; Evaluating Systems for Delivering Legal Services to the Poor: Conceptual and Methodological Consideration, with Gredd Ryzin, *67 Fordham L. Rev.* (1999) 2553; Litigation and Structural Change in Low-Income Communities: Toward a New Conceptualization of the Role of National Legal Campaigns, *Aspen Institute Roundtable on Comprehensive Community Initiatives* (July 1998). She received her B.A. *magna cum laude* from Cornell in 1984, her J.D. from Boalt Hall School of Law at the University of California Berkeley in 1987, and her M.A. in Politics from Princeton in 1989.

Simon Lazarus is Senior Counsel at Sidley Austin Brown & Wood. He counsels and represents companies and associations in legislative, regulatory, and policy matters affecting domestic and international issues. Mr. Lazarus also served as Associate Director of the White House Domestic Policy Staff under President Jimmy Carter, where he oversaw enactment of major initiatives including airline, trucking, and rail deregulation legislation, and ethics in government and civil service reform. He is the author of a number of articles including The Court Runs Amok, Review of Judge T. Noonan's Narrowing the Nation's Power: The Supreme Court Sides with the States, *Blueprint*, The Democratic Leadership Council (December 2002); The Most Dangerous Branch? *The Atlantic* (June 2002); and "Don't Be Fooled: They're Activists Too," *The Washington Post* (June 3, 2001), Outlook Section. Mr. Lazarus received his B.A. *magna cum laude* from Harvard University, and his L.L.B. from Yale Law School.

Julianna Lee is a third-year student at the University of Michigan Law School, where she is involved with the Asian Pacific American Law Students Association and the *Michigan Journal of International Law*. She has interned with the National Asian Pacific American Legal Consortium, working on hate crimes and race relations legislation as well as conducting historical research on Chinese school segregation and the 1927 *Gong Lum v. Rice* case. As a future voice of civil rights, Ms. Lee gave a keynote address launching the Voices of Civil Rights Project. She is also a former Asian Pacific American Institute for Congressional Studies Daniel K. Inouye Fellow with the Smithsonian Institute Asian Pacific American Studies Program. Following law school, she will be working as a law fellow with the Southern Poverty Law Center in Montgomery, Alabama. Ms. Lee received her B.A. in Japanese Studies and Economics from Wellesley College, and an M.A. in East Asian studies from Harvard University.

Arthur S. Leonard has been a member of the New York Law School faculty since 1982. He practiced labor law for five years before becoming a law professor. In 1978, he started the New York Law Group, which became the Bar Association for Human Rights in the mid-1980s and ultimately the Lesbian and Gay Law Association of Greater New York in the early 1990s. He has edited the Association's substantive newsletter, *Lesbian/Gay Law Notes*, since 1980. Mr. Leonard has served as a director or trustee on a number of nonprofit organizations. His publications include From *Bowers v. Harwick* to *Romer v. Evans*: Lesbian and Gay Rights in the U.S. Supreme Court, *Creating Change: Sexuality, Public Policy, and Civil Rights*, J.D'Emilio et al. eds. (2000) 57-77; *Homosexuality and the Constitution* (1997) (ed. and author of volume introductions); *AIDS Law and Policy: Cases and Materials*, 2d ed. (1995) (principal editor and co-author); The Gay Rights Workplace Revolution, *Hum. Rts.* (Summer 2003); *Boy Scouts of America v. Dale*: The "Gay Rights Activist" as Constitutional Pariah, *12 Stan. L. & Pol'y Rev.* (2001) 27; and *Lawrence v. Texas* and the New Law of Gay Rights, *30 Ohio Northern Univ. L. Rev.* (2004) 189–210. He is a contributing writer on legal topics for *Gay City News*. He is a graduate of Cornell University and Harvard Law School.

Susan Lerner is the Founder and Chair of the Committee for Judicial Independence, a grassroots organization dedicated to educating and activating Americans to the importance of an independent and open-minded federal Judiciary and to the threat posed by the radical Right's concerted effort to take over the federal courts. She spearheads the Justice for All Project, a California coalition of civil rights, feminist, and environmental organizations, working to educate members and lobby elected representatives on federal judicial nominations. Ms. Lerner has been an activist in progressive, feminist, and pro-choice issues for more than twenty-five years. She is the former Executive Director of the California Abortion and Reproductive Rights Action League-South and has chaired the Women Lawyers Association of Los Angeles' Pro-Choice Committee. As a staff attorney for the Federal Trade Commission, Lerner identified deceptive advertising aimed at women by a major consumer drug company, leading to the Commission's first-ever authorization to seek an injunction against ongoing consumer advertising. Ms. Lerner then entered private practice and was a trial lawyer specializing in complex commercial litigation and intellectual property for almost twenty years.

Emily J. Martin is a staff attorney at the ACLU Women's Rights Project where she litigates cases challenging gender discrimination in housing, employment, welfare administration, and public accommodations, with an emphasis on the needs of low-income women and women of color. One of her areas of focus at the Women's Rights Project is housing discrimination against victims of domestic violence. She was part of the team that litigated *Alvera v. CBM Group*, the first case to argue that housing discrimination against a woman who had experienced domestic violence constituted sex discrimination under the Fair Housing Act. Ms. Martin received a B.A. with highest distinction from the University of Virginia, and a J.D. from Yale Law School. She clerked for Judge T.S. Ellis, III, in the U.S. District Court for the Eastern District of Virginia, and for Judge Wilfred Feinberg in the U.S. Court of Appeals for the Second Circuit. As a recipient of the Rita Charmatz Davidson Fellowship through the Georgetown Women's Law and Public Policy Fellowship Program, she worked as an attorney at the National Women's Law Center, where she undertook legislative advocacy and policy analyses on issues affecting women's employment and economic security.

The late **Denise C. Morgan** taught Education Policy and the Law, Federal Courts, Civil Procedure, and a seminar on race and American History at New York Law School. Prof. Morgan was actively involved in public education in New York. Her activities included representing the Black, Puerto Rican, and Hispanic Legislative Caucus in *Campaign for Fiscal Equity v. New York State*. In 1995, she assisted the New York City Board of Education's Chancellor Search Office in its search for a leader for the City's public school system. Prof. Morgan also wrote extensively about civil rights and educational opportunity. Her publications include: The New Parity Debate: Congress and Rights of Belonging, *73 Cincinnati L. Rev.* (2005) 1347 (with Rebecca E. Zietlow); The Devil is in the Details: Or Why I Haven't Yet Learned to Stop Worrying and Love Vouchers, *59 N.Y.U. Ann. Surv. Am. L.* (2003) 477; Jack Johnson v. The American Racial Hierarchy, *Race on Trial: Law and Justice in American History*, Oxford Univ. Press (2002); The New School Finance Litigation: Acknowledging That Race Discrimination in Public Education is More Than Just a Tort, *96 Nw. U. L. Rev.* (2001) 99; Anti-Subordination Analysis After *U.S. v. Virginia*: Evaluating the Constitutionality of K-12 Single-Sex Public Schools, *1999 U. Chi. Legal F.* (1999) 381; The Less Polite Questions: Race, Place, Poverty and Public Education, *1998 N.Y.U. Ann. Surv. Am. L.* (1998) 267; and

What's Left to Argue in Desegregation Law? The Right to Minimally Adequate Education, *8 Harvard BlackLetter Journal* (1991) 99. She also co-authored *Breaking into the Academy*, a guide for aspiring law professors published by the *Michigan Journal of Race and Law*. Prior to joining the New York Law School faculty in 1995, Prof. Morgan practiced in the litigation department of Cleary, Gottlieb, Steen & Hamilton, clerked for Judge Marilyn Hall Patel on the U.S. District Court for the Northern District of California, and was a member of the Florida State Law School faculty. She received her B.A. from Yale College in 1986 and her J.D. from Yale Law School in 1990.

Joy Moses is a staff attorney with the Education Project at the National Law Center on Homelessness & Poverty. As such, she provides technical assistance and training to advocates, attorneys, families, and school, school district, and state administrators on issues related to homeless children and youth. She also engages in federal- and state-level policy and legal advocacy designed to increase educational and life opportunities for homeless students. Prior to joining the National Law Center on Homelessness & Poverty, Ms. Moses was an Equal Justice Works fellow at the NAACP LDF, where she worked on an assortment of education and federalism issues. She received her J.D. from Georgetown University Law Center, where she advocated on behalf of juvenile offenders, assisted special education advocates, and served on the board of a DC charter school. Ms. Moses received her undergraduate degree from Stanford University.

Lori A. Nessel is an Associate Professor and Director of the Immigration & Human Rights Clinic at Seton Hall University School of Law. In addition to directing the clinic, she teaches Immigration and Naturalization Law and an advanced seminar entitled Selected Topics in Immigration Law. She has also taught Gender and the Law and International Human Rights Law. Prof. Nessel received her B.A. in Latin American Studies from the University of California at Santa Cruz in 1987, and spent a few years working as a teacher and community organizer with refugee and inner city populations before pursuing a career in public interest law. After receiving her J.D. from the City University School of Law at Queens College in 1992, Prof. Nessel was awarded a Skadden Arps Public Interest Law Fellowship to represent migrant farm workers in upstate New York on labor, employment, education, and civil rights matters. After finishing her fellowship, Prof. Nessel worked on employment discrimination and police brutality cases at a civil rights firm in New York City before joining Seton Hall Law School in 1995. Prof. Nessel's interest in human rights and refugee issues dates back to 1984, when she spent a year living with Salvadoran refugees in Nicaragua and volunteering in local schools while studying the effects of war on children. Her publications include: "Willful

Blindness" to Gender-Based Violence Abroad: United States' Implementation of Article Three of the United Nations Convention Against Torture, *89 Minnesota Law Review* (2004) 71; Undocumented Immigrants in the Workplace: The Fallacy of Labor Protection and the Need for Reform, *36 Harvard Civil Rights-Civil Liberties Law Review* (2001) 345; and Migrant Farmworkers, Homeless and Runaway Youth: Challenging the Barriers to Inclusion, *13 Law and Inequality Journal* (1994) 99 (with Kevin Ryan).

Nathan Newman is Director of Agends for Justice, a non-profit supporting local and state campaigns for social justice and is a former Associate Counsel at the Brennan Center for Justice at NYU Law School. A lawyer and labor policy researcher, Mr. Newman provides legal and policy assistance for the Center's initiative to support living wage and other economic justice campaigns. Prior to joining the Center, Mr. Newman was an associate at a union-side law firm, and before going to law school, was a union organizer and co-directed a policy center at the University of California-Berkeley that assisted unions and low-income communities. He has published in *The Nation*, *The American Prospect*, and MIT's *Technology Review*, as well as in law and academic journals. He is the author of the book *Net Loss: Internet Prophets, Private Profits and the Costs to Community*, Penn State Press (2002). Mr. Newman earned his J.D. from Yale Law School, and has a Ph.D. in Sociology from the University of California-Berkeley. At Berkeley, he won a National Science Foundation Fellowship and a Jacob K. Javits Fellowship.

Barbara Olshansky is the Director Counsel of the Global Justice Initiative of the Center for Constitutional Rights (CCR). Ms. Olshansky's docket at CCR includes class action lawsuits concerning international human rights, immigrants' rights, race discrimination in employment, education, the environment and public health, and prisoners' rights. Among Ms. Olshansky's current cases are: a class action lawsuit challenging the unlawful arrest and detention of Arab and Muslim immigrants and visitors in the wake of 9/11 and the implementation of the decision in *Rasul v. Bush*, that challenged the detention without process of persons held in the U.S. naval base in Guantanamo Bay. Ms. Olshansky recently co-authored a book on America's detainees entitled *America's Disappeared*, and has written two other books: *Against War With Iraq*, analyzing the international law ramifications of the U.S. decision to go to war, and *Secret Trials and Executions*, assessing the military commissions scheduled for Guantanamo detainees. Ms. Olshansky received her J.D. from Stanford University, and her two undergraduate degrees, *summa cum laude*, from the University of Rochester.

Caroline Palmer is the Pro Bono Development Director at the Minnesota State Bar Association. Prior to this position, she served as a staff attorney at the Minnesota AIDS Project. Ms. Palmer was a 1999 recipient of a National Association for Public Interest Law/Equal Justice Works Fellowship, and was named one of ten "Up and Coming Attorneys" by *Minnesota Lawyer* as well as a "Rising Star" by *Minnesota Law and Politics*. Ms. Palmer is the author of: Falling Through the Cracks: The Unique Circumstances of HIV Disease Under Recent Americans with Disabilities Act Caselaw and Emerging Privacy Policies, *22 Law and Ineq.* (2003) 219 (with Lynn Mickelson); Many Rivers to Cross: Evolving and Emerging Legal Issues in the Third Decade of the HIV/AIDS Epidemic, *28 Wm. Mitchell L. Rev.* (2001) 455 (with Lynn Mickelson); The Risks of State Intervention in Preventing Prenatal Alcohol Abuse and the Viability of an Inclusive Approach: Arguments for Limiting Punitive Aid and Coercive Prenatal Alcohol Abuse Legislation in Minnesota, *10 Hastings Women's L.J.* (1999) 287; and Waiting For Democracy: Congress, Control Boards and the Pursuit of Self-Determination in the District of Columbia, *19 Hamline J. Pub. L. & Pol'y* (1997) 339. Ms. Palmer recently served as President of the Minnesota chapter of the National Lawyers Guild as well as Chair of the Human Rights Committee at the Minnesota State Bar Association. She was also Vice-Chair of Minnesotans Against the Death Penalty. She received her B.A. from Barnard College in 1989 and her J.D. from Hamline University School of Law in 1998.

Dennis D. Parker is the Bureau Chief for the Civil Rights Bureau of the Office of New York State Attorney General Eliot Spitzer, and is responsible for overseeing the enforcement of state and federal laws protecting New Yorkers from discrimination in housing, places of public accommodation, employment, voting, credit, law enforcement, and education. Prior to joining the Civil Rights Bureau, Mr. Parker served for fourteen years as Assistant Counsel for the NAACP LDF, where he headed its Education Litigation Program and supervised the education docket and trial and appellate work in cases involving affirmative action, school desegregation, and equal educational opportunity. Other legal experience includes the New York labor and employment discrimination firm Vladeck, Waldman, Elias & Engelhard, the New York State Department of Health, Office of Professional Medical Conduct, Assistant Attorney General in the New York State Attorney General's Office, Civil Rights Bureau, and a staff attorney at the Legal Aid Society, Criminal Defense Division. He has litigated scores of civil rights cases throughout the U.S., including the landmark Connecticut education case *Sheff v. O'Neill*. His publications include a book and numerous articles on housing discrimination, educational equity, affirmative action, and educational testing, and he is a frequent lecturer on civil rights issues at conferences and law schools. Mr.

Parker has served as an Adjunct Professor at New York Law School. He is a graduate of Middlebury College and Harvard Law School, where he was an editor of the *Civil Rights/Civil Liberties Law Review*.

Jane Perkins is the Legal Director at the National Health Law Program (NHeLP), a public interest law firm working to improve health care for low-income people, minorities, children, the elderly, and individuals with disabilities. Ms. Perkins directs NHeLP's Court Watch Project and focuses on Medicaid and discrimination in the delivery of health care. She has engaged in extensive litigation and policy advocacy, and has authored and co-authored numerous articles. She provides legal assistance and training to consumer advocates and health care consumers.

Olga Pomar is an attorney specializing in community development work at South Jersey Legal Services, where she represents numerous low-income community groups and non-profit organizations. She is lead counsel in *South Camden Citizens in Action v. NJ Dept. of Environmental Protection and St. Lawrence Cement*, a precedent-setting environmental justice case. Her co-counsel in that case are Luke Cole, Jerome Balter and Michael Churchill. She also represents local activists in other environmental justice struggles involving contaminated drinking water, Superfund remediation, open space and parks development, environmental enforcement, public health issues, and neighborhood planning. She has worked in legal services since 1984, having spent ten years as a housing specialist at the Legal Aid Society in Trenton, NJ. She also spent two years in private practice after graduating from the University of Pennsylvania Law School in 1982.

Alfred F. Ross is the Founder and President of the Institute for Democracy Studies. He is an attorney, and has been researching anti-democratic movements for over thirty years. He was a lecturer at Columbia University's School of International and Public Affairs, and an Associate Economic Affairs Officer with the United Nations Conference for Trade and Development in Geneva, Switzerland. From 1992-95 he directed Planned Parenthood Federation of America's Public Policy Institute, which was responsible for national and international research on anti-choice groups and movements. Mr. Ross is a graduate of Columbia University Law School.

The late **Herb Semmel** was Director of the Federal Rights Project of the National Senior Citizens Law Center. He formerly served as Director of the Center for Law and Social Policy and Litigation Director of New York Lawyers for the Public Interest. His areas of expertise were health law, disability law, and enforcement of federal rights. He wrote extensively on federal rights.

Rose Cuison Villazor is a Human Rights Fellow at Columbia Law School for the 2004-05 academic year. While at Columbia, she is working on an L.L.M program, researching issues concerning human rights, critical race theory, and immigrants' rights. Prior to her fellowship, Ms. Villazor was a staff attorney in the Access to Health Care Program at New York Lawyers for the Public Interest (NYLPI). At NYLPI, she litigated civil rights cases on behalf of people who had difficulty accessing health care services because of their limited proficiency in English, their disability, or their national origin. Ms. Villazor clerked for the Honorable Stephen H. Glickman of the DC Court of Appeals. She received her J.D., *cum laude*, from the American University's Washington College of Law, where she served as Notes and Comments Editor for the *American University Law Review*.

Brad Williams is the Executive Director of the New York State Independent Living Council, which provides technical assistance and training, increases public awareness about independent living, and pursues a public policy agenda that results in systematic change for people with disabilities. He is a past board member of the National Council on Independent Living. He has coordinated several media campaigns in support of systems advocacy efforts that helped leverage successful results on issues such as polling place access, Medicaid Buy-In for people with disabilities, and accessible housing construction. Mr. Williams earned a B.A. in Political Science from SUNY Albany and an M.A. in Public Administration from Russell Sage College.

Lisa Zeidner is a student at Columbia Law School and an active member of the Columbia Coalition to Restore Civil Rights. Prior to law school, she spent two years in Washington, DC working as the Legislative Correspondent for Health Care and Foreign Relations for U.S. Senator John Edwards (D-NC). Ms. Zeidner graduated *cum laude* from Duke University, where she served as student body president. She also chaired Duke's Inter-Community Council, leading a coalition of student organizations to address community issues, including the improvement of town-gown relations and campus race relations. Ms. Zeidner presented a workshop regarding campus organizing at the American Council on Education's 1999 Educating All of One Nation Conference.

Index

Table of Cases